NO SACRIFICE TOO GREAT

NO SACRIFICE TOO GREAT

The 1st Infantry Division in World War II

Gregory Fontenot
Colonel, US Army, Retired

UNIVERSITY OF MISSOURI PRESS
Columbia

Library of Congress Cataloging-in-Publication Data

Names: Fontenot, Gregory, 1949- author.
Title: No sacrifice too great : the 1st Infantry Division in World War II /
  by Gregory Fontenot.
Other titles: 1st Infantry Division in World War II
Description: [Columbia, Missouri] : [University of Missouri Press], [2023]
  | Series: American military experience | Includes bibliographical
  references and index.
Identifiers: LCCN 2022048757 (print) | LCCN 2022048758 (ebook) | ISBN
  9780826222848 (hardcover) | ISBN 9780826274892 (ebook)
Subjects: LCSH: United States. Army. Infantry Division, 1st--History. |
  World War, 1939-1945--Campaigns--Europe. | World War,
  1939-1945--Campaigns--Africa, North.
Classification: LCC D769.3 1st .F66 2023 (print) | LCC D769.3 1st (ebook)
  | DDC 940.54/1273--dc23/eng/20230103
LC record available at https://lccn.loc.gov/2022048757
LC ebook record available at https://lccn.loc.gov/2022048758

∞™ This paper meets the requirements of the
American National Standard for Permanence of Paper
for Printed Library Materials, Z39.48, 1984.

Typefaces: Acumin and Minion

THE AMERICAN MILITARY EXPERIENCE SERIES
JOHN C. MCMANUS, SERIES EDITOR

The books in this series portray and analyze the experience of Americans in military service during war and peacetime from the onset of the twentieth century to the present. The series emphasizes the profound impact wars have had on nearly every aspect of recent American history and considers the significant effects of modern conflict on combatants and noncombatants alike. Titles in the series include accounts of battles, campaigns, and wars; unit histories; biographical and autobiographical narratives; investigations of technology and warfare; studies of the social and economic consequences of war; and in general, the best recent scholarship on Americans in the modern armed forces. The books in the series are written and designed for a diverse audience that encompasses nonspecialists as well as expert readers.

Selected titles from this series:

Patton's War: An American General's Combat Leadership, Volume 2: August–December 1944
Kevin M. Hymel

Patton's War: An American General's Combat Leadership, Volume 1: November 1942–July 1944
Kevin M. Hymel

Patton: Battling with History
J. Furman Daniel

Lessons Unlearned: The U.S. Army's Role in Creating the Forever Wars in Afghanistan and Iraq
Pat Proctor

Loss and Redemption at St. Vith: The 7th Armored Division in the Battle of the Bulge
Gregory Fontenot

Military Realism: The Logic and Limits of Force and Innovation in the US Army
Peter Campbell

Omar Nelson Bradley: America's GI General, 1893–1981
Steven L. Ossad

The First Infantry Division and the US Army Transformed: Road to Victory in Desert Storm, 1970–1991
Gregory Fontenot

Bataan Survivor: A POW's Account of Japanese Captivity in World War II
Frank A. Blazich

Dick Cole's War: Doolittle Raider, Hump Pilot, Air Commando
Dennis R. Okerstrom

For Colonel Richard M. Swain, PhD. United States Army Retired Combat Veteran, Superb Historian, and Coach

Contents

Maps

Foreword

Carter F. Ham
General, US Army, Retired

GENERAL GORDON SULLIVAN, thirty-second Chief of Staff of the United States Army and a former Commanding General of the 1st Infantry Division, would often begin his talks by saying, "The history of the United States is the history of the United States Army." Given the Army's crucial role in gaining independence from Great Britain and subsequent contributions in exploration, engineering, and expansion, and in the emergence of America as a global power, General Sullivan's assertion rings true. In a similar vein, one might suggest that, "The history of the United States Army in World War II is the history of the 1st Infantry Division." While each Army Division has a storied history, my opinion is that none quite matches that of the 1st Infantry Division. My admittedly biased opinion stems from my service in The Big Red One, first in 1997–1999 in Wurzburg, Germany, as the G3 (the operations officer) then Chief of Staff. From 2005 to 2006, I was privileged to serve at Fort Riley, Kansas, as Division Commander.

The 1st Infantry Division holds the distinction of being the longest-serving active duty Division in the Army, having been on continuous active duty since 1917. The soldiers of the Division have distinguished themselves in combat and in peacetime for more than 100 years, but their service during World War II is particularly worth studying and honoring.

Distilling the WWII history of the 1st Infantry Division is no small task. Arriving in the United Kingdom in August 1942, the soldiers of the Big Red One fought through North Africa and Sicily, then assaulted Omaha Beach on D-Day, fighting through France and Belgium, and then into the heart of Germany and on to Czechoslovakia, remaining in Europe on occupation duty after V-E Day. Surprisingly, while several studies of individual battles or campaigns and biographies of many of the Division's WW II combat leaders have been written since the war's end, there's been no comprehensive history of the Division written since 1947. The undertaking by Colonel (Retired) Greg Fontenot, a notable historian, author, and teacher, and himself a combat veteran of the 1st Infantry Division in Iraq, has brought together a formal history of our Division's extraordinary service in World War II. This historical study of the Division's role in World War II could not have been told by a more credible, more committed, or more distinguished author.

This is a history about service and sacrifice, about Generals and young Privates, about deeds well-known and those previously untold. Each member of the 1st Infantry Division took great pride in their unit. They believed in the mystique of The Big Red One, they believed in their leaders, and they believed that they could defeat any enemy anywhere, anytime. Sometimes criticized for their combativeness and seeming indiscipline when not on the front, the soldiers of the Division earned wide respect for their extraordinary accomplishments on the battlefield. Senior commanders sought to have the 1st Infantry Division under their command; enemy commanders found out the hard way that they did not want to fight against them.

This is also a history about learning and improving, individually and collectively. Though most of the Division's senior officers had experienced combat in World War I, the character of war had changed dramatically in the inter-war years. Advancements in armored and mechanized warfare, the integration of air power, and the devastating effects of longer-range artillery fires, all of which were mostly pioneered by the Germans, rendered much of the combat experience of America's WWI veterans outdated, even obsolete. From its early battlefield experiences in North Africa, the 1st Infantry Division continually refined its tactics, techniques, and procedures. When not directly engaged in combat, the Division trained, then trained some more, a practice begun before the Division deployed from the United States in 1942 and continued throughout the war. They refined their combat practices, giving credence to their enemy, Field Marshall Erwin Rommel, who wrote, "The best form of welfare for the troops is first-rate training." This focus on applying lessons learned led the Division to increasing battlefield experience and set a precedent for the Army's future generations.

Colonel Fontenot's book comes at an important time for America's Army and for our nation. As today's Army studies the lessons of 20+ years of counterinsurgency operations and now returns its focus to major combat operations against near-peer competitors, the experiences of the 1st Infantry in

World War II show how a disciplined force led by imaginative leaders can adapt, even while in combat, to rapidly changing conditions. *No Sacrifice Too Great: The 1st Infantry Division in World War II* offers insights that help us better understand the crucial events of the past while providing useful insights that will help us prepare for an ever more challenging and rapidly evolving global security environment.

Mostly, though, Colonel Fontenot reminds us of the very human nature of war. As technology advances, as military capabilities continue to become ever more lethal, and as tactics evolve, this history reminds us of the incredible valor and the terrible human cost that have defined America's soldiers for generations. The soldiers of the 1st Infantry Division learn, recite, and inculcate values encapsulated in their Division Motto:

No Mission Too Difficult,
No Sacrifice Too Great…
Duty First!

It is to those soldiers … past, present, and future … and the families that support them, to whom we owe a debt that can never be fully repaid.

Carter F. Ham
General, US Army, Retired

Preface

My ABIDING INTEREST in the history of the US Army stems from my experience. I was born in an army hospital in Yokohama, Japan, in October 1949 to Staff Sergeant Ixon and Grace Fontenot. They raised four of us on army posts scattered across the United States, Japan, France, and Germany. My sister and I were born in Yokohama, one of my brothers at Fort Monroe, Virginia, and the other at Fort Rucker, Alabama.

I grew up in close proximity to the army. It was part of my everyday existence. My coaches, scout masters, and even some of my teachers were soldiers or married to soldiers. My father and his friends were all combat veterans of World War II. I started school in Rochefort, France. Bombed-out buildings, partially submerged merchant vessels sunk during the war, and nearby Roman ruins were among my earliest memories. Both of my parents valued education, so they made sure we took in the history and culture of Europe when we were overseas. They took us many places, including the Vatican and the Museo del Prado in Madrid.

But my parents also showed us the dirty underside of history. They took us to visit the village of Oradour-Sur-Glane, whose citizens had all been slaughtered by the 2nd SS Panzer Division. We visited the ossuary at Fort Douaumont, in Verdun, where the bones of thousands killed during the battle can be seen, as well as to the American cemetery at Saint-Miheil, the site of first major American battle in World War I. Finally, we saw Dachau—which I made sure my sons saw too when they grew up as army brats.

My father thought we should see these things, but I never remember him telling me why, exactly, or talking about his own experiences as a cruiser sailor escorting convoys in the Atlantic and supporting Operation Torch.

Nor did he say much about his five war patrols as a submarine sailor in the Pacific. Neither he nor his peers in the army said much about what they did in World War II or Korea, but occasionally I had insight. I met Bill Powers at a boy scout camporee at Fort Riley, Kansas, in the spring of 1964, and he remains to this day a close friend. His father, Walter E. Powers, landed with the 3rd wave on Omaha Beach. I recall one day asking Sergeant Powers—he was retired but I addressed my dad's peers and friends by their military title or "sir." In any case I asked Sergeant Powers what it was like and what had he seen. He looked at me for a moment—and then he said he saw the troops that landed ahead of him rolling back and forth with the breaking waves. He said no more and I never asked him a question about the war again.

I grew up with these men as role models and their kids as friends. I knew men who were captured during the Battle of the Bulge, parachuted into France, served in tank crews, yanked lanyards on cannons and in one case called naval gunfire in support of landings. They and other veterans mostly kept their own counsel until years later. Even today more of their stories remain to be told and can be told as their children and grandchildren donate diaries or letters or artifacts that enable us to understand their experiences.

My fascination with their story stems also from my own experiences as a soldier, my training as an historian and my conviction there is much still to be learned from that momentous and truly "awe" full war fought so long ago. I will examine their experience through the lens of the 1st Infantry Division. Justifiably renowned for its service since 1917 the Big Red One's operations during World War II offer the chance to understand how to adapt, innovate and cope with turbulence coming from a casualty rate of more than 200% exacerbated by reassignment and promotion.

The story of the 1st Infantry Division in World War II is similar to that of other divisions but at the same time unusual in several ways. It fought in North Africa, Sicily, France, Belgium, Germany and Czechoslovakia. The environment including weather and terrain was as varied as that confronted by any unit that fought in the Europe or Mediterranean theaters. For all of its renown there is no history other than its own early postwar product Danger Forward that tells its story from prior to Pearl Harbor until V-E Day. This is an effort to close that gap.

Acknowledgments

SEVENTY-EIGHT YEARS AFTER V-E Day the number of remaining Veterans of World War II are few. I had the privilege and great pleasure of speaking with several of them. I spoke with Ralph Lambert several times. He served as a medic in the 16th Infantry and made all three WWII landings the 1st Infantry Division executed. Badly wounded on Omaha beach, Ralph survived until this year. I communicated by email with Charles Norman Shay, who served with Ralph and lives near Omaha Beach. I interviewed Andy Anderson, Jerry Nauss, Jim Sharp, and Tommy Macdonnell. Jerry, Andy, and Tommy have passed. Only Jim and Charles remain. I found all of them bright and engaging, and I am grateful and honored to have had the chance to hear their stories firsthand.

The National Archives were closed but for a few weeks while I wrote this book. One wonders what archivists do when the archives are not open for the better part of two years. In any case, without access to the archives I needed help from a great many people. Some research institutions found ways to remain open, and their staffs always were helpful. The Ike Skelton Combined Arms Research Library is foremost among them. Rusty Rafferty is an invaluable member of that team, one who seemingly lives to assist researchers. I could not have completed this book without his help. Rusty is joined by the equally competent John and Liz Dubuisson. Andrew Woods, Research Historian at the Robert R. McCormick Research Center, assisted me throughout this process. The McCormick Research Center at the First Division Museum at Cantigny digitized the WWII record of the 1st Infantry Division. That is an invaluable resource and Andrew Woods is the navigator of choice. Dr. Bob Smith, Debbie Clark, and Ron Coyle at the Fort Riley

Museum Complex have a trove of records including personal papers and diaries unavailable anywhere else as well as a great collection of photographs. Unlike the National Archives, they soon opened for business. Prior to the outbreak of Covid and the ensuing quarantine, Toni Kiser at the National World War II Museum helped me navigate their archives.

Because travel was not feasible during the quarantine, collections one could access remotely were essential to my purpose. The McMaster University Library Map Collection made it possible for me to print maps and plot grid coordinates from reports. That enabled me to see the "battlefield." The Ohio University Archives' D-Day Project interviews can be accessed remotely, as can the Cornelius Ryan *Longest Day* surveys. Many universities have digital records, veterans interviews, memoirs, and other materials. The Veterans of the Battle of the Bulge Association collected accounts written by veterans and put them online. The Tank Destroyer Association has a plethora of resources ranging from after action reports to photos. The Army Heritage and Education Center has a collection of veterans surveys that address a variety of issues including reception and integration of replacements. Chuck Payne, Lieutenant Colonel USA Retired and a researcher at the Army Heritage Foundation, pulled those from 1st ID for me. Dr. Jim Scudieri, Colonel USA Retired Research Historian, and Geoff Manglesdorf, Colonel USA Retired Director of the Army Heritage and Education Center, helped me get documents that I needed while their institution was closed. The center has embarked on a project to scan its extensive collection and make it available digitally.

Authors and scholars willingly shared files they had collected. John McManus, who edits the series in which this book is published, shared with me V Corps After Action Reports. Steve Clay, the author of *Blood and Sacrifice,* a combat history of the 16th Infantry, shared his impressive collection of records. Dr. Adrian R. Lewis, author of *Omaha Beach: A Flawed Victory* and the David B. Pittaway Professor of Military History at the University of Kansas, shared his files. Steven Ossad, author of *Omar Nelson Bradley: America's GI General,* shared the Hanson Diary. Lieutenant Colonel William S. Nance, author of *Sabers Through the Reich: World War II Corps Cavalry From Normandy to the Elbe,* shared the reports of the 4th Cavalry Group. Dr. Christopher Rein, author of *The North African Air Campaign: US Army Air Forces from El Alamein to Salerno* and Managing Editor of the Air University Press, read four chapters and helped me think through the problems of establishing working air support in North Africa. The Army and Allied Air Forces performed brilliantly, but they and the ground forces had a lot of learning to do in North Africa and Sicily.

Don Patton from the Dr. Harold C. Deutsch World War II History Round Table introduced me to wireman Jerry Nauss and knows WWII history like few others. Relatives of Big Red One soldiers greatly assisted in telling this story. Jed Wyman, Willard Wyman's grandson, sent me Wyman's diary and photographs. Colonel Mike Corley USA Retired, also shared photos and ideas with me. In addition he conducted interviews of his father, Brigadier General John T. Corley, and Colonel Thomas Gendron. These are in the McCormick Research Center. Colonel Bill Ridley told me the story of his uncle, Staff Sergeant William A Becker, 18th Infantry, who was killed in action while leading his squad on 9 June 1944. Jill Moretto, the daughter of Rocky Moretto who served with the 26th Infantry, shared photos of Rocky and those with whom he served.

When I had questions on WWII equipment that my references failed to answer, I turned to Major John Donovan USA Retired. If John did not readily know the answer, he soon found it and never failed to provide supporting documentation. Colonel Bennett Dickson USA Retired helped me validate footnotes.

The University of Missouri Press has a wonderful team with whom it is a pleasure to work. They have been patient and always supportive. Mary Conley made sure the manuscript was ready for layout. Drew Griffith, as always, did a brilliant job with layout, including awkward maps. David Rosenbaum produced a great cover. Andrew Davidson read every page and provided useful advice. He is, however, profligate in the use of commas. Miranda Ottewell edited the manuscript and saved me from myself in several instances.

Finally, my old friend and critic Dr. Richard M. Swain Colonel USA Retired and the author of *"Lucky War": Third Army in Desert Storm*, read every page and offered cogent criticism and good advice. Thanks, Rick.

Any errors in fact are entirely my own, made despite the great efforts of all those who sought to help.

NO SACRIFICE TOO GREAT

Introduction

THIS BOOK IS based on a simple proposition: that the US 1st Infantry Division (ID), familiarly known as the Big Red One, adapted to dynamic battlefield conditions throughout the course of its employment during World War II by innovating and altering behavior including tactics, techniques, and procedures. The evidence shows that the division's leaders and soldiers did this by considering their experiences in combat critically and putting lessons learned to good use. Simply put, they learned on the job—including while in combat, in battle after battle—and did so quickly. For those in the 1st ID, learning, training, and adaptation were continuous processes because they had to be. Terrain, weather, and the enemy changed as the division fought its way through North Africa, Sicily, France, Belgium, Germany, and finally Czechoslovakia. Equally important constraints imposed by manpower shortages (some of them critical), structural changes, and even weapons capabilities required continual adjustment. In order to meet the challenges of a dynamic and deadly environment, the Big Red One's leaders at all levels, and soldiers from rifleman to clerk, had to learn and change.

It is common to read in histories of World War II that one unit or another was a veteran one and therefore particularly good. The 1st ID is one such storied unit, and with good reason. That said, the degree to which it was an effective unit and what underlay its success bears critical examination. The Division deployed overseas in August 1942. By May 8, 1945, the Big Red One "had served 443 days in combat" in nine discrete campaigns, with some 21,023 of its soldiers killed, wounded, or gone missing, so that the Army having had to provide it 28,892 replacements. To add to this turbulence, those not killed, wounded, or missing often moved on because they were promoted, reassigned to other units, or for one reason or another changed "jobs."[1]

In other words, the 1st ID may have been a veteran division in the sense of duration and even excellence in combat, but in every battle its ranks included a number of soldiers facing combat for the first time. Assimilating replacements required providing them adequate training, or at least attempting to do so. That was done both formally in a "division" school and informally in the field by the old hands. At the war's outset and throughout its duration, newly assigned officers, sergeants, and privates all had to learn their jobs and grow more effective at them over time. And those who managed to do so found they had to accept increased responsibility. Some privates rose to become senior sergeants and/or accepted commissions as officers. Some young officers began the war leading platoons and ended it commanding battalions. Older officers rose from battalion command to regimental command, or by the end of hostilities found themselves in general officer ranks.

The stories of how all of these men learned their jobs and how squads, platoons, companies, battalions, regiments, and the 1st Division operated will affirm or deny the central proposition herein. Mine is of course not the first effort to explore how the US Army learned and improved in World War II combat. Michael Doubler's *Closing with the Enemy: How GIs Fought the War in Europe, 1944–1945*, Peter R. Mansoor's *The GI Offensive in Europe: The Triumph of the American Infantry Divisions, 1941–1945*, and other works address the growth of the US Army. This work builds on those studies and others, including John Sloan Brown's *Draftee Division: The 88th Infantry Division in World War II*. What differentiates this effort from earlier contributions is explicit study of just how units and soldiers kept pace with the dynamic and usually dystopian conditions they confronted.

How the US Army writ large planned to wage war, including structure, doctrine, equipping, and training, provides context to the Big Red One's actions. The first two chapters consider the context of the interwar period, the strategic choices the Army made, tactical concepts, the organization of units, and methods to sustain the force. The second chapter focuses on how the army prepared the Big Red One for employment. During this period the army's convention for naming divisions changed from numbers only to number and type of division; thus the 1st Division became the 1st Infantry Division. In July and August 1942, the 1st ID deployed to the United Kingdom to complete its preparation for employment in combat operations.

The chapters that follow cover the 1st Infantry Division's combat operations from North Africa to Czechoslovakia. To the extent possible, I followed the chapter organization of the Society of the First Division's narrative history *Danger Forward* (1947). Like *Danger Forward*, this narrative unfolds in fourteen chapters covering the division's three assault landings in Algeria, Sicily, and most famously Omaha Beach in Normandy. The battle to encircle Aachen and then seize it warrants two chapters. Of the fighting in the Hürtgen Forest, journalist Cy Peterman, one of the collaborators in *Danger Forward*, wrote that "the Forest may whisper of death and carnage, and the 'green hell' in World War II." The Hürtgen Forest merits its own chapter, as does the Ardennes or Battle of the Bulge. Other chapters cover less famous but equally important combat in Tunisia and at Saint-Lô and Mortain, and Bonn and Remagen. The fourteenth chapter covers the march across Germany from the Harz Mountains to Czechoslovakia in the last month of the war. The last chapter offers conclusions.[2]

The history of the US Army's performance in World War II is spotty. It suffered a humiliating defeat at the Kasserine Pass. Some units struggled when they took to the field for the first time. The 106th ID famously lost two regiments in the Schnee Eifel. Self-aggrandizing memoirs and partisan accounts of the war established a tone of criticism that was not always well founded. Omar N. Bradley's *A Soldier's Story*, published in 1951, and Bernard Law Montgomery's *Memoirs,* published in 1958, are just two of a host of postwar memoirs that began an often contentious debate between two close allies. These and other accounts included recrimination and, in some cases, overstated criticism of the US Army. Of the early postwar histories, Chester Wilmot's *The Struggle for Europe* (1947) was among the first to appear and arguably the best balanced, and to this day remains one of the very best histories of the war in Europe. Wilmot found reasons to criticize the army, but did so in a way that accounted for the growth of the force during the conflict.[3]

For a time, historians and pundits opined that the US Army was not very good and played second fiddle to the vast Soviet armies. That reasoning includes an argument that one can largely attribute the victory of the Allies in the west to sheer numbers, the supposedly better but outnumbered German troops finally giving in to exhaustion. In any case, historians often disparaged the performance of each other's national armies. An example follows.

In March 1994, as the fiftieth anniversary of D-Day approached, the Cantigny First Division Foundation and the US Naval Institute sponsored a conference of eminent historians from several countries and two wartime participants—Brigadier General James L. Collins Jr. USA Retired, nephew of "Lighting Joe" Collins and one time *Stars and Stripes* correspondent Andy Rooney. More than once during the presentations, historians traded barbs. Stephen E. Ambrose, an unabashed advocate of the excellence of the US Army's troops, had terse exchanges with British historian H. P. Wilmott. In a paper delivered at the conference, Wilmott described one of Ambrose's assertions about the US Army's best being as good as the German Army's best as a "chauvinistic claptrap," because it insulted the Canadian forces performance against the 12th SS by comparison. Ambrose made no such comparison, but Wilmott's inference was not entirely without merit. He then went on to do just what he had accused Ambrose of doing by pointing out the US Army's struggles to break out of the bocage while comparing the GIs unfavorably to British Tommies.[4]

Examples of similar if less nasty exchanges can still be found. Thus to some extent this book is part of the corrective that illustrates the growth of the US Army from a very small force that often struggled early in the war to a much larger and highly effective one by the end of the war. Some of the eighty-nine divisions the US Army raised and deployed overseas were more famous than others, but every one of them contributed to its victory. This, then, is part of their story.

Notes

1. Wheeler, *The Big Red One*, 381–82.
2. Knickerbocker et al., *Danger Forward*, table of contents. The title comes from the code name for the 1st ID's forward command post. Code names normally were used in telephone communications. All 1st ID units' code names began with a *D*; thus the division artillery was called "Drumfire," the 16th Infantry was "Dagwood," and so forth. *Danger Forward* is a remarkable book published by a committee of veterans and journalists who served with the division at various points during the war. Knickerbocker, the chief editor, reported for the *New York Evening Post* and the *Philadelphia Ledger*. Hanson Baldwin wrote the introduction to *Danger Forward*, and Drew Middleton wrote its last section.
3. Bradley, *Soldier's Story*; Montgomery, *Memoirs*.
4. Weingartner, *Greatest Thing*, 181–82, 188–89.

CHAPTER ONE

Sidewalks of New York

As Human beings and raw material, they're the very best. . . . But they need a deal of training.

—French Army veteran,
speaking of the 16th Infantry, July 4, 1917

T HE 1ST DIVISION was the first of forty-five divisions the United States raised and trained between June 1917 and the armistice in November 1918. Forty-two of them deployed to France. More than two million soldiers manned those divisions, nine corps, and the services of supply. First over, the 1st Division was also the last to leave. On December 13, 1918, the division crossed the Rhine River and, with other American and Allied troops, began a tour of occupation near Koblenz. Nine months later, in mid-August, it headed home, arriving in New York Harbor on September 8, 1919. Subsequently the Big Red One, so named for its red shoulder patch, participated in national victory parades in New York and Washington. After the parades, the 1st Division demobilized the bulk of its troops at Camp Meade, Maryland.[1]

The experience of the 1st Division is illustrative of the state of the US Army during the period now described as the "interwar years." Few anticipated another world war on an even more monumental scale than what was then called the Great War (at the time, of course, no one thought of it as World War I). The scale and scope of World War II forced the United States and its army to operate or fight on every continent but Antarctica. To describe the state of the US Army as woeful in 1939 is too generous a description of its state of training and equipment. The story of the years following the victory parades is necessary to understand the experience of the 1st Division and those who served in it, as they emerged twenty years later to become one of the premier US combat divisions.

Following the armistice, the United States unburdened itself of this large army with breathtaking speed. In less than a year, the US Army discharged 2,608,218 soldiers and 128,436 officers. By January 1, 1920, only 130,000 soldiers remained on duty. Finally, the army bottomed out at 125,000 in 1925. In June 1920 Congress passed the National Defense Act. In the succeeding twenty years the army never reached 220,000, let alone the 280,000 imagined when Congress passed the act. Nor did the National Guard ever achieve more than half of its planned strength of 435,000. The Organized Reserve Corps, planned at 100,000, remained undermanned but provided the shell for mobilization and a training ground for would-be officers.[2]

For various reasons, Congress never funded the US Army in accordance with its expressed intention in the National Defense Act. Nevertheless the act achieved several important outcomes. It established in law three components of the army, including the regulars, the guard, and the Organized Reserve. It solidified the position of the guard by creating a militia bureau run by a National Guard soldier. The law enshrined another goal of the National Guard Association in the wake of the Spanish-American War, when regulars had reduced the National Guard's role through the artifice of raising US volunteers, by assuring that the guard would henceforth comprise both state militia and a reserve component of the regular army, thus preventing the regulars from going to war without it. The act also established the Air Service, originally a part of the Signal Corps, as a separate branch of the US Army, allowing it to compete for resources, develop concepts, and acquire aircraft on an equal footing with the other army branches.[3]

To improve the ground forces' training and readiness, the act eliminated the old administrative departments and replaced them with three field armies and nine army corps areas. Each of the nine army corps areas would have a regular US Army division, two National Guard divisions, and three Organized Reserve divisions, which streamlined training by associating regular army formations with divisions from the other two components. Theoretically this would improve readiness and preclude having to improvise divisions, corps, and field armies as the nation had done during the Great War. In 1932 the War Department created a fourth field army headquarters, though Congress failed to fund the army to support three, let alone four, field army headquarters. As late as 1936 the nine corps and the field army headquarters remained undermanned.[4]

Perhaps most importantly, the National Defense Act of 1920 provided for a "General Staff," supporting the broad powers conferred on the chief of staff to plan everything from recruiting to mobilization reporting to the secretary of war. This streamlined processes within the army and eliminated the cumbersome system of bureaus that had preceded it. The act also reaffirmed the principles of military officer training under the Reserve Officers' Training Corps (ROTC) as originally provided for in the Morrill Act of 1862. Section 47d provided for training camps both for reservists and civilians. The law provided for combat arms including infantry, cavalry, artillery, and coast artillery and affirmed two service arms, the Corps of Engineers and the Signal Corps, and number of largely administrative departments ranging from the Adjutant General's Department to the Ordnance Department. The act also created two new services, the Chemical Warfare Service and the Air Service, the latter on par with the combat arms branches, though not so identified. These provisions empowered the "branches" to administer their organizations and to procure and distribute equipment.[5]

In his seminal *History of the United States Army,* Russell E. Weigley reported that no less a personage than General of the Armies John J. Pershing "allowed himself unwonted expressions of enthusiasm for the National Defense Act." The new law, Pershing believed, "simply provides that our traditional citizen army be organized in time of peace instead of extemporized, as in the past, after danger had actually come."[6] Although Congress failed consistently to fund the army as authorized, the act enabled it to develop new concepts, doctrine, structure, and weapons during the lean years of the 1920s and '30s. This legislation provided the capability to mobilize rapidly. Finally, it provided the legal basis for the US Army until superseded by the National Defense Act of 1947.

Concepts, Doctrine and Structure

The US Army lacked sufficient funds to maintain readiness, let alone modernize, after the Great War. That did not prevent its leadership from attempting to learn from the institutional experience gained, and to consider how to fight in the future. Led by several effective chiefs of staff, the army developed concepts for modernizing the force, its structure, and its doctrine. General Peyton C. March, General of the Armies John J. Pershing, Major General John L. Hines, General Charles P. Summerall, General Douglas MacArthur, and General Malin Craig preceded George C. Marshall as the chief of staff. Their efforts, and those of the chiefs of the various branches and services, established the baseline that would support Marshall and the War Department at the outset of World War II. The National Defense Act of 1920, institutional decisions taken in the army before Marshall became chief of staff, and those made soon after would affect how the army fought that war.

Much of the army's work to anticipate modern warfare came from branches, departments, and services. These entities developed concepts, wrote doctrine, and recommended structure more or less independently. In 1923 the War Department published *Field Service Regulations 1923*, outlining how the army would organize for combat and how it would fight. That manual reflected early postwar thinking about the future but also retained concepts already in place to wage the Great War. *Field Service Regulations 1923* would remain in effect until the publication on May 22, 1941, of Field Manual (FM) 100-5, *Field Service Regulations, Operations*, which was informed by early assessments of the war in Europe.[7]

Each of the combat arms, departments, and services produced doctrine that reflected its estimate of the future and how it proposed to fight. The quality of the resulting field manuals varied, but they shared some basic notions. FM 100-5 highlighted two of these: the decisive quality of leadership, and the importance of initiative. Leadership on the modern battlefield would prove essential. Leaders had to understand the effect of "dispersion of troops in battle," a significant change from the environment of trench warfare, and be "cool thoughtful leaders with a strong feeling of the great responsibility imposed upon them." It followed logically that troops were "strongly influenced by the example and conduct of their leaders." The manual's authors believed that despite obvious advances in technology, the "worth of the individual man [was] still decisive." To take advantage of this fact, each man would "depend upon his initiative and action." The principles of leadership and initiative were consistent across the various branch manuals. The infantry battalion manual claimed that effective leadership stemmed from the "salient American characteristics of courage, self-reliance, initiative and vigor." However imperfect in execution, the US Army's basic doctrine reflected a belief in the value of the citizen soldier that extended back to the Revolution.[8]

The efficacy of "combined arms" is an important theme in the army's primary war fighting manual; in 1941 FM 100-5 stipulated that the "combat value of the infantry division derives from its ability to combine the action of the various arms and services." But the notion of combined arms is not followed up explicitly in the infantry's field manuals. This may be because infantry units already included important components of combined arms, including an antitank company and a cannon company at regimental level, as well as mortars and machine guns at battalion and company level. The field manuals of the branches, all written in parallel, reflect an intent to fight with combined arms but lack detail. FM 7-40, *Rifle Regiment*, discusses the formation of combat teams at regimental level by "grouping the regiment with artillery and other arms." Elsewhere the manual asserts that the "plan of fire support provides for effective cooperation" between the troops and supporting arms. Maybe the plan of fire support did just that, or did not, but the intention was to incorporate air, artillery, and even chemicals in support of ground troops. However, FM 7-40 offers little information about how to combine effects with tanks—less than half a page, to be precise—and none at all on how to employ tank destroyers. Some facets of combined arms operations would have to be developed in combat.[9]

The army produced a vast body of doctrine, ranging from prescriptive technical manuals as mundane as TM 20-205, *Dictionary of United States Army Terms*, to far more descriptive field manuals covering platoon tactical operations of the various branches. To grow an army of a few hundred thousand to one of millions required the means both to teach cognitive skills and train on basic tasks. Firing a weapon is one thing, but bringing to bear the effects of many weapons, dispersed across a lethal battle space, is quite another, and requires both training and education. Manuals devoted to small units, from platoon to battalion, included illustrations intended to help officers and noncommissioned officers grasp how a tactical evolution might look before trying it out on their units. Those writing these manuals had to take into account a "greatly expanded Army in which relatively few are familiar with the military vernacular," and write manuals "in clear, everyday language, with an emphasis on brevity and the use of illustrations."[10]

The Armored Force in particular used cartoonlike illustrations to show young officers, their sergeants, and soldiers just what "right" looked like. Lieutenant Colonel James C. Crockett modeled FM 17-30, *Tank Platoon*, on a German armor manual revised on the basis of "NAZI experiences in Germany," and the Armored Force followed his example for its company and battalion manuals as well. The other branches also liberally illustrated their manuals. FM 7-5, *Organization and Tactics of Infantry: The Rifle Battalion*, published in 1940, is as well illustrated as the Armored Force manuals. Several iterations of FM 7-5 succeeded the original as the army learned, as the Germans had in France, from experience in combat. The army, and for that matter the other services, also enlisted the support and methods of Hollywood to produce a large body of training films.[11]

Few soldiers wrote home extolling the clarity of the manuals, or the quality of their illustrations. But many read the manuals appropriate to their military specialty or were trained in the techniques described. In the months following the end of the war in Europe, US Forces European Theater convened a series of boards to publish studies under the rubric of the General Board. References to the utility of doctrine abound in these reports. Board members examined everything from ammunition consumption to tank gunnery, but they also studied how the army proposed to fight in the context of how it did fight to learn whether the doctrine and organizations built by the army worked effectively and as designed. General George S. Patton was the senior officer of the board that convened to put together General Board Study No. 3, *Organization, Equipment and Tactical Employment of the Infantry Division*, organizing it around the operational doctrine as envisaged in FM 100-5, as well as the doctrine pertinent to the division and its supporting arms.[12]

In *America's School for War: Fort Leavenworth, Officer Education and Victory in World War II*, Peter J. Schifferle argues convincingly that there was broad consensus on the requirements of future combat, but that is not to say there were no gaps between the branches. Indeed, there were critical gaps. There are two important examples. First, both the Armored Force and the infantry failed to develop combined arms tactics for tank-infantry operations. Equally significantly, the army failed to develop sufficient means to integrate air and ground operations because the Army Air Corps did not consider support of ground operations as important as its vision for strategic bombing.[13] It is fair to say that FM 100-5 did not adequately describe effective combined arms operations in 1941. The resolution of divergence among the branches would have to be resolved in combat.

The Context of Combined Arms Formations

The National Defense Act of 1920 assigned tanks to the infantry, an idea enshrined in *Field Service Regulations 1923* in accordance with the intent of the Congress. Doing so did not prevent the cavalry from experimenting with mechanization and tanks, although to avoid legal criticism they called their tanks combat cars. The Europeans, the Soviet Union, Japan, and others were fielding motorized and some mechanized formations that included tanks as their striking arm. The distinction, made at the time, between motorized and mechanized formations was simple. Motorized formations relied primarily on wheeled vehicles, while mechanized formations included tracked or half-tracked vehicles. Over time the distinction became less relevant.

The infantry perceived tanks exclusively as infantry support weapons, a view broadcast in the current *Field Service Regulations*: "The tank constitutes an armored infantry element. . . . Its essential mission is to assist in the progression of the infantry by overcoming or neutralizing resistances or breaking down obstacles that check the infantry advance." The cavalry's views on how to employ armor, and therefore what kind of tanks should be built, differed. Cavalrymen thought of tanks and armored units as an extension of traditional cavalry missions, but most importantly as a means to exploit success. Armored units, in their view, could operate independently with their own "armored infantry." Both perspectives reflected branch biases about future combat, and both had merit.[14] Thus thinking about mechanizing proceeded on two lines, and in the end, these differing perspectives affected combat operations.

During the Great War the US Army embraced mechanization and remained, with some exceptions, enthusiastic about exploiting it. In 1919 it undertook a well-publicized transcontinental convoy. According to Dwight D. Eisenhower, who participated as an observer from the tank corps, the convoy "would dramatize the need for better main highways"; furthermore, "the use of Army vehicles of almost all types would offer an opportunity for comparative tests." The convoy included a Great War light tank perched on a flatbed truck, enabling Americans along the route to see a tank for the first time. *Field Service Regulations 1923* devoted a chapter to movement generally, and a section exclusively to "Movements by Motor."[15]

Another step toward mechanization occurred in 1931, when the cavalry assigned its mechanized detachment to the 1st Cavalry Regiment with duty at Camp Knox, Kentucky. The rest of the 1st Cavalry remained at Fort Russell near the town of Marfa in West Texas, where it replaced its horses with vehicles. Later that year the War Department ordered the activation of the 7th Cavalry Brigade (Mechanized) at the newly renamed "Fort" Knox, Kentucky. In 1933 General Douglas MacArthur, then serving as chief of staff, moved to increase mechanization in the army and specifically to "motorize" half of the artillery. That same year the 1st Cavalry Regiment (Mechanized) convoyed 1,400 miles to Fort Knox to join the 7th Cavalry Brigade. Despite MacArthur's initiative, the lack of money forced the army and the artillery to mechanize incrementally. Still, by 1940 roughly 75 percent of the artillery was towed by trucks rather than horses. Equally important, the 7th Cavalry Brigade had the means to experiment with mechanized forces at scale.[16]

The cavalry's view won the day on July 10, 1940, when General Marshall established the Armored Force with Adna R. Chaffee, a cavalryman, in charge. First involved in mechanization efforts in 1931, Chaffee had commanded the experimental 7th Cavalry Brigade. From the outset Chaffee and his cavalry colleagues, including George S. Patton Jr., wanted a highly mobile force, light on its feet, and as a consequence light in armor. Patton was a charter member of the tank corps, which was subsumed into the infantry after the Great War. Patton commanded the sole US tank brigade at Saint-Mihiel and the Meuse-Argonne in September 1918. Martin Blumenson, who edited Patton's papers, noted that "because of Patton's influence, most of the early models [of tanks] were light tanks." Patton reprised his Great War influence in the new armored force when he assumed command of the 2nd Armored Division at Fort Benning, Georgia, in July 1940.[17]

Under Chaffee's direction the Armored Force developed armored divisions equipped and organized to exploit infantry penetration of enemy defenses, and built both light and medium tanks in accordance with its basic doctrine: that armored divisions' *"primary role is in offensive operations against hostile rear areas* [italics in the original]." The armored divisions that evolved from this concept proved agile and quick, but by the time US forces entered the war in North Africa, their tanks were outgunned by many of their German adversary's.[18]

The cavalry concept for the Armored Force ensured that US tanks were built not to fight other tanks but instead to attack soft targets in "hostile rear areas," or support infantry by direct fire against targets such as enemy "pillboxes" or fieldworks. Consequently the army, and infantry in particular, needed antitank weapons and organizations designed to fight enemy tanks. By the late 1930s the army included antitank units in the structure of divisions. In November 1941 it rationalized antitank units by withdrawing them from the various branches, in essence forming a new branch with the creation of the Tank Destroyer Tactical and Firing Center at Fort Meade, Maryland. General Lesley J. McNair, who commanded the General Headquarters of the Army (later the Army Ground Forces), played the decisive role in the design of the ground forces. McNair made the case for the tank destroyer in dollars and cents: "Certainly it is poor economy to use a $35,000 medium tank to destroy another when the job can be done by a gun costing a fraction as much." A combination of towed and self-propelled tank destroyer systems emerged as a result.[19]

Redesign of the infantry division, "the basis of the organization of field forces," was another important initiative undertaken during the lean years following the Great War. The square division, composed of two brigades of two regiments each, designed for trench warfare, proved too unwieldy for the warfare of the end of that war, characterized by rapid movement and maneuvering. It certainly was too large and unwieldy for the warfare the US Army imagined in the future, which favored smaller divisions. In late 1939, after the German conquest of Poland, several divisions, including the 1st, reorganized into three regiments, with no intervening brigade echelon between the regiments and their division headquarters. Following experimentation with this "triangular" organization, the army began shifting to that design in 1940. Although the infantry divisions did not fully mechanize, they were far more mobile than the infantry divisions in other armies. More importantly, they could be motorized by the simple expedient of attaching truck companies from higher-echelon formations.[20]

The field artillery also enjoyed the benefit of mechanization and motorization. But the artillery benefited from a second important initiative that improved its capability to mass fires, and shift them as necessary. Traditionally battery commanders owned the fires systems and directed fires in response to their own observers. In order to mass fires, forward observers provided target coordinates to their battery. Then each battery attempted to adjust on the target simultaneously, or nearly so. This resulted in the simultaneous impact of rounds from multiple batteries, making it very difficult to adjust fire. Massing effects, even after registering targets, took time—lots of it. Decentralized fire direction also assured minimal flexibility or agility in shifting fires unless it was planned well in advance. The solution came only after bitter opposition with conservatives in the branch. Lieutenant Colonel H. L. C. Jones, who became director of the gunnery department at the US Army Field Artillery School at Fort Sill, Oklahoma, in 1939, developed a battalion fire direction center and "centralized computation for observed and unobserved fire at the fire direction center." It would take nearly two more years to convince the chief of artillery of the efficacy of centralized battalion fire direction, which concentrated their batteries' fires in front of their supported infantry regiments. Dramatically improved wire and radio communications further enhanced performance, as did aerial observers flying light aircraft organic to artillery battalions.[21]

The artillery also streamlined support relationships by defining support missions. These included direct support—artillery dedicated to a specific unit, such as an infantry regiment; general support, designed to support all of the subordinate units of a formation; and reinforcing support, giving a higher-level battalion the mission to respond to calls for fire from divisional artillery units. The division artillery commander positioned artillery and managed fires, often supported by additional elements of corps and field army artillery. Corps artillery units generally took responsibility for counterbattery programs and preparation fires for major attacks. Effective communications and discrete missions of direct support, general support, or reinforcing fires enabled American artillery to quickly mass the fires of any number of battalions within the range of a target. The artillery could also shift fires just as rapidly, with devastating effect on the enemy. In the coming war, the army would use its artillery effectively and relentlessly.[22] Cannon battalions were never in reserve.

Contrary to myth, the US Army Air Service considered the future with the full support of succeeding chiefs of staff. In 1926 Congress elevated the Air Service to the US Army Air Corps, subordinate to the War Department in the same way that the Marine Corps was subordinate to the Navy. Army airmen were convinced that the United States required an independent air force, and that airpower would prove decisive in the next war. Italian airpower theorist Giulio Douhet's concepts dominated thinking among the airmen, leading them to focus on strategic bombing of enemy cities and factories as the key to winning the next war. That sharply drawn focus produced a concept for bombers: the Flying Fortress. These aircraft would be able to fly unescorted deep into enemy territory to carry out strategic bombing. The Air Corps' basic doctrinal manual clearly articulated its thinking in 1931, when it concluded, "Bombardment Aviation . . . is the basic arm of the Air Force." Ultimately this concept led to the acquisition of the B-17, B-24, B-29, and their postwar successors, down to the present-day bombers flown by the US Air Force. This focus had serious implications for supporting the army's ground forces.[23] In June 1941 the Air Corps was designated the US Army Air Force, led by General Henry A. Arnold as chief of air forces and deputy chief of staff for air, all but completing the transformation of the air arm into a separate service.

Professional Military Education

Effective education and training has proved essential to the American military experience as far back as Baron Friedrich Wilhelm von Steuben's effort to train Washington's Continentals. Everything about American history militates against large standing professional armies. Hastily raised forces, demobilized equally quickly, characterized the American military experience until the Cold War. After the Armistice in 1918 there was impetus to learn from that experience, as well as a short-lived but important discussion of creating a nation in arms on the Swiss model. In the National Defense Act, Congress affirmed its commitment to civilian military training and to creating the conditions for improved training of regular and reserve forces. Mobilizing a large army for war clearly required planning and education for that eventuality.[24]

The US Army also sought to learn from the bloody effort of the Great War. After all, there was much to learn. That war saw the first large-scale use of wireless communications in tactical command and control; of chemical warfare; of combat aviation, including strategic bombing; and of machine guns and tanks. For the first time the United States projected combat power in a major way onto another continent. Soldiers and sailors debated what should be learned, and what the character of war in the future might be. Learning resulted informally and within the institutional army at various army schools. Training for units and individual soldiers suffered because the army lacked adequate resources, but the schools served to narrow the gap in officer training and education.

The army had two "top level" schools: the Army War College, dating from 1901, and the Army Industrial College, established in 1924, which focused on "industrial mobilization problems." The Command and General Staff College, founded in 1881 as the School of Application, provided the next tier. Below that were the branch schools. The Infantry School is perhaps the best known of these for its renaissance in the 1920s, and the Command and General Staff College is the most relevant to this study.

The Command and General Staff College, and for that matter most of these schools, used the "applicatory method," combining theory and practice using large group lectures and smaller group conferences, supplemented by war games on maps and staff rides. Fort Leavenworth is perched on the palisades of the Missouri River and bounded to the west by rolling hills left by receding ice age glaciers. So ubiquitous were the instructional staff rides across this landscape of farms and small towns from the nineteenth century to the contemporary era that the names of some of these small Kansas towns made their way into doctrinal examples.

During the years after the Great War, course length at the college varied between one and two years but remained focused consistently on the operations of higher echelons, particularly division and corps. Learning to think and operate at higher echelons could be taught, and was, with reasonable success, though, as Dr. Peter J. Schifferle points out, Leavenworth failed in three important areas: planning and execution of mobilization, logistics, and airpower. Despite these shortcomings, Leavenworth graduates performed superbly in combat, and were praised by no less an authority than Field Marshal Gerd von Rundstedt. In a letter to President Truman, Secretary of

War Henry L. Stimson paraphrased a comment Rundstedt made to one of his captors, expressing surprise at the competence of US Corps commanders: "We could understand it if you had produced one superior corps commander, but now we find all of your corps commanders good and of equal superiority." The 1925 annual report of the General Service Schools at Fort Leavenworth provides a snapshot of officers who either taught at or were taught there. A cursory glance at the list of instructors, honor graduates, and distinguished graduates reveals the names of one army group commander, four field army commanders, two army corps commanders, and Marine Corps general Roy S. Geiger, who commanded an amphibious corps in the Pacific, and then Tenth Army, following the death of General Simon B. Buckner on Okinawa.[25]

The Infantry School at Fort Benning, Georgia, like the other service schools, played a vital role in preparing officers to lead in combat. It thrived in the years following the Great War, in part because of two particular officers. Lieutenant Colonel Frank Cocheu, who ran the school from 1925 to 1927, brought the concept of "demonstration—explanation—performance," a version of the applicatory method suited to teaching smaller unit operations ranging from company to regiment. Infantry officer students had to be able to explain what they had seen demonstrated, then be able to do it. George C. Marshall, who led the Infantry School from 1927 to 1932, reorganized the school and staffed it with first-rate instructors. These included Joseph W. Stilwell, who later served as chief of staff to the Chinese Nationalist forces and commanded first two Chinese field armies in the China-Burma-India theater and later Army Ground Forces Headquarters and Tenth Army in Okinawa, following the Japanese surrender on the island; Omar N. Bradley, who commanded two divisions in training, II Corps in Tunisia and Sicily, First Army and 12th Army Group in Europe; and J. Lawton Collins, who commanded the 25th ID at Guadalcanal and VII Corps from Normandy until after the end of the war.[26] Marshall aimed to produce flexible soldiers who could adapt rapidly to dynamic conditions. He did so in part by creating chaos and confusion. Often he ramped up the pressure on students by removing maps or critical information, and watched to see who still moved ahead to decision and who did not.

Under Marshall's auspices, in 1934 the Military History and Publications Section of the Infantry School published *Infantry in Battle*, which examined combat on the western front from the perspectives of the Allies and Germans, with an emphasis on the combat experiences of the American Expeditionary Force. This little book's first sentence establishes clearly its intention and reflects Marshall's view of combat: "The Art of War has no traffic with rules, for the infinitely varied circumstances and conditions of combat never produce exactly the same situation twice."[27]

Although the experience of officers in the school system varied, tracing the experience of one 1st Division officer through the system is of interest here. Norman D. "Dutch" Cota served in the 1st Division from November 1940 to January 1943 as executive officer of the 16th Infantry, assistant G-3 [operations officer], and chief of staff. After his promotion to brigadier general, Cota served as deputy commanding general of the 29th ID during its final preparation for the invasion of Normandy. On D-Day he landed on Omaha Beach about an hour after the first assault craft made it in. In large measure, the 116th Infantry got off Omaha Beach because Dutch Cota led them off the beach. He took command of the 28th Infantry Division on 14 August 1944, and led it through the rest of the war. He started his progress through the school system when he attended the company officers' course at Fort Benning from 1924 to 1925.[28]

Cota graduated the company officer's course just before Cocheu took over, and returned to take the advanced course in in 1928 with Marshall in charge. He thrived in the chaos Marshall savored and graduated first in his class, consequently going immediately to the Command and General Staff College. There he joined the first two-year iteration of the newly expanded course. The school system was not perfect, but it produced officers able to scale up rapidly from running small units to leading and maneuvering large units against formidable enemies around the globe.[29]

Sunset of the Old Army

The 1st Division's return from Europe, and the brief celebration the troops enjoyed, passed into memory quickly. After demobilizing most of its troops at Camp Meade, the division moved to Camp Zachary Taylor in Louisville, Kentucky. In August 1920 it moved again, this time to Camp Dix, New Jersey, to serve as the II Corps Area (New York, New Jersey, and Delaware) regular army division in accordance with the National Defense Act of 1920. There it aligned with the 27th Division of the New York National Guard, the 44th Division, composed of units from Delaware, New Jersey, and New York, and three Organized Reserve divisions, the 77th, 78th, and 98th, composed of units from the same three states.[30]

In 1922 the 1st Division relocated from the dilapidated temporary buildings at Camp Dix to small posts across the state of New York. In these posts, most of which dated to the early nineteenth Century, the Big Red One served for nearly twenty years. Life moved slowly, punctuated by buglers awakening the troops, calling them to various activities during the day, serenading them in the evening with tattoo, and putting them to bed with taps. The division had two infantry brigades, the 1st and 2nd. The 1st Brigade's two regiments (16th Infantry and 18th Infantry), and the division headquarters, occupied small posts in New York City. These included Forts Hamilton, Jay, Wadsworth, Schuyler, and Slocum. The 2nd Brigade was posted at Madison Barracks on Lake Ontario, adjacent to Sackets Harbor. Its commanders found it difficult to command, let alone control, the brigade's two infantry regiments, the 26th and 28th. The 26th Infantry, at Plattsburg Barracks in the extreme northeast of New York State, was some 150 miles away; the 28th Infantry, at Fort Niagara—a War of 1812 post across the Niagara River from an equally superfluous Canadian fort, whose buglers sounded their calls at different intervals than those of the Americans, irritating the 1st Division troops—was more than 200 miles away. The division headquarters shared Fort Hamilton with the 18th Infantry. Other units of the division composed the garrison at Camp Dix.[31]

Young men who joined the army during the Depression often did so as a means to an end—a paycheck. Often these men had little education and few opportunities at home. Some were illiterate, and a fair number had only grade school education. In 1940 Ralph Uffner joined a rifle company in the 26th Infantry as a second lieutenant. A year after Germany invaded Poland, the "old Army" had not faded away. Many of Uffner's soldiers had not completed grammar school. He also found quite a few long-service soldiers; the company first sergeant had been with the company since 1920. Thomas O. Beauchamp, a soldier in a different unit, who earned a Silver Star for valor on May 26, 1918, served with the Big Red One until he retired in 1955.[32]

Lieutenant Colonel Stanhope B. Mason joined the division in the spring of 1941, serving first as the operations officer, and later as chief of staff. Mason believed that "no other division had fared better during the period between the wars." By comparison to the other regular divisions, the Big Red One had remained more or less intact, with slightly more than half of its troops stationed in and around New York City. To Mason, "its recruits, its reserve officers, its public support had a definite stamp of Greater New York."[33]

A great many denizens of the city joined the 16th and 18th Infantry regiments during the Depression era. The ferry and the subway enabled New York soldiers to enjoy their city with the benefit of a paycheck, and the 16th came to be known as "subway soldiers." A. J. Liebling, one of the great reporters for the *New Yorker*, enjoyed his contact with the Big Red One in part because it "had many enlisted men from the sidewalks of the Bronx and Brooklyn," who spoke to him and around him with "a rich New York accent." In his recollection of the war, *The Road Back to Paris*, Liebling recounted an encounter he overheard between two New Yorkers serving in the Big Red One. These two soldiers spoke in the idiom he found comforting:

> "Give da passwoy," I once heard a 1st Division sentinel challenge.
> "Nobody told me nuttin," the challenged soldier replied.
> "What outfichas outuv?"
> "Foy Signals."
> "Whynchas get on da ball? Da passwoy is 'tatched roof.' "
> "What is it mean?"
> "How do I know? Whaddaya tink I yam, da Quiz Kids?"

New Yorkers abounded among the regulars in the 1st Division. The 16th Infantry commemorated its service in and its connection with New York City by adopting "Sidewalks of New York" as its regimental march.[34]

In a 1995 interview Thomas J. Gendron, who came from near Albany, recalled that he "went four summers in the Citizens Military Training Corps which was run by the 26th [Infantry] Regiment at its barracks in Plattsburg, New York. There I made some fine associations." Training for a commission, Gendron "fell in love with the Big Red One right away." He remembered being well treated by the old-timers even when he was a newly arrived rookie.[35]

Later famous as a Marine hero at Guadalcanal, for which he was awarded the Medal of Honor, "Manila John" Basilone, from Buffalo, was a first-generation Italian American who joined the 16th Infantry in 1934 and then served in Manila, the Philippines, with the 31st Infantry. Basilone left the army in 1937.[36] He enlisted in the Marine Corps in June 1940. In addition to the Medal of Honor, he was awarded the Navy Cross posthumously for heroism on Iwo Jima.

Like Basilone, Frank Beetle was one of many New Yorkers who enlisted in the 1st Division because it was his hometown unit. Born at St. Luke's Hospital at 115th and Amsterdam in New York City, he joined the 16th Infantry in October 1940. Though by then war clouds darkened the horizon, the army still trained as it had since 1919. Regiments trained their enlistees, with the result that training proved uneven. Beetle was unimpressed. In a 1998 interview he observed, "Well, needless to say, that it was a ragtag Army." The training lasted about three months mostly, "marching, doing short order drill, doing KP (kitchen police—washing dishes, cleaning grease traps, whatever had to be done) and all the rest of it." Training was unimpressive in part because "we didn't have enough equipment."[37] Beetle's recollection of his early service paralleled that of generations of young men who joined the army for a paycheck and a meal.

Gendron's positive experience training with the 26th Infantry and the Citizens' Military Training Corps (CMTC) was important to him. The CMTC training camps provided leadership and training opportunities for young officers and regular army noncommissioned officers. Paul Dickson argues in *The Rise of the GI Army, 1940–1941* that the Civilian Conservation Corps, organized in 1933, "became a driving force for improving the Army and facilitating the education and development" of officers. His argument is sound.[38]

CCC recruits provided the US Army a leadership laboratory that afforded officers and noncommissioned officers, and prepared the army for eventual mobilization. George C. Marshall, who would become chief of staff, believed the CCC to be "a splendid experience for the War Department and the Army." The 1st Division benefited both directly and indirectly. Major Alexander N. Starke Jr. won the first annual award for the best-run camp in the CCC. Stark commanded the 26th Infantry in North Africa, and then returned to the United States, where he was promoted to brigadier general.[39]

Whether they served in a CCC camp or in one of the small posts scattered around New York, young officers had similar experiences to those they led. Garrison life was not unlike what it had been in the nineteenth century. Lieutenant Charles Stone joined the 16th Infantry on July 1, 1937, at Fort Jay on Governor's Island in New York Harbor. Stone remembered that unit training proved difficult because there were so few troops on hand. It was "difficult to turn out more than fifty or sixty men [of about 200 authorized] for training on [a] given day so our training consisted primarily of classroom lectures and minor marching and small unit training on the parade ground and on the polo field." The 16th followed the routine practiced across the "old Army." Soldiers trained, more or less, in the morning and took the afternoons off for sports and/or housekeeping details. There were no ranges at Fort Jay, or for that matter at any of the posts in New York City, so units had to go elsewhere. According to Stone, the 16th did "rifle training and did our routine small unit training" at Camp Dix, New Jersey.[40]

Richard J. Lindo received a commission in June 1940 under the provisions of the Thomason Act, which permitted a limited number of reserve officers to serve for a year and selected fifty of them to accept regular army commissions. Nearly a year after the German invasion of Poland, and as France fell, the army continued on a peacetime footing. Lindo took great pride in becoming part of "the oldest and probably most famous outfit in the United States Army" when he joined D Battery of the 5th Field Artillery, at Madison Barracks. There, he recalled, "We wore our Smokey Bear hats, I carried a sabre at retreat parades, formal guard mounts and officer of the day." Along with seventeen other unmarried officers, Lindo "lived in bachelor officers' quarters with a very crusty old major, and for dinner at night we were required to wear a tuxedo or dress blues."[41]

Commissioned in 1940, Gendron noted that he was "fortunate, very fortunate" that when he applied for active duty, he was assigned to the 26th Infantry at Fort Benning, Georgia. On arriving he reported to the duty officer. That officer, John T. Corley, would become a lifelong friend. Gendron described his new friend as a "great Irish fighter, Brooklyn Irish," to be precise. Both served together until the fall of 1945. The sun had set on the "old Army."[42]

Notes

1. Wheeler, *The Big Red One*, 97–111. See also Coffman, *War to End All Wars*, 357. Coffman's book is the best single-volume history on the US war effort. For order of battle and units deployed, see Center of Military History, *Order of Battle*, 1:v, 2:445.

2. Wheeler, *The Big Red One,* 396, 599; Coffman, *War to End All Wars*, 357. Kreidberg and Henry, *History of Mobilization*, describes the various iterations of mobilization planning, ending with the Protective Mobilization Plan.

3. Weigley, *History*, 400–401; National Defense Act of 1920, Pub.L. 66–242, 41 Stat. 759, part 1. The act is fifty-six pages long, but unlike most contemporary legislation is readable, and well worth reading for those interested in the army as an institution. The legislation uses the terms *militia* and *National Guard* to distinguish between militia clauses of the Constitution and army clauses; active federal service is a National Guard function, whereas state service is technically a militia function, constitutionally. For field army headquarters funding, see Heller and Stofft, *America's First Battles*.

4. Weigley, *History*, 400; National Defense Act of 1920, sec. 3 and 3a, 759–60. The law is not as explicit regarding the number of units per corps area, but authorizes the president to determine these. The expressed intent of the Congress was to retain as many of the National Guard divisions "as practicable."

5. Weigley, *History*, 400. For chief of staff and General Staff, see National Defense Act of 2020, sec. 5, 762–64, sec. 47d, 779, and, for combat arms, etc., 765–71. Cline, *Washington Command Post*, 19–28, summarizes the act and the way the army and the secretary of war implemented it, including General Staff procedures.

6. Weigley, *History*, 400.

7. Chief of Staff, *Field Service Regulations 1923* (Washington, DC: Government Printing Office, 1923). See also War Department, FM 100-5, *Field Service Regulations: Operations* (Washington, DC: Government Printing Office, 1941).

8. War Department, FM 100-5; War Department, FM 7-5, *Organization and Tactics of Infantry: The Rifle Battalion* (Washington, DC: Government Printing Office, 1940), 4.

9. War Department, FM 100-5, 253; War Department, FM 7-40, *Rifle Regiment* (Washington, DC: Government Printing Office, 1942), 83, 100.

10. Keast, *Provision of Enlisted Replacements*, 194, 56.

11. Historical Section, Army Ground Forces, *Armored Force Command and Center*, 56. Manuals across the army used straightforward language and useful illustrations.

12. General Board, *Organization of the Infantry Division*, relies on doctrine and structure; see 1–8. Doctrine is mentioned throughout. Examples are readily apparent in General Board, *Organization of Separate Tank Battalions*, and General Board, *Study of Field Artillery Gunnery*.

13. Schifferle, *America's School for War*, ch. 2, "The Essence of Modern War." For consistency in doctrine, see 59–61. Schifferle's book is essential to understanding the value the US Army placed on education following the end of the Great War.

14. Chief of Staff, *Field Service Regulations 1923*, 13; Cameron, *Mobility, Shock, and Firepower*, ch. 5. Basil Liddell-Hart, J. F. C. Fuller, and Heinz Guderian are among advocates of mechanization, or "machine war," as Fuller described it. Fuller, *Machine War*, goes beyond the theory that he had considered in several earlier volumes to assess the German invasion and conquest of France and very brief introduction to Allied operations in North Africa. The distinction between motorized and mechanized is only important in that the US Army pooled fleets of trucks that could and did motorize infantry divisions.

15. Eisenhower, *At Ease*, 157. Major Sereno Brett accompanied Eisenhower as a second tank corps observer. When the tank corps folded, Eisenhower returned to the Infantry branch. Brett remained associated with mechanization; he was a charter member of the Armored Force and briefly commanded the 5th Armored Division. Medically retired, Brett did not deploy with the division. See also Chief of Staff, *Field Service Regulations 1923*, 66–67.

16. Cameron, *Mobility, Shock, and Firepower*, ch. 5.

17. Cameron, 35, 251–54; War Department, FM 17-100, *Armored Command Field Manual: The Armored Division* (Washington, DC: Government Printing Office, 1944), 2. Johnson, *Fast Tanks*, is the best study on the development of US Army armor concepts and the army air arm's fascination with strategic bombing. Both Dwight D. Eisenhower and George S. Patton Jr. had served with tanks during the Great War. During the interwar period both returned to their basic branches, infantry and cavalry respectively. Blumenson, *Patton Papers*, 9–10. In late summer 1940 Patton suggested to Eisenhower that he apply for a transfer to the Armored Force. Eisenhower apparently attempted to transfer without success. See Blumenson, 14–15. See also Daniel, *Patton*, 46–59.

18. War Department, FM 17-100, 2.

19. Gabel, *Seek, Strike, and Destroy*, 19.

20. Wheeler, *The Big Red One*, 129. Soon after World War I, the army reviewed the organization of the division. In the 1920s the army had tested a division structure of

three regiments, with no intervening brigade headquarters between the regiments and the division headquarters. Nothing came of the first tests. However, in 1936 the Army Modernization Board proposed a triangle division based on three infantry regiments. After continued study and revision, on September 14, 1939, the Modernization Board proposed a smaller version of the triangle division, which General Marshall, after further modification, approved. See also Wilson, *Maneuver and Firepower*, 125–23.

21. Dastrup, *King of Battle*, 196–99. Dastrup's work is indispensable to those interested in the development of field artillery and its employment in World War II.

22. On communications see Change 1, January 2, 1941 to War Department, FM 6-20, *Field Artillery Field Manual: Tactics and Technique* (Washington, DC: Government Printing Office, 1940). On aerial observation, see Dastrup, *King of Battle*, 206–8. Details on various support relationships are explained in chapter 3 of *Field Artillery Tactics and Technique*; see especially 69–74, 71.

23. Weigley, *History*, 411–13. It is no exaggeration to say that tension remains between the ground and air forces regarding how they can best support one another. See also Johnson, *Fast Tanks and Heavy Bombers*, 153. Johnson's critique of innovation in the US Army is excellent.

24. Colonel John MacCauley Palmer advocated for some form of universal military training; see Weigley, *History*, 395–400. As junior office Palmer served as a key advisor to Secretary of War Henry L. Stimson. He retired as a major general but remained associated with planning for mobilization throughout his career.

25. Schifferle, *America's School for War*, 193, 195.

26. Perret, *War to Be Won*, 10–16. Re teaching and working with Marshall, see Collins, *Lightning Joe*, 48–52. On Bradley and Stillwell at Benning, see Ossad, *Omar Nelson Bradley*, 67–74. On the effect of the school's system, see Gorman, *Secret of Future Victories*.

27. Harding, *Infantry in Battle*, 13.

28. Miller, *Division Commander*, 114. See chapter 4, "Life Between the Wars," 27–35, on assuming command of the 28th ID. Cota remained in command of the 28th ID until it was deactivated on 13 December 1945. Re Ridgway and Collins, see Miller, 27. At the Infantry School, Cota became reacquainted with West Point classmates, including Matthew B. Ridgway, who later commanded the 82nd Airborne Division and the XVIII Airborne Corps, and Mark W. Clark, who commanded II Corps, the Fifth US Army, the Seventh US Army, and 15th Army Group during the war. The advanced course, running in parallel with the company officers' course, included Omar N. Bradley, who later commanded two divisions, II Corps, First US Army, and ended the war in command of 12th Army Group. See also Ridgway, *Soldier*; Collins, *Lightning Joe*.

29. Miller, *Division Commander*, 30–33.

30. Wheeler, *The Big Red One*, 1117; Wilson, *Maneuver and Firepower*, map 1, 88–89, and table 9, 102.

31. Weigley, *History*, 121–22.

32. Uffner, "Recollections of World War." Re Thomas O. Beauchamp, see 1st ID, Public Information Office, September 15, 1955, release no. 9-75-55.

33. Mason, "Reminiscences," 21.

34. Liebling, *Road Back to Paris*, 333–34. *The Road Back to Paris* is a collection of articles Liebling wrote from the beginning of the war. As someone who soldiered alongside the 16th, was attached to it, or had units from it attached to mine, I have heard "Sidewalks of New York" played by army bands since I joined the 1st Infantry Division in 1971. When I gave up command of an armored brigade in Germany, I had it played as my last chance to hear it at my request. As an honorary member of the 16th Infantry, I love the connection between that great city and the dirty-faced infantry of the regiment.

35. Thomas J. Gendron, interview by John F. Votaw, August 10, 1995, Orlando, FL. Citizens' Military Training Camps stemmed from the Preparedness Movement led by Major General Leonard Wood, who served as army chief of staff from 1910 to 1914. The Preparedness Movement and the movement for universal military training together produced a number of voluntary citizens' military camps; the camp at Plattsburg Barracks was chief of among them. See Weigley, *History*, 422–23 and especially 657n2. The spelling of Plattsburg was later changed to Plattsburgh.

36. "Biography of Sgt. John Basilone," Buffalo Medal Park, https://buffalomedalof-honorpark.com/gunnery-sergeant-john-basilone/.

37. Frank Beetle, interview by Dr. Macklin Burg, January 15, 1988, Seattle.

38. Dickson, *Rise of the G.I. Army*, 23–42.

39. Dickson, 37. Dickson misspelled Stark's family name as Starke.

40. Charles Stone, "Oral History on 16th Infantry and 1st Division, 1937–1942," McCormick Research Center, Wheaton, IL.

41. Richard J. Lindo, oral history transcript, October 15, 1990, D-Day Project, National World War II Museum, New Orleans.

42. John Thomas Gendron, interview by John F. Votaw, Kissimmee, FL, August 10, 1995.

CHAPTER TWO

Preparing for War

Armies for the preparation of peace do not exist; they exist for triumphant exertion in war.

—Adolf Hitler, 1930

The German Army and Air Force, as of August 1939, were among the world's most formidable fighting machines.

— Military Intelligence Division,
Special Bulletin No. 3, February 1, 1940

ON FRIDAY, SEPTEMBER 1, 1939, Adolf Hitler used his army for what he believed was its exclusive purpose—war. Given a free hand by his fellow dictator in the USSR, Hitler's legions conquered Poland in less than a month. The German army that invaded Poland had grown from 100,000 in 1933 to 3.7 million. For most of the next three years Hitler's army seemed invincible. In the end, however, he had embarked on a course that led to the catastrophic destruction of his Thousand-Year Reich and much of Europe at the cost of millions of lives, including his genocidal "final solution" for Jews. A few hours after Germany invaded Poland, George C. Marshall became chief of staff of the US Army. With unwitting understatement Marshall commented, "My day of induction was momentous with the starting of what appears to be a World War."[1]

The Triangle Division
Brigadier General Walter C. Short commanded the 1st Division when Marshall became chief of staff. This is the same General Short who, along with

Admiral Husband E. Kimmel, took the blame for Pearl Harbor. In October 1940 Short gave up command to Major General Karl Truesdell, who with his troops continued the transition from peacetime to genuine preparation for war that began in 1939. In November the division moved to Fort Benning, Georgia, and established a tent camp at the Harmony Church cantonment area. Truesdell led the division at a critical time; with eight thousand troops, it had reached roughly 65 percent of its authorized strength of 15,245 but remained equipped with obsolete or obsolescent weapons.

Late that year the 1st Division reorganized as a triangular division composed primarily of the 16th, 18th, and 26th Infantry regiments, with no intervening brigade headquarters. Truesdell organized the three regiments into regimental combat teams, each with direct support artillery battalion, engineers, and service units that became standard over the next five years of training and fighting. The division experimented locally with the new design. In the spring of 1941, the 1st Division exercised with the 5th and 6th Infantry Divisions, attached to IV Corps, to test the triangular structure. The field exercises took place first at Fort Benning in April, and then in May the three divisions assigned to IV Corps maneuvered against the 2nd Division and the 1st Cavalry Division subordinate to IX Corps in Louisiana.[2]

When IV Corps took the field, it was the first corps to do so since the end of the Great War. The follow-on exercise that pitted corps on corps was the first ever in the army's history. In any case, the triangular organization proved more flexible and easier to manage than the square division, and the army adopted it quickly. About a year later, in May 1942, the army redesignated the division as the 1st Infantry Division to contrast it with armored, airborne, motorized, and other specialty formations that the army had built or proposed to build.[3]

The structure of the divisions remained dynamic as commanders and the General Staff learned more about the triangular design in subsequent exercises. Curiously, no division tactical manual was published, so tactics also remained dynamic and changed with each lesson learned. In fact, division organization, structure, and equipment remained dynamic throughout the war to respond to lessons learned, take advantage of new equipment, or account for reduced manpower. The key point of the "final" table of organization of August 1942 is the rule of three: three regiments of three battalions each, each of these with three rifle companies, each with three platoons of three squads each. The division artillery consisted of three 105-millimeter howitzer battalions to provide direct support to the three infantry regiments. The major exceptions to the rule of three include the presence of one cannon company in each regiment, and a 155-millimeter howitzer battalion that had the range to provide general support to the division as a whole. Each infantry battalion also had a weapons company. Combat support and service units rounded out the organization.[4]

During the spring of 1940, Hitler overran the Low Countries and much of France. By the end of June, France had collapsed. Despite sharp opposition to any warlike preparation, on 27 August Congress authorized calling up both the National Guard and the Organized Reserve. Later that summer Congress debated a proposed Selective Service Act. During testimony one senator accosted Marshall, saying that "the draft was the most stupid and outrageous thing that 'the generals' have ever perpetrated on the Congress." Yet the case for the draft held up, and on September 14 Congress passed the Selective Service Act. That solved the immediate problem of manpower, but much remained to be done. In an appearance before a house subcommittee, Marshall testified that the country confronted a "tragic shortage of time." Forrest Pogue, Marshall's biographer, noted that the chief of staff told "startled congressmen" point-blank that money would not buy time, and that it would require "one and one-half to two years . . . to show results."[5]

In August General McNair arrived in Washington to serve as the chief of staff of General Headquarters (GHQ), a vestige of the Great War. Pershing had commanded the GHQ separately from the authority of the chief of staff. In theory Marshall commanded the GHQ, which would develop the system for mobilization, training, and equipping the army, but he delegated the authority to run it to McNair. Thus the system for training and fielding divisions, including the 1st Division, would be largely McNair's creation. Eventually a detailed system for raising divisions emerged, based on the experiences of manning the regular army and mobilizing the National Guard. McNair also drove much of the development of weapons systems and supporting doctrine.[6] The Big Red One went through some facets of McNair's emerging plan, but deployed before it could be fully implemented.

Prewar Training

As the army and navy began to ramp up for combat operations, it was clear that assault landings on hostile shores would be necessary. In 1940 neither service had the means to execute large-scale landings, let alone against a defended beach, so the two agreed to form a joint force to "develop and test joint amphibious doctrine." The 1st Division would become the army's component of that force.

The slow pace of garrison life accelerated perceptibly during Truesdell's tenure, but not without resistance. On Thanksgiving Day 1940, recently commissioned second lieutenant Charles Hangsterfer reported to the 16th Infantry regimental adjutant. That worthy took umbrage with the new officer, asking, "Don't you know enough not to report for duty on a holiday?" A few days later the chastened lieutenant left with the 3rd Battalion of the 16th for Edgewood Arsenal. Situated on the banks of the estuarial waters of the Gunpowder River northeast of Baltimore, Maryland, the arsenal would serve as a base camp while the troops learned to execute assault landings on a hostile shore. There they were joined by the 3rd Battalion of the 18th Infantry.[7]

Hangsterfer described the training as "a riot." There were as yet no purpose-built landing craft available, so instead the troops would first learn to row boats that reminded him of "the whaleboat Captain Ahab used to chase Moby Dick." Everyone got soaked and, given it was winter on the Atlantic coast, felt frozen. The two battalions reprised their amphibious practice next in Puerto Rico. There they used ship's barges. "With all the makeshift equipment we had to use," Hangsterfer concluded, "we learned a lot about the problems of assault landings." [8]

Training for the early mobilizing divisions did not follow the sequence that McNair's staff had developed. As planning and mobilization proceeded apace, sequential efforts proved impossible for units that mobilized early. These units trained, equipped, reorganized, and shifted bases as required. Continuous change was the norm, not the exception.

Sidney "Hap" Haszard joined the division at Fort Devens, where he found himself helping to form the division's 1st Cavalry Reconnaissance Troop. To him, "These were thrilling days for a young soldier. The buildup of the division in the process of instilling esprit de corps in its units is an exciting time. . . . The presence of Word [sic] War I heroes of the division alive and moving around in the same unit, was an inspiring force." Haszard included among these heroes both Teddy Roosevelt—who, having commanded a battalion of the 26th Infantry in the Great War, was now back in the 1st Division commanding the 26th Infantry itself—and Haszard's own first sergeant, John Murphy, who had been decorated for valor in the first war.[9] Rapid change, the fielding of new gear, and organization of units characterized life in the army, especially in these early days.

While the two battalions doing amphibious training learned a lot about assault landings, the rest of the division trained at Fort Benning, Georgia, Camp Pine, New York (present day Fort Drum), and then returned to their original posts in New York. There the division became the recipient of largess from Congress.

Draftees and Officer Turbulence

For most of the twenty years after returning from occupation duty, the 1st Division had experienced little change. Now change occurred at light speed as the division doubled in size and its leadership turned over continuously, preparing for the possibility of war with large unit maneuvers, amphibious training, and constant change in unit organization. In the span of a few months during the fall and winter of 1940–41, some 5,500 draftees joined the division, raising its strength to 13,645. Turbulence among its officers became the norm as the army sought to spread experienced officers around to enable more effective mobilization of guard and reserve divisions. Charles E. Murphy, an officer in the 1st Engineer Battalion, organic to the division, described the effect: "They kept pulling the officers and NCOs, and then we would get replacements and start re-training all over again."[10]

In 1940 soldiers arrived in the 1st Division in droves. Their experiences in training and reception differed depending on when they joined and where they had trained. Wherever they came from, new arrivals had to be assimilated and trained. How a unit brings new troops into the "family" is important for two reasons; first, the receiving unit and the arriving soldier will make judgments about each other based on that first impression, and second, new soldiers are only as effective as the receiving unit enables them to be. If one assumes most new soldiers, whether drafted or enlisted, want to do their jobs, then they need to be treated that way. Small unit leadership is crucial to effective reception, but emphasis and support for new arrivals from senior leadership is nearly as important.

The draftees trained differently than their volunteer predecessors who joined as late as 1939. Soon after the Selective Service became law, the army established basic training centers around the country. The young men who went to them began their army career with thirteen weeks of basic training. Arguably the draftees had better initial training than those who joined in the 1920s and '30s. The experience of John Lebda, who served in Company D, 26th Infantry, was to him unique, but mirrored that of thousands of others.

Lebda registered for the draft in 1941, not long before the Japanese attacked Pearl Harbor. He took basic training at Camp Wheeler, near Macon, Georgia. Like all those who went through thirteen weeks of infantry training, he began with the disorienting process of moving through an assembly line that did everything from accounting for the new soldier to issuing him clothing and equipment. Lebda's new clothes, like nearly everyone else's, did not fit, but he exchanged with others until he had a uniform of proper size, more or less. Richard Colson recalled his clothing issue at Fort Thomas, Kentucky, where he drew a mix of Civilian Conservation Corps clothing and regular army uniforms. Others in his group drew World War I uniforms that still bore the divisional flash of the 42nd "Rainbow" Division. Adding to the disorientation for many was being required to strip down to their underwear or less. For teenage boys in an era of strict modesty, that proved unforgettable.[11]

Finally, clothed as a soldier, Lebda met his drill instructor or, more familiarly, drill sergeant, Sergeant Cummings, whose name he never forgot. That also is not unusual—nearly all old soldiers remember their drill sergeant forever. Lebda recalled that he never had time to rest—also a common complaint. Training on weapons and conditioning were the central pillars of basic. Forced marches of lengths of ten to twenty miles conducted day and night were de rigueur at Wheeler, as at every training base in the United States. Lebda learned, as did his peers, that the infantryman "was the vital cog in the Army. He had to be of the highest caliber and shouldered a heavy responsibility."[12]

Most of that was true. However, the US Army had evidently concluded that infantrymen did not in fact have to be of the highest caliber. The infantry did not get priority for the "highest caliber," as measured by the Army General Classification Test (AGCT), which measured "usable (rather than 'raw') intelligence." The best troops, by this measure, went first to the air forces to man the bomber crews who would be the first to strike directly at Germany, and then to the services of supply. The Army Specialized Training Program (ASTP) also diverted high-caliber draftees and recruits to study at the collegiate level or in highly technical programs. ASTP existed in part to assure a steady source of well-educated soldiers if the war proved to be a long one. Airborne units siphoned off still more high-caliber men. When William Lee took his AGCT, he was told by a sergeant, "You want to do the very best you can." Instead Lee determined "to do the very worst because though [sic] you could get out that way." Wrong! Lee went to Camp Croft, South Carolina, and trained to be an infantryman.[13]

Physical standards for the "vital cog" also seemed at variance with "highest caliber." The original draft was, in fact, selective. Geoffrey Perret in *There's a War to Be Won* reports, "The average draftee was brighter, healthier and better educated than the Average American." He "stood 5 feet 8 inches tall, weighed 144 pounds, had a 33 ½ inch waist and wore size 9 ½ D shoe." But the average declined quickly as manpower demands grew, and obviously did not describe everyone. A good many draftees and enlistees were not fit enough, not big enough, or could not see well enough to serve in the Marine Corps, the US Navy, or the Army Air Force.[14]

That did not make them unfit to carry rifle in Algeria, Tunisia, Sicily, Omaha Beach, and across France, Belgium, and Germany all the way to Cheb, Czechoslovakia. Standards for enlisting in the navy confounded Albert Mominee. At five foot one, he was too short for the navy, but it turned out he was just tall enough to carry a rifle in the 16th Infantry, where his lieutenant, who shared his vertical disadvantage, called him "little one." Because Ernest A. Hilberg had an overbite, the Army Air Force, the navy, the Coast Guard, and the Army's Enlisted Reserve Corps, all turned down. He was however, "accepted by ROTC [at Rutgers], in spite of my overbite." He left Rutgers after his freshman year, volunteered for the Army, and this time he passed overbite and all. Despite his handicap, Hilberg survived basic training, and joined the 18th Infantry in time to land with them on Omaha Beach.[15]

Standards for the Army Air Force and navy remained higher than that for the infantry at least in terms of fitness. Few who were turned down in 1939, or 1940, found it hard to enlist or easy to avoid the draft later on, despite their physical or educational differences. Both the Marines and the navy turned down Audie Murphy, but he did just fine in the 3rd ID and became the most decorated soldier of World War II.

After basic training, John Lebda joined the 26th ID, where he found that "everything was orderly; we were accepted even though we were draftees. The food was delicious [in contrast to what he ate at Camp Wheeler] and abundant and we had direction; we just fell right in and the regular army soldiers gave us additional guidance. Before long we were one of them." William Kent, another draftee, matriculated with Company L, 3rd Battalion, 26th Infantry, several months before Lebda joined Company D, 1st Battalion, 26th Infantry. Kent recalled that he was one of the first draftees to join the division. According to him, "It was kind of rough for about six months. I would say because we got all the shit! Nobody else was there. Until they got used to us draftees." Despite recalling their arrival in the same regiment differently, both believed they were fortunate to serve in the 26th Infantry. Kent was impressed with his sergeants, one of whom later accepted a battlefield commission and eventually commanded Company L.[16]

William Lee joined the 26th ID while the division was still at Camp Blanding, Florida. Assigned to Company A, Lee was impressed with his company commander, Captain Gerald C. Kelleher, who he remembered as "abrupt and military." Later, as the regiment sought to fill out spaces in other units, Lee was sent to interview for reassignment to Company D, 26th Infantry, and "got" the job of rifleman. Two weeks after he joined, his company commander called him to ask, "Lee, how do you like it in D Company?" Thinking like a civilian, Lee admitted without malice just how he felt: "I don't like it worth a damn." To which his commander opined, "Well, I don't give a damn whether you like it or not. You're in D Company to stay." And he stayed for the next thirty-nine months. His captain, however, did eventually leave Company D.[17]

Officer turbulence remained high throughout the period 1940–42, but the division dealt with it. As the army sought to spread the regulars around, their number drew down in the Big Red One. Ralph Uffner noted that by June 1942 there were very few regular army company commanders, but unlike most other divisions at this time, the Big Red One escaped being "cadred" to form new divisions. A "cadred" unit had to provide thousands of trained troops to new outfits. Doing so enabled the army to form thirty-six divisions, including all eighteen from the National Guard, by December 7, 1941, and thirty-eight more in 1942. Escaping a levy for cadre was a godsend, but it did not assure officer stability.[18]

Reserve officers who remained with the 1st Division, including Uffner, garnered considerable experience in running units and assumed greater responsibility. They had come together first at Benning in late 1939 to maneuver there and in Louisiana, and then maneuvered in Camp Pine, New York. In June 1941 they began training in earnest to conduct assault landings. These young officers and often very young sergeants trained, assimilated draftees, and rotated officers simultaneously. For the most part, everyone—officers, sergeants, and privates alike—accepted ambiguity and surprise about what came next with grace.[19]

Amphibious Operations and Large-Scale Maneuvers

Instead of returning to New York after the amphibious training in Puerto Rico, the 3rd Battalions of the 16th and 18th Infantry regiments went to Fort Devens, Massachusetts, where they prepared to receive the rest of the division. There, the Big Red One's battalions rotated through amphibious training at nearby Buzzard's Bay, suffering bitter cold. In January 1941 Truesdell fleeted up to command VI Corps. Major General Donald C. Cubbison, a combat veteran of the 1st Division in the Great War, assumed command in his stead. When the 1st Division joined the 1st Joint Amphibious Force with the 1st Marine Division, it built on its experience in assault landings. That spring Lieutenant Colonel Stanhope B. Mason joined the Big Red One at the behest of Brigadier General James G. Ord, assistant division commander. Ord and Mason knew each other from service in the Philippines.[20]

Ord commanded a task force organized around a regiment of the 1st Division, with the mission of seizing the French possession of Martinique in the Windward Islands of the eastern Caribbean, due to the possibility of Germany basing U-boats at Martinique. Ord assigned Mason, who served with the division from 1941 until December 1944, as assistant operations officer to Lieutenant Colonel George Taylor, who had long served in the 1st Division. Taylor would eventually command the 26th Infantry, and later the 16th Infantry, which he led ashore on D-Day. After a short hiatus with another division, Taylor returned as a brigadier general to serve as assistant division commander. Mason's task was to develop the tactics for ship-to-shore movement of troops using the newly developed "Higgins boats," named for their inventor, Andrew Jackson Higgins. Officially known as landing craft, vehicle, and personnel (LCVP), these flat-bottomed boats were of made of wood, except the ramp, which was steel. They bobbed up and down even in a flat calm and traveled at a stately ten miles per hour. It is difficult to see how anyone aboard could not have suffered *mal de mer* in any kind of chop or waves.[21]

Mason believed training had not progressed sufficiently to execute an assault on the island when the task force began to form at Brooklyn Army Base; "All in all it was a hastily made decision with a rudimentary plan with green forces for its execution," he wrote in his *Reminiscences*. An epidemic of measles broke out in the regiment earmarked for the attack, forcing a postponement while another regiment prepared to assume the mission. That regiment also suffered a measles outbreak, causing yet another delay. The division whistled up the last of its three regiments, but then, without explanation, the operation was canceled.[22]

Mason believed, though, that the effort to train for that mission "had incomparable value to the 1st Division and its subsequent participation in the World War II." First, the division had avoided an operation that Mason believed would have failed. Instead, the Big Red One spent the summer of 1941 training at the Marine Corps base at New River for amphibious assault. By this time sufficient numbers of LCVPs, or Higgins boats, were in service to train at scale. To all accounts the exercises demonstrated that the army, navy, and marines had learned a lot. The 1st Division ended the summer as arguably the most experienced division in the US Army at conduct of amphibious assault. Three assault landings later, the 1st Division still reported lessons learned.[23]

The Carolina Maneuvers that fall, so named because they were conducted across both North and South Carolina (following the better-known Louisiana Maneuvers of September), were part of the developing plan for training divisions. Equally important, the maneuvers enabled larger formations to train and the army to experiment with concepts and structure. They pitted Lieutenant General Hugh Drum's First Army, composed of three corps, including VI Corps, against IV Corps and I Armored Corps, the latter two led by Major General Oscar Griswold, acting as a de facto Army commander. The 1st Division was subordinated to VI Corps, commanded by Major General Truesdell, Cubbison's predecessor in the Big Red One. Lieutenant General Lesley J. McNair directed the exercise and the umpires who adjudicated "battles."[24]

At this time Marshall believed, as did McNair, in the utility of large-formation maneuvers to train units and their commanders. In his excellent study *The US Army GHQ Maneuvers of 1941*, Christopher R. Gabel let the chief of staff speak for himself. Marshall believed the maneuvers comprised a "combat college of troop leading." A senator who questioned the cost of the Louisiana maneuvers, given the mistakes reported, found Marshall unsympathetic. "My God, Senator," Marshall retorted, "that's the reason I do it. I want the mistake down in Louisiana, not over in Europe, and the only way to do this thing is to try it out, and if it doesn't work, find out what we need to make it work."[25]

The Carolina Maneuvers occurred in two phases, consuming most of November 1941. Eight infantry divisions "fought" as part of the First Army against two armored divisions, two infantry divisions, and a motorized division subordinated to General Griswold's "Red Army." For the second phase the opposing forces remained the same, but the combatants reset. Gabel describes the Louisiana and Carolina Maneuvers in rich detail. The army learned a lot, ranging from how to employ armor and antitank units to which of the commanders should be retained and which let go. Gabel's brief does not include detailing who was let go and who went on, but it is easily deduced from an appendix in which he lists the "Principal Officers" and what became of them. Cubbison did well enough to go on to command the Field Artillery Training Center at Fort Sill, but did not take the 1st Division to war.[26]

The division returned to Fort Devens after the Carolina Maneuvers and continued receiving and assimilating draftees and organizing in accord with the 1941 table of organization and equipment, often without the subject equipment. Hap Haszard's reconnaissance troop organized and began training without its scout cars, but Haszard remained unconcerned, remarking that this enabled the troop to concentrate on the "fundamentals of dismounted scouting and patrolling."[27]

Soon after returning to Fort Devens, the division learned of the attack on Pearl Harbor. War had been likely but theoretical. Now war was a fact. Steve Ralph, a draftee serving in the 16th Infantry, reflected on his group of draftees, "We were a patriotic bunch, happy to serve our country, but also fully aware of the neat proviso that our tours of duty were limited by our call-up orders to a term of one year." But, he added, "That little proviso sprouted wings and flew out the window on December 7, 1941." Ralph and his colleagues, whether volunteers or draftees, were going to war, and none would serve a one-year tour.[28]

Both as a practical matter and as the natural consequence of shared experience, the draftees and volunteers had become one. They had little time to consider their situation in any case. In February the 1st Division moved by train and convoy from Devens all the way to Camp Blanding in central Florida, midway between Gainesville and Jacksonville. At Blanding they met up with the 36th Division, composed largely of partisan Texas National Guard soldiers. Teddy Roosevelt was promoted to brigadier general as the assistant division commander of the 1st Division. He and Brigadier General Terry de la Mesa Allen, who held the same job in the 36th Division, did what they could to keep the peace between the Big Red One and the "Texas Division." It proved difficult. The 36th Division's pride in their state seemed boundless. According to Charles Hangsterfer, "their people were still fighting the Civil War." The 16th's "Subway Soldiers" from New York and elsewhere often irritated the southerners by refusing to stand at attention in various bars while the 36th sang "Deep in the Heart of Texas." In the end, "a joint parade of the two divisions was held, and it was explained to us, that the 1st and 36th were not enemies."[29]

The Command Team's Graduation Exercise

Still no one knew what would come next. They had trained for amphibious assault; now they also did "jungle training" in the wilds of central Florida. In May the 1st Division moved to Fort Benning, Georgia, to maneuver with the 36th Division and the 2nd Armored Division (AD). Just before the division left Blanding, the army reassigned Major General Cubbison to command the artillery replacement center, and Brigadier General Terry Allen assumed command in his stead. Unlike Cubbison and Truesdell, Allen had no previous service in the Big Red One.

Decorated for valor and badly wounded during the Great War, Terry Allen had commanded an infantry battalion of the 90th Division with distinction. He came to command the 1st Division because he had earned George Marshall's confidence when they served together at the Infantry School at Fort Benning, where Allen taught cavalry tactics. In Allen's efficiency report for 1931–32, Marshall wrote that Allen was ready to command a "regiment and in wartime a division." In addition to writing a glowing efficiency report, General Marshall added Allen to the list of worthy officers he kept in a black notebook.[30]

Teddy Roosevelt, like Allen, had served with distinction in the Great War, demonstrating courage in command of a battalion of the 26th Infantry. Indeed, Roosevelt commanded the regiment during the last weeks of the war, as the "first reserve officer to command a regular army regiment in action." Like his new boss, he had been badly wounded and cited for valor. Although the French government had proposed Roosevelt for the Legion of Honor for valor, the army did not act on this recommendation. As one staff officer said to him, "People might say you were promoted or decorated because you're the son of your father, and might criticize us."[31]

Brigadier General Clift Andrus also joined the division in May as the commander of the division artillery. Andrus—the son of a cavalry officer, Edwin Proctor Andrus, who served at Fort Apache in Arizona as commander and with the 3rd Cavalry Regiment from 1902 to 1904—had served on the Mexican border prior to the Great War and as an artillery instructor during the war. Terry Allen's father was an artilleryman assigned to Fort Apache. The two army brats knew each other as teenage boys there. A local Apache Chief invited the two boys to spend two weeks with him, and they did. Apparently life with the Apaches proved uncomfortable and no substitute for raising hell on the small post. The two are supposed to have sworn revenge on their fathers. If they joined the army, their oath committed each to choose the branch of the other's father—and that is what they did. Terry Allen's old friend proved himself a great artilleryman in combat.[32]

Norman D. Cota joined the 1st Division in November 1940, following a tour as an instructor at the Command and General Staff College. He served as executive officer of the 16th Infantry until March 1941 and then for four months as the intelligence officer of the 1st Division. Then he became the operations officer for the Big Red One. In June Allen chose him to be chief of staff.[33]

Stanhope Mason succeeded Cota as the operations officer. Other key staff officers were Major Paul Revere, personnel; Lieutenant Colonel Robert W. Porter Jr., intelligence; and logistics officer Lieutenant Colonel Clarence M. Eymer. The regimental commanders included Colonel Henry B. Cheadle in the 16th Infantry, Colonel Frank U. Greer in the 18th, and Colonel Alexander N. Stark Jr. in the 26th.[34]

The top tier of the leadership team that took the 1st Division overseas and led it through its early campaigns settled in soon after Allen assumed command. In mid-May the division left Blanding to return for maneuvers at Benning with the 36th Division and the 2nd Armored Division. These maneuvers proved to be a graduation exercise. At their conclusion the Big Red One moved to Indian Town Gap, Pennsylvania, to make final preparations to deploy. Whether their training was adequate would be tested in the coming months, but for the most part the troops felt confident. In March Joe Dawson, who graduated from officer candidate school in January 1942, reported to his parents that he believed only time would tell whether the division was well trained. But in July he wrote his father to say, "I cannot speak too highly of this division, Dad, for it is truly an excellent fighting unit." Many others shared Dawson's confidence. George Zenie, a rifleman in the 18th Infantry, perhaps said it best. Zenie joined the regiment in 1940. He thought well of his officers, who were mostly regulars in 1940, and of his sergeants, saying, "They drilled us and worked us very hard. Later in North Africa, Sicily, France and Germany, I thanked God they had pushed us." Now began the time Dawson believed would tell.[35]

Ready or Not, and Ready for What?

What the 1st Division learned collectively in large-scale maneuvers is debatable. Stanhope Mason thought the amphibious training produced "staff know-how unique in the Army." Furthermore, Mason believed Major General Arthur Cubbison, who commanded during most of division-level training, had handed over a well-trained and disciplined unit to Terry Allen, and that "professionalism and dependability characterized everything the 1st Div. did." Mason thought the division enjoyed a singular advantage because, despite officer turbulence, it "went overseas with a disproportionately larger number of Regular Army officers than any other division had."[36]

Large-scale exercises sweeping across multiple states had done much to prepare the Big Red One's senior officer leadership, as had amphibious training. Whether the troops learned much more than how to clamber down the side of a ship into an assault landing craft is less certain. Just what the troops had learned in the big maneuvers was equally unclear. General Paul Gorman in *The Secret of Future Victories* argues convincingly that by the end of the fall maneuvers in 1941, McNair had "concluded the large-scale free-play maneuvers contribute little to the development of proficiency in small infantry units." The absence of simulators, and for that matter equipment, hampered infantry training. In these "umpired" exercises, tactical execution mattered far less than adjudication, in which numbers mattered most. During the postmaneuver review of the Carolina Maneuvers, McNair voiced specific concerns, claiming on November 30, 1941, that the troops "could fight effectively. But it is added with heavy emphasis that the losses would be heavy, and the results of action against an adversary such as the German might not be all that could be desired."[37] Nevertheless, the big free-play maneuvers of 1941 led to those of the spring of 1942.

The 1st Division's preparations to deploy paled in comparison to other events in June 1942. The month began with the astounding defeat of the Japanese Navy in the carrier battle near Midway Island over the course of June 4–7. Later that month Winston S. Churchill led a delegation of senior British officers and diplomats to Washington to meet with President Roosevelt. Churchill had come to Washington "to reach a final decision on the operations for 1942–1943." The two allies had not reached consensus on strategy, and he had serious concerns in North Africa, where the Germans and Italians, led by Generalfeldmarschall Erwin Rommel, had besieged Tobruk. At sea, U-boats continued to savage convoys of vital supplies. Churchill was also concerned that the American chiefs might "consider a radical revision of the strategy of 'Germany First.' "[38]

The strategic conundrum was when to attempt a cross-Channel invasion of France, a decision made more difficult because the United Kingdom and United States had fundamentally different views of both strategy and timing. Marshall very much wanted to invade France as early as possible. Furthermore, he believed the US Navy's startling victory at Midway enabled the United States to focus on Europe, as the United Kingdom and United States had agreed. On the other hand, Admiral Ernest J. King, the chief of naval operations, saw the victory at Midway as providing an opportunity to mount an offensive in the Pacific. The British arrived with consensus. They wanted to invade North Africa, consistent with what they had proposed at the Arcadia conference not quite a year earlier. Marshall's biographer entitled the chapter devoted to the decision that followed "Marshall Loses a Fight." Marshall did lose, but he did so gracefully.

The British delegation arrived on June 18, 1942. The following morning Churchill flew to Hyde Park, where he began personal discussions with President Roosevelt. The next evening he and Roosevelt went to Washington together, where they learned that the British garrison at Tobruk had surrendered. Churchill was devastated; "Seasoned [British] soldiers had laid down their arms to perhaps half their number." Roosevelt asked what could be done, and the prime minister asked for tanks. Roosevelt agreed. There was some discussion of shipping the 2nd Armored Division, but that solution was infeasible. Instead, the army shipped tanks almost immediately—317 Sherman tanks off-loaded in Egypt less than two months later.[39]

On June 23 Churchill—along with his chief of imperial general staff, General Allan Brooke; Field Marshal Sir John Dill, chief of the British Joint Staff Mission in Washington; and Major General Hastings Ismay, chief of the staff to the minister of defense—traveled at Marshall's request to Fort Jackson, South Carolina, to "inspect" US troops. Marshall and secretary of war Henry L. Stimson hosted the visit. In blazing heat, the British visitors gamely watched demonstrations by troops from four US infantry divisions, including hundreds of tanks and other vehicles. The event culminated in airdrops of equipment and some six hundred paratroopers. Churchill asked Ismay what he made of the American soldiers. Ismay responded, "To put these troops against continental troops would be murder." Churchill said, "You're wrong. They are wonderful material and will learn very quickly."[40]

Churchill had to return home before he and Roosevelt reached a decision on operations for 1942–43. He went home to face a vote of censure over the loss of Tobruk and the general state of the war effort. Ultimately Roosevelt decided the course of affairs. Marshall remained hopeful of mounting a cross-Channel attack from the United Kingdom to France in 1942, aiming at the very least to secure a lodgment on the continent.[41]

Churchill's government surviving the vote of censure, and on its heels Roosevelt dispatched a delegation to the United Kingdom to make the decision that could not be made in June. The Americans included, among others, Ambassador Harry Hopkins, Marshall, and Admiral King, the chief of naval operations. They arrived in the UK with clear instructions from the president: if they could not persuade the British to support the cross-Channel invasion, they were to agree to one of the options developed previously that would get the United States into the war against Germany. The British planners would not agree to a cross-Channel invasion in 1942, with good reason. Operation Gymnast, a plan to invade North Africa, looked most likely to succeed, given the available troops and the situation in the field. The Germans held France securely while German armies rolled eastward in the USSR and from Tobruk eastward toward Cairo and the Suez Canal.[42]

Roosevelt confirmed Operation Gymnast as the operation the British preferred. An attack in North Africa would support "closing and tightening the ring around Germany." In any case, it is hard to see how any of the other options, mostly variants of a cross-Channel attack, had much chance of success. In 1942 the US ground troops got into the fight both in the Mediterranean and Pacific. Despite a herculean effort, only eighteen army divisions deployed in 1942. Of these eight went to Europe or the Mediterranean. The remaining ten went to the Pacific and joined the Marine Corps in combat against Japan.[43]

Overseas

During these machinations, of which its troops remained ignorant, the 1st Division—now styled the 1st Infantry Division—moved from Fort Benning to Indiantown Gap, where they prepared to deploy.

Despite having completed training for deployment, and escaping a large levy of cadre, the division still endured high turbulence among junior officers. On June 27, 1942, the Infantry Officer Candidate School (OCS) at Fort Benning, Georgia, graduated and commissioned eighty second lieutenants. The entire class—seventy-nine single officers and one married officer—joined the division. As a result, two of the four infantry platoon leaders in every rifle company were OCS Class 25 graduates. While the Big Red One had not suffered a large levy of sergeants and enlisted soldiers to provide a cadre, it had not escaped being ransacked for officers. Regardless, the division had done what it could, and would soon be on its way to fight.[44]

Everett Booth arrived with these newly minted lieutenants, becoming the platoon leader of the 3rd Platoon, Company K, 3rd Battalion, 16th Infantry. He was concerned about how he would fit in and handle infantrymen who, to his mind, were far better trained than he was. A sergeant by the name of Palowitz reported that he was Booth's platoon sergeant—second in command, so to speak. At six foot four and a sometime heavyweight boxing champion, Sergeant Palowitz seemed imposing to Lieutenant Booth, who knew as well that Palowitz had served eighteen years. He respected that experience, so he told his platoon sergeant, "Carry on just the way you have been doing things." Palowitz replied, "Sir, we'll do it just the way you want to."[45]

Absorbing new officers was one of many tasks associated with preparing a unit to move overseas. In addition to everything else that had to be done, the division continued organizing new formations authorized by the "final" table of organization. The 1st Reconnaissance Troop continued to field people, gear, and train. The three infantry regiments organized cannon companies, mostly without equipment. When they received that equipment, either in the States or overseas, it came in dribs and drabs, and was often not what had been authorized. The division ended up with diverse equipment that varied in some cases among the regiments. The new units had to make do.

Finally the time of departure arrived. An advance detachment left for England on July 1. They traveled in convoy on two British transports, the *Maloja* and *Duchess of Bedford*, arriving on July 13. The remainder of the division embarked on the *Queen Mary*, which "silently slipped out of New York harbor during the night the 1st–2nd August." The *Queen Mary* traveled alone because she was fast, able to cruise at twenty-four knots. Colonel Alexander N. Stark Jr., who commanded the 26th Infantry, had a more colorful way of describing the *Queen Mary* when he assembled his regiment in the post theater at Indiantown Gap, where he briefed his soldiers on the next stage of their army career: "They are going to put the whole GD division on the *Queen Mary*. They are going to shove a firecracker up its ass, touch it off, let it go; no escort, no nothing." And that is more or less what happened. The *Queen Mary* made a quick crossing, steamed up the Clyde River, and docked in Gourock, Scotland, on August 8, 1942.[46]

Notes

1. Cooper, *German Army*, 131. Cooper acknowledges the German mobilization achievement while highlighting the essential weakness of Germany's preparation for war; see ch. 12, "Unreadiness." For Marshall's comment, see Pogue, *Marshall: Ordeal and Hope*, 2.

2. Wheeler, *The Big Red One*, 128–30; Gabel, *GHQ Maneuvers*, 12.

3. Wheeler, *The Big Red One*, 128–30; Gabel, *GHQ Maneuvers*, 12. The official designation did not come until May 1942.

4. Reorganizing the division into a triangular structure required changes, based lessons learned in subsequent maneuvers. The table of organization remained in flux until 1942 and remained more or less dynamic until the end of the war. See Greenfield, Palmer, and Riley, *Organization of Ground Combat Troops*, 11, 271, and 276–77. On the development of the triangular division, see Wilson, *Maneuver and Firepower*, 125–27. See also chart 10, "Infantry Division, corrected to 1940," at page 124, and chart 15, "The Infantry Division, 1 August 1942."

5. Pogue, *Marshall: Ordeal and Hope*, 59–62. Marshall proved an effective advocate for the army, even after all that had happened in Europe and in Asia. Isolationist opposition was genuine and deep.

6. Pogue, 296. On reorganization of the War Department and the creation of the Army Ground Forces, see also Calhoun, *General Lesley J. McNair*, 214–45, 250.

Calhoun's biography of McNair is essential reading to understand the doctrine, structure, and training of the Army Ground Forces in World War II. McNair got some things wrong, but on the whole, thanks to McNair and his quite small staff, the army fielded reasonably well trained and equipped ground forces. McNair's staff developed a spreadsheet that laid the sequence of manning, equipping, training, and deploying divisions. See Wiley, *Building and Training of Infantry Division*. Troop basis, or the number of soldiers available, proved problematic throughout the war, with the result that divisions were manned at the lowest level possible. See Palmer, *Reorganization of Ground Troops*.

7. Finke, *No Mission Too Difficult*, 10–11.

8. Finke, 11–13.

9. Finke, 36–37.

10. Wheeler, *The Big Red One*, 132–33; Charles E. Murphy, interview by Stan Tinsley, September 5, 1990, Oak Ridge, TN.

11. Lebda, *Million Miles to Go*, 9–12. Lebda's well written and pithy memoir is compelling in a number of ways, providing insight into the dystopian life of the infantry. Lebda was grateful to the army for the life it enabled a poor coal miner's son to have. He believed he grew up in the army, and due to the GI bill he escaped the "miserable coal mining industry," as he put it, and found "a white collar job." Lebda, 184. See also Richard Colson, oral history, n.d., MRC 1998.168. Colson recalled more than fifty years after the fact his embarrassment at the induction center, "running around with all those people, bare-assed." The author remembers quite vividly his own embarrassment at being stripped down to jockey shorts while being measured by women for his uniform issue. At least the uniforms fit. In the summer of 1970, with hundreds of others I entered one end of the old riding hall at Fort Riley, wearing blue jeans and a short-sleeved shirt, and emerged from the other end in fatigues and carrying two duffel bags of gear. It was both amazing and embarrassing.

12. Lebda, *Million Miles to Go*, 9–11. The author did not go to "boot camp," but did go to ROTC Advanced Camp, which was similar but shorter.

13. Brown, *Draftee Division*, 13–18. Brown's history of the 88th delves into the issue of manning, training, and employment of a typical reserve infantry division. He examines personnel policy and the stripping off of talent to man higher-priority units and the Army Specialized Training Program. See also William M. Lee, interview by Colonel John Votaw, May 14, 1991.

14. Perret, *War to Be Won*, 124.

15. Albert Mominee and Ernest A. Hilberg, oral history transcripts, both D-Day Project, National World War II Museum, New Orleans.

16. Lebda, *Million Miles to Go*, 13; William Kent, interview by Colonel John Votaw, July 6, 1988, Cincinnati.

17. Lee interview. Kelleher was ultimately promoted to brigadier general. He ended the war serving the 104th Infantry Division with Terry Allen and alongside Hugh Carey, who became governor of New York. See https://www.legacy.com/obituaries/timesunion-albany/obituary.

18. Raphael L. Uffner, "Recollections of World War II with the First Infantry Division," n.d., MRC 1997.98, 159; Wilson, *Maneuver and Firepower*, table 12, 157, and table 13, 171.

19. Wheeler, *The Big Red One*, 134–36.

20. Wheeler; Mason, "Reminiscences," 3–9; Wheeler, *The Big Red One*, 133–35.

21. Mason, "Reminiscences," 10–11. Re Higgins boats, there are a number of easily accessible films that illustrate the development and use of the Higgins boat or LCVP. Of particular interest is a WWII Navy training film under fifteen minutes in length, "LCVP Higgins Boat 1944 U.S. Navy Landing Craft Training Film 29784," YouTube video, https://www.youtube.com/watch?v=4Mx8HDJx4ZI.

22. Mason, "Reminiscences," 11–13.

23. Mason, 11–13. Mason did not specify the sequence regiments. It is likely the 16th, 18th, and 26th, in that order, based on earlier training. The 3rd Infantry Division was training on the Pacific Coast.

24. Wheeler, *The Big Red One*, 134–35. See also Gabel, *GHQ Maneuvers*, ch. 8 and 9, which detail the Carolina maneuvers.

25. Pogue, *Marshall: Ordeal and Hope*, 89.

26. Pogue, appendix B.

27. Wheeler, *The Big Red One*, 136–37.

28. Finke, *No Mission Too Difficult*, 37, 45.

29. Finke, 16.

30. Astor, *Terrible Terry Allen*, 58, 77.

31. Jeffers, *Theodore Roosevelt Jr.*, 104 re valor awards, 114 re commanding 26th Infantry; Miller, *Division Commander*, 30–35.

32. Donald McBurney Curtis to Al Smith, November 3, 1980, Albert H. Smith Papers, MRC 1996.95. The reference to living together is apparently from a letter Curtis wrote in July 1980, also in the Smith Papers. For Clift Andrus, see also "Andrus, Clift," Generals of WWII, https://generals.dk/general/Andrus/Clift/USA.html. For Edwin Proctor Andrus, see "Edwin Proctor Andrus—Colonel, United States Army," Arlington National Cemetery, https://www.arlingtoncemetery.net/epandrus.htm, and "Col Edwin Proctor Andrus," https://www.findagrave.com/memorial/9150063 /edwin-proctor-andrus.

33. Miller, *Division Commander*, 36–41.

34. Knickerbocker et al., *Danger Forward*, 409. These officers proved successful. Mason, Porter, Cheadle Stark, and Greer all retired as general officers.

35. Kingseed, *Omaha Beach to Dawson's Ridge*, 17–21, 25; Astor, *Terrible Terry Allen*, 98.

36.Mason, "Reminiscences," 22.

37. Gorman, *Secret of Future Victories*, 2:23, 61.

38. Churchill, *Second World War*, 325–36.

39. Churchill, 327, 331, 332. In his account Churchill says the US shipped 300 tanks. Some 317 were delivered. See Blaxland, *Plain Cook*, 48. The shipment did not arrive without incident. The Germans sank one ship. Marshall made good by shipping another seventy tanks to make up the loss. The shipment also included a hundred 105-millimeter howitzers. See Pogue, *Marshall: Ordeal and Hope*, 333.

40. Churchill, *Second World War*, 336; Pogue, *Marshall: Ordeal and Hope*, 334–35.

41. Churchill, *Second World War*, 340–54; Pogue, *Marshall: Ordeal and Hope*, 336–49.

42. Pogue, *Marshall: Ordeal and Hope*, 340–49. Harry Hopkins played a central role in managing the histrionics of both the president and the prime minister. See 344. For the arc of planning and strategic principles articulated at the Arcadia Conference, see Matloff and Snell, *Strategic Planning*, 100. On the details of the decision see Leo J. Meyer, "The Decision to Invade North Africa (Torch)," ch. 7 in Greenfield, *Command Decisions*, 173–98. See also the excellent analysis of FDR's interest in North Africa in chapter 7 of Porch, *Path to Victory*, "FDR's Secret Baby"; the chapter title is taken from a phrase coined by Secretary Stimson. Stimson and Marshall both feared only distraction would come from operating in the Mediterranean. Porch, 326–32.

43. Matloff and Snell, *Strategic Planning*, 101. Re deploying divisions, see Wilson, *Maneuver and Firepower*, tables 15 and 16. The army divisions in Europe topped those in the Pacific by the end of 1943 but did not exceed the combined number of army and marine Divisions in the Pacific until early 1944.

44. Wheeler, *Big Red One*, 138; Baumer and Reardon, *American Iliad*, 14.

45. Finke, *No Mission Too Difficult*, 48–49. Just how many new lieutenants arrived that summer is uncertain. Booth recalled that his class graduated thirty-five, so he must have come from a different class; in *American Iliad* Baumer and Reardon report eighty from Class 25, which is accurate.

46. Lambert and DeFelice, *Every Man a Hero*, 44; Knickerbocker et al., *Danger Forward*, 6; John Kelly, interview by Michael Corley, April 20, 1977.

CHAPTER THREE

Torch Lights the Way Back

You men are the fuel that will ignite the torch of liberty. It will be the honor of the First Division to be the first to halt the tide of Nazism and stamp out the evil it represents.
> —*Major Richard Parker, commanding 1st Battalion,*
> *18th Infantry, November 7, 1942*

From the earliest inception of a plan for invasion of North Africa, the paramount enigma was probable French reaction to invasion.
> —*Danger Forward*

THE SCALE AND complexity of Operation Torch exceeded anything attempted in modern times, including the catastrophic British failure at Gallipoli during the Great War. The Allies' navies combined with merchant seamen to land invasion forces simultaneously on multiple beaches on the Atlantic and Mediterranean coasts of northwest Africa. Three separate invasion task forces embarked from ports in the United States and the United Kingdom. The operation required close coordination among allies whose views, means, and doctrine differed. Cultural differences further compounded difficulty. Finally, success depended, in part, on securing the acquiescence, if not the active cooperation, of Vichy France, given that the landings occurred on the soil of French colonial overseas territories and protectorates.

When they arrived in Scotland in August 1942, the Allied leadership and the troops of the 1st Infantry Division remained ignorant, if not blissfully so, of their objective. They expected to fight Germans somewhere in Europe. No one disabused them of that notion. None of them, from Terry Allen down to the last private to join the division, had any legitimate information. And despite months of training, the division still was not ready. The last intake of troops and new officers arrived too late to train with their units, something in need of remedy. The 1st ID boarded the *Queen Mary* with great excitement but with many of the newest replacements short of equipment. Many left without even mundane items such as their Class A uniforms—the army equivalent of a business suit, including, of course, a tie. That shortcoming led to confrontations with military police in the United Kingdom for being out of the uniform prescribed for visiting the local public houses. More important, some units, including the three regimental cannon companies, had not completed organizing and equipping, let alone training to do their mission. There remained much to do.[1]

Getting the Word

The 1st ID   arrived in the United Kingdom just days after Roosevelt and Churchill approved Operation Gymnast, renaming it Operation Torch. On August 21, Allen wrote to Mary Fran, his wife, "We [the 1st ID] are in fine shape and are now again undergoing very intensive training." Though as yet uninformed about the details of his mission, Allen knew it would involve an assault landing on a hostile coast. He continued, "I do not anticipate our doing anything but intensive training for a very long time." General Allen intended to get to know his division and train it. This he did with enthusiasm. His soldiers responded to his "infectious can-do enthusiasm and scrappiness."[2]

The division took up residence at Tidworth Barracks in the south of England. As Allen put it, "There was no indication of any specific operational mission in the offing, so activity again centered around combat training and reequipping." Despite having "graduated," the 1st ID still needed additional small-unit training and time to complete equipping. Rumors and false alarms abounded, the scariest being the possibility of "a cross channel invasion by the First Division unassisted on either flank and with no follow-up forces." On September 2, less than a month after arriving, General Allen was summoned to a conference in London. The next day he called his chief of staff, Colonel "Dutch" Cota, telling him to come to London "and bring the G-2 [intelligence], G-3 [operations] and G-4 [logistics] along with him." That day the key staff learned of their first combat mission of the war—invading Algeria.[3]

Terry Allen proved to be badly mistaken about the "very long time" he told Mary Fran he would have to train those under his command. As it turned out, the division, and for that matter everyone else involved in the execution of Torch, had less than two months to plan, train for, rehearse, and mount a profoundly complex operation requiring careful synchronization of forces on the move. In *The Path to Victory*, Douglas Porch succinctly describes the problem: some "65,000 troops divided into three 'Assault Forces' would sail from the United States and the United Kingdom in 370 merchant vessels escorted by 3000 warships." From start to finish the undertaking was joint—army, navy, and air force as well as combined, that is, forces from different nations. The Western Task Force planned to land on the Atlantic coast of Morocco as the Eastern Task Force descended on the Mediterranean coast of Algeria, twelve hundred miles to the east. The Center Task Force, the land component of which was US II Corps (including 1st ID), also intended to land on the Mediterranean coast of Algeria in order to seize Oran. There was little time to do everything that had to be done, and all of it had to be done with organizations formed on the fly and primarily composed of people who had never worked with one another. Often they came from different countries and thus sometimes miscommunicated. W. G. F. Jackson, a British veteran of the war in North Africa and prolific postwar author, may have said it best in *The Battle for North Africa, 1940–43*, in which he pointed out that among those who planned and executed Torch, "there were no professionals; all commanders, staffs and troops were amateurs groping into the unknown beyond the frontiers of known operational techniques."[4]

The II Corps staff originally deployed to the United Kingdom under the command of Major General Mark W. Clark to plan for a cross-Channel invasion. In September II Corps shifted to planning for an invasion of North Africa as part of the Center Task Force, which included the 1st ID and 1st Armored Division (AD) as well as other units. Stanhope B. Mason, Allen's G-3, found working with other units frustrating, remarking that they "as individuals, had no knowledge or experience in amphibious assaults." By the time planning began, Clark had moved on, and no officer had yet been identified to replace him. Eventually General Marshall selected Major General Lloyd R. Fredendall, who joined II Corps on October 10, 1942, just before the final rehearsal for Torch. Despite Mason's frustration, Allen and his division staff made effective use of their experience and won most points on the assault plan.[5] The remainder of the division remained in the dark but had plenty to do anyway.

Final Preparation

Equipping continued while the 1st ID trained in England. Before embarking for the United Kingdom, Ralph Uffner became leader of the 3rd Platoon of the 26th Infantry's cannon company. Newly authorized, the cannon company as yet had no cannons and few troops. Worse still, it had no doctrine to read and no equipment list. Not long after arriving in the UK, the company's first sergeant discovered six self-propelled 75-millimeter howitzers and two self-propelled 105-millimeter M7 howitzers sitting on a railway siding. The 75-millimeter howitzers were mounted on half-tracks, while the M7 was built on the M4 Sherman tank chassis. The soldiers called the ungainly self-propelled howitzers "Priests" because of the pulpit-like commander's station rising out of the right side of their chassis. The provenance of these howitzers remains uncertain to this day, but Uffner's platoon received both of the M7s.[6]

The "newly found" howitzers came with warm armored force winter clothing, gear the men of the cannon company relished. Now Uffner and his cannon crews became self-taught artillerymen. He recalled with pride, "The men had the aptitude and will to apply themselves. Soldiers with less than four years of grammar school did it." Uffner taught the instrument corporals "the principles of surveying and enough trigonometry to calculate the azimuth for pointing the howitzers in parallel." None of the division's three cannon companies had ever fired in practice before embarking for North Africa. And only once they were there did Uffner finally have access to the cannon company field manual, this during a visit to the cannon company of the 47th Infantry of the 9th ID. Because he had seen combat, II Corps sent Uffner to pass on his recently acquired wisdom. He found the affair ironic, given that "real artillerymen" manned the 47th's cannon company.[7]

The dilemma of the cannon companies was comparatively rare. There were other equipment shortages, but none so dire. For the rest of the division, small-unit training and fitness training continued apace. John Lebda recalled a march out and back from Tidworth to the ancient rock circle at Stonehenge, a distance of twenty-two miles. From Tidworth, Lebda and the 26th went north to Scotland, where they "lived in Quonset huts on the shore of Loch Ness." Ray Lambert, a medic in the 16th, remembered doing "live fire drills" in addition to the amphibious landings. According to him, "You practice and practice and practice trying to make everything automatic."[8]

There is nothing trivial about an assault landing, as it entails a great deal more than simply dropping men and their gear off on a beach. Ships to move troops, weapons, and still more ships to sustain the ships themselves are all necessary. But so too are naval escorts to prevent, if possible, losses of troop ships to submarine attack. U-boats remained numerous in 1942, and were reinforced by Italian boats. A discrete naval force also had to be found to provide over-the-horizon protection from Italian surface units. On arriving at the intended landing site, warships supported the landing with naval gunfire. Coordinating the whole affair occurred on flagships with facilities adequate for command and control. Yet getting to the beach is only the first step and not the mission.

In the fall of 1942, the incredible variety of landing craft and special equipment such as the DUKW, an amphibious 2.5-ton truck, had either not been fielded or fielded only in small numbers, and the flat-bottomed LST (landing ship, tank) had not yet arrived. The Royal Navy developed an extemporaneous solution by converting shallow-draft tankers designed to operate in the Venezuelan oil fields of Lake Maracaibo. These so-called Maracaibo tankers could cross over the many sandbars found in the lake. Only a devoted crewman would describe them as beautiful, but in North Africa, as in Venezuela, they proved their worth. Two of them, HMS *Misoa* and *Tasjera*, landed tanks from the 1st AD to provide armor support to the 1st ID. The availability of amphibious assault vessels determined the tempo and the feasibility of subsequent landings.[9]

Merely loading assault craft is a complex undertaking. Ralph Uffner kept copies of "boat" stations and diagrams of who went to which station and then who went where in the landing craft. Getting the troops from their bunks in holds to the various boat stations required careful sequencing. Everyone could not go charging up the stairs—or ladders, as sailors called them—at once. And as the green soldiers would soon find out, getting into a landing craft from a ship at sea is a difficult and dangerous exercise. Charles E. Murphy, an officer in the 1st Engineer Battalion, described the drill succinctly. First a soldier must get over the side and "climb down a 70 foot cargo net in the dark, full field equipment," and then "jump into a landing barge, with the sea, one minute it would be four feet below the net and the next minute four feet above the net, you had to scramble to keep from being crushed against the side of the ship."[10] What Murphy failed to mention is almost certain death to any soldier who fell into the sea laden with heavy equipment, or serious injury or death to anyone who fell from a distance onto the deck or gunnel of the craft.

Once a landing craft is loaded, it circles around, awaiting the loading of the remainder of the craft. Once assembled, a "wave" of loaded landing craft forms and then heads inshore based on the planned schedule. Assuming the surf fails to capsize the craft and enemy fire fails to sink it, the troops disembark, sometimes into water over their heads. If they manage to avoid drowning or getting shot while in the water, they wade onto the beach where, if they are not mowed down by entrenched machine-gun fire one or two steps onto dry land, they assemble and head inland to fight. Only then are they doing what they have risked death to do. An assault landing, no matter how complex or how long it takes, is merely a means of getting to the fight, not an end in itself.

Practicing the process of getting from ship to shore and rehearsing actions ashore could not be done too often. Iteration revealed mistakes that led to learning. The British Army supported unit training and passed on the bitter lessons learned from the Dieppe Raid, when the 2nd Canadian Division, accompanied by British commandos and a small contingent of US Army Rangers, assaulted Dieppe, France, on August 19, 1942. They mounted this ambitious raid hoping to cause mayhem among the German defenders, as well as to test concepts about best practices in an amphibious landing, but they failed, with horrific losses. Of the six thousand soldiers who tried to land or actually did so, more than half were killed, wounded, or captured. Survivors of the raid supported training of the 18th Infantry. The British passed on other lessons as well, including information on German tactics garnered in France, Crete, Greece, and North Africa. None of what the British and Canadians had learned and passed on about fighting the Germans could be applied, however, until the troops got ashore.[11]

The Plan

On August 14, 1942, General George C. Marshall selected Lieutenant General Dwight D. Eisenhower to serve as commander of the Allied Force Headquarters in the Mediterranean Theater of Operations. In that capacity Eisenhower served as commander for operations in North Africa. He proved a good choice, as he understood the contemporary limitations of the US Army and had been involved in negotiating Allied objectives from the outset. He forged a working combined staff despite the near-constant carping of British and American officers about their Allied counterparts. He also succeeded despite prejudice against Americans generally and him specifically from the British chief of the Imperial General Staff, Sir Alan Brooke. Equally impressive, Eisenhower achieved all this in the face of "help" from the British during the early going and throughout the war, as well as plenty of criticism from them. Winston Churchill, in particular, "helped" him nearly too much. The two men liked each other from the beginning and became fast friends. Nevertheless, they often had raised-voice discussions. But no matter how heated their debates became, they readily forgave each other. Of Churchill, Eisenhower said, "In countless ways he could have made my task a harder one had he been anything less than big."[12]

Competing strategic views between the British and Americans, combined with the complication of trying to deal simultaneously with "Free French" and Vichy French, further aggravated planning and accounted for considerable back-and-forth. In short, no one knew for certain what the Vichy French might do once the fighting began—support the Allied effort, offer resistance, or sit it out altogether. The Americans and the British did agree that the British should remain in the background as long as possible. The British had earned French enmity, first by evacuating the continent and then by attacking and sinking the French fleet at Toulon. Still, according to Stanhope Mason, "There was, on high, an optimistic expectation that the French in Algeria would welcome the invading forces as their liberators from the yoke of Nazi dominance—maybe with brass band and flags and champagne." But, he noted, "there was absolutely no intelligence estimate to support such thinking." Mason rightly suspected that some of the optimism stemmed from "state department types." He almost certainly had Robert D. Murphy in mind. Murphy, US chargé d'affaires to the Vichy, believed the French could be won over and genuinely attempted to do just that.[13]

Planning was problematic for Allen's staff for this and a great many other reasons. The chief irritation stemmed from the initial II Corps plan to land the division more or less evenly dispersed along the coast. Because of the terrain and the distances involved, that course of action effectively precluded concentrating forces to drive inland. In the end, "Gen. Allen had his way." The final plan assigned 1st ID two beaches on which to land: Y in the west and Z in the East. Beach Y lay adjacent to the tiny coastal village of Les Andalouses and north of a rocky ridge known in Arabic as Djebel Murdjadjo. Bounded on the south by Sebkha d'Oran (a dry lake except after heavy rains), the Djebel restricted movement to a very narrow corridor heading east toward Oran. The 26th Infantry Regimental Combat Team (hereinafter 26th Infantry) would come ashore at Beach Y, a bit more than ten miles west of Oran. Both the 16th and 18th combat teams would land at Beach Z, some twenty miles northeast of the small port town of Arzew. Once the infantry was ashore, a tank battalion task force from the 1st Armored Division would come ashore from the makeshift amphibious tank landing ships built on Maracaibo tankers. The plan required the 1st Ranger Battalion, organized and trained as commandos by their British counterparts and led by Lieutenant

Colonel William O. Darby, to land just north of Beach Z, directly on the quay of the small port town of Arzew. The Rangers were to seize the docks and destroy or capture two French coastal artillery batteries. Beach Z too suffered from narrow exits from the beach. Djebel Khar ran west to east, as did its counterpart on Beach Y. Units exiting Beach Z had to move westward with comparatively little maneuver room.[14]

The II Corps landings included two other important amphibious assaults. Combat Command B (more or less equivalent to a regimental combat team) of the 1st Armored Division, the other division in II Corps, would land at Beach X, some thirty miles southwest of Oran. Combat Command B formed the lead element of the 1st AD; the rest of the division would land later. Finally, troops from a battalion of the 1st AD's 6th Armored Infantry would attempt a *coup de main* to seize the docks in Oran, precluding the French from destroying cargo-handling facilities. The *coup de main* was under command of the Royal Navy, which proposed to land the assault force using onetime US Coast Guard cutters renamed HMS *Walney* and *Hartland*.[15]

Commodore Thomas H. Troubridge, Royal Navy, would command the naval task force and the landing until such time as General Fredendall believed he could "control the situation ashore." The task force included some sixty-one warships and forty-three transports. The HMS *Rodney's* nine 16-inch guns formed the centerpiece of naval gunfire supporting effort, but Troubridge also had one "Fleet Carrier," HMS *Furious*, and two auxiliary carriers. In addition to the carriers assigned to the Center Task Force, the US 12th Air Force would fly in land-based aircraft from Gibraltar. Other aircraft would launch from HMS *Archer*, one of the auxiliary carriers, once the ground troops seized the airfields and opened them up for Allied use. The 12th Air Force planned to have four fighter groups (about four hundred fighters), one air transport group (about one hundred aircraft), and two squadrons of B-17 bombers (about thirty-six aircraft) within days of the landing, and that was just the beginning.[16]

The plan included yet another wrinkle. Army Air Force colonel William C. Bentley would lead a parachute infantry task force based on the 3rd Battalion, 503rd Parachute Infantry, commanded by Lieutenant Colonel Edson D. Raff. C-47 Skytrain transports assigned to the 60th Troop Carrier Group, 51st Troop Carrier Wing, would fly the paratroopers 1,500 miles from the United Kingdom. On arrival in the area, a ship offshore of Oran would signal the aircraft. If the Vichy proved amenable, the paratroopers would not make their jumps but land in the aircraft in which they rode. If, on the other hand, the Vichy meant to fight, then the paratroopers would execute an airborne assault. Either way, the task was to seize or occupy the French air base at Tafraoui.[17]

The final iteration of the II Corps planning enabled Allen to employ a double envelopment of the French defenders of Oran. On October 5 the division published an embarkation plan and guidance for the tactical plan. The scheme of maneuver was quite clear: "The Division will make plans to land on two widely separated beaches executing a pincer movement on area between these beaches." The 16th and 18th Infantries would approach from the east along the road from Arzew through Saint-Cloud, while the 26th Infantry approached from the west via the coast road. Other II Corps units would land following after the 1st ID, including Task Force Red, composed primarily of 1st AD tanks. Once ashore, the task force's mission required it to head south some twenty miles to Sainte-Barbe du Tlélat to prevent outlying French troops from responding. Task Force Green, composed of Combat Command B, 1st AD troops landing at Beach X, would head southeast to Lourmel and then east before turning north toward Oran. The Corps plan had as many wrinkles as an old man's face.[18]

Three-quarters of Oran's two hundred thousand inhabitants were Pieds-Noirs—European French who made their homes in Algeria and lived much as they had before the Vichy took control. Arabs comprised the rest. The Oran Division's local garrison amounted to ten thousand soldiers readily available to defend the city. Within twenty-four hours nearby units could provide an additional eight thousand, and four thousand more within five days. Though not well equipped, if it chose to fight, the Oran Division would matter. The naval task force had also to contend with some forty-five coast artillery guns near Oran and another six at the small port adjacent to Beach Z. Finally, the French also had one hundred aircraft of varying capability. With the rugged djebels, mountain ridges extending nearly to the water's edge, the problem of getting ashore and seizing the beaches near Oran could prove difficult. The answer depended in large measure on what the French authorities and their military leadership chose to do.[19]

The Torch Is Lit

During one of the last rehearsals, General Roosevelt encountered Eisenhower "during the early morning hours" of October 19, 1942. Roosevelt, always effusive in the field, "gave a glowing account" of the exercise. Eisenhower, who had watched most of it, thought otherwise. In his view, "the whole demonstration was disappointing." Precisely what Eisenhower said to Roosevelt and/or Allen is unknown, but Allen either got the message directly or

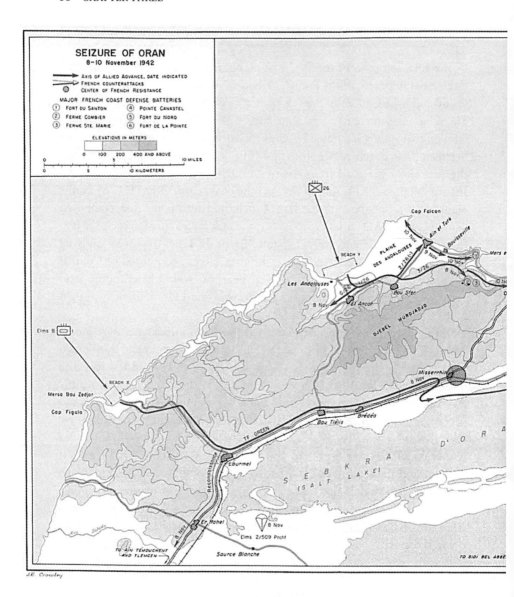

Map 1: Seizure of Oran, November 8–10, 1942. Reproduced from George F. Howe, *Northwest Africa: Seizing the Initiative in the West* (Washington: Center of Military History, 1957), Map IV.

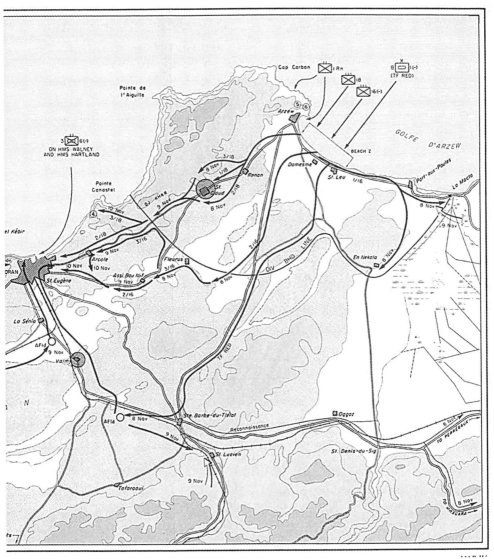

drew similar conclusions about the demonstration, because in their aftermath he relieved or reassigned some company-level officers and trained his men even harder. Terry Allen knew that his division, however lovely it appeared to him, was not yet ready to play at the varsity level. Not long before they embarked for North Africa, Allen shared, briefly, his concern about his troops' readiness with Mary Fran: "They are 1000% better than they were at Indiantown Gap. They are young but hard and fit. Only hope I have done all that could be done for them."[20]

What no one knew is just where they were "goin' a fightin'," but the troops believed they would be fighting Germans, likely in Norway or France. What they knew about fighting Germans, with few exceptions, they knew secondhand. Major Edwin Sutherland was one of those few Americans who had at least sniffed a battlefield. He got his whiff in Egypt courtesy of the British Eighth Army. Sutherland, an alumnus of the 16th Infantry, moved on to develop doctrine for tank destroyers. In that capacity he went to observe antitank operations in Egypt. After a harrowing and difficult journey from Miami to Africa via the Caribbean, Brazil, and various stops in Africa, he arrived in the aftermath of "the big battles of Knightsbridge and the Cauldron." These defeats had "severely wounded [the British] and Rommel was on the move." Sutherland survived the inevitable retreat and "observed" the British 22nd Armoured Brigade of the 7th Armoured Division—the Desert Rats. After a few weeks he made his way back to the States to codify what he had learned in US tank destroyer doctrine. Revealing an anglophile streak, he claimed that he had "a lovely experience there [with the 22nd Armored Brigade], and developed tremendous respect for the Tommy trooper. Hard as nails and resilient." Later he rejoined the division.[21]

The US Army learned how their enemies and friends fought, sometimes from reports but also through direct observation, as Sutherland, military attachés, and covert intelligence operatives did. Overt observations and insights appeared in the various professional journals published by branch associations. The army's military intelligence service contributed by collecting thirty "lessons" in three small volumes entitled *Special Bulletins from the 1939–1940 Campaign in Europe*. These thirty bulletins provided analysis of various campaigns, including the Soviet–Finnish War and German campaigns in Poland, France, and the Low Countries, providing important insights into how the Germans fought. Captain John T. Corley, then commanding a company in the 26th Infantry, thought the training had been pretty good, particularly the "commando training, with the commandos as aggressors and showing us all they knew about the German technique." But none of what the division had learned or been told about the Germans applied immediately.[22]

Eventually what the troops knew and their readiness for combat operations moved from the theoretical to the practical. Colonel Frank U. Greer, who commanded the 18th Infantry, put it succinctly when he announced to his assembled regiment, "Men of the 18th. We're goin' a fightin'!" Greer had orders not to share the destination or the enemy, but at least the troops were finally going to do what they had trained to do. Greer's regiment and supporting units loaded on six vessels that together styled themselves Transport Division 18. The remainder of the 1st ID loaded on five other vessels belonging to Transportation Divisions 16 and 26. The division headquarters sailed from Greenock, Scotland, with Greer, his staff, and the 18th's 3rd Battalion aboard the passenger ship *Reina del Pacifico*.[23]

Adversary Assessments

In 1942 George C. Marshall's vision of invading France exceeded his grasp of the possible to the point of hallucination. Getting into the war on the ground against the Axis powers in the west in 1942 was an important strategic objective. Henry L. Stimson agreed, disparaging the idea of invading North Africa as "FDR's secret baby," but there was nowhere else to go; North Africa offered the only feasible objective. A cross-Channel invasion at the time was simply out of the question. The United Kingdom's interests, apart from protecting the Suez and access to oil, included keeping at least some Germans tied down. Equally important, in 1942 the UK was the senior partner in the British–US alliance. The British had the preponderance of immediately available means, and thus they had influence. Hitler, for his part, considered the Mediterranean Theater peripheral to his interests, but the Italian possessions in Africa were vital to his much weaker ally. Supporting Mussolini in the Mediterranean also gave Hitler the use of an Italian field army in Russia and the addition of Italian troops to the German Army, which was poised to threaten the Suez.[24]

In May 1942 Adolf Hitler issued his appraisal of the looming Allied threat in the Mediterranean in Directive No. 42, "Instructions for operations against unoccupied France and the Iberian Peninsula," which began, "The development of the situation in unoccupied France, or in the French possessions in North Africa, may render it necessary to occupy the whole of French territory." Hitler wanted also to prepare to react to "enemy attempts to seize the Iberian Peninsula," and required the various arms of the Wehrmacht to assess the threat by June10. Subsequently the Wehrmacht would be authorized to coordinate the Reich's response with their Italian allies as appropriate. In other words, throughout the spring and summer of 1942, the Allies as well as the Axis powers were preparing for an Allied initiative in the Mediterranean or Africa. On October 7 Commander Harry C. Butcher, an old friend of Eisenhower and one of his aides, confided in his diary that Eisenhower was sure the Germans were aware of Torch, and that "the only question in [Eisenhower's] mind is what they are doing in order to meet it."[25]

While the Big Red One staged at Indiantown Gap, Generalfeldmarschall Erwin Rommel, commanding Panzer Army Africa, staged a tutorial on mechanized warfare. A prolific diarist, note taker, and letter writer, his appraisal and description of his undertaking can be read in *The Rommel Papers*. He advanced a theory of mechanized war and complained about his lack of resources and what he considered missed opportunity in Africa. Rommel wrote pithy assessments of his adversaries and found time to read and comment on Basil Liddell Hart's criticism of the British Army's operations in Africa. After the British defeat at Gazala in May–June 1942, Liddell Hart argued that the British defeat there stemmed from the British command's "close associations with infantry warfare." Rommel agreed. But after seizing Tobruk in June and advancing nearly to Cairo, the force commanded by the Desert Fox culminated near the small town of El Alamein, which lay astride the coast road to Cairo and the Suez Canal. Rommel described the physical and logistical exhaustion of his army in terms that Carl von Clausewitz had used more than one hundred years earlier. What had ensued was that which he most feared, "mechanized static warfare with a stabilized front, because that was just what the British officers and men had been trained for."[26]

Lieutenant General Sir Bernard Law Montgomery arrived on the scene to assume command of the British Eighth Army in August. No Allied soldier in Europe, other than perhaps George S. Patton Jr., proved more effective at self-promotion than Montgomery, even if both of them fell far short of Douglas MacArthur's efforts on that score. In *The Plain Cook and the Great Showman: The First and Eighth Armies in North Africa*, Gregory Blaxland, a British soldier who fought in North Africa, contrasted Montgomery with K. A. N. Anderson, who commanded the British First Army. Montgomery took advantage of the "mechanized static warfare" he found. He built up his forces and, like all who preceded him, laid mines in prolific qualities, wearing down the German and Italian forces in bloody battles of attrition. Rommel, it seems, had accommodated him. Whatever his faults, Montgomery proved very effective at inspiring the "Tommies," many of whom had fought in the seesaw battles across the deserts of both Libya and Egypt for two years, in

Eighth Army. His advantage in numbers and the nearing of Operation Torch afforded him the opportunity to plan a set-piece battle in the certain knowledge that the invasion of North Africa would require Rommel to withdraw. Montgomery planned no maneuver; instead, he would "blow a gap in Rommel's defense through which we could debouch." Montgomery and General Harold R. L. G. Alexander, the commander-in-chief, Middle East, worked to take maximum advantage of the threat to Rommel's rear that Torch would pose. General Alexander believed the ideal date for the offensive would be "minus thirteen of *Torch* [italics in original]."[27]

In the end, Eisenhower's blow landed four days later than originally planned. But it was the Vichy French authorities who held the hole card in this grand game. No one could say what they might do. Major General Mark W. Clark, Eisenhower's deputy, and Robert D. Murphy, chief American envoy in Algeria, undertook a clandestine operation they hoped would result in a cheap victory. Shortly after midnight on October 22, 1942, Clark and a small party landed on a beach near a fishing village called Cherchell, some sixty miles from Algiers. Clark disembarked from the British submarine HMS *Seraph* and paddled his way through the breakers in a two-man kayak manned by himself and a British commando. Six others in three kayaks made it ashore as well.[28]

There, Murphy met Clark and his associates to plan what Rick Atkinson described in *An Army at Dawn* as a mission both "courageous and daft." Murphy had worked for months with various Vichy military to hand over Algeria without a shot. Clark and Murphy had a confab the following morning with Major General Charles Emmanuel Mast, the deputy commanding general of the French XIX Corps, and five other officers. Both sides misled the other during the impromptu meeting, and no firm commitment emerged. Loyalty to Field Marshal Philippe Pétain, whose idea the formation of Vichy France had been, personal concepts of loyalty, and/or attempts to assess the German response would all play a role in their decisions. In any case, all the players in the game were ready to play their hands. Among those players were untried American troops.[29]

Intelligence about the Vichy forces was fairly accurate, although not shared beyond the planning staffs until the last minute. Terry Allen's intelligence officer knew the French order of battle and the officers who commanded their major units. General Pierre Juin, who commanded the French Army in North Africa, was reportedly "fundamentally Pro-Ally [sic]." The reports were true; later in the campaign Juin commanded French troops who fought alongside his erstwhile "opponents" in Algeria. French mobile forces included twenty tanks and twenty armored cars, a reconnaissance unit mounted on motorcycles, and three squadrons of horse-mounted cavalry amounting to no more than 2,200 troops of the 16,000 or so in the Oran Division. The division assessed the French troops as "2 [*sic*] or 3rd class" due to "restrictions on training imposed by the Armistice commission" and a lack of equipment and field training. This estimate of capability and capacity was sound. Still, what the French would actually do remained a mystery.[30]

As late as October, the German and Italian high commands believed that an Allied operation in the west was unlikely. They expected an effort eventually, but differed as to where the Allies would strike. The Germans feared that Dakar in Senegal was the most likely target, perhaps followed by a landing in Tunisia or even Libya to cut off Panzer Army Africa. The Italians thought a landing in French Morocco more probable followed by operations in Tunisia and then against the Italian mainland. Neither anticipated a landing in Algeria.[31]

Surprises of Varying Kinds

The British Eighth Army began its assault on Panzer Army Africa at 2140 hours on Friday, October 23, 1942. At about the same time in Norfolk, Virginia, troops preparing to embark learned they would land on the Atlantic coast of Africa in French Morocco. In the United Kingdom the Big Red One's rank and file remained ignorant of their destination. The following day they began heading to the ports of embarkation. On Monday, October 26, the *Reina del Pacifico*, bearing the division headquarters and part of the 18th Infantry, weighed anchor. Other transports left later but all eventually rendezvoused and moved in convoy. John Lebda, a soldier in the 26th Infantry, recalled that as the convoy sailed south, most aboard the ships assumed, "we were going to invade western France." They learned otherwise on 1 November, when unit commanders briefed the troops on their mission. Once briefed, the troops and their leaders studied reconnaissance photos, maps, and the plan.[32]

"On November 6, 1942," Lebda remembered, "we sailed east and that night we could see lights on our left from the Rock of Gibraltar and lights on our right from Spanish Morocco." More remarkably, none of the convoys encountered U-boats, or even bombers. As it turned out, the German U-boats and Italian submarines were patrolling farther east. The next day Lebda and his buddies were each issued the *Pocket Guide to North Africa*, a handy little pamphlet of forty-two pages that introduced the troops to the Arab Islamic culture they would soon encounter. The guidebook included advice on

"Dining with Moslems," "The Faith of Islam," "Warning the Women," and handy Arabic phrases. If they could follow the phonetic pronunciation guide, they could wish the inhabitants a good morning and other such pleasantries. They were also advised that North Africa "is not the continuous sea of sand such as is pictured in Hollywood movies about the French Foreign Legion." Quite the contrary, the guidebook described the coast as "almost as pleasant as Southern California, with hot, dry summers and consistently heavy rain." The Hollywood movies referred to undoubtedly included *Beau Geste* (1939), starring Gary Cooper, a film about the French Foreign Legion.[33]

The Big Red One would have its chance to encounter a *Beau Geste*-like desert soon enough. Before midnight the very evening Lebda received his booklet, he and the rest of the division began clambering down cargo nets to board assault craft. In accordance with doctrine proclaiming the hours of darkness best for amphibious assaults, the first troops waded ashore at approximately 0100 on November 8, 1942.[34]

H. R. Knickerbocker, a well-known journalist who wrote extensively about German politics during the rise of Adolf Hitler, was aboard the *Reina del Pacifico* along with Terry Allen. Knickerbocker's hard-hitting articles criticizing the Nazis won him sufficient fame that Hitler had him deported when he came into power. Waiting for the invasion to begin. Knickerbocker and Allen paced the deck in companionable silence. When Knickerbocker noticed lights in the distance, he asked Allen in a whisper what they were. "The shore," Allen responded; Oran was not in blackout. "At that moment," Knickerbocker recalled, "with hardly the rattle of a block, the first landing craft touched water. We could see it swaying far below and men climbing into it. This was H-Hour."[35]

The attached Ranger battalion, known as Darby's Rangers, after their commander, landed directly on the quay at Arzew. Taking the docks proved easy. The Rangers "scrambled on to the quay, overpowered two sentries in a brief exchange of gunfire, and caught the garrison asleep." Darby himself led the attack on the northernmost of the two coastal artillery batteries. The garrison at Fort du Nord, about mile north of the port, put up a fight. Nevertheless, by 0400 the Rangers had taken their objectives and signaled success by firing a green flare.[36] That night Darby's Rangers began a tradition of excellence and effective partnership with the 1st ID.

On Darby's left the 1st ID's main effort, composed of the 18th and 16th Regimental Combat Teams, landed abreast, with Colonel Greer's 18th on the right. The 18th began wading ashore at 0120. Greer sent his 3rd Battalion into Arzew to take the town and relieve Darby's Rangers. His 1st Battalion formed up and headed west toward Saint-Cloud, nearly ten miles west of the beachhead. Greer's 2nd Battalion trailed the 1st Battalion as both moved toward Saint-Cloud.

As Greer was stumbling around in the dark, looking for his units, one of his sergeants reminded him that they were supposed to have fired a pyrotechnic mortar that would produce an American flag fireworks display. Someone at higher headquarters during planning had apparently cherished the hope that the sight of the American flag would induce the defenders to lay down their weapons and accept the Americans as their liberators. Accordingly, Greer ordered the man carrying the mortar to fire it. Lieutenant Daniel Lyons thought the result "the most beautiful fireworks display I have ever seen in my life." Mason saw it differently: "Sparks changed darkness to light. From everywhere within rifle or machine gun range the French defenders could pin point the origin of the spark trails. By the time the US flag was displayed in its colorful glory with the added attracting bang, all the French defenders had at long last located the real target." Greer, according to Mason, experienced "a superfluity of incoming fire." Colonel Greer later maintained that "he had so flattened himself on the ground there could forever be imprints of his jacket buttons at that spot."[37]

Colonel Cheadle's 16th Infantry began landing at 0100. In the absence of resistance, the arriving troops experienced the familiar disorientation of wading ashore intermingled with other units and mucking about to get organized. Cheadle got his regimental combat team moving quickly. The 16th formed a column of battalions and headed west toward Oran. Lieutenant Colonel Frederick W. Gibb led with his 3rd Battalion. The 2nd and 1st followed in that order.

Meanwhile on Beach Y, Teddy Roosevelt and Colonel Alexander N. (Alec) Stark Jr. led the 26th Infantry ashore. They too landed more or less on schedule, at 0120. The 33rd Field Artillery, in direct support to the 26th, landed later. Quentin Roosevelt, a lieutenant in the 33rd, went to war alongside his father. The 26th's mission required them to scale a two-thousand-foot ridge called Djebel Murjadjo. They encountered resistance about 0600 as they struggled up the side of the ridge. The 3rd Battalion's Company K drew machine-gun fire and even turned back a cavalry charge in order to retain their position along the ridgeline, which they secured about 0800. John Lebda, an infantryman in the 26th, was disappointed to find that despite assurances to the contrary, the French had decided to fight. According to him, "the Vichy French Foreign Legion responded and gave us hell." At one point that morning Lebda was sheltered under a ledge on the djebel when a small man came up where he and others sheltered and announced, "The bastards can't hit the side of a barn, come on . . . follow me." Lebda did just that, as did others. Then someone yelled, "Hell that's Teddy Roosevelt." Indeed, it was: Teddy Roosevelt, Alec Stark, and young officers in their first fight kept the Blue Spaders, as the 26th styled themselves after the blue spade on their crest, moving uphill.[38]

The British have a long history of conducting special operations of heroic proportion that are often more akin to forlorn hope attacks than operations with a reasonable expectation of success. A forlorn hope is an attack in which the possibility of success justifies the likelihood of high casualties. Such attacks were nearly a shibboleth in the British forces. The British mounted a failed attack on the U-boat base at Zeebrugge in April 1918. They reprised it with better results in March 1942 against the U-boat base at Saint-Nazaire. Both were bloody battles but demonstrated incredible courage. The attack on the harbor of Oran would be of the same ilk, though with far less success. The 3rd Battalion, 6th Armored Infantry, who formed the assault force were aboard the former US Coast Guard cutters HMS *Walney* and *Hartland*. The two aging ships and two small cutters tagging along to lay smoke steamed straight in. At 0300 Royal Navy lieutenant Paul E. A. Duncan broadcast by loudspeaker, "Ne Tirez pas. Nous sommes vos amis. Ne Tirez pas." (Don't shoot. We are your friends. Don't shoot.) By this time the Allied landings had been underway for roughly two hours. The French were neither surprised nor did they believe the attackers were friends, a point they made by responding with fire from machine guns, shore batteries, and several naval vessels. While announcing that friends had arrived, Duncan was killed in midsentence. In less than two hours the forlorn hope ended with horrendous casualties. Of the 393 men that composed the 6th Armored Infantry's landing team, 189 died and another 157 suffered wounds. The Royal Navy lost 113 dead and 86 wounded. Five US Navy sailors were killed, and 7 wounded. Gallantry medals duly went to several, including the man who imagined the whole thing and presided over its failure.[39]

The two Maracaibo tankers (HMS *Misoa* and *Tasajera*) that served as tank landing ships Tank beached around 0400. Task Force Red disembarked tanks from them across pontoon bridges laid from ship to shore. The bulk of Task Force Red was ashore by 0800. Part of it landed later at the Arzew quay. The reconnaissance company of the 13th Armored Regiment headed out at 0829. Soon thereafter, Task Force Red tanks, armored infantry, tank destroyers, and supporting weapons moved off on the outer loop of the double envelopment of Oran. Task Force Red had two missions. First it had to seize the

Tafraoui airfield or link up with the paratroopers, depending on the results of the airborne effort. Part of Task Force Red had the mission of heading east to meet up with Task Force Green as it moved west. Task Force Red reached the airfield by 1112 and took it after a brief flurry of fire. They found no paratroopers Shortly after noon, they reported the airfield ready to receive friendly aircraft. Two squadrons of British Spitfires began landing at 1630.[40]

Terry Allen wrote to his son, "Forward group went ahead with me just in the rear of the assault battalions of the 18th Infantry. At that time the beach was under fire from a seaplane base and various shore batteries that had not yet been knocked out." Despite Vichy French resistance for which their navy set the standard, both the 1st ID and Combat Command B of the 1st AD made good headway throughout the day. Landing the 1st ID's artillery and vehicles did not proceed as well but did continue all day.[41]

Both the 16th and 18th Infantries had several skirmishes during the day. The lead battalion of the 18th passed through the village of Renan, not quite ten miles from the beach, at midmorning. Shortly afterward five charcoal-burning armored cars attacked the advanced guard. In short order, Company A of the 18th Infantry dispatched one of the armored cars and captured the remainder, having damaged all four. In the fight they took fourteen French prisoners, and one of their own was killed. Rifle grenades fired from the venerable M1903 Springfield proved their worth, as did the Browning automatic rifle. The 16th cleared its share of Beach Z quickly, enabling Task Force Red to come ashore. Just before 1230, the 2nd Algerian Infantry Regiment ambushed the 1st Battalion, 16th Infantry. Major William A. Cunningham mounted a coordinated attack supported by HMS *Farndale*, a destroyer, against the offending Algerian infantry. By 1330 the 16th Infantry owned the ground and the village of La Macta, five miles southeast of the beaches. The remainder of the regiment continued west.[42]

The airborne task force, an idea bold to the point of foolhardiness, played out over the course of the day. Thirty-nine transports took off on the evening of November 7, carrying Colonel Raff and his paratroopers (556, all told). Navigated by inexperienced young men using poor charts and British navigation equipment that did not work properly on US aircraft, many of the crews got lost. None received the message warning of French resistance, so all planned to land unimpeded. Some aircraft landed in Spanish Morocco, others in Gibraltar, and others in various dry lake beds in French Morocco. Only nine of the planes managed to arrive near the Tafraoui airfield. Raff and the other paratroopers in these nine duly "exited" the aircraft, believing they saw French armor moving on the airfield. Raff broke a rib on landing and then learned the tanks he had seen from the air belonged to Task Force Red and not the French.[43]

At the town of Saint-Cloud, the 2nd Algerian Infantry, a Foreign Legion unit, and a battery of 65th African Field Artillery bloodied the 18th Infantry. In short order the French stopped the lead battalion of the 18th with a number of casualties. Worse still, Vichy artillery produced panic in a number of the rookie infantrymen. Lieutenant Edward McGregor described what happened as "almost a rout." The troops "were terrified of artillery. I shouted, 'Stop, Stop.' " Indeed, he managed to stop them, round them up, and get them under control, but he was astonished by what he had just been through: "It never occurred to me that in the best trained division in the US Army that this could happen." As it turned out, he had to get the troops moving a second time, as their reluctance to face live fire endured. Later in the day, McGregor took command of the company when his commander was killed.[44]

Frank U. Greer, the regimental commander, set about reorganizing his newly bloodied regiment to mount an attack supported by a battery of the 32nd Field Artillery and his cannon company. Heavy surf had delayed unloading the artillery and the cannon company. The cannon company troops were nonplussed by the mission. They had been issued their two 105-millimeter self-propelled howitzers and their six half-track mounted 75-millimeter howitzers when they embarked for Africa. Until then they had not seen them, let alone fired them. When they finally did, they realized that the 75s lacked gunner's sights.[45]

The afternoon attack died out at sunset without success. The newly arrived cannon company lost one of its 105-millimeter howitzers to the surviving Vichy armored car. Friendly fire shot up the second howitzer as it was en route to the beach for ammunition. The "sightless" 75s literally could not fight. Captain Frank Colacicco, who commanded the cannon company, noted of his first day in combat, "It was a fiasco."[46] The second failed attack at Saint-Cloud serves as the mark for ending that first long day in combat, a grueling and frightening one for the young Americans. Most of them, however, had managed to conquer their fear, as did John Lebda when he got up and followed Teddy Roosevelt up the ridgeline.

A Day of Firsts

It was a day of many firsts. H. R. Knickerbocker ran into an old friend in Arzew when he encountered Edgar Guerard Hamilton, an American serving as an officer in the Foreign Legion. Captain Hamilton warned a party of soldiers with whom Knickerbocker was traveling that French infantry defending the barracks would resist. The Americans determined to press on with Hamilton along as an unofficial liaison to the 1st ID. Indeed, as Hamilton had predicted, the fusiliers defending the Arzew barracks fought. As the fight developed, Knickerbocker was joined by a young soldier from Brooklyn whom he did not know. The New Yorker observed in surprise, "Gee, do you know that a year ago in Brooklyn I never would have believed I could do this." Then, according to Knickerbocker, he proceeded to load and fire three clips of ammunition at the enemy.[47]

Young men also witnessed death, and ugly death at that, for the first time. More than anything, surprise describes their response. Daniel Lyons, a young officer in the 26th Infantry, recalled hearing a soldier say, "Hey they are killing people" as if somehow that was unnatural in combat. Also, on this same day of firsts, Ted Dobol, a young soldier who eventually served in every enlisted rank in the 26th Infantry, killed a sniper. He credited his training, saying he succeeded because he "was so well acquainted" with his rifle. But, he acknowledged, "the confusion on our first day of combat was evident. We were playing this game for keeps."[48]

Seeing your friends hurt badly is second only to seeing them killed. The eighth of November 1942 provided ample opportunity for this phenomenon. Clement van Wagoner, a platoon leader in the 18th Infantry, witnessed an oxcart run over several of his soldiers. The driver meant no harm; he merely wanted to avoid the confrontation the 18th was having with armored cars. In avoiding the fight, he ran over troops in the adjacent ditch. No glory in that. Lieutenant Wagoner did what he had to do; "I directed the medic to stay with the wounded, then we kept on going." One of the many great tragedies of combat is that there is little time for mourning the dead or consoling the wounded, which makes the memory all the more painful.[49]

Despite everything, Terry Allen's first day in command of a division in combat had gone tolerably well. His troops cleared the beaches, drove inland, fought several skirmishes, and mostly kept their heads about them. In the west, the 26th Infantry surmounted the high point of Djebel Murdjadjo and closed within five miles of Oran. In the east, Darby's Rangers held the ground just south of Cap Carbon. Although the 18th Infantry had been repulsed, they were not out of the fight. The 16th Infantry took La Macta, and its 2nd Battalion reached Fleurus some fifteen miles east of Oran. On the outer loop, Task Force Green had moved quickly to just west of the village of Misserghin, some ten miles southwest of Oran, while Task Force Red had taken the Tafraoui airfield.[50]

The End at Oran

The serious crisis occurred at Saint-Cloud, a situation that worsened on the second day, as the Zouaves continued to confound the 18th. Determined to take the town, Colonel Greer began the day with a fifteen-minute preparation fire from his supporting artillery. The regiment's three battalions then "jumped off again to take the town, at 7:00 AM." Mason described what followed: "Non-battle-experienced troops tend to converge on whatever is firing at them." The three battalions did indeed converge, and thus, "Greer found all three of his battalions pinned down by effective fire from the town." Greer regrouped his units, mounted a second attack, and failed yet again.[51]

At that moment Terry Allen was with the 16th Infantry near La Macta, "because of evident threat of an enemy-counter attack in that direction." The second failure "disturbed" him. And "one of the disturbing factors" that morning was the actions of General Fredendall, the II Corps commander. Because Fredendall was pressuring Allen to get into Oran, Allen turned up the heat up on Greer. Frustrated as hell, Greer proposed to concentrate the fires of all four of the 1st Division's artillery battalions on the town and level it if need be. Allen initially agreed, but on the advice of his staff reconsidered. Greer planned the attack for 1430. At 1350 on November 9, Allen arrived at the 18th's command post. He told Greer the division would not fire a major concentration on the town, as doing so would certainly kill and injure some of the four thousand civilians who lived there. The last point Allen made in turning off the artillery was to say, "We don't need the d—— place anyway. We can By-pass ST. CLOUD [emphasis in original], and take Oran at night."[52]

That evening Allen convened a meeting to issue orders for the division to continue the attack the following day. The II Corps operations officer attended, as did the commander of Combat Command B, the division artillery commander, the regimental liaison officers, and the staff. Colonel Cota, the chief of staff, recommended publishing a written field order. The resulting document, Field Order 3, was the first order issued in combat since 1918. Allen wrote an order of only eleven lines. Cota asked if there were "Any general instructions for all units?" Myth and even *Danger Forward*, the division history, proclaims that Allen stipulated, "Nothing in hell must stop the 1st division." In fact the order read, "Nothing in hell must delay or stop this atk." This order met the ideal imagined by both Marshall and McNair, who commanded the Army Ground Forces. It was short—both officers believed concise orders best. It included an overlay that showed the scheme of maneuver and reflected the growing confidence of the senior leaders.[53]

The following morning, November 10, the last of the gas escaped the Vichy French bag. Although French troops still held Saint-Cloud, most of the division advanced unopposed. Terry Allen entered Oran with a small escort. In a letter to his son he described what happened next: "On reaching the outskirts of [Oran—Allen left out names for security purposes] it was apparent that resistance had completely broken down and by making a hurried entrance we might forestall further resistance." Allen ordered his units to continue to advance but not to fire unless fired upon. Both Combat Command B of the 1st AD and the 26th Infantry had some fighting yet to do, even though the city capitulated at 1215. It took some time to get the shooting stopped, with the result that still more people on both sides died.[54]

Now the 1st ID transitioned quickly from combat to consolidating their position. That included jeep patrols westward to make contact with the Western Task Force and eastward to make contact with British forces at Algiers. They had some garrison duties as well but soon turned to "critiques." Contemporary American soldiers would recognize these as after-action reviews. They generally featured a map or perhaps sketches. On the basis of these critiques they hoped to shape training and/or devise techniques to improve.

An Assessment

Assessing the success of the invasion of North Africa depends on the denominator. It is hard to produce an objective assessment without determining the measure of success. And the assessment of performance should be done in context. In this case, the context included three widely separated amphibious landings under differing conditions. All three succeeded, and once ashore, all three ground elements took their assigned objectives. Doing so produced important consequences, chief among them being that those successes endangered the Axis units in Africa that were already under great pressure. On November 4 Rommel conceded defeat to Bernard Law Montgomery at El Alamein and began his long retreat to Tunisia—more than sixteen hundred miles for those troops who cut the corner of Cyrenaica, nearly two thousand for those who traveled along the coast road. That morning Rommel estimated that he had only twelve tanks left. In fact, he had eleven German tanks and ten Italian tanks. Neither Rommel's estimate of the situation nor the truth about it encouraged confidence. By November

7 his tattered legions had withdrawn more than seventy-five miles west to Mersa Matruh. The next day he learned that the Allies had landed. To Rommel, "That meant the end of the army in Africa."[55]

Officially the 1st ID declared its first mission a success, as indeed it was. It had not, however, come without cost. The division had 418 casualties, including 94 killed in action. Seventy-three soldiers went missing, while another 251 suffered wounds. Writing about Oran forty years later, Mason claimed that the division "had behaved in exemplary fashion," but he also noted "an understandable greenness." The division performed well enough to succeed against troops the division intelligence officer evaluated as second- and third-rate. They struggled against Foreign Legion and Algerian troops at Saint-Cloud. Carl von Clausewitz had himself experienced the vicissitudes of first battles and the effect of "moral elements" in battle. He concluded that the most vital moral elements in battle included "the skill of the commander, the experience of and courage of the troops, and their patriotic spirit." The 1st ID certainly could count on patriotic spirit among the troops, even if their lack of experience showed.

Lord Moran, a British veteran of the Great War who served as Churchill's physician in World War II, published a study of courage in 1945. In it he offered two important insights, concluding, "Courage is will-power, whereof no man has an unlimited stock; and when in war it is used up, he is finished." Training and discipline along with spirit played a role in developing willpower.[56] Still, success in building willpower depended far more on training and discipline than on patriotic fervor, given how easily patriotism wanes under fire.

Large maneuvers managed by umpires did little to train small units. There were too few opportunities to conduct live-fire training at small-unit level. Not every Big Red One soldier mirrored the performance of eager infantrymen from Brooklyn. Lieutenant Ted Antonelli, an officer in the 16th Infantry, observed that "the initial response of most of our people when we took fire was to hit the dirt." The problem, he believed, stemmed from a simple fact: "A lot of our training was on a rifle range, where you see a target and you shoot, but when fire is coming in your direction, what happens is people hit the dirt." Finally, "One of the shocks I had was that when the enemy is shooting at you, things don't work quite as they did in training." In combat, junior leaders like Antonelli and Edward McGregor had to lead. They had to get their troops in the fight. Others at higher levels, including Teddy Roosevelt, acted in ways that enabled soldiers to overcome their fear and find the willpower to do what had to be done.[57] The skill and willpower of leaders mattered in the 1st ID's first fight, just as it had during the Napoleonic Wars that shaped Clausewitz's famous theory of warfare.

The Royal Navy had done a brilliant job of getting the troops ashore safely and providing effective naval gunfire support as well as close air support from carrier-based aircraft. Once Task Force Red secured the Tafraoui airfield, twenty-six Spitfires wasted no time flying in, as did some of the C-47s carrying Edson's paratroopers. The chief contribution airpower made in taking Oran occurred on November 9, when Spitfires operating from the Tafraoui airfield strafed a column of Foreign Legion troops attempting to reach Oran via Tafraoui.[58]

Although airpower played a small role in the division's first fight, Terry Allen believed it was an important asset, with which more could and should be done. In his after-action report he offered one major observation and several recommendations regarding airpower. Probably as a consequence of the Spitfires fending off the reinforcing legionaries, he concluded that air "is especially effective against approaching enemy reserves." He recommended that air control parties be provided by the supporting air force unit.[59]

In a section of his report under the heading "Offensive Combat," Allen offered his mantra for offensive action: "Find 'Em, Fix 'Em, and Fight 'Em." To do that, he believed, "*Extensive* and *Aggressive* [italics in original] reconnaissance must be initiated without delay in order to locate the enemy and to ascertain the most favorable routes of approach." To ensure that Allen's unit understood his views, the 1st Division published a document called "Reconnaissance Pamphlet." He further directed his commanders and their units that they "must be thoroughly familiar with its contents," and added that the division needed additional reconnaissance assets, including a squadron headquarters and light tank troop of three platoons of four tanks each. He wrote at length on the importance of fire and maneuver as well as the best organization for regimental combat teams. Allen could look to the future with some satisfaction but without complacency.[60]

Lieutenant Joe Dawson was proud of his unit and of General Allen, claiming that "all who saw him felt the same gladness that we had such a wonderful courageous leader." Dawson was captivated by the Algerian countryside. The djebels "enabled the climate to be quite agreeable . . . the sky is almost unbelievably blue and the nights are a poet's dream. The stars shine in a manner that makes each one clearly visible." But Dawson had, like the rest of the division, experienced loss. "From now on 'til the end of the war," he advised his family, "the tenor of all these communiqués will doubtless be a reflection of all these aches and grief that result when men die for their country."[61]

Notes

1. Astor, *Terrible Terry Allen*, 102.

2. Astor, 103; Mason, "Reminiscences," 24.

3. Knickerbocker et al., *Danger Forward*, 8.

4. Porch, *Path to Victory*, 343. Porch's analysis and narrative on the operations in the Mediterranean takes advantage of important secondary sources not available when Howe's *Northwest Africa*, the army's official history, was written.

5. Mason, "Reminiscences," 23–24; Jackson, *Battle for North Africa*, 351. Howe, *Northwest Africa*, is the US official history. See also Porch, *Path to Victory*. There are a great many good histories from the British point of view. Moorehead, *March to Tunis*, is a useful narrative that includes civilian and military perspectives both.

6. Raphael L. Uffner, "Recollections of World War II with the First Infantry Division," n.d., MRC 1997.98, 161–62; Wilson, *Maneuver and Firepower*, chart 15, 162. Chart 15 shows the table of organization for the 1st Infantry Division as of August 1, 1942.

7. Uffner, "Recollections," 181, 190–94, 201, 213.

8. Lebda, *Million Miles to Go*, 17–18; Lambert and DeFelice, *Every Man a Hero*, 47. The author has spoken with Ray Lambert a number of times. Lambert made all three assault landings and was wounded in North Africa and Sicily, and finally on Omaha Beach. At the urging of many he published this memoir when he was ninety-nine.

9. Howe, *Northwest Africa*, 209–10.

10. Charles E. Murphy, interview by Stan Tinsley, September 5, 1990, Oak Ridge, TN.

11. Baumer and Reardon, *American Iliad*, 17.

12. Ambrose, *Supreme Commander*, 48–49, 78, 93. Marshall did not imagine to begin with that Eisenhower would remain in command in Europe until the war ended. Eisenhower did not either, but believed he was building a command post for Marshall. See Eisenhower, *Crusade in Europe*, chapters 3 and 5.

13. Mason, "Reminiscences," 3–4; Porch, *Path to Victory*, 342–43. See also Butcher, *Three Years with Eisenhower*, 87. Murphy, the US envoy in Algeria, traveled by a very circuitous route to the UK to provide advice to Eisenhower and his staff. Harold MacMillan later served alongside Murphy, arriving in Algeria in January 1943 as his British counterpart. Ambrose, *Supreme Commander*, 155–56. See also Boatner, *Biographical Dictionary*, 1996.

14. On the overall planning process, the best source is Howe, *Northwest Africa*, 46–50. See also Wheeler, *The Big Red One*, 143–49.

15. Howe, *Northwest Africa*, 47.

16. Howe, 48, 50. See also Maycock, *Twelfth Air Force*, 9. This study reports few aircraft because, as the author notes at p. 209, there was "a distressing lack of summary

material" Approximate numbers of aircraft surmised from HQ, US Army Air Forces, *Army Air Forces Statistical Digest*, December 1945.

17. Howe, *Northwest Africa*, 212–13. See also Blair, *Ridgway's Paratroopers*, 66–67. When the 503rd Parachute Infantry received orders to the Pacific instead of Europe, the army formed a new 3rd Battalion and renamed Raff's battalion the 509th Parachute Infantry Battalion.

18. HQ, 1st ID, Embarkation Memorandum 24, October 5, 1942, in RG 301-3.18: Embarkation Memoranda, Dec 41, Oct 42, Oct 43, MRC Digital Archives; Howe, *Northwest Africa*, map 5, 46–50. See also 1st ID, "A Factual Account of the Combat Operations of the 1st Infantry Division in N. Africa and Sicily during World War II," n.d., MRC 1988.31.

19. Howe, *Northwest Africa*, 47–48, 192–93.

20. Butcher, *Three Years with Eisenhower*, 147–48; Astor, *Terrible Terry Allen*, 106–8.

21. Finke, *No Mission Too Difficult*, 18–22, 56–64. Sutherland cut a distinguished figure as a long-serving professor of English at the US Military Academy. He was memorable not only as a teacher but also for his eccentric appearance, which featured an impressive handlebar mustache in a largely clean-shaven army. See Robert Mcg. Thomas, "Edwin Sutherland, 82, Officer and Scholar, Is Dead," *New York Times*, January 17, 1997, https://www.nytimes.com/1997/01/17/world/edwin-sutherland-82-soldier-and-scholar-is-dead.html.

22. Military Intelligence Division, *Special Bulletins from 1939–1940 Active Campaign in Europe*. Other sources, including the Army Ground Forces Command Observers Report and Allied reports, enjoyed wide distribution across the army.

23. Baumer and Reardon, *American Iliad*, 18; Knickerbocker et al., *Danger Forward*, 18.

24. Porch, *Path to Victory*, 327. Jackson's analysis of the United Kingdom's aims is useful as well. See Jackson, *Battle for North Africa*, chapters 1 and 2.

25. Fuhrer Headquarters, Directive No. 42, "Instructions for Operations against Unoccupied France and the Iberian Peninsula," May 29, 1942; Butcher, *Three Years with Eisenhower*, 135.

26. Liddell-Hart, *Rommel Papers*, 262; Clausewitz, *On War*, 528.

27. Blaxland, *Plain Cook*; Barnett, *Desert Generals*, 271. Barnett effectively disparages the myth-making around the Second Battle of El Alamein and Montgomery's alleged brilliance as a political contrivance by Churchill, with Montgomery as an enthusiastic participant. Britain needed a hero, and Montgomery served that purpose well. Montgomery, *Memoirs*.

28. Atkinson, *Army at Dawn*, 42.

29. Atkinson, 42, recounts the almost ludicrous discussions with French officers that followed in the section entitled "Rendezvous at Cherchell," 42–49.

30. HQ, 26th Infantry, "History of the 26th Infantry in the Present Struggle," n.d., MRC 1988.38, 17–18.

31. Howe, *Northwest Africa*, 72–77.

32. Lebda, *Million Miles to Go*, 21. The troops of the 1st ID were kept in ignorance until November 1 because of their greater vulnerability to submarine attack as they made their way south, or so the command maintained.

33. War Department, *A Pocket Guide to North Africa* (Washington, DC: Government Printing Office, 1923), 9. See table of contents for section headings, and pages 42–44 for phrases.

34. Lebda, *Million Miles to Go*, 21. Re time of landing, see Howe, *Northwest Africa*, 198, 199, 207.

35. Knickerbocker et al., *Danger Forward*, 38. Knickerbocker was one of a group of journalists who served alongside the 1st ID and developed an affinity for the Big Red One. Knickerbocker was killed in an airplane accident near Mumbai, India in 1949.

36. Howe, *Northwest Africa*, 205–6; Atkinson, *Army at Dawn*, 78–80.

37. Mason, "Reminiscences," 27–28; Daniel Lyons, interview by Colonel John Votaw, June 17, 1994, First Division Museum at Cantigny, Wheaton, IL.

38. 26th Infantry, "History," 1–3; Lebda, *Million Miles to Go*, 25–26.

39. Atkinson, *Army at Dawn*, 69–77.

40. Howe, *Northwest Africa*, 209–12.

41. Astor, *Terrible Terry Allen*, 117.

42. Howe, *Northwest Africa*, 207–9; Knickerbocker et al., *Danger Forward*, 24–27; Wheeler, *The Big Red One*, 143–49.

43. Just how many aircraft arrived near the airfield may be uncertain. Clay Blair reported six, while Rick Atkinson reports nine. The author believes Atkinson is right. Blair, *Ridgway's Paratroopers*, 66; Atkinson, *Army at Dawn*, 88–90.

44. Baumer and Reardon, *American Iliad*, 30–31. On 35 Baumer and Reardon report a fourth French battery, this one of 155-millimeter howitzers.

45. Baumer and Reardon, 31.

46. Baumer and Reardon, 34.

47. Knickerbocker et al., *Danger Forward*, 43–44.

48. "Theodore L. Dobol, Command Sergeant Major United States Army (Retired): Autobiography," ms., n.d., MRC 1991.24, 10–11.

49. Baumer and Reardon, *American Iliad*, 28–29.

50. 1st ID, "Factual Account," 5–6. This remarkable document was developed to enable Samuel Fuller to develop a screenplay starring Lee Marvin, released in 1989 as the *Big Red One*. Fuller served in the 1st ID with the 16th Infantry during World War II. He was devoted to the 1st ID. His wife Christa produced a documentary called *A Fuller Life*, directed by his daughter Samantha. The author spoke with Samantha at the 2019 reunion of the Society of the 1st Division.

51. Baumer and Reardon, *American Iliad*, 28–35. On 36 Baumer and Reardon mistakenly cite 1st ID's FO 2 as providing orders for November 9, 1942. The order was published at 2115 on November 9, 1942. See 1st ID, "Factual Account," 6.

52. 1st ID, "Factual Account," 6.

53. 1st ID, 7. Re FO 3, the entire eleven lines may be seen at http://www.ibiblio.org/hyperwar/USA/rep/TORCH/1InfDiv_FO-1/.

54. Howe, *Northwest Africa*, 223–28; Mason, "Reminiscences," 30.

55. Liddell-Hart, *Rommel Papers*, 335–36, 345, 347.

56. Moran, *Anatomy of Courage*, xvi.

57. Finke, *No Mission Too Difficult*, 71–72. See also Marshall, *Men against Fire*, which argues that no more than 25 percent of soldiers fired their weapons in combat, and often without aiming. There is room to doubt Marshall's conclusions; he

extrapolated results from a small number of interviews (around one hundred) and applied them to the US Army as a whole. In 1988 army historian Roger J. Spiller debunked Marshall in the *RUSI Journal*. It is quite likely that Marshall exaggerated his evidence, but his case is no without merit.

58. Center for Air Force History, *AAF in Northwest Africa*, 17–19. See also Maycock, *Twelfth Air Force*. Maycock's word is the basis of the official history of the campaign and details the build-up of Army Air Force assets and employment in North Africa.

59. 1st ID, after-action report, December 5, 1942, annex 2, 4, in 301-0.3: After Action Report, 4 Sept–10 Nov 1942, MRC Digital Archives.

60. 1st ID, 2. See also annex 1, "Amphibious Training of Regimental Combat Teams," August 24, 1942, 1, and annex 2, "Offensive Combat," November 23, 1942, 1.

61. Kingseed, *Omaha Beach to Dawson's Ridge*, 55–56, 58.

CHAPTER FOUR

Tunisia: The Wehrmacht as Tutors

> I hope that every fighter's efforts are crowned with Success. To all I wish a victorious return to a free, great and strong homeland.
> —*Generaloberst Jürgen von Arnim, Fifth Panzer Army*

> At Kasserine Pass, we got the hell kicked out of us.
> —*Robert L. Bogart, medic, 16th Infantry*

AFTER SEIZING ORAN on November 10, 1943, the Big Red One turned to preparing for whatever came next as the Vichy French transitioned from enemies to allies. The 1st Division's units took some time to rest/refit and conducted "critiques," which, as mentioned, were the precursors to the contemporary army's after-action reviews. These had become routine during training but took on new meaning after seizing Oran. The 26th Infantry, for example, claimed to have learned lessons in tactics but also in the more mundane operations of "supply, transportation and communication." The Big Red One also "detailed a policing force for the City of Oran." But any notion of long occupation and relative peace soon vanished. Within days of the cessation of hostilities in Oran, Lieutenant General Dwight D. Eisenhower's Allied Force Headquarters began committing the division piecemeal in an effort to seize Tunis, the strategic gem in North Africa. The 5th Field Artillery moved first, leaving Oran on November19, but other units soon followed, attached either to Allied formations or the 1st Armored Division. From the day it rolled out of Oran until mid-March, the 1st ID fought in parcels rather than the way they had trained to fight—as a division. This chapter follows the escapades of individual units, as there is no coherent 1st ID story to tell until the last few weeks of the campaign.[1]

Allied Assessment and Intentions

In *Crusade in Europe*, Dwight D. Eisenhower declared that the major mission for the invading Allied Forces required "co-operating with General Harold R. L. G. Alexander's forces, then twelve hundred miles away at the opposite end of the Mediterranean." Alexander's command included Bernard Law Montgomery's Eighth Army. The aim was to destroy "all axis forces in northern Africa and reopen the sea for use of Allied shipping." To assure the destruction of Generalfeldmarschall Erwin Rommel's Italian and German troops, Eisenhower's forces had to seize Tunis, indeed, all of Tunisia. Located in Algiers, Lieutenant General K. A. N. Anderson's "Eastern Task Force" composed of two British Divisions and the US 34th Infantry Division was closest. However, the Eastern Task Force lay some five hundred miles west of Tunis, and was inadequately supplied; General Anderson had not yet landed all of his troops.[2]

Carl von Clausewitz described the predicament Eisenhower was facing when he observed that "war does not consist of a single short blow." War plays out in a series of blows, almost in spasms of violence, often followed by periods of apparent calm. These lulls occur when one or both sides are doing things other than engaging in direct combat but necessary to sustain the fight, such as refitting, maneuvering, or reinforcing. That proved true in North Africa in 1942, just as it had during the Napoleonic Wars. Seizing French Morocco and Algeria necessarily preceded the real objective—the seizure of Tunisia and Tunis as the means to turn the Axis out of Africa. The possibility of destroying a large portion of the Axis armies advanced the aim of supporting Russia, which had its hands full staving off the Wehrmacht on the eastern front. Logistics, terrain, and the troops available forced the Allies to use a series of blows rather than a single decisive action. In order to seize Tunisia before the Germans could reinforce it, they had to act quickly. Anderson accordingly headed east with the forces immediately available. As resistance in Oran and Algeria collapsed, Eisenhower cabled Anderson to say that he had ordered Major General Lloyd R. Fredendall, at II Corps, to "reorganize rapidly and be ready to assist to eastward with anything he can make available on your call." The resulting extemporaneous haste had a Keystone Kops quality characterized by frantic, even frenetic, activity that achieved little. Wanting to go quickly guaranteed neither speed nor, more importantly, the momentum enabled by adequate forces.[3]

The Allies could not get to Tunis quickly for several reasons. Foremost, Torch forces landed much farther west of Tunis than desirable because the very thing that gave Tunis strategic value made it unsuitable as a landing site. Located just south of Cape Bon, the city's port lay less than a hundred miles southwest of Sicily and within the radius of German and Italian air bases on the islands of Sicily, Sardinia, and Pantelleria. Prudence ruled out landing much nearer to Tunis. Landing farther west meant depending, in part, relying after landfall on the Algerian road and rail "network." The single narrow-gauge railway from Algiers to Tunis could not handle large numbers of combat vehicles. The roads south of the coast also proved inadequate to sustain the volume of traffic necessary to move thousands of troops. The same day Anderson received Eisenhower's cable, Major General Charles S. Ryder, commanding the 34th ID, negotiated the handover of Algiers with French general Alphonse Juin. That reduced the immediate threat to Anderson's rear so that he could move on the main objective. [4]

Axis Assessment and Intentions

French dithering further muddled things in Tunisia, as it had elsewhere. The most important development occurred when General George Barré, the Vichy ground forces commander, withdrew westward toward Algeria, out of reach of the Germans, but did not commit to the Allies. On November 5 the Axis had detected part of the invasion force as it sailed from Gibraltar. Yet Hitler failed to react. Finally, on the 7th, he ordered the Luftwaffe to reinforce its units in the theater. He also ordered Generalfeldmarschall Gerd von Rundstedt, who commanded in France, to prepare to execute Operation Anton, the occupation of Vichy France. *Der Führer*'s newfound concern did not prevent him from leaving his Prussian command post in the hands of a colonel and taking his closest advisors with him to Munich to "celebrate the anniversary of the Beer Hall putsch."[5]

While Hitler fiddled, Generalfeldmarschall Albert Kesselring, in command in the Mediterranean theater, acted decisively, albeit with a free hand from the führer. With Anton underway, Kesselring dispatched two staff officers to Tunis immediately. They arrived at Vichy headquarters in Tunis on the day of the landings and politely but firmly demanded the use of Tunisian airfields to bring in German reinforcements. These worthies, who maintained that they were merely reinforcing their Vichy allies, made their threats sufficiently convincing that the French opened their air bases to the Luftwaffe on November 11. Air and ground units began arriving that same day.[6]

Frustrated with Barré's dissimulation, Kesselring ordered Stukas to attack French ground forces, noting that "in war it is futile to bargain with unreliable auxiliaries." The so-called race for Tunis followed. The Germans won the first leg when the Luftwaffe airlifted Kampfgruppe Schirmer into the city. Formed with an understrength parachute regiment and a security battalion, Kampfgruppe Schirmer effected control of Tunis by November 12. Kesselring flew in still more ground forces. The German high command also reinforced Kesselring's theater air transport by pulling transport squadrons out of Russia. In the moment, Kesselring could move troops faster than could Alexander.[7]

The Battleground

Tunisia stretches three hundred miles east from the Algerian frontier to the bulge on the Tunisian Sahel, or eastern coast. It extends roughly five hundred miles from Bizerte on the northern coast to its southern extremity on the shared frontier with Algeria and Libya. North of a large salt lake called Chott el Fejaj, the country is mountainous, with two chief ranges. The Western Dorsal extends southwest–northeast for two hundred miles. The Eastern Dorsal runs north–south for a hundred miles, merging with the Western Dorsal in east-central Tunisia. The Sahara Desert of *Beau Geste* fame extends north into southern Tunisia nearly to the port of Gabès. Inland the terrain is dry most of the year, offset by winter rains. The coastal climate is mild, but rain falls often during the winter months. Temperatures in the mountains and desert drop precipitously at night, assuring that no one living outside enjoys winter in Tunisia. US troops had not yet experienced *Beau Geste*'s desert, but they would see the northernmost reaches of the Sahara in southern Tunisia.

The Dorsal range restricted east–west movement to the defiles that cut through it, so fighting for control of these passes dominated the campaign. The Tunisian roadways compared unfavorably to the execrable roads in Algeria. Rain and the resultant mud made them impassable, exacerbating soldiers' already dystopian life. The rail network, such as it was, stemmed from a single standard-gauge track that originated in Casablanca in French Morocco and ran through Algeria and ultimately to Tunis. Off this branched several narrow-gauge single-track lines. One ran southwest from Tunis to the Algerian town of Tébessa, with a spur off it running south to Kasserine and northeast to the east-coast port of Sousse. From Kasserine still another line ran south and then generally east to the port of Sfax. From there a line ran south to Gabès. Roads ran parallel to these lines, defining the chief avenues of approach.[8]

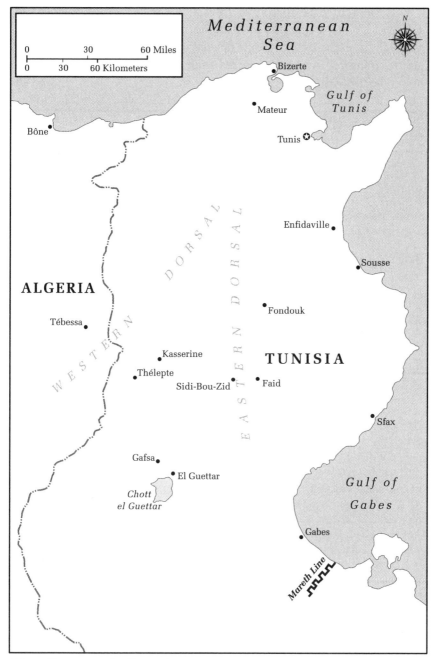

Map 2: Tunisia. Map by Chris Robinson.

Both sides dribbled troops into Tunisia for similar reasons. Neither had sufficient forces. Neither had adequate sealift—each lost ships to the other, although the exchange rate greatly favored the Allies. Neither had sufficient ground transport. And both suffered from the winter rains, which Eisenhower described as "unreasonable." In Tunisia the Axis generally enjoyed air superiority, although they could not have achieved what they did without both German and Italian airmen. Not only did the Axis airmen bring in reinforcements but they made Allied movement difficult as well. On November 11 the Luftwaffe sank three lighters supporting the transshipment of cargo and damaged the British carrier *Argus*. Of air support, one officer summed up the view of most American ground troops: "The Luftwaffe controls the sky here."[9]

Lurching into Tunisia

Both sides improvised, with resulting confusion. Alan Moorehead, an Australian correspondent for the London *Daily Express* who had previously covered the Desert War, described what he found on arriving in Tunisia: "For a month I could not get used to this front. The geography baffled me. The tactics were an endless riddle." Many of the troops were baffled as well. The only thing not hard to follow in the winter of 1942–43 was that the Axis stymied the Allies' helter-skelter attempt to reach Tunis. In a cable to General Thomas T. Hardy sent on the anniversary of the Japanese attack at Pearl Harbor, Eisenhower noted that his operations "have violated every recognized principle of war . . . and will be condemned in their entirety, by all Leavenworth and War College classes for the next twenty-five years."[10]

Eisenhower's choices have been criticized legitimately, but such is not the purpose here; rather it's to form an understanding of how the 1st ID learned in combat, and in the context of the larger operation. This is important. Anderson and Fredendall used American units, including the 1st ID, in ways that army doctrine did not intend. Fighting by battalion or occasionally at regimental level is not how the army organized or trained its divisions. Several battles illustrate the growth of the division's units, if not the division's coming of age. The 18th Infantry's fight at Longstop Hill, the first encounter between 1st ID troops and the Germans, is critical, as are the operations of the 26th Infantry and other divisional units in and around Kasserine. These actions are the focal points of this chapter.

In the race for Tunis, General Anderson, in command of the British First Army, led the Allied ground forces. Gregory Blaxland, who served under him, described Anderson as "blunt and uncompromising." Eisenhower thought him a "gallant Scot" but "blunt to the point of rudeness." Anderson certainly demonstrated these traits, and did so often, as well as displaying his distinct lack of confidence in American troops. With Allied units spread out from the Atlantic coast of Africa to Algiers, he had few forces available to attack toward Tunis. Still, he did what he could, beginning with an amphibious and airborne strike to seize the port of Bône, Algeria, roughly 125 miles west of Tunis. He followed up with additional airborne landings to seize passes through the Western Dorsal.[11]

This effort fizzled for lack of troops by the end of the first week of December. Eisenhower then worked with Alexander to mount a second attack, this time with more troops, including the 18th Infantry, but with no more success. The Germans and Italians, though caught by surprise, had reinforced quickly, sending five divisions across the short sea gap between Sicily and Tunisia. Robert M. Citino notes in *The Wehrmacht Retreats* that none of these five divisions arrived intact. Some had to leave equipment behind, while others lost equipment to Allied air and submarines.[12]

The saga of the veteran 10th Panzer Division illustrates the Axis effort as well as their central problem. Units of the 10th PZ entered Czechoslovakia in 1938. Then the division fought in Poland in 1939, France in 1940, and Russia from June 1941 to April 1942. Worn down from fifteen thousand troops to eight thousand, the 10th PZ redeployed to France to refit and reequip, rebuilding, drawing new equipment, reorganizing, and retraining the core of veterans it had brought out of Russia. The division completed training in the fall and remained near Abbeville, France, expecting to return to Russia. On November 8 the 10th PZ received orders to support Operation Anton. Later that day they moved south to occupy Marseille, arriving on the November 12. The high command then ordered them to Tunisia the following day. Ten days later two motorcycle companies of infantry embarked from Naples. The motorcycle units made it to Tunisia, but a British submarine sank the first shipment of tanks. At the end of November Generalleutnant Wolfgang Fischer, the 10th's commander, had only seven hundred of his own troops, a handful of tanks, and four thousand soldiers attached from other units.[13] More followed as they made their way from France to Italy and then to Tunis.

Blooding the Vanguard Regiment

Styling themselves the Vanguards, the 18th Infantry had a long and proud history. On May 4, 1941, the regiment held a review to celebrate eighty years of service. The reviewing officer, Brigadier General William H. Bisbee, a veteran from the original regiment, then 101 years old, spoke of their history.

Bisbee had joined the 18th in July 1861. During the Civil War he rose to the rank of lieutenant colonel and took command of one of the battalions. Colonel Ely P. Denson, the contemporary regimental commander, responded to Bisbee, riffing on the regiment's motto, "In Omnia Paratus" (ready for all things). Denson asserted that the present-day Vanguards "will see that the Regiment is always ready." The successors to Bisbee's regiment did well against the Vichy French but now would face the "first team."[14]

Colonel Frank U. Greer's 18th Infantry started east by convoy on December 8, bound for Medjez el Bab in Tunisia to serve attached to the British 78th ID of British V Corps, a journey of four hundred miles as the crow flies. Medjez el Bab straddled the main road to Tunis some thirty miles northeast. V Corps made the main effort in the renewed offensive. The 18th arrived on 23 December. That very night the 78th required one battalion to relieve the 2nd Battalion Coldstream Guards on a hill the British called Longstop, after a cricket position designed to backstop the wicket. Longstop Hill (or more formally Hill 290) overlooked the Medjerda River and stretched eastward along the highway. Although the British perceived Longstop as a single hill, it did in fact have two main peaks (Hills 290 and 243), with a low saddle between them and a number of other undulations or knobs. Longstop Hill is slightly more than six miles north of the village of Medjez el Bab. Sparsely covered with gorse, Longstop rose gently, yet whoever held this muddy ridge with its two peaks and knobby prominences controlled movement along the highway and valley that led toward Tunis. A small railway stop lay just downslope from Hill 290, on the rail line that ran parallel to the highway.[15]

The 10th PZ had operated in the area of Longstop Hill since mid-December; on December 13 they occupied the hill, and then were relieved in turn. They were back in position on or about December 19. A well-dug-in force composed of an engineer battalion and a rifle company defended the hill when the 2nd Battalion Coldstream Guards attacked. The engineer battalion improved its defensive positions by using jackhammers to dig a series of trenches. The German troops had eighteen machine guns, giving them considerable firepower. They fought until they burned up their ammunition. Only then did they withdraw in good order, from their forward positions only, and even then not until just after midnight on the 23rd. The guard's battalion had failed to clear all of Longstop, nor had it maintained contact with the enemy. Thinking they had done more than they had, the guardsmen awaited relief. The 1st Battalion, 18th Infantry, clambered up the hill in a winter rainstorm, arriving to relieve the British at 0300 Christmas Eve.[16]

Major Robert H. York, the battalion commander, arrived late, having lost his way. Then the Germans pinned him and his command group down with accurate machine-gun fire. Eventually York stumbled upon the Coldstream Guards' command post. There he was told that only a few Germans remained on the hill. York and his battalion knew nothing about the ground. Worse still, the British had not identified, let alone cleared, the second peak. At dawn York discovered that much of Longstop—all but the peak at Hill 290—remained in German hands. The Germans had also reoccupied some of the positions the Coldstream Guards left prior to their relief. Enemy prisoners freely advised York that a battalion of the 69th Panzergrenadier Regiment remained on the eastern end of the saddle formed by Longstop and the slightly lower Hill 243, just over two hundred yards east.[17]

The Germans then did what German units strove to do throughout the war—they counterattacked. The 10th's operations officer personally led a Kampfgruppe formed on the 1st Battalions of the 69th Panzergrenadier and 7th Panzer regiments, supported by 88-millimeter flak guns and artillery. The Germans did not realize that Americans had relieved the British. It did not matter. Incompatible radios and concern about location resulted in little artillery support for the beleaguered Americans. Daniel Lyons, a lieutenant in the 18th, recalled Coldstream Guards guides that brought them up claiming that "the hill was unoccupied. We got up on the hill, middle of the night and there were more Germans there than there were of us." When the Germans counterattacked, Lyons admitted, "Most of the men ran. I was one of those that stayed because I didn't know where to run and besides, I had this one thing ingrained in me that [running was] the one thing that won't do." In fact, most of the battalion did not run. They fought hard all day but eventually were driven off. York's battalion suffered heavy losses, including the complete destruction of Company A. During the attack Generaloberst Jürgen von Arnim, commanding the newly formed Fifth Panzer Army, visited the hill that the Germans came to call "Christmas Hill" and took a briefing from Oberst Rudolph Lang, who commanded the 69th.[18]

Hans Lüke, a veteran of the 69th, wrote in *Grenadier Regiment 69* that the Americans "defended tenaciously and persistently . . . using machine guns, mortars and small arms." The American "freely employs artillery and is unwilling to be driven from machine gun nests and fighting positions carved out of the rocks." Nevertheless, the Panzergrenadiers drove the York's troops off. Lüke concluded that the Americans "had probably not expected such a violent and rapid counterattack." Probably not, but York and his troops learned fast.[19]

Map 3: The Battle for Longstop Hill, December 22–26, 1942. Reproduced from Howe, *Northwest Africa*, Map 7.

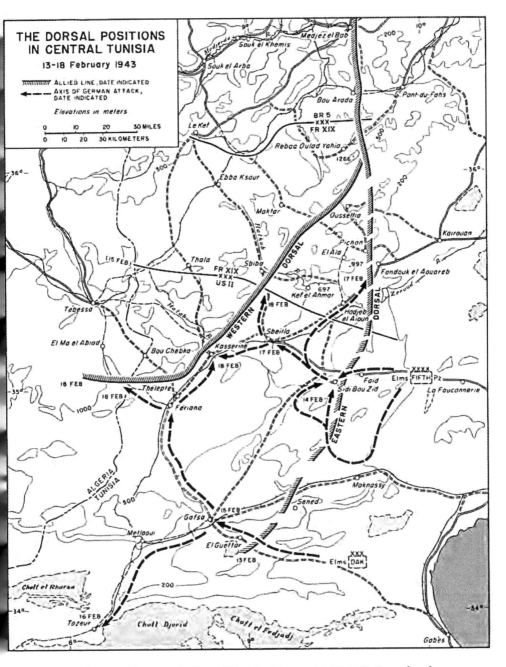

Map 4: The Dorsal Positions in Central Tunisia, February 13–18, 1943. Reproduced from Howe, *Northwest Africa*, Map 10.

Late Christmas Eve the 2nd Battalion Coldstream Guards and York's 1st Battalion retook part of the hill and defended the right of the line. Later that day Wolfgang Fischer climbed the hill himself to size up the situation. Forthwith he prepared to retake all of Longstop Hill. On Christmas Day the 10th PZ attacked in regimental strength. Panzergrenadiers, supported by tanks from the 7th Panzer Regiment, turned the right flank of York's battalion by attacking from the railway stop below Longstop Hill.

Although the Americans "fought with stubborn courage," Hans Lüke reported, the battle seesawed back and forth, both sides fighting hard. It was, he observed, "a bloody slaughter on both sides." Eventually, however, the Germans drove the Americans back, putting the entire force at risk. Accordingly, the British withdrew both battalions. In three days the 18th suffered 356 killed, wounded, or missing—nearly half of the battalion's assigned strength.[20]

Nearly continuous rain rendered the Tunisian battlefield a sodden, muddy mess. On Christmas Eve Eisenhower visited Lieutenant General Charles Alfred Allfrey at his V Corps headquarters to assess the situation for himself. While at V Corps he watched four soldiers attempt to retrieve a motorcycle mired in the viscous mud. They struggled manfully but eventually gave up, and so did Eisenhower. He called off the offensive to wait for better weather. Mud and the Germans stopped the second attempt to take Tunis.[21]

The fighting on Longstop Hill did not add to the luster of the Big Red One or the 18th Infantry. Lieutenant Franklyn (Frank) Johnson, who led a platoon in the 18th Infantry's cannon company, believed the "fight for Longstop will go down as one of the worst for the 18th Infantry." To restore the battered 1st Battalion to some semblance of combat readiness, Colonel Greer drafted replacements from his other two battalions. Recriminations about the performance of the Americans from the Coldstream Guards and the British command followed, to which the 18th responded angrily. Terry Allen, frustrated at being sidelined and then hearing his units maligned, lost his patience. Ernie Pyle put it bluntly: "Allen not-so-quietly went nuts." Allen was furious at the losses suffered by the 18th and the British commentary that followed, including a report from British V Corps that reflected poorly on the 1st Battalion. Allen went forward with his intelligence officer, Lieutenant Colonel Robert W. Porter Jr., to learn for himself what had happened.[22]

He first met with Allfrey, whose report tipped the scale of his patience. Allen listened to Allfrey's account and then advised the corps commander that Porter would investigate the matter. Porter dutifully interviewed "the battalion commander, staff and company commanders (the three that survived—one was killed and another captured)." His report detailed a number of serious problems with the relief, most of which stemmed from two fundamentally different tactical systems, different communications, and inadequate preparation. There was more, including indifferent reconnaissance by the British troops, and guides who did not know where they were to go. Porter found nothing malicious, but the Coldstream Guards had done little to assure a tactically sound relief. After reading Porter's assessment, Allfrey was alarmed that Allen might use the report to embarrass him. Instead Allen tore it up, telling the corps commander that he would not make "an international incident over this." He went on to say, "I expect if that if I get any British Troops under my command, I'll give them a lot better treatment than you have given my men." Taking care of others even better than you do your own remains good advice.[23]

The Winter of Discontent

At the end of December 1943, Allen's division was scattered from hell to breakfast. Allen proposed to do something about that. Not long after his contretemps with Allfrey, Allen visited Eisenhower in Algiers and asked to have the division reassembled. Eisenhower promised to look into it. On his way out, Allen met with Eisenhower's chief of staff, Major General Walter Bedell "Beetle" Smith. Allen vented his frustration by telling Beetle he forgotten to ask the commander in chief one question: "Is this a private war in Tunisia or can anybody get in on it?"[24]

After Eisenhower conceded the race for Tunis to the Axis, he turned to marshalling resources to resume the offensive after the winter rains. His first two efforts to take Tunis failed for several reasons, but inadequate resources and a lack of tactical excellence rose high on the list. The Allied effort culminated for all the reasons Clausewitz imagined in his theory of war. According to him, culmination occurs when attacks reach a point where "the remaining strength is just enough to maintain a defense." At the end of December, the Axis enjoyed the edge in both airpower and forces on the ground, and the Allies had most definitely culminated.[25]

On New Year's Day, Anderson's Eastern Task Force officially became the British First Army. Soon thereafter more troops began moving east. Fredendall's II Corps headquarters did so on January 4. Ten days later, Allied Force Headquarters ordered Allen to assemble what remained of the 1st ID (the 16th Infantry and little else) at Guelma, Algeria, an old Roman town near the Tunisian frontier. There it would constitute the First Army reserve. Anderson, at Eisenhower's behest, sought to hold the passes through the Eastern

Dorsal while II Corps concentrated four US divisions to defend the southern flank against the inevitable arrival of Rommel's German-Italian Panzer Army as it retreated through Tripolitania. The II Corps would have the 1st AD immediately, the 34th ID as soon as French troops relieved them from securing the lines of communication, and the 9th ID when it completed its thousand-mile journey from French Morocco. The 1st ID would reunite "as quickly as it could be assembled from its scattered positions on the front and brought to this sector." These dispositions reflected Eisenhower's concern over the possibility of an assault on his flank by the combined resources of both Fifth Panzer Army and Panzer Army Africa.[26]

From north to south, British V Corps, French XIX Corps, and US II Corps defended two hundred miles with fewer than six divisions. Given that well-equipped infantry division could manage about ten miles of frontage, Anderson had too few troops to hold the ground, let alone contemplate an offensive. Tunisia is compartmented by hills, mountains, and forests. Compartmented terrain reduces line of sight and the effectiveness of weapons, necessitating more rather than fewer troops to defend. Only the British V Corps units operated in cohesive formations. The French colonial soldiers of XIX Corps were neither equipped nor trained for conventional operations. Moreover, the Americans and some of the British remained relatively inexperienced. Alan Moorehead aptly described the mishmash of differing means, tactics, and equipment as an "uncertainly balanced three-decker cake."[27]

Unity of command, despite being viewed among the Allies as a principle of war, proved ephemeral. Piecemeal commitment of units made for confusion in determining who reported to whom. General Eisenhower owned both the problem and the failure to find a solution. The British official history, very kindly, describes the Allied command system as "creaking." The French complicated matters by refusing to serve under British officers. Finally, on January 18, the Allied chiefs established the 18th Army Group under the command of British general Harold R. L. G. Alexander. First Army and Montgomery at Eighth Army would report to him. On January 28 Eisenhower swept the decks cleanly when he explicitly assigned "command of all Allied Forces on the Tunisian Front" to Anderson, including the French XIX Corps.[28]

Terry and Friends

The XIX Corps moved into the Ousseltia Valley in late December. It undertook "two limited offensives," seizing two exits from the Ousseltia Valley on the Eastern Dorsal at Karachoum Gap and Kairouan Pass. The Germans could not let this stand. Holding the passes could enable the Allies to cut off the roads north to Tunis, which would trap Rommel's German-Italian Panzer Army, now nearing Tunisia. Fifth Panzer Army's tasks included to keep "open the road to Tunis for Rommel's Army, and to hold the ports at his disposal." Accordingly, von Arnim assembled a large Kampfgruppe formed on parts of the 334th ID, 10th PZ, and half of the Italian 1st Superga Division. He ordered this task force to clear both passes in an operation code-named Eilbote I. The German-Italian Kampfgruppe fielded a relatively small number of tanks, but these included at least four Panzerkampfwagen (PKW) VI Tiger tanks as well as a few PKW III and IV medium tanks. The better-armed and -equipped Germans and Italians attacked on January 18 and soon drove the French troops from the passes and back across the valley.[29]

This quashed the effort to consolidate the Big Red One. Instead Anderson ordered British troops south to restore the situation, and II Corps to send troops north. Fredendall attached Colonel Alexander N. Stark Jr.'s 26th Infantry to Colonel Paul Robinette's Combat Command B of the 1st AD. On January 19 the 26th Infantry departed Guelma to join Robinette. To react quickly, the division violated local custom and moved during daylight; doing so all but assured a German air attack. Alec Stark's troops fought off two fighters, with only one soldier killed in action; Private First Class Leslie Gauthern, who "stuck to his guns and tried to bring the raider down," paid for this bravery with his life. The 26th arrived near the village of Ousseltia before dawn on January 23. Robinette immediately ordered Stark to seize the high ground on the south side of the Kairouan Pass, the crossroads west of the pass, and to "close the ousseltia-kairouan Pass."[30]

Stark's troops attacked the Italians defending the pass before dawn on January 25. Lieutenant Colonel Clarence E. Beck, commanding the 2nd Battalion, preceded his attack with infantry platoon to scout the route and the objective. The remainder of Beck's battalion and Lieutenant Colonel Gerald C. Kelleher's 1st Battalion moved out at 0900. The scouts duly reported that more than one company defended the pass. Based on this intelligence Beck employed two artillery battalions and his mortars to pound the Italians defending along the crest and reverse slopes of the hills either side of the pass. The two battalions then cleared the pass against sporadic fire—a term best used by people who have not experienced it. One of the Italian defenders who survived the artillery and mortars described the process succinctly: "When the men [Americans] fixed bayonets and charged up the hill, moving fast, some of us broke and fled down the slope: some just threw up their hands and surrendered."[31]

The 26th Infantry and Robinette's combat command restored the situation in Kairouan Pass, while the British 36th Brigade took care of the northern penetration. Following the action at Kairouan Pass, First Army ordered Allen's headquarters to take over the southern part of the XIX Corps sector controlling the 16th Infantry as well as various French troops. This "international" organization reported to General Jean-Louis Koeltz at XIX Corps. Allen's French and American contingent defended an area from the village of Ousseltia south along a frontage of roughly thirty miles. The sector remained quiet, characterized by patrolling and exchanging artillery fire with the Axis. That changed when the counterattacks that became known collectively as the Battle of Kasserine Pass began. When the depth of the German penetration grew, 1st ID withdrew, under orders, from the Eastern Dorsal across the valley floor during the course of two nights on February 17 and 18.[32]

During the fighting to stabilize the XIX Corps, Anderson cabled Eisenhower to report that First Army had "a very exposed southern flank." He suggested withdrawing, and Eisenhower agreed. II Corps then withdrew from outposts at Gafsa and other positions along the Eastern Dorsal to defend along the Feriana-Sbéitla line along the Western Dorsal. That same day Eisenhower cabled Marshall, admitting that he had attempted too much with the forces available, with the result that Anderson had not been able to "reestablish divisional organizations." Eisenhower believed the problem affected, in particular, the 1st and 34th ID. He may as well have added the 1st AD.[33] The resulting weakness of the bottom layer of "three-decker cake" would soon be revealed.

Moorehead's comparison of the Allied line to an unbalanced three-layer cake remained valid. The British V Corps included two infantry divisions, the 46th and 78th, as well as the 6th Armored Division. These divisions defended an area from the coast west of Mateur to the village of Bou Arada. V Corps retained Greer's 18th Infantry in reserve. V Corps, unlike the other two corps, was concentrated and comparatively well positioned. Koeltz's XIX Corps defended sixty more miles, from Bou Arada south to the village of Hadjeb el Aiouan, with a single understrength French division composed of four infantry battalions and a few smaller infantry detachments as well as Allen's 1st ID, composed of the 16th Infantry and five battalions of French infantry. Robinett's Combat Command, 1st AD, served as the corps reserve. The US II Corps in the south defended the largest sector with the fewest troops. Fredendall had Combat Command A and C of the 1st AD, the 34th ID's 168th Infantry, less one battalion, and the understrength French Welvert

(Constantine) Division. Positioned just west of the Faid Pass, Combat Command A, 1st AD, hung like a ripe fruit on the eastern tip of the line.[34]

Between them, Jürgen von Arnim and Erwin Rommel, now nearing the end of the long retreat Rommel had led from El Alamein, enjoyed several advantages. They had interior lines, formidable armor forces, and control of the air. Both saw opportunity and both needed the other, but neither would play second fiddle. Kesselring too perceived opportunity. Since the Axis controlled most of the passes through the Eastern Dorsal, they could attack at will. Kesselring brought his two prima donna commanders together long enough to arrange the series of engagements to penetrate key passes known by the name of only one—Kasserine. He believed that "a bold thrust into the enemy's offensive preparations held out the greatest promise of success." Rommel saw it the same way. According to him. the "the first aim had to be to break up the American assembly areas in southwest Tunisia." The two commanders would share the 10th PZ from Fifth Panzer Army and 21st PZ from Rommel's Panzer Army Africa. Von Arnim would begin the operation using both Panzer divisions but then turn them over to Rommel for the next phase. Rommel articulated a second aim: "to instill in [the Americans] from the outset an inferiority complex." Kesselring hoped the Panzers could drive all the way to Tébessa. Taking the important supply dump and road junction there might force the Allies out of Tunisia altogether.[35]

Von Arnim named 5th Panzer Army's part of Operation Frülingswind (Spring Wind). The 10th PZ, now commanded by Oberst Fritz Freiherr von Broich, attacked through the Faid Pass at 0400 on Saint Valentine's Day. By 0600 his Panzergrenadiers, supported by a company of Tiger tanks, had advanced eight kilometers west of the pass. The 10th PZ war diary reported, "At 0830 our tanks advanced southward on Sidi bou Zid." After a hard day's fighting ably supported by the Luftwaffe and organic artillery, the 10th PZ drove off Combat Command A, 1st AD, seized Sidi bou Zid, and opened the way to the passes through the Western Dorsal.[36] The first phase of the counteroffensive set the conditions for Rommel to begin the next phase.

On the evening of February 18, General Fredendall reacted to the threat developing toward the Kasserine Pass. At 2000 he called Alec Stark at his 26th Infantry command post. Without ado he told Stark, "I want you to go to Kasserine right away and pull a Stonewall Jackson. Take over up there." Stark wondered if he meant literally right away, to which Fredendall replied, "Yes, immediately; stop at my CP on the way up." Stark had little to work with. The 19th Engineer Battalion was the only unit defending the pass that night, and

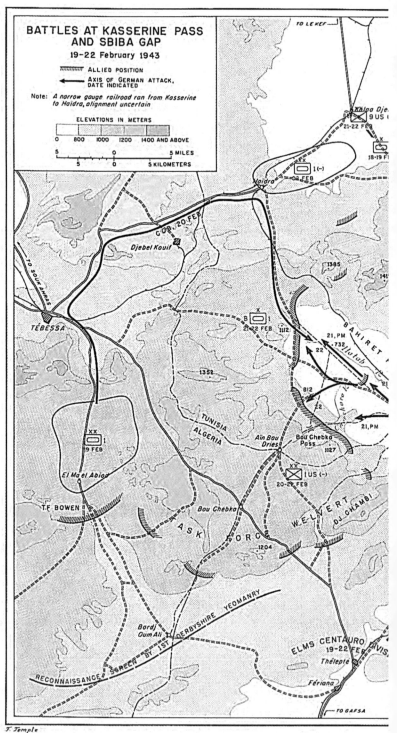

Map 5: The Battles at Kasserine Pass and Sbiba Gap, February 19–22, 1943.
Reproduced from Howe, *Northwest Africa*, Map VIII.

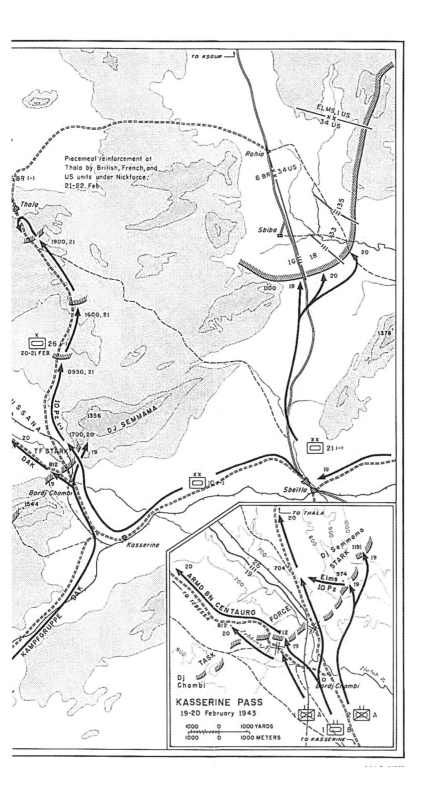

Piecemeal reinforcement at
Thala by British, French, and
US units under Nickforce,
21-22 Feb

TO KSOUR

ELMS, I US
XX
34 US

Rohia

6 BR · 34 US

Thala

1900, 21

Sbiba

1600, 21

26 (-)
20-21 FEB

0930, 21

1356

DJ SEMMAMA

1700, 20

TF STARK

Bordj Chambi

Kasserine

Sbeïtla

KAMPFGRUPPE

DAK

KASSERINE PASS
19-20 February 1943

1000   0   1000 YARDS
1000   0   1000 METERS

TO THALA

Dj Semmama
STARK

Elms
10 Pz

ARMD BN CENTAURO FORCE

TO TEBESSA

TASK

Dj Chambi

Bordj Chambi

TO KASSERINE

Stark's regiment had not yet concentrated. Eisenhower's fears were about to be realized.[37]

Stark and his command post moved at midnight, arriving just west of the pass at 0730 on February 19. His 1st Battalion arrived soon after that and just ahead of the German elements of the justly famous Deutsches Afrikakorps made the main effort through Kasserine Pass. As Sergeant John Lebda described it, "Kasserine Pass in the southern part of Tunisia was a valley about a mile wide. It had two mountain ranges on each side about a thousand feet high. Mountains converged to form a narrow pass half through the stem of an hourglass." A river bed cut a swath thirty-five feet deep and forty feet wide over which an arched stone bridge and a narrow-gauge railway trestle passed. This defile and others nearby that cut through the Dorsals attracted Germans, Americans, Italians, and Brits like moths to a flame.[38]

Mines, the 19th Engineers, Stark's units, and various others thrown into the fight slowed the Axis attack. Stark's amalgamation of units held on throughout the 19th. Meanwhile, Terry Allen and his headquarters controlled only the 16th Infantry, but he, along with Teddy Roosevelt and Clift Andrus, did what they could going forward to encourage soldiers and seeing to the provision of their supplies. The division's units fought whomever, with whoever and wherever Fredendall sent them. Allen described what happened: "The German panzers came boiling out of the west end of the Pass and with a whiplash of tanks, guns and men, knocked the American Forces reeling back behind the mountain passes at Sebeitla and Kasserine 40 miles west of the Faid Pass."[39]

Lieutenant Johnson's 18th Infantry cannon company was ordered south from Teboursouk when V Corps committed them. They departed at dusk of February 17 on a trek of about a hundred miles south to Sbiba, a village forty miles north of Kasserine, to backstop yet another pass in the Western Dorsal. They arrived at 0830 the following morning. Of the situation, Greer said, "Don't call me for help—I haven't any. If they attack us in force we cannot hold, but by god we will. We must." The 18th fought a bitter fight alongside British troops. Johnson thought it only a matter of time before the Germans surrounded them, yet like the troops in the Kasserine Pass, they bent but held on. Along with British troops, they managed to stop Rommel's 21st PZ on February 19.[40]

The division headquarters and 16th Infantry joined the fight on February 19. Fredendall ordered Allen to "assume command of the kasserine [emphasis in original] sector, including the Constantine (Welvert) Division and various separate American units." Not surprisingly, the division operations summary concluded that "there was considerable confusion," alleging that the Germans attacked wearing French and American uniforms. The confusion stemmed from chaotic fighting among mixed units, as the Deutsches Afrika Korps attacked along with the 10th and 21st PZ. In bitter fighting the Germans "captured one battery of the 33rd Field Artillery," which Allen had assigned to support Combat Command B of the 1st AD, one of the "various separate American units."[41]

On the night of February 20 John Lebda found himself behind enemy lines. He despaired of surviving, noting that "we had no planes in Tunisia; therefore, we knew that no one was aware of our plight." Allen, with the 16th Infantry and Combat Command B, 1st AD, held the western shoulder of the burgeoning German penetration while British troops held the eastern shoulder. The remainder of 1st AD and the 9th ID, arriving from French Morocco, built bulwarks farther north. By the afternoon of February 21, Allied efforts began to tell. The following morning Rommel concluded that "the enemy had grown too strong for our attack to be maintained." At 1300 he met with Kesselring, who agreed to break off the attack. Of the Americans he said, "The tactical conduct of the enemy's defense had been first class. They had recovered very quickly after the first shock and soon succeeded in damming up our advance by grouping their reserves to defend the passes and other suitable points." The German-Italian forces withdrew from Kasserine on February 23. The weather cleared that day, and the US Army Air Force delivered, according to the Desert Fox, "hammer-blow air attacks."[42] Having gained the edge, Allied air forces retained it from then on.

The right thing to do tactically when the Germans and Italians withdrew would have been to maintain contact, and better yet to pursue with sufficient force to force the Germans to wage a fighting withdrawal. Instead, II Corps allowed the retreating Germans to break contact. Fredendall may not have been able to do much else, as he still lacked coherent divisional formations and had no reserve. Not concentrating his forces had a battlefield effect. The 1st AD alone had more tanks than the Germans and Italians had in the Kasserine fights, but Anderson had never permitted the 1st AD, or for that matter any US formation, to fight as a unit. The exigencies of the campaign alone do not explain his tactics. Part of what happened must be attributed to Anderson not seeing the potential of massing armor and his lack of confidence in the Americans.

Respite and Learning

On March 1, II Corps ordered the 9th ID to relieve the 1st ID. The Big Red One then assembled at Marsott west of Tébessa. Refitting and planning to resume the offensive occupied most of the ten days during which the division "rested." The troops had learned some hard lessons, as had their officers up to and including Dwight D. Eisenhower. Both Eisenhower and Allen realized they had some training deficiencies that ranged from the absurd—the cannon companies never having fired before they entered combat—to more mundane problems, including patrolling and maintaining security. Soldiers summed up the lessons from the bottom up that would have sounded familiar to one of Caesar's legionaries. Those legionaries would also know that if behavior is not changed, then the lesson goes unlearned.

Corporal Sam Fuller, later famous as a movie producer, summed up the combat experience: "Civilized wars just don't exist." To that he added that soldiers, "become a killing machine" who worry about "simple but basic things" like "dry socks, edible chow, fresh water, the runs." Ernie Pyle witnessed this change. He found the troops talked about killing in a "casual and workshop manner." Ralph Berry, who joined the 16th Infantry in the fall of 1943, admired and appreciated his squad leader, Sergeant Zigmund Kirdzik. Kirdzik had fought in both North Africa and Sicily, which taught him, among other things, to "dig in fast below the level of the ground." George Zenie, who learned that lesson firsthand in North Africa, added that he looked to "dig foxholes in the sides of hills and cover the tops for protection against artillery fire." Jarvis Moore, a platoon leader, discovered that he was exhilarated "before a fire fight but badly depressed afterward with severe shakes that lasted for hours on occasion." There is a perfectly reasonable biochemical explanation for both the exhilaration of combat and the depression that often follows. It is difficult to explain but happens even when the soldier knows why it does.[43]

Lessons bubbled up from the bottom, but others came top down. Chief of staff Stan Mason concluded that "rigid interpretation of a written order" could and did cause time lost and casualties. He also learned when he made the move from operations officer to chief of staff that he needed a succession plan. Commenting on the air battle, Mason claimed there were "absolutely no Allied fighter planes to contest the air space and no surcease day or night." To be fair, for much of the time the weather precluded either side from flying. The division increasingly "used field telephones for command and staff messages," and to afford some level of security, the Big Red One used code names for units and their commanders. The division became Danger, and the command post Danger Forward.[44]

At Allied Force Headquarters Eisenhower reached several important conclusions in his first few months in command. He also used observer reports provided by Army Ground Forces observers and others. Quite apart from recognizing that his decision to attempt to take Tunis *à outrance* had produced confusion and a lack of coherence that contributed to the disasters during the Kasserine Pass battles, he found discipline in the American forces unsatisfactory. Early in the fighting he found that units had not dug in and were indifferent to noise and light discipline—lessons 1st ID soldiers reported having learned by mid-March. He found air-ground coordination not up to par, which he blamed on inadequate training.[45]

Major General Omar N. Bradley submitted an important Army Ground Forces observer report on the 1st AD, which ran to thirteen pages and reflected numerous interviews that he conducted personally with soldiers and officers. The tankers and armored infantrymen reported in detail on what Allies sometimes called the PAK defense, the name coming from the German acronym for antitank guns (*Panzerabwehrkanone*). The German PAK defense featured guns in depth and others hidden on either flank. If an attacking unit maneuvered to avoid the guns positioned in depth, it would be ambushed by those on the flanks. Like their colleagues in the Big Red One, 1st AD troops learned the discipline Eisenhower had worried about. One junior leader reported to Bradley that his boys got it: "Every time they hit the ground [from now on], you'll find them digging a helluva big hole." His troops would also correct anyone, regardless of rank, who violated light discipline. The armor troops wanted photo reconnaissance of the kind they believed the Germans enjoyed—"We must put greater emphasis on good reconnaissance."[46] Training was part of the solution, so it became a central theme in the Mediterranean Theater. In a cable to General Marshall transmitted the day after Rommel withdrew, Eisenhower asserted, "I am going to make it a fixed rule that no unit from the time one reaches this theater until this war is won will ever stop training. This includes units in the front line." He noted in that same cable that Terry Allen agreed. And indeed Allen did. On December 23 the division published a plan for testing 81-millimeter mortar squads to assess their training. Specifically, the testing would rate mortar squads, recommend further training as needed, and determine "defects in weapons or ammunition." Training without evaluation does not ensure learning.[47]

Although he embarrassed the Americans at Kasserine Pass, Rommel recognized them as apt pupils. They "could not yet be compared with the veteran troops of the Eighth Army," he said, "yet they made up for their lack of experience by their far better equipment and their tactically more flexible command." He added that "the tactical conduct of the enemy's defence had been first class. They had recovered quickly after the first shock and had soon succeeded in damming up our advance by grouping their reserves to defend the passes and other suitable points." Not bad marks from the man widely acknowledged to be the master of desert warfare.[48]

Notes

1. HQ, 26th Infantry, "History of the 26th Infantry in the Present Struggle," n.d., MRC 1988.38; Knickerbocker et al., *Danger Forward*, 58–59; Wheeler, *The Big Red One*, 155. See Ambrose, *Supreme Commander*. Chapter 10 details the confusion, missteps and political difficulties Eisenhower confronted in his first campaign. See also Douglas Porch's assessment of decision making on both sides, *Path to Victory*. Robert M. Citino contrasts German assessments and actions with those of the Allies in *Wehrmacht Retreats*, 24–30.

2. Eisenhower, *Crusade in Europe*, 235. The Eighth Army began its pursuit of Erwin Rommel's Panzer Army Africa on November 5. See Montgomery, *Memoirs*, 129.

3. Clausewitz, *On War*, 79. See also 216–19, which lays out why combat tends toward spasmodic activity rather than steady pressure.

4. Howe, *Northwest Africa*, ch. 15 and 16, 277–310. See also ch. 20, 373–400.

5. Howe, 233–55; Shirer, *Rise and Fall*, 922.

6. Howe, *Northwest Africa*, 253–55. See also Kesselring, *A Soldier's Record*, 168, which identifies Loerzer and Oberst Harlinghausen as Kesselring's messengers but does not provide their first names. They almost certainly are Bruno Loerzer and Martin Harlinghausen, who, like Kesselring, were Luftwaffe officers.

7. Howe, *Northwest Africa*; 168–69; Citino, *Wehrmacht Retreats*, 24–27. See also Boatner, *Biographical Dictionary*, 272–73.

8. Bykofsky and Larson, *Transportation Corps*, map at 138–39. This book is essential to understanding the scale and scope of operations in North African, and for that matter the global fight the Transportation Corps supported.

9. On the problems shared by both sides, see Eisenhower, *Crusade in Europe*, 116. Eisenhower was describing what he saw as General Anderson's problems rather than those of both sides. In fact, he could have been writing about the Germans. On vessels sunk, see Maycock, *Twelfth Air Force*, 11. On Luftwaffe control of the air, see Johnson, *One More Hill*, 13. Most veterans' surveys and soldier memoirs from the North African campaign share Johnson's view. See also Butcher, *Three Years with Eisenhower*, 188–89. Butcher believed that four transports, rather than two lighters, had been sunk or damaged. Butcher's diary also reported the loss of one transport sunk and two damaged at Casablanca, as well as two British transports sunk while returning to Gibraltar. In the same entry he described three other successful attacks, including two "outside Med" and one just north of Algiers.

10. Moorehead, *March to Tunis*, 469; Eisenhower, *Papers*, no. 698, 2:81. Moorehead earned the right to form operational judgments. He reported on fighting in North Africa from beginning to end, with a brief respite in the United States, returning to North Africa in time to witness the end there from the vantage point of British First Army. Among the many things that proved troublesome is that the French XIX Corps did not have tactical control of its units. Some reported to British V Corps, and others to the US II Corps.

11. Howe, *Northwest Africa*, 277–79.

12. Citino, *Wehrmacht Retreats*, 24–27.

13. Schick, *History of the 10. Panzer*, 1–13, 94–95, 210, 414–31.

14. Baumer and Reardon, *American Iliad*, 1–3.

15. Wheeler, *The Big Red One*, 160. The slope of the hill is easily seen in maps that feature contours, as well as in photographs of the area.

16. Wheeler, 159–62; Schick, *History of the 10. Panzer*, 447–49. The author is indebted to historian Mark Reardon for his insights on the fighting at Longstop Hill.

17. Schick, *History of the 10. Panzer*, 448–49; Atkinson, *Army at Dawn*, 240–45.

18. Schick, *History of the 10. Panzer*, 448–49. See also Baumer and Reardon, *American Iliad*, 48–61; Knickerbocker et al., *Danger Forward*, 411. There is confusion on just who commanded the 1st Battalion, 18th Infantry, at Longstop Hill. Atkinson and Knickerbocker both list Robert H. York as commanding; Baumer and Reardon report George Fricke as the commander. The author believes it was York, a choice borne out in York's obituary. See also Daniel Lyons, interview by Colonel John Votaw, June 17, 1994, First Division Museum at Cantigny, Wheaton, IL.

19. Lüke, *Grenadier Regiment 69*, 412–13.

20. Citino, *Wehrmacht Retreats*, 36–37; Blaxland, *Plain Cook*, 140–41. Re casualties, see HQ, 1st ID, "Summary of Activities of 1st Infantry Division," March 8, 1943, Record Group (RG) 301-0.5, MRC, 1. See also Astor, *Terrible Terry Allen*, 153. Blaxland reported 356 casualties, as does Astor, but the division cited 344. Lüke, *Grenadier Regiment 69*, 413.

21. Eisenhower, *Crusade in Europe*, 123–24.

22. Astor, *Terrible Terry Allen*, 133–35; Johnson, *One More Hill*, 29.

23. Astor, *Terrible Terry Allen*, 136.

24. Astor, 136.

25. Clausewitz, *On War*, 528. On comparative strengths of the two sides, Eisenhower's estimate of December 15, 1943, is good; see Memorandum: Eisenhower Mss., "Butcher Diary," December 15, 1942, no. 721, in Eisenhower, *Papers*, 2:842–43. Strengths reported in the official history were collected postwar. At the end of January 1943, the total Axis strength reached 100,000, including 26,000 Italian soldiers. Rommel's forces arrived with another 78,000 troops. Italians outnumbered Germans in Rommel's formation, with 48,000 troops. See Howe, *Northwest Africa*, 371.

26. HQ, Allied Force, conference memorandum, January 21, 1943, no. 787, in Eisenhower, *Papers*, 2:918–19; Eisenhower, *Crusade in Europe*, 125. The January 21 memorandum is explicit: "General Fredendall retains responsibility for the general protection of the right flank of the Allied Forces." See also "From El Aghelia to Tripoli," ch. 9 of Playfair and Molony, *Destruction of the Axis Forces in Africa*, which traces

the continued retreat of Panzer Army Africa along the Libyan coast. Montgomery allowed what Rommel called a reprieve that lasted from December 28 to January 15, but then Rommel headed west again. See Liddell-Hart, *Rommel Papers*, 381–85.

27. Howe, *Northwest Africa*, 349–50; Moorehead, *March to Tunis*, 463.

28. Playfair and Molony, *Destruction of the Axis Forces in Africa*, 270; Howe, *Northwest Africa*, 383–84. Howe reported in the US official history that Anderson had traveled "more than 1,000 miles" in the first days of his time coordinating rather than commanding the forces. For Alexander's biography, see Boatner, *Biographical Dictionary*, 4–6.

29. Wheeler, *The Big Red One*, 164; Knickerbocker et al., *Danger Forward*, 60. See also Howe, *Northwest Africa*, 376–83. The Germans styled their operation Eilbote. Translations vary; Citino translates it as "messenger" in *Wehrmacht Retreats*, 80. Robert Edwards, who translated Schick, *History of the 10. Panzer*, uses "special delivery." Cassell's dictionary makes it "express delivery," which this author likes. The order of battle for Kampfgruppe Weber can be found in Schick, 454. Re Fifth Panzer Army task, see Alfred Gause, "German-Italian Army Group Africa, Nov 1942–13 May 1943," 1953, ms. D-385, N17500.902, Combined Arms Research Library, Fort Leavenworth, KS (henceforth CARL), 6.

30. 26th Infantry, "History," 2–4, 5.

31. 26th Infantry, 9–10.

32. Re 36th Brigade Operations, see Jackson, *Battle for North Africa*, 415; Howe, *Northwest Africa*, 374–83; 1st ID, "Summary of Activities," 1.

33. Howe, *Northwest Africa*, 423; Eisenhower, *Papers*, 2:953.

34. Playfair and Molony, *Destruction of the Axis Forces in Africa*, map 27. The order of battle shows the Welvert Division. French general J. E. Welvert commanded the French Constantine Division, manned by colonial troops. It may have had as few as five battalions by this point. Playfair and Molony, 396, 399.

35. Kesselring, *A Soldier's Record*, 178–79; Liddell-Hart, *Rommel Papers*, 397–401. Rommel agreed with Kesselring, but von Arnim opposed driving as deep as Tébessa. Rommel claimed it was because von Arnim wanted to use the 10th PZ "for a small private show of his own." See also Cirillo, *Kasserine Pass Battles*, which contains after-action reports for pertinent US Army units, German unit diaries, maps, and doctrinal references for both combatants, including the 10th PZ war diary, vol. 1, pt. 2, "Readings," sec. 23; Schick, *History of the 10. Panzer*, 463–81.

36. Oberst von Borich took command of the 10th PZ following Fischer's death, along with that of his operations officer, when he drove into an Italian minefield on February 1. Claus von Stauffenberg, later famous for the attempted assassination of Hitler, joined the 10th PZ later in the month as the senior staff officer. 10th PZ war diary, in Cirillo, *Kasserine Pass Battles*; Schick, *History of the 10. Panzer*, 463–65.

37. Howe, *Northwest Africa*, 447.

38. Howe, 423–81; Lebda, *Million Miles to Go*, 33.

39. Astor, *Terrible Terry Allen*, 145; 21st PZ war diary, in Cirillo, *Kasserine Pass Battles*, vol. 1, pt. 2, "Readings," sec. 24.

40. Johnson, *One More Hill*, 39; Howe, *Northwest Africa*, 452–53.

41. 1st ID, "Summary of Activities," 3.

42. Liddell-Hart, *Rommel Papers*, 406.

43. Samantha Fuller, dir., *A Fuller Life: The Story of a True American Maverick*, documentary film, 2013. See also Fuller, *A Third Face*, 120; Ralph A. Berry Sr. and Jarvis Burns Moore, veterans surveys, n.d., box 2, US Army Heritage and Education Center, Carlisle, PA; Astor, *Terrible Terry Allen*, 163; Ernie Pyle, "Brave Men, Brave Men!" *Pittsburgh Press*, April 22, 1943, reproduced at https://erniepyle.iu.edu/wartime-columns/brave-men-brave-men.html.

44. Mason, "Reminiscences," 45, 47, 48.

45. Eisenhower to his deputy commander in ETOUSA, his subordinate US commanders, and Allied Force Headquarters staff, in Eisenhower, *Papers*, no. 770, 2:904.

46. Major General Omar N. Bradley, "Notes on Operations of the 1st Armored Division," May 13, 1943, N602, CARL, 3.

47. Eisenhower, *Papers*, no. 840, 2:984; 1st ID, entry 179, December 23, 1943, in RG 301-3.2: G-3 Journal, Tunisian Campaign, MRC Digital Archives.

48. Liddell-Hart, *Rommel Papers*, 407.

CHAPTER FIVE

Lessons Learned: The End in Tunisia

Nineteen forty-three will be the year of the Anglo-American effort.
　　　　　—Mussolini to Count Ciano

We're a hell of gang to tangle with, just stick with us and see. The 1st
Division will lead the way from hell to victory.
　　　　　— Terry Allen, quoting from Song of the Fighting First

THE PERFORMANCE OF the US Army and the 1st ID showed promise and
problems. Lieutenant General K. A. N. Anderson and Major General Lloyd
R. Fredendall ordered units hither and yon with little regard for unit integ-
rity or US doctrine. Big Red One soldiers and leaders showed adaptability,
agility, inexperience, and occasional panic. Rommel's plan to instill a sense
of inferiority succeeded to some degree, causing most American soldiers to
concede German tactical excellence. Raymond E. Zerfass, a soldier in the
16th Infantry, put it simply: "The German troops in the Desert were tops."
But he also pointed out that the Germans were more than "five years ahead
of us in experience."

Gaining experience takes time. The US Army managed to land four divisions in North Africa, along with their supporting arms, less than a year
after the Japanese attacked Pearl Harbor and just over two years after the institution of a "peacetime" draft. There had been little time to absorb lessons
learned in training. The soldiers who landed on the beaches of North Africa
on November 8 had already learned a great deal from their German tutors,
and lessons would continue.[1]

Allied Assessment and Intentions

General Harold R. L. G. Alexander, slated to command the 18th Army Group and serve as Eisenhower's deputy, visited the Tunisian front on February 18 at the outset of the Kasserine Pass fight. Alarmed by what he saw, Alexander took command the next day before his headquarters activated. At the end of the Kasserine crisis, Alexander undertook to organize formations along national lines, coordinate the operations of Allied troops in Tunisia with those of Bernard Law Montgomery's Eighth Army as it closed on the Mareth Line, and plan the Allied invasion of Sicily.[2]

By mid-March, Alexander had reorganized as Eisenhower directed. The US II Corps assembled with four divisions assigned: the 1st, 9th, and 35th Infantry Divisions and the 1st Armored Division. II Corps reported directly to Alexander. The British First Army retained the British V Corps, composed of three infantry divisions, and the French XIX Corps, with two infantry divisions. First Army also had an armored division in reserve. Montgomery's Eighth Army, composed of four corps comprising nine divisions and several separate brigades, provided the second main force. The moment of Axis advantage had passed.[3]

Concluding the campaign required joining the two field armies and II Corps, followed by a final offensive to drive the Axis from Africa. The balance between the burgeoning American army and the still more numerous British forces required sensitive handling. Alexander and Anderson, like many senior British officers, had low regard for the fighting skills and leadership of the US Army. Alexander formed his impression of US troops based on what he saw in the February battles. Not surprisingly, he claimed that his "main anxiety is the poor fighting value of Americans." His original intention to bring the campaign to conclusion caused him to assign II Corps supporting roles that would not tax troops he considered inferior. To his credit, Alexander responded decisively and with alacrity to quiet counseling from Eisenhower to the effect that his intention to relegate American troops to supporting roles would not do.[4]

Eisenhower had one more command and control issue to resolve: Who would command II Corps? His view of Fredendall evolved rapidly during the first week of March. On March 2 he sent Fredendall a note of congratulations on managing the difficult Kasserine Pass battles, but tempered his praise with advice on managing his subordinates. Specifically, Eisenhower told Fredendall to assign missions and then let each person "do his job." He warned the II Corps commander that it was sometimes "difficult for a superior to keep his fingers out of the subordinate's pie." The following day he cabled General Marshall to express concern over managing personnel, say-ing, "As you know, I have had moments of doubt about Fredendall." Chiefly, Eisenhower believed Fredendall was not good at "getting the best out of sub-ordinates." His cable reeks of indecision and genuine concern over how best to deal with a problem that, he wrote, "plagues me all of the time." Cables sent during this period suggest that Eisenhower was testing the limits of his authority with respect to men Marshall had chosen. On March 5, he relieved General Fredendall and assigned George S. Patton Jr. in his place. From that date forward, Eisenhower showed no indecision about personnel manage-ment, even faced with difficult men like Patton and Montgomery.[5]

On March 6 the Germans sortied from the Mareth line to attack Eighth Army. After El Alamein, Montgomery methodically followed Rommel, occasionally attempting envelopments, but he took no risks. In *The Desert Generals*, British historian Correlli Barnett stirred up a hornet's nest by char-acterizing Montgomery's "pursuit" of Rommel after El Alamein as "showing the bustling confidence of an archdeacon entering a *maison clos* [brothel]." Barnett added that during the long march of some fifteen hundred miles to the Mareth Line, in "mobility and maneuver, Montgomery was as lost as a dray horse on a polo field." Rommel's rearguard entered Tunisia on Febru-ary 12. Montgomery followed, prepared for an Axis riposte and waiting for Anderson's troops to help him end the campaign. Barnett's criticism is valid, but elegance in victory is an unnecessary luxury for those who have the big-gest battalions. Montgomery understood that the tide had turned, and took advantage of the Axis ebb. His inelegant pursuit might not win staff college approbation, but was it was certain to work.[6]

The endgame in Tunisia required two stages. To begin, II Corps would attack through the same passes in Western Dorsal through which the Axis attacks had come in February. Once through the passes, II Corps would con-tinue generally southeast to clear the Eastern Dorsal. Alexander wanted II Corps to draw off Germans and or Italians, thus weakening the enemy's hold on the Mareth Line. II Corps success would assist Montgomery's troops. For his part, Montgomery planned a set-piece battle, but he did order the New Zealand Corps around the left or western flank of the Mareth Line.[7]

Once through the Mareth, Eighth Army would turn north, attacking par-allel to the coast to link up with II Corps and ultimately First Army. The final stage envisioned II Corps moving to the western or left flank of the Allied forces and attacking northward abreast of First and Eighth Armies. The tide in the air had turned as well. The Allied air forces now enjoyed superiority in numbers and the advantage in the air over Tunisia.

Axis Assessment and Intentions

Despite the failure of the counteroffensive in February, Generalfeldmarschall Albert Kesselring still believed that "the chances of a successful defence of the 'fortress of Tunisia' were not altogether unfavorable as long as the two Allied Armies could be kept apart and their air forces prevented from coordinating." Rommel, who briefly commanded the newly formed Army Group Afrika, departed March 9 on sick leave. General Giovanni Messe replaced him in command of the German-Italian Panzer Army, now styled First Italian Army, and by Generaloberst Jürgen von Arnim at Army Group. General Gustav von Varst succeeded von Arnim at Fifth Panzer Army.[8]

Soon after taking command of Army Group Afrika, Rommel asked von Arnim and Messe for their estimate of the situation. After considering his subordinates' assessments, he summarized their views and added his own analysis. Concluding that the Army Group could not defend the line it held and should withdraw, he proposed to defend a frontage of about one hundred miles extending from Enfidaville, across the Eastern Dorsal to Bou Arada, and then more or less north to the coast through Mateur. Since Bou Arada remained in Allied hands, he believed that town should be taken, as well as Medjez el Bab to the north. Rommel asked that his proposal be addressed quickly, given the "gravity of the situation."[9]

Kesselring did not agree. He believed that the 10th, 15th, and 21st PZ enabled sufficient mobility for Army Group Afrika to defend nearly 350 miles, from the Mareth Line through the mountains to the northern coast of Tunisia. He presumed that, somehow, fuel and ammunition would arrive in sufficient quantity; Rommel, on the other hand, believed they would not. In any case, Hitler said no to any withdrawal. Walter Warlimont, deputy chief of operations to Generaloberst Alfred Jodl at the Oberkommando der Wehrmacht, characterized German strategic policy succinctly. According to him, Hitler's "every thought and action became increasingly centered on holding what had been won, winning back what had been lost and never giving up anything anywhere." The standfast orders issued for Stalingrad, El Alamein, and Tunis became de rigueur.[10]

With few options, Rommel ordered a spoiling attack on Montgomery's positions at Medenene just west of the Mareth Line. On March 6 the 10th PZ attacked with some early success. Halted at noon by determined defenders, the 10th regrouped, attacked a second time, and failed again. Rommel concluded that "instead of facing a weakly-defended assembly area, his corps ran into a fully-prepared defense." That discovery cost the axis fifty-two tanks, with nothing but insight in return.[11]

On March 10, 1st ID intelligence (G-2) published a reasonably accurate order of battle for the remaining German forces. The division's analysts reckoned that the Panzer divisions retained perhaps 276 tanks, including the light PKW II, with a 20-millimeter cannon, as well as the PKW III, which fired a 50-millimeter main gun, although some had been refitted with 75-millimeter cannon, and the PKW IV, with a 75-millimeter cannon. The Germans also had as many as nine PKW VI Tiger tanks and ten PKW III tanks assigned to a heavy tank battalion, the 501st. Even with the handful of tanks assigned to the two Italian armored divisions, the Axis had fewer tanks than the US 1st AD, let alone British V Corps and Eighth Army, which had more than eight hundred of their own.[12]

The Germans also had five infantry divisions and a Fallschirmjäger (parachute) brigade. The 1st ID estimated that Fifth Panzer Army could field 52,000 combatants supported by 8,000 services and logistics troops, while the Italian First Army's German contingent included 40,000 combatants with 13,000 service and logistics troops. In addition, Army Group Africa included five Italian infantry and two armored divisions, as well as supporting and some independent combat formations, approaching a total strength of about 60,000 combat troops and 11,000 services and logistics troops. Rommel made his final estimate in early March. He believed the Army Group confronted just over 200,000 Allied soldiers equipped with 1,600 tanks, 1,100 antitank guns, and 850 pieces of artillery.[13]

Rest, Refit, and Reorganize

Sustaining combat operations requires systematic means to reconstitute units that have taken a beating. For example, Colonel Frank U. Greer reconstituted his 1st Battalion after it lost almost half of its strength at Longstop Hill by moving troops from his other battalions. His improvisation is clearly not the best way. Other 1st ID units also paid the "butcher's bill." "Reorganization was badly needed," according to *Danger Forward*. By the time the Germans savaged Greer's troops, the US Army had mobilized seventy-two divisions, although most had not completed training. It had become obvious that the soldiers required to man the two hundred divisions imagined in prewar planning could not be found. In fact, the army mobilized only sixteen more divisions. The United States simply could not man the units required to afford unit rotation or unit replacement, as well as manning the other services and equipping US and Allied forces. Moreover, building airpower took priority through the next year, as that was the quickest way to carry the war to the enemy in Europe and the Pacific.[14]

Rotation or unit replacement gave way to assigning individuals directly from the training base, or disbanding units deemed unnecessary. General Eisenhower, who commanded both the Allied Force Headquarters in Algiers as well as all US forces in North Africa, also reassigned soldiers within the theater. The 3rd ID, for example, provided some experienced soldiers to the 1st ID and received soldiers from the training base in their stead. Walter Ehlers, who hailed from Junction City, Kansas, near the old cavalry post at Fort Riley, enlisted in 1940. He made the amphibious assault in North Africa assigned to the 30th Infantry, 3rd ID. During the Casablanca conference, he served on the honor guard for the president. When Roosevelt trooped the line, Ehlers heard him say, "These are mighty fine looking troops. They would make good replacements for the First Infantry Division."[15]

Whether Ehlers had heard right or not, he joined the 18th Infantry in the assembly area at Marsott, Tunisia. The unit welcomed him, as well as soldiers arriving fresh from training in the States, with open arms. Jarvis Moore joined from the training base as a replacement platoon leader. His journey to the 1st ID reads like the outline for a heroic odyssey. He went from Fort Benning, Georgia, to Camp Wheeler, also in Georgia. From there he traveled to Camp Gordon Johnston in Florida and finally to Camp Kilmer, close to the port of embarkation in New Jersey. He then crossed the Atlantic, disembarking in French Morocco. His odyssey continued with more than a thousand more miles on the French colonial railway to Tunisia, where he finally joined the 1st ID.[16]

Traveling in a combat zone is much less than half the fun. On arrival, Moore believed his new platoon "seemed sincerely glad to have a replacement who had a little smarts and didn't have to be led. They protected me as much as they could and really adopted me." Richard Cole was one of those receiving the replacements. Of them, he said, "We tried to make replacements feel accepted." The old saw seen in movies where replacements are not welcomed was generally not the case. Cole admitted, however, that "combat wise soldiers are always wary of replacements not because they don't like them but because they don't want to get hurt by some replacement's dumb action." In the 1st ID, replacements went "for a week of our orientation if possible." On February 23, amid the Kasserine Pass fighting, the division tasked the 18th Infantry to provide seven officers, fifteen noncommissioned officers, and five cooks to support the six hundred replacements scheduled to arrive on the 26th, after which they would "be classified, equipped and trained."[17]

The division titled this effort the 1st Division Battle School, in emulation of the infantry battle school that had supported preinvasion training in the

United Kingdom. The regiments all provided cadre in rotation to the school, where veterans like Ehlers and new replacements alike received an orientation on the history and traditions of the 1st ID. Training tasks included "intensive physical conditioning-special instruction in infantry weapons-scouting and patrolling-*night combat* [italics in original] and platoon combat exercises."[18]

In addition to classifying, equipping, and training replacements, divisions reorganized and issued new equipment when in a "rest" area. While in Marsott, the 1st ID issued the 2.34-inch rocket launcher, familiarly known as the bazooka, entailing changes to the tables of organization and equipment throughout the division. Units drew, issued, and trained on 462 bazookas while turning in sixteen 37-millimeter antitank guns and more than a hundred M1903 Springfield rifles equipped with grenade launchers. These changes affected literally every unit from the division's headquarters to the light maintenance company. This was not the first time a division in the field had changed its organization and equipment, nor would it be the last.[19]

The old soldiers—"old" because they had been in combat since November—trained as well. Some went to the First Army Battle School; others went to signal training or weapons training. The curriculum was broad and encompassed observations from the preceding months and experiences as well as lessons passed on by the British Army. On March 4 Eisenhower issued a commendation to the US units that fought the Kasserine Pass battles. He congratulated the troops but then admonished them, saying, "Let us make sure the new men coming up quickly absorb the lessons that the front line units have learned, so that every pound of ammunition and equipment that is brought to you, may be most effectively employed in the destruction of the forces opposing us."[20]

On March 8, First Army published First Army Training Instruction No. 3. In thirteen tightly written paragraphs, the First Army training staff offered observations, lessons, and recommendations on everything from choosing defensive positions to "Control of the Battle." First Army explicitly argued that inexperienced soldiers "go through their baptism of enemy fire without committing errors of judgment. . . . [They] must first be taught to realise as far as possible what it is like to work under fire." Accordingly, First Army prescribed live-fire training and hands-on learning through multiple iterations. Although soon relieved of assignment to First Army, the 1st ID applied much if not all this guidance at the Battle School. Resting and refitting were on the schedule, but so too was learning tactics and techniques based on the trials at Longstop Hill, Ousseltia Valley, and Kasserine Pass.[21]

Routine changes occurred within the leadership. Colonel Alexander N. Stark Jr., who had taken command of the 26th Infantry from Teddy Roosevelt, turned the regiment over to Lieutenant Colonel George A. Taylor on March 3, 1943. Stark went home, with Eisenhower's recommendation for promotion. Eisenhower opined that he would make a good assistant division commander, but that he might "not be of the caliber to go higher." Taylor's previous service with the division in the 16th Infantry made his transition comparatively easy. He too assisted in the transition of leadership days later, when he met with five officers commissioned from the ranks, "who had proven themselves on the field of battle." Rotating commanders helped pass on lessons learned in combat and afforded talented officers an opportunity to command.[22]

Patton and Operation Wop

George S. Patton Jr. landed on II Corps like a ton of bricks. The exigencies of terrain, Germans, and too few troops combined to produce tactical defeat and confusion in Tunisia. But it was as clear to Eisenhower as it was to Alexander and Anderson that the US Army needed more and better training, as well as better discipline. This was equally clear to Major General Terry Allen. On March 4, Allen issued guidance on training and discipline in a memorandum sent to every unit in the 1st ID. He made several points, ranging from proper wear of the uniform to saluting. According to Allen, "*Discipline means thorough teamwork and cooperation and the prompt, cheerful execution of orders and instruction* [italics in original]." Two days later Patton issued orders that some thought unnecessary, even petty. He required soldiers to be in the full prescribed combat uniform, and, yes, that included ties. Patton thought it "absurd to believe that soldiers who cannot be made to wear the proper uniform can be induced to move forward in battle." A few days later he reflected on his order and the fines he issued to those who disobeyed it, confiding to his diary on March 13, "If men do not obey orders in small things, they are incapable of being led in battle. I *will* [italics in original] have discipline—to do otherwise is to commit murder."[23] Although Terry Allen had no argument with that thinking, his troops remained unconvinced on the utility of ties in combat.

Alexander planned the operation to affect the juncture of the two field armies, to begin on March 15. II Corps would attack with 1st AD in the north, from the Kasserine Pass to first Station de Sened and then Maknassey, to prevent Fifth Panzer Army from threatening the II Corps flank. The 1st ID would move south from Fériana and attack to seize Gafsa, for two reasons: first, because roads and the rail line emanating from Gafsa suited it as a base for Eighth Army; and second, because seizing Gafsa was likely to draw a reaction from the Italian First Army that would weaken the defense of the Mareth Line. Just east of Gafsa two passes opened and the highway divided. One road led northeast to Maknassy and the other southeast to Gabes. The 18th Army Group would coordinate the attack to support Eighth Army's fight to penetrate the Mareth Line, while the New Zealand Corps flanked the line south of the Salt Lake and marshes at Chott el Fejaj.[24]

That it was the Italian Centauro Armored Division defending the passes in the Eastern Dorsal that II Corps planned to attack led the staff to name the effort Operation Wop. The corps would enjoy robust air support and supporting ground arms. The army designed the triangular division to fight three combined arms regimental combat teams by assigning to the division headquarters three regiments and an organic division artillery, intending these formations to be augmented by additional artillery, tanks, tank destroyers, and antiaircraft artillery attached as needed. For the first time during the war, the 1st ID would fight as the army intended and as it had been trained.

Combat support provided to II Corps included the 1st Tank Destroyer group with seven battalions. Five of these fought with 75-millimeter howitzers mounted on half-tracks, and two with M10 self-propelled tank destroyers mounting three-inch high-velocity guns. Corps artillery included two field artillery brigades and a regiment. The 13th Artillery Brigade boasted four battalions of 155-millimeter howitzers and one 105-millimeter howitzer battalion. The 5th Field Artillery Group provided two battalions of M7 Priest 105-millimeter self-propelled howitzers. The 17th Field Artillery Regiment fielded three 155-millimeter battalions. An antiaircraft artillery group with five battalions and several separate batteries of short- and long-range antiaircraft artillery assured ample defense against marauding Stukas. II Corps' occupation of poverty row had come to an end. During the Kasserine Pass battles, Rommel observed that the "Americans were fantastically well equipped"; a month later they were even more lavishly so.[25]

On March 8 Patton convened a commanders' conference to review the plan. Division commanders attended with their deputies and key staff. Stanhope B. Mason recalled that Patton began with "a brief introductory remark to the effect that we were about to hear a plan of attack which he had not devised, but had inherited, and that there was not now time available for him to give us a better plan." After hearing his staff brief the plan, Patton harangued those present to say if they—and here he used "deprecatory terms such as cowards, yellow-bellies, etc."—would only fight, the corps "just might get away without getting the hell kicked out of us." With the benefit of those dubiously inspiring words, his commanders and staff went forward to complete their planning for an operation for which the corps commander took no ownership.[26] Such was Patton's idea of leadership.

Allen asked to attack at night rather than midmorning, as the corps specified, but corps denied the change, believing that the approach march of almost fifty miles couldn't be completed prior to dawn. Moreover, the corps commander had arranged an air bombardment as part of the preparatory fires. H-Hour therefore remained set for 0930 March 15 until Alexander delayed the attack by forty-eight hours to accommodate Eighth Army. Accordingly, 1st AD made its approach during daylight on the 16th, while 1st ID did as it was wont to do, and moved by truck during the night of March 16–17 on a tightly controlled schedule, over routes the 1st Engineer Battalion had reconnoitered and cleared of two thousand mines. Nearly fifteen thousand 1st ID soldiers, with their necessary impedimenta, arrived in their attack position before daylight on the 17th. There, as Stanhope B. Mason put it with smug complacency, they "began the wait."[27]

Corps estimated that the Centauro AD defended Gafsa and the nearby hills with no more than two battalions of infantry and two of artillery, supported by perhaps two companies of tanks. Allen planned a converging attack on the oasis town consistent with the two general forms of maneuver described in the operations manual. According to that document, "attack maneuvers are classified as envelopments and penetrations." In this instance Allen planned a double envelopment, with the 18th Infantry attacking from the northeast and the 16th from the northwest. The 26th followed. Some of the troops in the 26th had been to Gafsa once already, but had withdrawn under orders in February. According to Ralph Uffner, the 3rd Battalion, 26th Infantry, was "aching to return to Gafsa after leaving it in February without firing a shot."[28]

Soaked by rain, the Tunisian desert remained as it had since December, a muddy morass. Fog caused the bombers to miss their planned time, but they arrived overhead at 0945, dropped their bombs, and moved on, as did the Big Red One. With unintended understatement, II Corps' after-action report noted that units from the "Centauro Division withdrew without offering serious resistance," just as the Italians and a German reconnaissance battalion had the day before.[29]

Mines, road craters, and mud from rains the night before provided the only resistance. Clearing mines is not without risk, but it is comparatively easy when not under fire. The 26th Infantry antitank company cleared sixty of the dangerous Teller antitank mines from one road. Teller mines were especially lethal because they came with what is euphemistically called an antihandling device, designed to blow up anyone handling the mine. Shortly after noon, the 16th Infantry entered Gafsa. Not long after, they reached the tiny village of Lala, where the highway forked. Allen then issued a one-page order that set the stage for defending Gafsa and continuing the operation. The division commander wanted to gain and maintain contact with the enemy—a basic tactical "rule" much abused by II Corps previously.

Finding the enemy was not only a matter of sound tactics; Allen anticipated that Patton would order the corps forward, because the taking of Gafsa would not satisfy Alexander's intention. The attack had not drawn a response from Italian First Army or Fifth Panzer Army. Now the 16th Infantry prepared a hasty defense of Gafsa, supported by the 601st and 899th Tank Destroyer (TD) Battalions. The tank destroyers occupied firing positions northeast of the town from which they could take flank shots at any counterattack that developed, and their men also reconnoitered routes to "counter [any] enemy mech. thrust." The 18th Infantry occupied defensive positions to the southeast of the town. The 26th assembled west of Gafsa to serve as the division's reserve and reconnoitered routes to reduce any penetrations of the defense or to reinforce the forward regiments. Brigadier General Clift Andrus positioned his artillery to range targets on both the Sfax and Gabes roads.[30]

Allen ordered 1st Reconnaissance Troop toward El Guettar, ten miles farther east, to make contact and establish a screen, but the recon troop, "bogged down by heavy rains," failed to reach the village. Allen, however, had another option. At 1910 he wrote a letter to Lieutenant Colonel William O. Darby, commanding the attached 1st Ranger Battalion. In his letter/order to Darby, Allen provided an overview of the situation. He admitted that Patton's directive "suspended any immediate coordinated attack on EL GUET-TAR [emphasis in original]: however, it is vitally necessary to resume close contact with the enemy who has withdrawn to EL GUETTAR, to develop his full strength and maintain the initiative." He ordered Darby to move out after nightfall, and amplified his intent by adding, "You will keep your battalion in hand, will act aggressively but will not be committed into any action from which you cannot properly extricate yourself."[31]

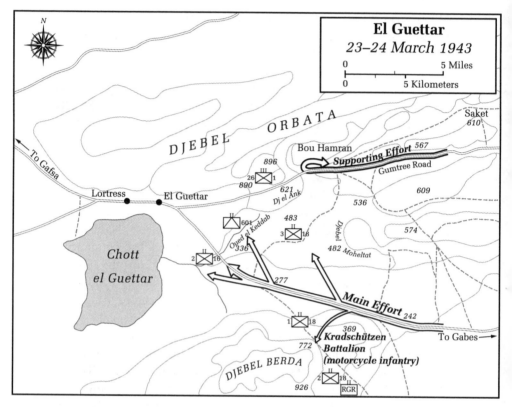

Map 6: El Guettar, March 23–24, 1943. Redrawn and annotated from Major Sam Carter's Personal Experience Monograph Map.

The Ranger battalion arrived on the high ground above El Guettar the following afternoon at 1625. Darby's scouts discovered that the enemy had decamped, so the Rangers moved in. The next day, the division moved forward in heavy rain to establish defensive positions around El Guettar and prepare to renew the corps attack when ordered. The 18th Infantry called the division's movement forward on February 19 a "pursuit, which lasted through the 20th." The rain, mud, and the fact that the enemy had outpaced the "pursuit" made it just what Allen believed it was—a movement to contact. Stanhope Mason thought of it as a tactical movement, and "exactly on the strategic axis to the Gulf of Gabes where we would cut off Rommel's retreat into Tunisia, or failing that, make contact with Montgomery's advancing Eighth Army."[32]

The division caught up with the enemy just east of El Guettar. According to Mason, "We found them in rather strong defensive positions in rugged hills (really low mountains) on both sides of a wide open, treeless valley of sand and widely scattered red flowered weeds." The Italians chose to make their main effort on the north side of the valley on a particularly rugged chain of peaks "extending eastward toward the Gulf of Gabes." There the ridge or hill named Djebel Ank rose roughly two thousand feet above the valley floor. The Italians believed it would be impossible "for an attacking force to scale the bare and rocky peak to get at their flank," Mason surmised. The Centauro Division also defended a ridgeline called Oued el Keddab that rose only nine hundred feet above the valley. Infantrymen in the 18th Infantry referred to unpronounceable Oued el Keddab after Fredendall's code name, Wop Hill.[33]

At 1630 on March 20, Allen received a letter order from Patton. Written in florid language, it began, "My dear General Allen." The first sentence required Allen to "Please make all necessary plans, including areas for the emplacement of your artillery, for an attack along the axis Gafsa-Gabes." Patton expected to order execution on the 21st. The new corps commander wanted very much to go all the way to the coast and thus rupture the Axis defense and divide Fifth Panzer Army from First Italian Army. Alexander, however, restrained him; he thought the Americans should be used carefully and kept to tasks he believed they could handle without a great deal of risk. General Allen issued his order for the attack later that day. Montgomery's Eighth Army began its attack that evening.[34]

Allen planned a frontal attack on three rocky hills/mountains the natives called *djebels*. From north to south they included Djebel Ank, Djebel Moheltat, and Djebel Berda. He directed Darby's Rangers to climb a steep range of mountains called Djebel Orbata, then make their way ten miles east along the range of mountains to flank the main Italian position at Djebel Ank. The 26th Infantry would attack along Gumtree Road and clear the pass below Djebel Ank. Once the 18th cleared Wop Hill, they would continue east to take Djebel Moheltat, a ridge that extended some fifteen miles eastward. Clearing this ridgeline could not be done in a day. The western tip of the ridge was called Horseshoe Hill, after its shape. Because the division had laid protective minefield across the Gabes road, Allen planned to take Djebel Berda from the north rather than clear a large lane in his own minefield. The 16th Infantry garrisoned Gafsa with a single battalion, leaving two battalions as the division reserve. At 1800, II Corps ordered execution at 0600 on March 21.[35]

Darby's Rangers, with Company D, 1st Engineers, attached, began their trek after dark on the 20th. Ralph Ingersoll, onetime editor of *Fortune* and the *New Yorker* and general manager of *Time*, made the grueling approach march along the razorback ridge that led to Djebel Ank with the Rangers. Ingersoll, who had enlisted at age forty and was now a forty-three-year-old lieutenant of engineers, described the footing as "impossible," the ground littered with "small and medium pebbles and rocks the size of two or three fists held together." Walking on the steep slopes meant that as the ground rose, "it seemed to weave and tilt from side to side." *Beau Geste* had dealt with dunes and blowing sand. In the mountains of Tunisia, the troops confronted rugged ground as well as blowing sand, intense cold, and/or torrential rains. Some of the Rangers doubted that Ingersoll could keep up with the Rangers, most of whom were half his age. Even Darby would not turn thirty-two until April. Yet when the Rangers arrived on the flank of the Italians, high above Gumtree Road, Ingersoll was still with them.[36]

Colonel Greer maneuvered two battalions of the 18th Infantry to attack the Italians on Wop Hill by enveloping their position from the north during the predawn hours of the 21st. Because corps issued the order to execute at 1800, the orders came down from division to regiment, and finally to battalions, two or more hours later. Lieutenant Colonel Courtney P. Brown returned to his 3rd Battalion with the regimental order at 2030; the other two battalion commanders could not have returned to their units much earlier. Planning based on anticipation proved essential in the operation that followed. Brown's 3rd Battalion had to seize the center of Wop Hill while the 2nd Battalion began the day in reserve. The 1st Battalion had the most difficult task, crossing open ground along the Gabes Road to seize the left or southern end of the hill. The regiment shuttled the troops closer to their attack positions by truck, and then the infantry did what infantry does: they walked the rest of the way. The 3rd Battalion hunkered down in a wadi about one mile east of El Guettar. The wadi stretched from the Gafsa-Gabes road toward the northeast and was approximately perpendicular to the direction of attack, and on the flank of the Italian position.[37]

The Rangers, supported by their own 60-millimeter mortars and the engineer company's 81s, humped ten miserable miles before they began their attack at 0500, when their bugler sounded the charge. Ralph Ingersoll, moving toward the action, reported that "rifles cracked and popped almost continuously," and thought that "but for the helmets, the men on the firing line, from the postures they took, might have been from a print of the Civil War." Later, when the Rangers and engineers had "won," Ingersoll glanced at his watch, feeling that he "had been on that hilltop for a long weekend. It was a few minutes after eight o'clock in the morning." Ingersoll now understood Civil War veterans' euphemism: he had seen the Elephant.[38]

The rest of the division had not been idle. The 26th got underway at midnight, as it had to go about as far as the Rangers, albeit on an easier path. The 18th started out at 0200, and achieved "complete surprise." At 0550 Greer reported the 18th in position to assault Wop Hill. Approaching the pass below Djebel Ank, Taylor's troops could hear the Rangers fighting above the pass. At 0630 the 601st TD cleared El Guettar heading east. Both American and Italian artillery weighed in. Italian gunners brought down heavy fire on the 18th as it scaled Wop Hill. Allied and Axis air forces fought overhead. Despite American fighters, Stukas got through and scored.[39]

At 0730 Teddy Roosevelt advised Allen, "Reaction to our attack is dying down." The 18th, despite intense artillery fire, took Wop Hill around 0800, and with it a slew of prisoners. From the hill Greer could see Italian reinforcements coming in from the east, as well five to seven tanks. Soon after, the division operations officer reminded Greer that "Mohelta [sic] is your next objective." Greer asked who would cover his "open flank," as he could see enemy activity on Djebel Berda to the south. Allen ordered Lieutenant Colonel John H. Matthews's 3rd Battalion, 16th Infantry, forward to relieve Greer's troops on Wop Hill so Greer could care for his flank himself.[40]

At 0901, the 601st TD overwatching the 18th reported excitedly, "Whole Italian army in bag." Well, maybe not all of them, but the division had captured quite a few. By noon the Big Red One had taken all but one of its objectives and brought its artillery forward. The regiments worked to consolidate their positions, either to defend against a counterattack or to continue the attack.[41]

In addition to Wop Hill, the 18th Infantry had taken the western edge of Djebel Moheltat, capturing a total of 17 officers and 398 soldiers. Later that night they reached Djebel Berda and captured 198 more prisoners, but had not cleared all Djebel Berda. Taylor's combat team cleared the defile on Gumtree Road below Djebel Ank, and seized the village of Bou Hamran on the southern slope of Djebel Orbata. The 1st Division held both roads and the tip of the ridgeline that separated them. Patton, his deputy Omar Bradley, and Allen survived a near miss from artillery while forward with Greer. Despite that, it was a good day, but the job was not yet done.[42]

On March 22 the division continued the attack to finish what they had started the day before. Matthews's battalion of the 16th didn't close on Wop Hill until fifteen minutes after midnight that morning. At 0745 Greer reported firing on five tanks on the Gabes Road. A minute later the 601st TD confirmed Greer's report, but believed there were seven tanks. Although neither report included grid coordinates, it is clear that these tanks were on the Djebel Moheltat ridge, and neither road from El Guettar could be used if the enemy held part of the ridge. At 0930 Patton called and chastised the G-3, Lieutenant Colonel Frederick W. Gibb, because the 18th had not completed clearing Djebel Berda. Gibb heard from the corps commander several more times during the day. Patton had forgotten that everything takes too long in combat. As Clausewitz notes, "Everything in war is very simple, but the simplest thing is difficult." Friction gummed up the best theoretical plan.[43]

About 1800, Greer's troops heard firing in the valley to the northeast of Djebel Berda. The colonel sent a "strong mtz [motorized platoon] patrol" to discover the source. Fired on by an Italian unit, the patrol dismounted and began digging in, harassed by machine gun and artillery fire. Allen, who was at the 18th's command post, assessed the enemy position as held by two or three companies. The fight built up to the point that Lieutenant Colonel Robert H. York's 1st Battalion needed some help from the adjacent 2nd Battalion, commanded by Lieutenant Colonel Ben Sternberg. Elsewhere the enemy probed the boundary between the 26th and 18th.[44]

Allen and General Andrus believed the Italians and Germans had moved artillery forward, a logical step if they planned to counterattack. Andrus commented, "It looks like another atk and after defense of this area yet. (Environs of El Guettar) We have nothing." The division artillery commander needed to move his own artillery up, beginning with the 32nd Field Artillery (FA). He was concerned about providing support forward, either to support an attack or defend against counterattack—and for good reason: "In the midnight hours of March 22–23, messages began to come in to the Division CP [command post] telling of a strong counterattack on all forward positions."[45]

Patton's irritation with the delay in taking Djebel Berda was not unreasonable. Clearing Djebel Berda was as important as clearing Djebel Moheltat. That night Lieutenant Colonel Percy W. Thompson brought his 32nd FA up to Wop Hill, with Lieutenant Colonel Hershal D. Baker's 601st TD serving as escort and protection, once the artillery established their firing positions. With artillery, Greer's 1st and 2nd Battalions finished the job on Djebel Berda and captured 190 more Italians. Enemy activity elsewhere continued throughout the night. At midnight, a 26th Infantry combat patrol that had gone out shortly after 2000 captured twenty-two Italians at the tiny hamlet of Saket, about five miles east of Bou Hamran. The enemy, despite heavy losses during the day, had not withdrawn. Taylor ordered the motorized platoon that took Saket to establish an outpost in the town to provide early warning in the event "any heavy mechanized attack was pushed by the enemy from that direction."[46]

El Guettar

Despite the difficulty getting through the muck, 1st AD took Sened Station on the 21st and closed on Maknassy. General Orlando Ward perceived a chance to take the town by coup de main but, mindful of General Alexander's imperative about minimizing risk, did not exercise initiative. He determined instead on a deliberate attack the following day. Then, and certainly ex post facto, Patton believed Ward missed an opportunity. Maybe things could have gone better for the Allies if Ward had taken Maknassy on the 21st, but Kesselring thought they were bad enough, calling that day and those that followed "crucial days for the interior wings, the seam of the two Axis armies." Patton's corps looked as if it might drive a wedge between Fifth Panzer Army in the north and Italian First Army in the south. Doing so would assure the destruction of the troops in the south caught between II Corps and Eighth Army.[47]

At this point, the 10th PZ constituted the chief Axis mobile reserve. After the disastrous attack on Medenine on March 6, it was withdrawn to rest and refit. The 10th moved twice during its refit period in response to variations in planning as von Arnim came to grips with his new duties as an army group commander. On March 9 he directed the formation of a mobile strike group composed of his three armored formations, the 10th, 15th, and 21st PZ, but vacillated over whether they would be controlled by army group, Fifth Panzer Army, or Deutsches Afrikakorps.[48]

When the II Corps offensive got underway, the 10th PZ was near Sousse, preparing defensive positions to back up the Mareth Line. On March 20 von Arnim ordered the division to assemble at Al-Maharas, a town on the coast south of Sfax. From there they could respond to the 1st AD or 1st ID. The threat to eight Luftwaffe bases located south and west of Sfax and the rear of Italian First Army had to be addressed. Most of the 10th PZ assigned to the Deutsches Afrikakorps moved to squelch the 1st ID while the remainder responded to the developing threat posed by Ward's armor.[49]

The 10th PZ main body assembled ten to fifteen kilometers east of El Guettar. The division's 7th PZ Regiment had both of its battalions, but no more than fifty tanks between them. The attacking force included the 10th Kradschützen (motorcycle) Battalion, two battalions of Panzergrenadiers

(one each from the 69th and 86th Panzergrenadier regiments) and supporting units, including engineers, antitank, antiaircraft, and an assault
gun battery of the 90th Panzer Artillery Regiment. Altogether, about six
thousand troops were available. The mission was to retake the Italian positions and drive on to El Guettar, and then Gafsa. The 10th PZ planned to
attack up the Gabes Road with the bulk of its tanks, the Panzergrenadier
battalion, and the motorcycle battalion. As they advanced, various units
would peel off to the north to attack Djebel El Ank, Moheltat, and Wop
Hill. The motorcycle infantry would sweep left to take Djebel Berda. The
Germans moved out at 0300 on March 23, hoping to reprise their success
in the Kasserine Pass.[50]

Whether or not Allen thought a counterattack possible, he still had work
to do to assure that both Gumtree Road and the Gabes Road could be used
without interference. Under the light of a full moon, the division started
early. The 601st TD moved into positions on the eastern edge of Wop Hill
around 0230. The 5th, 32nd, and 33rd FA followed the 601st, taking positions in the lee of Wop Hill. The 3rd Battalion, 18th Infantry, defended the
western edge of Djebel Moheltat. The 3rd Battalion, 16th Infantry, arrived
after midnight and occupied positions that extended north from the defile
at the southern edge of Wop Hill. The two battalions of the 18th, on the
eastern slope of Djebel Berda, proposed to push a bit farther east. The Ranger battalion had moved from Djebel Ank to a position on the south side
of Djebel Berda. Elsewhere Montgomery's attack, despite his methodical
approach, had not gone well. Weather and strong opposition led him to ask
for help wanting II Corps to continue to attack east. Alexander remained
concerned about letting Patton get too ambitious with troops in which Alexander had little faith. He would allow Patton to continue the attack with
1st AD, while Allen improved his position.[51]

Taylor's troops began the day by crossing their line of departure just fifteen minutes before 10th PZ crossed theirs. What transpired over the next
eighteen hours exemplified the validity of Oliver Wendell Holmes's assertion
that war is an "incommunicable experience"—incommunicable for more
than the horror that Justice Holmes recalled. Incommunicable because it
is impossible for leaders to make exact sense of a battle, let alone for soldiers at ground level to discern what is happening. To "see" the battle, commanders above company level depended on telephones, radios when they
worked, and seeing for themselves when they could. Platoon and company
commanders depended on runners, radios, and, when they could lay wire,

telephones. Confusion caused by error, fear, smoke, dust, and occasional deception generated chaos, in the midst of which Allen and his leaders, from Teddy Roosevelt to the young men leading squads, had to surmise the next right thing to do or pay the price. To decide what to do they depended on how well they could "see" the battlefield using their eyes and ears, and use their means of communication to understand what others saw.

At Taylor's command post, when the attack started, "the ordeal of waiting began until reports trickled in. . . . Radio could not be depended upon for steady contact with the battalions." Nothing happened until 0350, when soldiers at the command post saw two "amber flares" to the southeast beyond, where no Americans happened to be, noting that "these were not sent up by our troops." The Germans may have detected movement. Nevertheless, the two battalions making the attack continued east, while the enemy on the south side of the ridge continued west on the Gabes Road heading for El Guettar.[52]

As the 10th rolled west, it divided into two groups. One, formed on the 69th Panzergrenadier regiment, turned off the road toward Djebel Ank, behind Brown's battalion, while the main body continued astride the Gabes road and on the ridge to take Wop Hill. Both battle groups included tanks. The main body, composed of the 7th PZ and the 86th Panzergrenadiers, attacked the 601st, while the 10th's motorcycle infantry battalion attacked Djebel Berda.[53]

When the enemy tanks and infantry reached Wop Hill, only the 601st TD stood between them and the artillery. The tank destroyer troops' lightly armored 75-millimeter half-track "Purple Heart Boxes" were outnumbered and outgunned. Tom Morrison, an assistant gunner in Company A, remembered that the attack came at the "break of day." The 601st reported at 0510, "We are having an atk [attack]; 10 tks [tanks], 2 Cos [companies] Inf. Think we can handle it." Company C occupied positions well north of the Gabes Road, while Company B occupied positions just north of the road. Company A was to their rear and nearly adjacent to the road.[54]

Although they arrived at different times, ultimately all the artillery was at risk. From south to north the 7th, 33rd, 32nd, and 5th Field Artilleries all occupied positions to the rear of the tank destroyers. Just before the sun rose, Sam Carter, an officer in the 1st Battalion, 18th Infantry, saw "red, white and blue tracers" across the valley toward Djebel Moheltat. Later there were "green, purple, yellow and orange tracers." As the sun rose, it revealed the full panoply of German tanks—or, as Carter put it, "before us in the valley was an entire panzer division." The Germans moved "with infantry interspersed among the tanks and self-propelled guns."[55]

The number of tanks observers report varies from thirty to a hundred. German sources have some variation, but Albert Schick's *Combat History of the 10. Panzer Division, 1939–1943* is probably the best. If so, no more than fifty tanks attacked that morning. Despite reports to the contrary, the 10th PZ had Mark II, III, and IV tanks, but no Tiger tanks that day. The confusion in the number of tanks results from observer perspectives, miscounting, counting the same tanks more than once, and most likely observers confusing self-propelled antitank and assault guns with tanks; the 10th PZ did indeed have a company of antitank guns and a battery of assault guns. There may have been as many as two dozen of these weapons, both of which could be mistaken for tanks. Whether there were fifty or a hundred tanks, the thirty-one tank destroyers in the 601st were not going to get all of them.[56]

Panzergrenadiers, accompanied by some tanks, overran Brown's infantry, crushing some of the soldiers by driving over their foxholes. The survivors fought back, supported by the 32nd. Company K used a surprising technique to confound the Panzergrenadiers. Lieutenant Astor Morris, a platoon leader, withdrew his troops from the military crest of the hill they were on to the reverse slope, leaving a single observer peering over the crest. What he and his soldiers did next worked quite well: "When the enemy approached to grenade throwing distance, the observer gave a signal to indicate the direction of the enemy approach." Then everyone "volleyed" their grenades. Morris's innovation enabled Company K to hang on to their piece of Djebel Moheltat, preventing the Germans from clearing the hill and taking Djebel Ank. Soon "hand grenades were rushed to company K from every available source in the battalion." By the end of the day, they had thrown 1,300 grenades.[57]

Farther west, the battle for Wop Hill began in earnest for the 601st. Lieutenant Frederick C. Miner's platoon straddled the defile at the southern end of Wop Hill through which the Gabes road passed. When his platoon arrived at the pass at 0300, Miner placed three guns north of the road and one gun south of it. When the 7th PZ hove in sight, the destroyer men waited until the lead tanks closed to eight hundred yards before firing. Nearby units to the south and artillery joined in the fight. The Panzers stopped, withdrew a bit, and began "circling the high ground," looking to flank Miner's position. About noon, Miner's platoon destroyed an American half-track manned by Germans towing an antitank gun. That concluded their fight for the morning.[58]

The 69th Panzergrenadier clashed with Company B, 601st TD, just before daybreak. Sergeant Adolf I. Raymond of the 601st began the festivities by killing an enemy tank, probably a Mark IV. It took six rounds to do so because the first four "ricocheted off the tank." Raymond proceeded, however, to kill a second Mark IV with one round. The Germans then hit Raymond's half-track three times, setting it on fire, with Raymond and his crew escaping on foot. Three other tracks in the platoon fired steadily and with apparent impunity. Lieutenant John D. Yowell believed the Germans could not locate his tracks, as they were firing from defilade. He was mistaken. The platoon drove the Germans off, but they soon returned and destroyed a second track. Two more tank destroyers ran out of ammunition, including one from Company C. Out of ammunition, Yowell withdrew.[59]

By 0700 the situation had deteriorated to the point that Allen began moving reserves. He ordered the 16th Infantry forward to El Guettar, preceded by their antitank company. Corps sent in the 899th TD as well. The 899th boasted the M10 tracked tank destroyer, mounting the highly effective three-inch naval rifle. Allen alerted Darby to be prepared to move by truck to wherever he was needed. Two platoons of Company B, 601st TD, including Yowell's, had withdrawn from their positions, exposing the 32nd and 5th Field Artilleries. At Djebel Berda the 18th held, but the motorcycle battalion got close enough to shoot mortars at Greer's command post, where he and Teddy Roosevelt were running the fight. Looking into the valley, the Rangers reported that artillery had stymied the Panzers, reporting three tanks "definitely hit." Even that good news came with a caveat; "On the extreme right flank," the Rangers added, "there is at the present time a tremendous amount of small arms fire."[60]

II Corps did what it could vectoring in fighters and medium bombers, and also moved corps artillery forward of El Guettar. Despite everything, the 10th PZ reached the defile at Wop Hill less than three miles from El Guettar. Alerted at 0730, and on the move soon after, the 899th traveled thirty miles and arrived at El Guettar at 0845 during a Stuka raid on the town. Undeterred, the destroyer men continued to the defile, where they met their own commander, Lieutenant Colonel Maxwell A. Tincher, who was with Colonel Baker of the 601st. Teddy Roosevelt joined the gathering soon thereafter to ensure that everyone knew what they needed to do.[61]

Company B, 899th TD, passed through the defile to counterattack and ran into what was almost certainly a "friendly" minefield, leaving the counterattack stillborn. The mine strike killed killed Lieutenant Alvin F. Koch. Lieutenant Gerald D. Coady, the only officer left with the two platoons, who had gone through the defile led the surviving tank destroyers off the road and up onto Wop Hill into defilade. Teddy Roosevelt described the 899th TD as "Gallant but Green." They were gallant. An 899th tank destroyer platoon moving up encountered infantrymen who urged them not to "go up there we were just run out by German tanks." The tank destroyer platoon leader countered, "That's what I am looking for; show me the tanks." Company C arrived next and took positions to support Coady. Captain Thomas W. Hackworth, commanding Company A, arrived last. Under Teddy Roosevelt's direction, Hackworth placed two platoons on the reverse slope of the defile or pass at Wop Hill, with a platoon on each side of the road and one in reserve. Hackworth's crews kept their destroyers in defilade, or, as they termed it, hull down.[62] The German tide began to recede.

Although the fighting for Wop Hill had not stopped, there was a lull while the Germans sought a way to get at the two artillery battalions on the reverse slope. They eventually found their way and cut off a battery of the 5th FA. Division artillery reported that the 32nd "has had a hard time but is still firing." The antitank companies of the 18th and 26th converged on the fight with good effect. Company C of the 26th attacked south into the enemy's flank. Taylor sought and received permission to reposition his 3rd Battalion to cover the gap between his regiment and Greer's. Effective air support played an important role as well. Although the Panzergrenadiers got in among the guns, they and their supporting tanks withdrew around 1100.[63]

The 10th PZ withdrew and, to the amazement of their opponents, recovered damaged equipment under fire. Just after 1100, Mason spoke with the II Corps operations officer, noting that "things are getting reorgd [sic] on both sides." By noon the fighting had ended for the moment, but Mason was right; the 10th PZ had withdrawn to reorganize and prepare for a second "spasm." The 1st Division had the same problem. In the early afternoon Gibb spoke with Lieutenant Colonel Russell F. Akers Jr., the assistant operations officer at II Corps. Akers advised that the 9th ID was on the move, and that its 84th FA would reinforce Andrus's artillery. Furthermore, two bombing missions were planned for later that afternoon. He then asked for a situation report. Gibb reported briefly, "Lost no positions." To which Akers responded, "The big chief is pleased to hear that."[64]

Gibb's report was not all that accurate. In fact, the Germans had swept aside the 601st TD and overrun part of the 5th and 32nd FA battalions. The artillerymen fought hard but finally abandoned their guns and withdrew, taking their howitzers' breech blocks with them. Lieutenant Colonel Joseph B. Crawford's 2nd Battalion, 16th Infantry, reclaimed the artillery firing positions. The grateful artillerymen restored their breech blocks and pre-pared for whatever came next. Bringing ammunition forward, recovering damaged equipment, and evacuation of wounded and any prisoners were occupying both sides. Teddy Roosevelt, still forward with Greer, claimed "24 Tks [tanks] knocked out." Roosevelt further reported that Greer's troops had captured one hundred Germans. He identified the prisoners as assigned to the reconnaissance battalion of the 10th PZ and the 7th Panzer Regiment.[65]

At 1515 II Corps reported a radio intercept noting units and the time that the 10th PZ planned to make their second effort. Half an hour later, II Corps reported a second intercept that read "Angriff bis 1640 verschoben"; literally, the attack is delayed until 1640. In a fit of hubris Allen ordered his signal officer to send the following message on the German command net: "What the hell are you guys waiting for? We have been ready since four p.m. Signed, First Division." Patton, who was forward with Allen, asked rhetorically, "Terry when are you going to take this war seriously?"[66]

The 10th PZ renewed the attack at 1645, or, as the 18th Infantry report-ed awkwardly but accurately, "This thing broke about amounting to the schedule" (per intercept). The attack began with a Stuka attack that did little damage. German artillery did not rate comment. Panzergrenadiers led the second attack. It was as fierce as the first, but the artillery savaged the Ger-man infantry, employing "scissors and sweep," a technique that required per-fect timing, good communications, and centralized fire direction. Some of the artillery shifted fires from near to far, while other units shifted from far to near. The 10th pressed the attack, but it was beaten back. Patton, Allen, and Roosevelt shared a grandstand view of the second attack from Horseshoe Hill, shown with its peak at 536 meters on maps of the area. At 1848 Allen advised Brigadier General Hugh Gaffey, Patton's chief of staff, "Enemy tks [tanks] withdrawing, enemy inf atk [infantry attack] has been driven back."[67]

It had been a hell of fight. Tank destroyers, field artillery, and determined infantrymen had carried the day. The 601st TD alone fired 2,911 seventy-five-millimeter rounds. It had entered the fight with thirty-one guns, all but ten of which were damaged or destroyed. With stowage for fifty-nine rounds, the destroyers averaged eighty-eight rounds per gun. As it had been beaten to a pulp, the 601st was withdrawn by II Corps to refit. The troops were proud of their success. The artillery and regimental cannon companies had fired 9,590 rounds. The consumption of infantry ammunition seems implau-sible, at more than 500,000 rounds fired by rifleman and machine gunners—but projectiles are a lot cheaper than people. The 1st ID suffered 51 killed in action, 309 wounded, and 57 missing. These figures don't include attached units such as the 601st, the 899th, and the 110th Coastal Artillery Battalion (Antiaircraft). The 601st alone accounts for another 72 killed, wounded, or missing.[68]

Despite this US success, the 10th PZ, though beaten, did not give up, and neither did Army Group Afrika. The heart had gone out of the Italians, but they fought on, with some exceptions. An American guard ridiculed an Italian for giving up; undaunted, the Italian replied, "Yes but I am going to America and *you* are going to Italy or Germany." The 10th PZ continued the fight east of El Guettar until April 6. The following day, 1st AD linked up with the British 8th Army. Eisenhower, aware of Alexander's misgivings about II Corps, cabled him the same day the 10th PZ attacked at El Guettar. In his cable, Eisenhower told Alexander "to make a real effort to use the II US Corps right up to the bitter end of the campaign." Political fallout from Kasserine and backbiting among the Allies in this case superseded any bias Alexander may have felt.[69]

The End in Tunisia

The 1st ID withdrew for a short rest on April 8 but reassembled for the final effort to drive the Axis out of Tunisia. II Corps moved from the right flank of the British First Army to the left or northern flank, moving with their habitual speed, "motorized" by their own "deuce and half" trucks. On April 12, 1943, Patton left II Corps to return to command of I Armored Corps and plan the US part of the invasion of Sicily. Patton and Allen had a long history of more less friendly rivalry. In Tunisia they exchanged views loudly and often, but they respected each other. Major General Omar N. Bradley succeeded Patton at II Corps. He and Allen had never served together. Bradley thought Allen cavalier and crude. Allen, as profane as Patton, loved bourbon, perhaps more than he should have; Bradley had no use for profanity or bourbon. Worse still, he thought Allen far too devoted to the 1st Division and insufficiently devoted to the corps as a whole. Their different attitudes produced difficulty almost immediately.[70]

On May 5, II Corps ordered an assault crossing of the Tine River near Chouïgui, a small town less than twenty miles west of Tunis. Once across, Corps directed the 1st ID to "contain or destroy enemy forces contacted in that area immediately east of the Tine." The attack did not go well. The next day Allen asked permission to withdraw west of the Tine, since the assigned mission was a "holding mission." In *A Soldier's Story*, Bradley asserted that the "1st Division pushed brashly into the Chouïgui foothills," and then, "on May 7, Terry withdrew, chastened and with heavy losses." Allen may well have exceeded his intent, but Bradley had indeed ordered the attack. How far he meant Allen to go is subject to speculation, as that had not been made clear. Major John T. Corley, executive officer of the 3rd Battalion, 26th Infantry, agreed with Bradley: "We got the shit beat out of us," he said, blaming the beating on "my bloody foolish commander, Terry Allen." When the German-Italian army group surrendered, the 1st ID was still on the banks of the Tine.[71]

What did the fighting in Tunisia, and at El Guettar especially, mean to the 1st Division, and for that matter to the United States and the alliance? El Guettar showed dramatic improvement in performance over Longstop Hill and Kasserine. Big Red One soldiers conceded German excellence, but in the context of experience, they were now gaining. The division's ability to move rapidly, employ sophisticated firing techniques, and transition quickly from offense to defense and back demonstrated that predeployment training, despite shortcomings in tactics at small-unit level, had merit. The organization and basic doctrinal intention for the triangle division, if not yet proven, seemed effective and inherently flexible.

El Guettar demonstrated learning—that is, the adjustment of behavior based on experience. That nearly every unit journal rejoiced in the reunion of the division reflected the sense of cohesion developed in training, sustained while orphaned under First Army. That feeling grew at El Guettar. In late April Eisenhower visited II Corps, where he chatted with a veteran British soldier serving as a liaison officer in Bradley's headquarters. In a cable to Marshall, Eisenhower reported with satisfaction that this officer "stated categorically that the 1st US Division is one of the finest tactical organizations he had ever seen." The US Army was learning.[72]

As for what the battle meant for the United States and the alliance, A. J. Liebling, a writer for the *New Yorker*, said it best: "If one American division could beat one German division, I thought then, a hundred American divisions could beat a hundred German divisions." It meant the Allies would win the war, and the United States would carry its share of the load.[73]

Notes

1. Raymond E. Zerfass, veteran's survey, n.d., US Army Heritage and Education Center, Carlisle, PA. See also Schrijvers, *Crash of Ruin*, which is revealing about both Germans and Americans. Schrijvers believes that American views were very much informed by the American experience in the Great War.

2. Playfair and Molony, *Destruction of the Axis Forces*, 304. Playfair and Molony are the best source for understanding the British view, the Allied order of battle, and the theaterwide context. See also Howe, *Northwest Africa*, chart 2, following 486.

Howe shows Eighth Army with seven divisions. Orders of battle varied day to day, so the disparity is almost certainly based on when during the campaign the data is taken.

3. Playfair and Molony, *Destruction of the Axis Forces*, 303, quotes Eisenhower's directive. Eisenhower wrote a detailed memorandum for Lieutenant Commander Harry Butcher, his diarist, to capture his thinking on his directive, the overall situation in Tunisia, and his detailed instruction of Alexander on the campaign, including an important role for II Corps. Eisenhower, *Papers*, no. 843, 2:987–93.

4. Playfair and Molony, *Destruction of the Axis Forces*, 303. See also Ambrose, *Supreme Commander*, 177–90, on the conclusion of the campaign and Eisenhower's effort with Alexander. General Alexander understood that relegating II Corps to a small role would not do.

5. Eisenhower, *Papers*, no. 857, 2:1002, no. 860, 2:1006, and end note at no. 861, 2:1007. See also Ambrose, *Supreme Commander*, 179.

6. Barnett, *Desert Generals*, 287, 290.

7. Montgomery, *Memoirs*, 144–45; Eisenhower, *Crusade in Europe*, 150. On the details of Eighth Army's plan for the Mareth Line, see Playfair and Molony, *Destruction of the Axis Forces*, ch. 13 (map 30 shows the route taken by the New Zealand Corps); Jackson, *Alexander of Tunis*, 181. I have used Montgomery's description of the orientation of the Mareth Line.

8. Rommel took command of Army Group Africa on February 23. Liddell-Hart, *Rommel Papers*, 408, 418; Citino, *Wehrmacht Retreats*, 99; Kesselring, *A Soldier's Record*, 182.

9. Liddell-Hart, *Rommel Papers*, 416–18.

10. Kesselring, *A Soldier's Record*, 182; Warlimont, *Inside Hitler's Headquarters*, 277.

11. Liddell-Hart, *Rommel Papers*, 414–16. Rommel believed the Axis lost forty tanks. Montgomery's number is likely more accurate. Montgomery, *Memoirs*, 143; Schick, *History of the 10. Panzer*, 493.

12. HQ, 1st ID, RG 301-2.7: German Order of Battle in Tunisia, MRC Digital Archives. Estimated numbers of tanks are at 1, 4, 5, 6; summary numbers at 10. The British official history focuses on the forces opposing Montgomery, but they too account for all the German armor. Their estimate is that the Germans had 142 operational tanks. Conceivably the number of tanks on hand was higher. They do not offer an estimate for Italian tanks. See Playfair and Molony, *Destruction of the Axis Forces*, 333. See also HQ, Allied Force, G-2 estimate no. 4 of Axis battle order, strength and disposition as of February 14, 1943, N6214-B, CARL.

13. 1st ID, German Order of Battle, 10. For Italian strength, see Allied Force, G-2 estimate no. 4. Assessing Italian strength is problematic, but the number of divisions can be deduced in both the US and British official histories by reading the index and seeing what role each unit played.

14. Greenfield, Palmer, and Riley, *Organization of Ground Combat Troops*, table 2, 211. This source is the best on the "troop basis" driving the number of divisions that could be built. On the evolution of division structure, see also Wilson, *Maneuver and Firepower*.

15. Walter D. Ehlers, interview by Colonel John Votaw, January 20, 1996, First Division Museum at Cantigny, Wheaton, IL.

16. Jarvis B. Moore, veteran's survey, n.d., US Army Heritage and Education Center, Carlisle, PA.

17. Moore, Veterans Survey; message signed "Ware," dated February 23, 1943, in RG 301-INF(18)-0.3: 1st Inf Div, Reports of Operations, Hq Combat Team 18, 23 Dec 42–9 Mar 43, MRC Digital Archives. It is not clear whether each of the regiments received this tasking.

18. HQ, 1st ID, "A Factual Account of the Combat Operations of the 1st Infantry Division in N. Africa and Sicily during World War II," n.d., MRC 1988.31.

19. HQ, 26th Infantry, "Basis of Issue," enclosure to II Corps message dated March 7, 1943, in RG 301-INF(26)-0.3: Operations Report, November 8, 1942–May 9, 1943, MRC Digital Archives.

20. 1st ID, RG 301-0.3: Summary of Operations, 8 Nov 1942–9 Mar 1943, MRC Digital Archives.

21. 1st ID, First Army Training Instruction No. 3, Mar 8, 1943, MRC Digital Archives.

22. 26th Infantry, "History"; see section on move to Marsott and departure of Stark. For battlefield promotions, see "The First Contact," box 301, MRC 1988.38, 2. This history, written during the war, amplifies the unit journals and may have been intended to provide the basis for a postwar history that was never written. It is not paginated throughout. Eisenhower, *Papers*, no. 910, 2:1059.

23. Blumenson, *Patton Papers*, 181, 188–89.

24. Howe, *Northwest Africa*, 543–47. The 9th and 34th ID were tasked to defend the passes through the Western Dorsal and preclude a threat to the Corps line of communication.

25. HQ, II Corps, operation report, Tunisia, April 10, 1943, N2652-A, CARL, 2. Re 13th Field Artillery Brigade order of battle, see A. J. Rance, "Corps Artillery: How It Was Employed," *Field Artillery Journal* 33, no. 12 (December 1943): 886; Howe, *Northwest Africa*, 571n.

26. Mason, "Reminiscences," 65–66. Re the date of the conference, see Blumenson, *Patton Papers*, 185. Patton does not mention his inspiring words in his entry. See also II Corps, operation report, Tunisia, 1–5.

27. Mason, "Reminiscences," 69; II Corps, operation report, Tunisia. On mine clearing, see Thomas E. Bennett, "Gafsa-El Guettar," in RG 301-INF(18)-0.3: Reports of Operations–18th Inf Regt–1st Inf Div (Tunisian Campaign), 12 Apr 43–8 May 43, MRC Digital Archives.

28. HQ, II Corps, G-2 periodic no. 63, March 10, 1943, in RG 301-3.2: G-3 Journal and File, 1st Inf Div, 14 Jan 43–13 Mar 43, MRC Digital Archives; Raphael L. Uffner, "Recollections of World War II with the First Infantry Division," n.d., MRC 1997.98, 276. On forms of maneuver, see War Department, FM 100-5, *Field Service Regulations: Operations* (Washington, DC: Government Printing Office, 1941), 99–101.

29. II Corps, operation report, Tunisia, 5.

30. Untitled order, March 17, 1943, in RG 301.3.2: G-3 Journal, Tunisian Campaign, MRC Digital Archives. The 601st TD Battalion provided their overlay plan to

G-3 at 2330, entry 44 in the day's journal. See also Darby and Baumer, *We Led the Way*, 68–69.

31. Allen to Darby, sent at 1910, March 17, 1943, in G-3 Journal, Tunisian Campaign. Darby did not receive the letter from Allen until 20 minutes after midnight.

32. Anonymous, "Draft Regimental War Time History," n.d., Stanhope B. Mason Collection, MRC 1994.126, 35; Mason, "Reminiscences," 70.

33. Mason, "Reminiscences," 70.

34. Terrain description is based on satellite imagery and map B in Sam Carter, "The Operations of the 1st Battalion, 18th Infantry (1st Division) at El Guettar, Tunisia, 17–25 March 1943, Tunisian Campaign," Advanced Infantry Officers Course, 1947–1948, Fort Benning, GA, n.d., WWII Student Papers, DRL. See also Patton to Allen, March 20, 1943, in G-3 Journal, Tunisian Campaign. Re British attack on Mareth line, see Playfair and Molony, *Destruction of the Axis Forces*, maps 30 and 31, 320. Meanwhile in the north, Fifth Panzer Army launched Operation Ochsenkopf at V Corps. The corps stopped the attack the same day, after the Axis made relatively small gains.

35. FO 4, March 20, 1943, in G-3 Journal, Tunisian Campaign. What is legible in the file is Brigadier General Andrus's order, which mirrors the division order. II Corps, operation report, Tunisia, 7. On the time the letter arrived, see Bennett, "Gafsa-El Guettar."

36. Ingersoll, *Battle Is the Payoff*, 133. Ingersoll was moving with D Company, 1st Engineers, as a II Corps observer. A proven writer, he describes the sheer difficulty of the march compellingly. See also Atkinson, *Army at Dawn*, 346.

37. Herbert A. Smith Jr., "The Operations of the 3rd Battalion, 18th Infantry (1st Infantry Division) at El Guettar 17–23 March 1943 (Tunisian Campaign)," Advanced Infantry Officers Course, 1948–1949, Fort Benning, GA, WWII Student Papers, DRL, 8–9. Smith was the executive officer of the 3rd Battalion weapons company. On the time of the order, see Bennett, "Gafsa-El Guettar." Anonymous, "Draft Regimental History," places the three battalions differently than does Smith, as does Sam Carter, who served in 1st Battalion, in Carter, "Operations of the 1st Battalion." The author has chosen Smith's view of where 3rd Battalion fought, given that he served in it.

38. Ingersoll, *Battle Is the Payoff*, 149–57.

39. G-3 Journal, Tunisian Campaign, March 21, 1943; 1st ID, "Factual Account," 22–23.

40. G-3 Journal, Tunisian Campaign, March 21, 1943.

41. G-3 journal.

42. G-3 journal; 1st ID, "Factual Account," 36. For a sense of the level of combat at the battalion level, see 1st Battalion journal, 43, in 26th Infantry, Reports of Operations, 8 Nov 42–9 May 43. For the roundabout way Bradley became Patton's deputy, see Bradley, *Soldier's Story*, 15–19, 30–35, 45–46.

43. G-3 journal, March 21, 1943. See also Anonymous, "Draft Regimental History," 35–36. There were numerous reports of tanks seen during the day, although none prosecuted an attack. It is likely these were Centauro Division tanks. On friction, see Clausewitz, *On War*, 119.

44. G-3 journal, March 21, 1943.

45. G-3 journal; Mason, "Reminiscences," 81.

46. G-3 journal, March 21, 1943; 26th Infantry, "History," 46. The Italian soldiers had fled 1st AD by crossing over the Djebel Robata Ridge.

47. Howe, *Northwest Africa*, 552; Blumenson, *Patton Papers*, 196–99; Kesselring, *A Soldier's Record*, 185.

48. Schick, *History of the 10. Panzer*, 496–98. The 10th PZ had still not received all its equipment. On March 1, 1943, some seventy vehicles remained in Sicily, where the Allies bombed them. That day the Germans moved the equipment, only to have them bombed again the next day. One artillery battalion remained committed elsewhere and did not support the division during the fighting near Maknassy and at El Guettar.

49. Schick, 498–99. On Luftwaffe bases, see Walther Nehring, "Des Leiters der Arbeitsgruppe Nordafrika zu Band 3, Geschichte des Feldzuges in Nord Afrika, 1941/1943," March 1948, ms. D-086, N-17500.812, CARL, sketches 1, 2. These are hand-drawn sketches made by either Nehring or a member of the working group.

50. Schick, *History of the 10. Panzer*, 499.

51. Jackson, *Alexander of Tunis*, 182; Astor, *Terrible Terry Allen*, 165–66; 26th Infantry, "History," 46.

52. G-3 journal, March 23, 1943; 26th Infantry, after-action report (Torch Operation), in Reports of Operations, 8 Nov 42–9 May 43; HQ, 601st Tank Destroyer Battalion, after-action report, March 28, 1943, http://tankdestroyer.net, 2. The 601st report cites the four-digit grid coordinates given for the thousand-meter grid square for the artillery. In fact, the artillery organized positions north and east of grid square YT 29 69.

53. Carter, "Operations of the 1st Battalion," 18–19; Schick, *History of the 10. Panzer*, 499. Several personal experience monographs have beautifully done maps that illustrate most of the 1st Division's positions. All of them agree on attack axis.

54. G-3 Journal, Tunisian Campaign, March 23, 1943. Thomas E. Morrison, statement and sketch, n.d., at http://tankdestroyer.net.

55. Carter, "Operations of the 1st Battalion," 18. Just when the 7th and 33rd FA battalions moved in is unclear. Their positions are taken from a 1:100,000 map in HQ, 26th Infantry, unit report (Torch Operation), November 8–11, 1942, in Reports of Operations, 8 Nov 42–9 May 43.

56. Carter, "Operations of the 1st Battalion," 18.

57. Anonymous, "Draft Regimental History," 38; Smith, "Operations of the 3rd Battalion," 38; Carter, "Operations of the 1st Battalion," 20.

58. Frederick C. Miner, supporting statement, March 26, 1943, in 601st TD, after-action report.

59. John D. Yowell, supporting statement, March 27, 1943, in 601st TD.

60. G-3 Journal, Tunisian Campaign, March 23, 1943.

61. II Corps, operation report, Tunisia, 7–8; G-3 Journal, Tunisian Campaign, March 23, 1943; Clarence A. Heckethorn, typewritten statement, n.d., at http://tankdestroyer.net, accessed August 4, 2020.

62. Roosevelt quotation from Atkinson, *Army at Dawn*, 441; HQ, 899th TD, unit history, January 1–December 31, 1943, 4, 6, http://tankdestroyer.net. See also 899th TD, combat report, March 15–April 15, 1943, 1, and Thomas Hawksworth, personal

statement, n.d., 106, both at http://tankdestroyer.net. Hawksworth's account is labeled "Chapter 14, Gafsa and El Guettar," and is likely from a battalion history.

63. G-3 Journal, Tunisian Campaign, March 23, 1943 (report on the artillery received at 1050); 26th Infantry, "History," 50–51; Robert W. Young, "Armored Support of Infantry," Armor Advanced Officers Class No. 2, Fort Knox, KY, May 5, 1948. 4.

64. Schick, *History of the 10. Panzer*, 500; G-3 Journal, Tunisian Campaign, March 23, 1943.

65. Schick, *History of the 10. Panzer*, 500. The 32nd FA lost six of twelve 105-millimeter howitzers, and the 5th FA, six of twelve 155-millimeter howitzers. 1st ID, G-4 after-action report, El Guettar Operation, April 17, 1943, in RG 301-4: G-4 Operations Reports, 8 Nov 42–14 Apr 43, 18 May–31 Aug 43, Oct–Dec 43, MRC Digital Archives, 9.

66. This quotation appears in just about every account of the battle of El Guettar. 1st ID, "Factual Account," 24. The signal company broadcast the taunt at 1615, March 23, 1945. Re Patton's query, see Atkinson, *Army at Dawn*, 442.

67. G-3 Journal, Tunisian Campaign, March 23, 1943. Re scissors and sweep, see Mason, "Reminiscences," 89; Atkinson, *Army at Dawn,* 442.

68. 1st ID, Division Artillery, after-action report, March 2–April 9, 1943, in RG 301-Art-0.3: Artillery Operations Reports, 1 Jun 44–May 45, 7, MRC Digital Archives; 601st Tank Destroyer Battalion, after-action report, March 28, 1943, Tank Destroyer Net, 6; G-4 after-action report, April 17, 1943, in RG 301-4: G-4 Diary, 23–24 March 1943, MRC Digital Archives.

69. 1st ID, "Factual Account," 24; Eisenhower, *Papers*, no. 906, 2:1056.

70. Butcher, *Three Years with Eisenhower*, 46, 284–85. The change in command was not made public. See also Ambrose, *Supreme Commander*, 184–18; and Ossad, *Omar Nelson Bradley*, 72, 89, 139–41, which shows clearly the fundamental differences between them. For Bradley's decision to relieve Allen in Sicily, illustrating the fundamental difference in how each approached leadership, see Bradley, *Soldier's Story*, 154–57, and caption at 108.

71. 1st ID, "Factual Account"; Bradley, *Soldier's Story*, 98; Astor, *Terrible Terry Allen*, 175–78.

72. Eisenhower, *Papers*, no. 959, 2:1104.

73. Liebling, *Road Back to Paris*, 468. Liebling is frequently quoted in narratives about North Africa because he really did say it best.

CHAPTER SIX

Husky: The Invasion of Sicily

I want those sons of bitches.
—*George S. Patton, asking to use 1st ID for Husky*

It's okay to go AWOL as long as you go toward the enemy.
—*Thomas Gendron on the 1st ID ethos*

THE TUNISIAN CAMPAIGN ended, as many do, with a whimper rather than a bang. General Jürgen von Arnim, commanding the German-Italian Army Group, gave up at noon on May 12, 1943. The actual end came the following day when Giovanni Messe, just promoted to field marshal, surrendered his Italian First Army to Sir Bernard C. Freyberg, who commanded the New Zealand Corps. As many as 275,000 Axis troops went into captivity. Some on both sides referred to the surrender as "Tunisgrad," likening the achievement to that of the Russians at Stalingrad. Although Italian soldiers comprised the majority of those taken in Tunisia, the analogy held. The western Allies had suffered far less for their victory than had the Soviets for theirs. Total Allied casualties for the North African campaign amounted to 70,341, with just over 10,000 killed in action. The US Army, including the Army Air Force, lost 18,221, including more than 2,770 killed. The 1st ID "butcher's bill" amounted to 3,916, including 634 killed in action. These numbers don't include nonbattle casualties such as those who died in accidents or contracted malaria, typhus, or other diseases common to the region.[1]

The Allies celebrated their victory with a parade in Tunis in which French troops figured prominently, but the attention of planning staffs, and for that matter most of the American troops, had already shifted. At Casablanca in

January, Roosevelt, Churchill, and their respective staffs had decided on invading Sicily as the next step in the prosecution of the war in Europe. General Eisenhower had established a target date for executing Operation Husky, the invasion of Sicily between July 10 and 14, 1943. With barely six weeks to prepare and launch a landing in Sicily, the largest amphibious operation conducted up to that point, there was little time to waste. General Omar N. Bradley headed west on May 13, followed soon thereafter by the II Corps staff. General Harold R. L. G. Alexander's 18th Army Group returned to Algiers and disbanded on May 15. There they were folded into Force 141, the planning staff created for Husky, and became 15th Army Group. The next day General Bernard Law Montgomery and the Eighth Army staff headed to Tripoli, Libya.[2]

"Those sons of bitches" in the Big Red One spent four days or more traveling just under nine hundred road miles to assembly areas near Oran, to rest, refit, reorganize, and train for Husky. French colonials greeted the troops with cheering and flowers, but best of all, they "offered wine in liberal quantities." The 1st ID arrived in its assembly areas over the course of May 16 and 17.[3]

Already veterans of multiple landings while preparing to deploy overseas, for the Big Red One, Husky would be the second of three amphibious assaults. In terms of numbers of troops landed during the first phase, the invasion of Sicily is arguably the largest ever accomplished. Three US and four Commonwealth divisions crossed the beach. (By contrast, two US and three Commonwealth divisions would assault Normandy.) Two regiments of paratroops crash-landed in gliders or leaped from aircraft, hoping to land safely. The 116th Infantry from the 29th ID landed as attached to the 1st ID. Two US and one British airborne division did airborne assaults.[4]

These assaults, despite their difficulty, are, as asserted in an earlier chapter, not objectives in themselves but only the means to employ forces ashore. From the perspective of a ground commander, there are three phases to an amphibious assault—the landing, expanding the lodgment to assemble forces, and finally the breakout. This chapter focuses on these three phases as they occurred. Transition from one phase to another, despite the crisp blue arrows that illustrate these discrete operations on a map, are not clearly defined in practice. Instead, they are messy, often come as surprise to both sides, and are always contested.

The Second Liberation of Oran

After six months in the field, 1st ID troops believed they had earned a respite, even a return home. To the chagrin of most, however, rumors that the division would go home proved false. Instead, to train for Sicily, the troops returned to Oran, Algeria, where, as Stan Mason put it, the division moved into "bivouac areas about ten miles east of Oran, still wearing wool uniforms in an early summer climate about like that found in Alabama at that season"—that is to say, hot and humid. On arriving, the combat troops found the area "teeming with Army units, mostly service types, who were freshly arrived from the States and wearing Khaki." By comparison, the veterans of Longstop Hill, Kasserine Pass, El Guettar, and the fight to finish the Axis in Tunisia were clad in woolen field uniforms both uncomfortably hot and shoddy by comparison with khaki.[5]

Since time immemorial, or at least since Caesar's legionaries, combat soldiers have taken umbrage at the comparative comfort of those who serve in the rear. In Vietnam, combat troops used the acronym REMFS—rear echelon soldiers of dubious sexual practices—for those who did not share their hardships. In the forever wars in Iraq and Afghanistan, they referred to those who lived full-time in forward operating bases, or FOBs, as Fobbits. The combat veterans of the 1st ID had little use for those assigned to the rear or, according to its official title, Mediterranean Base Section. It grated that these creatures were now making the rules in Oran, which they had taken in the first place. In Oran, as in Vietnam and more recently, support installations had established rules that front-line troops found onerous, even unbearable.

Worst of all, the 1st ID could not meet the Mediterranean Base Section dress code. Ralph Uffner had a surreal experience with these uniform requirements. Sick with malaria, he visited the 7th Station Hospital. After waiting for some time in his woolen ODs (olive drabs), he was told he would not be seen unless he was in the proper uniform, "suntans" (khakis). The 1st ID literally fought back. General Bradley complained that Allen's troops made it so "sweaty woolen uniforms were the only assurance of safe-conduct in the city's streets." Worse still, "the theater," meaning Eisenhower, "sternly directed [Bradley] to order the division to stay out of Oran. At one point, Eisenhower sent deputy theater commander Major General Everett Hughes to investigate an allegation against the 1st ID. Hughes concluded that the allegation of rampaging through a vineyard was false, and added that the division's military courtesy was excellent. Yet there is no question that 1st ID soldiers harassed or did worse to those who wore khakis.[6]

John Finke, then a lieutenant in the 16th Infantry, remembered his own run-in with none other than Colonel Edmund H. Leavey, Mediterranean Base Section chief of staff. Finke, just released from a hospital following treatment for a wound suffered at El Guettar, rejoined the regiment in its bivouac near Oran. On arrival, he was instructed to report to the regimental commander, Lieutenant Colonel George A. Taylor, who had moved from commanding the 26th Infantry to the 16th, where he served previously. Taylor took Finke to task: apparently, when Finke and another officer encountered Leavey while on pass from the 2nd Convalescent Hospital, they had failed to salute the base section chief. Just as bad, they appeared scruffy in their wool field uniforms and the stocking caps issued for wear under their helmets. The good colonel (Leavey) tongue-lashed the two and made disparaging remarks about Terry Allen. He concluded his lecture, "You may be all right at the front but you're not so hot back here."[7]

Looking back on their time "resting" near Oran, most 1st ID soldiers understood that their behavior, whatever the justification, had been beyond the pale. In reflecting on their conduct, Thomas Gendron admitted, "We had tremendous spirit but we were not disciplined." Patton and Bradley were both incensed. In *A Soldier's Story*, Bradley, the so-called GI's General, described the 1st ID as "brawling." He admitted that the trouble seemed to begin with the rear-area troops closing "their clubs and installations to our combat troops from the front." Bradley further admitted that "the episode resulted partly from our failure to prepare a rest area." But he considered the real problem a lack of discipline. Bradley also knew that part of the irritation stemmed from the hot, uncomfortable woolen uniforms that he preferred combat troops to wear. He defended his decision not to issue khakis to the fighting troops as "impractical for field wear," adding that it would have "unnecessarily burdened supply." There is no evidence that he ever explained why lightweight uniforms, especially considering the weather conditions, were impractical, or just how supplying khakis to combat troops could be a burden, when supplying them to the more numerous support troops was not.[8]

Terry Allen did not, as Bradley implied, do nothing in response. He took appropriate action, but he also fought for his troops. Allen and Mason drove fifty miles to Patton's headquarters, where Allen made the case for issuing his soldiers cotton khaki uniforms to wear in the stifling heat. Patton opined that there was no point in issuing khaki, since most of the Big Red One would be killed in the fight for Sicily. Not content with just saying no—and crudely at that—he threw in a few more criticisms, including that he thought the division's soldiers were "sloppy looking, thought they were heroes didn't salute properly, wouldn't fight." In the midst of this harangue Allen "turned his back to Patton" and left. Patton never referred to the incident; blustering and then forgetting was, it seemed, his style. Later, however, just before the invasion of Sicily, Patton defended the 1st ID to General Eisenhower, denying that it had a discipline problem.[9] The GI General, on the other hand, neither forgave nor forgot the fact that the Big Red One had behaved badly and, worse still, embarrassed him.

Training and Lessons Learned

Samuel Fuller, known to his soldier peers as "Sammy," later famous as a novelist, screenwriter, and Hollywood producer, took pride in his service as an infantryman in the Big Red One. Fuller was offered a way out as an army journalist, but he chose instead to carry a rifle, with all that entailed. Recollecting his service, he spoke for infantrymen everywhere when he observed that "survival was the one thought that held dominion over everything in a doggie's universe." *Doggie, doughboy,* or just plain *dough* are honorifics applied to the soldiers who operated at the sharp end. In Tunisia they learned to kill, to dig deep, and to adapt or die.[10]

Carl von Clausewitz described the key to adaptation and learning in his treatise on the theory of warfare. In chapter 5, book 3, of *On War* he wrote about military virtues. Clausewitz served during a time in which communications and weapons technology required massed formations and strictly enforced drill. Yet even with those constraints, he argued that war required each soldier to apply "his intelligence to every detail; who gains ease and confidence through practice, and who completely immerses his personality in the appointed task." He believed professionalism essential. "Soldiers," he wrote, "will think of themselves as members of a kind of guild, in whose regulations, laws and customs the spirit of war is given pride of place." That philosophy, stemming from a man writing from the perspective of the Napoleonic era, obtained in the US Army with good reason. According to Fuller, a soldier had to learn how to become a "killing machine."[11]

The performance of the US Army and the 1st ID improved in North Africa but reflected inadequate training and shortfalls in weapons systems, organization, and doctrine. Post operation critiques, assessments by observers recorded in reports, provided the means to adapt based on experience. Adapting required training, evaluation, and practice. General Eisenhower identified the problem early on, as did the British, and for that matter US, commanders in the field. In his own report, Eisenhower noted that "Our mistakes some of which were serious . . . should be subjected to dispassionate analysis," thus setting the tone for the theater and for US troops. To that end, in mid-May Bradley, now commanding II Corps, convened "a post mortem" in order to "profit from what we learned in Tunisia." That process played out with more or less formality down to the lowest levels, including a good many written reports at company level.[12]

There were some missteps, but the effort to prepare for the invasion of Sicily—and doing so with the lessons just learned from the campaign in North Africa—paid off. The theater established the Infantry Training Center, "designed to refresh troops' basic infantry skills, including minefield removal." This idea, while useful, could have been better implemented. Ralph Uffner, more or less recovered from malaria, believed that the center "served its purpose up to a point." According to Uffner, the instructors of the 36th ID ("the Texas Division"), which ran the center, "had zero combat time." Despite that criticism, the idea to afford training to the 1st ID supported by someone else made sense.[13] It relieved the division of the task, and allowed the new division to benefit from the experience of the veterans they were training.

1st ID units also rotated through amphibious operations training at the Fifth US Army Amphibious Training Center, located at Port aux Poules (in Arabic, Mers el Hadjadj) on the coast near Oran. There veterans relearned some things and had the opportunity to practice with the improved amphibious capability provided by new tools. Getting ashore rapidly is the key to success in amphibious operations, and now the Allies began to enjoy the means to do just that.

The first purpose-built oceangoing LST (landing ship, tank) replaced the Maracaibo improvisations used to seize Oran. At 328 feet long, these LSTs could run up on a beach and unload over a ramp. They were capable of carrying a prodigious cargo, including up to eighteen tanks, 160 troops, and small craft as a deck load. Still another new vessel, the LCT (landing craft, tank), was 112 feet long. At 45 feet, the LCM (landing craft, mechanized) could carry as many as a hundred troops or a single tank, while the 150-foot LCI (landing craft, infantry) could carry two hundred troops and sustain them for forty-eight hours. The LCVP (landing craft, vehicle, personnel), known simply as the Higgins boat after its inventor, reprised the role it played in Torch. Finally, the DUKW, a 2.5-ton amphibious truck, debuted during Husky and became ubiquitous as a lighter that could travel inland as needed.[14]

Despite an intensive training schedule and the contretemps with the rear area authorities, the 1st ID assimilated still more replacements, rested veterans, and welcomed back wounded and sick soldiers from hospitals. The division also dealt with routine officer turbulence. Colonel D'Alery Fechet, who took over the 16th Infantry from Henry B. Cheadle after the Torch landing, was wounded in action on March 30, and Taylor moved over from the 26th Infantry to replace him. Colonel John W. Bowen fleeted up in Taylor's stead. Colonel Frank U. Greer was promoted out of the 18th Infantry in June, with Colonel George A. Smith Jr. replacing him. Turnover was brisk among the battalions and tumultuous at company and platoon. Joe Dawson, writing home, observed that in one company there had been four commanders during the six months in North Africa, "whereas turnover in battalion commanders . . . has not been but a bit over 50 percent."[15]

Allied Assessment and Intentions

As noted, the Allies decided to invade Sicily at the Casablanca Conference in January 1943. The Americans, General Marshall in particular, remained unenthusiastic about operations in the Mediterranean; Marshall worried that they would delay a cross-Channel invasion of France. Nevertheless, "General" Logistics dictated the strategic course of action; in short, the Allies still lacked adequate means to invade France in 1943. The Americans had too few trained troops ready to deploy. Shipping, ranging from transports to the various amphibious craft, determined the size of the force that could be landed anywhere, whether that was Sicily in 1943 or Normandy in 1944. Moreover, when it came to the allocation of amphibious craft, plans in the Pacific competed with those in Europe.[16]

As it had at nearly every step of the way, strategic planning involved differing strategic views and philosophies and various levels of mistrust among the Allies, and even between the different US services. Samuel Eliot Morrison asserts in his *Two-Ocean War* that the US Air Force was "fighting its own war," a view not limited to navy observers. As a result, the "amphibious expedition sailed and landed with no promise of tactical support from the air, and almost none did it obtain." Patton, the Seventh Army commander, was more explicit, saying to Admiral H. Kent Hewitt, "You can get Navy planes to do anything you want but we can't get the Air Force to do a goddam thing." Hewitt lacked the means to do as Patton would have liked, and in any case believed that supporting the army was the Air Force's job.[17]

Finally the British insisted that Montgomery's Eighth Army headquarters carry the British share of the load. Patton had given up II Corps to Bradley and returned to his original command, I Armored Corps, to plan and execute the American effort. Montgomery remained in the field with his headquarters until the end in Tunisia. His intervention late in the planning for

Husky drove the final result, but not before some angst during which Montgomery admitted, accurately, that he was regarded "by many people as being a tiresome person." The US Army official history concluded that the final plan "reflected" Montgomery's view, and "like him it was cautious." And, it added, "No one except Montgomery was particularly happy with it."[18]

The last iteration of Husky did indeed reflect Montgomery's wishes. There would be no attempt to destroy Axis forces on Sicily; rather, the operation would minimize risks by pushing them out of the island. Patton would land US Seventh Army (built on I Armored Corps staff) with Joss Force, 3rd ID reinforced, commanded by Major General Lucian D. Truscott, and Bradley's II Corps. Montgomery's Eighth Army would land on II Corps' right with British XIII Corps. Seventh Army's assault formations included General Truscott's 3rd ID landing on the left, near Licata. Terry Allen and 1st ID, dubbed Dime Force, would land in the center. The planners drew the boundary with 3rd ID about ten miles west of Gela. The Acate River defined the right boundary with the 45th ID. Major General Troy Middleton's 45th ID, arriving directly from the United States, would land on the right, oriented on Vittoria. Colonel James M. Gavin's 505th Parachute Infantry Regiment (PIR) would conduct the first ever night parachute assault just inland of the beaches.[19]

The British planned to land 1st Canadian Division on the 45th ID right flank, just west of the village of Pachino, and three more divisions along nearly twenty miles of beach from Pachino to the ancient city of Syracuse. British glider troops intended to seize two inland objectives. Both field armies retained a reserve. Patton's reserve included Combat Command B, 2nd Armored Division, afloat. The remainder of the division would land as part of the follow-on force. The 18th provided the infantry contingent of the floating reserve. Follow-on forces included the 9th Infantry and the 82nd Airborne Division, less the 504th Parachute Infantry Regiment (PIR), which was still in Tunis. Eighth Army retained two divisions in reserve, with a corps and an airborne division in the follow-on forces.[20]

Axis Assessment and Intentions

Allied planning for the Husky invasion is an example of exemplary comity, collegiality, and collaboration compared with the Axis effort. Trust between the Germans and Italians had eroded to the barest minimum. After Tunisia, the Germans began assessing the effect of an Italian surrender or, worse still, an outright defection. Hitler continued to insist on the perimeter of

Nazi-held Europe being defended everywhere. The transcript of a May 20 conference chaired by Hitler, and attended by Generalfeldmarschall Wilhelm Keitel, chief of staff of the high command (OKW), Generalfeldmarschall Erwin Rommel, and Generalleutnant Walter Warlimont, deputy director of operations (OKW), yields insight into the state of the Axis "partnership." German diplomat Constantin von Neurath briefed the conferees on his visit to Italy and Sicily. His account was candid and grim: the Italians lacked the stomach to fight, he reported, and the civilian population in Rome and Sicily was hostile. Hitler wondered aloud whether the Italians "wanted to defend [Sicily]." He further concluded that Mussolini was in political trouble.[21]

Despite the obvious mistrust between the Axis powers, they assembled a reasonably potent defense. Mussolini withdrew the Italian Army from the war in the east, thus freeing up troops to defend Italy and Sicily. The Germans moved a handful of divisions from France to Italy and reconstituted the 15th Panzergrenadier (PZG) Division in Sicily and the Herman Göring PZ in Italy. Both eventually took positions in Sicily. The Axis established a defensive plan for the island under the command of Generale d'Armata Alfredo Guzzoni, an officer of proven competence who had sound relations with the Germans.[22]

Guzzoni assumed command of the island's defense in May. He not only believed the Allies would invade Sicily as their next step but also anticipated that they would land in the southeastern part of the island. He and Kesselring disagreed over the concept of defense: Guzzoni believed the solution was a powerful mobile force that could destroy the enemy once it came ashore, while Kesselring wanted to fight right at the shoreline. Moreover, Kesselring would not permit Guzzoni to concentrate the best available mobile forces, the 15th PZG and Herman Göring PZ.[23]

The Axis order of battle included Italian Sixth Army, commanded by Guzzoni, who also commanded the German-Italian Armed Forces Command, Sicily, along with the Italian XII and XVI Corps, the German XIV Corps, and a separate antiaircraft command. XII Corps defended the western half of Sicily, while XVI Corps, commanded by Generale di Corpo d'Armata Carlo Rossi, defended the eastern half of the island. The 1st ID would fight various of Rossi's troops. Rossi's ground combat forces included five coastal divisions, one coastal regiment, and two coastal brigades. Four first-line Italian divisions and three mobile groups rounded out the Italian contingent. The two German Panzer divisions, one German Fallschirmjäger (parachute) division, and one Panzergrenadier division formed the balance.[24]

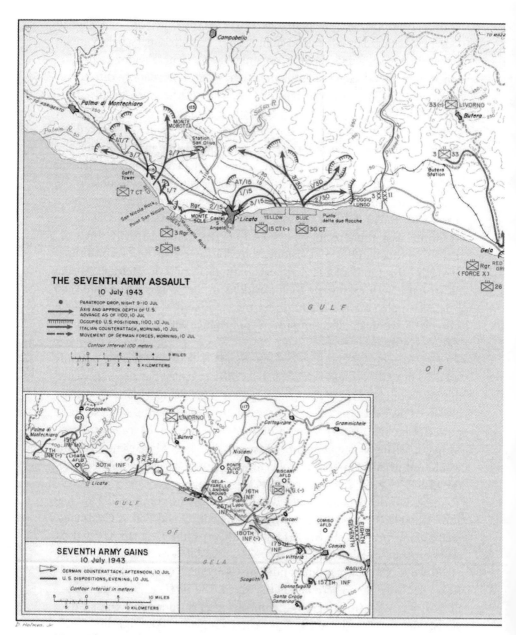

Map 7: The Seventh Army Assault and Gains. Reproduced from Lieutenant Colonel Albert N. Garland and Howard McGaw Smyth, assisted by Martin Blumenson, *Sicily and the Surrender of Italy* (Washington: Center of Military History, 1965), Map III.

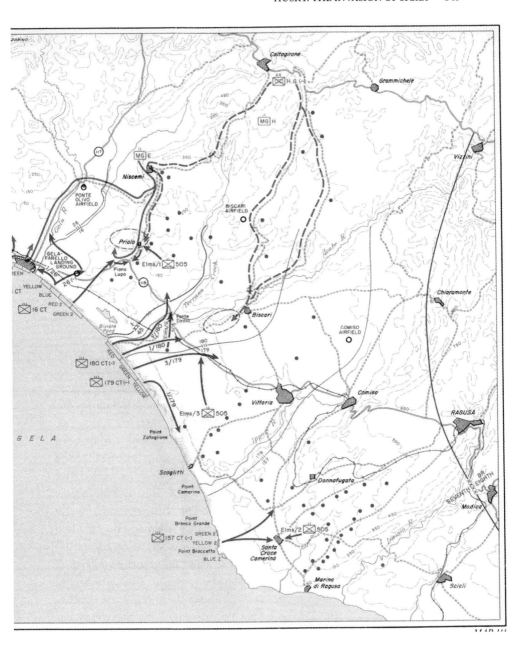

The 1st ID Plan

Despite squabbling among the Allied and service planners, far better intelligence and more effective processes in the senior headquarters enabled II Corps and 1st ID to prepare for Husky far more effectively than they had for Torch. Brigadier Kenneth W. D. Strong at Allied Forces Headquarters, Colonel Oscar W. Koch at I Armored Corps, and Benjamin A. "Monk" Dickson at II Corps were all talented officers and highly effective intelligence officers. The lessons on amphibious operations garnered in Torch and operations against the Axis in Tunisia did not go unremarked. Lieutenant Colonel Robert W. Porter Jr., another talented officer who Allen had hand-picked as his intelligence officer, compiled a first-rate Sicily terrain study that took advantage of good products provided by all three of the senior headquarters.

Porter's voluminous study covered every conceivable aspect of Sicily, including culture, politics, and personalities among local political, police, and military authorities. The study covered infrastructure, including highways, rail networks, airfields, and water and electricity in detail. The navy supplied equally impressive detail on the beaches, including the matter of false beaches created by tidal currents that piled up sand, often creating a "false" beach well short of the actual shoreline. The topographical study assured that there were few illusions about how difficult the fighting would be, given the rugged hilly country that covered virtually all of the island, dominated by its active volcano. At nearly eleven thousand feet and liable to erupt at any moment, Mount Etna loomed over the terrain on the east coast.[25]

Porter's study included a detailed order of battle with enemy dispositions that he updated over time on his own intelligence notes and those he received from senior headquarters. Photo reconnaissance and detailed perspective sketches of the beaches further aided the division staff. Together the enemy dispositions and the mission to seize the Ponte Olivo airfield some twelve miles north of the beaches defined the problem that Allen and his staff had to solve. In addition to confronting the Italian coastal defenses, the 1st ID had to reckon with the Herman Göring PZ as well as the Livorno and Napoli divisions, all three of which enjoyed reasonable mobility. The Livorno and Herman Göring divisions were located within twenty miles of the beaches designated as landing sites for the 1st ID. Fortunately, Allen had robust capability. Although he had given up the 18th Infantry so that it could serve as part of the floating reserve, he received in its stead Lieutenant Colonel William O. Darby with the 1st and 4th Ranger Battalions, supported by two combat engineer battalions and a 4.2-inch chemical mortar battalion. The 1st ID regarded Darby and his Rangers as "old friends," even as their own.

In addition, the division received, attached, the 70th Tank Battalion (Light), with its Stuart tanks, the 105th Coast Artillery (antiaircraft), and various other supporting arms formations.[26] There was nothing elegant about the assault plan—Allen planned to land two Ranger battalions and four infantry battalions abreast. Seizing a beachhead is hard and inelegant work.

In addition to seizing the airfield at Ponte Olivo, II Corps required the 1st ID to take the town of Niscemi, located just east of the airfield, which was essential for the use of the Allied air force. Gavin's 505th PIR aimed to land close enough to provide "further assistance toward the rapid seizure of the 1st Div. objectives." Allen planned to land the two Ranger battalions (styled Force X) directly into the town of Gela, with the 26th and 16th Infantries landing in several waves on Darby's right. The 26th would attack generally northwestward in support of Darby should he need help, but aimed ultimately at the airfield. The 16th focused on Niscemi. The navy identified six beaches on a narrow frontage of less than five miles. From there, the 1st ID would work its way generally along Highway 117, which ran from Gela north across the island, fighting, as Stan Mason put it, from "hill top to hill top." First, however, they had to get ashore and cross the narrow open plain north of Gela.[27]

A week before the landings, Porter updated the Axis order of battle based on intelligence passed downward. The order of battle identified 15th PZG but called it the Division Sicilien, which indeed was its nom de guerre. The order of battle accurately defined the composition of most of the Herman Göring PZ's units; the update estimated that the PZ fielded 124 tanks, of which 16 were Mark VI Tiger tanks. There was no estimate of the number of tanks assigned to the 15th PZG. Porter knew the division would confront a static coastal division on the beach, but he wasn't sure of its designation. The order of battle accurately identified all four Italian mobile or "field divisions" but mistook units on the east coast for a fifth field division. Although unsure of all of the Herman Göring positions, the order of battle provided good locations for both the Livorno and Napoli divisions. All three of these divisions occupied positions from which they could quickly intervene against the landings.[28]

No Way to Travel: Amphibious Assault

Perhaps there are good ways to arrive on a battlefield, but amphibious assault is decidedly not among them. To begin with, soldiers had several phases to endure before they reached the point of almost certain seasickness while pitching, yawing, rolling, and maybe sinking along with the craft they rode to the beach. The navy shuttled most of the 1st ID from the port of Algiers to Tunis, although some troops sailed to Sicily directly from Algiers. The operation began on June 26. Many troops made the short voyage to Tunis aboard an LCI or LST. Once in Tunis, troops and equipment disembarked and, when called forward, reembarked on various assault transports.

All were aboard transports or LCIs or LSTs soon after July 5. The transports served as "mother" ships for the various landing craft that would actually deliver the assault troops to the beach. Larger vessels such as LCIs and LSTs landed the bulk of heavy gear, including howitzers and light tanks. Although General Allen commanded the landing force, Rear Admiral "Jimmy" Hall commanded the Western Task Force of transports and combatants, and he, not Allen, executed the landing operation. Allen would assume command only once he could establish himself ashore and accept a "handoff" to which he and Hall agreed. The US Navy and its partners performed with precision and without serious incident.[29]

Allied naval and air forces devastated their opposition. Whether or not the airmen put the ground commanders' minds at ease, they bombed airfields, ports and cities in accordance with their strategic perception. Along with naval forces, the Allied airmen removed the Royal Italian Navy from the board. One Italian admiral complained that "there no longer existed a harbor or naval base in Sicily where ships great or small could remain in safety." Bombing airfields prevented the defenders from enjoying air superiority as they had in North Africa. Siegfried Freytag, an experienced German fighter pilot, reached a grim conclusion a few days before the invasion, complaining to his commander, Major Johannes "Macky" Steinhoff, "In [a] day or two we won't have a single aircraft to fly. And they will leave us behind. . . . This time the trap's going to close with a snap." Of greater importance, the Axis air forces provided practically no air cover over the beaches.[30]

Although Freytag's misgivings were legitimate, the invasion turned out differently than he feared. Husky began with the weather changing for the worse, just as it had for Torch. Even so, at 1842 on July 9, 1944, British and American transport aircraft began taking off, towing 144 gliders carrying the British contingent of the airborne assault. At sunset, some two hours later, Gavin's 505th PIR, augmented by the 3rd Battalion, 504th PIR, took off from Kairouan, Tunisia, aboard 246 C-47 transports. The plan, Gavin recalled, "was simple." The transports were to fly nearly due east over the island of Linosa to Malta and then turn left at a beacon on Malta and fly a heading just short of 360 degrees to drop zones north of the 1st ID beaches.

Just before takeoff an airman arrived at Gavin's transport, asking for Colonel Gavin. Gavin identified himself, and the airman advised, "I was told to tell [them] that the wind is 35 miles an hour west to east." The planners intended the airborne insertion to generate depth to enable the 1st ID to break out more readily from the beach head. A lack of aircraft required the 82nd to arrive in serials.[31]

Then, as now, a breeze of fifteen miles per hour exceeded safety parameters for training. Gavin took off knowing there was nothing for it but to hope for the best. The storm-born wind played havoc with both the airborne and amphibious assaults. The US contingent of the landing force, less the 45th ID, sailed for Sicily on July 8, 1943. Staff Sergeant Lawrence Manley, writing in the 26th Infantry's wartime journal, reflected on the not uncommon view that waiting to go to a fight is but a miserable prelude to the fight itself: "The endless days of training," he wrote, "were behind combat team 26 when they drew near Gela, Sicily." On a 16th Infantry transport, Sam Fuller recorded events for the journal he kept for Colonel Taylor. Fuller's attempt to avoid army journalism proved temporary. Taylor shanghaied him from the 26th Infantry to be the regimental scribe. Fuller recorded that boat crews began to assemble at 2340. At 2349 the first wave of troops got the call to head to their boat stations. Next, at 2351, came the call for "scouts and scout teams." The scout teams were composed of infantrymen trained to guide the assault forces to the right beach.[32]

Fuller's description of the landing is apt, although embellished by references to other invaders, including Greeks, Romans, and Vandals. "The elements are against us," he wrote. "The sea is furious." Nonetheless, at 0057 hours the first wave set off to cross nearly five miles of tumultuous seas. Finally, Fuller's LCI shoots "into the sand, comes to a sudden halt. Many of us are thrown. The ramp drops [there are actually two—one on each side of an LCI]. Machine gun bullets crack past us. Doggies splash forward, death-dealing figures we are, soaked waist-high, guns held aloft, dashing through the surf, sprinting across the sand toward the enemy." If only every "doggie" had that experience. A soldier near Fuller was killed before he even reached the LCI's ramp. Some boats broached; others struck sandbars, after which some of their troops drowned in deep water short of the actual beach. Four soldiers drowned trying to land with the 18th Infantry, even though it arrived after the assault forces had secured the beaches.[33]

Tracers, artillery, searchlights, and various exploding things lit up the night, but the division journal reported the landing with what reads like insouciance. The second through fifth entries for the journal of July 10 are the epitome of brevity, to the point of providing little information: "0243 1st Wave Rngr force landed successful, 0245 1st Wave CT 26 ditto and finally 0247 1st Wave CT 16 ditto with little opposition." Teddy Roosevelt went ashore with that wave and spent the day doing whatever had to be done. In *The Day of Battle*, Rick Atkinson writes of Roosevelt bellowing "Get into battle!" and directing troops to beach exits. He visited every beach during the day and went everywhere he believed he was needed. The fifth entry reports that at 0700 "Adv CP [command post] opened at 277262 [map grid coordinates]. Terry Allen and small staff occupied a makeshift command post barely two hundred yards from the surf breaking on the soft sand of one of the 16th Infantry's beaches.[34]

Two and a half miles northwest of the CP, Darby and his Rangers fought their way into Gela, where they were joined by two companies of the 26th Infantry that looped around to the north of the town and then turned south. They helped with the house-to-house clearing of Gela. Soon after landing, the 16th Infantry reported that they had "surrounded strong pts . . . and reduced pill boxes and MG [machine gun] posns." Sam Fuller recorded that the infantry used the "famed bazooka, long-secret rocket anti-tank gun" to deal with them. Later in the day, in response to a query about Gela, the CP watch officer responded, "We have it entirely." These laconic reports bely the violence required on both sides. The Italians, dispirited, ill-trained, undermanned, poorly equipped, and for the most part badly led, did not give up without a fight. Darby's two Ranger battalions and an attached engineer battalion took most of Gela before daylight with hand grenades, rifles, and six-inch guns fired by the USS *Savannah*.[35]

Bowen's 26th Infantry and Taylor's 16th Infantry each landed with two battalions abreast. Lieutenant Walter H. Grant commanded Bowen's 1st Battalion, and Lieutenant Colonel Derrill M. Daniel commanded the 2nd. The 16th Infantry's 2nd Battalion, commanded by Lieutenant Colonel Joseph B. Crawford, landed on their right. On his right Lieutenant Colonel Charles J. Denholm led the 1st Battalion, 16th Infantry. But before they could fight, each of the four assault battalions first had to get off the beach, which proved problematic. The landing beaches were covered in soft sand and well mined, just as those at Gela had been. Fortunately, the surprised coastal defense troops had not all reached their positions, so all four battalions crossed the beaches primarily "harried by artillery fire from the hills," north and east of the Gela plain that stretched from three to nearly ten miles of wide-open ground. Eventually all four regiments managed to cross the beaches, as well as the railway that ran east from Gela to the coastal highway.[36]

At 0900 the 1st Infantry Division was arrayed, with Darby's Force X in Gela, 26th Infantry advancing north, adjacent to Gela, and the 16th Infantry heading toward the small crossroads that lay about six miles south of Niscemi. Known locally as Piano Lupo, the crossroads linked a secondary road from Niscemi with Highway 115. From there, Highway 115 ran more or less parallel to the coast toward Gela to the west or Vittorio (in the 45th ID sector) to the east. Landing the first wave of troops with relative ease confirmed the G-2's estimate. Porter believed the division would "get ashore alright. The critical time will come when the Germans size up the situation and throw their counterattack to break the beachhead." Porter believed the counterattack "will come within forty-eight hours after we land."[37]

Late in the morning, the 1st ID made radio contact with some of Gavin's widely scattered paratroops, who, despite few of them having landed where intended, had begun a great tradition of the airborne, sowing confusion upon the enemy. These troopers belonged to the 1st Battalion, 505th, many of whom had congregated on a ridgeline about three miles north of the beach. They and their colleagues created chaos and havoc among the enemy, not least by cutting Axis telephone lines whenever they came upon them. The effect greatly exceeded the number of paratroopers actually on the scene. One group led by Captain Edwin B. Sayre reduced an Italian strong point on the Niscemi road north of the Piano Lupo crossroads, capturing the occupants and a few Germans from the Herman Göring Division. It took Sayre's paratroops two tries. He made the first attempt soon after landing, with about a dozen soldiers. In the succeeding hours, he found enough paratroopers to grow his "force" to forty-five. Sayre's troops took the stronghold at 0430.[38]

Getting across the beaches all along the shoreline required clearing mines, or at least attempting to avoid them. The division lost equipment and people to mines despite confronting relatively light resistance. Once off the beach, Allen's troops needed to get inland far enough to do two things. First, they needed to create space to land follow-on troops and equipment. To do that, they had to drive the enemy direct-fire weapons far enough inland to enable unloading of supplies and heavy equipment with beach parties under "only" artillery and air attack, which the Italians and Germans continued throughout the day. Presuming the division could complete downloading and assembling, it could then proceed with the reason for landing—taking Sicily from the Axis.[39]

Axis Reaction

Alfredo Guzzoni had adequate warning to execute a planned riposte to the landing, thanks to Luftwaffe reports received during the afternoon and evening of July 9. Poor communications and the assumption that rough seas and high winds would force a delay of the landings assured that the static coastal units, as well as others, were surprised. Thanks to Gavin's paratroopers, who cut telephone wires wherever they found them, the already atrocious Axis communications system could not function when it mattered most. Both Generalleutnant Paul Conrath and his counterpart in the Livorno Division intended to counterattack as planned. Indeed, his division was supposed to be subordinated to XVI Corps, but he may not have known that salient fact; he had no communications with XVI Corps or the Livorno Division. Thus, he had no idea that part of Mobile Group E, a battalion-sized armored force, had orders to attack and planned to use the same route he did. Sicily's mountainous terrain generally forced armor onto roads. One of two Mobile Group E columns planned to pass through the crossroads at Piano Lupo. As it happened, Rossi proved unable to coordinate the operations of his corps.[40]

Mobile Group E, organized in two "columns," fielded approximately fifty obsolescent or obsolete tanks, ranging from French-built Renault light tanks to some whose provenance dated from the Great War. One column moved south on Highway 117. The other headed south from Niscemi toward Piano Lupo. Additionally, the Livorno Division launched a truck-mounted battalion on a secondary road that led southeast to Gela. Conrath had alerted his division the night before and began moving at 0400, planning to strike the beaches east of Gela before 0900. Conrath organized two Kampfgruppe. His Panzer Kampfgruppe had ninety tanks. He formed the second with his two infantry regiments, bolstered by seventeen Tiger tanks. Both Kampfgruppen had artillery and other support.[41]

Defending the Beach

Conrath could not get his units on the road. His division demonstrated the inutility of Göring's creation, which reflected his vanity rather than necessity. This "crack" division was green, neither well trained nor well led. On July 10 the much-maligned Italians proved far better soldiers than those of the Herman Göring Division. Still, Mobile Group E's two columns would have posed little threat if the division's cannon companies, artillery, and tanks had been unloaded. As it stood, however, very little of the division's artillery had unloaded, and no tanks. The 7th Field Artillery (FA) had two batteries ashore, but both remained within a few hundred yards of the shoreline.

Without tanks to support the beachhead, the quality of Italian tanks was irrelevant. The division's troops had bazookas, some 37-millimeter antitank guns, and, even better, the support of the US Navy. The 18th Infantry, still part of the Seventh Army reserve, did have a platoon of Sherman tanks from 2nd AD that got into the first iteration of the counterattacks.[42]

Naval gunfire, artillery, and the determined "doggies" won the day. Scouting floatplanes launched by USS *Savannah* and *Boise* managed to survive the day despite frequent attacks by German fighters, and the American cruisers wreaked havoc on the various attacking columns. At 0830 Lieutenant C. G. Lewis, flying one of *Boise's* planes, spotted the eastern column of Mobile Group E. At 0910 *Boise* opened up with its six-inch guns. The 16th Infantry, along with some of Gavin's paratroops at the Piano Lupo crossroads, dealt with what few tanks got through *Boise's* fire, the surviving tanks withdrawing north shortly after 1100. USS *Shubrick,* a destroyer, pounded the western column, but some of that column reached Gela. Darby believed six Italian tanks got into town. His Rangers polished them off with a combination of bazookas, "sticky" grenades, and a 37-millimeter antitank gun. The Rangers destroyed at least one tank by dropping fifteen-pound blocks of TNT onto it from a rooftop. Darby himself got another one with a 37 "borrowed" from one of his companies. Later the Rangers, supported by 4.2-inch mortars, beat off the battalion of Italian infantry attacking from the northwest.[43]

At 0945 the 26th Infantry reported seeing tanks from what proved to be Conrath's western column, lumbering down the road from Niscemi toward Piano Lupo. At 1145 paratroopers and infantrymen from the 16th Infantry, bolstered by naval gunfire, drove off the German armor. It is fair to say that neither the Italians nor the Germans pressed their attacks. Across the Acate River, Conrath's infantry task force of two mechanized battalions and fourteen Mark VI tanks fared even worse at the hands of an infantry battalion with the 45th ID. Lieutenant Colonel William H. Schaefer's 1st Battalion, 180th Infantry, augmented by paratroopers, drove the Germans back. However, once Conrath arrived on the scene, Panzergrenadiers mounted a second, more successful attack, capturing Schaefer and most of his battalion. This attack opened a way to flank the 1st ID, but the 3rd Battalion of the 180th restored the situation by routing Conrath's inexperienced and badly led infantry Kampfgruppe. The 45th's "green" infantry saw the Germans off twice, despite losing most of Schaefer's battalion.[44]

Roosevelt and Allen had gone ashore before these attacks played out. Roosevelt landed at 0500, and Allen soon after. Allen used Roosevelt to run the close fight—that is, to go where the fighting seemed thickest or to the most

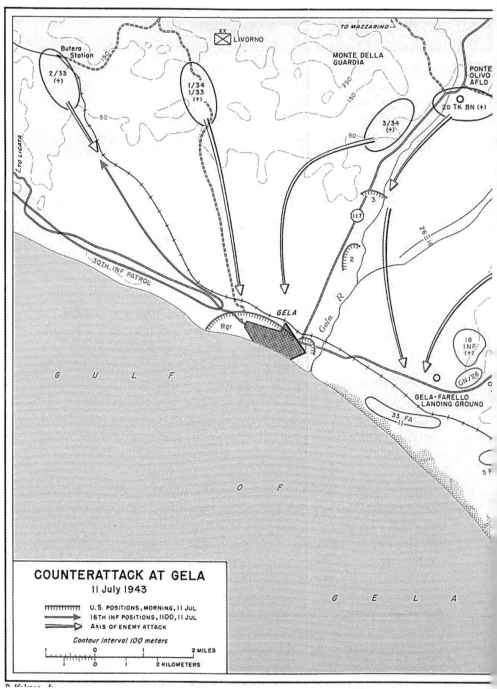

Map 8: Counterattack at Gela. Reproduced from Garland and Smyth, *Sicily and the Surrender of Italy*, Map V.

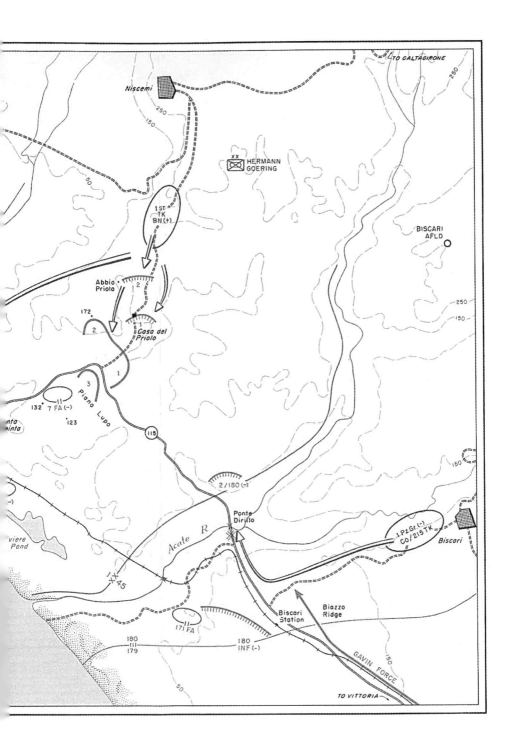

TO CALTAGIRONE

Niscemi

250

150

HERMANN
GOERING

BISCARI
AFLD

1ST
TK
BN(+)

Abbio
Priolo   2

172·
2   Casa del
               Priolo

250
150

3
132· 7 FA (-)   1
nta
inta   ·123   Piano Lupo

115

2/180 (-)

150

Ponte
Dirillo

1 PzGr(-)
CO/215TK   Biscari

viere
Pond   Acate R

1 X 45

Biazzo
Ridge

171 FA

Biscari
Station

GAVIN FORCE

150

180   180
111   INF (-)
179

50

TO VITTORIA

important objective. On July 10 that meant operating with the 26th Infantry as it supported Darby's ersatz regimental combat team. Allen operated at his advanced CP, worked alongside Stan Mason and the staff to sustain the fight while also keeping II Corps aware of the situation on the 1st ID beaches. Allen also sent repeated requests to land the tanks identified to support the division as well as his artillery. The G-2 journals reflect what Allen heard from II Corps, his own units, shore parties, and adjacent units. From sight, sound, and hearing within his CP, he developed a perception of the battle, as did Bradley and Patton. Seeing the battle from message traffic and phone calls shows that Allen had clarity on the situation in Gela and with the 26th Infantry. The situation was less clear near Piano Lupo and along the boundary with the 45th ID.[45]

Like Allen, Patton expected to encounter more Axis armor. To deal with that, he committed both the floating reserve and Major General Hugh Gaffey's 2nd Armored Division (AD), less one combat command. Gaffey's remaining two combat commands and the 18th Infantry began landing in the 1st ID zone. The threat to the beachhead was clear, given the absence of any American tanks or tank destroyers. Bradley visited Allen's CP on the beach, arriving during the converging, albeit uncoordinated, Axis armor attacks. He asked, "Do you have it in hand, Terry?" Allen replied, "Yes, I think so," but added that they would "have a helluva' time stopping [the Axis tanks] until we get some anti-tank stuff ashore."[46]

Allen and Bradley both expected another counterattack by Italian and German armor. The question was when, not whether. The corps commander also watched Teddy Roosevelt clearing the way to get one of the cannon companies ashore to provide additional antitank resources. Roosevelt visited each of the six beaches assigned to 1st ID, found two mined, and closed them, further inhibiting, or at least slowing, the landing of more troops.[47]

Crisis on the Beaches

Wind, beach conditions, and continuous air bombardment made getting equipment and men ashore difficult and dangerous on July 10 and 11. Donald J. Hunt bore witness to perhaps the worst incident on Husky's D-Day. Hunt, a sixteen-year-old sailor serving on a Higgins boat assigned to LST 313, watched "with horror" the destruction of his ship. The 33rd FA lost twenty-seven killed or wounded, as well as equipment, with LST 313. When 313 went down, so too did all of the antitank guns belonging to the 26th Infantry. In addition, two of the 33rd's howitzers went to the bottom when the DUKWs carrying them sank. To compound matters further, the battalion headquarters was put ashore two miles from their assigned beach. It had not been a great day for the 33rd. Yet most of the division did get ashore, and the Rangers held Gela. The 26th was adjacent, and the 16th had reached Piano Lupo, nearly four miles inland.[48]

Perceptions and behavior in the Big Red One showed a marked difference from the landings in North Africa and the long and difficult campaign in Tunisia. Little things showed in the behavior of the troops and their leadership. Perhaps most important, the division had grown from the post-Tunisia hubris played out in the streets of Oran to sober confidence. John T. Corley with the division since before the war and a newly promoted Lieutenant Colonel described the change succinctly: "We were a different Army after Kasserine. And then when we went into Sicily there was all the difference in the World." He believed the division fought "with a lot of push and drive. And it was push and drive that we gained from North Africa."[49]

Experience manifested itself in several ways. Reports and orders from the Sicilian campaign reflect improved estimates. Short, clear situation reports accompanied by an overlay of positions demonstrate that the 1st ID understood that contiguous front lines, nearly standard in the Great War, no longer applied or were even feasible. Very short orders accompanied by an overlay reflected common understanding born of practice; so few words suffice only if some tactical functions are reduced to standard operating procedures, as automatic as drills.[50]

John Finke demonstrated growth as an officer and confidence on D-Day. As the headquarters commandant of the 16th Infantry, he chose Taylor's command-post locations. A brigadier general he did not know arrived with Major General Matthew B. Ridgway. Finke found Ridgway friendly and courteous, but the brigadier disparaged the location of the command post and made unflattering remarks about Colonel Taylor on that basis. Finke confronted the general and advised that he had chosen the location based on criteria he learned at the Infantry School. Trivial perhaps, but an exemplar of confidence. Finke believed he knew his job and preferred to take credit for his choices rather than have his commander's name sullied.[51]

In response to Patton's order to land the reserve, Colonel Smith's 18th Infantry began landing in the middle of the night. High surf and the presence of false beaches/sandbars prevented the LCIs carrying the bulk of the 18th Infantry from reaching the shoreline, so the infantry and their equipment had to be shuttled ashore in smaller craft. Friction produced by currents and confusion caused one LCI to deposit its load of seasick soldiers some twelve miles east of the assigned beach, well into the 45th ID's beachhead.

Between 0030 and 0600 on the morning of 11 July, the 18th Infantry came ashore. Ten medium tanks landed to support the division but then could not cross the soft sand. With the exception of the tanks and Colonel I. D. White's command post, Combat Command B, 2nd AD, did not get ashore that night.[52]

At 2000 on July 10, Guzzoni issued orders for XVI Corps to counterattack to reduce the British beachhead, using the Napoli Division and Kampfgruppe Schmalz. That evening Conrath was called to the corps command post, where he learned that his division had been subordinated to XVI Corps. Rossi, the corps commander, ordered Generale di Divisione Domenico Chirieleison, commanding the Livorno Division, and Conrath to mount a coordinated attack to retake Gela and reduce the American beachhead at 0600 the following morning.[53]

Rossi's plan featured a feint on Gela by a few tanks from Conrath's Panzer regiment, with a tank-heavy Kampfgruppe attacking the beachhead across the Gela plain. A second tank-heavy Kampfgruppe would attack south through Piano Lupo and then roll up the American beachhead from its eastern flank. The Livorno Division would attempt the same from the west. Conrath had fired both commanders who led the attack on July 10 and organized three Kampfgruppen, each with both tanks and Panzergrenadiers. His infantry-heavy Kampfgruppe would come down the eastern bank of the Acate River and then attack to join the main effort at Piano Lupo. Then, in the early morning hours, Guzzoni changed the plan. Now, if Conrath had success, he was to turn to the east and flank both the 45th ID and the British beachheads, leaving the Livorno Division to cope with the 1st ID. The infantry-heavy Kampfgruppe would turn and seize high ground near the village of Biscari to secure the flank.[54]

At sunset on July 10 the 1st ID had reached positions that ran east from a point some three miles north of Gela. From there, the "front" extended to the Acate River and the boundary with the 45th ID. Darby and his Rangers were in and around Gela, Bowen and the 26th on Darby's right, and Taylor's 16th on Bowen's right. Allen's command post moved up the same highway and tucked in behind the 16th, adjacent to the road. Roosevelt, with a small "liaison team," spent the night with the 26th, where he could work with Darby and Bowen as needed. Thus both generals could "see" the battlefield along the major avenues of approach into the beachhead. When the 18th Infantry came ashore, it took positions adjacent to Highway 115 southwest of Piano Lupo. That first night passed peacefully.[55]

Terry Allen's concern about another armored counterattack perhaps stimulated him to attempt a preemptive attack that might inhibit an Axis effort, or even forestall it. Allen also needed to generate some depth, and he had not taken the airfield at Ponte Olivo. In his memoir, Bradley argues that this attack was ill advised and occurred at Patton's behest, claiming that Patton had harangued an exhausted Allen about not having taken the airfield. That might be so, though there is no record of such an encounter in the division journal, and Patton did not go ashore on D-Day. Attacking at night, or at least predawn, had become *comme d'habitude* in the 1st ID. And Allen was nothing if not aggressive. In any case, the 26th and 16th attacked at midnight. Corley's 3rd Battalion, 26th Infantry, attacked up Highway 117 toward Ponte Olivo. About three miles south of the airfield, they were stopped cold by German tanks and Panzergrenadiers. Now Corley went on the defense astride the highway. The 2nd Battalion, commanded by Derrill M. Daniel, assumed a defensive position a mile south of the 3rd Battalion.

Colonel Crawford's 2nd Battalion, 16th Infantry, got as far as Abbio Priolo, north of Piano Lupo on the Niscemi road. Charles J. Denholm's 1st Battalion, 16th Infantry, seized Casa del Prio, a mile south of the 2nd Battalion. At 0400 the 16th Infantry reported "confused fighting." Like the 26th, they had "found" one of Conrath's Kampfgruppen. Company G, 2nd Battalion, 16th Infantry, withdrew without orders, uncovering the first battalion. Crawford, supported by paratroopers, drove ahead. The infantry of two separate regiments in two different divisions together took the high ground at Abbio Priolo, overlapping the Niscemi road. There the attack ground to a halt; the 1st ID had come in contact with two of the Panzer-heavy Kampfgruppen. At 0600 division issued a veiled warning, veiled in the sense that no specific intelligence accompanied it. Later the division asked the 16th to report the status of its antitank guns, as no tanks or tank destroyers had yet been unloaded. At 0700 the 16th reported that it had four of its 57-millimeter guns at regiment and some others within the battalions. The 26th Infantry still had none. The division was now fully alert.[56]

Soon thereafter, the Italians and Germans made their appearance. Soldiers in Corley's 3rd Battalion, 26th Infantry, observed two tanks reconnoitering to their front. Allen's concern was being realized. At 0900 he ruminated about what to do and issued a warning order to the 18th Infantry to be prepared to act "as buffer to surprise the Germans," enabling the 16th Infantry to "atk [attack] them on the flank." Immediately after that conversation, the G-3 helpfully advised, "Tk atk coming your way, alert your men. Give them all you got." Great idea, but with no tanks, all they had might well prove insufficient.[57]

Once again unable to communicate with the Livorno Division, Conrath attacked at 0615, preceded by air and artillery support. The Italian infantry battalion on Conrath's right flank moved out when they saw their allies attack. Axis aircraft supported the corps-level attack by pounding Allied positions, ships, and amphibious craft throughout the day. By contrast, the Allied air forces flew just one mission in support of Patton's ground troops. D+1 proved to be a long day. Allen's assertion that the division would have a "helluva time stopping them" proved all too accurate.[58]

The XVI Corps attack developed into six more or less coordinated thrusts. The Livorno Division attacked on three axes with four truck-mounted infantry battalions, supported by light tanks and supporting arms. Two columns aimed to retake Gela, with the easternmost column aimed at the beachhead. Conrath attacked with all three Kampfgruppen, the westernmost headed south toward Gela. Conrath's center Kampfgruppe continued south on the Niscemi road. His easternmost infantry Kampfgruppe, formed on a Panzergrenadier battalion, reinforced by a company of Mark VI Tiger tanks, attacked inside the 45th ID sector, close to the thinly defended seam with 1st ID. Conrath tasked that Kampfgruppe to protect his eastern flank. The Panzergrenadiers and tanks of that Kampfgruppe encountered Jim Gavin and a handful of paratroopers defending the Biazza Ridge, near the town of Biscari. That Gavin, the regimental commander, fired a bazooka from within ten feet of a Tiger indicates just how badly things were going. Worse still, the rocket bounced off the Tiger's steel hide. The Germans stopped only because they had reached their objective. From there they blazed away at the paratroopers all day, and with good effect.[59]

Conrath's center Kampfgruppe, southbound on the Niscemi road, aimed at Taylor's 2nd Battalion, intending to hit hard enough to enable a rapid bypass. The battalion slowed the attacking Germans but could not prevent them from flowing around the infantry on both sides. The majority of this column sheared off to the southwest, across the plain toward the beach. The sole battery of the 7th FA ashore banged away over open sights with their 105-millimeter howitzers. During the day four howitzers fired 561 rounds, "mostly at tanks."[60]

Just before 0700 Roosevelt spoke with Allen, saying, "Terry, look, the situation is not very comfortable out here." At this point Roosevelt had not yet seen the expected German attack developing. He was still thinking about taking the airfield, but he also knew there were German tanks between it and the 26th. He gave Allen a rough trace of Corley's front and argued that to take the airfield, they had to have medium tanks. None were available yet, and the 26th had no antitank guns. Roosevelt's perception soon changed as Conrath's right-hand Kampfgruppe hit Corley's battalion a glancing blow as it headed south. When that occurred, Roosevelt spoke succinctly, if profanely, with Stan Mason about getting tanks forward. Allen was en route to the developing crisis at Gela. Roosevelt was no longer thinking offensively but instead about being overrun, telling him, "God damn it, I'll come back and pull those tanks out myself." And he meant it, saying he would return "as the situation becomes clarified." But neither Allen nor Mason could do anything other than move what few antitank assets they had. At 1000 hours, the 18th Infantry reported forty tanks on the Gela plain, and still no US tanks had cleared the beach.[61]

Patton came ashore at 0930 in full regalia, including his ubiquitous pair of ivory-handled pistols, riding boots, and jodhpurs, as pukka sahib as a Victorian cavalryman in India. He went into Gela, where he met Darby, who was directing mortar fire on one of the Italian columns. Patton asked for Darby to point out the counterattack, to which the Ranger commander replied, "Which one do you want to see?" From the second floor of the Ranger command post, Patton could see for himself the attacks by Livorno Division's infantry, supported by tanks. The army commander encouraged the naval gunfire officer "to drop some shell fire on the road." That officer needed no stimulus, as he had the USS *Savannah* working the Italians over. Soon after, Patton departed, but not without telling Captain James B. Lyle to "kill every one of the goddam bastards." The *Savannah* savaged the Italians, shooting nearly five hundred 6-inch rounds at them.[62]

Patton continued his tour, his column of three vehicles, including a "command-car with a three-star general's flag," narrowly avoiding mortar rounds fired by Ralph Uffner's mortar platoon. He "stood the mortars down and examined the column" as it reversed course, seeing "the livid face General George Patton Jr. looking in my direction." Uffner and his weapons company of 1st Battalion, 26th Infantry, were where they should have been and doing their job. In this instance, Uffner's mortars were shooting their "sheaf" to "determine the spread" after registering a target. Patton, for all his bluster, was not the man to seek revenge for his own error, so Uffner continued about his business.[63]

By late morning the center and western German Kampfgruppen had gotten past both of Allen's forward regiments but had not reached the beach. Darby, elements of the 26th Infantry, and the US Navy stopped the Italian contingents about noon. A company-sized combat patrol from the 3rd ID played a hand in the fight as well. After stopping the Italians, Rangers rounded up some four hundred dazed Italian survivors of the failed attack. According to Captain Lyle, "There were human bodies hanging from trees and some blown to bits." Things did not go as well in the 16th. Charles J. Denholm, captured and then freed in Tunisia, was wounded seriously while manning an antitank gun. The medics evacuated him "despite protest." Denholm's executive officer, Major Edmund F. Driscoll, took command. Soon after, Taylor ordered his troops to hold fast, saying, "Under no circumstances will anyone be pulled back." Accepting that some enemy tanks would get through, he added, "Don't let anything else get through."[64]

The 16th fought hard, but despite Taylor's order it slowly withdrew toward Piano Lupo. Around noon, Taylor reported to Allen, "We are being overrun by tanks. In Crawford's area [2nd Battalion] the enemy has ten tanks in front of the Battalion and ringed them with an additional thirty. We have no idea what is going on east of us. The 3rd Battalion is covering main road [Highway 115 at Piano Lupo]." Crawford had not exaggerated. Captain Edward F. Wozenski described the conundrum of fighting tanks with none of your own: "A tank went over my foxhole. But then it seemed to me tanks went over almost everyone's foxhole." His company, Company E of the 16th, did not bolt. Wozenski said his "boys were shooting pistols, rifles, tommy guns and bazookas and throwing grenades," admitting ruefully that "some of the men ran off when the tanks came in. I wanted to take off too, but then my men were looking at me and I couldn't run."[65]

Soon after that, the 33rd FA joined the fight, and according to Captain John B. Kemp of the 18th Infantry demonstrated "a beautiful exhibition of direct fire." Kemp claimed the artillery destroyed fourteen German tanks. The 18th Infantry, the division's command-post defense platoon, the 106th Coast Artillery, the 531st Engineer Shore Regiment, the 5th FA, and the 26th Infantry all played a role in the close fight. The 1st Battalion, 41st Armored Infantry Battalion (AIB), from 2nd AD did as well.[66]

At the height of the crisis, Allen joined the 18th Infantry, where he found Roosevelt also drawn to the critical point. A staff officer wondered aloud whether they should pull back. Don Whitehead, an associated press correspondent who was at the CP, described what happened next. Allen, channeling John Paul Jones, exclaimed "Pull back? Hell! We haven't begun to fight. They haven't reached the beach yet." Then he announced, "We attack tonight at ten o'clock." Seeing surprise on the faces around him, he explained, "It's like this. We will stop this attack. We'll break it up, and that will be the psychological time attack. It's good tactics."[67] (In the end, as it happened, the attack would take place at midnight.)

Four of the ten 2nd AD tanks that had been stuck in the sand finally crossed the beach. Combat Command B, 2nd AD, commander Colonel I. D. White sent them and part of the 32nd FA up to Highway 115, where they too got into the fight. At 1330 Roosevelt appeared in the 16th Infantry command post to tell Taylor four tanks were on the way. "We have them licked," Roosevelt opined, but then called the G-3, saying that "many more were sorely needed." When additional tanks became available, White ordered them into the fight as well. One of White's officers asked what the plan was. Colonel White, not given to hysteria, replied, "Plans hell! This may be Custer's last stand." The German attack finally stalled under a hail of fire of all kinds. In midafternoon the Germans began to withdraw, leaving a goodly number of hulks behind. Just how many is unclear; the US Army official history estimates at least twenty-six, and perhaps as many as forty-five. The number is uncertain because the Germans recovered some of the damaged ones. Of the seventeen Tiger tanks employed in the 45th ID zone, the Americans dispatched ten of them by various means.[68]

During the latter stages of the fight, Allen and his operations officer, Lieutenant Colonel Frederick W. Gibb, visited the 16th Infantry to hear Taylor's assessment and ask how they could help. On their way back to the CP, they encountered Patton, whose entourage had grown to include tanks. Patton was "very 'wrought up' " because the division had not taken the airfield at Ponte Olivo, "scheduled to be taken on 'D+1.'" Allen, though his original plan to attack at ten o'clock had been pushed back at some point, reminded the army commander that D+1 would not end until midnight, and that the 1st ID would attack at that very time. Furthermore, he insisted, "the attack would go, 'Come hell or high water.' "[69]

Plenty more happened that afternoon and evening. At 1540 a German air raid of at least twenty bombers appeared overhead and did considerable damage. Several bombs hit the Liberty ship SS *Robert Rowan*, which was loaded with 18th Infantry equipment, about four hundred troops, and tons of ammunition. Fortunately the navy got the troops and sailors off the *Robert Rowan* before it blew up. The wreck settled in shallow water, and the structure left above the surface burned for hours, sending up a huge pall of smoke. The 18th Infantry lost more than sixty wheeled vehicles when the ship blew up.[70]

One more horrific event occurred later that evening. Although the ground troops ashore allegedly knew that the 504th PIR (minus its third battalion), arriving from Tunis, would make an administrative jump onto the Gela plain to reinforce the engaged forces, the navy received the warning at 1740.

Orders warning the ships were received soon after. At 2150 the largest air raid of the day began, an attack that did not abate until 2300. As the enemy bombing abated, 114 C-47s carrying the 504th began arriving overhead. Just who in the anchorage fired first is not known, but twenty-three of the Allied transports were either shot down by Americans or hit by German bombs. Ralph Uffner, who watched the tragedy unfold, observed, "We on the ground were horrified at the carnage."[71]

Back on the Attack

True to his word, Allen ordered his tired soldiers back on the attack at midnight. Along with the order, he announced his intention to "sock the hell out of those damned Heines, before they can hit us again." During the evening before the attack, the division learned from the chief of the Niscemi carabinieri that the Germans intended to withdraw. Local farmers made the same claim. Indeed, that was so, as Guzzoni, who wanted the Herman Göring Division to move northward and assemble at Caltagirone to be committed against the British, did order XVI Corps to cease its attack. Apropos of German-Italian collaboration, Frido von Senger und Etterlin, the German liaison to Guzzoni and senior German Army officer in Sicily, still believed success possible and ordered Conrath to attack east into the 45th ID. Conrath was inclined to agree until he learned of the beating his infantry Kampfgruppe had taken at the hands of Gavin's paratroopers. Conrath decided to do as Guzzoni and XVI Corps preferred, and retire in stages.[72]

Despite what the 1st ID heard from Italians, there was no physical evidence to support their assertions. On the contrary, the 16th Infantry repulsed an attack in the later afternoon and battled with Axis patrols throughout the night. Not surprisingly, the leadership remained concerned that the Livorno Division and Conrath's tanks might yet reappear. At midnight the division attack got underway, with Darby's ersatz regiment heading north along a secondary road toward Butera. The 26th Infantry (including 3rd Battalion, 18th Infantry), reinforced with a company of tanks, headed up Highway 117, bent on seizing the airfield. The 16th fought its way north along the Niscemi road. The division's post action summary exulted, claiming that "by 3:30 AM, July 12th the division attack was rolling along in high gear, with an *upsurge* of *combat morale* [italics in original]."[73]

When the sun came up, Darby's Rangers held positions astride the road to Buter, some five miles north of Gela. Colonel Bowen, in the 26th Infantry, used his main body to seize high ground just west and overlooking the airfield, while the 3rd Battalion, 18th Infantry, took the airfield itself. Attacking

against the bulk of the Herman Göring Division, the 16th did not take Niscemi until the following day. Lieutenant Colonel Robert H. York's 1st Battalion, 18th Infantry, supported by 2nd AD tanks, fended off three Panzer
counterattacks against the right flank of the division.[74]

General Alexander's lack of confidence notwithstanding, Patton's Seventh
Army, II Corps, and the 1st ID had done all that had been asked of them and
more. Alexander and Montgomery intended that US troops would protect
the flank of the main effort, Eighth Army. Allen's regiments had withstood
two days of counterattacks from XVI Corps' Italian and German troops. Despite obsolete tanks and truck-borne infantry, the Italians had pressed their
attacks bravely, with at least as much courage as their German counterparts.
Frido von Senger und Etterlin observed that "Italian soldiers are neither better nor worse than the soldiers of any other nation," and no less a personage
than Generalfeldmarschall Rommel found occasion to praise them. Italians
had showed guts under the horrific condition of Alpine fighting in the Great
War. Often badly led, and always badly equipped, some of the troops folded,
but they deserve better than they get in many histories and almost all casual
discussion. German troops, on the other hand, are routinely credited with
herculean achievement under horrible conditions.[75]

For their part the American troops, including those of the 1st ID, Gavin's
paratroopers, and the rookie 45th ID, demonstrated tactical acumen and
initiative on July 10 and 11. Some wearing the Big Red One shoulder
patch panicked on Longstop Hill and at Kasserine Pass. At El Guettar they
demonstrated what disciplined, well-led infantry could achieve, even if only
supported by under gunned though bravely fought half-track-mounted
75-millimeter tank destroyers. The doughboys' confidence in their leaders
showed with their stubborn refusal to give up or run on July 10 and 11. Bazookas in the hands of the infantry, howitzers firing over open sights, and
US Navy gunfire won the day on the Gela plain. Even Bradley, despite his
disdain for Allen and Roosevelt, acknowledged the division's excellence. Not
long after the war, he asked "whether any other US division could have repelled that charge in time to save the beach from penetration." But then he
answered his own question: "Only the perverse Big Red One with its no less
perverse commander was both hard and experienced enough to take that
assault in stride."[76]

Generalleutnant Conrath, chagrined by the performance of his troops,
lashed out at them in a letter published for their benefit on July 12, 1943: "I
had the bitter experience to watch scenes, during these last few days, which
are not worthy of a German soldier particularly not a soldier of the Panzer

Division Herman Göring." Conrath's assessment of his soldiers went downhill from there. Don Whitehead, who covered the British Eighth Army in the fall and winter of 1942 and 1943, reported on the 1st ID during the campaign in Sicily. He recorded his observations on combat and combat leadership in his diary. Of the 1st ID he wrote, "Watching Allen and Roosevelt at work, along with their staff, I began to understand why the First was recognized as the greatest fighting outfit in the American Army at the time. These men [including the staff] formed an inspired team and they had the trick of inspiring those who fought with them." Soldier historian Carlo D'Este quoted a verse from "Song of the Fighting First" that captures what happened on the Gela plain:

> The Panzers came with all their tanks
> and thought we were sunk.
> Bazookas, guts and one-oh-fives
> Turned them into junk.[77]

Notes

1. Howe, *Northwest Africa*, 654–65. On casualties see table 5, 675. On nonbattle casualties and disease, see also Porch, *Path to Victory*, 411–14. According to Porch, the Italian High Command promoted Messe on May 12, 1943. His concluding chapter, "The Pivotal Theater," is essential to understanding the strategic value of the Mediterranean Theater. The campaign did irreversible damage to Germany, weakened Hitler's principal ally, and aided materially the Soviet effort in the east. Playfair and Molony, *Destruction of the Axis Forces*, 460, reports 238,000 Axis prisoners.

2. Howe, *Northwest Africa*, 667. The 15th Army Group activated July 10, 1943.

3. Baumgartner et al., *16th Infantry*, 33. This remarkable little book was written and edited by John W. Baumgartner, Al de Poto, William Fraccio, and Samuel Fuller. De Poto and Fraccio reflect the New York Italian connection with the 16th Infantry; Hollywood producer, screenwriter and novelist Fuller represents the draftees who came from all over America. Fuller turned down the opportunity to serve as an army journalist to serve in the infantry. See Fuller, *A Third Face*, 109.

4. The Normandy operation grew far larger than Sicily during the expansion of the lodgment. The argument here is based on the initial landings.

5. Mason, "Reminiscences," 95.

6. Mason, 95; Raphael L. Uffner, "Recollections of World War II with the First Infantry Division," n.d., MRC 1997.98, 305; Astor, *Terrible Terry Allen*, 185. Hughes, head of the US Army's North African Theater, served as Eisenhower's deputy commander. Eisenhower, *Papers*, no. 811, 2:945; Bradley, *Soldier's Story*, 110. There are numerous references to contretemps in interviews, surveys, and memoirs of 1st ID veterans.

7. Finke, *No Mission Too Difficult*, 122–23; Mason, "Reminiscences," 36.

8. Bradley, *Soldier's Story*, 109–10. Bradley damns both Allen and Roosevelt in his memoir as good soldiers, effective leaders but poor disciplinarians. His argument is weakened by his desire to have the poorly discipline 1st ID on his troop list.

9. Mason, "Reminiscences," 96–97; Blumenson, *Patton Papers*, 2:272.

10. Fuller, *A Third Face*, 122. Veterans interviews, surveys and memoirs are replete with accounts of accepting the need to kill and above all to learn.

11. Clausewitz, *On War*, 187. Clausewitz did distinguish between military virtues in "regular" armies and what he called "natural qualities of a people mobilized for war," 188.

12. HQ, Allied Force, Eisenhower Report on "Torch," n.d., N7290, CARL, 48; Fuller, *A Third Face*, 123.

13. Uffner, "Recollections," 308.

14. *Encyclopaedia Britannica* articles accessed at https://www.britannica.com, December 20, 2020. The author also consulted several veterans' associations, including the USS Landing Craft Infantry National Association at usslci.org, December 20, 2020, and the LST 325 Memorial at https://lstmemorial.org, December 20, 2020. LST 325 landed troops in Sicily, Salerno, and Normandy, and is now moored in Evansville, Indiana, where she was built. Morrison, *Sicily–Salerno–Anzio*, 30–33. Re LCMs, see http://www.ibiblio.org/hyperwar/USN/ships/ships-slc.html. The LCMs used in Sicily were first-generation; the next generation of LCMs were fifty-six feet long.

15. On turbulence at regiment and battalion, see Knickerbocker et al., *Danger Forward*, 409–12. Re Greer, see Eisenhower, *Papers*, no. 1007, 2:1143. In that same message he proposed promoting Clift Andrus as well. Greer was promoted on June 3, 1943. He returned to the United States, where he became assistant division commander of the 79th Infantry Division, and served with it until the end of the war. Kingseed, *Omaha Beach to Dawson's Ridge*, 83.

16. On the availability of shipping, see Coakley and Leighton, *Global Logistics*, 33–41.

17. Morrison, *Two-Ocean War*, 247. Re Patton and Hewitt, see Morrison, *Sicily–Salerno–Anzio*, 22. Morrison believed Lieutenant General Carl "Tooey" Spaatz called the shots as commander of the North African Air Forces (Allied Air Forces). Patton blamed the British generally and air chief marshal Sir Arthur W. Tedder in particular. Perhaps what is most indicative is that while the British placed an air vice marshal in support of Montgomery, Spaatz provided Colonel L. P. Hickey to Patton.

18. Both Montgomery's admission and the quotation from the official history are as cited in Ambrose, *Supreme*, 209.

19. Garland and Smyth, *Sicily*, 89–93. On details of the Seventh Army plan, see 96–105. On air operations planning, see 105–11. See also Molony, *Campaign in Sicily*, 32–36. Molony does not address the squabble between the air and ground forces for the obvious reason that the British official histories were "all services," or joint.

20. D'Este, *Bitter Victory*, appendix B, 585–89. The 18th INF, with two platoons of tanks from Company I, 67th Armored Regiment, 2nd AD attached, comprised the floating reserve and went by the code name "Kool Force." HQ, 2nd AD, "Historical Record—Operations of the US Second Armored Division (Kool Force)," August 5, 1943, R11274.1, CARL, 2.

21. Warlimont, *Inside Hitler's Headquarters*, 319–31. Hitler's quotation is at 326. See Boatner, *Biographical Dictionary*, 268, 391–92, for biographies of Keitel and Neurath.

22. Garland and Smyth, *Sicily*, 27–51.

23. Garland and Smyth, 75–87; Kesselring, *A Soldier's Record*, 189–95.

24. Garland and Smyth, *Sicily*, 75–87.

25. 1st ID, "Sicily General," in RG 301-2.10: G-2 Terrain Study, May 1943. The Sicily study is not paginated. The map showing the mountainous topography of Sicily is numbered 89 by pencil.

26. HQ, 1st ID, "A Factual Account of the Combat Operations of the 1st Infantry Division in N. Africa and Sicily during World War II," n.d., MRC 1988.31, 33–34; Knickerbocker et al., *Danger Forward*, 411–12, 424–27. Attachments ranged from additional medical support to the 2637th QM Battalion (TRK[truck]) DUKWS. The perspective sketches were almost certainly done by Ensign Edouard Sandoz, UNSR. Most were focused on the beaches just west of Gela and so of only general interest to 1st ID. Sketches of coastal batteries were of even greater interest. Morrison, *Sicily–Salerno–Anzio*, 22. See also Garland and Smyth, *Sicily*, 83–84; Darby and Baumer, *We Led the Way*, 85.

27. 1st ID, "Sicily General." Most of the products in the G-2 Terrain Study came from either the Allied Force Headquarters or, for 1st ID beaches, the US Navy. Garland and Smyth, *Sicily*, 99–100.

28. 1st ID, "Sicily General," order of battle map, intelligence notes, no. 6, July 3, 1943. The notes include a map entitled "Disposition of Italian Forces as Known 30 May 1943." The field divisions had not moved.

29. Morrison, *Sicily–Salerno–Anzio*, remains the best source on naval operations in support of Husky. Re embarkation, see Knickerbocker et al., *Danger Forward*, 102.

30. Holland, *Sicily '43*, 132.

31. Garland and Smyth, *Sicily*, 115–19; Atkinson, *Day of Battle*, 76. See also Ridgway, *Soldier*, 68.

32. Lawrence P. Manley, "26th Infantry History," MRC 2005.144, 52. The 26th named their team the Seaton Scout Force after their commander, Lieutenant Seton. Baumgartner et al., *16th Infantry*, 34. The 45th ID sailed in June from the United States.

33. Baumgartner et al., *16th Infantry*, 38.

34. Multiple sources report an impressive light show of different colors of tracers and searchlights illuminating the beaches. See Baumgartner et al., *16th Infantry*, 34–35; 1st ID, G-3 journal, July 10, 1943, in RG 301-3.2: G-3 Journal and File, Sicilian Campaign, 1st Infantry Division, 1 Jul 43–13 Aug 43, MRC Digital Archives; Atkinson, *Day of Battle*, 98.

35. Baumgartner et al., *16th Infantry*, 38. USS *Savannah* (CL-42) was a Brooklyn-class light cruiser armed with fifteen 6-inch guns in five 3-gun turrets. The author's father served on the USS *Brooklyn* (CL-40) and remembered with pride that he shared a battle station with Samuel Eliot Morrison. *Savannah*'s sister ship the USS *Boise* (CL 47) also supported the 1st ID landing. For Brooklyn class, see https://www.naval-encyclopedia.com/ww2/us/brooklyn-class-cruisers.

36. Mason, "Reminiscences," 53–54; Knickerbocker et al., *Danger Forward*, 102–3; G-3 journal, Sicilian campaign, July 10, 1943.

37. Whitehead, *Combat Reporter*, 162.

38. First contact was by radio, but Gavin himself was reported visiting the forward line of the 16th at 1708. Re Gavin's first day in combat, see Gavin, *On to Berlin*, 24–34. He makes no specific mention of encountering the 16th, but his visit is recorded in the journal. Holland, *Sicily '43*, 215–17.

39. G-3 journal, Sicilian campaign, July 10, 1943, entries 13, 18.

40. D'Este, *Bitter Victory*, 195–204 and 248–53. See also Garland and Smyth, *Sicily*, ch. 2, "The Axis on the Defensive." In a note on page 253, D'Este quoted Kesselring's OB South war diary, which reports that paratroops had delayed units and were the cause of "considerable casualties." See Garland and Smyth, *Sicily*, 147–48, for Axis communications. The Livorno Division formed part of the Sixth Army reserve, but the attack was by the Livorno.

41. For German tank strength, see Garland and Smyth, *Sicily*, 148. For Italian tank strength, see D'Este, *Bitter Victory*, 284. Mark VI tanks were not known as Tigers until 1944. Senger und Etterlin, *Neither Fear Nor Hope*, 131.

42. Senger und Etterlin, *Neither Fear Nor Hope*, 132.

43. Morrison, *Sicily–Salerno–Anzio*, 102–3; Baumer and Reardon, *American Iliad*, 90–91; Baumgartner et al., *16th Infantry*, 39; 1st ID, G-2 journal, July 10, 1943, in RG 301-2.3: G-2 Journal and File, 1st Infantry Division (Sicilian Campaign), 10 Jul 43–23 Jul 43, MRC Digital Archives.

44. D'Este, *Bitter Victory*, 282, 289; Garland and Smyth, *Sicily*, 147–56. The division received multiple reports indicating a counterattack, the first reported by the division artillery at 0835. The 26th Infantry reports came through the G-3. G-2 and G-3 journals, July 10, 1943.

45. The G-2 and G-3 journals, as well as the those of the 16th and 26th Infantries, are the chief source of data for this analysis. For Darby and the Rangers, see Baumer and Reardon, *American Iliad*, 89–90 .

46. Astor, *Terrible Terry Allen*, 199.

47. Astor, 199; Garland and Smyth, *Sicily*, 158.

48. Donald J. Hunt, *USS LST 313 and Battery A—33rd Field Artillery, 26th Regimental Combat Team of the 1st Division* (self-published, 1994), 2–9; HQ, 33rd Field Artillery Battalion, Report of Action, July 10–21, 1943, August 12, 1943, RG 301-FA (33)-0, s, 1.

49. John T. Corley, interview by Michael Corley, March 6, 10, 13 and 20, 1977, Fort Jackson, SC, MRC; Tom Gendron, interview by John F. Votaw, Orlando, FL, August 10, 1995, MRC.

50. Based on the author's comparison of orders and reports in Algeria, Tunisia, and Sicily. Detailed plans and orders with strict timetables remained the standard for motor marches, landings, and timings of any kind. The 1st ID required position reports each day. These were provided by overlay. These documents show positions as ellipses rather than lines.

51. Finke, *No Mission Too Difficult*, 137.

52. HQ, 18th Infantry, after-action report, July 1943, n.d., in RG 301-INF(18)-0.3: Reports of Operations–1st Inf Div (Sicilian Campaign), 1 Jun 43–31 Dec 43, MRC

Digital Archives. Garland claims the 18th was ashore soon after midnight. The regiment's after-action report shows them in position no sooner than 0600. Garland and Smyth, *Sicily*, 198–99.

53. Garland and Smyth, *Sicily*, 164.

54. Garland and Smyth, 161–64.

55. Locations determined from 1:100,000 map and unit reports. See also 1st ID, "Factual Account," 34.

56. G-3 journal, Sicilian campaign, July 11, 1943; Manley, "26th Infantry History," 57.

57. G-3 journal, July 11, 1943.

58. Garland and Smyth, *Sicily*, 164–65.

59. D'Este, *Bitter Victory*, 293–95.

60. D'Este, 296–97; Garland and Smyth, *Sicily*, 166–67. Garland wrote that the 2nd Battalion, 16th Infantry, was attacked from the west by Conrath's right-hand Kampfgruppe. His map 4 suggests otherwise. The author believes the evidence favors the illustration and not what Garland wrote on 166. The attack from the west is more likely by Conrath's right-hand column bypassing the 2nd Battalion and hitting Casa del Priolo from east and west. The 16th's after-action report is not clear about this. The 7th FA does claim the attack came from the west.

61. 26th Infantry journal, July 11, 1943, in RG 301-Inf(26)-0.3: Reports of Operations, 10 Jul–31 Dec 43, MRC Digital Archives. There are contradictory accounts of this conversation. Knickerbocker et al., *Danger Forward*, 105, says that Corley had been penetrated before 0700, but that is not what is recorded in either the G-3 journal or the 26th Infantry journal. This error is repeated in other sources, including Morrison's well-documented work. Garland reports that Company K was driven back, but the battalion was not penetrated. Company K withdrew in good order and interfered with the Italian column advancing on the west side of Highway 117. Garland and Smyth, *Sicily*, 166; for antitank guns, 111.

62. D'Este, *Bitter Victory*, 296; Darby and Baumer, *We Led the Way*, 92.

63. Uffner, "Recollections," 312.

64. Garland and Smyth, *Sicily*, 164–68 and, re Lyle, 170; 1st ID, "Factual Account," 34, 42. Sequence and times are primarily taken from unit journals. There are contradictions between sources, for the understandable reason that a great many things happened at once. Garland and Smyth, *Sicily*, and D'Este, *Bitter Victory*, are the best sources on sequence.

65. G-3 journal, Sicilian campaign, July 11, 1943. The exact time of the Wozenski incident is unknown, but it occurred earlier than the time of Crawford's report. Whitehead, *Combat Reporter*, 161.

66. 1st ID, "Factual Account," 34.

67. Whitehead, *Combat Reporter*, 169. Whitehead, Jack Belden of *Time*, and H. R. Knickerbocker came ashore together and witnessed Allen's assessment alongside the 1st ID staff.

68. 1st ID, "Factual Account," 36; HQ, 16th Infantry, Invasion Journal, Sicily, July 5–16, 1943, 30. This "journal" is a narrative account, and not the US Army record. It is likely the work of Fuller, as much of it appears in Baumgartner et al., *16th Infantry*.

Garland and Smyth, *Sicily*, 171–72 fn. Garland's analysis takes into account US reporting as well as that of the Hermann Göring Division.

69. 1st ID, "Factual Account," 36.

70. Garland and Smyth, *Sicily*, 177.

71. Morrison, *Sicily–Salerno–Anzio*, 119–21. Morrison's account includes the postmortem Eisenhower ordered. It proved impossible or, in the author's opinion, inconvenient to assign blame. It appears that the C-47 stream was also off course; they were not supposed to fly over the invasion fleet. See also D'Este, *Bitter Victory*, 307–9. At 308 D'Este points out that Ridgway visited six antiaircraft crews in the area of the drop zone and learned that five crews knew of the drop, but one did not. Uffner, "Recollections," 313. See Anonymous, "Draft Regimental History," and, for the 504th's operation, Ridgway, *Soldier*, 69–73.

72. 1st ID, "Factual Account," 36; Baumer and Reardon, *American Iliad*, 150; Garland and Smyth, *Sicily*, 172.

73. 1st ID, "Factual Account," 36; Garland and Smyth, *Sicily*, 186–89. The collaboration with Darby and his troops ended soon after. The 16th and 26th Infantry reports each claim a tank company from the 67th Armored Regiment, 2nd AD; Knickerbocker et al., *Danger Forward*, lists only two platoons. The 2nd AD afteraction report lists two platoons each attached to the 16th and 26th Infantries to support the attack planned for midnight. These platoons belonged to Companies G and H of the 67th Armored.

74. Garland and Smyth, 186–89; Baumgartner, *The 16th Infantry Regiment*, 40–44.

75. Senger und Etterlin, *Neither Fear Nor Hope*, 49; Liddell-Hart, *Rommel Papers*, 147, 249, 325, 373.

76. Bradley, *Soldier's Story*, 130; quoted also in D'Este, *Bitter Victory*, 306.

77. D'Este, *Bitter Victory*, 301, epigraph, 290; Whitehead, *Combat Reporter*, 163. The verse is from "Song of the Fighting First."

CHAPTER SEVEN

Troina: The End for Terry and Teddy

We are fighting in the area where Hannibal and Scipio fought.
—*16th Infantry, Invasion Journal, Sicily*

Upon moving to the high ground, we were surrounded on all sides, it
was nerve racking to receive fire from the front and rear.
—*Staff Sergeant Ted Dobol, on Troina*

STAN MASON DESCRIBED the campaign in Sicily as "a hard onerous fight,
from hill top to hill top." He did so with good reason. Lieutenant Colonel
Robert W. Porter Jr.'s Sicily terrain study describes the terrain north of the
Gela plain as "Bold Hills—Strong Relief." The ground transitioned near
Enna, the capital of Sicily, to the Caronie Mountains or, according to the
terrain study, "high relief." At more than ten thousand feet, and not without danger of erupting, Mount Etna towered over the approaches to the real
prize in Sicily—the port city of Messina, fewer than one hundred miles from
the Italian mainland and the only feasible way off the island for Axis forces.
The road network, such as it was, supported east-west movement far better
than it supported movement north.[1]

No one had illusions about the ground. The hills could be seen from the
beaches across the five miles of the plain. Having fended off a nearly fatal
counterattack, the division needed to expand its lodgment. Doing so would
force Axis artillery, especially the particularly effective Italian guns, out of
range of the beaches. That would greatly facilitate the unloading of supplies
and advancing inland. After driving the Axis artillery back, the division
received medium tanks from the 2nd AD's 67th Armored. II Corps also

attached the 70th Tank Battalion (Light), the 91st Cavalry Reconnaissance Squadron, several antiaircraft artillery battalions, and additional artillery. Taking the air field at Ponte Olivo would enable better air support by permitting basing on Sicily. The 1st ID seized the airfield on July 12. Allied air forces deployed eighteen squadrons to that airfield and others in just four days. These included specialized ground-attack aircraft.[2]

As promised, the 1st ID attacked the night of July 11–12, but did not do so until just after midnight. Patton's badgering of Allen on the afternoon of July 11 amounted to an order that bypassed Major General Omar N. Bradley, who was justifiably unhappy. A gap had developed between the 1st and 3rd ID. The corps commander wanted to close it before undertaking a general offensive, to reduce the risk of a German counterattack along that seam. Allen, like Patton, was not worried about the gap, and happily accommodated the army commander. Aggressive, perhaps to a fault, Allen believed that a rapid transition from defending to attacking would surprise the Livorno and Herman Göring Divisions. Alarmed, Bradley inserted part of the 2nd AD to cover the gap. Not given to forgiving, he certainly did not forget Patton's overstepping. Now tension existed between Seventh Army and II Corps. Nor did Allen's enthusiasm for the attack endear him to his corps commander.[3]

The remainder of the campaign unfolded just as Mason said, "hard and onerous." Fighting in mountainous terrain is problematic for any unit. Carl von Clausewitz noted that mountainous terrain allowed the commander "little real command over his scattered units and he [was] unable to control them at all." Successful fighting in the mountains relied on the division's ability to sustain the effort, but platoons and companies would decide the outcome. The division attacked day and night, which led one German soldier to observe to a friend that the Americans "fight all day, attack all night, and shoot all the time." 1st ID fought its way north, usually attacking with two infantry regiments abreast and a third in reserve. They attacked day and night, and sought to envelop the enemy where feasible. Rugged terrain enabled Axis troops to exact a stiff price to take the hilltop towns along Highway 117 and the few other northbound roads in the Big Red One's zone. Once the division reached the village of Gangi, it turned east. From there the "doggies" fought their way along Highway 120 to Troina, which, like most Sicilian towns, sat atop a hill at an intersection of several roads and adjacent to the western slope of Mt. Etna. Any unit maneuvering west of the volcano had to pass through Troina. It attracted the belligerents as surely as light attracts moths.[4]

Allied Assessment and Intentions

The transition from expanding the lodgment to breaking out and pursuing retiring Axis troops is central to understanding the conclusion of the 1st ID's campaign in Sicily. Organized for the first time as the combined arms team the army had intended it to be, the Big Red One would employ tanks, cavalry, a large body of artillery, and even a battalion of rugged Moroccan horse cavalry. Clift Andrus and the division artillery played an outsize role. And for the first time in its combat experience, the Big Red One also enjoyed considerable air support.

There was no meeting to determine the course of action unless Patton's "wrought up" discussion with Allen on July 11 counts as such. Nor was there any need for one. The "plan" required 1st ID to seize the airfield at Ponte Olivo and the town of Niscemi on D+1. Patton, Bradley, and Allen shared a common understanding of the doctrinal requirement to maintain a running or continuing estimate of the situation. All three had graduated from the staff college at Fort Leavenworth, Kansas. Bradley and Allen, having taught at the Infantry School during Marshall's tenure, understood the utility of doctrine in a citizen army. FM 100-5, *Field Service Regulations*, was clear and succinct: "The commander's estimate of the situation is based on the mission of the unit, the means available to him and to the enemy, the conditions in his area of operations including terrain and weather, and the probable effects of various lines of action on future operations." Patton and Allen shared the conviction that 1st ID should attack, and do so immediately. Allen had two goals in mind: to exploit success and maintain contact.[5]

In any case, General Harold R. L. G. Alexander did not revisit his plan, which amounted to adjusting it as matters developed. His general scheme called for the Eighth Army to make the main effort north along the coast to take Messina. In *Alexander of Tunis*, soldier historian W. G. F. Jackson argues that Alexander came to respect the US Army during this campaign. Perhaps so, but that had not yet come to pass, and in the moment he sought to relegate the Americans to holding Montgomery's coat.[6]

That lack of trust manifested itself in an operational directive that created problems and bitterness at II Corps and Seventh Army. Jackson contends that the problem stemmed from the Americans taking the view that "orders are orders," whereas British officers felt free to continue to debate them. Bradley, in *A Soldier's Story*, asserts that in the US Army's "instant compliance" was required. Not so, as FM 100-5 makes it clear that initiative is requisite for effective leaders as well as soldiers. The manual advises commanders to act on the "intentions of the higher commander"; it issues no imperative for anyone to obey instantly and without question. Commanders were to issue "clear and concise orders, which gives them [subordinates] freedom of action appropriate to their professional knowledge, to the situation, to their dependability and to the teamplay desired." That means that in a highly coordinated effort, compliance with specifics should be instant. In practice, officers did debate plans and even orders, depending on the situation. Certainly Patton and Allen did not share Bradley's view that orders required strict adherence and instant obedience.[7]

Meanwhile, Bernard Law Montgomery concluded that Eighth Army needed Highway 124, located in the zone of the 45th ID. Without so much as a by-your-leave, he ordered his XXX Corps to use that highway. Ex post facto, in the spirit of "it's better to ask for forgiveness," General Montgomery sought Alexander's approval. In fact, Montgomery had recognized weeks too late that the road network in his zone would not support maneuvering west of Mount Etna, and that he had too little room to take Messina by moving north along the coastal highway east of the volcano. Patton did not object when Alexander "forgave" Montgomery and assigned him the highway on July 13. Jackson misinterpreted Patton's failure to complain as a cultural artifact, believing that US officers did not argue with their superiors. In fact, Patton believed that Eisenhower was looking for an excuse to fire him, so he did not demur when Alexander conceded that Montgomery could use Highway 24, though doing so forced the 45th ID, which was about to get on the highway, to break contact, maneuver across the 1st ID's rear, and then come up on the left flank of the Big Red One.[8]

Martin Blumenson explains Patton's failure to complain differently than did Jackson. According to Blumenson, "Patton was outraged, but he restrained his temper and practiced cunning." What Blumenson does not mention is Patton's genuine fear that pushing back at the British was good for getting you sent home. Patton was genuinely afraid that Eisenhower could fire him over the airborne tragedy. In any event, he had little interest in the order to protect Montgomery's left flank. He asked Alexander to allow Seventh Army to seize the port town of Agrigento, which lay "beyond the line specified for the front of Seventh Army," twenty-five miles west of Licata, believing that the port there would suffice to supply Seventh Army. That would open up what he really wanted to do, which was to seize Palermo. Patton received permission two days later, when Alexander allowed him to clear out the western half of the island and seize Palermo.[9]

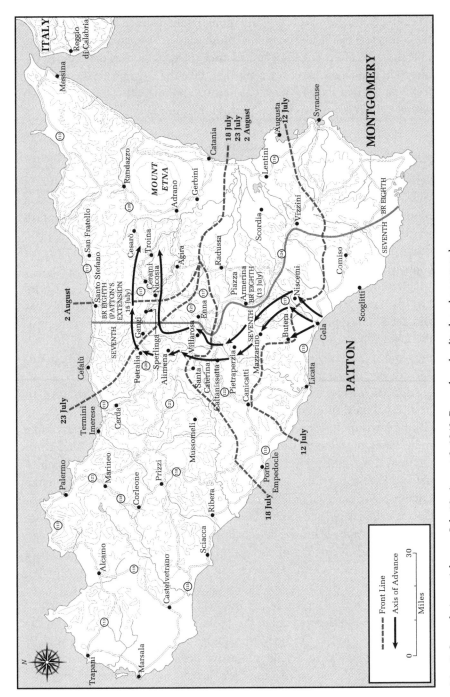

Map 9: Seventh Army Advance, July 12–August 2, 1943. Reproduced, edited, and annotated from the Sicily base map in Garland and Smyth, *Sicily and the Surrender of Italy.*

The tactical echelons of corps, divisions, regiments, and below operated in the context set by the "deliberations" of Alexander, Montgomery, and Patton. Like the gods of the Greeks who had once ruled Sicily, they determined the direction and character of the campaign. Like the Olympians, they periodically intervened in the fate of GIs and Commonwealth "Tommies," often without much thought as to the effect on their minions.

Axis Assessment and Intentions

Guzzoni at the Italian Sixth Army had a more difficult problem than his adversaries. He rightly concluded that the American landings on either side of Gela were more dangerous than the British landings, for precisely the reason Montgomery believed he need Highway 124. Highway 117 from Gela north was the quickest path to Messina on D-Day simply because the Gela plain enabled the Allies to use more than one route north through the rugged country west of Mount Etna.

Guzzoni had played his best card by counterattacking with XVI Corps' Livorno and Herman Göring Divisions, and their defeat led to an immediate and decisive reappraisal. Late on July 12, he issued an order that contained the following assessment: "In view of the situation resulting from the enemy's known advances, it is considered inadvisable for the time being to undertake any further offensive operations."[10]

Guzzoni, however, still believed that a part of Sicily could be retained, so he directed the disposition of his forces accordingly. He ordered the Herman Göring Division to concentrate initially along Highway 124, the very same route Montgomery intended to use, and named the towns of Caltagirone, Grandmichele, and Vizzini as forming the line he wanted the division to defend. The highway ran east through these towns and then southeast to the Catania plain. Guzzoni ordered the Livorno Division to defend the Herman Göring's right flank, and required the rest of XVI Corps, the Napoli Division, and Kampfgruppe Schmalz, detached from the Herman Göring, to defend against the advancing Eighth Army. Finally, he ordered 15th PZG to move east, but retained it as army reserve. Late on July 13, Allied bombers pasted Enna, the site of the Sixth Army's headquarters. Guzzoni moved his headquarters north that night. He repositioned the Assietta Division to block the approach to Palermo but left the Aosta Division in place along with the coastal defense forces. On Sicily all roads led not to Rome but to Messina.[11]

Guzzoni planned to defend successive positions south of Mount Etna while he built the so-called Etna Line farther north. In that scheme, the

Herman Göring Division would defend along the Dittaino River from the coast just south of Catania to the village of Catenanuova some twenty kilometers west. The Livorno Division would defend the center, continuing westward along the river to just northeast of Enna. The 15th PZG would defend on the right of the line, south of Enna.[12]

Frido von Senger und Etterlin, Generalfeldmarschall Albert Kesselring's liason to Guzzoni, generally agreed, but what little trust and comity remained between the Axis partners faded quickly. On July 13, Hitler ordered XIV Corps, commanded by General der Panzertruppen Hans Valentin Hube, to Sicily to assume command of German troops, and announced he would assume personal command in Sicily from his headquarters. By July 15 Kesselring no longer bothered to issue orders through Guzzoni. Hube and his corps headquarters arrived on the island that same day with instructions that required him "unobtrusively to assume overall command of the Sicily Bridgehead himself, cutting out all Italian Headquarters." Guzzoni, then, would be superfluous.[13]

The command arrangements and mutual distrust extended from the top to the bottom. In the conference on May 20, discussed in the previous chapter, Constantin von Neurath, Hitler's adviser on Italian affairs, reported that Sicilians were hostile toward the German troops. German soldiers reported that hostility, which included not only Sicilian civilians but also Italian soldiers. Many German troops, and most of their leaders, believed the poor performance of Italians in general and the coastal defense units in particular made a successful defense of the island unlikely. One soldier, fighting in Sicily, received a letter from a friend in officer training who had fought alongside Italians in Russia and claimed, "I really got to know those Italian 'Shysters,' " adding that he had attended a lecture by an officer who fought with the Italians in Africa who felt as he did. Another soldier's parents wondered in a letter whether the Italians would do their part. Soldiers in Sicily, those who fought with Italians elsewhere, and even the folks at home had doubts about their allies. For that matter, Italian prisoners reported that they did not trust their German "colleagues," and that the Germans felt the same way about them. Cohesion among the Axis forces was not high.[14]

Night Attack July 12, 1943

Shortly after the end of the war, Terry Allen produced a tightly written twenty-one-page manuscript titled "Situation and Operations Report of the First Infantry Division during the Period of Its Overseas Movement, North

African and Sicilian Campaigns, from 8 August 1942 to 7 August 1943," as a contribution to data gathered for the division history *Danger Forward*, published in 1947. Allen had access to the record as well as those papers he kept. His report covered the highlights as he saw them. It is a useful artifact of the tactics he employed during the campaign, and often takes entire phrases from wartime reports. Terry Allen makes no mention in the report of his own role, but his imprint is on everything the division did. Allen operated from his main command post but visited his forward units daily.[15]

Of special interest is Allen's recollection that he used Roosevelt to co-ordinate close-combat operations. He cited the fight at Gela in which the assistant division commander supervised the operations of Darby's rump regiment of Rangers and Colonel John W. Bowen's 26th Infantry. In his account Allen contended that the division's campaign occurred in four phases, starting with the landing on D-Day and concluding with the night attack that began just after midnight on D+3 (July 13). Phase II was the "Advance North to Petralia (13–23 July)"; in Phase III, the division turned and executed the "Advance East from Petralia to Troina (23–30 July)"; and the campaign ended with Phase IV, "The Battle for Troina (30 July–6 August 1943)."[16] Allen accounted for the transition from landing to expanding the lodgment as well as the breakout in Phase III, but the terrain did not permit a genuine exploitation of the breakout. Rather the division fought as Mason had foretold, from hilltop to hilltop.

Although the Allies had the initiative, the Germans and Italians had the advantage of defending heavily mountainous terrain. The 1st Infantry Division, like all of the Allied forces, confronted an "uninterrupted slugging match against stubborn defenders of inaccessible hill tops." Joe Dawson, who left the G-3 to return to the 16th Infantry, spoke for most when he noted, "The hills rise here, and as usual we force our way ever upward. Someday, I hope we shall be able to fight downhill for a change."[17]

According to Allen, the division "picked itself up by its boot-straps and launched an aggressive *coordinated attack at midnight* [of July 12; italics in original], with concentrated artillery and naval gun fire support." This is true, except that approach marches to reach the line of departure began well before midnight for some units. The actual attack got underway fifteen minutes after midnight. There was some blundering around in the dark despite the division's habit of attacking at night. In the era before infrared projectors, let alone passive night vision and ubiquitous thermal imaging systems, getting around in the dark, let alone fighting in it, was very difficult. Nevertheless Darby's Rangers and Bowen's 26th Infantry, with a battalion of the

18th attached, and Taylor's 16th, attacked as planned. The 1st Battalion, 18th Infantry, moved early in the evening of July 11 to cover the gap on the right flank between the 1st ID and Major General Troy Middleton's 45th ID. They were in position by midnight. Shortly thereafter, the Rangers and the 26th moved forward with alacrity against what was characterized as moderate to light resistance, bearing in mind that no resistance is light to those under fire. The Rangers attacked up the Gela-Butera road, while the 26th attacked north along Highway 117.[18]

The Rangers advanced without pause toward Butera, supported by USS *Savannah's* six-inch guns, firing from seven miles away. Darby claimed to have formed his estimate of the town's defenses when he discovered a bottle of cognac abandoned by Italian troops forward of the town; "You don't leave cognac behind unless you are in a hurry," he opined. After he passed the bottle around with the officers in the lead company, the attack continued. The Rangers took Butera before noon on July 12, though despite Darby's estimate, the Italians did not give up without a fight. At 1240 he could report also that he had made contact with the 3rd ID on his left.[19]

The 26th Infantry had less trouble. An Italian strongpoint held up Lieutenant Colonel Ben Sternberg's 2nd Battalion, 18th Infantry, for a short time, but otherwise the 26th advanced against light resistance. Sternberg's infantry reduced the Italian strongpoint at 0400, taking some three hundred prisoners. The 26th took the airfield at Ponte Olivo shortly before noon. Soon after, they repelled a "local" counterattack. During the day, Smith's troops observed the enemy blowing up installations near the airport. From these observations, all concerned drew the obvious conclusion—the Livorno Division would withdraw.[20]

Lieutenant Colonel Joseph B. Crawford's 2nd Battalion, 16th Infantry, mixed it up with both German tanks and Panzergrenadiers, eventually supported by Sherman tanks from the 2nd AD's 67th Armored Regiment. At 0615 Crawford reported, "Jerry tanks cut us off. Lot of tanks ahead." Another voice on the regimental net reported "Messerschmitt 109s dropping bombs on our tanks." To compound the problem, German armor counterattacked south from Niscemi with a body of tanks, including six Mark VI Tigers. None of the 2nd AD supporting tanks had yet reached Crawford.[21]

Lieutenant Colonel Frederick W. Gibb, who had just left as G-3 of the division to command the 7th Field Artillery (FA), reported that "Red [1st Battalion] is ringed by German infantry on 3 sides." Red, with Major Edmond F. Driscoll in command, then sent flash traffic: "Enemy tanks coming. Bn will withdraw." Lieutenant Colonel George A. Taylor, as he had on the

Gela plain, "flashe[d] right back the succinct order: 'Do not withdraw any under cicumstances [sic].' " All of this happened in just under an hour, from 0615 to 0713. The fight wore on with no less excitement throughout the day. Crawford was wounded half an hour after Taylor ordered Driscoll to stand fast. Captain Bryce Denno, Crawford's executive officer, assumed command. Denno, like Driscoll, was in trouble, but he told the regiment he could hold if he had some tanks. Taylor advised they were trying to get him some. About twenty minutes into his command, Denno replied, "If we don't get tanks—we're sunk."[22]

Sherman tanks from Company G, 67th Armored Regiment, arrived in time to be ambushed by antitank fire. They retired promptly. Lieutenant K. E. Beichley, whose tank had mechanical problems, remained behind. Fortuitously he was perfectly placed to destroy three German tanks as they attempted to pass by. The fight continued until noon, with the Germans subjected to the combined effects of the 16th's cannon company, tanks, and artillery. They pulled back, leaving three Tigers and two 75-millimeter Mark IV tanks behind.[23]

The Germans continued to resist fiercely throughout the day. Just before dusk, the 16th closed in on Niscemi. Lieutenant Colonel Robert H. York's 1st Battalion, 18th Infantry, fended off three German tanks attempting to penetrate the division's right flank. That night, 16th Infantry reconnaissance patrols detected the Germans blowing up one of their own ammunition dumps. Here, as at Ponte Olivo, all concerned drew the obvious conclusion—the Herman Göring intended to withdraw. Guzzoni's orders to pick up the pace to get to the initial delay positions were taking effect. Nevertheless, German armor remained in Niscemi for at least part of the night.[24]

The following morning the evidence of withdrawal seen the evening before proved out. Most of the enemy had withdrawn sometime during the night. The 16th advanced into Niscemi, "where little resistance is met, and a few prisoners are taken." The infantry regained contact with the Germans three miles north of town, covering the ground between themselves and the town with tank guns. Taylor's 1st and 2nd Battalions had taken a beating, so he sparred with the Germans, doing just enough to retain contact. The regiment suffered 309 casualties in the four days of the campaign, including 24 officers. With an authorized strength of 151 officers and 3,100 noncommissioned officers and soldiers, the 16th had literally been decimated.[25]

During the early stages of the attack on July 12, the 16th obtained a copy of Conrath's letter chastising his soldiers for their poor performance during their attack on the beachhead. That missive, or at least its gist, raced through the division. The 16th's journal exulted in the news. Interrogation of German and Italian prisoners revealed the deepening rift between the Axis powers. Prisoners shared their misgivings about the outcome of the campaign. German soldiers professed surprise at the "amount of material which was available to us so soon after the initial landing operations." Their officers, noncommissioned and commissioned alike, "openly expressed their views as to the impossibility of defending and holding Sicily successfully." They believed this to be so because of the "disharmony existing between the Italian and German forces and the animosity shown to them by the native population." Conrath's letter and the apparent decline in Axis morale were both good news to the troops in the field.[26]

The reports across the 1st Division and II Corps all point in the same direction. Prisoners captured by the division bore out Allen's contention that attacking at midnight would produce surprise and success. He and the staff believed the attack had not only met its physical objectives but also renewed confidence and morale. Post campaign after-action reports jubilantly made that very claim. Indeed, *Danger Forward* contends that "however bitter the fighting was thereafter, the issue was never in doubt after July 12, D + 2."[27]

Onward to Troina from Hilltop to Hilltop

On July 13, Lieutenant Franklyn "Frank" Johnson led his antitank platoon onto the airfield at Ponte Olivo. Johnson, like nearly every soldier in the 1st ID, knew that capturing the airfield had been the D-Day objective. With some irony he described the airfield that had "sent aloft fighters and light bombers to strafe our troops and sink our ships" as "only a mass of shredded aircraft and crazily swaying hangars that have no military value."[28]

Johnson led his platoon a mile farther north, where he found a field in which to disperse. To add to the surreal nature of this first day of doing something besides fighting for the lodgment, along came Teddy Roosevelt to wish the antitanks troops well. Shirt open, helmetless, and, according to Johnson, "being kidded that his shiny bald pate may give away our position," Roosevelt was as usual upbeat and friendly. Nevertheless, he pointed out to the lieutenant that he had occupied a field rife with Teller mines, including some surface-laid. Johnson was surprised that the "cussing out I should have received becomes merely a 'You'd better be more careful, Lieutenant Johnson,' and a cheery wave as the general and slyly grinning driver roar off in cloud of dust." Humiliated, but grateful that he and his tired soldiers had missed what an equally tired and much older man had not, Johnson thought Teddy "one of the very best [officers] in the business."[29]

The boundary change ordered by Alexander at 2000 on 13 July had little effect on the Big Red One, largely due to the professionalism of the comparatively green 45th ID. The Thunderbird Division took full advantage of the spectacular mobility of American infantry divisions. With expertise developed in large-field exercises in the states, the 45th crossed through the 1st ID rear with so few hiccups that no notice is taken in unit journals. The Big Red One had orders now to advance north across the island to Cefalu on the northern coast. Only two significant changes occurred as a consequence of this directive. First, instead of the 45th ID, the 1st Canadian Division attacked on the 1st ID's right. Second, the zone of operations north narrowed a bit. The roads north from Niscemi were abysmal, so some constriction would have been necessary no matter where the boundary lay.

From July 13 to 23, the 1st ID attacked north with two regiments abreast, rotating them as possible with battalions bounding forward. Colonel Bowen described the tactics in his order published late on the evening of July 13: "The Regiment will leapfrog battalions forward, keeping one battalion in position at all times to cover the battalion on the move." The division fought several sharp engagements along the way, well supported by artillery, tanks, and air. The 26th Infantry took Mazzarino, twelve miles northwest of Ponte Olivo, on July 14, while the 16th Infantry took Caltagirone, twelve miles northeast of Niscemi, the same day. After a hell of fight the 26th seized Barrafranca on July 16. The Germans defended the town with a company of fourteen Mark IV tanks well supported with mortars and artillery. Lieutenant Colonel John T. Corley's 3rd Battalion, supported by the 70th TB, finally fought their way into Barrafranca in the late afternoon. The 70th's Lieutenant Colonel John Welborn managed to support both of the advancing regiments by moving his battalion back and forth between them. The 91st Cavalry Squadron provided security between the two attacking regiments.[30]

As the division moved north, it found paratroopers who had been dropped far from the planned drop zones but still in the fight. A 16th Infantry soldier shared a most unusual story about one group of paratroopers with Colonel Taylor and his S-2, Captain John H. Lauten. Eighteen paratroopers, some of whom were wounded, were being held in a house in a village just forward of the 1st Battalion, 16th Infantry, by the crews of two Tiger tanks. One of the tankers had been wounded as well. As the 16th approached, the Germans and paratroopers concluded a "gentlemen's agreement." The Germans would release the paratroopers and their officer on the condition that he would seek aid for the wounded German soldier."[31]

Sergeant Earl L. Willis, a 1st Battalion medic, recounted their tale. The paratrooper lieutenant made his way to the 1st Battalion and asked for help. Willis accompanied him to the courtyard of the house in which the prisoners were being held. The sergeant said, "I got kind of worried but before I showed it, I treated the wounded. 3 doggies and one German. And all the time the prisoners were having a hell of a time eating and drinking, and joking, with the Germans." Once the wounded were treated, the parties to the agreement were to go their own way. "Then," according to Sergeant Willis, "the Jerries—they wept." "Why," asked Captain Lauten, "did they weep?" Willis responded, "Because they were going to blow up their own two Mark VI tanks." They intended to claim when asked about it that they had lost the Tigers in combat.[32]

Sergeant Willis prudently did not remain to see if the Germans were true to their word. Instead he brought the wounded, "including the Jerry," back to the aid station. Incredulous, Taylor told his S-2, "By God, get into a jeep and investigate that story right away." Lauten did as Taylor ordered. He confirmed the tale by following Willis back to the site, where indeed they found the two Tigers had been destroyed. The intelligence officer then went looking for the paratroopers, whom he found trudging toward friendly lines under the leadership of their officer, Lieutenant Fred E. Thomas. The 16th Infantry's invasion journal concluded, "Yes, war touches the S-2 in the damndest way and now we are waiting for word when the Mark VI crews and the Yank paratroopers meet once again this time as enemies—when the 'gentlemen's agreement' is cold and forgotten."[33]

With the 82nd Airborne ashore, paratroopers who "joined" the 1st ID now began making their way back to their own units. The paratroopers earned the respect of their doggie colleagues by their aggressive action: "Even small detachments, and in some cases individuals, ambushed enemy troop movements, disrupted land communications, and caused alarms without number, all deep within enemy lines."[34]

The advance north continued with almost no rest, attacking day and night. Even when the attackers did pause for a short rest, they sent patrols forward and to the flanks. After the 16th took Caltagirone, the division shifted farther west, as now Highway 117 belonged to Eighth Army. Montgomery needed that road, too, since Highway 124 joined 117 a few miles northwest of Caltagirone. This was fallout from the boundary change, which Bradley and Patton believed stemmed from a malicious intent to slight Seventh Army and the Americans. Carlo d'Este is kinder. He argues that in the absence of leadership from Alexander, Montgomery filled the vacuum as he honestly thought best. Montgomery, according to D'Este, viewed the campaign naively, "across a spectrum that did not include an equal division of the spoils and battle honors." If being squeezed westward bothered Allen and the 1st ID, there is no evidence of it in the journals or post-operation reports.[35]

A second kerfuffle occurred at Enna, where the Germans stopped 1st Canadian Division cold. General Sir Oliver Leese, commanding British XXX Corps, ordered the Canadians to bypass Enna exposing the 1st ID's right flank. Incensed, Bradley sent a sharp note to Leese, advising that II Corps would seize the city and that, he assumed, "we have the right to use any of your roads for this attack." Leese replied promptly and apologetically, so the 16th Infantry, supported by the 70th TB, drove on to Enna on July 20. That morning a patrol from Company K, 16th Infantry, reported their belief that the Germans had withdrawn. At 1100 the 2nd and 3rd Battalions entered Enna and cleared the capital of Sicily with "little difficulty." Of course, that evening the BBC reported that the British had captured Enna, which did little to assuage Bradley.[36]

Three days after taking Enna, Allen's second phase ended with the capture of Petralia by the 18th Infantry, "after several hours of *sharp night fighting* [italics in original]." Allen claimed the 18th Infantry's night attack "caught the enemy completely off guard." Colonel Smith adapted to the 1st ID preference for night attacks as if to the manor born. That same day Frank Johnson read a three-day-old copy of the *Stars and Stripes* that reported with great jubilation the successes garnered thus far in Sicily. Johnson noted also that German prisoners "blame our withering artillery fire" for their defeat.[37]

While the 1st ID fought its way north, an extemporized corps, commanded by Major General Geoffrey Keyes, drove across the western half of Sicily largely unopposed aside from Assietta Division. With the 2nd AD, 3rd ID, 82nd Airborne, and two battalions of Rangers, Keyes's corps made short work of clearing the bulk of the island. Palermo, the jewel in Patton's eye, surrendered on July 22. The "corps" finished clearing more than half of Sicily four days later. Suffering only 272 casualties, Keyes's troops captured 53,000 Italians and killed or wounded another 2,900.[38]

Monty Can't Do It Alone: II Corps Turns East

On July 23, Seventh Army issued a new directive to II Corps to attack Messina from the west. The II Corps plan called for the 1st ID to attack along

Highway 120, while Middleton's 45th ID would advance on Highway 113 along the coast toward the city. The 45th ID had reached Palermo, so heading east toward Messina would necessitate Middleton turning his division nearly 180 degrees. Montgomery's concept of taking Messina by attacking on either side of Mount Etna had proved infeasible. On July 23 the 15th PZG, the remnants of the Livorno Division, the Herman Göring Division, and the newly arrived 29th Panzergrenadier Division defended the Etna line. The 29th PZG was moving in to close what little gap remained between the 15th PZG and the northern coast. Two days later Patton met with Montgomery in Syracuse, where they agreed on the final direction of the campaign, with the Army Group commander as an observer. Patton now formally expressed his intention to take Messina from the west. To his surprise, Montgomery agreed. Montgomery remembered the discussion differently, but both agreed to Patton's using highways 120 and 113.[39]

In his semiofficial diary, Commander Harry C. Butcher summarized the decisions taken as he understood them. Fundamentally, Montgomery's belief that the Eighth Army could achieve success via the Catania plain or the "left hook" had proved mistaken. Eisenhower had a more accurate estimate of the difficulty than either Alexander or Montgomery, but he had not overruled them. Now the Army Group "plan" would make II Corps and the Canadians the main effort, with Montgomery poised to "deliver a wallop no doubt simultaneously with or shortly after the attack of the Americans and Canadians." In fact, the Etna line was short enough that the Germans expected to be able to hold it long enough to enable an orderly evacuation of Sicily. Defending the Etna line became critical not to winning in Sicily but to living to fight another day.[40]

Petralia, a town dating at least to the medieval era, is located in the southern reaches of the Caronie Mountains and is perched roughly 2,700 feet above sea level. From Petralia, Highway 120 led east toward Troina through Gangi, Nicosia, and Cerami. Gangi and Cerami reached elevations of 2,700 and 2,800 feet, while Nicosia rose only to 2,000 feet on a steeply sloped "hill." North of Highway 120 lay two ridges that ranged above 3,000 feet. From their slopes, water ran downhill, forming several rivers that emptied into the Tyrrhenian Sea on the northern coast. From the hills along Highway 117, water drained southeasterly toward the Catania plain, forming streams and rivers that eventually emptied into the sea on the east coast of Sicily. To reach Troina, which sat at 3,300 feet, the 1st Infantry Division had to attack across the grain of the terrain. German troops comprised the bulk of the opposition, and understood things were going badly for them. They fought with desperation.[41]

The folks at home also knew that the war was going badly for the Axis powers. Jacob Wagner's mother wrote him from Michelbach, a small town in what was then known as the Rhein-Pfalz. None of her news was good. First, she had no idea where her son was. "Those beautiful Rhein cities are nearly all gone [to bombing]," she lamented, and there was too little rain, from which she concluded, "We probably don't deserve any." She closed hoping for a letter from Jacob. The division G-2 summarized cumulative prisoner-of-war reports, noting that morale of the Germans fighting in Sicily "has deteriorated remarkably and in exact ratio to our successes." Prisoners who had served in Russia believed the war there was lost. Aerial bombardment at home and in Sicily took a toll as well.[42]

Declining morale did not, however, manifest itself in surrender. One counterintelligence officer concluded from his interrogations of German soldiers that it required more courage to desert than to stay and fight. According to Terry Allen, the division fought eastward using the 26th Infantry, "as a pivot of maneuver, on the axis of advance; while the *18th and 16th* [italics in original], operating on the north and south flanks, aggressively outflanked the enemy centers of resistance." The division commander admitted that these flanking maneuvers "were exhausting operations, made largely at night, over mountainous terrain." He used the 91st Cavalry to screen his southern flank, and the 4th Tabor of Goums (a French Moroccan irregular cavalry force, roughly equivalent to a battalion) to screen his northern flank.[43]

The division made two unpleasant discoveries just before making the turn to the east. First, they began to capture Germans assigned to what was variously identified as the Sicilian Division or 15th Panzer Division, but which was in fact the well-led and well-equipped 15th Panzergrenadier Division. These were the likely owners of the second discovery—the six-barreled 210-millimeter Nebelwerfer 42. This nasty weapon, fired electrically, launched projectiles with a twenty-eight-pound bursting charge to a range of 4,500 yards and produced a frightening sound that earned it the sobriquet "Screaming Meemie."[44]

Jean Peltier, a lieutenant in the 32nd FA, had already endured a rough campaign. He headed ashore from the ill-fated LST (landing ship, tank) 313 in a DUKW loaded with ammunition. Long before reaching shore, he had to abandon the amphibious truck as it sank. He finally reached the shore on the only remaining DUKW of the four that had headed toward the beach in a group that morning. Later in the day, he saw the LST 313 blow up with the

rest of his battery's gear. Peltier was one of the first to encounter the Screaming Meemie. He recounted the experience in his diary: "At dark we suddenly
saw several red balls that looked like tracers from a 50-caliber machine gun
rise from behind a hill far to the front of us. We watched as the balls arched
up into the air—six of them at about one second intervals. They went higher
and seemed to be coming in our directions [sic] in the gathering dusk with
a terrifying wailing sound. It actually made your hair stand on end. They
landed with six terrific explosions somewhere to our rear." The impact of
six projectiles of more than eight inches diameter proved frightening but
not devastating. The warheads produced significant blast but relatively few
fragments, so they were less effective than they might have been.[45]

The continued fighting proved as exhausting as Allen claimed. During
one of the inevitable night attacks, Staff Sergeant Ted Dobol took over his
Company K, 26th Infantry, platoon when his lieutenant was wounded. The
platoon had been hit hard with rocket and artillery fire. Dobol "reorganized
the remnants and pushed on to the objective." By 25 July "the steady grind,
day and night, started to show on the men." The next day Dobol and his
dwindling platoon continued the attack. Taking artillery fire again, a piece
of shrapnel struck him. "As it was not a serious or dangerous wound," he
remained with his platoon. They went into "reserve" for a rest but soon rejoined the fight. They carried on despite losses and little rest because, according to Dobol, morale was high in the 26th. He attributed the high morale
to his battalion commander, twenty-nine-year-old John T. Corley, and his
regimental commander, thirty-two-year-old John W. Bowen. According to
Dobol, the regiment stopped just long enough "to reorganize and catch a
breather before continuing on like goats over the hills of Sicily."[46]

It took four days of hard fighting to reach Nicosia, and six more to reach
the outskirts of Troina. The 1st ID needed to control Highway 120 in order to
move heavy equipment, including tanks and the trucks, to sustain the fight.
The mountainous terrain and the bitterly resisting Germans exacerbated the
problem. German artillery proved galling at Nicosia. John Hersey, a correspondent for *Time*, reported on Captain Edward F. Wozenski's reaction to
the steady artillery duel between the antagonists. Preparing for an attack,
Wozenski's company absorbed German counterfire and wisely took to their
"holes." Wozenski, who had not, observed "sadly," according to Hersey, "This
hill's a little too crowded for my liking." After the German barrage, Wozenski's soldiers took the next hill on the way to Troina.[47]

Bowen's 26th found the approach in the mountains before Troina difficult
as well. In his history of the regiment, Staff Sergeant Lawrence Manley noted

that "the Infantryman had to plunge ahead from the hollows, up the precip-
itous sides of the hills in the face of heavy enemy fire," and then repeat the
process for miles on end, or so it seemed. During that time Colonel Bowen
reluctantly concluded that the regiment's morale and combat efficiency had
declined and could be rated no better than fair. The other regiments were
feeling the pain as well.[48]

The 15th PZG Division's Kampfgruppe Fullriede produced the symptoms
the division experienced—heavy direct and indirect fire, good tactics, and
frequent counterattacks. Oberst Fritz Fullriede commanded the 129th Panzergrenadier Regiment (PGR) on which his battle group was formed. A career soldier, Fullriede had fought in the Great War and, with distinction,
in the current one. One of the survivors from Africa, he rebuilt the 129th
PGR from remnants withdrawn from the 22nd PZ that had been destroyed
in Russia. During the campaign, the Germans redesignated the 129th as the
3rd PGR. Although not fully equipped or manned, Fullriede's Kampfgruppe
fought well under his leadership. Kampfgruppe Fullriede and the 15th PZG
fought an effective delaying action to the Etna line.[49]

The 26th made headway by "bounding battalions," as absurd as that
sounds, given the terrain. That, however, is the actual term of art, rather
than "leapfrogging," the term Bowen used. The 33rd FA and other artillery
provided effective fire support for the "bounding" unit. Soon after his frightening encounter with the Nebelwerfer, Peltier left his job as executive officer
of A Battery and joined Lieutenant Colonel Derrill M. Daniel's 2nd Battalion, 26th Infantry, as his artillery liaison officer, becoming in effect Daniel's
fire support coordinator. He positioned forward observers or assigned them
to support specific units. The liaison officer, according to Peltier, "stays with
the battalion commander and gives him observation and fire through his
forward observers. He also get [sic] and prepares defensive fires requested
by the infantry company commander and relays them to the artillery C. P.
[command post]." He also kept track of patrols so that he could support the
infantry with harassing fires. Most important, Peltier and those who did his
job sought to maintain accurate current locations of their infantry to avoid
fratricide. Whether by shoe leather or vehicle, he moved with the battalion
commander.[50]

On July 24, Peltier moved with Daniel's command group. The battalion
struggled up and down hills from Gangi, finally attacking to seize Hill 937,
also known as Monte Caolino. Despite the imposing name, Monte Caolino
was a bare rocky ridge just on the south side of, and overlooking, Highway
120, about three miles east of Gangi. Bowen wanted the hill so he could

bound the next battalion forward and bring up the 70th TB. Throughout the day, Peltier kept up periodic fires in support of forward observer Lieutenant Bernard I. Cody, who was moving with Company G. The Germans fought skillfully. They would wait just on the far side of the hilltops until the American infantry approached the crest, and then "walk up from the reverse slope and throw hand grenades at them." This worked quite well, and despite the division raining artillery on them, the Germans held the hill until about midnight.[51]

During the night, Rodt reinforced Fullriede and ordered him to retake Hill 937. Fullriede's attack began around 0830 with what seemed at first to be a firefight rather than an attack. The Panzergrenadiers followed up and drove off the infantry platoon on Hill 937. At 0952 Bowen ordered Daniel to "work hard on it—get it back." With a nose for trouble, Roosevelt arrived at Bowen's CP at 1017. Just after 1100, Roosevelt spoke with Danger 6, Allen's radio-telephone call sign. Allen was clear he wanted Bowen to take Hill 825 and retake Hill 937—both of which had to be held to secure the highway. At 1116 Bradley weighed in with the same order. By late afternoon, the 26th had done as ordered, supported by six 105-millimeter artillery battalions and two 155 batteries.[52]

Rodt's step-by-step delay, exacting whatever price he could, went well to start with. He noted, however, that on July 22 the road from Petralia east came "under artillery fire from new enemy forces, coming from the west." Andrus and the division artillery was having an effect. Kampfgruppe Fullriede bore the brunt of the artillery fire, along with a Fascist "Blackshirt" battalion that defended on Fullriede's right. The 15th PZG continued to fight effectively, forcing a stiff fight for every hilltop.[53]

Bowen also ordered Major Walter H. Grant to seize Hill 825 with his first battalion. Also called Monte Cannella, 825 was still another bare hill, this one north of the highway. Grant had earlier advised against taking 825. Bowen had agreed then, but now he insisted. "There is no place to put anyone if [we] did have it," Grant complained. Bowen ordered the attack, believing it would force the Germans out—and it did, with a bit more artillery.[54]

Peltier and the artillerymen supporting Grant's battalion pounded Hill 825 courtesy of Brigadier General Clift Andrus and the division artillery. In a masterpiece of traffic management and careful positioning, Andrus brought six battalions of 105-millimeter artillery and two batteries of 155 and literally smothered the hills and the Germans on them with exploding shells. With artillery keeping the Germans' heads down, Bowen maneuvered Corley's 3rd Battalion south of 937 and took Monte Barnagiano, Hill

962, in the German rear. Andrus's artillery, at the behest of Peltier and his colleagues, rained down three thousand rounds on the Germans that day, and that was to drive the Germans from the latest hilltop. In a postwar monograph, Generalleutnant Eberhard Rodt noted the efficacy of American artillery. In the middle of all this, the Italian monarch and the Fascists deposed Mussolini.[55]

Il Duce's departure made little difference to the 1st ID. Life, such as it was, went on. On July 27, the division closed in on the town of Sperlinga. There Allen brought up the redoubtable 70th Tank Battalion, with twenty-eight tanks still running and the six M3 medium tanks from the 753rd Tank Battalion. Allen sent the tankers on a sweep down the highway at 2030. The tanks were to "clean out the enemy pocket in that area (west of Nicosia) and then to withdraw to the west." The tanks roared off, shot up the defenders, and returned to friendly lines by 2130. The "sweep" cost the 70th TB three light tanks and six casualties. The 15th PZG's Kampfgruppe Ens decamped soon after and moved all the way back, then through Nicosia. They failed to advise the Italian soldiers defending the town.[56]

Guzzoni hoped to form a defense at Nicosia with his troops and the 15th PZG. On the morning of July 28, the 16th Infantry attacked and after a stiff fight took the town and captured some seven hundred Italians assigned to the Aosta Division and a handful of Germans. Guzzoni's last attempt to slow the Americans west of Troina failed because of the continued decline in coordination with the Germans. Allen crowed about the relative success of the sweep and taking Nicosia. The tank sweep Allen ordered also cheered the infantrymen peering down on the fight from the high ground either side of the highway.[57]

Captain James L. Pence, commander of Company A, 1st Battalion, 16th Infantry, described what all infantry company commanders and their soldiers confronted fighting eastward along Highway 120. Pence and his company reached Nicosia at 1600 hours on July 28, "a very tired, dirty, thirsty, hungry organization." No one had slept or eaten in thirty-six hours. Yet Pence believed spirits were high because they had "the enemy on the run." Soon after Company A closed in, the battalion commander, Driscoll, assembled his company commanders. At 1615 he led them to a point on the eastern edge of town from which they could scan the ground ahead. Here he gave orders to seize a nondescript hill with an elevation of 731 meters some 3,000 yards east. The "reconnaissance" and carrying out of the orders took all of five minutes.[58]

The regimental intelligence and reconnaissance (I & R) platoon provided the only information on the objective. The I & R platoon leader advised Driscoll that east of Nicosia he had "drawn heavy machine gun fire," and that the bridge some 2,000 yards east had been blown. Driscoll had a single map. He allowed each of his platoon leaders to look at it, then issued his order. The battalion would attack in column with Company A leading down the highway until just past the blown bridge, and then would leave the road and take to the hills. From there the battalion would advance across the hilltops with Company A on the right and C on the left. B and Company D would follow A. Finally, Driscoll planned to establish his CP at the bridge.[59]

Driscoll's order required the battalion to move as soon as company commanders returned to their companies. Pence briefed his platoon leaders on the plan, such as it was, while on the move. The company first sergeant handed him a box of K rations and returned his canteen freshly refilled. A messenger arrived with a roll of maps, from which he extracted two sheets and gave them to Pence. A delay ensued while he sorted out which sheet actually covered the ground they were traversing. Pence kept his commander informed by telephone, transmissions conducted over wire laid on the move.[60]

Soon after getting back in motion, the machine guns the I & R platoon had encountered took the column under fire. Pence, with Driscoll's approval, stopped the advance to await sunset. Resuming the advance after dark, the battalion encountered no resistance—apparently the machine gunners had withdrawn. Pence halted when he believed he had arrived at the top of Hill 731. He verified this looking at his map by the "flickering flame of a zippo lighter." Company A covered this last mile in five hours of careful movement. Satisfied, Pence positioned his troops and sent out two patrols, one to assure contact with Company B, and a second to patrol forward to be sure the company owned the hill. Pence then went to sleep. Two hours later, at dawn, one of his platoon leaders awakened Captain Pence to show him that that the company was about two hundred yards short of the peak, and within seventy-five to eighty yards of the Germans who shared the hill with them. The fight that ensued took the rest of the day.[61]

Within the first hour, Pence had fired all of his 60-millimeter mortar ammunition. Eventually soldiers humped more ammunition up several hundred feet of hillside. The battle swung back and forth all day, with failed attempts by both Companies A and C to clear the hill. Late in the day, Company B drove the Germans off, supported by fire from Companies A and C. The battalion took about one hundred prisoners and Hill 731. After a day-long effort, they were three thousand yards closer to Troina. Now they were only five or six miles away for crows, and a hard hump for the doggies. And they were more tired, dirtier, thirstier, and hungrier than they had been the day before. At least they had slept some.[62]

In the pages of a paper written at the Infantry School after the war, Pence recalled what he had learned on Hill 731. He understood the need for haste that led to attacking the hill. Colonel Taylor and Major Driscoll believed they were pursuing the enemy. In fact, the Germans had decided to defend Hill 731. In hindsight, Pence believed a few more minutes scanning the ground would have helped. Company C had fallen behind, and one of his own platoons did not arrive on the hill with the company. He remained a believer in the utility of night attacks, but concluded that "strict discipline must prevail and stricter supervision must be exercised in night movements, even though it only be a movement in column." Finally, he believed he had failed to supervise adequately, as his forward patrol had not established that the company had reached the hilltop.[63]

Troina and the End for Terry and Teddy

The climactic fight for the 1st Division on Sicily began on August 1, 1943. The 15th PZG had fought a skillful delay and exacted a heavy toll on the Big Red One. After capturing Nicosia on July 28, the division closed on Cerami northeast of Captain Pence's Hill 731 and organized for a deliberate attack. The 16th Infantry occupied positions on the north side of the highway, and the 18th on the south. Cerami lay several tortuous hairpin turns and rugged mountains west of Troina, where the 15th PZG defended, with Kampfgruppe Fullriede on the right and Kampfgruppe Ens on the left. The 15th PZG had tenuous contact with the Herman Göring on its left, and the beat-up Aosta Division on its right. The Big Red One brought up supplies and repositioned artillery. Andrus now had eleven battalions of artillery with which to support. Moving the artillery forward on the single road and finding positions from which to fire was no mean feat.[64]

On the night of the 28th, Rodt had withdrawn nearly fourteen miles to his positions on the Etna line. He assumed the Americans would follow, so the division's pause did not go unnoticed at 15th PZG. However, Rodt surmised the 1st ID had not pressed the attack "because of cloud bursts that made the valleys impassable." On 29 July Colonel Harry A. "Paddy" Flint, commanding the 9th ID's 39th Infantry, joined the 1st ID with his unit as an attachment. With his regiments worn down to about half strength, Allen needed fresh troops. Paddy Flint, like Allen and Roosevelt, was a charismatic leader who led from the front. Flint's motto for the 39th proved as viral as a contemporary social media trend: "Anything, Anywhere, Anytime Bar Nothing" appeared literally as a cattle-brand-style logo, rendered as AAA with a horizontal bar through the As. Although both the 16th and 18th Infantry regiments had nearly reached Cerami, they did not attack. Paddy Flint's 39th Infantry would have that honor.[65]

Allen's G-2, Colonel Porter, believed that Kampfgruppe Fullriede, along with some Italian forces, defended Troina. In fact, Rodt also had Kampfgruppe Ens and two Italian artillery battalions that he claimed volunteered to support the 15th. Rodt wrote after the war that the Italians had "proved themselves well." Porter believed the Germans would continue to fight stubbornly but delay rather than defend. His periodic reports show that he believed German morale and combat capability was in decline. Bradley's II Corps was emphatic: "Indications are Troina lightly held." Moreover, the Allied air forces had, as a practical matter, taken control of the air over Sicily. That too promoted optimism. Flint believed his troops could take both Cerami and Troina. Allen agreed, and let him have it. Conventional wisdom among the Allies was that the Germans were delaying back to the ferry sites on the Straits of Messina. With Moroccan cavalry in support, Flint attacked on July 31 to seize Cerami and Troina.[66]

The 39th took Cerami, but the 15th PZG stopped the attack by midnight, August 1, "west of Troina." Meanwhile the 91st Cavalry Reconnaissance Squadron seized the village of Gagliano, eight miles south of Troina. Gagliano would afford room for units to assemble later. Rodt's boundary with the Herman Göring ran through the town. Sergeant Gerry H. Kisters, assigned to B Troop, took two machine-gun nests by himself, killing three Germans and capturing four, despite having been shot five times. For his courage Kisters was eventually awarded the Medal of Honor. The day ended with mixed results. Teddy Roosevelt coordinated a second attempt in the early hours of August 2. That attack began with the 26th Infantry passing through the 39th. The two regiments planned to continue the attack, with the 26th on the left, the Moroccans now supporting them while the 39th attacked straight east into Troina. In his field order Bowen described the mission after the passage of lines as "attack Troina at 0500 hours. Capture Troina and Hill 872. Cut road from Troina to Cesaro." Bowen's order reflects the common belief that the Germans would delay. The 26th's contemporary history noted, "The terrain was rugged," and supported only "by elementary trails through the heights held by the enemy artillery." The division brought against the Germans delaying in this ideal terrain its considerable artillery and supporting air units.[67]

Mule trains led by erstwhile truck drivers sustained the operation. Both sides sweltered during the daylight hours but renewed bitter fighting at nightfall. The rugged terrain surrounding Troina, atop the highest occupied elevation in Sicily, assured that the fighting devolved not on the division, or even regiments and battalions, but on the company level and below. Individual effort mattered as much as massed fires.

On July 31, when Paddy Flint's infantrymen began what would prove to be seven days of brutal fighting, General Eisenhower agreed to allow Patton to relieve both Allen and Roosevelt. A week earlier, General Alexander had rid himself of a major irritant in the person of Major General Clarence R. Huebner. Huebner pushed back at perceived slights by the British against the American soldiers, which limited his utility as 15th Army Group's deputy chief of staff. Patton believed that Huebner was dismissed because "he stood up for American interests." Whatever the reason, Alexander had a right to have officers in whom he had confidence. For Patton, it was a godsend; now Huebner, an old friend, was available. He believed that Allen was worn out and needed to rotate home. In his opinion, Roosevelt was "brave, but otherwise no soldier." He too should go. But the army commander wanted them relieved without prejudice. In their stead he wanted Huebner and Colonel Willard G. Wyman. Bradley had no qualms about relieving either Allen or Roosevelt. He believed both had to go because the two of them and the 1st ID were too independent and too full of themselves. Finally they had to go for "loving the division too much." And go they would, but not until they took Troina and could be relieved by the 9th ID.[68]

With no idea what awaited them, Allen and Roosevelt soldiered on. As always, Roosevelt coordinated the fight forward while Allen gave direction and assured resources. Andrus managed to crowd eleven battalions of artillery among the mountains extending some three miles either side of Highway 120. II Corps planned to relieve the 1st ID with the Manton Eddy's 9th ID on or about August 4. Allen believed that it was "the moral obligation of the division to button up the capture of Troina." Accordingly, he issued Field Order 30, in which he stated a complex mission succinctly: "The 1st US Inf Div with 39th CT attached, atks 0300, 3 August, captures TROINA [emphasis in original] cuts the roads leading from TROINA to AGIRA and develops the sit in the direction of CESARO and ADRANO." The accompanying overlay illustrated Allen's return to his preferred method, enveloping to create the means to conduct a concentric attack that might trap the defenders in Troina. The scheme of maneuver was complicated.[69]

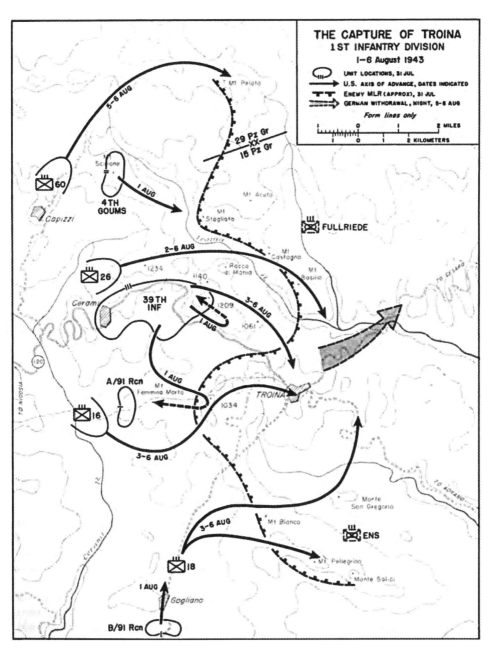

Map 10: The Capture of Troina, August 1–6, 1943. Reproduced from Garland and Smyth, *Sicily and the Surrender of Italy*, Map 5.

During the first stage of the bloody fighting that followed, 1st ID and Paddy Flint's troops fought to take the high ground around Troina. Bowen warned Allen that the enemy defenses seemed more powerful than the division estimated, and the outcome proved him right. His 26th Infantry fought its way along the outside loop, with the 39th on his right. The 16th attacked more or less due east. The 18th attacked from Gagliano, looping well to the east aimed at the rear of Troina. The 26th did drive in Fullriede's outposts and took ground adjacent to Troina at approximately the same elevation, but could go no further. At 1240 that day, Andrus had seven battalions of artillery firing to assist the hard-pressed infantry. Even with that help, the 26th could not press on, and neither could the 39th. Rodt's troops resisted fiercely and counterattacked frequently. Colonel Gibb, Allen's G-3, admitted, "We are afraid of counterattacks," because they might catch units off balance if they had just concluded a fight.[70]

Coordinating the attack based on the proximity of friendly forces converging on Troina became problematic. On more than one occasion the division artillery refused missions because no one could provide with confidence the location of "friendly" forces. The paucity of forward observers played a role as well. Coordinating with the 1st Canadian Division became critical as it approached Troina from the south.

Eberhard Rodt saw the crisis unfolding with "the critical point of the battle always more on the heights west and northwest of Troina." Still Rodt's troops fought on. According to Allen, "the Germans were fighting desperately, and counter-attacked viciously, to recover lost ground." The division renewed the attack the following day. He committed the rest of the 18th Infantry to the attack in the south and weighted the attack with two additional artillery battalions. What Rodt described as the "Grossangriff," or main attack, began at 0300 on August 4 and hit the 15th PZG all along its line that ran along hilltops in an arc around Troina. He remembered the fighting as hot, with hilltops changing hands frequently.[71]

For most of August 4 the Grossangriff went nowhere, but at 1345 Gibb advised the regiments that the division had "something cooking here." That something included seventy-two A-36 bombers that would attack targets in Troina in two flights, one striking at 1700 and the second at 1715. The division had also planned three discrete concentrations of artillery fires that would last just over half an hour and conclude with smoke rounds at 1730. These would signal a general attack. All Gibb needed was "all the targets you would like hit." All of this came together. At 1803 the 26th Infantry advised, "Air and arty [artillery] bombardment lovely." Bowen's troops were on the move and reported that "the enemy is completely unnerved, arty fire practically nil." There was a tone of relief, even exultation, in reporting. Gibb found himself offering artillery concentrations to units who appeared not to need it, at least for the moment.[72]

All four regimental combat teams closed on Troina on August 5, as did the 1st Canadian Division. By far the most important event that day occurred when York's 2nd Battalion, 18th Infantry, took Monte Pellegrino, less than two miles from Troina. York's troops had fought hard for the ridge since the previous afternoon and gotten on it about 0800. They did not finally take it for good until 2015. Even then the battalion admitted that the mountain was "not too secure." They did not report it secure until 0930 the next day. At more than 6,300 feet in elevation, Mount Pellegrino towered nearly 3,000 feet above Troina. This elevation enabled observed artillery fire into Troina and, more important, opened artillery position areas to the rear of the town.[73]

The actions on August 5 were decisive. Two things made the 15th PZG's defense of Troina untenable. Toward the end of the day, the 26th Infantry threatened Highway 120 from Troina to Cesaro, and with it the 15th's only withdrawal route. A local counterattack on the initiative of the 15th PZG's tank battalion commander held the road open. In Rodt's view, after the "enemy also took possession of the dominant heights southeast of Troina [Monte Pellegrino], the fate of the position was sealed."[74]

The next morning, patrols from Taylor's 16th Infantry entered Troina and found that the enemy had withdrawn. At 1115 the 1st ID journal trumpeted to II Corps and the 1st Canadian Division, "TROINA ours." Allen had planned another envelopment for August 6, but the German Rückzug (retreat) rendered that plan unnecessary. Allen immediately issued orders for the division to continue the attack toward Cesaro, farther along Highway 120. Instead, over the course of the next several hours II Corps issued orders for the 9th ID to relieve the 1st ID. Three other orders also arrived from Bradley's headquarters, none of which were supposed to have been transmitted quite yet. The first relieved Allen, the second relieved Roosevelt, and the third announced that General Huebner would assume command of the 1st ID effective at 0001, August 7, and Colonel Wyman, on the list for promotion to brigadier general, would replace Roosevelt.[75]

Clift Andrus, Terry Allen's childhood friend, witnessed Allen's reaction to the message ordering him to give up the Big Red One. According to Andrus, "Terry read the thing, said nothing for a while, and then burst into tears like a high strung school girl." Harsh for an old friend, but then Andrus noted, "It came as a terrible shock." It was a shock to Teddy Roosevelt as well. Stan Mason believed the relief left Teddy "hurt despondent and mentally in a black cloud." After a tear-filled farewell to his old regiment, Roosevelt was packed off to Seventh Army. Allen recovered himself immediately and proved a gracious host to Huebner, who arrived soon after the bad news. The next day Allen began to make his way back to the United States, via Algeria and the United Kingdom.[76]

In his memoir Bradley claimed that "to break the news as gently as I could . . . I called Allen and Roosevelt to my CP in Nicosia." It is true that he called the two back to Nicosia. It is unlikely it was meant as a kindness, given that both men knew they had been fired before being ordered to II Corps' CP. Bradly also claimed that firing these two officers "was one of my most unpleasant duties of the entire war." Maybe so. Teddy Roosevelt observed to the Corps commander, "Brad we get along a helluva lot better with the Krauts up front than we do with your people back here in the rear."[77]

The end for Terry and Teddy was hard for the staff, commanders, and troops. Terry and Teddy had led the Big Red One for fifteen months, in peace and war. The bonds forged in combat in Algeria, Tunisia, and Sicily were strong from the bottom up. In Ray Lambert's view, Allen was "a great leader, and his firing wounded us deeply." Writing about the relief years later, Lambert might have been speaking for all of the troops. His words sound as angry in 2019 as he must have felt in 1943. Morale, he recalled, was "sliding," given the 500 casualties the division had suffered in the fight to take Troina, and the troops' depression on learning of the relief of two popular generals turned to anger. Patton's high jinks and nasty antics, including urinating in Allen's slit trench in Tunisia, were well known. Soon after the relief, word came that he had slapped Charles Kuhl, a 26th Infantry soldier likely suffering from shell shock, or what is known now as post-traumatic stress disorder, during a visit to an evacuation hospital.[78]

Many soldiers shared Lambert's opinion. Stan Mason believed that "throughout the division there was a sense of hurt at the loss of Allen and Roosevelt, who were respected and beloved leaders." Feelings ran high on the division staff as well, for they were closest to the three "stars" Allen, Roosevelt, and Andrus. Clarence M. "Pop" Eymer, the division G-4, asserted that the staff in particular were shocked and angry over Allen and Roosevelt being relieved. "We all without justification or reason, transferred our anger and sense of frustration to [Huebner]," Eymer recalled. For all of these reasons, "Huebner's problem was to turn this loyalty, pride and affection from

Allen and Roosevelt to himself." Ironically, Allen made the cover of *Time* magazine in the edition published two days after his relief.[79]

The New Sheriff and His Deputy

Stan Mason assumed that he and the entire general staff of the 1st ID would be replaced, given the army tradition of new brooms sweeping clean. Huebner chose not to do that. Eventually Mason asked him why he had not done so. Huebner explained, "I have known Terry Allen all my life and I know he never paid attention to details. I have known Ted Roosevelt all my life. . . . I fought World War I with him in the First Division . . . and I know that Ted, while a great leader, still wouldn't be a technician in the way of running a division." Huebner concluded that given the division's demonstrated performance, he believed the staff was solid, and he would reserve judgment rather than sweep clean the old guard.[80]

Bradley was pleased to have Huebner, who he described as a "flinty" disciplinarian, take over the Big Red One. Like both Eisenhower and Bradley, Huebner was a midwesterner. Bradley was from a small town in Missouri, whereas Eisenhower and Huebner hailed from small Kansas towns. Huebner was born in November 1888 on a homestead granted his grandfather in May 1884. The Huebner homestead was near Bushton, a tiny farm village in central Kansas near the town of Ellsworth. He left home in 1905 to attend Grand Island Business College in Grand Island, Nebraska, where he learned accounting, stenography, and typing. In 1908 he took a job as a clerk for a railroad, but he seemed to have been marking time until he reached twenty-one, the legal age for enlisting in the army.[81]

Huebner joined the 18th Infantry in 1910. He found his skills as a typist made him a valuable commodity, and rose rapidly to sergeant. He passed the examination for commissioning and accepted an infantry commission in 1916. A charter member of the 1st Division when it formed in 1917, he went to war with the 28th Infantry. Like Allen and Roosevelt, he compiled a brilliant record. Wounded in March 1918, he returned to command a company. As a captain he took command of the 2nd Battalion when his commander was badly wounded in the first hour of the attack to seize the village of Cantigny in May 1918. He commanded the 2nd Battalion throughout the rest of the war, fighting at Soissons and the Meuse Argonne. He ended the war as a major, decorated with the Distinguished Service Cross.[82]

Huebner continued to excel in the interwar period. He graduated from both the Command and General Staff School and the Army War College.

Like Bradley and Allen, he taught tactics at the Infantry School under the tutelage of George C. Marshall. He also served at the Command and General Staff School, where he taught, among others, Omar Bradley. Huebner had a succession of command and training jobs and rose in rank rapidly after World War II began. He commanded a training center briefly until he went overseas in 1942, ultimately to serve as Alexander's deputy chief of staff, where his flinty personality made him available to command the 1st ID.[83]

Huebner had a mandate to "to clean out the whole Division . . . that the Division was a bunch of people who were sorry for themselves." Willard G. Wyman, a lanky cavalryman, understood the mandate as well. Wyman, who graduated with an accelerated class from the Military Academy in November 1918, had a remarkable career. A horseman of Olympic quality, he mapped a thousand square miles of the Gobi Desert in 1928 while on assignment in China for language training. In 1933 he went back to China. Assigned as G-3 in support of the Chinese Fifth Army, he hiked out of Burma with Lieutenant General Joseph Stillwell and a handful of British and American survivors of the mauling the Allies received at the hands of the Japanese. Wyman, in a word, was a hard man. Stan Mason described him as "energetic, knowledgeable," and by comparison to Huebner, "more relaxed and had an outgoing, optimistic personality." Together he and Huebner took on the task of "re-bluing" the 1st ID.[84]

Huebner oversaw the last few days of his division's active combat in Sicily. That included taking Randazzo east of Troina. Smith's 18th Infantry accomplished this final task, attached to the 9th ID. The 18th encountered few Germans, but their task was complicated by the Germans' prolific use of mines. These included the Teller antitank mine, the S-mine or "Bouncing Betty," and the really nasty Schu-mine—nasty because it was encased in wood and therefore particularly hard to detect. Situated practically on the slope of Mount Etna, Randazzo and the approaches to it are covered in volcanic slag laden with iron ore. Finding metal mines in soil of that composition proved difficult, with the result that the division suffered many casualties from mine strikes. The 32nd FA lost more soldiers to mines than to any other cause during the campaign. The 18th Infantry completed this last mission on the evening of August 16, ending active combat in Sicily for the 1st ID, and was withdrawn on D+37. During the thirty-seven days of the campaign, the 1st ID suffered 294 killed in action, 23 died of wounds, 1,485 wounded, 2 captured, and 337 missing. Sixty-nine of the missing turned up. These numbers don't include several thousand more who suffered malaria, dysentery, some other sickness, or nonbattle injury.[85]

Huebner formed several impressions that required correction. First, he believed the division relied too much on Andrus's artillery. Whether that view would stand the test of time remained to be seen. He believed the division's infantry did not employ small arms effectively. Auditing records, Huebner discovered that some two thousand soldiers had not qualified with their rifles. Rushing hither and yon, practicing landings, testing new tables of organization, and the arrival of incompletely trained replacements had produced the unforgivable result of infantrymen in combat inadequately trained to use their primary weapon—the very source of their inherent power.[86]

Huebner and Wyman took the reins firmly from their first day on the job. Teaching and training began even before the shooting stopped. Major Joseph W. Sisson Jr. encountered Huebner not long after Troina fell but before his 3rd Battalion, 18th Infantry, advanced on Randazzo. Huebner asked Joe Sisson if he knew of the "squatting position for rifle marksmanship." Learning that Sisson did not, Huebner, who claimed to have invented the position, had an impromptu range set up and demonstrated it himself. Sisson admitted what nearly every combat veteran of the Big Red One felt: "We 'combat soldiers' didn't think too much of starting basic training on the outskirts of a town just taken from the enemy."[87]

Frank Johnson's first encounter with the new commanding general came right after he and his antitank platoon completed a firing practice with their 57-millimeter antitank guns. He and the platoon had adopted comfortable positions of repose in the grass near an improvised gunnery range. "Get up Lieutenant," Huebner ordered, and Johnson forthwith rose, assumed the position of attention, and directed his platoon to fall in, something they had not done "since leaving Africa." The result did not endear Johnson to his commanding general. Next Huebner discovered that Johnson and his ragtag platoon could not salute properly. Johnson remedied the problem under the division commander's supervision.[88]

Huebner and Wyman went through the division like a dose of salts. Wyman kept a journal of his efforts. His entry for August 14–15 covered visits to the 16th and 18th Infantry, as well as observations on the work of the 1st Engineers. Over the next four days, the division moved from assembly areas back to Licata, west of where it had landed on July 10. The assistant division commander commented or intervened in twenty-one areas of particular interest to him. Swimming, sports, and recreation were all of interest to him and to Huebner. Both wanted the focus on training and restoring fitness, but also recognized the need for their tired soldiers to rest and relax. Of import too was how to receive replacements. "Plans are underway for a ceremonious reception for the newly arrived replacements," Wyman noted. Reception included greetings from General Huebner and awarding "the Divisional shoulder insignia."[89]

The two new generals knew, too, that many of the troops had just completed two grueling campaigns virtually back to back. They were exhausted, and their morale was brittle. Colonel John Bowen described the problem in a letter to Huebner. Bowen believed that "in general individual and unit morale is excellent," due to "the long unbroken string of victories." However, Bowen argued that the troops were exhausted, and "Many of the 'old timers' are depressed to find so few of their old comrades still with them. Too many the thought of continued combat without respite is disturbing."[90]

For the first several months of their tenure, Huebner and Wyman seemed to be hard-nosed, but in fact Bowen's assessment was not lost on them. They focused on taking care of their soldiers. In June 1944, just before the invasion of Normandy, Huebner did an interview with Colonel Julian S. Dayton, an Army Ground Forces observer. General Huebner shared with Dayton his philosophy for resting, training, and preparing the 1st ID after its two campaigns in the Mediterranean theater. He believed the most important thing was not to describe rest and retraining as a "rest period." Instead, "Let the officers and men know they are reconditioning for the next fight." Immediately after arriving in the rear, Huebner believed getting "the men bathed and cleaned up" was job number one. Replacing lost articles ranging from toothbrushes to clothing was also essential.[91]

Huebner recalled that he focused on physical conditioning, marksmanship, and small unit training. If time permitted, as it had since Sicily, "combined training with supporting units" was essential. Physical conditioning included sports but also a daily five-mile speed march. Finally, he believed in allowing for "approximately one-half day of training and one-half day for recreation." Ted Dobol recalled that they "held extensive rifle fire" because, according to Huebner, "the Germans were complaining because they had so many wounded." "The General thought they should all be dead," Dobol claimed, "shot between the eyes."[92]

Not satisfied with slapping the hapless Private Kuhl, Patton found occasion to strike another soldier. On August 10 he pulled his revolver on a soldier whose unit had sent him to be assessed for combat fatigue. Patton threated Private Paul G. Bennett with his revolver but satisfied himself with slapping him instead. This second incident ensured that neither offense would simply go away. Ultimately Patton visited each of his major units to apologize. He did so with the 1st ID on 27 August. The division listened but greeted him with "stony silence" rather than the three cheers of approval Patton had experienced elsewhere. There are any number of explanations for the frosty reception. Few Big Red One soldiers knew of the slapping incidents. The most likely explanation is that after the firing of Allen and Roosevelt, the troops held the army commander in low regard.[93]

In any case, Huebner carried out his program, and the division came around. By August 28 the 1st ID had closed on its new home at Palma di Montechiaro, west of Licata, where 3rd ID had landed on July 10. Soon after, Mason came "to realize that our new commander," despite the way he treated everyone from staff to private, "really had a great deal of pride in what we had done and what we are doing." One afternoon General Huebner shared his vision for how to move forward, saying, with what Mason called a "puckish smile," "Stan one of us is going to have to be a son of bitch." Although he knew who the son of bitch was, Mason played along, claiming he had played that role. Then he asked, "How about you being one for a while?" Huebner laughed and agreed: "That's the way we'll work it. I'll knock 'em down, scare hell out of 'em. Then you pull them up, dust them off and make sure we don't lose anybody worth saving."[94]

In *Masters of the Art of Command*, Martin Blumenson and James L. Stokesbury proffer a more dispassionate assessment. They understand that at first the troops resented Huebner, "who abolished the informality of his predecessors." But "within a brief time Huebner had overcome this handicap, won the affection of his troops, and placed his own stamp on them." Just when that happened is debatable. Huebner himself thought it was not until after Omaha Beach.[95]

Decisions taken at the Trident Conference in May 1943 made Omaha Beach central to the division's accepting Huebner. Soon after securing Sicily, the Allies intended to attack the Italian mainland, but 1st ID would not be part of that effort. Instead, the Big Red One would redeploy to the United Kingdom to prepare for the cross-Channel invasion of France. Although the division received more than seven hundred replacements in July, it remained understrength. As of September 1, the G-1 had "requisitioned" 45 officers and 1,539 enlisted soldiers. On September 5, Seventh Army advised it would not act on these requisitions and that none were to be resubmitted for at least ninety days.[96]

Just as the 3rd ID had helped fill out 1st ID to invade Sicily, so now the 1st ID became the bill payer for units headed to Italy. Between September 8 and

17, II Corps levied 1st ID for 1,251 soldiers of various specialties to fill short-ages, primarily in the 3rd and 45th ID. These transfers had to occur quickly. The largest transfer orders arrived on September 10 and required that 969 sol-diers be transferred to 3rd ID no later than 1700 hours on September 15. On September 17, II Corps required that 2,379 enlisted soldiers be transferred to the 9th ID, but Seventh Army intervened and stopped the bleeding.[97]

Sending off soldiers, many of whom had made both landings with the 1st ID, was wrenching for those who went as well as for those charged with ordering them to go. Lieutenant John P. Downing, an officer in the 18th Infantry, watched his company commander struggle with what Downing thought the "toughest" order "to comply with." Those who went to other units left the one they knew, were not going to the United Kingdom with the rest of their buddies, and were going back into combat almost imme-diately. His captain asked for volunteers but eventually had to consult with his officers, first sergeant, and platoon sergeants. They too struggled, but "the list was finally made up mainly on the basis of those joining late in the campaign."[98]

Casualties, illness, levies to other units, and finally routine reassignment produced considerable turbulence in the division. Colonel Bowen, who commanded a battalion in the 26th and the regiment, contracted malaria and jaundice and had to give up the regiment. Colonel J. F. R. "Jeff" Seitz re-placed Bowen as the third officer to command the 26th during World War II. Several staff officers also turned over, including Bob Porter, the G-2 through North Africa and Sicily. Porter went to II Corps, with Major Robert F. Evans replacing him. Routine changes rippled down through the division. Captain Joe Dawson was one of many reassigned, taking command of Company G, 2nd Battalion, 16th Infantry. Like Huebner, Dawson succeeded a brave and much loved commander, in Dawson's case in the person of Ed Wozenski. Now Dawson, like Huebner, had to win his spurs.[99]

From October 18 to 21, those who remained in the 1st Infantry Divi-sion embarked on transports. The division sailed to Algiers on October 23, remaining there for two days. The transports then departed for the Unit-ed Kingdom, arriving without incident on November 5. By then General Huebner had earned the not entirely affectionate nickname "Coach" for his close personal supervision of marksmanship training. The derisiveness of the nickname can be discerned from its appearance in the sixty-fourth verse of the 1st Division's song cum epic poem, written during the long months of World War II:

Under Terry and Teddy
The gang was plenty rough.
But now it's "Take me out coach,
I think I have had enough."[100]

Notes

1. 1st ID, "Sicily General," G-2 Terrain Study, May 1943, RG 301-2.10, MRC Digital Archives. The study is not paginated. The map showing terrain is labeled "Sicily Topography" and dated June 1943. The route map is untitled. It does show both provincial main highways, all numbered with three digits, and secondary roads, which are numbered and circled.

2. Mason, "Reminiscences," 126; HQ, 1st ID, "A Factual Account of the Combat Operations of the 1st Infantry Division in N. Africa and Sicily during World War II," n.d., MRC 1988.31, 37. Re other attached units, see Knickerbocker et al., *Danger Forward*. See also Craven and Cate, *Europe: Torch to Point Blank*, re Air Force planning and execution in Sicily.

3. Terry Allen, "Situation and Operations Report of the First Infantry Division during the Period of Its Overseas Movement, North African and Sicilian Campaigns from 8 August 1942 to 7 August 1943," N17371, CARL, 12–13. Allen wrote this document at the behest of the committee writing *Danger Forward*. HQ, 1st ID, "Factual Account," 36; Astor, *Terrible Terry Allen*, 201.

4. Clausewitz, *On War*, 186; Allen, "Situation and Operations Report," 13–18; Bradley, *Soldier's Story*, 141.

5. War Department, FM 100-5, *Field Service Regulations: Operations* (Washington, DC: Government Printing Office, 1941), 25.

6. Jackson, *Alexander of Tunis*, 219–221. Garland reference is from Jackson, who quoted the official history.

7. War Department, FM 100-5, 18–19 and 30–33. There is no requirement in doctrine for unquestioning obedience. Bradley, *Soldier's Story*, 138. Bradley himself expected once he issued an order it would be followed without question. Nevertheless, his subordinates did push back even after receiving his orders. For example, see John S. D. Eisenhower, *Bitter Woods*, 100. For example, Troy Middleton, then commanding VIII Corps, complained to Bradley about the orders for his sector the Ardennes. Middleton wanted to shorten his line or be reinforced because he believed that the Germans might counterattack through the Ardennes. Bradley heard him out but claimed, "Don't worry Troy they won't come through here." Middleton pointed out they had come through three times already. Of course, they did attack in the Ardennes on 16 December 1944.

8. Blumenson, *Patton Papers*, 283–85.

9. Blumenson, 285–86.

10. Senger und Etterlin, *Neither Fear Nor Hope*, 139. See also Garland and Smyth, *Sicily*, 243–44. 217

11. Senger und Etterlin, *Neither Fear Nor Hope*, 139–40; Garland and Smyth, *Sicily*, 217– 222 and maps 5 and 6. The author learned to his chagrin that Carlo D'Este made use of the phrase, "All Roads Lead to Messina" as a chapter title in *Bitter Victory*. With apologies to his memory the phrase is used again.

12. Senger, 139-146. See also Garland and Smyth 204-205.

13. Warlimont, *Inside Hitler's Headquarters*, 336.

14. German and Italian observations cited here come primarily from prisoner interrogation reports from II Corps, 2nd AD and 1st ID. See, for example, HQ, 1st ID, interrogation report, July 24, 1943, 2, in RG 301-2.13: Interrogations Reports, 1st Inf Div, Jul–Aug 1943, MRC Digital Archives. The letter cited was written by E. Schomber to a soldier named George on May 1943 who was serving in Sicily. The letter was found near Troina on August 7, 1943. Günter Baumgart's parents wrote about their doubts on July 11, 1943. They referred to the landing as a "Schlamassel"— literally, hassle or scrape. The letters cited are at RG 301-2.1: Intelligence Notes, 1943, MRC Digital Archives. Others can be found in RG 301-2.13: Interrogations Reports, as well.

15. Allen, "Situation and Operations Report."

16. Allen, "Situation and Operations Report," 11, 13, 15, 17.

17. Mason, "Reminiscences," 173; Kingseed, *Omaha Beach to Dawson's Ridge*, 101.

18. Allen, "Situation and Operations Report," 12. In his narrative Allen reports that 18th INF returned to division control on the 11th. The 18th's journal suggests it came at midnight. HQ, 18th Infantry, after-action report, July 1943, n.d., in RG 301-Inf(18)-0.3: Reports of Operations–1st Inf Div (Sicilian Campaign), 1 Jun 43–31 Dec 43, MRC Digital Archives, 2. Re Bowen, see Knickerbocker et al., *Danger Forward*, 111.

19. Knickerbocker et al., *Danger Forward*, 108.

20. Lawrence P. Manley, "26th Infantry History," MRC 2005.144, 59–62; HQ, 26th Infantry, S-3 journal, July 12, 1943, 6–9, in RG 301-Inf(26)-0.3: Reports of Operations, 10 Jul–31 Dec 43, MRC Digital Archives. The report of Darby's liaison with 3rd ID cited above is from the S-3 journal. The journal is not explicit on when the regiment cleared the airfield nor is their report of operations. See report no. 3, 2000 July 12 to 2000 July 13, 1943, in RG 301-Inf(18)-0.3, Sicilian Campaign, 1. The report says merely they accomplished assigned mission with no time offered.

21. HQ, 16th Infantry, Invasion Journal, Sicily, July 5–16, 1943, 44. In the author's opinion, this journal—a combination of excerpts from the official 16th Infantry S-3 journal, coupled with narrative and often detailed transcriptions of conversations— shows the hand of Sam Fuller.

22. 16th Infantry, 44–46.

23. Time of arrival for the tanks is uncertain. The 16th's invasion journal gives various times for the tanks approaching the fight but does not report the time of engagement by Beichley or the other 2nd AD tanks. See also Houston, *Hell on Wheels*, 167–68.

24. 16th Infantry, Invasion Journal, 66–70.

25. HQ, 16th Infantry, after-action report, July 1943, in RG 301-INF(16)-0.3: Reports of Operations, 1 Sep 43–31 Dec 44, MRC Digital Archives, 8. On July 12,

1943, the regiment reported 82 casualties, including 28 killed in action, 11 missing, and 33 evacuated with wounds. The regiment suffered another 14 casualties on July 17, including 4 killed in action. The 1st ID organized under Table of Organization and Equipment (TO&E) 7–11, July 15, 1943. See Bellanger, *Army Infantry Divisions*, 1:25. The division reorganized before Sicily, but the author cannot be certain they had organized with the July 1943 TO&E. At worst the numbers in the text are close.

26. HQ, 1st ID, "Consolidated Interrogation Report on German PW's Captured since July 10, 1943," in RG 301-2.13, Interrogation Reports, July–August 1943, MRC Digital Archives.

27. Knickerbocker et al., *Danger Forward*, 110.

28. Johnson, *One More Hill*, 101.

29. Johnson, 101.

30. Allen, "Situation and Operations Report," 14–15. See also Walt Nechey, "3rd Battalion 26th Inf. Regiment Journal, Nov. 1, 1942–May 1945, in Memory of BG John T. Corley," MRC 1988.32.6, 22. This document includes the unit journal as well as narrative points and enclosures made by Nechey.

31. 16th Infantry, Invasion Journal, 81.

32. 16th Infantry, 82.

33. 16th Infantry, 82–83.

34. Knickerbocker et al., *Danger Forward*, 109. Although this assessment was made postwar, the regiments' journals report similarly during execution.

35. D'Este, *Bitter Victory*, 326.

36. Bradley, *Soldier's Story*, 143. Both Bradley and to a lesser extent Allen trumpeted taking Enna. Germans defended Enna from outside the old walled city and in fact withdrew the morning of July 20, so there was no grand fight to take the city. Allen, in "Situation and Operations Report," 15, asserts that the city was taken by "quick sharp maneuvering."

37. Allen, "Situation and Operations Report," 15; Johnson, *One More Hill*, 112.

38. Garland and Smyth, *Sicily*, 250–57, and maps 6, "The Fight for Fratello," 362, and 7, "15th Army Group Gains," 381.

39. D'Este, *Bitter Victory*, 443–51. For Patton's account, see Blumenson, *Patton Papers*. See also Hamilton, *Master of the Battlefield*, 319–27. Hamilton and others, including Montgomery, saw no value in Patton's exploitation in the western half of Sicily. However, eventually western Sicily also needed to be cleared. Given that Alexander gave the Americans little to do, it is hard to see his point. Montgomery's assessment is particularly hard to understand, given that he is the one who cut the Americans out of the operation. Montgomery says nothing about this meeting in his memoir. D'Este and the author have relied on Hamilton's account. In a letter to General Marshall sent on July 21, 1943, Eisenhower advised that Alexander was considering reorienting 7th Army to take Messina. Eisenhower, *Papers*, no. 1129, 2:1272.

40. Butcher, *Three Years with Eisenhower*, 369–70; Warlimont, *Inside Hitler's Headquarters*, 345. Even Kesselring, the persistent optimist, wrote in his memoir that as of July 16 he was committed to evacuating the island and told Hube as much. Kesselring, *A Soldier's Record*, 197.

41. Satellite imagery linked to elevation maps and the legacy 1:100,000 maps, along with the terrain study 1st ID, "Sicily General," form the basis of this terrain analysis.

42. "German Morale," annex B to G-2 periodic report no. 27, August 7, 1943, 1–2, and J. Wagner to son Jacob Wagner, July 18, 1943, both in RG 301-2.1: G-2 Periodic Reports, Nov 42, 10 Jul–14 Aug 43, Sep 44, MRC Digital Archives.

43.Allen, "Situation and Operations Report," 15–16.

44. There are multiple accounts of first experience with the Nebelwerfer. It produced significant blast effect but relatively little fragmentation. War Department, TM-E 30-451, *Handbook on German Military Forces* (1945; repr., Baton Rouge: Louisiana State University Press, 1990), 395–98. For the rocket weapons produced by the Germans, see 396–402.

45. "World War II Diary of Jean Gordon Peltier," August 2, 1942–July 5, 1945, MRC 1998.79, 105. The assertion that the Nebelwerfer proved comparatively ineffective stems from various accounts. All agree the weapon was frightening.

46. "Theodore L. Dobol, Command Sergeant Major United States Army (Retired): Autobiography," ms., n.d., MRC 1991.24.

47. "Major General Terry Allen of the 1st Division; The Infantry with Dirt behind their Ears," sidebar story in John Hersey, "The Hills of Nicosia," *Time*, August 9, 1943, 30; Manley, "26th Infantry History," 70; Eberhard Rodt, "Studie über den Feldzug in Sizilien bei der 15. Pz. Gren. Divi. Mai–August 1943," Karlsruhe, June 15, 1951, ms. C-077, N17500.765, CARL, 45. Rodt's study lists the 15th PGD's order of battle and commanders.

48. Manley, "26th Infantry History," 70.

49. There is comparatively little written about the organization of the 15th Panzergrenadier Division, or Fullriede. There are numerous internet sources, the accuracy of which the author could not confirm. Rodt is the best source for the 15th PGD. See also Mitcham, *German Order of Battle*, 3:105; re 22nd Panzer Division, see 61. Eberhard Rodt commanded the 22nd Panzer Division when it was disbanded. He rebuilt and commanded the 15th Panzergrenadier Division.

50. Peltier, diary, 106, 109.

51. Peltier, 109–10.

52. 26th Infantry, S-1 journal, July 25, 1943, in Reports of Operations, 10 Jul–31 Dec 43.

53. Rodt, "Studie über den Feldzug in Sizilien," 25. That artillery fire forced the continued "step by step" delay by the 15th PZG. Rodt, 29.

54. Rodt, 25.

55. Rodt, 110, 25. After particularly effective artillery fire on the night of July 22–23, 1943, on the Petralia-Gangi section of the highway, Kampfgruppe Fullriede withdrew to get out from under the American artillery.

56. Allen, "Situation and Operations Report," 17; Garland and Smyth, *Sicily*, 312–15.

57. Garland, 312–15.

58. James L. Pence, "The Operations of Company A, 16th Infantry (1st Infantry Division) Near Nicosia, in Northeast Sicily, 28–29 July 1943 (Sicily Campaign)," Advanced Infantry Officers Course, 1948–1949, Fort Benning, GA, WWII Student Papers, DRL, 6, 8.

59. Pence, 7.

60. Pence, 9–11.

61. Pence, 13–14.

62. Pence, 14–20.

63. Pence, 20–22.

64. Allen, "Situation and Operations Report," 17.

65. Rodt, "Studie über den Feldzug in Sizilien," 29; Allen, "Situation and Operations Report," 17. For Paddy Flint, see "COL Harry Albert 'Paddy' Flint," Find a Grave, https://www.findagrave.com/memorial/42924752/harry-albert-flint.

66. Garland and Smyth, Sicily, 333; G-2 periodic reports no. 19 and 20, in G-2 Periodic Reports, Nov 42, 10 Jul–14 Aug 43, Sep 44; prisoner of war interrogation report, July 22, 1943, in RG 301-2.13: Interrogations Reports, 1st Inf Div, Jul–Aug 1943, MRC Digital Archives. The bulk of the prisoners covered in this report came from the Fullriede's 3rd PGR. See also Astor, Terrible Terry Allen, 214–215; Atkinson, Day of Battle, 153.

67. Allen, "Situation and Operations Report," 18; Manley, "26th Infantry History," 72–73.

68. Carlo D'Este and the author tend toward Patton's view on why Alexander rid himself of Huebner. Holland, Sicily '43, argues that Huebner had been disloyal. For Patton's view, see Blumenson, Patton Papers, 301, 303, 309. Bradley's assessment has merit, though he clearly did not like Allen. Bradley, Soldier's Story, 155. See also Butcher, Three Years with Eisenhower, 376. Butcher's view reflects Eisenhower's intent. Neither officer was to be discarded.

69. HQ, 1st ID, "Situation Overlay, as of 2400 2 Aug 1944, 1:100,00, 1–13 Aug 43," and HQ, 1st ID, FO 30, August 2, 1944, both in RG 301-3.2: G-3 Journal and File, Sicilian Campaign, 1st Infantry Division, 1 Jul 43–13 Aug 43, MRC Digital Archives.

70. Rodt, "Studie über den Feldzug in Sizilien," 30. Rodt admitted that his outposts were driven back earlier than he wished. G-3 journal. The journal shows some progress in the 26th but little anywhere else. See also D'Este, Bitter Victory, 463.

71. Rodt, "Studie über den Feldzug in Sizilien," 30; Allen, "Situation and Operations Report," 19.

72. G-3 journal, Sicilian campaign; Allen, "Situation and Operations Report," 20.

73. Monte Pellegrino changed hands several times. The 1st ID's G-3 journal reports fighting on Pellegrino throughout the day. G-3 journal; 18th Infantry, S-1 journal, 052015, MRC Digital Archives. See also Baumer and Reardon, American Iliad, 162.

74. Rodt, "Studie über den Feldzug in Sizilien," 31.

75. G-3 journal, August 6, 1943; Atkinson, Day of Battle, 159; D'Este, Bitter Victory, 470.

76. Atkinson, 159–60; Astor, *Terrible Terry Allen*, 218–19; Jeffers, *Theodore Roosevelt Jr.*, 225–26.

77. Bradley, *Soldier's Story*, 155–56.

78. Lambert and DeFelice, *Every Man a Hero*, 120–22. The author had the good fortune to know Ray Lambert and to have interviewed him. He was not given to histrionics. If he said with fervor in 2019, he meant it that way in 1943. Charles H. Kuhl, Company L, 3rd Battalion, 26th Infantry, is one of two soldiers Patton abused in the 15th Evacuation Hospital. In response to Patton asking what was wrong with him, Kuhl responded, "I guess I can't take it." Patton slapped Kuhl with the leather gloves he was carrying, ordered him from the tent, and kicked him for good measure. D'Este, *Bitter Victory*, 484. Kuhl had a "diagnosis of psychoneurosis anxiety state." Apparently, he truly couldn't take it. He also had dysentery and malaria. Garland and Smyth, *Sicily*, 426–27. The incident occurred on August 3, 1943.

79. Mason, "Reminiscences," 186–87; Hersey, "Hills of Nicosia," 29–36.

80. Arthur L. Chaitt, "Clarence R. Huebner, Lieutenant General USA (Retired), 1888–1972," *Bridgehead Sentinel*, March 1973, Bridgehead Sentinel Collection, MRC, 1–21, 6.

81. Bradley, *Soldier's Story*, 156; Steven Flaig, "Clarence R. Huebner: An American Military Story of Achievement," MA thesis, University of North Texas, 2006, 8–18. Flaig's thesis is the best biographical source available.

82. Flaig, "Clarence R. Huebner," 14–18.

83. Flaig, 67–81. Huebner taught at the Infantry School twice. Flaig writes that Huebner spent five years teaching or going to school, from 1922 to 1927.

84. Chaitt, "Clarence R. Huebner," 6; "Wyman, Willard Gordon," Generals of WWII, https://www.generals.dk/general/Wyman/Willard_Gordon/USA.html, accessed March 4, 2020.

85. Chaitt, "Clarence R. Huebner," 6; HQ, 1st ID, after-action report, in RG 301-1: G-1 Operations Reports, 8 Nov 1942–14 Apr 1943, Jul 1943–Mar 1944, Jun 1944–May 1945, 1 Jul–31 Dec 1948, MRC Digital Archives.

86. Chaitt, "Clarence R. Huebner," 6.

87. Chaitt, 8.

88. Johnson, *One More Hill*, 127–28.

89. Wyman, "Journal of Events," entries for August 17, 18, 19.

90. Wheeler, *The Big Red One*, 260.

91. HQ, FUSAG (1st Army Group, later renamed 12th Army Group), Immediate Report no. 10 (Combat Observations), July 24, 1944, box 1, N3080, CARL, 1.

92. FUSAG, Immediate Report no. 10, 2; Dobol, "Autobiography," 19.

93. There is no clear-cut explanation for the 1st ID reaction. In "Reminiscences and Anecdotes," Mason discusses Patton at length and mostly critically, but says nothing about this incident, leaving it to the reader's inference. Carlo D'Este covers the incident thoroughly: D'Este, *Bitter Victory*, 483–96.

94. Mason, "Reminiscences," 197. See also Mason, "After-Dinner Talk by MG (Ret) Stanhope B. Mason, Chief of Staff 1st Inf Div., WWII," n.d., Albert H. Smith Papers,

MRC 1996.95.1, 7. On more than one occasion Mason reflected on Huebner and Allen, who, despite their differences, both came to love and be loved by the 1st ID.

95. Blumenson and Stokesbury, *Masters of the Art of Command*, 170; Stanhope after-dinner speech is on 9.

96. Trident demonstrated the continued divergence among the Allies; it did maintain commitment to invading France, but focused the next step on taking Italy. Matloff, *Strategic Planning*, 126–45, covers the main points of difference and agreement. See also Ambrose, *Supreme Commander*, 210–18. Ambrose's account of the visit of a high-powered British delegation led by Churchill but accompanied by Marshall to provide support for Eisenhower is enlightening on the machinations of Allied policy-making. HQ 1st ID, G-1 after-action report, annex 5, July 31, 1943, in G-1 Operations Reports.

97. G-1 after-action report, September 1–20, 1943, in G-1 Operations Reports.

98. John P. Downing, "No Promotion," n.d., MRC 1994.41.1, 250.

99. Mason, "Reminiscences," 194; Kingseed, *Omaha Beach to Dawson's Ridge*, 108.

100. On embarkation and redeployment to United Kingdom, see Wheeler, *The Big Red One*, 262. Re "Song of the Fighting First," see Chaitt, "Clarence R. Huebner," 7.

CHAPTER EIGHT

Preparing for the Longest Day

I believe we'll be able to beat off the assault.
—Erwin Rommel, January 19, 1944

**We did quite a number of mock invasions along the Slapton
Sands area.**
*—Jerry W. Eades, 62nd Anti-Aircraft Artillery supporting
16th Infantry on training for D-Day*

GEORGE S. PATTON Jr., according to Stan Mason, had two characters. In one
version he demonstrated probity and good manners. In that rendition, Patton "would measure up to the critical standards of Lord Chesterfield." In his
other persona, he was "boorish, overbearing, rude, coarse, and a blustering
braggart." The latter was the Patton with which the soldiers of the 1st Division were familiar. During his tenure in command of II Corps and Seventh
Army, Patton routinely and publicly made disparaging remarks about the
division's leadership and its performance in the field. The stony silence with
which the Big Red One greeted the apology he made to the entire division
apparently had no effect on him. Just before the division departed for the
United Kingdom, Seventh Army notified 1st ID that Patton intended to bid
farewell to the troops by cruising around the transports at anchor in Augusta, Sicily. The implication was that applause or even a cheer from the troops
would not be amiss.[1]

Major General Clarence R. Huebner knew what was expected, and as
an old friend, he intended for Patton to receive a fond farewell from the

division. However, what followed demonstrated that he had not yet come to know and understand his men. Huebner instructed Mason to have the troops line the rails of the transports and cheer as Patton cruised past. Mason demurred, suggesting that the soldiers would certainly line the rails but were unlikely to cheer, based on their history with the Seventh Army commander. Huebner listened carefully, but disagreed. Mason, who thought Huebner generally "knew soldier thinking," this time got it "completely wrong." When the day came, Huebner, Colonel Willard G. Wyman, members of Patton's personal staff, and the general himself boarded a launch and cruised the harbor so that the army commander could be seen and presumably witness acts of approbation from the troops. Instead, "Silence was total. Every ship had its rails solidly lined with soldiers as deep as space permitted. But not a cheer was heard. No applause. Nothing was heard but sepulchral silence."[2]

Mason met his boss afterward, making sure he exhibited no sign of an inherent "I told you so," visually or otherwise. For his part, Hueubner was "quiet, thoughtful, with mixed emotions running all the way from anger and chagrin to deeply felt embarrassment." According to Mason, Huebner held no one to blame for a "regretful outcome of what was in reality a well intentioned gesture." The silence with which the division responded to Patton spoke loudly about the way the general had treated the 1st ID. Ernest A. Hilberg, who joined the 1st ID in time for the Normandy invasion, trained with the veterans of North Africa and Sicily. Of them he said, "They hated Patton." Whatever the depth of their feelings toward Patton, the silence of the division spoke clearly about Huebner's relation with his command. Clarence "Coach" Huebner and the 1st Division would come to know and understand each other in the coming months. Their relationship bore fruit on D-Day.[3]

This chapter describes the strategic challenge, but focuses narrowly on the 1st Infantry Division's retraining, reequipping, and otherwise preparing for the invasion of France. The division needed to reconstitute itself, given the number of casualties suffered and troops transferred to 3rd ID to plump the latter up for the invasion of Italy. The Big Red One's preparation and its role in the landing in Operation Overlord are considered in the context they occurred and at the tactical level. The deception efforts, the Allied air forces' successful campaign to defeat the Luftwaffe, and many other important topics are discussed here only as they apply to what the division did and experienced at Omaha Beach and subsequent operations, eventually leading to their breakout at Saint-Lô.

Back to the United Kingdom

The Big Red One sailed from Augusta, Sicily, on October 23 in the company of transports headed for the States and others bound for the United Kingdom. In Algiers, October 25–26, the ships divided into two convoys. Additionally, 1st ID troops aboard the HMS *Stirling Castle* transshipped to HMS *Franconia*. Both convoys sailed from Algiers on October 27. After passing through the Strait of Gibraltar, the convoy bound for the United Kingdom turned north. That course change disabused most of those aboard of the idea that the 1st ID might be going home. The bulk of the division arrived in Liverpool, England, on November 5. Rumors abounded about what would come next, but General Huebner personally informed his soldiers of their destiny as soon as possible after they disembarked.[4]

Addressing the 16th Infantry in a crowded warehouse, Huebner began by saying, "We will not participate in the invasion of Italy." The 16th responded with cheers. But then he applied the wet blanket. He reminded the assembled infantrymen of their combat record and its costs, but assured them that they would finish the job that those who were killed and wounded could not complete. That could mean only one thing—participation in a cross-Channel invasion. He piled it on, asserting, "You're going to train like you've never trained before." Previously he had denied his men their pride of place. Before arriving in England, Huebner had required the veteran soldiers to remove their patches and paint over the 1st ID flash that adorned their helmets. Now he added insult to injury. If asked, they were not to admit they were combat veterans of the 1st ID. Instead, they were to claim they were assigned to the nonexistent 314th Anti-Airforce Regiment, newly arrived from the States. The purpose, he asserted, was to "keep Hitler guessing about what the First Division is going to do next."[5]

The regiment then boarded trains bound for the county of Dorset, on the south coast of England. Dorset would be their home for the next several months. Dorchester in south Dorset lay more or less at the center of the small villages and hamlets in which the division's units settled. Some soldiers lived in resort towns along the coast, including Weymouth, Bournemouth, and Swanage. Accommodations ranged from Nissen huts to the homes of British citizens, who, unlike the Americans' ancestors, generally did not object to housing foreign soldiers.[6]

Frank Johnson and the antitank company of the 18th Infantry settled in Winterborne Saint-Martin, near Dorchester, where Johnson found the inhabitants "friendly and genuinely happy to have us in their midst." Jean Peltier and the 33rd Field Artillery made their home in recently built barracks near the village of Piddlehinton. Peltier thought the camp was "very nice." The amenities included a British military canteen, run by "a very efficient Mrs. Little and a group of volunteer girls who wore uniforms," which "supplied doughnuts, tea, coffee, 'canned' music, beer, etc.... to us this was next door to heaven." Richard Colson, assigned to Company H, 26th Infantry, lived in a house in Swanage in which he slept on a mattress cover "stuffed with corn husks." Everything else, including the food, was good.[7]

The soldiers in the 1st ID enjoyed the comforts of the United Kingdom, including the time to rest and enjoy an occasional night on the town. To their credit, they were generally well behaved, although there were incidents of serious misbehavior, including rape and scuffles with black troops. The great majority of Americans plunked down in rural England, however, comported themselves well. Ernie Pyle said it best: "Actually the Americans weren't bad and English reception was good." Both sides made genuinely entertaining cracks about the other. One joke the Americans liked to repeat was the comment of one to another—"These English are beginning to act as if this country belonged to them."[8]

The Allies Decide

In the United Kingdom, training remained oriented on the basics, with some effort to retrain amphibious operations, but the focus on assault landings did not begin until the planning for the invasion solidified. Allied decisions taken at the end of the Sicily campaign presumed that opportunity existed in Italy. Generalfeldmarschall Albert Kesselring Kesselring, on the other hand, perceived opportunity for a defense in depth that would prove costly to the Allies. The Allies landed in Italy because they could, and because doing so kept the pressure on the Germans, whose major ally was collapsing. Kesselring's assessment proved valid.[9]

Conferences at Cairo and Tehran at the end of November settled the question of the next steps for the Allies. Although Churchill argued for invading anywhere but France, Stalin sided with the American view that the time to land there had come. Their views prevailed. In December 1943 President Roosevelt chose Eisenhower as Supreme Commander, Allied

Expeditionary Forces. Air chief marshal Sir Arthur Tedder served as his deputy. Eisenhower had three component commanders: Sir Trafford Leigh-Mallory, who commanded the Allied Expeditionary Air Force; Sir Bertram Ramsay, the naval component commander; and Sir Bernard Law Montgomery, who as commander of 21st Army Group would lead the land component. The landing would occur on the Calvados coast of Normandy, adjacent to the Cotentin Peninsula.[10]

Availability of LSTs (landing ships, tank) and other landing craft determined what could be done amphibiously and so drove planning. Though the Allies had an enormous collection of amphibious craft, the number remained finite. The shortage of smaller landing craft was even more severe than the shortage of LSTs. Competition for LSTs and other craft denied Eisenhower a simultaneous landing in the north and south of France. Churchill expressed his own frustration quite clearly: "The destinies of two great empires . . . seem to be tied up in some God-damned things called LSTs." Eisenhower would have to do as Carl von Clausewitz suggested in his magnum opus, achieving "skillful concentration of superior strength at the decisive point." Shortages of LSTs or not, the Normandy landing was a go.[11]

The Calvados coast faces nearly due north on the Bay of the Seine. The landing zone itself extends from Caen on the Orne River to Quinéville on the Cotentin Peninsula. Caen lies 110 miles southeast of Portsmouth, England. Cherbourg, the first port the Allies proposed to seize, sits at the northern tip of the Cotentin Peninsula. The planners assigned code names to landing beaches: from east to west, Sword, Juno, Gold, Omaha, and Utah. General Montgomery had five assault divisions and three airborne divisions assigned to execute the landings. Two field army and four corps headquarters would exercise tactical command and expand the "bridgehead to receive follow on forces and necessary material to continue the attack."[12]

Montgomery's concept for the invasion required Commonwealth forces to establish a firm left flank at Caen, given that German reserves were positioned generally east and south of Normandy, and the ground to the east favored mobile operations. He intended Bradley's First Army to expand the lodgment south, clear the Cotentin Peninsula to the north, and seize the port of Cherbourg. The plan bore Montgomery's stamp. It was, as Hans Speidel, Rommel's chief of staff, observed, "tactically and strategically methodical . . . it sought to eliminate every risk, keep casualties down to a

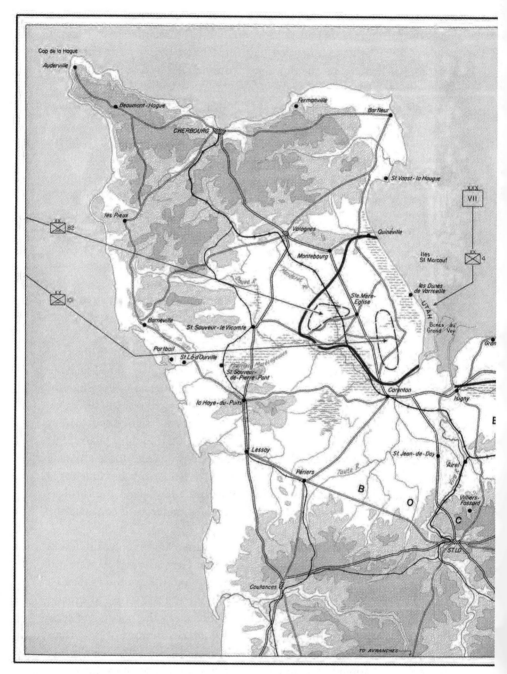

Map 11: The Final OVERLORD Plan. Reproduced from G. A. Harrison, *Cross-Channel Attack* (Washington: Center of Military History, 1951), Map II.

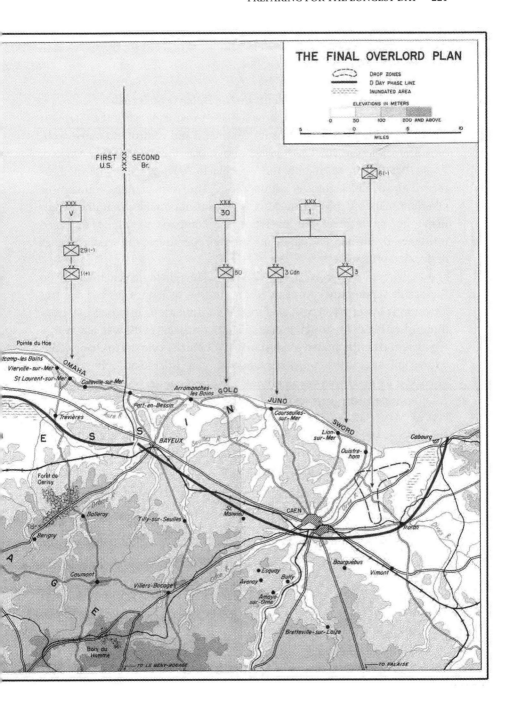

THE FINAL OVERLORD PLAN

minimum, and put into practice the attack *a coup sûr.*" Fair enough, and why not? The stakes were too high to gamble. Whether Montgomery's plan worked, as he claimed and others have disputed, is irrelevant.[13]

German Assessments on the Defense of France

Despite having no Vichy French or Italians to wrangle with, the Germans still managed to produce ineffective command and control in France. Robert Citino argues in *The Wehrmacht's Last Stand: The German Campaigns of 1944–1945* that in Normandy the Wehrmacht "opened badly and then careened into complete disaster within weeks." The German high command, or Oberkommando der Wehrmacht (OKW), did not establish a unified command, nor did it direct joint operations. By comparison, despite continued resistance by airmen to supporting ground operations, the western Allies performed brilliantly.[14]

As Oberbefalshaber West, or OB West, Generalfeldmarschall Gerd von Rundstedt supposedly commanded the defense of France. In fact, he had little control over naval and air forces, and limitations imposed by Hitler diminished his ability to act. Worse still, other theaters of the war, but mostly the eastern front, siphoned off resources. Not much occurred to change conditions in France until a series of raids prompted Hitler to order the building of coastal defenses that became known as the Atlantic Wall. His program, ambitious to say the least, required the completion of fifteen thousand bunkers by May 1943. In October 1943, Rundstedt reviewed Germany's defensive posture in France, from bunkers to troops. He reported accurately but pessimistically about what he found. Frontages for divisions were beyond his force's means. Most lacked the transport to react quickly. In short, there were too few troops to defend the coast and no means to fight *Bewegungskrieg*, or war of movement. Finally, construction of the Atlantic Wall fell short of Hitler's goals.[15]

Rundstedt submitted his report on October 25. On November 3 Hitler issued his Directive 51, which rightly concluded that there was operational space in the east but none in the west. Accordingly, he ordered the main effort to be shifted from east to west, writing, "I have therefore decided to reinforce its [France's] defenses, particularly those places from which the long range bombardment [V1 and V2 rocket attacks] of England will begin. For it is here that the enemy must and will attack, and it is here—unless all indications are misleading—that the decisive battle against the landing forces will be fought."[16]

Hitler's directive made a difference, but not that which he imagined. The demands of the war in the east and success of the Allied air campaign made it difficult to shift the main effort. Still, the effort to improve defenses bore fruit, as did the arrival of Generalfeldmarschall Erwin Rommel. Rommel originally organized Army Group B in preparation for assuming command of the Italian theater. Instead, Hitler appointed Kesselring to command in Italy and moved Rommel and Army Group B's staff to France. In May 1944 Rundstedt organized Army Group G, commanded by Johannes Blaskowitz, to defend the South of France.[17]

Rommel arrived in France on December 14 and acted with characteristic energy. After meeting with Rundstedt, he spent nearly a month inspecting his new command. On his return, Rommel concluded that the Germans could fend off a landing, but only if they won the fight at the landing site. He put it simply: "If we are not at the throat of the enemy immediately, he lands there will be no restoring the situation." Firepower and obstacles to the landing forces' ability to get off the beaches, including a vast number of mines laid, were in his view essential. By May 1944 the Germans had laid nearly five million mines along the Channel coast alone. They also built formidable defenses around concrete fighting positions and obstacles, including air-landing obstacles. Obstacles along the coast were well fortified, covered by fire, and supported by artillery. To have armor reserves positioned close to the coast was also essential to his concept, but this, however, did not come to pass. It is important to note that Rommel had not completed preparing the defenses before the Allied landings. Accordingly, the strength of his defenses was uneven.[18]

Rommel had the Seventh and Fifteenth Armies assigned to Army Group B. Generaloberst Friedrich Dollmann commanded Seventh Army. His sector extended from the just east of Caen to the Loire River. Generaloberst Hans von Salmuth's Fifteenth Army defended from Caen to the Netherlands. His sector included the Pas de Calais, perceived Rommel, and OKW, as the most likely invasion site.[19]

Huebner Sets the Standard

Huebner and his commanders had a number of tasks to complete without the luxury of knowing how much time they had before returning to combat. And in so doing they had to contend with combat veterans, many of whom had served together since 1940 or earlier. These soldiers had trained hard to execute amphibious assaults, and had actually performed two of them, fought in Algeria, then across Tunisia and Sicily. They had hoped for a break or even a rotation home. After nearly a year in combat, they were experienced but also exhausted. Sam Fuller typified how many, perhaps most of them, felt. He arrived in England in "a foul mood," with reason to feel that way. As he put it, "My nerves were strained to the breaking point. I'd had my fill of combat."[20]

To add insult to injury, the veterans of North Africa and Sicily continued to suffer recurrent malaria and/or jaundice and various secondary illnesses. They were genuinely sick and tired. Robert L. Bogart's experience was not unusual. On the way to England, Bogart endured two malaria attacks because, like many others, he was run down. Shortly after arriving in England, he came down with pneumonia and spent six weeks in the hospital. Training, however important, had to account for the need to rest and rebuild strength.[21]

The division also had to reequip, since it had left the majority of its equipment, less "motor vehicles," behind in Sicily. In the end, that exception did not matter; the 1st ID transferred "a great amount of its transportation" to other units in September. What few trucks it retained were turned in just before embarking for England in October. Receiving new equipment was welcome, but nothing excess to the tables of organization would be issued, and equipment excess to the tables of organization had to be turned in.[22]

The division also departed Sicily short of junior officers. That meant new platoon leaders had to be assimilated and learn their jobs at the same time. Huebner and Wyman took advantage of the turnover to incorporate lessons from the division's previous operations, as well as setting standards for the basic tactical formation of the division—the platoon. Less than two weeks before sailing, Huebner issued a two-page memorandum for platoon commanders that listed what he believed were the functions of "platoon command." The commanding general listed fourteen, with the last being the most important: "The above instructions will be carried out whenever applicable by placing the responsibility for their observance and enforcing their observance upon the appropriate noncommissioned officers of the platoon." The memorandum stipulated that platoon commanders might decide what to do, but sergeants ran platoons and supervised execution.[23]

Platoon leader functions ranged from the mundane—personally inspecting the feet of each soldier weekly—to the more esoteric—"study all training literature to the type of platoon to which assigned." The latter, of course, included the appropriate field manuals. Each platoon leader had also to know "the name of every man in their respective platoon," and do so within ten days of taking charge of a platoon. Other functions addressed equipment readiness and assuring the welfare of the troops.[24]

The second and final paragraph of two sentences stated that "frequent checks will be made by company, troop or battery commanders, battalion commanders and staff officers to insure [*sic*] compliance." Finally, checking would "include the questioning of enlisted men as well as platoon commanders." This short memorandum established the fundamental standard of operation for the entire chain of command. Just as Allen, Roosevelt, and Andrus visited or inspected their units almost daily, so too would the new team. Establishing standards and enforcing them are essential to imprinting a commander's views on his unit. Huebner was not unusual in that way. Wyman's efforts in support, apparent in Sicily, came to bear fruit in the months leading to the Allied invasion of France.[25]

Huebner's method went further than functions and imperatives. He followed the memorandum for platoon commanders with a pamphlet produced at his direction entitled "Notes on Leadership." The cover of the pamphlet asserted that it was "intended to point out that certain common errors and omissions occur in training and in battle as well in as in your daily life as a leader, which may have escaped your attention." At fourteen pages, it is a pithy and still useful primer on leadership. It included basic advice such as "*never bluff!!* [emphasis in original]." But it goes deeper, arguing that to bring cheerful obedience to their orders young officers needed to show "*personal initiative, decision,* and *courage.* Without these attributes, no man can expect to lead." The definition of *courage,* according to Huebner's pamphlet, included "moral courage," such as the willingness "to assume responsibility for your own acts."[26]

Huebner, his two generals, and his commanders turned to training, but with limitations that often led to frustration. Reequipping affected training, as did personnel shortages and competing demands for time, such as attendance at special schools. Shortages of ammunition and insufficient training in landing compounded matters. Training in a combat zone led to other issues—and make no mistake, in 1943–44 the south of England remained a combat zone. Nearby units often trained at night, necessitating warnings of the use of pyrotechnics and flares. Mistaking training for an actual attack by the enemy was ever possible. Occasional enemy air raids also affected training. Finally, with illness, injury, and other commitments competing for their attention, commanders could almost never count on having their entire unit available for training.

Despite distractions, Huebner's assertion to the 16th Infantry the very night it came ashore made it plain that the division would be part of the cross-Channel invasion. Reflecting on the eight months in England, Huebner wrote later that the division concentrated on "the development of skills and techniques of our weapons, the training of specialists, and the molding of our battle teams. . . . To assist in these aims, we had the services of many combat-wise and experienced leaders who could impart to our new replacements the know-how of battle." He recalled rehearsing the "infantry-tank-team" as well as planning and training with the air force and navy, "for there was a triphibious landing to be made."[27]

Lessons learned or at least collected and internal observations identified training requirements. Eisenhower's Allied Force Headquarters training memorandum no. 50, "Lessons from the Sicilian Campaign," rolled up key observations from subordinate units. Perhaps the most important lesson stemmed from the Seventh Army's after-action report, which claimed, "It is the general consensus of opinion of all officers who have actually participated in battle that our men do not shoot enough." The troops had been taught not to shoot "unless the target was seen and was a profitable one." The report concluded, however, that in retrospect "this was a mistake." Instead, "continuous fire" should be directed at positions from which enemy fire is emanating. Aimed fire at clearly visible targets does not take advantage of suppressive fire.[28]

The 1st ID's faith in envelopment and night attacks received prominent mention, with high marks going to the field artillery. Of sixty-five pages, lessons learned on artillery consumed twenty-three. The training memorandum included an excerpt of a letter home written by young German artilleryman captured by the 1st ID. He wrote at length of the misery of receiving what felt like continuous barrages. The artilleryman reported the observation of a veteran sergeant who said "he had never experienced anything like it [US artillery] in France, Poland, or Russia." American artillery proved sufficiently ubiquitous for this soldier and his mates to call it "magic fire." Clift Andrus, the division artillery, and II Corps Artillery set a high standard.[29]

There were many more lessons, ranging from maintenance of tanks to air-ground coordination. This report and others like it, along with Huebner's own assessments and those of his subordinates, formed the basis of training of the 1st ID for the eventual campaign in France. They understood that no lesson is learned until it results in a change of behavior. In particular, teaching soldiers the utility of providing suppressive fire, rather than firing only at visible targets, would take time and iteration. The means to practice would come in live-fire exercises. Later on, rehearsing assault landings took precedence. Working with the various units that were attached for the invasion came both in rehearsing the landing and in war games that attempted to anticipate the fight beyond the beachhead, also featured prominently in training schedules.[30]

Huebner Coaches

Marksmanship and field firing topped the list of Huebner's training priorities. Accordingly, field firing began in November, while the field artillery began practice firing in Wales on December 1. As units began to stabilize assigned strength, qualification firing began. Field exercises for small units from squad to company included street fighting, night fighting, and a range of exercises to train in coordination with regimental antitank and cannon companies. Nearly four hundred soldiers trained on antiaircraft firing from truck cabs against rocket-propelled targets.[31]

Huebner's insistence on focusing on discipline and the basics irritated many of the old soldiers. The "Coach," as it turned out, knew his stuff, and could personally intervene in marksmanship training with good effect. Huebner's approach was often Socratic: he asked questions in such a way as to inspire in his subordinates an effort to get ahead of him. He wanted his young officers to learn from these discussions, and ultimately to anticipate him. In *The Dead and Those About to Die*, John McManus recounts an example of Huebner's hands-on approach. An infantryman watched him participate in one of their drills. Huebner held his position in a foxhole while a tank drove over him. The soldier observed to Brigadier General Clift Andrus, "The 'Old Man' surely knows his business."[32]

The division's low-density support units, known collectively as "Special Troops," got their training underway, but not without problems. Lieutenant Paul Skogsberg, commanding the 1st Reconnaissance Troop, complained that replacing radios in the troop's M8 armored cars "greatly hindered" his unit's training. The upgrade caused the troop to lose "almost the entire month." Worse still, two M8s lacked telescopic sights for their 37-millimeter cannons, rendering them "useless." The 1st Signal Company complained of similar problems. The division headquarters company commander reported that he could obtain no training ammunition to shoot his rocket launchers. Even the infantry regiments experienced problems.

The 26th Infantry reported that training in January had gone very well, but then rated efficiency at 90 percent because 10 percent of the command was hospitalized. A shortage of rifles for replacements also hindered training.[33]

In the first weeks of training for the inevitable return to combat, both physical illness and sheer exhaustion incumbered progress. Combatants had experienced "shell shock" in the Great War and would confront it again in this second iteration. In World War II "neuropsychiatric" conditions emerged from long-duration combat. Generally, medical officers used the term "combat exhaustion" to describe the problems stemming from pro-longed combat. Allied medical officers learned a great deal about the phe-nomenon from the campaigns in North Africa and Sicily and gleaned some of what their colleagues in the Pacific were learning. The stress of combat could and often did induce in once brave and effective soldiers an unrelent-ing condition of stress that hindered ability to fight, or function, normally, so that what was abnormal in peacetime, "insomnia, trembling, recurrent nightmares—became normal in combat."[34]

Despite what some were seeing and experiencing in the field, many if not most officers at the time shared Patton's dim view of the validity of the neuropsychiatric diagnosis; still, and to its credit, the army acted. These actions included assigning a psychiatrist to divisions, including the 1st ID. Although Bradley described him as "a flinty disciplinarian," Huebner found merit in the attempt to mitigate neuropsychiatric conditions emerging from long service in combat. Dr. Joseph Bradley joined the 1st ID as its psychi-atrist in January. For a month in January–February, he attended the Euro-pean Theater of Operations School of Military Psychiatry. On return, Dr. Bradley educated his medical staff and "all infantry officers in the division" on combat exhaustion.[35]

That the doctor had access to "all infantry officers" demonstrates Hueb-ner's confidence in the utility of studying how to identify, mitigate, or treat a problem. In this case, doing so could stem the loss of tactical effective-ness and unit cohesion that could result from combat fatigue. The division mandated that every soldier processed for trial by general court-martial be screened for symptoms or behaviors that put them at risk. Dr. Bradley de-scribed the effort as a "weeding out process." The focus then turned to how to handle combat exhaustion "in the coming of the invasion." Among other things, this meant convincing officers and noncommissioned officers that combat exhaustion was not "malingering," and that the only certain way to extend a soldier's usefulness was treatment, which often meant no more than sufficient rest.[36]

Richard Colson bore witness to what may have been a consequence of combat exhaustion when he campaigned in North Africa and Sicily with the 26th Infantry. His platoon sergeant, whom he admired, accepted a battlefield commission and now led the platoon as a lieutenant. One morning a soldier found the lieutenant dead, attired in "full dress" uniform. He had killed himself with his pistol. Of the dead lieutenant Colson observed, "He was a good officer."[37]

The Assistant Coach

Huebner let the division know what he expected and required. Like Allen before him, Huebner was well known to the troops, if not yet well liked. The first planning meetings for the Normandy landing began in December; in February he learned that his division would be one of the assault divisions. Planning consumed more and more time for Huebner, Mason, and a small core of the staff. That meant Huebner could no longer interact daily with his troops, and therefore increasingly looked to Wyman to act in his stead. In the months leading to the invasion, Wyman led the training effort while Huebner led the planning effort. Wyman approached training with the same level of energy as had Roosevelt but with a different style. Bill Wyman personified the imperturbable laconic Mainer. Fluent in Mandarin, Wyman admired Chinese culture and enjoyed living in China, but he was equally at home with the young Americans soldiering in the Big Red One.[38]

The 1st ID had a very high opinion of itself, mostly well earned. But in some ways the attitude that it had developed had gone too far, manifesting itself in what Wyman called a lack of "punctilious" military courtesy and bearing. Soldiers in the division, like nearly all young men everywhere, got away with what they thought they could. Wyman set about altering that habit. Speeding trucks and jeeps, regardless of who drove them, found the assistant division commander playing highway patrol. A large American truck barreling down the narrow roads through towns as old as the Middle Ages or even Roman Britain was dangerous to all and sundry. On November 15 the assistant division commander caught up with a deuce and a half (two-and-a-half-ton cargo truck) driven by a corporal named Watkins. Wyman ordered Watkins to report to his company commander, tell him about the incident, and report that he was now a private. Of course, Wyman followed up to make sure Watkins had done as he was told; he had. Neither were officers exempted from the general's enforcement of traffic rules.[39]

Wyman did more than terrorize speeders. Like Huebner, he was a coach. He did not intervene in training if it was going reasonably well, or if doing so would undermine the trainer. Only after training and the unit "critique" ended would he offer ways to improve or his congratulations. He believed the most important thing was to "create realism." He and General Huebner believed live-fire exercises should do everything within the limits of safety to approach "realistic conditions." Wyman met frequently with regimental and battalion commanders and coached them on how to improve training. He was concerned, too, that subordinate commanders be allowed "to develop their own initiative."[40]

Huebner set a high standard for his officer leadership. He took the role of harsh taskmaster, while Mason ensured that those worth saving were saved. In this early version of "talent management," Wyman played a critical role, keeping notes of his assessments of officers he encountered from the outset of his tour as assistant division commander. In particular, he spent a lot of time with the 1st Reconnaissance Troop. The troop commander and his platoon leaders had no intervening headquarters between them and the division, so Wyman worked closely with them to assure they were prepared and had someone to turn to. He identified underperforming officers but also kept notes on top performers. For example, in December he commented very favorably on Captains Edward F. Wozenski and Joe Dawson, who both led companies on D-Day.[41]

General Wyman's approach worked. Commanders from company to regiment were not squeamish about asking him for help. He freely took on their concerns and followed up with the division staff and elsewhere as necessary. He served as inspector, assistant coach, enforcer, and interlocutor for General Huebner and the division. That is the job of an assistant division commander, and it was precisely what the 1st ID needed. In Wyman, Huebner had a worthy partner.

Assimilating and Training Replacements

The Hollywood depiction of cynical and worn combat veterans remaining aloof from replacements, or telling them they do not even want to know their names, has a basis in fact. However, the narrative is overstated. The 1st Infantry Division, like most divisions, attempted to receive replacements in at least a humane way. As noted in chapter 5, just getting to the division often entailed a long and miserable odyssey. Replacement depots worked on an industrial scale. That resulted in few niceties and no tolerance for variation. "One size must fit all" would have been a worthy motto for the "repple depots."

How replacements came to the 1st ID reflected manpower problems as well. In August 1943 the War Department warned of "a breakdown in the replacement system." The Army Specialized Training Program and the Army Air Force, along with specialty schools, skimmed off the top of volunteers and draftees, both with the recognized result that the "quality of men received by the Ground Forces declined."[42]

Furthermore, the replacement system could not keep up with the requirements of the infantry. Undersize soldiers like Albert Mominee, mentioned in chapter 2, arrived in time to make all three assault landings of the 1st ID. His colleague Eddie Steeg measured just over five feet, nearly an inch shorter than Albert, but Eddie was tall enough to carry an M1 Garand rifle, some forty-eight inches long, less the bayonet, or only twelve inches shorter than he was. Samuel E. Dixon's poor eyesight and a ruptured eardrum prevented him from volunteering, but later in the war he was good enough to be drafted and sent to the 1st ID in time for D-Day. Many replacements who came to the 1st ID were transferred from units in training, and therefore had endured the disorientation of joining a new unit more than once. The replacement system could not keep up with the need. At the end of March, only four of the division's twenty-seven rifle companies had reached full strength. Despite everything, once replacements arrived in 1st ID, they were generally well received. Of the replacements, veteran soldier Joseph A. Rowley said, "We welcomed them as brothers."[43]

In February 1944 the War Department directed that no eighteen-year-old soldiers or pre-Pearl Harbor fathers (literally men who had a child born before December 7, 1941) should not be sent overseas with less than six months' service. Drafted on April 2, 1943, eighteen-year-old Charles Dye met the criteria to join 1st ID. To him, "the veterans of the 1st Division were a good bunch." John H. MacPhee joined Ed Wozenski's Company E, 16th Infantry. He realized Company E was understrength and asked his platoon sergeant "where everybody was." The sergeant responded, "Dead or wounded or in the hospitals." Soldiers returned after recovering from wounds, new men arrived, and the company trained hard. Of Wozenski, Dye said, "I had the greatest confidence in my Captain."[44]

Samuel E. Dixon joined the 26th Infantry in Swanage, where, he said, "my sergeant took me under his wing." He recalled stories about how heroic his company commander was. Small things made for confidence and reduced the feeling of strangeness, even foreboding, in arriving at one's first unit. Isadore R. Berkowitz joined the 16th Infantry. His company employed a "buddy system" to integrate replacements. Small kindnesses made a difference. Miller Bellich, who made all three landings with the 18th Infantry, observed that his battalion commander, Major Henry V. Middleworth, knew the name of every soldier in the battalion. Ralph J. Gordon, who also served in the 18th, in England came to admire his company commander, Captain Herbert A. Scott-Smith Jr., known in the company as Scotty. But it was the competence of the platoon sergeants that sold him on the company. They were "old Army men who had fought in Africa and Sicily and were the kind of men you would follow to the edge of the world."[45]

The Plan

Overlord, the code name for the overall invasion of France, envisaged US First Army landing V and VII Corps ashore with the 1st ID and 4th ID in the initial assault and the two US airborne divisions parachuting in several hours earlier. 1st ID's assault echelon would be made up of one 1st ID regimental combat team and one from the 29th ID. Although the 1st and 29th ID were both assault divisions, Huebner controlled the landing to assure unity of command. Eventually D-Day was set for June 5, 1944, with H-Hour planned for 0630. The naval component had responsibility for Neptune, the code name for the amphibious assault. Rear Admiral Allan G. Kirk, commanding the Western Naval Task Force with First Army embarked, owned the landing at Omaha and Utah beaches. As conditions allowed, the 29th ID command post would come ashore and assume control of its units, as would V Corps. Finally, Omar Bradley would take command of forces ashore as soon as he could reasonably move the First Army command post ashore.

Adrian Lewis in *Omaha Beach: Flawed Victory* argues convincingly that the plan had several basic flaws. Landing in daylight was perhaps chief among these. Professor Lewis points out that there were two tried and proven doctrines on assault landings, one developed and practiced in the Mediterranean and the other developed and practiced in the Central Pacific. The Mediterranean method developed by the British "relied on night landings, surprises, and stealth against poorly defended coast line." That used in the Pacific "relied on daylight assaults, mass and fire power against strongly defended beaches." The planners determined to land at daylight despite the opposition of Major General Leonard T. Gerow at V Corps and Huebner at 1st ID.[46]

Rear Admiral John L. Hall, commanding Assault Force O, would land Huebner's troops and ultimately General Gerow's V Corps. The navy also provided gunfire support and beach-clearing teams to scrub the beaches clean of water obstacles, including Belgian gates, tetrahedrons, and wooden obstacles with Teller mines attached. Naval gunfire support provided for Force O included the battleships *Arkansas* and *Texas*, as well as three British and one French light cruisers, and an even dozen destroyers (nine US Navy, three Royal Navy). Naval gunfire units available to support the landing were significantly less than the navy used in the Pacific to support smaller efforts.[47]

The air component planned prodigious effort in support of the landings. Eisenhower wanted, and despite resistance, obtained from the airmen the so-called transportation plan that aimed to destroy the railway network in France and Belgium to interdict, delay, or even stop movement forward of German reserves. The Royal Air Force's 2nd Tactical Air Force and the US Ninth Air Force had the mission of providing tactical air support to the ground forces. Major General Lewis H. Brereton, commanding the Ninth Air Force, built a robust capability that included troop-carrier aircraft, bombers, fighter bombers, fighters, and organic antiaircraft artillery to protect expeditionary airfields. The airmen were on board for Overlord. General Bradley's faith in them was such that he told a gathering of troops that they would "pulverize the beaches."[48]

There are no elegant maneuvers associated with an assault landing, and Omaha Beach was no exception. The 1st ID proposed to land with two V Corps regimental combat teams abreast—the 116th (29th Division) on the right or west, and the 16th on the left or east. With months to plan, the invaders knew a lot about the beach and a fair amount about the defenders. They had detailed data on beach gradients, tides, currents, and the general lay of the land. Landing at low tide, the troops would have to cross roughly three hundred yards of sandy beach to reach the shingle (gravel of up to three inches in diameter). The shingle lay several yards deep before a seawall. In some places there were dunes. When soldiers left the cover provided by the seawall, they had to cross a flat open area of about two hundred yards to reach the palisades or escarpment that rose 170–200 feet. Perhaps most importantly, the stretch of the coast still known as Omaha Beach is shaped like a crescent, so it is concave. The crescent shape afforded the enemy the means to employ enfilading fire from nearly every defensive position.[49]

Five draws or exits led from the beach through the high ground. The easternmost debouched near Colleville-sur-Mer, the second midway between

Colleville and Saint-Laurent-sur-Mer. The others were at Saint-Laurent it-self and Vierville, nearly two miles west of Saint-Laurent. The Omaha land-ing zone included six discrete sub-beaches. The 16th would land from east to west on Fox Red, Fox Green, and Easy Red. Easy Green, Dog Red, White, and Green were assigned to the 116th RCT (29th Division), with the 5th Ranger Battalion attached. Farther west the 2nd Ranger battalion planned to land at beaches Baker and Charlie in order to assault the sheer cliffs of Pointe du Hoc.[50]

Photo reconnaissance showed a prodigious belt of obstacles. The three main beach obstacles included tetrahedrons, Belgian gates, and ramp-like obstacles that would snag landing craft and of course had mines attached. As of May 13, 1944, Rommel's troops had emplaced "517,000 foreshore obsta-cles . . . 31,000 of which were fitted with mines." To clear these obstacles the planners created "gap assault teams." Working in tandem, naval teams would clear those obstacles lying short of the waterline while army engineers dealt with those forward of the waterline. The intended outcome was that these sweeps would free the boat sections to focus on the wire and mine obstacles and fortifications.[51]

Photo reconnaissance and maps allowed the 1st ID to develop detailed models of the terrain as well as elaborate "sand tables" on which to orient troops and work through the assault planning and sand-table rehearsals. The invaders had a fairly clear idea of the locations of obstacles and minefields. Complex obstacles covered by fire from "pillboxes" and elaborate *Wider-standsnesten*, or strongpoints, required special means to overcome. Some fifteen of these strongpoints had been completed along Omaha Beach. In the gaps between the *Widerstandsnesten*, the Germans emplaced minefields and wire. To deal with these formidable obstacles, the plan required the assault divisions to build teams equipped with the means to blow their way through mines, cross antitank ditches, and reduce pillboxes.[52]

These assault teams organized based on the capacity of the LCVP (landing craft, vehicle, personnel). A team therefore had thirty men or about three-quarters of an infantry platoon (one officer and forty enlisted soldiers). With just over two hundred officers and men, rifle companies could organize six teams but did so by reorganizing from the standard structure. The assault teams had Bangalore torpedoes to breach wire and/or clear lanes through mines, flame throwers to discommode the occupants of bunkers, and satchel charges to blow up bunkers and/or obstacles, as well as rocket launchers, rifle grenades, machine gun, mortars, and their personal weapons. In short, they were armed to the teeth.[53]

Tanks, antiaircraft artillery, field artillery, engineers, and a host of other units were attached to or coming ashore in support of the two lead regimental combat teams. The 16th's end strength with attachments reached 9,828, or roughly three times its normal size. Additionally, the 16th would bring ashore 985 vehicles. At 11,076, the 116th (29th ID) had even more combat power. The 116th had 976 vehicles to bring ashore. The landing tables called for 1st ID to land 31,768 troops and 3,306 vehicles on D-Day. With that level of combat power, V Corps intended to seize the coastal highway that ran along the heights above the beach from Arromanches in the British zone through Colleville, Saint-Laurent, and Vierville to Grandchamp, and then south to Isigny at the junction of the Aure and Vire Rivers. The ground east of Isigny is marshy and not readily traversable for any vehicles, let alone armored vehicles. To achieve this objective meant getting about five miles inland, thus preventing the defenders from being able to fire on the beach and probably denying them observed artillery fire.[54]

On May 17, 1944, G-2 Lieutenant Colonel Robert F. Evans published his estimate of the enemy situation. He reported seven Panzer divisions, two Panzergrenadier divisions, seven infantry divisions, and one parachute and three training divisions that could possibly influence the fight. The Panzer divisions included the reincarnation of the 10th and 21st Panzer Divisions, against which the 1st ID had fought in the Mediterranean. The 21st Panzer Division moved several times in the spring of 1944. Unknown to Evans, they were now near Caen. With more than a hundred tanks, they were the most powerful nearby German reserve formation. The G-2 placed the 709th ID on the Cherbourg Peninsula and the 716th ID as defending Omaha Beach. Evans believed the 352nd ID was located near the Saint-Lô area and thus a threat as a counterattack force. He had no means to generate an independent estimate. Instead, his estimate reflected the analysis of the theater from sources as varied as the French resistance and Ultra.[55]

Assault landings are frontal attacks that require the assault forces to fight their way ashore, penetrate obstacles, reduce fortifications, and get far enough inland to permit the main force to come ashore. The 1st ID's plan reflected that problem, as the assigned mission read simply:

The 1st US Infantry Division, less Regimental Combat Team 26 [V Corps reserve] with Regimental Combat team 116 [29th ID] and other troops attached will make the initial assault on Beach OMAHA at H-Hour on D-Day with two Regimental Combat teams abreast, reduce the beach defenses in its zone of action, secure the Beachhead Maintenance

Line [essentially the coastal highway], secure the D-Day phase line by two hours before dark on D-Day.

H-Hour and D-Day would be determined based on tides, moon phase, and other considerations. Although the plan went through various iterations, the general outline was straightforward: get ashore, take the high ground, and expand from there.[56]

The plan specified that the 16th and 116th land two battalion landing teams abreast. The 16th Infantry had to seize the coastal highway and extend patrols out to Trévières, located south of Colleville and some five miles inland. The 116th Infantry would land on the right. Rangers, attached for the landing, would land on Dog Green to seize Pointe du Hoc and destroy the coastal artillery battery believed to be located there. The 116th Infantry had to seize its portion of the coastal highway and Isigny, nearly seven miles from the beaches. The 1st ID would determine when to land the 18th Infantry and the 29th ID's 115th Infantry in order to expand the beachhead.[57]

Although the base plan was settled, the planners continued to iterate the plan over time. By April 1944 photo reconnaissance showed the results of Rommel's intervention and energy in the improvements to the Atlantic Wall. This concerned both Bradley and Gerow, so the planners developed gap assault teams composed of army engineers and naval combat demolition units. The gap assault teams had the task of creating sixteen gaps—each of them fifty yards wide—through the beach obstacles. The Provisional Engineer Support Brigade Group, composed of the 5th and 6th Engineer Special Brigades, would assume the tasks of the four engineer combat battalions, clearing obstacles and preparing for the beach landing of follow-on troops that had landed with the assault battalions.[58]

To provide immediate armor support, 1st ID had 3rd Armored Group attached. The 3rd Armored Group's 741st and 743rd tank battalion, equipped with Duplex Drive Sherman tanks, were attached to the 16th and 116th, respectively. Duplex Drive (DD) tanks had flotation collars that enabled them to "swim" ashore, propelled by two screws powered by the tank's engine. A third tank battalion, the 745th, equipped with conventional Sherman tanks, formed part of the division reserve. If all went well, 112 tanks would land with the assault battalions.[59]

Amphibious Training and Rehearsals

Between them, the staff at First Army and 1st ID had considerable experience in amphibious operations. Bradley brought key members of his II

Corps staff with him to First Army. Like the 1st ID staff, they had planned and executed two previous landings. The 1st ID was not among the assault divisions in early iterations of the plan. Bradley wanted Huebner's troops because, of the eleven American divisions in England, only the 1st ID had executed an assault landing. He understood that many of those assigned to the Big Red One considered this unfair, but he did what he felt had to be done.[60]

Training hard in the cold, wet months of an English winter is no treat. Joe Dawson described the hardest part when he wrote his family to say that "the many duties of comprising army life are most heavy when a period of preparation occupies the main center of our stage life." He added, "How demanding [preparation is] upon our nerves cannot be easily explained." As bad as it likely was for those who had not done an assault landing, training for the third who had must have been an order of magnitude harder.[61]

The British, Eisenhower's Supreme Headquarters Allied Expedition Force (SHAEF, pronounced "Shafe"), and the US Army did all that could be done to facilitate preparation and training. In April 1943 the European Theater of Operations US Army established the Assault Training Center at Woolacombe. The 16th trained at the Assault Training Center, as did the 18th. The training combined classroom instruction, hands-on drills, and exercises. Full-scale rehearsals occurred at Slapton Sands in south Devon on ground very much like that on the Calvados coast of Normandy. In March, 1st ID executed Exercise Fox, which rehearsed the landing with both the 16th and 116th RCTs.[62]

Infantryman F. L. Mutter recalled a practice landing in February. The Channel surf was both wet and cold. One sergeant complained that "if hell is any worse than this I don't want to go there." Charles Dye remembered that in addition to amphibious training, the division conducted live-fire reduction of bunkers. Live-fire training comes with risks. Steve Kellman, a rifleman, carried a gap-crossing ladder in his assault team. He described the dangers of practicing an assault landing: "With live ammunition being fired overhead, we sustained several casualties on the beach." Worse still, the soldier "immediately to my left was struck with shrapnel in the head and killed." On the night of April 27–28, much worse happened when German E-boats (fast motor torpedo boats) got in amongst LST landing units of the 4th ID during Exercise Tiger. The E-boats sank two LSTs and damaged six others, killing 749 soldiers and sailors. Another three hundred men suffered wounds.[63]

Over the course of that winter and spring, the troops heard from their commanders. In January Montgomery visited and spoke to most of the division. Bradley visited more than once. Not long before the invasion he gave what Charles Hangsterfer called a "little pep talk for the officers of the 16th Regiment." Bradley said that "he would give anything if he could be in the first wave going ashore with us." Hangsterfer wanted to offer up his place but lacked the courage to do so. Eisenhower visited in April. According to Theo Aufort, "He laid the whole bill of fare on us. We were going to land on the coast of France. A place called Normandy." "Ike" told the soldiers that their officers would brief the details. They did so and advised "that a lot of men would die." LeRoy Hermann received more explicit information. He was told that "if we didn't make it, we were expendable and there was another division to take over." With those words of cold comfort, the troops turned to final preparations for the landing.[64]

For much of February and March, Huebner and his key planners had been either in the "BIGOT" room, the code name for top-secret planning of Neptune, in conferences with V Corps, or in other planning cells. Many details, varying from combat loading to uniforms, were hammered out long before the division plan could be finished. The division briefed its plan to the V Corps commander on March 25. Published on April 16 as Field Order 35, it was more than four hundred pages. In some ways publishing the order, or any order for that matter, was anticlimactic, as all orders are artifacts of planning. By the last iteration of the plan, the commanders knew the details cold. As always, the learning that preceded the order mattered more than did the order itself.

Once the troops were in the marshaling areas, sand tables, models, and photo reconnaissance images specific to the beaches became available to them, enabling them to better absorb the last details. William H. Jones remembered being required to cite the details of the beach from memory and receiving feedback on how he did. Ernest Deeds spoke for most when he said that he "studied maps, studied maps, studied maps." Studying maps and doing sand-table "walk-throughs" involved those of all ranks and of all echelons. Knowing where you were to land, as well as where others would, could enable initiative in the event something went wrong.[65]

By the spring of 1944 the veterans of the 1st ID understood that something always went wrong. Chance and friction would play their roles on the beach, just as they had in North Africa, Sicily, and points in between. The combat soldiers, some of whom were still tired, understood these matters as surely as did the Prussian theorist Carl von Clausewitz, who claimed about combat, "No other human activity is so continuously or universally bound up with chance." Even the replacements were coming to understand that "everything in war is very simple, but the simplest thing is difficult." Small things could change everything. Most of all, what Clausewitz called the military machine "is composed of individuals, every one of whom retains his potential for friction." Getting ashore, getting off the beach, and taking the planned objectives would occur only if those who landed overcame friction, confounded chance, and took matters in hand.[66]

Coping with fear and anxiety over not knowing just when the landing would occur proved easier when soldiers could talk to someone about it. Richard H. Conley joined the 18th Infantry as a replacement officer. He put it this way: "My platoon and I, we talked." Those talks included discussing their fears. Ralph Burnett was nineteen years old on D-Day. He joined the 1st ID in November 1943, but by D-Day his squad had shared the hardships and their fears so that "they had become very close." When asked by one of his soldiers about the role of Company G, 16th Infantry, Joe Dawson responded, "We will have a one shilling seat." In British theaters the cheapest seats were up front and cost one shilling. Indeed, Dawson's troops and thousands of others would be in the front row on Omaha Beach. To get through that longest of days, they would rely on their training and each other.[67]

Notes

1. Mason, "Reminiscences," 54. It is clear from diaries from the time as well as postwar memoirs and interviews that a significant number of troops who heard Patton's "apology" did not take it to be such.

2. Mason, 54, 55.

3. Mason, 55; Ernest A. Hilberg, oral history transcript, D-Day Project, National World War II Museum, New Orleans, 16.

4. HQ, 1st ID, after-action report, November 1943, 1, in RG 301-3: G-3 Operations Reports, Jun 43–Mar 44, MRC Digital Archives. The report notes that not all of the four transports docked in Liverpool, but it does not say where any of them docked explicitly. They unloaded over the course of several days as space opened up at docks in the harbor.

5. Fuller, *A Third Face*, 146–47.

6. Wheeler, *The Big Red One*, 262.

7. Johnson, *One More Hill*, 142; "World War II Diary of Jean Gordon Peltier," August 2, 1942–July 5, 1945, MRC 1998.79, 118; Richard Colson, oral history, n.d., MRC 1998.168. Peltier's observations are quoted more fully in Wheeler, *The Big Red One*, 262–63.

8. Fussell, *Boys' Crusade*, 21; Pyle, *Brave Men*, 297–98. Fussell recounts the most serious racial incident. It occurred in Bristol when some four hundred white and black Americans engaged in a riot/brawl that required 120 military policemen to subdue. Several men were injured and one soldier killed. Fussell's account reveals the bitterness of a man writing in his old age about the misery of combat, military

nonsense, and social injustice. Nevertheless, *The Boys' Crusade* is an important addition to the story of the greatest generation. .

9. Kesselring, *A Soldier's Record*, 199–200. As late as July 24, Hitler still believed operations in the Mediterranean could yet produce "decisive events." Warlimont, *Inside Hitler's Headquarters*, 341. See also Porch, *Path to Victory*, 677–83. Porch makes an interesting argument to the effect that the Allies gained more from fighting in Italy than did the Germans, and points out that George Marshall's fear that the United States, once entangled in the Mediterranean and Middle East, would find it hard to disengage seems prescient.

10. See Matloff, *Strategic Planning*, 355–87, for US–British preparations as well as the debate and decisions taken at Tehran. British lieutenant general Frederick Morgan, chief of staff to supreme Allied commander (COSSAC), led a small staff that chose the landing zone and wrote the basic plan. Harrison, *Cross-Channel Attack*, 46–82. On adjustments, see Ambrose, *Supreme Commander*, 331–409.

11. Eisenhower, *Papers*, no. 1516, 3:1688, and no. 1536, 3:1711; Morrison, *Invasion of France and Germany*, 28. Morrison defends Admiral King regarding the shortage of landing craft, but in the end there were not enough LSTs to go around. Clausewitz, *On War*, 197.

12. For troop list and general operations planning, see D'Este, *Bitter Victory*, ch. 12, "Ends and Means." See also Hastings, *Overlord*, for Commonwealth order of battle. Both authors ably sort through the historiography of the battle to arrive at a balanced assessment of the planning and the plan.

13. Speidel, *We Defended Normandy*, 168–69.

14. The Allied Air Forces had taken control in the air over Europe by virtue of a determined and bloody attrition. See Craven and Cate, *Europe: Torch to Pointblank*.

15. Citino, *Wehrmacht's Last Stand*, 110–13.

16. Citino, 114; Harrison, *Cross-Channel Attack*, 148, 464. At appendix D Harrison has included the entire directive.

17. Wilmot, *Struggle for Europe*, chart at 735. Re Blaskowitz, see Boatner, *Biographical Dictionary*, 43–44.

18. Speidel, *We Defended Normandy*, 76. Re preparations, see Liddell-Hart, *Rommel Papers*, 459; McManus, *Those About to Die*, 49.

19. Harrison, *Cross-Channel Attack*, 154, 230. See also maps 6 and 14.

20. Fuller, *A Third Face*, 147.

21. Robert L. Bogart, oral history transcript, D-Day Project, 4–5. See also Cowdrey, *Fighting for Life*, 132–33. Between July 10, when the invasion of Sicily began, and August 20, 21,000 American soldiers were sick with malaria, dysentery, or some other disease. Given that there were only five thousand hospital beds, most suffered in "quarters," generally a tent in their unit's rear area. Those with a fever of less than 101 degrees were returned to their units. There were approximately ten thousand American malaria cases in Sicily, versus eight thousand battlefield casualties.

22. 1st ID, G-4 after-action reports, October 1–November 30, 1943, 1, and December 1–31, 1943, 2, both in RG 301–4: Operations Reports, 8 Nov 42–14 Apr 43, 18 May–31 Aug 43, Oct–Dec 43, MRC Digital Archives.

23. HQ, 1st ID, "Platoon Command Functions," October 11, 1943, George Taylor Papers, MRC 1960.3.599, 2.

24. 1st ID, 1.

25. 1st ID, 2.

26. HQ, 1st ID, "Notes on Leadership," October 14, 1943, cover, 7, 10.

27. *Memorial Album: Pictorial History of the 1st Division* (San Diego, CA: Society of the First Division, 1950), cited in Weingartner, *Blue Spaders*, 46.

28. HQ, Allied Force, "Lessons from the Sicilian Campaign, 20 November 1943," training memorandum no. 50, N2248-4, CARL, 14.

29. Allied Force, 12–13, 18, 27. Re artillery section of the report, see 24–47.

30. Allied Force, table of contents.

31. G-3 after-action reports, December 31, 1943, 1–4, and January 31, 1944, 1–6, both in G-3 Operations Reports, Jun 43–Mar 44.

32. McManus, *Those About to Die*, 25–31.

33. Subordinate unit reports to 1st ID, G-3 after-action report, January 31, 1944, 1–6, in RG 301-3.2: G-3 Journal and File–1st Inf Div–European Campaign, 1 Jan 45–31 Jan 45, MRC Digital Archives. See also 1st Reconnaissance Troop, S-3 report, January 28, 1944, 2–3; First Signal Company, S-3 report, January 27, 1944, 1; 1st ID, S-3 periodic report, February 1, 1944; 26th Infantry, S-3 report, January 28, 1944, all in RG 301-Inf(26)-0.3: Reports of Operations, Jan 44, MRC Digital Archives.

34. There are several good sources on military psychiatry in World War II. Cowdrey, *Fighting for Life*, 143, is cited here. See also Moran, *Anatomy of Courage*, an early standard on the matter of shell shock or combat exhaustion. More on Lord Moran in a later chapter.

35. HQ, 1st ID, Office of the Division Surgeon, "Annual Report of the Medical Department Activities," Division Psychiatrist Annex, January 19, 1945, MRC 1960.88.3214, 1. The copy of the psychiatrist's annex cited here is one that Colonel George A. Taylor kept. The complete annual report is at https://history.amedd.army.mil/index.html. Bradley joined as part of the change to table of organization dated July 9, 1943. In October the army added the position of neuropsychiatrist. See Bellanger, *Army Infantry Divisions*, 1:21.

36. Bellanger, *Army Infantry Divisions*, 1:3.

37. Colson, oral history. Colson did this history on his own. No interviewer questioned him on why the lieutenant committed suicide. What he did not say in his oral history speaks volumes.

38. Jed Wyman, grandson of General Wyman, to the author, April 12, 2021. Mr. Wyman was born after his grandfather's death. The comment on Mandarin and General Wyman's regard for Chinese culture is secondhand from Jed's father. Re notification of assignment as assault division, see HQ, 1st ID, after-action report, July 10, 1944, 7, in G-3 Operations Reports, Jun 44–Dec 44.

39. Wyman, "Journal of Events," entry for November 15, 1943. There are several instances of Wyman pulling over speeders or even convoys.

40. Wyman, entries for November 11, on both coaching in marksmanship training and his initiative, and February 15, among numerous others, re coaching fire movement with BAR. With respect to initiative in training, Wyman is not clear about what echelon he had in mind. It is likely he was thinking that battalion commanders were not affording enough flexibility.

41. Re Wozenski and Dawson, see Wyman, entry for December 10. Wyman's observations and notes on officers over time show his growing comfort with the division. The author's inference is that Wyman was an effective mentor of commander from company up.

42. Keast, *Provision of Enlisted Replacements*, 16.

43. Albert Mominee, oral history transcript, D-Day Project; Whitlock, *Fighting First*, 46; Samuel E. Dixon Sr., interview by Christopher Kelly, November 20, 2009, Veterans History Project, Library of Congress, http://www.loc.gov/vets/; Joseph A. Rowley, oral history transcript, D-Day Project, National World War II Museum, New Orleans. For strength in rifle companies, see Clarence R. Huebner, diary, March 3, 1944–September 26, 1944, April 2, 1945–September 6, 1945, Stanhope B. Mason Collection, MRC 1994.26, entry for March 30, 1944.

44. Charles E. Dye, interview by Douglas E. Clanin, July 16, 1992, Indiana Historical Society, Indianapolis.

45. Dixon, interview; Isadore R. Berkowitz, veteran's survey, n.d., US Army Heritage and Education Center, Carlisle, PA; Miller Bellich, interview by Christine Bellich, January 8, 2003, Richyville, PA, Veterans History Project; Gordon, *Infantrymen*, 22–23.

46. Lewis, *Omaha Beach*.

47. Morrison, *Invasion of France*, appendix 1, shows the complex naval package to support the landing, ranging from minesweepers to the shore party that included the US Army 1st Engineer Special Brigade and naval units that would clear obstacles.

48. Craven and Cate, *Argument to V-E Day*, 72–79, 108–21, organizational chart at 111; George K. Folk, interview by unknown interviewer, October 3, 1999, donated by Colonel Gerald K. Griffin, MRC 2004.85. See also George, *Ninth Air Force*.

49. HQ, 1st ID, "Tactical Study of Terrain," March 25, 1944, in RG 301-0.13: Operation Plan "Neptune," Mar–May 1944, MRC Digital Archives; Harrison, *Cross-Channel Attack*, map 12. The terrain study includes tidal charts, beach gradient, and other terrain data as well as obstacle overprints.

50. Harrison, *Cross-Channel Attack*, maps 12 and 15. Some sources list Pointe du Hoc as Pointe du Hoe. Pointe du Hoe is the Parisian spelling, while Pointe du Hoc is the Norman usage.

51. Morrison, *Invasion of France*, 47.

52. Severloh, *WN 62*, 16; 1st ID, "Tactical Study of Terrain."

53. Bellanger, *Army Infantry Divisions*, 1:65. Rifle platoons had one officer and forty enlisted soldiers organized with a platoon headquarters of one officer, one platoon sergeant, one platoon guide, and two messengers. Three rifle squads were authorized twelve men each. The Browning automatic rifle was the base around which the squads organized.

54. HQ, 1st ID, FO 35, "Neptune" Force O., April 16, 1944, troop list 1-5, in RG 301-3.9: Field Orders, Apr–May 44, Jul–Sep 44, Nov 44, Jan–Apr 45, MRC Digital Archives.

55. HQ, 1st ID, "Order of Battle Selected German Divisions," April 6, 1944, in RG 301-0.13: Operation Plan "Neptune," MRC Digital Archives. See also Edgar Feuchtinger, "21st Panzer Division in Combat against American Troops in France

and Germany," n.d, ms. A-871, MRC 1960-88.4.4, 8; Feuchtinger, "21st Panzer Division 1942–Jul 44," n.d., ms. B-441, N17500.332-A, CARL, 7.

56. 1st ID, FO 35, 2.

57. 1st ID, FO 35, 2–5.

58. 1st ID, FO 35, annex 13, Engineer Support Plan. Re Provisional Engineer Support Brigade task, see 3. Annex 14 spelled out their tasks but is missing from the MRC Digital Archives copy of FO 35. See also McManus, *Those About to Die*, 49–51.

59. 1st ID, FO 35, annex 3.

60. Bradley, *Soldier's Story*, 236.

61. Kingseed, *Omaha Beach to Dawson's Ridge*, 136.

62. Wheeler, *The Big Red One*, 264.

63. F. L. Mutter, oral history transcript, D-Day Project; Dye interview; Steve Kellman, oral history transcript, D-Day Project; Ambrose, *D-Day*, 139.

64. Finke, *No Mission Too Difficult*, 179.

65. William H. Jones, oral history transcript, D-Day Project; Ernest J. Deeds, interview by John Hayes, February 24, 2009, Irving, TX, Veterans History Project.

66. Clausewitz, *On War*, 85, 119; Theo G. Aufort, oral history transcript, D-Day Project; LeRoy Hermann, responses to questionnaire, box 11, folder 3, Ryan Collection, https://media.library.ohio.edu/digital/collection/p15808coll15/id/6770.

67. Richard H. Conley, Ralph R. Burnett, and Mutter, oral history transcripts, D-Day Project.

CHAPTER NINE

Omaha Beach and the Lodgment

Being in the first wave was like committing suicide.
—*Ted Lombarski, First Wave on Omaha Beach*

It was a horrible slaughter.
—*Helmut Machamer, 352nd ID*

After long delay the Allies yield to pressure of the Soviets.
—*Joseph Goebbels*

The Landing

During his research for *The Longest Day*, Cornelius Ryan asked soldiers what rumors they heard as the time of the landings approached. Although most of them believed what their leaders told them, they naturally did hear and pass on rumors. The old saw that after this invasion the 1st ID would surely be rotated home came up for the third time and proved as false, just as it had in Sicily and before that in North Africa. Lieutenant Colonel Herbert C. Hicks Jr., who commanded the 2nd Battalion, 16th Infantry, at Normandy, took exception to the very idea. Of rumors, he asserted there were "None—we were a combat ready Bn. [battalion] who had fought through Africa including the invasion of Oran—made the invasion at Gela, Sicily and fought without relief through Sicily. We had a job to do and had no time for rumors."[1]

General Omar N. Bradley, not given to rumormongering, stated as fact that prior to the landings the air force would "pulverize the beaches." Intense preparation and the immense scale of the effort seemed to promise success.

At least that's what Donald Wilson a soldier in the 16th Infantry, thought. He, like many others, found the enormous quantity of shipping astonishing, saying, "Surveying the panorama convinced me that victory would ultimately, unquestionably be ours."[2]

This chapter addresses the assault landing focused on achieving a lodgment from which a breakout could occur. It doing so, it tests Bradley's assertion as well as Wilson's conclusion. The chapter concludes with the preparation for the breakout at Saint-Lô. During what turned out to be a tumultuous interval, the troops of the 116th Infantry fought under the 1st ID, so their story is told as context; the focus, however, remains on the Big Red One. As at Oran and Gela, the landing in Normandy was not the mission but rather the means to an end. Two themes that emerged in North Africa continued in Sicily and would do so in France. First was the importance of initiative, both from top down and bottom up; second, that combat operations are dynamic and chaotic.[3]

Brigadier General "Dutch" Cota, assistant division commander of the 29th ID, landed with the 116th Infantry. Like Willard Wyman, his counterpart in 1st ID, Cota would bring the 29th ID's forward command post ashore and run the operation, reporting to Huebner until the 29th's main command post could come ashore and enable the Blue and Gray, as the division was known, to operate on its own. Dutch Cota had considerable first-hand experience with amphibious operations in the 1st ID and had served as an instructor of amphibious tactics. While assigned to the Big Red One, he participated in training landings in 1940 and 1941. And as Terry Allen's chief of staff, he played a key role in planning and executing the landing on the Algerian coast.[4]

On the afternoon of June 5, Cota outlined for his command-post staff what they should expect and do on this, their first amphibious assault as well as first taste of combat. He reminded them of what they knew instinctively but needed to hear one last time before executing the plan. Things, he told them, would not go as planned. Timing would not be right. Landing craft would land at places other than where desired. The operation would tend toward confusion. As he succinctly put it, "The enemy will try and will have some success in preventing our gaining a lodgment. But we must improvise, carry on and not lose our heads, nor must we add to the confusion. You all must try to elevate the confusion, but in doing so be careful not to add to or create more. Ours is not the job of actually commanding but of assisting." Generals Huebner and Wyman, and the veteran officers of the 1st Division, understood the case Cota made. The job for combat leaders on D-Day was to do what they could to mitigate confusion by improvisation, and above all to help wherever they could.[5]

As they well knew, just reaching the beach would be problematic. Even if no one shot at them as they tried to land, getting more than thirty thousand men and three thousand vehicles ashore would be quite an achievement. Success depended literally on flowing troops ashore more rapidly than the defending Germans could kill them. Doing so depended not only on the initiative of the landing soldiers but the sailors manning LSTs, LCIs, and LCVPs. Samuel Elliot Morrison, the navy's official historian, considered the scheme "a little too neat. Its success depending on every boat's beaching within fifty yards of the right spot and on there being, not-too-stout defenses on the [exits]." The scheme did prove to be "a little too neat."[6]

The sequence of landing was precise. Duplex Drive tanks, then infantry, were to land first, followed by army and navy engineers to clear obstacles, and finally the main body of the assault force. Because the small-craft skippers charged with guiding the landing craft had no time to rehearse the plan and too much sea to cross, they had little chance of navigating as accurately as the plan required to get the soldiers and equipment within fifty yards of the designated landing spots. As Morrison opined, they were "little better than the blind leading the blind." Furthermore, the weather conditions that had led Overlord's planners to scuttle landing on June 5 had not improved much by the next day. June 6, 1944, dawned overcast and cool, with rough seas and a three-knot current running parallel to the beach from west to east. Although it would burn off as the morning wore on, haze reduced visibility. As amphibious craft closed on the beach, the smokescreen generated to preclude the onshore defenders from seeing the approaching boats also precluded coxswains from seeing landmarks and precisely where the defenders lay in wait. Dust and additional smoke cause by gunfire made poor visibility worse. Even had there been good visibility and no Germans defending the beaches from fortified positions, finding the designated landing spots and delivering troops to them would have proved daunting. But visibility was bad, and there were Germans—plenty of them.[7]

Combat tends toward pulses of violence rather than long periods of sustained horror. But even though there are necessarily lulls between pulses, veterans know that nothing good happens during a lull, as this is typically the time during which one side or the other is maneuvering to a position of advantage or preparing some nasty tactic. Clausewitz describes war as a series of blows, an observation valid in his own time, in 1944, and today. The acme of tactical success is finding a way to reduce the intervals between blows, and reducing those intervals is the role of commanders, including those running the complex logistics of modern warfare. Logistics are the essential ingredient of success at both the operational and high tactical level.[8]

The Antagonists

Despite fighting on two fronts and facing manpower shortages, the German Army remained quite capable. In *We Defended Normandy*, Hans Speidel, Rommel's chief of staff, noted that Rommel "commanded two field armies, eight corps, twenty-four infantry divisions and five Luftwaffe field divisions." He did not control the mobile reserves. The defenders of the Atlantic Wall had serious advantages over those attempting to land. Rommel had not won the argument for coastwise defense over mobile battle inland, but he had gotten half a loaf, and his efforts to improve the fortifications and obstacles along the coast paid dividends. Speidel observed of his commander, "It was an effort of will for Rommel to prepare a static defense when his mind worked on a mobile solution."[9]

The field marshal believed Allied airpower did not permit a mobile battle inland. He believed the Allies' advantage in the air required a defense along the coast with powerful local Panzer reserves. He did not, however, get control of the Panzer reserves. He did get the 2nd, 21st, and 116th Panzer Divisions, although they reported to Geyr von Schweppenburg, commander Panzer Group West, for training. These divisions were far enough forward to serve Rommel's purpose. OKW controlled the theater reserve, which included the I SS Panzer Corps with the 1st, 12th, and 17th SS PZG. The Panzer Lehr Division, reporting directly to OKW, was also in reserve. Although Generalfeldmarschall Gerd von Rundstedt at OB West was the theater commander, he could not commit the theater reserve without OKW approval.[10]

General der Artillerie Erich Marcks's LXXXIV Corps defended the Norman coast from the army boundary east of Caen to the Vire River in the west. His defensive arrangements reflected Rommel's energy and insistence on improving fortifications and obstacles. Nevertheless, Marcks had a problem: to defend forty miles of coast, he had just three divisions. Older soldiers and eastern "volunteers" manned his two "static" divisions, the 709th ID and the 716th ID, which had almost no transport, rendering them literally static. Many of the so-called volunteers had chosen to serve in German units as an alternative to prisoner-of-war camps. None was considered particularly reliable. Marcks had two other divisions. The 319th ID, garrisoned on Guernsey Island, played no role in the coming battle. The 91st Air Landing Division joined the corps on May 2, 1944, occupying positions on the approaches to Cherbourg. Finally, Marcks had the 352nd ID, originally stationed at Saint-Lô. What no one at SHAEF, 21st Army Group, First Army, V Corps, or 1st ID knew until too late to act on the information was that in March Marcks had repositioned the 352nd to defend the beach. Germany offset its manpower shortage in part by increasing the number of automatic weapons in its units. The 352nd benefited from having a great many automatic weapons, including the MG 42 machine gun, which boasted a cyclic rate of fire of 1,200 to 1,400 rounds per minute.[11]

Although other units joined the fray, the 352nd ID and the 726th Grenadier Regiment of the 716th static division were the chief antagonists on Omaha Beach and during the early part of the campaign in Normandy. Generalleutnant Dietrich Kraiss assumed command of the 352nd in November and built the division from the bones of four that had been shattered on the eastern front. The remnants of 321st ID, which arrived from the east in December 1943, provided the bulk of the division's veteran soldiers. Kraiss and Oberstleutnant Fritz Ziegelmann, his 1a or chief operations officer, organized the 352nd on the 1944 infantry division plan. Authorized 12,500 soldiers, the Wehrmacht 1944 type infantry division fielded three infantry regiments of two battalions each. The equipment included just over two thousand automatic weapons. The division artillery included 75-, 105-, and 150-millimeter howitzers organized in four battalions. A fusilier battalion mounted on bicycles, as well as antitank and antiaircraft units and support troops, rounded out the 352nd ID.[12]

The conscription classes of 1925 and 1926 provided the bulk of infantrymen assigned to the 352nd, so it had younger men than did the 716th. However, these recruits arrived undernourished due to "food shortages in Germany." The 352nd contracted with local farmers for whole milk to "improve the nutritional status of the young people." Only about half of the officers had combat experience, and the 352nd was short in noncommissioned officers. Despite problems, the division reached its assigned strength in March, in time to take positions on the coast. With thirty miles of frontage, the 352nd was stretched, but given that they occupied positions from which they could sweep the beaches with fire, their situation was not as grim as Ziegelmann claimed in a postwar interrogation. He did admit that where the static 716th Division had defended with a single battalion, there were now regiments. Although in each case a battalion defended the same amount of beach, it now had a second battalion in reserve.[13]

The 352nd divided its time between preparing for the invasion and improving the defenses. Kraiss focused on individual training, including marksmanship. The division trained to mount counterattacks in accord with German custom codified in doctrine; improving defenses consumed about half the available time. Most of the obstacles the Americans encountered on Omaha Beach had been built and emplaced in April and May by the 352nd. Most of these required wood harvested from the Forêt de Cerisy, some thirty kilometers away, the troops hiking to and from the forest. The division also replaced mines laid two years earlier with some ten thousand new ones delivered that spring. Kraiss's Landsers (the German equivalent of GIs, or doughboys) installed trip-wired booby traps and various other devices to impede their enemy. They also repaired or replaced water obstacles damaged by storms or merely silted up. Improving and maintaining the defenses could itself have been a full-time job. The 352nd received remote-controlled Goliath tracked vehicles that carried enough explosives to disable or destroy tanks, but these did not arrive until June 5, too late to use.[14]

When Rommel visited the 352nd in May, the reserve battalions were not as close to the shoreline as he believed they should be. Kraiss was away at the corps command post, so Rommel tore a strip off Ziegelmann's hide. That rankled sufficiently that the 1a complained about it in a postwar monograph written for his captors. But whether or not the 352nd had done exactly as Rommel specified, it had done all that it could within the limitations imposed by lack of transport, lack of fuel for transport, lack of munitions, and lack of time.[15]

By the end of May the Germans expected the invasion any day. They did not, however, expect it to come in less than optimal weather. Cornelius Ryan, writing in *The Longest Day*, may have said it best: "the continuing bad weather acted like a tranquilizer," distracting the Germans from the growing evidence that the cross-Channel attack would soon be underway. Ryan's account of the absence of corps, division, and regimental commanders for Generaloberst Friedrich Dollmann's Seventh Army war game in Rennes is justifiably famous, the implication being that the absence of senior officers explains, in part, what happened in the following days. In *The Wehrmacht's Last Stand*, Robert Citino asks the right question: Would the presence of these commanders have made a difference? That judgment can come only after examining what happened.[16]

D-DAY

The trip to the beach began in May, when the units earmarked for the cross-Channel attack moved into their marshaling areas. The movement of tens of thousands of troops and thousands of vehicles did not go unnoticed in Britain. British citizens lined the streets in Devon to watch the 1st ID and other American units march or ride to where they would be briefed, waterproof vehicles, and make last-minute preparations. Similar numbers of troops in the British Second Army moved to their marshaling areas as well. The Germans also "saw" this movement and understood what it meant. The troops remained sequestered in their marshaling areas until they moved to the ports at the end of May. Jean Peltier and C Battery, 33rd FA, moved to the port on May 31 and "boarded LST 494 about 1700." The following night, battery officers reviewed the plan with their section chiefs. LST 494 sailed on June 3, but turned back when General Eisenhower postponed the invasion. Like thousands of others confined to amphibious craft, they spent an uncomfortable night in driving rain.[17]

The convoys formed and moved again on June 5, this time committed to carrying out the attack. Once across the Channel, troop ships anchored in the "transport area" some 23,000 yards, or just over thirteen miles, off shore. The troops in LSTs, LCIs, and LCTs plodded on in seas of five to six feet. Beginning around 0300, soldiers on the transports began to clamber over the side, down the nets, and into the LCVPs and LCAs. With a best speed of twelve knots, the trip from the transport area generally took three hours based on sea state, organizing columns, and so forth. Vessels at sea move in three dimensions; amphibious craft did so with gusto. They pitched, rolled, yawed, and sometimes moved in ways that combined all of these movements, with the result that virtually everyone aboard was cold, wet, and violently seasick.[18]

Normandy is at a comparatively high latitude, so much of the trip to the shore occurred in daylight. Nautical twilight came at 0517, and sunrise forty minutes later. The landing occurred in full, albeit overcast daylight. Allied bombers and paratroopers crossed the Channel during the night. The paratroops began landing about 0130; glider-borne troops arrived about two hours later. As Bradley promised, Allied planes bombed Utah Beach shortly after 0600. B-24 heavy bombers slated to "pulverize" the beaches came in perpendicular to the coast and, because of weather, bombed on instruments. The air force fudged the drop point to avoid bombing short, with the result that they missed the beach altogether. The infantry had hoped to be able to seek cover in bomb craters on the beach. Instead they found none, causing Colonel Hicks to conclude, "The Air Corps might just as well have stayed home for all the good that their bombing concentration did." The airborne assault and bombers also caused confusion, and alerted the defenders; the Germans occupied their coastal defense positions hours before the assault began.[19]

Landing craft approached Omaha Beach on boat lanes swept for mines and marked with buoys. At twelve thousand yards offshore, the boats passed the USS *Texas*, anchored in her firing position. Heavy units of the bombardment group rode at anchor between there and the beach. Armed with ten 14-inch guns, the *Texas* packed a wallop. A second battleship, the USS *Arkansas*, operated on the opposite or left side of the boat lanes, some six thousand yards from the beach. The *Arkansas* had five twin turrets equipped with 12-inch guns. Two British light cruisers, two French light cruisers, and thirteen destroyers, including three Royal Navy vessels, completed the bombardment unit. Sixty modified landing craft provided "close gunfire support."[20]

In *Omaha Beach: A Flawed Victory*, Adrian Lewis shows that the naval gunfire support provided for the landings was inadequate and far less than that provided in the Pacific. He acknowledges that Bradley and Eisenhower wanted more, but he is equally clear that Bradley chose to divide naval gunfire assets equally, even though he had certain knowledge of heavier defenses at Omaha. Lewis notes that the officer responsible for supporting the landing believed he had inadequate resources; Admiral John L. Hall, who commanded the assault force, told Chief of Naval Operations principal staff officer Admiral Ernest J. King, "It's a crime to send me on the biggest attack in history with inadequate support."[21]

Despite the shortage of naval resources, the bombardment was nevertheless impressive. The fire planning had great expectations from LCT (R)— landing craft, tank (rocket). These craft fired five-inch rockets, each with a twenty-nine-pound warhead. Each of those supporting Omaha Beach carried 1,064 rockets. There were several other small craft equipped to fire everything from 4.7-inch guns to 40-millimeter pom-poms. Adrian Lewis reports that the "shock power" of the rocket-firing platforms was estimated to be "two and a half times the salvo power of a battleship." Sadly, that proved mistaken. The other small gunfire platforms also failed to perform as expected.[22]

Jerry W. Eades, an artilleryman trained to fire the 105-millimeter self-propelled howitzer from the doubtful platform of an LCT at sea, was shocked by the intensity of the shore bombardment. Eades's howitzer and the rest of the 62nd AFA went in with 3rd Battalion, 16th Infantry. At eleven thousand yards, the 62nd and the 58th AFA began firing unobserved fire at maximum elevation, adding to the already prodigious din. Of the bombardment, Eades remembered, "All I could see was some tremendous gun flashes." As the LCTs closed in on the beach, enemy return fire became a problem. Eades spoke for many when he observed that he was "Just waiting to be hit." Unlike the infantry, he and his gunners "felt like we were doing something. We were shooting back."[23]

Those GIs who were not too seasick—and there were few of them—and able to see the invasion armada found the sight amazing. Robert Vogt, a young German infantryman who saw the invasion fleet from near Arromanches, was equally impressed. Vogt saw "ships as far as the eye could see, an entire fleet," and thought, "Oh god, we're finished now."[24]

What so impressed Vogt provided little assurance to the troops aboard the boats as they approached the line of departure, four thousand yards from the beach. There, at the line of departure, the columns of landing craft peeled off either to port or starboard, formed assault waves, and headed inshore. Some sixty-four Duplex Drive tanks were scheduled to land just ahead of the first wave. Those tanks were to launch six to ten thousand yards from the beach, sea state permitting. It did not. Captain James Thornton, commanding Company B, 741st Tank Battalion (TB), and Captain Charles Young, commanding Company C, believed they were duty-bound to launch their thirty-two tanks and did so without consulting their naval counterparts. They ordered the launch, and their coxswains complied, which led the other boats to do the same. Only two tanks managed to "swim" ashore. Unable to launch at sea, LCT-600 beached three other tanks. The rest were lost, although most of the tank crews escaped drowning.[25]

Don Whitehead, an Associated Press correspondent, accompanied General Wyman and the Danger Forward staff. They bucked and reeled inshore in the company of LCVPs crowded with seasick, wet, and cold GIs. As they approached Easy Red Beach, Whitehead and the others could see "a hellish inferno of battle. Shells exploded in the surf and sent up small geysers, while bullets whipped up ugly little spouts of water. The thunder of our naval gunfire and the explosion of shells rolled over us now. Above the crashing shells and the sharp slap of the waves against our boat was a murderous hissing of flying shells."[26]

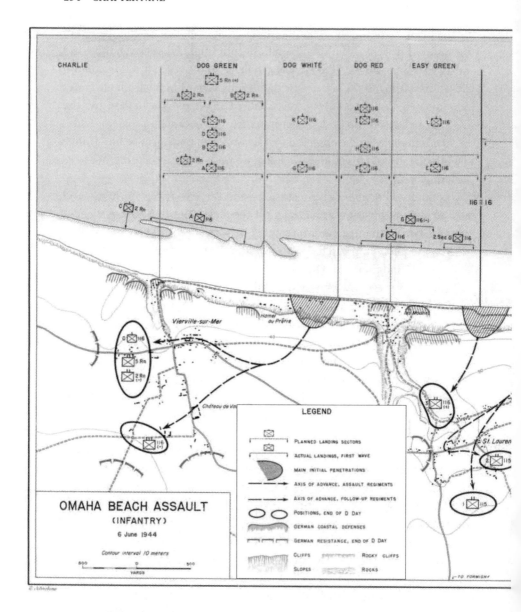

Map 12: Omaha Beach Assault, June 6, 1944. Reproduced from Harrison, *Cross-Channel Attack*, Map XII.

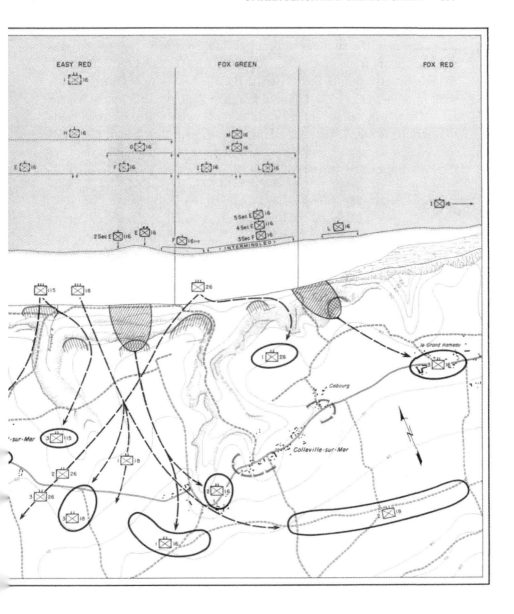

To take advantage of the tide—landing so the water obstacles could be seen—required the landings to occur at different times. The tide receded at earlier hours from west to east. Thus the 4th ID landed on Utah Beach roughly twenty minutes before the 1st ID. The first wave at Omaha Beach went in the water at 0635, followed less than a minute later by the second wave. Once "ashore," the infantry had to wade two or three hundred yards to reach the beach. Some went ashore in water over their heads. Burdened with equipment and ammunition, many of those who went into water over their heads drowned. Ernest A. Hilberg found himself in water deeper than his six feet four inches. In addition to his carbine, grenades, and personal gear, he carried six 81-millimeter mortar rounds. He pushed off the bottom and bobbed to the surface, where he heard a GI screaming "I can't swim!" Hilberg "grabbed him," and "we bounced ashore."[27]

The 29th ID's 116th Infantry, the 5th Ranger Battalion, and two companies of the 2nd Ranger Battalion landed on the western half of Omaha Beach, with the Rangers at the extreme western edge of the beach. Three companies of Rangers from the 2nd Battalion climbed the cliff face at Pointe du Hoc to destroy a battery of artillery believed to be located there. They got ashore and up the cliff face, only to discover that the guns had withdrawn. No matter, the Rangers eventually caught up with them. The 5th Battalion landed near Vierville-sur-Mer to clear the heights out to Pointe de la Percée, west of the village.[28]

In the 116th zone, four companies were to land abreast. From west to east, they were A, F, G, and E. Captain Taylor N. Fellers and the company headquarters of Company A, 116th Infantry, landed more or less on time and within 250 yards of their planned objective. Machine gunners, riflemen, and mortars from the 352nd ID's 916th Grenadier Regiment wiped them out in minutes. The thirty men in Fellers's boat team died before they could fight. Well-sighted machine guns effectively decimated the male population of Bedford, Virginia. The remainder of Company A fared little better. The Germans sunk a boat, killing two more and drowning one. The remaining three teams reached the shore but suffered as well. Within half an hour Company A's "combat effectiveness was almost zero." The other three companies of the 29th's first wave fared little better. Company F shared Company A's fate. Companies E and G landed well away from their assigned beaches.[29]

The 16th also landed four companies abreast. From west to east, Companies E and F aimed to land on Easy Red, while I and L were bound for Fox Green. The 16th got off to a rough start. Captains Edward F. Wozenski and John Finke commanded Companies E and F. On the twelve-mile trip to the beach, their boats drifted east with the current. All of them came under fire five hundred yards offshore. Despite the current and enemy fire, John Finke's LCVP landed almost on target at the junction of Easy Red and Fox Green. His boat section landed at 0640, late but not by much. The rest of his company landed some four hundred yards east of him on Fox Green. Wozenki's Company E landed on the heels of Company F's main body, as did Company E of the 116th, hopelessly out of sector. All were under heavy fire.[30]

Wozenksi and Finke's battalion commander landed under fire as well. Hicks and his operations officer, Captain Fred Hall, managed to get to the seawall, where the two "opened our map case wrapped in canvas, containing our assault maps showing unit boundaries, phase lines and objectives." Hall thought it "a bit incongruous under the circumstances." Perhaps so, but Hicks and the 2nd Battalion were in business. Wozenksi and Finke, both proven officers, were moving west to reach their objectives. Both did so, although Finke was wounded near Coleville. Ted Lombarksi, his first sergeant, took over the ten men who survived the onslaught on the beach. Only Finke among Company F's officers made it off the beach.[31]

Captain John Armellino, commanding Company L, lost one boat immediately after it loaded, the craft swamping and going to the bottom. That left him with five boat sections. On the way in, artillery struck another boat twice, killing nineteen of his soldiers. Company L reached the shore at 0700, four hundred meters east of where they intended. The company suffered sixty-four casualties before it could begin attacking toward its objective. Captain Kimball R. Richmond and Company I had similar luck. As his boats neared the beach, Richmond realized they were off course. He ordered the navy coxswains to head west, parallel to the beach, toward Fox Green, where he was supposed to land. On the way, two of his boats swamped and sank. He advised Lieutenant Colonel Charles T. Horner Jr. of his predicament. Horner sent Company K in to take over for Company I.[32]

At 0700, only Company L, 16th Infantry, was ashore more or less intact. Of the 116th's four companies, Company A was hors de combat. Company E made it ashore but well east, on the 16th's part of the beach. Company F landed east of where it intended, but at least it was in the 116th's zone. G Company was a thousand yards east of its intended landing site. The Rangers were in better shape, given that a V Corps observer did see a visual signal that Pointe du Hoc had been taken. Armellino and the survivors of Company L managed to get across the beach and into the lee of a cliff of just over twelve feet high. The cliff, such as it was, lay immediately adjacent to Widerstandsnest (WN) 60, northeast of Coleville. Here Armellino attempted to reorganize and get his company underway. All of these actions remained opaque to both his regiment and the division.[33]

"There are only two classes of men that may be found on the beach, those who are already dead and those who are about to die," is rightly attributed to Colonel George A. Taylor. In *The Dead and Those About to Die*, John McManus points out that Taylor had this on his mind long before D-Day. Taylor best articulated the notion that getting off the beach was essential, but it was commonly held among those who had executed assault landings. D-Day and the next several days demonstrated the practicality of this view. Getting off the beach is step two of an assault landing.[34]

Wyman and Danger Forward had not yet landed. Huebner and Danger Main remained aboard the USS *Ancon* and knew little of what had transpired since 0635. What they did hear did not sound good. At 0655 Patrol Craft 552, one of the control vessels positioned at the start line for assault waves, reported that "the first wave foundered." Similarly gloomy reports came from the 116th. Huebner, aboard the *Ancon*, could do little to help. Wyman and Cota, although closer, were equally helpless.[35]

WN 62 lay about mile west of WN 60, where Armellino's boat section came ashore. Hein Severloh, a veteran of the Russian front, served with 1st Battery, 1st Battalion, of the 352nd Artillery Regiment. He manned an MG 42 machine gun at WN 62, where he had a panoramic view of Fox Green. His job was to defend the 1st Battery's observation post. Severloh and six other artillerymen, including his battery commander Oberstleutnant Bernhard Frerking, manned the post. Twenty-seven soldiers from the 726th GR rounded out the garrison. The men had been on full alert since shortly after midnight. All of them survived the inaccurate bombardment of the Allied B-24s that came about 0500, as well as naval gunfire. Severloh's MG 42, two 50-millimeter antitank guns, mortars, and other machine guns overlooked the beach. Finally, Frerking could call for fire from his four 105-millimeter howitzers.[36]

For the landing parties, reducing or bypassing WN 62 would not be easy. An LCI carrying infantry provided Severloh his first target. He followed instructions to "wait until the G.I.s were only about 400 meters from the upper beach, and in deep water." Severloh scythed down the wading US troops and proceeded to kill, wound, or suppress all of the troops in his sight. Within a minute or two, none were standing, and those still alive were hugging the ground or scrambling for cover at the shingle, a bed of gravel, along the seawall. "Gravel" suggests small pebbles, but some of these stones were the size of a softball. It was hard to walk on or even drive a truck over the shingle.[37]

Widerstandsnesten covered all of Omaha Beach. Accordingly, the Germans savaged the first wave. From offshore it did appear to be foundering. Yet even as more troops joined the growing confusion on the beach, individuals and small units began to act with the initiative encouraged in army doctrine, the inclination of experienced soldiers, and in accordance with a well-rehearsed understanding of the plan. FM 100-5, *Operations*, advised commanders that when they were unable to exert direct influence, "initiative of subordinates must be relied upon to a great extent." The conditions on Omaha Beach were just what the authors of 100-5 imagined they might be. Small groups of men set out to breach obstacles, defeat local defensive positions, and secure the exits from the beach. Doing so would permit following units to penetrate farther south, beyond the heights to the coastal highway. More important, getting off the beach and on with the job ensured the survival of some soldiers, at least for a while.[38]

Armellino's Company L found that their cliff provided little effective cover. Case in point, an artillery round struck nearby, wounding Armellino badly. Now command passed to Lieutenant Robert Cutler. Company L had nowhere to go except up the Cabourg Draw, named on the invasion overlays as exit F-1. Cutler announced, "Come on we[']re moving out." He intended to move by bounds. Lieutenant Jimmie Monteith, who led the second boat section, would bound first. Monteith had a well-deserved reputation for bravery earned in the Sicilian campaign. His platoon sergeant, a career soldier, said of him, "He was a man I had the utmost respect and admiration for." And to get off the beach, Company L needed help.[39]

Jimmie Monteith sprinted through machine-gun fire to reach two Sherman tanks sitting on the beach. Once there, he showed the tankers the targets they needed to shoot and returned once again through machine-gun fire to his section. Monteith got his men underway through a wire obstacle breached by one of his sergeants. He then had to reprise his race to the beach to bring the tanks up. On foot he led the tanks up the draw, where they helped clear the way. Monteith clearly led, but he did not act alone. Soldiers in Company L breached other obstacles, reduced machine-gun nests, and used fire to suppress the opposition so they could maneuver to advantage. Progress came slowly and with costs. Eventually Company L got through the obstacles, both wire and mines, and made it up the draw to a position from which they could reduce WN 60. Monteith was killed soon after, during an enemy counterattack on the high ground just south of exit F-1.[40]

Lieutenant John Spalding, one of Wozenksi's platoon leaders, was in business on the extreme right or western flank of the 16th Infantry. Spalding's boat grounded on a sandbar and unloaded immediately. Once over the sand-bar, the doggies discovered water over their heads and a strong current. Spalding, on the verge of drowning, grabbed at an eighteen-foot ladder two of his men were carrying, to use for crossing antitank ditches. Sergeant Philip Streczyk, his section sergeant, and one of the men carrying the ladder told Spalding they didn't need any help. Spalding was not trying to help but rather grabbing the ladder to stay alive. He did manage to avoid drowning, and his boat section reached the beach with no one killed or wounded—a rare achievement on D-Day. They did, however, lose their flame thrower, their mortar, one of two bazookas, and some of their rockets.[41]

Spalding collected his troops, and the boat section moved out. His soldiers were so waterlogged that it looked to him as if "they were walking in the face of a real strong wind." They moved as quickly as they could. First, they used a Bangalore torpedo to breach a wire obstacle, thereby permitting them to get off the beach. Spalding saw no mines other than antitank mines. He attempted to use his SCR-536 "handie talkie" radio to contact Wozenski, but the radio would not work. Looking down, Spalding "saw [that] the mouthpiece [of the radio] was shot away."[42]

The boat section reached a beach house en route to the company objective (later Spalding discovered this house was some fifteen hundred yards east of the house he sought). Here they encountered mines and heavy fire. Here too they lost Private First Class Lewis J. Ramundo, killed by machine-gun fire, and captured a Polish soldier who may well have been manning the machine gun that killed Ramundo. They continued, encountering Captain Joe Dawson and a boat section of Company G about 0800. Dawson and his section turned toward Coleville while Spalding turned toward Saint-Laurent. The section reached the top of the ridge overlooking the beach at 0900, the first to do so. Spalding and his boat section reduced WN 64. Wozenski and the rest of Company E joined them at 1045.[43]

Colonel Taylor brought his headquarters ashore around 0800. Sam Fuller, who went in with Taylor's team, remarked on how familiar the beach looked, "What we saw was exactly what we were trained to see all those months in England. The draw, the house, the spire." Any satisfaction he felt dissipated when he and his mates landed in neck-deep water. German machine-gun fire killed Lieutenant Colonel John Matthews, the regimental executive officer, the moment the ramp of the landing craft lowered.[44]

Troops kept coming ashore despite the fact that the beach was continuously swept by fire, with the result that a great many men were pinned down.

Taylor's headquarters team included his regimental surgeon, Major Charles E. Tegtmeyer, and his medical assistants. Dr. Tegtmeyer is arguably the best source for understanding the role George Taylor fulfilled on D-Day. When the surgeon reached the beach, he lay facedown on the slope formed by the shingle. The shingle sloped at about thirty degrees, so it provided a degree of defilade from German machine guns and rifles. As he swiveled his head to look around, Tegtmeyer could see the living and the dead "as tightly packed together as a layer of cigars in a box." Engineers, infantry, indeed everyone ashore, joined the tightly packed mass of men on the beach.[45]

Taylor rallied his headquarters, including Tegtmeyer, and they began moving along the beach, exhorting some, encouraging others. Taylor focused on organizing small groups and getting them off the beach. Tegtmeyer's medical team followed, caring for the wounded and pulling soldiers out of the surf. They also encountered the commander of the 741st TB, who had three of his surviving DD tanks firing on targets of opportunity. At one point Taylor and his three radiomen moved up the crest of the shale, where they immediately drew fire. Tegtmeyer yelled at him, "For Christ's sake, Colonel get down you're drawing fire." Taylor grinned at him and responded with his now famous line, "There are only two kinds of men on this beach, those who are dead and those who are about to die." They headed back the way they had come, to continue the work of getting men off the beach.[46]

Wyman brought Danger Forward ashore at Easy Red not long after Taylor had gone in. Wyman and his staff also took advantage of the defilade provided by the slope of the shingle. Don Whitehead saw what Tegtmeyer had seen earlier and concluded, "This time we have failed. God, we have failed!" He believed that if the Germans counterattacked, they would drive the Americans into the sea. Wyman stood erect and did as Taylor had. "Calmly, he began moving lost units to their proper positions, organizing leadership for leaderless troops. He began to bring order out of confusion and to give direction to this vast collection of inert manpower waiting only to be told what to do, where to go."[47]

Wyman's responsibility as assistant division commander extended beyond what Whitehead recorded. Required to coordinate follow-on forces, Wyman made his first report to Huebner at 0907, advising that movement off the beach was slow. At 0950 he asked Huebner to stop sending vehicles and instead "send combat troops." In the 116th zone, the beachmaster there reached the same conclusion. Not long after, the 18th Infantry began landing at 1031 as planned. Soon after, Wyman called for 18th to "reinforce 2nd

Battalion 16th at once." John McManus concludes in *The Dead and Those About to Die* that "Wyman's influence was cerebral and logistical." McManus argues further that the actions of Taylor and Wyman complemented each other.[48]

Wyman and Taylor, on Omaha Beach East, and Cota and Colonel Charles Canham on Omaha Beach West, did what senior leaders had to do. Canham, commander of the 116th Infantry, went ashore armed with a Browning automatic rifle and used it. Cota rallied the troops and started them inland. In the end, it was individual effort that got the job done. Private Tommy Macdonnell demonstrated individual expertise. Staff Sergeant Ray Lambert exemplified noncommissioned officer leadership.

Tommy Macdonnell, an antiaircraft artillery gunner assigned to Battery A, 467th AAA, manned a "quad fifty," four 50-caliber machine guns mounted in an open turret on a half-track. He came in on an LCT, carrying three other half-tracks and a jeep. Together they comprised a section. A master sergeant led the section, while a sergeant, named Duke, served as Macdonnell's track commander. Like many others, Macdonnell's craft landed well east of its mark. The section went ashore at the junction of Fox Green and Easy Red, below the heights on which the Coleville American cemetery is situated.[49]

Macdonnell had the assistance of two infantrymen from the 16th Infantry aboard his quad fifty to handle ammunition, which came in ninety-six-round magazines. The infantrymen would assure rapid reload, so Macdonnell could use his weapon in direct support of the infantry coming ashore. Sergeant Duke's section also had a mission to destroy an artillery observation post. When the ramp went down on their landing craft, machine-gun fire killed both sailors manning the vessel, but the section still managed to disembark successfully. Minutes later, however, enemy fire damaged or destroyed the other three half-tracks, in which "most of those boys were killed." Under intense fire, and unable to get off the beach, Macdonnell destroyed three machine-gun nests and killed a handful of Germans. He destroyed one of the nests by scoring hits directly through the firing aperture of the pillbox in which the enemy was fortified. In the midst of all this, a sniper killed one of the two infantrymen with Macdonnell and a shell fragment penetrated deeply into Macdonnell's hip.[50]

Still fighting, Macdonnell literally fired all of the onboard 50-caliber ammunition, at which point Duke ordered everybody out. Duke and the driver dismounted through the doors. Macdonnell and his remaining ammunition handler went over the side of the track and took cover behind driftwood.

When the survivors of the section, fewer than ten men, were ready to move, Macdonnell discovered that the second ammunition handler, a veteran of Sicily, had been killed by a shot in the head.[51]

Now fighting on foot, Macdonnell silenced another enemy machine gun with a rifle grenade. He fired his first round short, but his second apparently killed, wounded, or drove off the crew as the firing stopped. Although the section failed to destroy the artillery observation post, Macdonnell did take out the spotting scope. His day ended on a low note when he took cover in a slit trench that turned out to be a latrine trench.[52]

Ray Lambert led a medical team that supported the 2nd Battalion, 16th Infantry. Lambert had joined the army in 1940; by D-Day he was a staff sergeant and had been awarded three Purple Hearts and two Silver Stars. He made his third assault landing on Omaha Beach. Wounded both in North Africa and Sicily, he knew that this landing and the subsequent campaign would cost more lives.[53]

Lambert and his team landed with the first wave. He stepped from the ramp of his team's LCVP into chest-deep water and was hit by a shell fragment that made "a clean tunnel where once had been bone and muscle." Lambert eventually got ashore between the firing arcs of two machine guns near Hein Severloh and WN 62. He and his team began the work of pulling wounded from the water and treating those hit on the beach. Lambert found a chunk of concrete left over from the construction of an obstacle and made that his base. Immortalized as "Ray's rock," it remains on the beach, replete with a plaque listing the names of the 2nd Battalion's medics. Lambert and his team did yeoman work that day, right up until the ramp of an LCVP hit him, breaking his back. Lambert spent the rest of the war in various hospitals, but his team soldiered on.[54]

Monteith, Spalding, Macdonnell, Lambert, and other soldiers on that day reduced obstacles, pillboxes, and strongpoints in order to get off the beach and establish themselves far enough inland to permit landing follow-on forces. Boat sections were organized and trained to clear obstacles and reduce fortifications. They had trained hard to do just that, the key to these tasks being suppressive fire. Fire buys time to employ Bangalore torpedoes or throw a satchel charge into a bunker. Tommy Macdonnell did some of that, as did as did other soldiers and tanks that reached the beach. But naval gunfire, especially that supplied by Destroyer Squadron 18, composed of both US and Royal Navy vessels, was crucial and likely decisive.[55]

Unlike the big ships firing from farther offshore, the destroyers could move quite close to the beach and fire on targets of opportunity. The destroyer men also fired on targets they perceived as being suppressed by the infantrymen on the beach. This technique proved effective. Each of the destroyers fired hundreds of rounds in support of the ground troops; while the big ships had done so, too, many of the troops on the ground believed the destroyers won the day. Writing to the Naval Task Force commander on behalf of the 1st ID, Colonel Mason opined that without naval gunfire "we positively could not have crossed the beaches." When Major General Leonard T. Gerow, commanding V Corps, landed, the first message he sent to General Bradley at First Army was simple: "Thank God for the United States Navy."[56]

German Assessments

Hans Speidel, Rommel's chief of staff, reacted with alacrity, despite admitting that the situation was "not at all clear." He alerted all of Army Group B, including its Panzer reserve. Accordingly, the 2nd, the 21st, and the 116th Panzer Divisions prepared to move. Speidel also asked Sepp Dietrich, who commanded the I SS Panzer Corps, "to keep in contact with General Erich Marcks [LXXXIV Corps]." He also ordered 21st PZ to move toward Caen. Barely twenty miles away, the 21st PZ was by far the closest of the Army Group B reserve. The 2nd PZ located near Amiens was more than 120 miles north. The 116th PZ, located between Chartres and Le Mans, had to travel more than 110 miles to reach Caen. Speidel reported his actions both to OB West and OKW. Between 0600 and 0630 he spoke with Rommel, who agreed that the invasion finally had begun. Now the Generalfeldmarschall headed back, reaching Army Group B at La Roche Guyon before 1700.[57]

Alerted not long after midnight, the troops of the German Seventh Army were in position or on the move before daylight on June 6. Generaloberst Dollmann reacted quickly to the airborne landings, which played havoc with his rear area and communications. He sought control of the 21st Panzer Division to counterattack in the zone east of the Orne River. Army Group B released the 21st to Seventh Army at 0645. Dollmann ordered a Kampfgruppe formed on Panzergrenadier Regiment 125 to "eliminate enemy airborne forces on both sides of the mouth of the Orne River." He also concluded that a landing would occur soon. Seventh Army estimated that although the landing would occur in the Bayeux-Caen region, the Allies likely intended to include the Cotentin Peninsula in their lodgment and ultimately needed to take Cherbourg.[58]

Around 0645 the commander of the 916th Grenadier Regiment reported seeing "a large number of enemy landing crafts, [sic] some of which were also engaging the fortified defense system." That and "continuous fire from naval artillery" compelled the conclusion at the 352nd command post that the invasion had started. British and Canadian troops broke through the 716th Static Division near Caen. Meanwhile the 916th GR seemed to have the landing near Coleville and Vierville under control. The 352nd moved its reserve, the 915th GR, toward Bayeux to protect the right flank. Although casualties in the 916th GR increased through the morning, the regiment was holding. The 916th GR also reported the loss of Pointe du Hoc. The 352nd remained concerned about penetration of the 716th, in particular the adjoining 726th GR. Finally, losses in the 916th led Kraiss to commit a battalion of his reserve, 915th GR, to reinforce the 916th.[59]

Generaloberst Dollmann alerted Seventh Army units stationed in Brittany for movement. Initially he ordered 266th and 275th ID to send regimental-sized Kampfgruppen immediately. Both had more than a hundred miles to travel just to reach Saint-Lô. He also ordered the 77th ID to prepare to join Marck's LXXXIV Corps. Located near Saint-Malo, the 77th had only sixty miles to travel. At 0230 Generalleutnant Günther Blumentritt, Rundstedt's chief of staff, ordered the 12th SS Hitler Jugend to reconnoiter toward the coast. Later, at 0500, despite no release from OKW, Blumentritt released 12th SS to Army Group B. Speidel assigned them to Marcks. Blumentritt also released Panzer Lehr, and reported his actions to OKW. At 0730 OKW overrode these orders. The 12th SS stopped, while Panzer Lehr had not yet moved. All in all, the Germans responded with alacrity even though many of their key leaders had been away from their posts. Still, their response reflected confusion, and was thus uneven; they were aggressive in some places and not in others. The intervention of OKW to override Blumentritt added to the confusion. Nevertheless, the effort to reinforce and apparent success on Omaha Beach gave Marcks some confidence. At 1300 he reported concern about the landings near Bayeux but considered "the landing near Vierville as good as repulsed."[60]

Omaha Beach

The tenor of the 1st ID's G-3 journal on D-Day remained matter-of-fact, even when reporting grim tidings. Nevertheless, the laconic journal revealed a subtle change in affairs ashore. Ambiguity had been the order of the day, but as that horrible day wore on, it became clear that the efforts of the assault companies and following waves were having effect. By midmorning reports noted enemy fire on the exits, meaning that some of the landed forces had managed to reach them. The entry for 1031 read, "Smith landing as planned. Use where needed." This from Huebner for Wyman. The 18th Infantry was coming ashore. At 1106 Cota called in, requesting that infantry be sent in faster—indicating room on the beach as well as urgent need.[61]

At 1131 the 115th Infantry headed ashore. Huebner wanted them to clear the "high grd [sic] SW beach Easy Red in 16th Inf sector. Coordinate with Co CT 16, Co CT 18 Gen Wyman." Next, he called for the 18th and 115th Infantry landings to be expedited. At 1144 he noted "Reinf [sic] being employed." At 1146 the Ranger commander, Lieutenant Colonel James Rudder, reported from his vantage point at Pointe du Hoc, "Germans leaving prepared positions and surrendering." As the situation began to clear, General Gerow committed the 26th Infantry, the corps reserve, to assume, eventually, the mission of the battered 16th Infantry. The 745th Tank Battalion came ashore in the 1st ID zone. Direct-fire support from the surviving tanks of the 741st, some artillery, and, most of all, the destroyers was turning the tide.[62]

Various naval vessels began reporting seeing troops atop the heights or climbing them. At 1213 USS *Harding* repotted that troops "previously pinned down to beaches now adv [sic] up heights behind Easy Red Easy Green and Fox Red and Fox Green." *Harding* could see the 16th taking the heights and clearing the beach. At 1315, the 16th reported that it had Coleville. At 1341 the navy, whose landing this was, reported that Dog Green and White read "entirely clear of opposition" and noted the same conditions on Easy Green and Red. Don Whitehead's fear of failure would not be realized on D-Day. The 18th Infantry got on the heights and secured a section of the coastal highway. The 115th Infantry cleared the Saint-Laurent Draw and took the town.[63]

The first step had been taken. The lodgment was less than a mile deep in the 16th's zone, and even shallower in what would soon be the 29th ID's zone of action. The Rangers held the promontory at Pointe du Hoc, but that was all. Bradley described the situation on Omaha concisely: "They are digging in on Omaha with their fingernails." VII Corps had done far better, taking a beachhead more than five miles deep and just over five miles wide from Sainte Mère Eglise to Carentan. The British and Canadians had gotten four miles inland, just short of Bayeux, their lodgment extending from that point to just north of Caen. They held a second sliver of beach and ground taken by the 6th Airborne along the Orne River.[64]

Ralph R. Burnett came ashore with Company K, 18th Infantry. He landed on Easy Red. "It was Omaha," he said, "and it was red. But there was nothing easy about it." As night fell, he and his buddies stood "guard back to back. Nobody slept. If we sat, we sat back to back with our rifles ready." Ralph Uffner, commanding Company M, 26th Infantry, landed around 1600. Coming across the beach, he discovered "dozens of black soldiers." They were ashore to unload cargo from landing craft. Their officers had disappeared, and they had no cargo to unload. One of their sergeants volunteered the information that they had all trained as infantry, "before they were made into baggage handlers." Uffner asked if they were willing to fight. They said they were, and so joined Company M until the following day.[65]

Arthur G. Heidrick kept a meticulous journal that went as far back as the North Carolina amphibious exercises. A messenger in the 16th, he recorded his journal entries on the backs of message forms in the message book he carried. For obvious reasons he wrote little on D-Day, noting only that the 16th had two command-post locations, one on the beach and the second "on ridge to left of cut." The cut he wrote of was the exit leading to Coleville. The fight for Normandy was by no means over. Heidrick concluded his entry, "Jerry bombs at night."[66]

Heidrich's terse entries are a clear statement of what was achieved on D-Day, yet much remained to be done. On Omaha Beach not all of the intended objectives had been taken, but still the troops of the Big Red One had reached the coast road. More importantly, they had opened the beach exits. They had succeeded in doing so, according to the Australian correspondent Chester Wilmot, because of the "unquenchable spirit and drive of the 1st Division. The lodgment was barely adequate to receive follow on forces, so the next task at hand required expanding inland and making contact with units on the right and left."[67]

During the late afternoon and evening more combat troops came ashore, as did the main command posts of 1st and 29th ID. Huebner came ashore with Danger Main at 1900. The 29th ID main command post landed that same evening. General Gerow brought his V Corps command post ashore at 2030. The cost in lives had been high in both the 16th and the 116th. The 16th Infantry lost a fourth of its strength, or 972 killed, wounded, or missing, although as many as 241 soldiers reported as missing turned up later. The 116th suffered just as badly, but on their first day in combat its soldiers proved heroic.[68]

Expanding the Lodgment

Late on the afternoon of D-Day, the 745th TB and the 16th Infantry began a partnership that remains in effect to this very day. Of that partnership Lieutenant Bud Spencer, a platoon leader in the 745th, wrote, "we considered ourselves lucky to be with an experienced outfit that knew what they were doing." Unlike the ill-fated 741st, the 745th TB trundled ashore from LCTs. Captain Donald E. Honeman's Company B landed at 1500 on D-Day and "inched its way precariously through the defenses losing but three tanks by mines." The tankers, led inland by the 16th Infantry intelligence and reconnaissance platoon, spent the night adjacent to Coleville-sur-Mer, "between the crossfire of our own troops and those of the enemy." In part the "crossfire" stemmed from Joe Dawson's Company G fighting its way through the town.[69]

Generals Gerow and Bradley visited Danger Forward at 0630 D+1. Gerow chatted with Huebner and took control of the beachhead, which freed Huebner and General Gerhardt of the 29th ID to focus their efforts on expanding the lodgment, while Gerow managed the continuing landing, including bringing the 2nd ID ashore. Bradley arrived before Gerow left. Communications remained "iffy." Coach Huebner expressed his frustration with continued pockets of resistance, noting that "these Goddam Boche just won't stop fighting." The First Army commander sympathized, allowing, "It'll take time and ammunition."[70]

Huebner issued orders at 0730 requiring the division to secure the ground along the beachhead maintenance line that coincided with the coastal highway. Taylor's 1st and 2nd Battalions worked to complete clearing Coleville. Honeman's tankers joined Horner's 3rd Battalion to attack east toward the coastal village of Port-en-Bessin to "link up" with the British 50th Division. Lieutenant Colonel Francis J. Murdoch Jr.'s 1st Battalion, 26th Infantry, attacked along the Bayeux highway to take Tour-en-Bessin. Together these two attacks would shore up the left flank and assure contact with the British. Late in the afternoon a patrol from the 16th did move through Port-en-Bessin.[71]

The 18th Infantry made the main attack on June 7. In reserve, Seitz's 26th served as a force provider, so he played no role in the attack. Instead, he gave up a battalion to the 16th Infantry, as noted above, and one to the 18th. To reach its objective, the 18th had to cross the Aure River, which flowed westward to Isigny, where it joined the Vire. The division artillery had twenty-one guns among three battalions to support the various attacks. Naval gunfire support was available, and air "was 'laid on' for requests every 45 minutes." In other words, the 18th Infantry had plenty of support.[72]

Smith attacked on the division's right flank south to take Formigny, Engranville, and Mandeville. He attacked with the 1st and 2nd Battalions abreast, with the 3rd in reserve. Lieutenant Colonel Robert York's 1st

Battalion, supported by a tank platoon from Company A, 745th, crossed the Bayeux highway to Isigny west of Formigny, where they "ambushed cyclists" from the 352nd's fusilier battalion. Lieutenant Colonel John T. Corley's 3rd Battalion, 26th Infantry, attacked along the right flank of the 18th Infantry and the division. Seitz's remaining battalion, the 2nd, commanded by Derrill M. Daniel, attacked to clear the ground along the Bayeux highway between Formigny and Tour-en-Bessin. The attack got underway shortly after 1100.[73]

Mines, snipers, and the occasionally bypassed small unit enhanced the 352nd's defenses despite a growing number of casualties. A "bypassed Jerry" wounded John Lebda's company commander in Company K, 26th Infantry, and the lieutenant who replaced him was killed the next day. According to Lebda, the Germans often mined the sides of roads and pulled up their markers as they withdrew. It was so common in Normandy that if Lebda saw disturbed ground, he probed for mines. Seeking shade from trees growing along a road could result in death or injury. Ralph J. Gordon witnessed just such an incident, "when one of the fellows stepped on a mine. He was blown apart. The three fellows that were near him got it, too." "Things like that really start to mess with your mind after a while," Gordon observed.[74]

Corley's battalion spent most of the day "trying to develop more than two platoons." Snipers from the 916th GR harassed the battalion throughout the day. The unit journal opined that the attack was like "hunting quail." Looking for snipers, the battalion slowed to a crawl and achieved little. In midafternoon the 3rd Battalion culminated just north of Formigny. Ziegelmann, the 1a for the 716th, graded Corley's paper and found that the battalion fought "stubbornly and skillfully" in the villages, but "in open terrain" Corley's battalion "met with strong German defense. Then infantry fighting was replaced with heavy weapons, with materiel." This is a typical criticism of the US Army by German officers cooperating with the historical studies conducted by the army after V-E day.[75]

Ziegelmann's criticism has merit, but it is disingenuous, given the application of materiel by the 352nd. Ziegelmann expressed no qualms about laying some ten thousand mines and improving fortifications or removing markers. These were and are legitimate actions of war, but he takes a querulous tone when the Americans apply their materiel advantage. Ziegelmann also takes pains to show the great disadvantage at which the Landser fought. They were tired, he suggests, and their "determination" was no longer enough in the face of overwhelming materiel superiority. Despite their own advantages on D-Day, they were beaten, and yes, the Allies applied their materiel advantage. That is not, as Ziegelmann implies, unfair or unprofessional; it is rather the point.

This "weakness" of the 3rd Battalion is nevertheless noteworthy because it illustrates a legitimate critique of the division's preparation. John Corley was an experienced battalion commander. He began his service with the 1st ID as a lieutenant in 1940, took command of the battalion in Algeria in 1942, and led it in Sicily. Corley knew his battalion and was more than competent. He and his troops trained to overcome beach defenses and to fight in towns and in open terrain. But their training did not account for everything.[76]

In the attack on Formigny, the battalion confronted two new problems. Well-camouflaged German snipers, ensconced in trees, performed effectively. Second, despite Ziegelmann's claim about open country, the fighting occurred in the northern edge of the bocage. The division had not prepared for the bocage, but neither had anyone else. The G-2 tactical terrain study published in March notes that the "low-lying hills in the northern part of this area have less abrupt slopes and are extensively cultivated." True, but these smallholdings were marked with dense hedges along their property lines. The 3rd Battalion was prepared for neither the proliferation of snipers nor the bocage. Corley and his company commanders had difficulty concentrating their efforts, and so failed that day. They and the rest of the troops fighting in the bocage would have to adapt.[77]

Huebner spent most of the day on the move, on foot, visiting the 16th and 18th Infantry and V Corps. He met with Smith shortly before the 18th began its attack. He met at length with the 1st Medical Battalion commander and staff, who, along with the engineer support brigade, were handling medical evacuation for both the 1st and 29th. At the end of the day, the division still had not taken all of its objectives. Forced to use Seitz's 26th to make up for the great loss in Taylor's regiment, he would next have to clean up his rear area.[78]

The division had identified the 726th, 915th, and 916th Grenadier Regiments as well as most of the other units assigned or attached to the 352nd. The 16th Infantry reported German prisoners' morale "very low, and most of them don't give a damn." A lot happened that day. The 2nd Infantry Division came ashore and was preparing to enter a zone between the 1st and 29th ID. At 0102 on D+2 the 16th Infantry reported British commandos in Port-en-Bessin. There was plenty yet to do, including returning two boat sections of troops who landed far off course to the 116th Infantry, but the situation was improving. In fact, the battle of the beachhead was over. The Allies had won it decisively.[79]

Decision in Calvados

The 352nd ID took a singular prize on June 7. That morning the Pioneer Battalion counterattacked in the 29th ID zone to retake the village of Vierville-sur-Mer. In what Ziegelmann described as "fierce fighting," the battalion succeeded. In doing so they killed a young officer, probably assigned to the 29th. On his person, the Pioneer troops found the V Corps operations plan. For the rest of the campaign in Normandy, the 352nd and presumably all of the German command had access to Gerow's plan. Coupled with radio intercepts, the 352nd generally knew what the Americans intended. Ziegelmann thought the order of great importance, but believed too little use was made of the information. The most likely explanation is that offered by Robert M. Citino in *The Wehrmacht's Last Stand*: the OKW continued to believe that the landing in Normandy was a diversion.[80]

Certainly OKW denied the timely release of the Panzer reserves. Release finally came at 1500 on June 6. Ordered to move, the mobile reserves then had to run the gauntlet of Allied airpower. Rommel described the result clearly and concisely: "During the day, practically our entire traffic—on roads, tracks and in open country—is pinned down by powerful fighter-bomber and bomber formations, with the result the movement of our troops on the battlefield is almost completely paralysed while the enemy can manoeuvre freely." Fritz Bayerlein, Rommel's close friend and onetime 1a, began moving his Panzer Lehr Division toward the front at 1700 on D-Day. Bayerlein tried, unsuccessfully, to convince Dollmann at Seventh Army to let him move after nightfall. Denied permission to wait, Panzer Lehr moved on five routes under almost constant air attack. According to Bayerlein, "There was no question that the advance had been identified by the enemy's air reconnaissance. Soon, the bombers were loitering over the roads, destroying crossings, villages and cities that were along the advance route and diving on the snaking columns." Panzer Lehr lost five tanks, forty fuel trucks, eighty-four half-tracks or self-propelled guns, and ninety other vehicles en route to the fight.[81]

Panzer Lehr and the 12th SS Hitler Jugend, commanded by SS Oberführer Fritz Witt, finally reached assembly areas near the front on June 7. They arrived duly harassed and diminished by air attack. Sepp Dietrich, commanding I SS Panzer Corps, had hoped to coordinate a corps-level counterattack that included the 21st PZ. That could not be done. Instead the Germans attempted, according to Hubert Meyer, the 1a of the 12th SS, to employ small mobile *Kampfgruppen*, a tactic that had worked in Russia. The 12th SS struck at the Canadians in the Caen zone of action, where they discovered that the tactic "had not resulted in the expected success here against a courageous and determined enemy who was ready for defense and well equipped."[82]

Air attacks, naval gunfire, and determined Allied soldiers stymied the Germans at Caen and everywhere else. The fighting settled into grinding action against armored forces in the British and Canadian zone and bitter fighting in the bocage for most of V Corps. Allied airpower and artillery also savaged German commanders. On June 10 the RAF struck the Panzergruppe West command post, killing a number of the staff, including the 1a, and wounding Geyr. Panzergruppe West was out of action for two weeks. Allied artillery or air attacks killed four division commanders, and Marcks of LXXXIV Corps, within the first two weeks. Bayerlein dove for cover more than once but managed to avoid being wounded. Rommel was nearly killed on July 17.[83]

Troops and equipment continued to come ashore. The 1st Division and the rest of the Allied force continued to encounter stubborn defenses and various tactical problems, but they overcame them, in part by sheer weight of materiel and troops but also by innovations and adaptation. Experiences in North Africa and Sicily and training in the United Kingdom influenced the outcome, but the division and its units learned new lessons, with the Germans doing some of the teaching as they had "tutored" Corley and his 3rd Battalion on June 7.

At 1015 the next day, Corley's battalion, supported by a tank platoon from Company C, 745th TB, headed out to cover the four miles south to Formigny, intent on redeeming themselves. The tankers had just gotten ashore on the afternoon of D+1. Company K infantrymen, who were in the lead, entered the village at 1320, when they discovered that the Germans had withdrawn. Next, they were ordered east along the road to Bayeux to rejoin the regiment on the left or eastern flank of the division. The battalion walked seven miles to Mosles. Here they were ordered to move through the tiny village of Tour-en-Bessin, held by the 1st Battalion, to seize the even smaller village of Saint-Anne. Corley rested his troops a short while. They moved out at 2115 in a column of companies heading east on both sides of the road. Company K led, just as they had all day. This march would take them three miles more for a total of fourteen, with almost no rest since landing, and they expected a fight at Saint-Anne. Sniper fire and intermittent artillery marked their path eastward.[84]

The battalion passed through Tour-en-Bessin at 2230. Because of fighting earlier in the day, several houses were ablaze, and there were snipers about.

A tank from the attached tank platoon moved to the center of town and began firing more or less in the direction of the enemy, who were firing from nearby woods. Buttoned up, the tank crew really could see nothing for certain. The 745th and 1st ID still had work to do on fighting combined arms effectively. To remedy the problem, a lieutenant named Baker "jumped on the tank and took control of the gun and directed fire into the trees where there was at least possibility of hitting the enemy."[85]

The battalion then drove on through Saint-Anne and consolidated defensive positions. The battalion immediately sent out patrols. Company K platoon sergeant Ted Dobol received the order to lead a patrol eastward to make contact with the British. Corley personally briefed him on the sign/countersign for making contact, as well as a summary of the 3rd Battalion's situation to provide his counterpart. Because his platoon "was being depleted by the hour with no replacements," Dobol took only two privates with him. The patrol set out at 0230 along the Bayeux road. Other patrols went out to assure contact among the companies and thus security for the battalion.[86]

Dobol was confident in his knowledge of the ground because he had "undergone special training on a large, well detailed, rubber terrain map." With morning approaching, the patrol "came upon a German squad moving into position." Although the Germans killed one of Dobol's soldiers, he and Private Merritt "made quick work" of five German infantrymen. Dobol and Merritt next encountered a single German, whom they captured. He was of Polish descent, as was Dobol. From this Polish German, Dobol learned of an imminent German counterattack, and sent Merritt back to warn the company and the battalion. Next a German truck came down the road. Dobol dispatched an officer standing on the running board and killed the driver. From beneath the tarpaulin covering the truck, German troops threw several grenades, one of which wounded Dobol, rendering him unconscious. Apparently he looked dead, or the Germans never saw him.[87]

The German counterattack Dobol had warned of came soon after. Perhaps as many as three hundred German infantry, supported by Tiger tanks from the 518th Panzer Battalion, made the attack. Ralph Uffner had attached his machine-gun platoons to the rifle company but retained his weapons company headquarters and his mortar platoon. The battalion occupied positions in Saint-Anne, much as they had rehearsed in a war game, "using remarkably accurate three dimensional maps," like the one on which Dobol had learned. Company I occupied positions on the right or south side of the Bayeux road, on the eastern edge of the town. Company L occupied positions north of the road alongside Company I, while Company K lay in reserve in positions on the western edge of town. Visibility was limited because the battalion found itself among "fields enclosed by dense hedgerows"—or, simply stated, the bocage. Uffner had his command astride the road to the rear of a 745th TB Sherman, which was blocking the road.[88]

The fight began with the tank shooting a German truck and then quickly descended into chaos. The Germans overran Company L, causing significant casualties. Uffner less kindly claimed that "L Company broke and fled," leaving Uffner's machine-gun platoon to its fate. In the ensuing melee, the machine-gun platoon scythed down a goodly number of Germans. Uffner shot a German and was wounded in return. Company C, 745th, helped drive the Tigers off in its "first heavy counterattack of its combat history," or for that matter its first counterattack of any kind. The fighting at Saint-Anne continued until daybreak, which comes early in Normandy in June, when naval gunfire ended the German efforts to retake Saint-Anne. Dobol, after having been knocked unconscious by the grenade attack, came to in "excruciating pain. It was daylight by this time and I could not pull myself together or concentrate." Fortunately for him, Corley, leading a patrol of his own, found Dobol, who was evacuated with this, his fourth wound in combat.[89]

At 1300 the battalion attacked again, this time turning ninety degrees to head south to take still another small village seven miles farther south. The mission to contact the British was lifted, as they had not gotten as far south as Saint-Anne. Moving against "light resistance," the 3rd Battalion occupied the area at 2000. It had been "a busy day." Ralph Uffner, lightly wounded himself, saw the Company I commander killed. Corley's battalion lost eleven soldiers and two officers killed, as well as thirty-six soldiers wounded and seven missing. The battalion learned a new lesson. When defending from buildings, Corley's battalion would henceforth create "mouseholes" to enable the infantry to move from room to room, or building to building, without using doors—a lesson that remains valid to this day.[90]

At the end of D+1, the battle for the province of Normandy remained to be decided, but the struggle for the *département*, or county, of Calvados was in hand. The British had by no means decided the battle for Caen, which drew German reserves like swallows returning to Capistrano. Getting ashore at Gold, Sword, and June was comparatively easy, but taking Caen and Bayeux was not. Beach exits at Utah and Omaha led into the bocage, with no maneuver space for armored forces. Caen lay on the boundary between German Seventh and Fifteenth Armies, but more importantly led directly to ground across which armored formations could be employed with advantage.

For several more weeks the Commonwealth struggled against such mobile reserves as the Germans could send their way. A battle of attrition emerged that neither side wanted but that the Commonwealth troops ultimately won. The hard fighting in the Commonwealth lodgment produced casualties that are particularly bitter, given the price Canadian and British troops had paid in the Great War. In the American zone, securing the beaches led to no immediate advantage. Marck's LXXXIV Corps declined daily, but reinforcements, including the 30th Mobile Brigade ("mobile" because it had bicycles), kept the corps in the fight. The Germans used the small fields enclosed by ancient hedges to great advantage. Focused on getting ashore, none of the Allied planners had paid adequate attention to the defensive potential of the bocage, despite terrain studies supported by air reconnaissance. In *Breakout and Pursuit*, Martin Blumenson points out that "air photos gave no real appreciation of what they [hedgerows] were like."[91]

On D+3, June 9, V Corps attacked south with three divisions—from west to east, the 29th, 2nd, and 1st ID. Huebner put the eviscerated 16th Infantry in reserve. By June 13 the Big Red One had fought its way through nearly twenty miles of rugged bocage country, learning the skill of reducing the bocage even as it attacked. That same day Major General Joe Collins turned VII Corps to the task of cutting off German forces in the Cotentin Peninsula. Tactics to reduce the German defenses in the bocage brief easily, but are more difficult to execute in the field. Suppressive fire to "pin down the enemy" was already part of infantry doctrine. Breaking through the hedges came with experience and application of means with which to blow holes in them and drive through while using "hedges parallel to the line of advance . . . to serve as covered approach routes."[92]

On that first day of the attack, Staff Sergeant William A. Becker lost his life. He, like many others, had received his draft notice in December 1941, but President Roosevelt decreed that those drafted in this tranche would report after Christmas. So Bill departed from Union Station in Bethlehem, Pennsylvania, on February 2, 1942, for basic training at Fort Meade in Maryland. From there he joined the 18th Infantry. He deployed from Indian Town Gap with the 1st ID to the United Kingdom. He then fought across North Africa and Sicily. On D+3 Becker was leading a rifle squad in Company B when, in the fight to seize an objective astride the road to Bayeux, he was killed. By this point in the war Bill Becker knew his business, but experience no more guaranteed his survival than it had that of Jimmie Monteith or the thousands of others who died fighting in the Big Red One. The division drove on.[93]

Even during the fighting, replacements came forward over the beach. Jerry Nauss came forward to join the 1st ID three days after Bill Becker died. His journey to the front paralleled Carl von Clausewitz's description of a "novice" going forward during the Napoleonic Wars. From comparative peace in the rear, when the novice goes forward, he hears the sounds of battle and then comes upon the detritus of fighting and the din of shelling and firing. Jerry Nauss experienced this same surreal journey. He crossed the Channel on the *Devonshire*, a converted liner, with other replacements on the night of June 11. On the twelfth, as the *Devonshire* approached the shore, Nauss could see "bits of American uniforms floating on the surface . . . and all sorts of debris bobbling in the rough sea."[94]

The replacements waited several hours for LCVPs to come alongside to ferry them ashore. Like those of many who had landed or tried to land earlier, their boat grounded on a sandbar. Nauss and his comrades stepped into hip-deep water and "struggled to reach the beach," enduring German artillery fire as they waded ashore through the jetsam of the prior fighting. Once having done so, they were led inland to a bivouac among the hedgerows. As they settled in, they could hear the "roar of gunfire in the distance," see gun flashes, and hear the horrendous noise of the supporting warships firing. The following morning the newly arrived troops were led farther forward. Along the way they saw their first combat dead—the bodies of two charred Germans in a destroyed scout car.[95]

Finally arriving at the replacement center, Nauss and the others who shared his specialty—he was signalman—were formed in a line and counted off by twos. With the application of superb military logic, the "ones" went to 1st ID and the "twos" to 2nd ID. Lieutenant Elton P. Smith took Nauss and the other new Big Red One soldiers under his wing. He began his orientation by assuring the new men that they "didn't have a worry in the world" because they were joining the 1st Division. Smith bragged about the division and its current success, assuring the replacements, "You are as safe in the Signal Company as if you were home." It did not immediately occur to Jerry that he was a replacement for a reason.[96]

The 1st ID took the tiny village of Caumont-l'Eventé on June 13, the same day Jerry Nauss made his way to the replacement center. Commonwealth attacks south from Bayeux had not gone well, so Huebner now had an open left flank. Gerow therefore ordered him to go over on the defense. The 1st ID remained on the defense in the vicinity of Caumont until relieved on July 15. The 635th TD battalion and the 745th TB rejoined the division a few days later, and remained as routine attachments for the remainder of the war. The division spent a month defending the ground they gained while the buildup of forces continued. The buildup enabled VII Corps to cut across the Cotentin Peninsula and then turn north to clear the Cotentin and take Cherbourg. The German commander of Fortress Cherbourg surrendered on June 26. VII Corps finished clearing the city the following day.[97]

A month defending the lodgment did not pass without incident. All three regiments patrolled actively and with effect. On the evening of July 4, the 18th Infantry sent out an ambush patrol forward of its positions. The regiment reported that the patrol "got a scout car with rifle and hand grenades and killing two Germans." They also dug in deeply. Engineers built "bombproof shelters" for battalion command posts. Despite the burgeoning efforts of the Allied air forces, antiaircraft artillery engaged a number of German fighters, including "56 ME [Messerschmidt] 109s, 76 FW [Focke-Wulf] 190s and 1 ME 210." The division artillery and tanks fired in support of the front line units, albeit with limits imposed by insufficient supplies. Sustaining combat operations over the beaches and in the artificial harbors encumbered by a gale in mid-June remained problematic. On July 7 enemy tanks probed the division but were seen off by artillery fire.[98]

On July 13 the 5th ID began the relief in place of the Big Red One, after which the latter withdrew to rest, refit, and prepare for its next mission. The division leadership knew they would have little time to do so. Huebner met with 3rd AD leadership to discuss Operation Cobra, the breakout plan, on July 15. It now appeared that the 1st ID only had a matter of days to refit and prepare. As they had throughout the fighting, replacements continued to stream in. These new men had to be assimilated—that is, assigned a job and oriented on their new unit. Many felt fortunate to join the Big Red One, like Jerry Nauss, who believed that because of the division's three campaigns, "Their methods were well established and worked." He did admit, though, that it took some time for the old-timers to accept the new men. Along the way Lieutenant Smith, 1st Signal Company commander Captain Herbert H. Wiggins, and Lieutenant David R. Wood all took time to orient and instruct the new men on their mission and the tactical situation. Wood even briefed them on the history of the three infantry regiments and the mission of his platoon in support of Danger Forward.[99]

There is no means to extrapolate from Nauss to others who joined in June and July, but his story is similar to theirs. Pride in the division's recent achievements and friendly if reserved acceptance by the seasoned soldiers seems to have been the rule. When asked about assimilating replacements, Nauss himself admitted that once he had some combat experience under his belt, he felt the same way as had the older veterans; "Until they got to be battle tested and doing things our way, we would be kind of leery of them." Assimilation requires effort on both sides, and for both to recognize that their lives depend on one another.[100]

The 16th Infantry remained in reserve for most of June and July, Taylor using the time to rebuild his unit. On July 2 Eisenhower visited the 1st Division to award the Distinguished Service Cross to twenty-two of its soldiers. During the ceremony he said, "I am beginning to think of the First Division as a sort of Praetorian Guard which goes along with me and gives me luck." Three days later Eisenhower wrote to Marshall to report on his visit to the beachhead, praising the "fighting quality of the German soldier" operating in the close terrain of the bocage as well as commenting on his corps commanders and providing his estimate of the divisions ashore. Eisenhower thought of the 1st and 9th Divisions as "tops."[101]

Refitting and resting were an important part of the 1st ID's time out of the line. The division had received some sixteen hundred replacements since D-Day, so rebuilding units and training were also important. While out of the line, Huebner met with Colonel Julian S. Dayton, a combat observer, gathering lessons for Eisenhower's supreme headquarters. "Coach" made several points. He recommended that time out of the line not be called "rest period"; troops were not out of the line to rest but to undergo "reconditioning for the next fight." The first task should be to "get the men bathed and cleaned up." That meant replacing or issuing basic equipment ranging from toothbrushes and toothpaste to clothing. He asserted that the "best available facilities for bathing, messing living be provided." As a rule, he thought each day should be divided equally between "recreation and training."[102]

In the short time Huebner knew he had available, he focused on marksmanship and squad, platoon, and "small tank infantry team" training. In this instance, that included preparing for further fighting in the bocage. He also mandated short, fast marches of no more than five miles to recondition troops who "have been in fox holes in cramped positions." Although he expected to be back in the fight soon, he offered ideas for units that might have more time out of the line. These units, he believed, should be afforded training areas that permitted "combined training with supporting units."[103]

Coach Huebner had an armywide reputation as man who knew his stuff, trained hard, and demanded the best from his units. He was thought, accurately, to be a disciplinarian. But this hard man also argued for provisions for "organized recreational games . . . moving picture equipment . . . [and] stage show entertainment as is available." Finally, he believed these facilities should be prepared so that soldiers "reconditioning" for combat would be free "to enjoy recreation" or to train.[104]

Colonel Charles H. Coates, assigned as a War Department observer, interviewed George Taylor on the exploits of his regiment on D-Day. The narrative in the report is detailed on the terrain, the obstacles, and the strongpoints. Coates reported, "*On the main walls of the pillboxes over each aperture was placed a sketch showing our landing craft and tanks by type, with ranges and ammunition to be used on them* [italics in original]." Over ten pages of single-spaced type, Coates detailed the courage of Jimmie Monteith and others, writing that "this observer considers the three prime reasons for the 16th Infantry's successful landing leadership, small unit fire and maneuver." Those conclusions speak for themselves, and apply equally to the 116th and the rest of the Big Red One.[105]

There was less turbulence after this operation than after Husky. George Taylor was the only officer from battalion commander and above who departed, receiving a well-deserved promotion to brigadier general and moving to the 4th ID as assistant division commander. There was also a sad loss for the 26th Infantry. Teddy Roosevelt, after visiting with his son Quinton, died of a heart attack in the early-morning hours of July 12, 1944. Quinton, an artilleryman in the 1st ID, and Teddy had both gone ashore on D-Day, making them the only father and son to do so. Colonel Jeff Seitz and his staff attended the funeral of the former regimental commander of the 26th Infantry and combat veteran of the Big Red One over two wars. Roosevelt was buried on July 14, with Bradley and other senior officers in attendance.[106]

In a letter home, Joe Dawson wrote that he had "become a bit calloused by the innumerable spectacles of war that have etched themselves upon my memory." He went on to describe his disillusionment about the war but also his wondrous admiration of the men with whom he served, describing the lot of the infantry succinctly: "No one is indispensable in this world, and how expendable we infantrymen really are is reflected by the ever growing list of comrades who have fallen."[107]

Notes

1. Herbert C. Hicks Jr., responses to questionnaire, box 11, folder 39, Ryan Collection, https://media.library.ohio.edu/digital/collection/p15808coll15/id/393.

2. For Bradley quotation, see George K. Folk, interview by unknown interviewer, October 3, 1999, donated by Colonel Gerald K. Griffin, MRC 2004.85; Clay, *Blood and Sacrifice*, 183.

3. For an overview of the operation, see Hastings, *Overlord*. Wilmot, *Struggle for Europe*, remains an important overview of the war in Europe and reasoned criticism

of the American plan for the invasion. See also Lewis, *Omaha Beach*. Professor Lewis's contribution to the historiography of the invasion is to bring forward Wilmot and British criticism of US Army planning. He expands that critique with careful analysis of development of amphibious doctrine as it differed between the Americans and British and between the Atlantic and Pacific. McManus, *Those About to Die*, and Whitlock, *Fighting First*, tell the details of the 1st ID at Omaha Beach.

4. Chapters 4–8 of Miller, *Division Commander*, cover the interwar years and Cota's service until he joined the 29th ID.

5. Norman D. Cota, questionnaire, box 6, folder 15, Ryan Collection, https://media.library.ohio.edu/digital/collection/p15808coll15/id/921. In the Cota file are two documents: an undated, unattributed questionnaire filled out with handwritten responses, and an unpaginated, undated manuscript written by Lieutenant Jack Shea, with three illustrations. Shea was an army historian assigned to the 28th. He and Cota became lifelong friends, according to Cota's biographer. Miller, *Division Commander*, 192.

6. Just how many troops and vehicles were to land is debatable. The landing tables for the 1st ID are the chief source here, although the precise numbers are taken from Knickerbocker et al., *Danger Forward*, 172, and Morrison, *Invasion of France*, 131.

7. Morrison, *Invasion of France*, 131.

8. Clausewitz, *On War*, 79. Later in his opus Clausewitz discusses in some detail the reasons that war, and thus battle, are "spasmodic," arguing that *immobility* and *inactivity* are the norm in armies, and action demands overcoming inertia. Clausewitz, 216–19.

9. Speidel, *We Defended Normandy*, 56, 76. Speidel's account reveals Rommel's inner tension quite clearly.

10. Speidel. See also Harrison, *Cross-Channel Attack*, 244–45.

11. Fritz Ziegelmann, "History of the 352nd Infantry Division," n.d., ms. B-432, Sturmpanzer, 6. Marcks issued his order on March 15, with March 20 as the date by which the 352nd had to be in position. Ziegelmann wrote thirteen separate short monographs on the 352nd ID that cover the time from organizing through July 30, 1944, by which time the 352nd had become combat-ineffective due to losses. War Department, TM-E 30-451, *Handbook on German Military Forces* (1945; repr., Baton Rouge: Louisiana State University Press, 1990), 308. The 1944 infantry division was authorized more than two thousand automatic weapons, ranging from submachine guns to heavy machine guns; see War Department, figures 5 and 6. The 352nd had close to its authorization of automatic weapons, and it is likely they had some captured weapons as well. The author found the formidable MG 42 still in use in Bosnia in 1995; if not limited to short bursts of fire, it will consume ammunition at a huge rate and risks barrel-drooping from overheating. Bradley learned the actual position of the 352nd on June 5, too late to act on it. A lengthy discussion of how this may have come to pass in Harrison, *Cross-Channel Attack*, curiously occurs in a footnote, 319n. Re 91st Air Landing Division, see Harrison, *Cross-Channel Attack*, 186; Reardon, *Defending Fortress Europe*, 25.

12. Very few units in any army are manned and equipped precisely in accordance with their tables of organization and equipment. These documents are aspirational and

depend on availability of troops and equipment. See War Department, TM-E 30-451, figs. 5 and 6; Ziegelmann, "History," 3; Mitcham, *German Order of Battle*, 2:60–62.

13. Ziegelmann, "History," 4, 6, 8.

14. Ziegelmann, 9–13. Re German doctrine on counterattacks, see Condell and Zabecki, *German Art of War*, 128, para 463.

15. Ziegelmann, "History," 8.

16. Ryan, *Longest Day*, 79, 80–83; Citino, *Wehrmacht's Last Stand*, 136–40.

17. "World War II Diary of Jean Gordon Peltier," August 2, 1942–July 5, 1945, MRC 1998.79, 137. See also Smith, *Eisenhower's Six Great Decisions*, 51–55.

18. See HQ, 1st ID, FO 35, "Neptune" Force O., April 16, 1944, annex 6, p. 4, in RG 301-3.9: Field Orders, Apr–May 44, Jul–Sep 44, Nov 44, Jan–Apr 45, MRC Digital Archives. This sketch shows marked boat lanes and planned positions for all naval gun fire units.

19. Harrison, *Cross-Channel Attack*, 278. For US Army airborne operations on June 6, 1944, see 278–300; Craven and Cate, *Argument to V-E Day*, 186–95. See also prologue in Atkinson, *Guns at Last Light*, an excellent and succinct account that describes scale and scope of the cross-Channel attack. Re Hicks, see McManus, *Those About to Die*, 16. Re sunrise, see https://skyandtelescope.org/astronomy-news/astronomy-d-day-sun-moon-tides/, accessed May 14, 2021.

20. Morrison, *Invasion of France*, 335–36. A large minesweeper group composed of British and Canadian vessels swept the boat lanes and naval gunfire support areas.

21. Lewis, *Omaha Beach*, 225–31.

22. Lewis discusses the many platforms developed for use on D-Day, as well as the problems each added; see 218–20, and 244 on results obtained.

23. Jerry W. Eades, 62nd Armored Field Artillery Facebook page, accessed March 21, 2021, also available on YouTube.

24. Steinhoff, Pechel, and Showalter, *Voices from the Third Reich*, 255.

25. McManus, *Those About to Die*, 67–70.

26. Don Whitehead, "Normandy as I Saw It," in Knickerbocker et al., *Danger Forward*, 211.

27. Ernest A. Hilberg, oral history transcript, D-Day Project, National World War II Museum, New Orleans.

28. Ambrose, *D-Day*, 398–417.

29. Kershaw, *Bedford Boys*, 129; Ewing, *Twenty-Nine, Let's Go*, 41, 39–42.

30. Clay, *Blood and Sacrifice*, 187.

31. Ambrose, *D-Day*, 148–49; Finke, *No Mission Too Difficult*, 193.

32. Clay, *Blood and Sacrifice*, 184–93.

33. McManus, *Those About to Die*, 110–17. Re 116th, see Ewing, *Twenty-Nine, Let's Go*, 39–42. Re overall narrative through midmorning, see 1st ID, G-3 after-action report, May 31–June 30, 1944, in RG 301-INF(16)-0.7: Journal, Jun 44–Aug 44, MRC Digital Archives, 9–13. The 16th Infantry journal records calmly what the regimental main command post knew—which was very little.

34. McManus, *Those About to Die*, 177. Taylor served on the planning staff for Torch and made the assault landing at Sicily. He was well schooled in the vulnerability of the early hours ashore.

35. G-3 journal, June 6, 1944, in RG 301-3.1: G-3 Periodic Reports–1st Inf Div, Feb–Mar 44, Jan–May 45, MRC. The file label is misleading.

36. Severloh, *WN 62*, 50–85. Severloh had suffered frostbite while serving with the 321st ID. For that and other illness he was out of action for some nine months. He returned to his unit in December 1943 to discover it had been renamed.

37. Severloh.

38. Visitors to Omaha Beach are often puzzled to find no shingle on the beach today. Army engineers used all of it to create fill for roads exiting the beachhead. War Department, FM 100-5, *Field Service Regulations: Operations* (Washington, DC: Government Printing Office, 1941), 507, 514. Individual initiative is discussed in several other places as well.

39. McManus, *Those About to Die*, 115–16, 164–68.

40. McManus.

41. Several historians have written about Spalding's boat section. Most of what is described comes directly from the postcombat interviews done by Master Sergeant Forest C. Pogue and Staff Sergeant J. M. Topete. I have relied on the Pogue interview: John Spalding, interview by F. C. Pogue and J. M. Topete Herve, Belgium, February 9, 1945. The interview is sixteen pages long and includes a list of the thirty-two soldiers assigned to the boat section. Surprisingly, only two were killed in action that day; six were wounded in action, and five were awarded the Distinguished Service Cross. The MRC has a copy, as does the Military History Institute at US Army Heritage and Education Center, Carlisle, PA. It can also be found in RG 319 at the National Archives and Records Administration. A sketch map done by Topete for the Navy Neptune Monograph can be found both at NARA and MRC.

42. Spalding, interview, 4–6. This radio is often called mistakenly a walkie-talkie; it was the SCR 300 backpack radio that was known as a walkie-talkie at the time.

43. Spalding, 9–12; McManus, *Those About to Die*, chart at 201.

44. Samuel Fuller, "Impressions of Normandy on D-Day," *Bridgehead Sentinel*, March 1984, Bridgehead Sentinel Collection, MRC, 8, 26.

45. Charles E. Tegtmeyer, "D-Day-H-Hour," 2–4, chapter 20 of "Personal Wartime Memoir of Major Charles E. Tegtmeyer, Medical Corps Regimental Surgeon, 16th Infantry Regiment, 1st Infantry Division," n.p., MRC (no accession number per Andrew Woods, MRC archivist).

46. Tegtmeyer, 4.

47. Whitehead, "Normandy as I Saw It," 213.

48. McManus, *Those About to Die*, 193.

49. Tommy Macdonnell, phone interview by the author, September 19, 2019. The author confirmed facts and asked Macdonnell to review paragraphs on May 16, 2021.

50. Macdonnell, interview.

51. Macdonnell.

52. Macdonnell.

53. Lambert and DeFelice, *Every Man a Hero*, flyleaf. The author met Ray Lambert at the Society of the First Division Reunion in 2016 and spoke with him at length several times. Lambert was unpretentious and open about his experience in the US Army and at war.

54. Lambert and DeFelice, 169.

55. See Kirkland, *Destroyers at Normandy*. Kirkland served as the gunnery officer of the USS *Doyle*, one of the destroyers that fought at Omaha Beach.

56. Morrison, *Invasion of France*, 149–52.

57. Speidel, *We Defended Normandy*, 92–93. In a postwar manuscript done at the behest of his captors, the 21st PZ commander, Generalleutnant Edgar Feuchtinger, wrote that he sent his Panzergrenadier regiment toward Caen without orders. Feuchtinger, "21st Panzer Division 1942–Jul 44," n.d., ms. B-441, N17500.332-A, CARL. Re Panzer Reserve locations, see Guderian, *From Normandy to the Ruhr*, 20.

58. Reardon, *Defending Fortress Europe*, 38. Reardon had carefully translated and edited the war diary of the German Seventh Army, which is invaluable for understanding Seventh Army's role in the battle for Normandy. The 21st PZ did mount a counterattack with the 215th PGR early on June 6 against the British 6th Airborne Division.

59. Ziegelmann, "History," 21–22.

60. Reardon, *Defending Fortress Europe*, 39–40; Reynolds, *Steel Inferno*, 54–55; Carell, *Invasion!*, 97; Harrison, *Cross-Channel Attack*, 301, 333. Harrison wrote that Blumentritt ordered both 12th SS and Panzer Lehr to move between 0330 and 0430. Jodl overrode that order at 0730.

61. G-3 journal, June 6, 1944, in RG 301-3.2: G-3 Journal and File, 1 Jan 44–11 Jun 44, MRC Digital Archives.

62. G-3 journal, June 6.

63. G-3 journal, June 6. Re casualties, see Clay, *Blood and Sacrifice*, 202. Using unit morning reports, Clay arrived at 972 casualties in the 16th Infantry.

64. Chester B. Hansen, diary, June 6, 1944, 3, in Hansen, "Summary of Activities of General Omar N. Bradley," June 1–15, 1944, folder 13, "Official Papers–Reports," Chester B. Hansen Collection, US Army Heritage and Education Center, Carlisle, PA, author's copy courtesy of Steven L. Ossad; Ossad, *Omar Nelson Bradley*.

65. Raphael L. Uffner, "Recollections of World War II with the First Infantry Division," n.d., MRC 1997.98, 386–88.

66. Arthur G. Heidrick, diary, June 13, 1942–February 1, 1945, Fort Riley Museum Complex, Fort Riley, KS, entry for June 6, 1944.

67. Wilmot, *Struggle for Europe*, 261.

68. McManus, *Those About to Die*, 341n4; McManus, *Those About to Die*, 286; Clay, *Blood and Sacrifice*, 202. Huebner left the USS *Ancon* at about 1700. Ewing, *Twenty-Nine, Let's Go*, 57, reports only that the *Gerard* came ashore that evening.

69. Mygatt, *Return to La Roche-en-Ardenne*, 462–63, 537; Knickerbocker et al., *Danger Forward*, 190–93. "History of the 745th Tank Battalion," a bonus section at the end of Mygatt's novel, is on pp. 420–522 inclusive.

70. G-3 journal, June 7; Bradley, *Soldier's Story*, 280. According to Harrison, Gerhardt did not take over until 1700. Cota ran the 29th until then. Harrison, *Cross-Channel Attack*, 336.

71. Baumer and Reardon, *American Iliad*, 225; Lebda, *Million Miles to Go*, 83–84; Gordon, *Infantrymen*, 35–36.

72. G-3 after-action report, May 3–June 30, 1944, 14, 16.

73. G-3 after-action report, 14–15; G-3 journal, June 7, 12; Knickerbocker et al., *Danger Forward*, 191–93. Precise time of the attack is uncertain. The G-3 journal is unclear on the time of the attack. Baumer and Reardon report the time of the attack as "set at 1100." *American Iliad*, 225.

74. Lebda, *Million Miles to Go*, 84; Gordon, *Infantrymen*, 35–36.

75. Nechey, "3rd Battalion 26th Inf. Regiment Journal," 44–45; Fritz Ziegelmann, "The Battles of 7 June 1944," ms. B-433, N17500.483-B, CARL, 12. Harrison, *Cross-Channel Attack*, also cites Ziegelmann at 337n3.

76. defender.west-point.org Eulogy at West Point.org the West Point Connection. See also John Thomas Gendron, interview by John F. Votaw, Kissimmee, FL, 10 August 1995, 2–3.

77. HQ, 1st ID, "Tactical Study of Terrain," March 25, 1944, 1–2, in RG 301-0.13: Operation Plan "Neptune," Mar–May 1944, MRC Digital Archives.

78. Clarence R. Huebner, diary, March 3, 1944–September 26, 1944, April 2, 1945–September 6, 1945, Stanhope B. Mason Collection, MRC 1994.26, entry for June 7.

79. Identification of enemy units began on D-Day. All three regiments took prisoners on June 7. Citation here is from HQ, 16th Infantry, journal for June 7, in RG 301-INF(16)-0.7: Journal, Jun 44–Aug 44.

80. Fritz Ziegelmann, "Additional Information about the Operational Plan of V (US) Corps, Capture on & Jun 44, in the Sector of 352 Infantry Division," September 3, 1947, ms. B-636, N17500.615, CARL, 1; Ziegelmann, "Battles of 7 June," 8–9; Citino, *Wehrmacht's Last Stand*, 228.

81. Speidel, *We Defended Normandy*, 96; Kurowski, *Elite Panzer Strike Force*, 27, 33. Some accounts claim release came at 1600. This one-hour difference occurs among several sources, likely reflecting the difference between Greenwich, which is time zone A, and Normandy in time zone B, a gap exacerbated by British daylight saving time. Rommel offered this assessment in a paper published on June 10, 1944. Liddell-Hart, *Rommel Papers*, 476–77.

82. Citino, *Wehrmacht's Last Stand*, 236–37; HQ, 26th Infantry, after-action report, June 7, 1944, 2, in RG 301-INF(26)-0.3: Reports of Operations, Jun 44, MRC Digital Archives. Citino's account uses Milner, *Stopping the Panzers*, an important addition to the historiography of the Normandy campaign, as it corrects the lack of coverage of Canadian operations. See also Meyer, *12th SS*, 1:186.

83. Citino, *Wehrmacht's Last Stand*, 238.

84. 26th Infantry, "History of 26th Infantry in France, 6 June 44–30 Jun 44," 2, in Reports of Operations, Jun 44.

85. "K Company History 26th Infantry," an anonymous wartime history written from the company log, MRC 1991.25, 24–26. See also Nechey, "3rd Battalion Journal," 45.

86. "K Company History," 25; "Theodore L. Dobol, Command Sergeant Major United States Army (Retired): Autobiography," n.d., MRC 1991.24, 23–25.

87. Dobol, "Autobiography," 23–25.

88. Uffner, "Recollections," 394–97. The number of Germans attacking cannot be determined from the reports. The estimate here is from Mygatt, *Return to La Roche-en-Ardenne*, 463.

89. There are variations on just what happened that night, depending on the source. The author has deferred to Dobol, "Autobiography," on his part of the story. The 26th Infantry after-action report for June 1–30, 1944, 2, claims that a Tiger tank participated in the attack. Mygatt's "History of the 745th Tank Battalion" says only that they took antitank hits on a single tank. The 518th Tiger Battalion was in the area, but the attack may have been made by self-propelled antitank guns. Uffner believed the Germans were withdrawing west. The regimental after-action report claimed that they were attempting to break out to the west. Either way a fight ensued.

90. Uffner, "Recollections," 2:397, 399. On June 12 Uffner was evacuated, as his wound had become infected. See also Nechey, "3rd Battalion Journal," 45.

91. Blumenson, *Breakout*, 40–41.

92. Wheeler, *The Big Red One*, 288–91; Harrison, *Cross-Channel Attack*, 366–77.

93. Edward P. Becker, "Profile of S/SGT William A. Becker: A World II Veteran Who Gave His Life for His Country," ms., June 6, 2004.

94. Nauss, *Troubleshooting All the Way*, 27–28.

95. Nauss, 29–31.

96. Nauss, 32–33.

97. Collins, *Lightning Joe*, 27–28, 218–25.

98. 1st ID, G-3 after-action report, July 1–31, 1944, 2–6, in RG 301-3: G-3 Operations Reports, Jun 44–Dec 44, MRC Digital Archives.

99. Huebner diary, entry for July 15, 1944; Wyman, "Journal of Events," entry for July 15, 1944; Lovern "Jerry" Nauss, interview by author, December 9, 2019, Minnetonka, MN.

100. Nauss, interview, 33–41.

101. Kingseed, *Omaha Beach to Dawson's Ridge*, 166; Eisenhower, *Papers*, no. 1796, 3:1971.

102. HQ, First US Army Group, Immediate Report No. 10, July 24, 1944, //N-3080, CARL, 1.

103. First US Army Group, 1–2.

104. First US Army Group, 3, 4.

105. HQ, Army Ground Forces, Observers Report 130, "Operations of the 16th Infantry on the Normandy Beachhead, D to D+2," July 21, 1944, N7323, CARL, 1, 2, and attached sector sketch.

106. Quinton Roosevelt visited with his father in the latter's sleep van from 1930 to 2200 the evening of July 11. Jeffers, *Theodore Roosevelt Jr.*, 262–63.

107. Kingseed, *Omaha Beach to Dawson's Ridge*, 162.

Photo Essay

THE FOLLOWING PHOTOGRAPHS were selected to tell the story of the 1st Infantry Division as it learned to fight, wage war, and sustain excellence over time. There are very few photographs of German and Italian soldiers or their generals. This is not their story. Most of the photographs shown here were taken by Army photographers.

Prewar Training

The 1st Infantry Division went through the training system that all of the Army's divisions did, but the Big Red One focused along with others on amphibious operations. At one point the Division was earmarked to seize Vichy-held Martinique. Obviously an amphibious assault of NAZI-held Europe had to be undertaken.

Figure 1: 16th Infantry Soldiers at their boat station aboard the USS *Wakefield* (converted SS *Manhattan*) preparing for a practice amphibious landing near New Bern, North Carolina. Soldier photo, courtesy of the Robert R. McCormick Research Center, 1st Division Museum at Cantigny, Wheaton Illinois. (Hereinafter MRC)

Figure 2: Infantrymen making their way down cargo nets from the *Wakefield* to a US Navy launch in the summer of 1941. Using a launch, normally utilized to support ship-to-shore and shore-to-ship traffic, to land troops illustrates how bereft the US Navy was of amphibious craft. Note the descent to the launch is some 30 feet or more. Soldier photo, MRC

Figure 3: An early amphibious craft seen from the *Wakefield*. Note the rails on the ramp for unloading vehicles, in this case a light tank. Soldier photo, MRC

Figure 4: The menagerie of different craft being used to train amphibious operations. Soldier photo, MRC

Figure 5: Troops in the chow line aboard the *Wakefield*. Note that they are wearing "fatigue" uniforms which were made of blue denim. Their trays are well laden with food. The sconces in the background reflect the *Wakefield*'s history as a luxury liner. Soldier photo, MRC

Figure 6: Colonel Teddy Roosevelt Jr. (in the passenger seat), then commanding the 26th Infantry, chatting with Lieutenant Colonel McClure the G-4 (logistics officer) of the Division. Soldier photo, MRC

Figure 7: An officer conducting classroom training at Fort Devens, Massachusetts. Soldier photo, Fort Riley Museum Complex

North Africa and Sicily

In August 1942, the Big Red One deployed to the United Kingdom, where it planned and trained for Operation Torch, the invasion of Northwest Africa. The Division began its shooting war on November 8, 1942. The British First Army committed the Division piecemeal with unsurprising results. At the Kasserine Pass, the Germans taught some hard lessons. The Division recovered and showed growth at El Guettar. After the fighting ended in North Africa, Terry Allen's troops became the bane of rear area commanders with some reason. Even so, their behavior went beyond the pale. Given time to integrate replacements and train them, the Big Red One demonstrated excellence in Sicily. The troops clung to the beach at Gela because they learned they could survive tank attacks by doing so. Aided by naval gunfire, they turned the Germans back.

After the end of the campaign in Sicily, Clarence R. "Coach" Huebner and Willard Wyman took over from Terry and Teddy. The newcomers cleaned house, but did so with an eye to training as well as rest and recreation.

Figure 8: 1st Infantry Division soldiers aboard a British landing craft heading for the beach near Oran, Algeria, on November 8, 1942. They all look young but perhaps the youngest is the baby-faced soldier in the center of the photograph. He was Donald C. Wright. He earned two Silver Stars and survived the war. Wright passed on May 27, 1988. Photo by F. A. Hudson, Lieutenant Royal Navy, Wikimedia Commons, accessed May 2022. See also *Bridgehead Sentinel*, Spring 1990

Figure 9: Thomas O. Beauchamp supervising the unloading of 33rd Field Artillery equipment on the beach in Algeria. Beauchamp served in the Big Red One from 1917 until he retired as a Warrant Officer in 1955. Photographer unknown, MRC

Figure 10: M-7 "Priest" self-propelled howitzer assigned to the 16th Infantry's cannon company near Tébessa, Algeria, on the Tunisian border. Soldier photo, MRC

Figure 11: "Official" link-up point for the First and Eighth British Armies. US II Corps sign notes its command post has moved to Gabes, Tunisia. The truck seen in the photograph is hauling a SOMUA S35 French tank. Soldier photo, MRC

Figure 12: 2nd Battalion 18th Infantry positions east of Djebel Berda at El Guettar. These positions are being prepared on the south side of the valley. This is a pre-battle photograph as there is no combat detritus. The ridge on the far side of the valley is the one the Rangers moved along in the early stages of the battle. Signal Corps photo, MRC

Figure 13: 16th Infantry post-operation critique in Tunisia. Ernie Pyle can be seen toward the back with his ubiquitous stocking cap (just below the arrow). Soldier photo, MRC

Figure 14: On 11 July 1943, D+1 of Operation Husky, Ju 88s (German fighter bombers) struck the SS *Robert Rowan*, a liberty ship carrying soldiers and equipment from the 18th Infantry and tons of ammunition. The ship was heavily damaged and on fire. The Captain concluded that the ship was doomed and ordered it abandoned. Shortly after he had evacuated all hands the *Robert Rowan* blew up. No lives were lost but the 33rd Field Artillery lost most of their equipment. The author believes this to be a Signal Corps photo, MRC

Figure 15: View of the Herman Göring Fallschirmjäger Panzer Division counterattack in Gela. In the foreground, two US soldiers are looking out from a rooftop. In the background, dust and smoke from artillery and tank rounds obscure the Gela plain. The 1st Infantry Division repulsed the attack with the support of naval gunfire. Photographer unknown, MRC

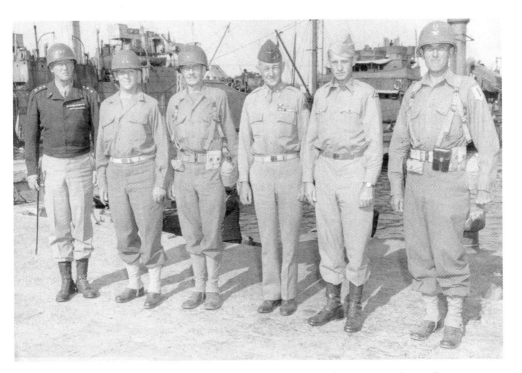

Figure 16: From left to right, Patton, Huebner, Brigadier General Clift Andrus, Hugh J. Gaffney, an unidentified Seventh Army Staff Officer, and Wyman just prior to Patton's farewell to the 1st Infantry Division. The Division sailed for the United Kingdom to prepare for the invasion of France on October 23, 1943. The author believes this to be a Signal Corps photo, MRC

Overlord, the Breakout and Pursuit

In October 1943, the Division returned to the United Kingdom, where it planned, integrated replacements, and rehearsed for the invasion of Normandy. Courage from top to bottom, naval gunfire, and small unit excellence assured the outcome on Omaha Beach. After fierce fighting in the Bocage, First Army broke out during Operation Cobra in August 1944. The 1st Infantry Division played a key role during the exploitation and pursuit, including hard fighting at Mons. In September, the Big Red One reached the Siegfried Line, where it culminated. Hard fighting followed.

Figure 17: An 18th Infantry half-track from the regimental antitank company moving to a "dewaterproofing site" following a practice landing. Signal Corps photo, MRC

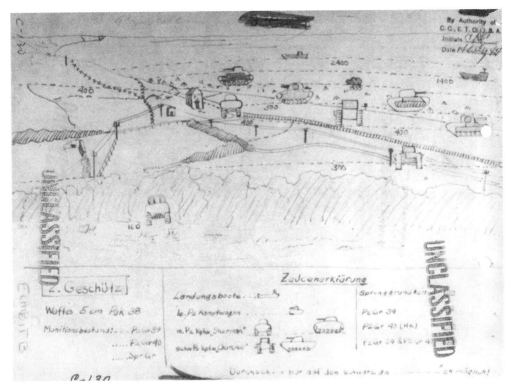

Figure 18: A German range card/sector sketch taken from a bunker on Omaha Beach. The sketch shows the crescent shape of Omaha Beach as it extends to the west, permitting enfilading or flanking fire along its entirety. Ranges are in meters. This sketch was made for a 50 millimeter antitank gun. MRC

Figure 19: Wounded men from the 3rd Battalion 16th Infantry waiting to be evacuated from the beach on June 6, 1944. Signal Corps photo, MRC

Figure 20: Willard G. Wyman and part of his command-post team sheltering in defilade among reeds inland from the beach. General Huebner's scrapbook, MRC

Figure 21: Mulberry Harbor at Omaha Beach. General Huebner's scrapbook, MRC

Figure 22: Huebner briefing Eisenhower and Bradley on 1st ID operations. Andrus can be seen between Huebner and Eisenhower. Bradley is on Eisenhower's left. Although he cannot be seen, the record shows that Leonard Gerow, the V Corps commander, accompanied Eisenhower and Bradley. This photograph was probably taken on July 2, 1944, the same day Eisenhower awarded a number of Distinguished Service Crosses to 1st Infantry Division soldiers. General Huebner's scrapbook, MRC

Figure 23: 3rd Armored Division troops, attached to the Big Red One, celebrate with newly liberated French civilians during the breakout. General Huebner's scrapbook, MRC

Figure 24: Unidentified "liberated" French town in Normandy, summer 1944. General Huebner's scrapbook, MRC

Figure 25: Huebner chatting with troops in Normandy. General Huebner's scrapbook, MRC

Figure 26: Major General J. Lawton Collins, (Lightning Joe) conferring with 1st ID troops during the pursuit. The sign in the background points to Danger Forward, the 1st ID Command Post. The Army caption for the photo reads in part "conferring with cavalry." This is mistaken. This is a photograph of Joe Collins using a Greyhound Armored Car marked with the VII Corps flash on right fender, just above number 9, signifying weight classification as 9 tons. Given the direction he is heading, it is likely he has just left Danger Forward. Photographer unknown, MRC

Figure 27: During the pursuit the Big Red One "motorized" on anything that rolled, including tanks. This tank, carrying at least 12 infantrymen, is rolling through the town of La Ferté Macé, France on August 14, 1944. The tank and its passengers are about 20 miles east of Mortain almost certainly heading east. Signal Corps photo, Fort Riley Museum Complex

Figure 28: One of the many river crossings during the pursuit across France. The soldier on the "handie talkie" radio (Signal Corps Radio set 536) is calling forward the next unit to cross. The soldiers crossing the bridge are from one of the regimental antitank companies. General Huebner's scrapbook, MRC

Figure 29: An Infantry squad using defilade cover. One of them appears to be high enough to see over the rise ahead. Photographer unknown, MRC

Figure 30: Terry Allen, fourth from the left, now commanding the 104th Infantry Division, and soldiers who had followed him from the 1st Infantry Division visiting the grave of Teddy Roosevelt Jr. in September 1944. Soldier photo, MRC

Aachen and the Forest Battles

The 1st Infantry Division fought on the edge of the Hürtgen Forest in the early fall, avoiding the decimation that other divisions faced. It too had its hard share of fighting to seize Aachen, the first German city to fall to the Allies. Afterward the 1st ID entered the maw of the Hürtgen, where it suffered attrition in breaking out of the forest.

The Division began withdrawing by regiment as they were relieved from the Hürtgen on December 6. The 16th was the last regiment to come out, withdrawing on December 13. In the midst of being relieved, Major General Huebner departed on December 11, 1944 to take command of V Corps. Brigadier General Clift Andrus assumed command of the 1st ID that same day.

All of the regiments needed time to bring on replacements and equipment. However, on 16 December both the 16th and 18th Infantry Regiments were detached from the Division while the 26th was ordered to Camp Elsenborn in Belgium. The 26th Infantry Regiment headed south on December 17 and entered the line at Bütgenbach, where it helped hold the northern shoulder of the German penetration. Andrus and Danger Forward moved the next day. Ultimately, the Division played a key role in retaking St. Vith, Belgium, and reducing the German penetration. By the end of January 1945, the Germans had been driven back to their start line.

Figure 31: A 745th Tank Battalion Sherman firing in Aachen, October 1944. The author believes this to be a Signal Corps photo, MRC

Figure 32: Corporal Eugene McKay observes from the turret of his C Company 745th Tank Battalion Sherman as an M-10 tank destroyer from the 634th Tank Destroyer maneuvers forward in Aachen, October 20, 1944. Signal Corps photo, www.tankdestroyer.net, accessed September 20, 2020.

Figure 33: Oberst Gerhard Wilck in the passenger's seat of the jeep that will take him to captivity. Members of his staff are in the back seat. This photo was taken shortly after his surrender of Aachen at 1300 on October 21, 1944. The three Americans in the background are from K Company 26th Infantry, including the company commander, his executive officer, and First Sergeant Ted Dobol. The author believes this to be a Signal Corps photo, MRC

Figure 34: Huebner, Colonel J. F. R. Seitz (commander of the 26th Infantry), and Lieutenant Colonel John T. Corley in Aachen after the surrender. Note the German prisoners of war to their left. Huebner is carrying Corley's M-1 and Corley is carrying an airborne version of the carbine. Huebner was trying to convince Corley that he should carry the folding stock carbine. Corley remained unconvinced. Photographer unknown, courtesy of Michael Corley.

Figure 35: The 3rd Battalion 18th Infantry advancing through the Hürtgen Forest. Photographer unknown, MRC

Figure 36: In the late winter, the road in Hürtgen Forest was deep literally. Note the cobweb of telephone wires to the left of the halftrack. Signal Corps photo, MRC

Figure 37: 18th Infantry troops taking a break in Bütgenbach, Belgium, on January 24, 1945, before continuing the attack to reduce the bulge. Telephone wires festoon the building in the foreground. Photographer unknown, MRC

Figure 38: M-10 Tank Destroyers firing as artillery on January 26, 1945. The M-10 in the foreground is using propellant designed to reduce the flash. The one in the background is firing with far less stealthy propellant. Signal Corps photo, Fort Riley Museum Complex

Figure 39: L Company 3rd Battalion 26th Infantry on the march, January 31, 1945, during operations to reduce the bulge. The lead solider in file on the right is wearing the new shoe pac outerwear. He was likely a replacement who received the shoe pac en route to his unit. Soldiers in the file on the left are wearing combat boots that provided little protection against cold or wet weather. The second soldier in that file is carrying a half mile reel of WD 1 telephone wire. Signal Corps photo, MRC

Figure 40: A soldier from L Company 3rd Battalion 26th Infantry receives treatment after being wounded by a mine on January 31, 1945. Signal Corps photo, MRC

Figure 41: Rocco J. "Rocky" Moretto (on the left) and friends during the Battle of the Bulge. The soldier in the center is Rocky's best friend, Robert (Bob) Francis Wright. Wright was killed in action on January 25, 1945, and was interred in Henri-Chapelle American Cemetery in Belgium. Moretto ended the war as a Staff Sergeant. He was one of only two soldiers assigned to C Company 1st Battalion 26 Infantry to fight all the way from Omaha Beach to V-E Day. Soldier photo, courtesy of Jill Moretto

Figure 42: 18th Infantry soldiers chatting beside a 28th Infantry Division Reconnaissance Troop armored car, which was captured by the Germans and then recovered by the 18th Infantry in Faymonville, Belgium. Photographer unknown, MRC

The Battles for the Roer and the Rhine

In February 1945, the 1st Infantry Division returned to the same ground where it fought in the battle to take Aachen. Next, the Division crossed the Roer River at Kreuzau, Germany, on February 25. From there it took ten days to reach the Rhine River at Bonn, which it took on March 7. On March 16 the Big Red One began crossing the Rhine, where it formed part of the force that broke out of the bridgehead. The Division raced north, where it helped encircle German Army Group B. Once the circle was closed, the Division turned east with VII Corps to clear the Harz Mountains.

Figure 43: Brigadier General Clift Andrus, sporting a brand new field jacket, leads 12th Army Group commander Omar N. Bradley into a dugout. This photo was likely taken in the Hürtgen Forest in mid-February 1945. Signal Corps photo, MRC

Figure 44: 18th Infantry bivouac back in the Hürtgen Forest on February 19, 1945. PFC Joseph Porcarelli of C Company 2nd Battalion 18th Infantry reading his hometown paper is in the foreground. Signal Corps photo, MRC

igure 45: Private Michael Swinkin f B Company 1st Battalion 16th nfantry waiting to make the assault rossing of the Roer River to seize reuzau, Germany, on February 5, 1945. He is carrying at least ree fragmentation grenades. Two ares can be seen just under his ght hand and above a bandolier f ammunition. Part of his lifebelt an be seen just below the grenades. le has placed a box, possibly from K Ration Meal, atop the barrel of is M-1 Rifle to keep rain or the oer River out. He has the look of a eteran—ready to go. Signal Corps noto, Fort Riley Museum Complex

Figure 46: Soldiers from E Company 2nd Battalion 26th Infantry sleeping or resting on 27 February 1945 near one of the Sherman tanks supporting them. They are in Soller, Germany, a little more than a mile east of Kreuzau. Signal Corps photo, Fort Riley Museum Complex

Figure 47: C Company 1st Battalion 18th Infantry moving forward through the village of Frauwüllesheim after crossing the Roer River on February 28, 1945. The 16th Infantry made the initial assault crossing, repulsed a counterattack, and with the 26th Infantry broke out of the bridgehead. The 18th followed to exploit success. Frauwüllesheim is five miles northeast of Kreuzau. The jeeps are returning to the crossing site, possibly after delivering supplies to the forward units. Signal Corps photo, Fort Riley Museum Complex

Figure 48: 745th Tank Battalion Sherman moving through a German village, en route to the Rhine River on March 1, 1945. Signal Corps photo, MRC

Figure 49: C Company 1st Battalion 26th Infantry .30 caliber light machine gun crew watching for enemy movement in Bonn, Germany, on March 7, 1945. Signal Corps photo, MRC

Figure 50: B Company 1st Battalion 16th Infantry soldiers watching the approaches to the bridge over the Rhine in Bonn, March 9, 1945. They are adjacent to a German Panther Tank. Signal Corps photo, Fort Riley Museum Complex

The Harz Mountains and the Last Yard

The Big Red One crossed the Weser River and began what led to the final campaign of the war in Europe. The Division along with other VII Corps units cleared the Harz mountains. Near the Elbe River, the Division was assigned to Huebner's V Corps, fighting its last battles of the war in Czechoslovakia.

Figure 51: Private Michael Di Carlo, H Company 2nd Battalion 16th Infantry, hauling 81 millimeter mortar ammunition with a "captured" German wheelbarrow in Weiler, Germany, on March 5, 1945. Weiler is south of Bonn. Signal Corps photo, MRC

Figure 52: 1st Infantry Division troops crossing the Weser River on April 8, 1945 at the start of the Harz Mountains campaign. Signal Corps photo, MRC

Figure 53: A photo from the Harz Mountains, April 14, 1945. The 1st Infantry Division caption reads, "Scattered shots by Germans disturb the stillness of St Andreasberg, Germany. Tank swings broadside across street and offers cover as they see[k] out snipers in buildings." The tank on the left is the long-barreled 76 millimeter variant of the Sherman. Photo by 1st Infantry Division, MRC

Figure 54: 1st ID soldier with POWs at war's end. Signal Corps photo, MRC

Figure 55: 1st ID MPs welcome the 100,000th POW taken by the Big Red One. Signal Corps photo, MRC

Figure 56: Staff Sergeant Tommy Macdonnell home after the war. Photo courtesy of Tommy Macdonnell, MD

Figure 57: Staff Sergeant Tommy Macdonnell in Normandy for the fiftieth anniversary of D-Day. Tommy is standing next to an M-16 Gun Motor Carriage mounting a quad fifty like the one he fought with on D-Day. Photo courtesy of Tommy Macdonnell, MD

CHAPTER TEN

The Breakout and Pursuing "Le Sale Boche"

> Weather warm and rain in the afternoon. Rumors of early peace con-
> tinue to circulate.
> —*Sergeant Forrest C. Pogue Jr., diary, entry for July 26 (D+50)*

> Only a great division can make tough going look easy.
> —*A. J. Liebling*

At the end of July 1944, the US Army in France transitioned from the comparatively small operations that characterized the Mediterranean and Pacific theaters to operations far beyond those in scope and scale. The landings in Normandy created new and fundamentally different opportunity for the Allies. Within the compact frame of western Europe, the western Allies would finally rise to the level of coordinated multi–Army Group operations conducted in depth against the forces of Germany. More importantly, together with the Soviet Armies, the Allies in the West now had the means to bring the war to the Germans in ways they could not in Italy.

For the 1st ID, that meant participating in what army doctrine called the strategic breakthrough. Doctrinally, the purpose of a breakthrough was to "advance deep into hostile territory to encircle and destroy or capture large hostile forces or to seize strategically important areas." From the outset of Overlord, Bernard Law Montgomery had intended that Americans would affect the breakthrough and then pivot on the Commonwealth forces at Caen-Bayeux. It was Omar Bradley who conceived the breakthrough plan to which his operations officer assigned the code name Cobra. A break-through in the west would enable an envelopment of the German Seventh

Army as US forces turned toward the Seine and Paris. Then the greatest all of prizes would be within the reach of the Allies—pursuit of a beaten enemy.[1]

Gethsemane of the Hedgerows

The marshy ground just south of Utah Beach, the marshes west of Carentan, and the bocage canalized movement and so favored the defenders. The Germans used ground effectively. To break free of the bocage and through the Germans required First Army to secure the road from Bayeux through Balleroy, through Saint-Lô to Coutances. The 1st ID learned to fight in the bocage in the successful attack to seize Caumont. In taking Caumont, 1st ID cleared part of the bocage and secured the road from Bayeux to within ten miles of Saint-Lô. Once south of the road, First Army would be out of the low marshy ground, although still among the hedgerows. Farther south, the Americans would finally be able to maneuver at corps level rather than fighting bloody company-level battles for tiny patches of pasture protected by dense hedges atop berms built up over hundreds of years.

On July 1 First Army attacked south to fight its way through the bocage and seize Saint-Lô, from which eight roads radiated. Some went east and west, as does that from Bayeux to Saint-Lô to Caumont, but others went north-south, including one that led to Avranches, out of Normandy, and into France proper. By then Bradley had four corps ashore, including V, VII, VIII, and XVIII, as well as thirteen divisions, including the 2nd and 3rd Armored Divisions, the 82nd and 101st Airborne Divisions, and nine infantry divisions. Of these the 1st, 2nd, 4th, 9th, 29th, and 30th ID were battle tested, the 79th, 83rd, and 90th less so. Three more, including the 5th, 8th, and 35th ID, came ashore in early July. The 4th, 5th, and 6th Armored Divisions came ashore mid- to late July.[2]

Finally, on July 18, Saint-Lô fell to a combination of bloody assaults by the 29th and 35th Infantry Divisions under the control of XIX Corps, led by Major General Charles H. Corlett. Much of the city was reduced to rubble, but what remained still controlled the roads. The Germans continued to resist, keeping the town and roads under fire for another week. The Seventh Army diary reported laconically, "In the bitter fighting that took place during the evening of 18 July, St Lô was definitely lost." But the diarist went on to add with pride that the troops had held the city since fending off American tanks on June 9. The diary continued, "Our men stubbornly defended the city along a ten mile line of resistance and dealt the enemy heavy losses in personnel."[3]

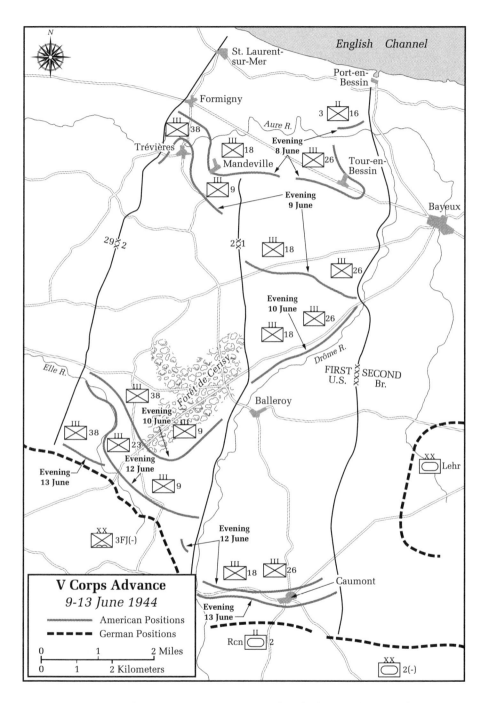

Map 13: V Corps Advance, June 9–13, 1944. Reproduced, edited, and annotated to focus on the 1st ID, from Harrison, *Cross-Channel Attack*, Map XVIII.

Meanwhile a New York City cavalryman, Sergeant Curtis G. Culin Jr., built a four-pronged gadget that enabled a tank to plow through a hedgerow covered in a "canopy of dirt" rather than exposing its belly by bulling over the top. Gerow invited Bradley to see a demonstration of the sergeant's invention on July 14. Duly impressed, the army commander had his engineers and ordnance men mass-produce the device. First Army equipped "three of every five tanks in the breakout" with Culin's gizmo. Tanks so equipped took the appellation "Rhino" for the hornlike prongs. On its next attack, 1st ID employed Rhinos.[4]

Despite being pounded from the sea, air, and ground, Seventh Army made the Americans pay dearly, exacting some forty thousand casualties across the entire front. Of these, thirty-six thousand infantrymen were killed, wounded, captured, or missing. In return, First Army had advanced all of seven miles and taken over the rubble that remained at the road junction that had once been Saint-Lô. But at last the conditions could be set to break through and out. Writing about the fighting in *A Soldier's Story*, Bradley observed that "the German has shown an astonishing capacity for recuperation." The "German" would show this resilience again and again. Executing the breakthrough, the exploitation, and the pursuit are the focus here.[5]

The Germans

Both sides suffered during the landings and in the bocage. One correspondent described the fighting there as "the Gethsemane of the hedgerows." Thanks to the Allied air forces as well as naval and army artillery, the German Landsers had little peace. Nearly every entry in the Seventh Army war diary remarks on artillery and/or air attacks. The tone of the diary is just this side of complaining about American profligacy with ammunition. Even in defeat, the enemy remained arrogant about their capabilities viz their opposition. An Austrian infantry lieutenant was "very emphatic" in his criticism. He claimed that "Modern War consists of fire and movement. The Americans have fire but no movement." Perhaps, but the Austrian still went to the cage. On his way to a prisoner-of-war camp, Obersturmbannführer Reinhardt, a battalion commander in the 17th SS Division, whined that American infantry "never attack until the artillery and air force have blasted the area."[6]

True, but his argument misses the mark. World War II was not a friendly competition between the American GI and his Axis counterpart, although one German soldier allowed that the Americans were "good sports but poor soldiers." War is not a sporting event, so fighting "fair" is foolish; one should always bring at least one gun to a knife fight. The Allies fought, to use a fashionable term, asymmetrically. The US Army has a saying, "Send a projo [projectile] so Joe don't go." Even if inelegant, the massive application of fire reduced the loss of life among the "poor bloody infantry." As soldier historian and combat veteran Richard M. Swain puts it, "there are no style points" awarded in combat. His assessment applied then as it does now. The effect of American firepower on the Germans is indisputable. "By far the heaviest casualties were produced by artillery," a German medic noted. An officer prisoner observed that artillery made it impossible to "hold a line of defense."[7]

In mid-July Generalfeldmarschall Erwin Rommel summed it up: "The situation on the Normandy front is growing worse every day and is now approaching a grave crisis." Rommel continued his assessment, listing the losses in Army Group B against replacements. Perhaps most telling, Army Group B had received only 17 replacement tanks against 225 lost. Rommel argued that in the face of the Allies' materiel superiority, "even the bravest army will be smashed piece by piece, losing men arms and territory in the process." Equally important, no new forces could be brought forward without weakening defenses elsewhere. "In these circumstances," Rommel concluded, "we must expect that in the foreseeable future the enemy will succeed in breaking through our thin front, above all, Seventh Army's, and thrusting deep into France."[8]

Rommel might also have mentioned the decapitation of the German Army in Normandy. Several division commanders and the LXXXIV Corps commander succumbed to bombs, artillery, or guns. Seventh Army lost its commander to a heart attack. Not long after, Hitler fired Gerd von Rundstedt for advising Generaloberst Alfred Jodl to "Make peace you fools." Four days later, on July 5, he fired Geyr von Schweppenburg for defeatist sentiments voiced in a situation report that Rommel endorsed. The damning sentence read, "The choice now is between tactical botching combined with rigid defense, which leaves the initiative to the enemy, and an elastic strategy that would at least seize the initiative." Rommel's report of July 15 shattered Hitler's faith in him. British planes then rendered him hors de combat on July 17. Rommel's involvement in, or at least awareness of, the July 20 attempt to assassinate Hitler led to his being offered on October 14 the choice to commit suicide rather than face charges, which he took. Generalfeldmarschall Günther von Kluge, who replaced both Rundstedt and Rommel, survived only until August 19, when he too committed suicide after receiving a summons to return to Berlin in the purge after the assassination attempt. Herr Hitler did not include elasticity among his tenets. He did, however, value loyalty.[9]

Cobra

In *The Panzer Killers*, Daniel P. Bolger takes Patton's view that Bradley could not read terrain. As proof he cites Bradley's failure to see the problem posed by the bocage. But then no one else appreciated the challenges posed by the bocage either. Arguably those involved in Overlord were so focused on getting ashore that they could not see beyond the beach. Bolger is right; Bradley was no Patton. But then who would trust Patton with an army group? Pedestrian he may have been, but it was Omar Bradley who conceived Cobra.

On June 20, at the height of the horrendous gale that largely destroyed the artificial harbors, Bradley turned his attention southward. Able to do more than one thing at time, he also turned J. Lawton Collins and VII Corps loose in the Cotentin Peninsula. The corps attacked north toward Cherbourg, which it took on June 26. Taking the port was a first step toward improving the logistics, but the Allies also needed the Atlantic ports in Brittany and the major port at Antwerp. On July 8, Bradley began planning Cobra.

Despite Patton's criticism, his onetime subordinate got it right.[10] Bradley settled the details during a conference on July 12. He envisioned using as the line of departure the Saint-Lô–Périers road, which ran generally northwest from Saint-Lô. VII Corps, with five divisions assigned, would make the breakthrough. After a massive air bombardment, the 4th, 9th, and 30th ID would break through. The "motorized" 1st ID, followed by the 3rd AD, would exploit southwest to Coutances, with 2nd AD joining the fight to protect the corps' left flank. Major General Troy H. Middleton's VIII Corps attacked on the right or western flank of First Army with the 79th ID, 8th ID, 90th ID, 4th AD and 83rd ID from right to left. XIX and V Corps remained in place. Seizing Coutances could turn the Germans out of their position in Normandy. The British Second Army would support First Army by mounting an attack as well. Bradley chose Collins, who did well during the landing and very well in taking Cherbourg, to lead the main effort for First Army.[11]

Ambitious and smart, J. "Joe" Lawton Collins joined the faculty of the Infantry School in the same year that George C. Marshall arrived. He became a member of the "inner circle of officers" who met at Marshall's home for informal seminars on a range of topics. That put him in the famous black book. When Bradley began looking for corps commanders for Overlord, Marshall recommended Collins. General Bradley readily agreed. Collins came to Europe from the Pacific, where he had led the 25th ID, known as Tropic Lightning, in concluding the Guadalcanal campaign alongside the 2nd Marine Division. He brought with him the nom de guerre Lightning Joe, claiming, with little supporting evidence, that his troops had accorded him that

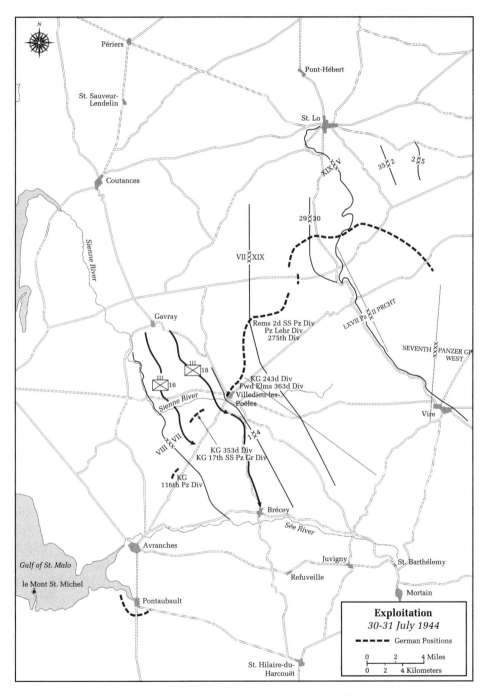

Map 14: Exploitation, July 30–31, 1944. Reproduced from Martin Blumenson, *Breakout and Pursuit* (Washington: Office of the Chief of Military History, 1961), Map VII.

nickname. Whether they did or not it, stuck. Writing about Lightning Joe in his memoir, Bradley observed that he had "boundless self-confidence . . . tolerable only when right and Collins, happily, almost always was."[12]

With Bradley's approval, Collins revised Cobra in several ways. First, he asked for and received the 4th ID, for the simple reason that three divisions attacking on a narrow front improved the odds. He also shifted the vector of the attack even more toward Coutances. Both Bradley and Collins claimed credit for assigning the "motorized" division role to 1st ID. In any case, on 14 July, Huebner learned from Major General William B. Kean, First Army chief of staff, that the Big Red One would deliver the "Sunday Punch." That same day Huebner attended a VII Corps conference regarding Cobra. Later that day Bradley, Patton, and Huebner served as honorary pallbearers at Teddy Roosevelt's funeral, along with Lieutenant General Courtney H. Hodges, who had been designated to succeed Bradley at First Army; Major General Raymond O. "Tubby" Barton, commanding the 4th ID; and Brigadier General Harold W. Blakely, 4th ID Division Artillery commander.[13]

Things moved quickly after Roosevelt's funeral, or rather as quickly as the weather permitted. On July 20, VII Corps issued Field Order 6, which described the mission succinctly: "The Corps will penetrate the enemy's defenses." It designated initial objectives that would cut off enemy forces confronting Middleton's VIII Corps, whose divisions could then exploit the penetration toward the town of Avranches at the southwestern corner of the Cotentin Peninsula.[14]

Huebner had to pass 1st ID through Major General Manton Eddy's 9th ID, "turn rapidly southwest, and block and assist in destroying forces in front of VIII Corps." The 3rd AD would follow. As the breach expanded, the exploitation was to include 3rd AD and then 2nd AD. Success required good communications, effective coordination and rapid transitions. Curiously, the corps order did not use the word *exploitation* in the maneuver paragraphs, but it did direct that corps artillery "support the attack and exploitation."[15]

Being the Sunday Punch meant that 1st ID, moving on trucks and supported by tanks, would drive through the gap created by the penetration with the intention of enveloping the left flank of the German Seventh Army, thus extending the same opportunity to the entire First Army. Huebner would have to act quickly once committed, and do so with little time to develop intelligence. VII Corps attached the 4th Cavalry Reconnaissance Squadron, Combat Command B of the 3rd Armored Division, the 745th TB, and the 634th and 635th TD as well additional field and antiaircraft artillery units. Planning for the breakout began a partnership between Collins and Huebner that lasted until December, when Coach assumed command of V Corps. The partnership between the 1st ID and Lightning Joe would last for most of the rest of the war.[16]

LXXXIV Corps, now under the command of Generalleutnant Dietrich von Choltitz, occupied the line opposite VII and VIII Corps. His units, most of them whittled down since D-Day, confronted Middleton's VIII Corps from the west coast of the Cotentin Peninsula to just west of Saint-Lô. Opposite VII Corps, he had part of the 5th Fallschirmjäger Division (FJD) and Panzer Lehr, with the three weakened battalions of the 275th ID in reserve. The corps G-2 estimated that there were no more than seven thousand German troops, with no more than thirty-five or forty tanks in their zone. The planned saturation bombing area stretched roughly four miles wide and half a mile deep, encompassing the entire front line of the Panzer Lehr Division, along with the easternmost part of the German parachute division. The westernmost part of the 352nd ID, located on Panzer Lehr's right but subordinated to the II SS Panzer Corps, would also be struck. Collins's order identified the ridgeline north of Marigny and the town itself as key terrain to be taken in the early stages of the attack.[17]

Breakthrough

Rain and occasional gales lashed Normandy throughout that summer. Rain postponed the attack on July 21 and again the next day. During the second delay, Huebner visited VII Corps with General Andrus in tow, and they discussed the operation with Collins, Eddy, and Barton. Collins, perhaps frustrated by the weather, chided Huebner on his division's lack of salutes and indifference to wearing helmets. Given Huebner's views on discipline, this criticism stung. The planned air bombardment finally began in hazy weather on July 24, "but the heavies couldn't bomb through the haze so the attack was postponed" yet again. Nevertheless, some of the bombers dropped their loads before they could be recalled. Unfortunately, they had not flown as Bradley believed the air force had promised; rather than flying parallel to the line of departure, they flew perpendicular, with some bombs falling short, killing and wounding Americans. The false start shook up the assault troops and served to alert Seventh Army, including Panzer Lehr Division, the first major target of VII Corps.[18]

To do what his corps commander wanted done "rapidly," Huebner would have to "see" the battlefield. Seeing the battlefield required judgment and intuition, based on what he could see, what he could hear, what he was told, and what his staff believed might be so. Seeing the battlefield meant accepting what Clausewitz learned in the late eighteenth and early nineteenth centuries: "War is the realm of uncertainty." According to the Prussian theorist, "danger, exertion, uncertainty and chance" together establish the "climate" of war. On July 24, things had not gone as planned perfectly, influencing this climate. Moreover, the scale of operations now required tactical commanders to do more than organize and encourage small units. Massing fires, maneuvering troops, and arranging logistics at scale amidst the confusion and friction of combat within a multidivision operation would require Huebner, his two generals, his staff, and his subordinate commanders to demonstrate their ability to see the battle in an instant and demonstrate the determination to act on it.[19]

At last the weather cleared, and the attack went ahead. Huebner moved up to collocate with Manton Eddy at the 9th ID command post and facilitate passage forward. The two division command posts were about mile north of the line of departure formed by the Saint-Lô–Périers road. More than 2,400 aircraft struck the "Bomb Saturation area" south of the line of departure. Once again some of the bombers dropped short, killing or wounding 601 soldiers, including Lieutenant General Lesley J. McNair.[20] The shock of two days of short bombing unnerved the attacking units, but Barton, Eddy, and Major General Leland S. Hobbes got their outfits moving. Still not clear of the bocage, the assault divisions made steady but slow progress, reaching no more than three to four thousand yards depth by sunset.[21]

As horrific as the bombardment seemed to the Americans, the Germans endured far worse. The bombers drubbed the Panzer Lehr and the 275th ID in particular. A Panzer Lehr soldier claimed the only way to escape the bombing was to run into the American lines as he had done. According to his commander, Fritz Bayerlein, "digging in of the infantry was useless and did not protect against bombing." He believed that a number of his troops "who survived the pattern bombing—because of the great morale effect—surrendered soon to the attacking infantry or escaped to the rear." Bayerlein, who was at the center of the carpet bombing, remarked, "For me, who during this war was in every theater committed at the points of the main efforts, this was the worst I ever saw." Even better, the bombers knocked out German tanks. The Australian correspondent Chester Wilmot counted twenty-two of them destroyed by bombs.[22]

Although Bayerlein believed his first line to have been annihilated by the bombing, his division resisted nevertheless by committing reserves. Panzer Lehr's reserve formations not only fought back but, with typical German resilience, mounted local counterattacks. The defense put up after the bombing reflects a great truism of combat—if it did not happen to me, it may as well not have happened. Soldiers and combat vehicle crews not struck fought back and counterattacked when ordered to do so. Making effective use of the bocage, Panzer Lehr and the 5th FJD put up what Collins described as "surprisingly dogged resistance." Accordingly, he committed his exploitation force, the 1st ID and 3rd AD, the next day rather than waiting for the breakthrough.[23]

Ralph J. Gordon, an infantryman in the 18th Infantry, moved out at 0700 on July 26. He and his buddies saw "what a wonderful job the Air Corps had really done. There wasn't a German soldier to be found for the first couple of miles, as every ten feet there was a bomb crater, and no one could live through that—not even the so-called supermen." Even so, the Germans managed to shell Gordon's company, which was in reserve and traveling well to the rear of the lead formations. Some German somewhere could see them and had not given up. Still, Gordon remained confident as "Our Air Force" strafed two hedgerows ahead, enabling the 18th to roll forward. The 18th reached Marigny and fought on until 2300, but could not take the entire town.[24]

For the infantry fighting through the bocage, that day went much like the earlier attack to Caumont, but they were now enabled by operating motorized, lavishly supported by artillery, air force, and armor. General Bill Wyman kept things moving, resorting when required to clearing congested roads personally and urging units "to go across fields and not stay on the road." Wyman spent a good deal of time with Colonel Truman E. Boudinot and Combat Command B, 3rd AD. He was unhappy with the tankers' liaison efforts and tendency to bunch up. Finally, he wanted the Combat Command B commander to be where he could communicate.[25]

Under attack from the air, and by the newly committed 1st ID and 3rd AD, Bayerlein understood that the jig was up. The Americans drove Panzer Lehr well back from the line of the Saint-Lô–Périers road. Indeed, the Americans had driven the division south of the road to Coutances. At 1800 that sultry Norman evening, Bayerlein received an *Oberstleutant* from OKW who officer stood to attention and announced, "Herr Generalfeldmarschall von Kluge demands that the St Lô-Périers line be held!" Good thinking, but far too late. The staff officer issued other orders on Kluge's behalf. When he was done, Bayerlein said only, "Tell the field marshal that the *Panzer-Lehr-Division* [sic] is destroyed. Only the dead can continue to hold up front." That evening the 116th Panzer Division began arriving to relieve what was left of Panzer Lehr.[26]

Huebner ordered Combat Command B and the 16th to continue forward while the 18th cleared Marigny. To cut off the LXXXIV Corps, Coutances had to be taken. While Wyman operated at the front, Huebner sustained the fight, working with Eddy as the 1st ID passed forward and coordinating support with Collins. Both understood the need for speed. Exploiting the efforts of the assault divisions was their purpose, and that depended on speed. On July 27 Huebner too went forward to the 18th Infantry, where he found Colonel George A. Smith Jr. and his operations officer dead on their feet. Neither had been sleeping, and both were exhausted. He ordered them to sleep for at least four hours. Exhausted regimental commanders and operations officers slow things down. That same morning Smith's regiment took Marigny.[27]

Meanwhile Combat Command B bypassed Marigny and headed toward Coutances. During the day Boudinot's tankers and armored infantry took the village of Comprond, four miles west of Marigny That afternoon a 16th Infantry patrol discovered a gap in the German defenses at Marigny and a path that paralleled the road from Saint-Lô. Huebner and the 16th's commander, Lieutenant Colonel Frederick W. Gibb, sensed opportunity and launched the entire regimental combat team down the trail through the gap. Once south of Marigny, the 16th would turn west and follow Combat Command B.[28]

Pete Lypka, a soldier in the 16th's intelligence and reconnaissance (I & R) platoon, described what followed: "As it got dark we moved out, with a patrol out ahead, followed by Engineers to clear the mines." With little reaction from the Germans, the 16th accepted the risk of attacking in column across the front of the Germans on their left or southern flank. The 1st Engineer Battalion committed bulldozers to improving the route so the infantry could remain motorized. Huebner reported to his diary for that day, "The breakthrough is a success." The Germans perceived the breakthrough as well. A Panzer Lehr company commander observed that the "entire front began to stagger."[29]

Now the Germans found themselves in the position they had often placed their adversaries—responding to conditions that no longer obtained. Although Bayerlein rallied Panzer Lehr, it lacked the capability it had just days earlier. With both VII and VIII Corps attacking, Choltitz's LXXXIV Corps confronted the possibility of being cut off. Although the 18th Infantry took Marigny, the town remained under observation by German field artillery observers. German artillery impeded the use of the road junction, slowing the developing exploitation of the breakthrough. German units counterattacked from both north and south or simply tried to slip through the attacking columns to escape. A good many got through.

The 1st ID fought through the night, trying to reach Coutances. At sunup, Combat Command B, 3rd AD, and the 16th Infantry were about five miles west of Marigny. Compartmented terrain and determined German resistance slowed their attack to a snail's pace. Congestion compounded the problem. Lieutenant Colonel Edmund F. Driscoll, commanding 1st Battalion, 16th Infantry, recalled particularly heavy fighting among the hedgerows just south of the road from Marigny to Coutances. Driscoll's 1st Battalion and Lieutenant Colonel Charles T. Horner Jr.'s 3rd Battalion, 16th Infantry, suffered 140 casualties and lost eight tanks in fighting that devolved into "squad actions with the enemy who appeared to be fighting a delaying action so as to allow the main body to get out of the trap [cut off at Coutances]." The opposition came from the 4th SS Panzergrenadier Regiment of the 2nd SS Panzer Division. According to Driscoll, the Germans made good use of their artillery as well. Indicative of the close-quarters fighting, Americans killed the 2nd SS Division commander at a road intersection south of Coutances.[30] In the end neither the 1st ID or the 3rd AD, Collins' exploitation units, took Coutances. Instead 4th AD, assigned to VIII Corps, seized the town late on July 28.

From Coutances the attack would continue toward Avranches, where VIII Corps could turn toward Brittany and join Patton's Third Army when it activated at 1200 on August 1. At the same time, 12th Army Group would activate with Bradley in command, while Hodges assumed command of First Army. Huebner and 1st ID had not achieved all that Collins wished, but they had produced, along with the rest of VII Corps, the desired breakthrough. From here, the Bradley planned for First Army to wheel eastward, with his corps abreast from north to south but oriented east. Third Army would enter Brittany with a single corps but continue south and then east with two.[31]

To Choltitz the danger was obvious. He asked to withdraw LXXXIV Corps before Coutances fell. Oberststurmgruppenführer Paul Hausser, now commanding Seventh Army, agreed and pressed Kluge for permission. In command now of both Army Group B and OB West, Kluge instead ordered Hausser to conduct a fighting withdrawal to the Seulles River. This order, like an increasing number of them, was overcome by events. Nevertheless, most of LXXXIV Corps managed to retire south, eluding the 1st Division. To compound his problems, Hausser barely escaped with his life that day when American troops overran his command post. The army commander "and his operations staff . . . escaped to the south by infiltrating overland, re-crossing the roads between serials of American tanks and trucks like so many fugitives.[32]

Exploitation—The Advance to Mortain

Collins ordered Huebner to clear up the detritus of cut off German units between Coutances and Marigny. On July 29 the division reported it had ' "cleaned out' enemy resistance to the soulle [Seulles] River and was awaiting further orders to continue the exploitation of the break-through." Traffic control proved to be the biggest problem for the next few days. Limited roads and the sheer number of combat vehicles trying to get out of the bocage compounded the problem. The 3rd Armored Division found, for example, that if it moved on two parallel routes with its logistics following, it required more than fifty miles of road space on each route, assuming fifty yards per vehicle, not including trailers. When motorized, an infantry regiment moving on about 240 trucks needed nearly as much space. No wonder generals like Wyman and notably Patton wound up directing traffic.[33]

Traffic management and march discipline proved every bit as important as tactical acumen. Clausewitz himself devoted an entire chapter to marches. Marches, he opined, "are the principal basis for the modern order of battle, as well as being its principal beneficiaries." What seems trivial to a casual observer is understood as essential to the professional. The 1st ID established high standards in precombat training and honed these skills in North Africa and Sicily. The Big Red One could produce and publish detailed march tables rapidly and adhere to them. Their military courtesy may have fallen short of perfection, but their march discipline approached it. The 1st Engineer Battalion prepared overlays that showed slope, road condition, and primary routes, and did so almost every day. As the combat forces moved forward, these overlays served to facilitate movement of logistics and supporting arms that moved behind them. Lessons learned in four years of training and combat paid dividends; mobility is about more than vehicles.[34]

An opportunity yet existed to turn the German withdrawal into a rout. When VIII Corps seized Coutances, it effectively severed LXXXIV Corps and Seventh Army from the Cotentin coast. Despite the difficulty Patton claimed Bradley had with maps, the army commander understood this. He realized also that for both sides, the road junction at Avranches was key terrain, as was the town of Mortain. Possession of Mortain expanded the corridor, afforded access to more roads, and included easily defended ground. On

July 28 Hodges ordered VIII Corps toward Avranches and VII Corps toward Mortain and Brécy. Accordingly, Collins turned his corps southeast, with 3rd AD and 4th ID now leading.[35]

At the outset, 1st ID constituted the corps reserve but joined the attack on July 31, reinforced by CCA 3rd AD and a plethora of attached combat and combat support formations. That same day, Third Army seized Avranches and the entrance to Brittany. The division made an assault crossing of the Seine River at Gavray and headed southeast just after 0800. The Big Red One attacked in three parallel columns led by armored-infantry task forces, called X, Y, and Z, formed on CCA formations. The 26th Infantry trailed the eastern column on the division left flank. The 18th Infantry trailed the center column. In reserve, the 16th Infantry trailed the western column. Motorized and/or clinging to tanks, the reinforced 1st ID had more trouble with CCA's task force columns than they did with the enemy. At one point CCA reported that one of its task force columns stretched twelve miles. The corps attacked on a narrow frontage, bypassing Germans as it headed south and southeast.[36]

Although the Allied air forces had achieved air superiority, the German Luftwaffe operated when able. Usually, the Germans attacked at night using flares to illuminate targets. The Luftwaffe appeared over the 1st ID at 0015 hours on August 1, and bombed across the division. The bombers killed two and wounded twenty-nine at Danger Main alone. There were casualties throughout the division as well as destroyed and damaged equipment. Nevertheless, the 1st ID resumed the attack that morning. Task Force X formed on the 32nd Armor Regiment, led by the regimental commander Colonel Leander L. Doan, entered Brécy about noon. That day and for the next several, the infantry marched, rode tanks, tank destroyers, and/or trucks with little rest in order to "seize the high ground and rail centers west of MORTAIN [emphasis in original]."[37]

Lieutenant Colonel Francis J. Murdoch Jr., commanding the 1st Battalion, 26th Infantry, described the attack as "day-to-day fighting. We were given . . . a line of march you might say, but it was 'Push, push push.' " Murdoch's battalion used every means of transportation from boots to riding on tanks. Pushing killed Murdoch's driver when his jeep "detonated a Teller mine near Brecy." John Lebda took the unlucky driver's place. Soon after, he and Murdoch encountered Germans, on foot, crossing the road ahead of him. According to Lebda, "The Colonel grabbed My BAR [Browning automatic rifle] and I got on the machine gun." Lebda and his colonel dispatched some of them and moved on. The division maintained its inclination to fight, or at least move, at night. According to Murdoch, "losses were less" when fighting at night. When he planned an attack on a town, Murdoch and his direct support artillery planed defensive concentrations in anticipation of the German doctrine of immediate counterattack.[38]

Fighting at night may have lessened casualties, but despite the best efforts of good people, confusion reigned. German and Americans mistook each other for friends and mistook friends for enemies. Artilleryman Jean Peltier learned of a weird incident from a CCA. Peltier and his column from the 32nd FA had halted at 0400 on August 1 when they encountered a CCA supply company an orchard. A lane ran through the orchard. There, "an enemy tank sat in the lane and a German officer lay stretched out on the front of the tank. He was very much dead." When the supply troops moved in earlier that night, the German officer had apparently mistaken them for friendly troops. Although his crew apparently knew better, since they ran off into the orchard, the German officer dismounted, confronted an American lieutenant, "shouted Heil Hitler," and gave the Nazi salute. Whereupon the American officer picked up an ax lying on the tank and hit the German in the head, killing him instantly." An M16 quad fifty antiaircraft mount then sprayed the orchard, setting fire to several nearby German trucks. Fighting at night had its ups and downs.[39]

Working with familiar units at night is difficult enough. Learning to work effectively with unfamiliar units takes time. The comparatively inexperienced 3rd AD and the 1st ID developed an effective relationship, but it took some effort. The 3rd AD tended to bunch up in column and at first did not clear the roads when stopped. One evening, after CCA coiled for the night, its commander confronted Murdoch with "Where the hell are your men?" To which Murdoch responded, "They're out protecting you for the night." After some more terse discussion, Murdoch explained that the infantry did the job best by being dispersed and out of sight rather than guarding the tanks. Ultimately the two divisions learned to fight together effectively.[40]

As the pace quickened, coordination and communications became increasingly important. Wire, radio, messengers and liaison officers were the glue that held the attack together. The road network south of Brécy led out of the bocage country but was inadequate to support the VII Corps attack. On the night of August 1, Jerry Nauss and his wire team set out to find CCA and lay wire back to Danger Forward. Laying wire, repairing wire, and making the clunky radios of the era work consumed a lot of time and energy. Early on August 2, the 18th Infantry complained that it was "having a hard job . . . coordinating with other units." Communicating left and right, and with units ahead and behind, grew more problematic as the day wore on. The whole of VII Corps and nearly all of US forces ashore were on the move. Radios and messengers had to suffice until telephone communications could be established.[41]

The attack continued, with Wyman and Huebner both working coordination. The pace remained hot at the tip of the attacking columns but slowed farther back. At the 16th Infantry command post, Arthur A. Heidrich found himself collecting German corpses as he had on July 31, when he "loaded German stiffs in a trailer like cordwood." That day the command post moved by echelon. Heidrich remained in the rear with the second lift. Germans ambushed the first lift, killing and wounding several soldiers. Fifteen others went missing.[42]

Late in the afternoon, as the division fought its way south, Huebner issued specific orders to keep things moving. At 1830 he told CCA, "I want all tanks thrown off the road to clear the road to get infantry up there. I want the 26th in back of TF 'X'. Tell your CG [Brigadier General Doyle O. Hickey] the situation." Twenty minutes later he ordered CCA to send guides to bring the infantry up. Hickey had broken through the weakening German units, including elements of the 363rd ID, 2nd PZ, and 116th PZ, but needed more infantry. At 1910 Huebner ordered the 18th Infantry as follows: "TF 'X' has broken through. . . . I am taking both of your battalions and attaching you to the 3rd Armored Division [CCA]." Located just north of CCA, in the village of Reffuveille two miles north west of Mortain, Colonel Smith and his regiment along with his direct support artillery and the 5th FA, joined Hickey's CCA to secure the Mortain road.[43]

The attack continued through the night. The division overran elements of the 275th ID and the 2nd PZ, taking Mortain and, as required, outposting the high ground north of the town from Reffuveille to Juvigny-les-Vallées and Hill 317 to the east. That same afternoon Lighting Joe encountered Huebner south of Brécy (probably at Reffuveille). In his memoir, Collins recalled that he "pointed on my map to Hill 317, above Mortain, which dominated the country side for miles to the east. 'Ralph,' I said, 'be sure to take Hill 317.' 'Joe, I already have it,' he replied with a grin."[44]

For its rugged beauty, the area is known as "Norman Switzerland." Hill 317, known by the thirteen hundred or so inhabitants of Mortain as Mont Joie, provides a panoramic view to the north, west, and south. The view to the east is not as good, as the ground is nearly as high as Hill 317 and extends about nine miles. The high ground is readily defended, however. The view to the south is far better, with no hills of even 250 meters altitude. The ground is lower to the west and north. Mortain was important for the seven roads that ran out of it, especially the major roads leading east and south. With Avranches and Mortain in hand, 12th Army Group had decided advantages. Chief among these, the army group had a twenty-mile-wide corridor with a path into Brittany and the ports on the Bay of Biscay as well as others to the south and east. The Americans' breakthrough opened Seventh Army's flank and perhaps could lead to enveloping LXXXIV Corps. However, the corridor remained too narrow. It needed to be widened lest it be cut by a German counterattack, which would stop the burgeoning exploitation.[45]

Collins and his corps staff had an effective routine for directing operations. During the day, Jayhawk 6 (the VII Corps commanding general's call sign) traveled the corps' zone in an M8 Greyhound Scout Car, often issuing orders on the road. The corps staff then codified these orders in operations memoranda. When the conditions warranted, the corps issued an operations or field order that reflected updated planning. On August 4 Collins ordered Huebner to "initiate reconnaissance at 1030 along the frontage from Domfront in the north to Mayenne in the south."[46]

Domfront lay twenty-five miles east of Mortain, while Mayenne lay some twenty miles southeast along a frontage of more than twenty miles. The corps follow-up documentation, Operations Memorandum 57, promised help. The 9th ID's 39th Infantry would be attached at 2015, and Combat Command B, 3rd AD, at 2200. Combat Command B was to secure a crossing on the Sée River north of Mortain to support an attack by 39th Infantry from Juvigny-le-Tertre northeast to Gathemo. Huebner ordered 4th Cavalry Group to seize Le Teilleul and Barenton to secure his right or southern flank. A cavalry squadron from 4th Cavalry Group eventually took Le Teilleul after a skirmish with a handful of infantrymen from the 275th ID and two tanks from Panzer Lehr. Later the 4th Cavalry Group's remaining squadron moved to the southwest. This widespread set of missions would widen the corridor, create more room for Third Army's XV Corps, and find out just what German units were southeast. Doing so would enable Collins to close up the corps and prepare for a possible counterattack or a turn eastward. The mission reflected the corps commander's confidence in Huebner and the 1st ID.[47]

Combat Command B attacked north, and the final consolidation got underway on August 4. That day the division artillery fired 105 missions in support of operations in three directions. During one fight the 18th Infantry exulted, "We are having quite a show. The enemy is east of 317 in a draw. . . .

There are two batteries of artillery, vehicles and a lot of jerries. They can't get out." Air support came to further pound the trapped Germans, with the proviso that they "watch for the 1st Battalion 18th Infantry which is east of Mortain on the high ground." That battalion had struggled at Longstop Hill but came of age in Sicily and showed excellence in Normandy. It had a field day on August 4 under the command of Henry G. Learnard Jr. The 1st Battalion showed its mettle and experience that day. Robert H. York had taken command in Algeria and led the battalion until July 12, when he rotated to take command of an infantry regiment in another division. Joseph W. Sisson Jr., another old hand, assumed command. Sisson was wounded on July 26. The systems developed over time enabled the new commander and his unfamiliar command to function like a well-oiled machine.[48]

Once again Wyman coordinated details focused on the attached units. He oriented Lieutenant Colonel Van H. Bond, who commanded the attached 39th Infantry, helped settle the regiment, and worked with Combat Command B and the 4th ID as well. The attack north toward Chérencé-le-Roussel occurred August against five bypassed units. The rest of 1st ID prepared to continue operations to the southeast.[49]

At midnight, August 5, 1944, the division issued Field Order 42 to resume the attack southeastward "in parallel columns." That could not occur until the 30th ID assumed the mission of defending Mortain and the road network. The 30th ID began relieving the 16th Infantry about 0800. The 16th's lead unit moved motorized just after 0900, led by the I & R platoon. The 2nd Battalion 18th Infantry, also motorized, moved out at 0845, trailing the 3rd AD's Task Force X. The 2nd Battalion of the 120th assumed the defense of Hill 317. The 26th Infantry followed when the 117th Infantry relieved it at 1500. Wyman remained to help the 30th ID settle in. The 16th Infantry occupied Mayenne without resistance. Indeed the 1st ID as a whole advanced against minimal resistance. Attacking motorized east and southeast in columns supported by armor, the division fought German infantry units supported by tanks in "2s and 3s." At sunset the division had secured crossing sites on the Mayenne River, preparing to turn east and continue the attack.[50]

That night it became apparent that the 16th Infantry had cut off elements of the 9th PZ. Horner's 3rd Battalion bore the brunt of attacks from the 9th PZ, aiming to get past his infantry heading south and east. Gibb remained cool, as did Horner. They had good artillery support. Just after midnight, the 16th allowed as how they would let the "situation develop to see what happens." The situation remained unclear. Horner, not a man easily shaken, said

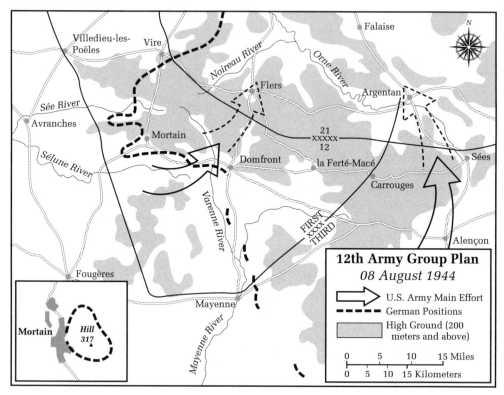

Map 15: 12th Army Group Plan, August 8, 1944. Reproduced and edited with inset showing Hill 317 and Mortain from Blumenson, *Breakout and Pursuit*, Map 14.

it best earlier in the evening when he told his regiment, "I don't feel secure in any direction." The German attacks petered out by sunup.[51]

The 26th Infantry reviewed their role in the move during a commanders' meeting early on August 6. Colonel J. F. R Seitz assigned the main mission to seize the crossing on a secondary highway three miles north of Mayenne to John T. Corley's 3rd Battalion. Derrill M. Daniel and his 2nd Battalion had orders to seize Oisseau, four miles northwest of Mayenne, while Murdoch's 1st Battalion had to take a crossing near Oisseau. The meeting concluded with the regiment issuing march tables. Wyman arrived later to review the scheme with the operations officer. The 26th moved out at 1548 and closed in without opposition at 2300. Jean Peltier, leading his battery in the 33rd FA, moved with the 26th. Of the move, Peltier reported to his diary that "it was worthy of note that it was the first area we had seen since the breakthrough that wasn't burned and completely pitted with shell and bomb craters."[52]

Although infantry could ford the Mayenne and did, the division needed bridges for vehicles to cross. During the day the 1st Engineer Battalion repaired bridges across the Mayenne in the town of the same name, repaired road craters, demined one bridge, and cleared the streets of the village of Ambrières-le-Grand. The 1st ID had now arrayed north to south oriented east, prepared to cross the Mayenne River (which becomes the Varenne north of the town of Mayenne) and continue the exploitation on order. Major General Wade Haislip's XV Corps from Patton's Third Army was moving in on the division's southern flank. The 12th Army Group could now complete the turn east.[53]

From the lofty heights at SHAEF, Eisenhower reported to General Marshall his satisfaction with current operations and confidence in the future. He told the chief of staff that he now saw no reason "to detach large forces for the conquest of Brittany and would devote the great bulk of forces to the task of completing the destruction of the German Army, at least that portion west of the Orne, and exploiting beyond that as far as we possibly could." Annihilating Seventh Army seemed possible.[54]

The German Estimate of the Situation

Generalfeldmarschall von Kluge's confidence, shown on assuming command, soon dissipated. The day Avranches fell, he declaimed, "It's a madhouse here." With VIII Corps moving south of Avranches and VII Corps attacking southeast, he declared the situation "completely unclear." Worse, his corps commanders could not communicate effectively with their subordinates. In short, he could not see the battlefield. Attacks on German command posts, disruption of communications, constant air attacks, and close fighting in which the Americans killed a division commander effectively blinded him. Furthermore, Kluge, Hausser at Seventh Army, and the high command at OKW continued to believe the breakthrough attempt would come at Caen rather in the west. Their estimate of the situation was dead wrong, with deadly results.[55]

Kluge had no readily available mobile reserve to react to surprise or breakthrough because Hausser had deployed his Panzer formations in the line opposite the British and Canadian field armies. In postwar debriefings, Hausser claimed that he intended to build mobile reserves, but his "opinion was not approved." This ex post facto account does not ring true. Soon after taking command of Army Group B and OB West, Kluge ordered Hausser to withdraw the 2nd SS PZ and Panzer Lehr to generate a reserve. In *Breakout and Pursuit*, Martin Blumenson shows that Hausser dissembled, delayed, and even disobeyed because he believed that " 'the defensive capabilities of the infantry divisions are less' than those of an armored division."[56]

The inability to see the battlefield extended well downward, where at least the local situation should have been fairly clear. Generalleutnant Gerhard Graf von Schwerin and his 116th PZ joined the defensive battle on July 29. Like other units, the 116th moved in increments and, when possible, at night to mitigate against air attack. According to the division's history, they got through thanks to fog, after a difficult 150-kilometer march from their Panzer Group West assembly area. Seeking information, Schwerin stopped at the II Panzer Corps command post. The corps commander was out, and the staff could tell him nothing. Next he visited the XLVII Panzer Corps, where General der Panzertruppen Hans von Funck told him that the 116th was subordinated to his corps. Even so, Funck could tell him little other than that he wanted Schwerin to counterattack. Schwerin did learn a bit more from Bayerlein at Panzer Lehr but found Bayerlein "visibly impressed by the destructive blows his division had been exposed to."[57]

The instability and lack of clarity in Kluge's command and control apparatus was acerbated by his commanders' tendency to look over their shoulders. Since the attempt on Hitler's life, those who were involved, even on the periphery, had reason to be nervous, while those who had not been wondered if there were traitors in their midst. Blumenson suggests as much concerning Kluge's relationship with Hausser. Kluge had good reason to be dissatisfied with Hausser, who had not carried out his orders effectively and had shown an inadequate grasp of the situation. In the end, Hausser survived because he was Heinrich Himmler's creature. Instead, Kluge fired Hausser's chief of staff, Generalmajor Max Pemsel, and replaced him with Generalmajor Rudolf-Christoff von Gersdorff, who was in fact one of the conspirators. Generalleutnant Otto Elfeldt replaced Choltitz, who then took command in Paris, where he defied Hitler's orders to raze the city. Sudden changes of command and casualties among commanders contributed to unease and confusion.[58]

General Montgomery compounded the German problem by waging a bitter attrition fight against the Panzer divisions defending the Bayeux-Caen sector. Montgomery's two field armies fixed seven of the nine Panzer divisions in the Seventh Army. He described the intention of these operations quite clearly: "To engage the German armour in battle and 'write it down.' " This his troops did in series of horrific tank fights. The 21st Army Group wrote down the 9th, 10th, and 12th SS Panzer Divisions as well as the 2nd Panzer Division. By the end of July, Hausser counted eight other divisions destroyed including Panzer Lehr. The British and Canadians field armies helped create the conditions for Cobra at great cost.[59]

Surprise, according to Clausewitz, "confuses the enemy and lowers his morale." The Allies achieved surprise on D-Day both in time and place. The landings occurred in foul weather at a place where the Germans believed the Allies would not come. From June through early August at least, the high command clung to the idea that the Allied main effort would either come north of the Seine estuary or from Caen. Clausewitz believed surprise stemmed from two factors, "secrecy and speed." In July and August the Americans in Normandy acted with greater speed in decision and execution than the Germans. The US Army and the Allies enjoyed a great many advantages in midsummer of 1944, ranging from Ultra intercepts to air superiority. Nevertheless, during the exploitation of the breakout the US Army proved apt pupils of the lessons they had learned at the hands of Wehrmacht in North Africa, Sicily, and Normandy. They now taught their tutors a thing or two about *Blitzkrieg*.[60]

Operation Lüttich: The German Counterattack at Mortain

Bradley, a beneficiary of Ultra intelligence, anticipated the German counterattack at Mortain. Collins did not have that advantage, but he did as well. The counterattack was standard for German units. If they lost ground, they counterattacked as soon as possible, hoping to catch their opponent before they consolidated their positions. Hitler and Kluge did not disappoint. Robert M. Citino has written the best contemporary account of German thinking and operations at Mortain. According to Citino, OKW developed a plan, codenamed Operation Lüttich, "in all its particulars on a map table hundreds of miles behind the lines." The plan focused on taking Avranches, which would cut off VIII Corps in Brittany and the rest of Third Army south of the town. Hitler specified "all available Panzer units" to participate, "regardless of their present commitment."[61]

Kluge received the OKW order on the morning of August 3.[62] Warlimont, Jodl's deputy, was visiting Army Group B headquarters in La Roche–Guyon when the order arrived. He told Kluge he had not known of the order. In his memoir he concluded that once again Hitler "had taken a snap decision." Over the next several days Army Group B worked with Seventh Army to develop the operation and withdraw what they could from opposite Montgomery. The Panzer and Panzergrenadier units then had to move laterally behind the thinned-out German lines. On August 7 Montgomery launched Operation Bluecoat, an attack of six divisions on the very formations Kluge planned to use in Lüttich. The Germans estimated that the attack included six hundred tanks. Of the attack, Heinrich Eberbach, in command of Panzer Group West, told Kluge, "I have always expected it and looked toward the morrow with a heavy heart."[63]

Seventh Army planned to attack northwest through Mortain, aiming to take Avranches and restore the line held in July. Hitler intervened with grandiose ideas and some additional tanks. It became clear that where Kluge envisaged a counterattack, Hitler had in mind a multi-corps counteroffensive. Heinz Günther Guderian, the operations officer and postwar historian of the 116th PZ, observed that "in theory, this order [counterattack] was correct, but it came too late." The time had passed when the Panzers could be withdrawn from the Caen sector. *Bewegungskrieg*, or war of movement, would not prove advantageous to the Germans.[64]

The counterattack began shortly after midnight on the morning of August 7, with four Panzer divisions; from north to south, the 116th and 2nd PZ and the 1st and 2nd SS. Of these formations, Gersdorff, Hausser's chief of staff, believed only the 116th PZ had adequate strength. The attackers made limited gains but were savaged by air and artillery and determined resistance from the 30th ID. On the periphery of the defense, the 1st ID encountered elements of the 9th PZ's 10th Panzergrenadier Regiment. The Germans probed 1st ID positions east of the Mayenne River. The only direct contribution 1st ID made to repelling the Germans came at 1845, when Collins ordered 1st ID to "send one battalion at once to hold GORRON (670840). Enemy has launched a Major Counterattack to separate First and Third Armies. Our front is holding." The front did hold. Robert M. Citino says it best: "Lüttich was a case of the Wehrmacht putting its head in the Allied noose."[65]

Falaise—the Happy Time

The Germans persisted in trying to break past Mortain, with no success. By the end of the day on August 12, the 30th ID had retaken what ground they lost. Hausser, who thought the "possibilities [for the counterattack] entirely favorable," was disappointed. But he also believed the attack had gone on too long He opined that the high command called off the attack only when success was clearly "no longer possible." Five days of fighting to break through had left the committed units overextended and nearly surrounded. On August 8, during the height of the counterattack, Bradley's confidence and vision was such that, with Eisenhower present, he proposed to Montgomery that the two army groups collaborate to encircle the German forces south of Caen, with the 21st Army Group seizing Falaise and the 12th Army Group taking Argentan. Doing so would destroy the Seventh Army and the recently renamed 5th Panzer Army.[66]

The Big Red One played a peripheral role in the effort to close the Falaise gap. On August 9 Collins ordered Huebner to turn north. Still motorized, the division "attacked" northward through Bagnoles de l'Orne and then La Ferté Macé about twenty-four miles south of Falaise. *Danger Forward* described this operation breezily: "Supply was working nicely. Gasoline was on hand. Rations were ample. Action was not severe. Casualties were almost nil. Sweat was taking the place of blood and the undamaged countryside in its late summer greenness was little indicative of war." But running into "isolated detachments of Jerries" dispelled "any attitude of inattention." Still, according to *Danger Forward*, "Joe was happy; his morale was high and the world was a pleasant place to be." Corporal Sam Fuller spoke for the doggies: "Our outfit was in high spirits. Every time the convoy passed road signs that said, 'Paris,' there were shouts and whistles. Paris! The very word aroused us, sending a jolt through every guy."[67]

On the other side, things did not look so bright. On August 15, Seventh US Army began landing troops on the French Riviera. Kluge's time had come. Two days later Generalfeldmarschall Walter Model arrived with orders to relieve him as soon as Model could familiarize himself with the current situation. Kluge's relief came as no surprise to him, and certainly not at OKW. Of the failed counterattack, Hitler told Jodl and Warlimont, "with a harsh edge to his voice . . . the attack failed because Field Marshal von Kluge wanted it to fail." The following day at 0600, Model convened a conference with his senior commanders, including Eberbach as commander of Panzer Group Eberbach and Oberstgruppenführer Josef "Sepp" Dietrich, who assumed command of Fifth Panzer Army when Eberbach left to command the Panzer Group. Gersdorff attended as Hausser's representative, as that officer was trying to save what remained of Seventh Army. On the basis of this conference, Model issued orders for Seventh Army and Panzer Group Eberbach to escape the Falaise pocket with what could be saved on the night of August 19.[68]

Following the conference with his commanders, Model relieved Kluge, who committed suicide that evening rather than returning to Berlin. Oblivious to all of this, "The Division pulled back all along the front for a bath and a rest." During the respite Huebner, a skilled man with a knife who could whittle interlocking chains, "whittled most of the day" on August 21. He also worked on getting replacements. Practically nil did not actually mean nil; Wyman did some coaching with the 16th and 18th Infantry on "anti-tank holes."[69]

Training and learning continued in other ways. On August 21 J. F. R. Seitz, commanding the 26th Infantry, brought in his three battalion commanders, his direct support artillery commander, and his routinely assigned tank destroyer and tank company commanders. They met to work out "a more suitable formation in the use of tanks and TD in working in coordination with the infantry in this type of warfare." By "type of warfare," Seitz meant mobile warfare with the infantry motorized. The discussion evolved into a far-ranging critique or postcombat review of what worked and did not.[70]

Seitz led the discussion. Each of the three battalion commanders offered an opening statement. Major Francis W. Adams, newly in command in place of the recently wounded Lieutenant Colonel Murdoch, said that in the 1st Battalion tanks led, followed by TDs, then infantry. Derrill M. Daniel led with infantry, then tanks, then a second infantry company followed by the TDs. John T. Corley had a third way. He mounted a company of infantry on a tank company and another on the TD company. The commanders also discussed how they fought with combined arms. The tank destroyer company commander believed that the three-inch rifle on his M10s proved effective in support of the tanks. The tank company commander reported that, once the infantry deployed, using the TDs on the flanks and his tanks up front in direct support of the infantry worked best.[71]

The conversation included Seitz's concern that "the men are looking for a target to shoot at instead of sweeping the area [with fire]." Corley acknowledged that he could "find that in my Bn." Teaching the troops to fire unaimed suppressive fire went against the marksmanship training they had undergone. Training units to use suppressive fire would be an ongoing concern. The commanders also reviewed techniques for improving the means to call for fire. This kind of far-ranging postcombat review occurred frequently in the 1st ID, but generally informally; more formal discussion occurred only in short rest periods.[72]

During the division's short hiatus, a good many Germans managed to escaped the Falaise pocket. Recrimination followed, but there were more reasons to celebrate than remonstrate. The 1st ID rested, watched USO shows, trained, and began compiling its G-3 after-action report for August 1944. At sixty-six closely typed pages, the report reflected the attention to detail that Colonel Mason and Huebner expected. Lieutenant Colonel Clarence E. Beck, who succeeded Gibb, compiled his first report as G-3 operations officer. His conclusions reflected the division's growing maturity in combined arms operations, and in employing tanks in particular. Tanks, according to Beck, "can seize terrain features, but they can not [sic] hold them against enemy counter-attacks." Getting infantry forward, motorized if possible, was vital and that meant that "armor must be side-tracked to make room on the road."[73]

On seizing an objective, the infantry had to consolidate rapidly and " 'tie in' with artillery and other supporting weapons for the defense of the captured area," according to Beck, who said that "the 1st US Infantry Division emphasizes this coordination." He cited artillery coordination on Hill 317 as an example of getting this right. The use of cavalry in security and reconnaissance also received attention.[74]

Beck also argued that "the Division has become adept at the use of supporting Arms. Each battalion is a complete task force." To support this conclusion, he reviewed routine task organizations that two of the regiments used. In the 16th Infantry, each battalion task force organized on variations that included infantry, engineers, tanks, tank destroyers, mortars, medical support, and support from the regimental antitank company. The task forces organized for differing missions. The 3rd Battalion appearsed to have organized as an advanced guard, including an entire company of combat engineers, the 745th TB reconnaissance platoon, two tank platoons, two tank destroyer platoons, and two of the regiment's antitank platoons. Of the models employed by the 16th and 26th Infantry regiments, Beck concluded that the battalions that each organized "had so much fire power that they were considered as a battalion combat team capable of 'knocking out' any enemy resistance." The report concluded with fifteen paragraphs examining various aspects of tank-infantry combined arms operations.[75]

On August 25, after a few days' rest, the Big Red One returned to pursuing retreating German forces. The division galloped forward, motorized, moving as much as thirty or more miles a day against light resistance. Elsewhere, Paris fell on August 25 to the French 2nd AD, more or less under the control of V Corps, supported by 4th ID. Once east of Paris, VII Corps turned northeast. The 1st ID crossed the Seine east of Paris on August 27, heading northeast. Two days later Lightning Joe made "a gesture of respect for my old friend and added incentive for the 1st Division," assigning a route that took the 1st ID through Soissons, where their division, and for that matter their commander, had fought during the Great War. The 1st ID took Soissons on August 30. That day Huebner visited "the First Division monument from the first war."[76]

On August 31 General Hodges called Collins to say, "Joe you've got to change direction at once toward Mons to help cut off the German Seventh Army." To do as Hodges wanted required the corps to turn through about forty-five degrees and head north. As the right-flank corps in First Army, Collins had to maintain contact with Haislip's XV Corps in Third Army. He asked Hodges who would fill the gap that opened when the corps turned north. Hodges answered, "Joe, that's your problem." With that exchange, 1st ID, following 3rd Armored Division, with Maurice Rose now in command, headed for Mons, Belgium, 110 miles north of Soissons.[77]

Notes

1. War Department, FM 100-15, *Field Service Regulations: Larger Units* (Washington, DC: Government Printing Office, 1942). Just what Montgomery intended has been debated ever since. The assessment of the debate in Hastings, *Overlord*, 231, 249–50, is succinct and objective. See also Bradley, *Soldier's Story*, 330.

2. Re First Army order of battle, see Blumenson, *Breakout*, 37, 90. All of the divisions cited arrived in June, less the 35th ID, which landed at the beginning of July. For the German view see Paul Hausser, "Seventh Army, 29 June to 20 August 1944," ms. A-974, N-175000.1104, CARL. See also *Defending Fortress Europe*, Seventh Army Diary for the period.

3. Blumenson, *Breakout*, 147–75; Reardon, *Defending Fortress Europe,* 217. The 275th ID comprised the Seventh Army reserve through the end of July. By July 24 Hausser reckoned his reserves at three battalions of the 275th at Marigny and five weak battalions of the 353rd. See Hausser, "Seventh Army," 38.

4. Bradley, *Soldier's Story*, 342. See also Blumenson, *Breakout*, 206.

5. Bradley, *Soldier's Story*, 343.

6. Reardon, *Defending Fortress Europe* (see, for example, entries for July 8–12, 162, 163, 168, 171, 174); HQ, Army Ground Forces, "Comments of German Prisoners Concerning American Employment of Infantry and Artillery," August 2 1944, CARL, N7313, 1–2. Reinhardt commanded the 1st Battalion of the 37th SS Panzergrenadier Regiment. Afiero, *17th Waffen-SS Panzergrenadier Division*, 57. A great many of the postwar manuscripts written by German officers make similar criticisms; Dupuy, *Genius for War*, argues similarly, and Van Creveld builds on Dupuy's argument in *Fighting Power*.

7. Bolger, *Panzer Killers*, 24n. Lieutenant General Daniel Bolger, a proven commander in combat who has keen insight on the nature of leadership under fire, credits Andrew Krepinevich with coining the phrase "send a bullet not a man." The author has no argument with Bolger's assertion that Krepinevich can lay claim to first using the phrase in a publication, but he heard the phrase long before 1986. It is an old idea. Colonel Richard M. Swain, personal communication to the author. For the effect of artillery on German troops, see Army Ground Forces, "Comments of German Prisoners," 2.

8. Liddell-Hart, *Rommel Papers*, 486–87.

9. Boatner, *Biographical Dictionary*, 284, 466, 478; Speidel, *We Defended Normandy*, 124–27. Speidel considered Rommel's July 15 report an ultimatum. Kluge endorsed Rommel's report, putting him at risk as well.

10. Bolger, *Panzer Killers*, 19–24. See also "The Port Discharge and Shipping Problems," ch. 3 of Ruppenthal, *Logistical Support of the Armies*, vol. 1. Sustaining the troops ashore required ports that could process and discharge cargo far faster than the damaged artificial ports and the small Norman ports. Despite heroic efforts, Cherbourg was inadequate to the task. More ports were needed.

11. Hogan, *Command Post at War*, 104–5; Blumenson, 213–23 and map 10; Wilmot, *Struggle for Europe*, 395–98; Montgomery, *Memoirs*, 227–28.

12. Winton, *Commanders of the Bulge*, 53–57.

13. Hogan, *Command Post at War*, 104–5. For 1st ID and assigning 4th ID, see Bradley, *Soldier's Story*, 332. See also Collins, *Lightning Joe*, 233–35; Huebner diary, entry for July 14, 1944. Re Blakely, see "Blakely, Harold Whittle," https://generals.dk/general/Blakeley/Harold_Whittle/USA.html, accessed July 9, 2021. See also D'Este, *Decision in Normandy*, 342–43. D'Este quotes at length Weigley, *Eisenhower's Lieutenants*, accepting Weigley's argument that attacking a narrow front was not normal US practice; Weigley's full passage is at his pages 137–38. This argument is overstated, given that the army had mounted very few corps-level attacks on this scale. Collins cleared the Cotentin by using converging and, yes, frontal attacks. North Africa and Sicily do support this assertion. It is hard to see how the argument applies, even in Italy.

14. HQ, VII Corps, FO 6, July 20, 1944, n.p., R13343.6, CARL.

15. VII Corps, FO 6, 1–3.

16. FO 38 is included in full in HQ, 1st ID, G-3 after-action report, July 1–31, 1944, 9–13n, in RG 301-3: G-3 Operations Reports, Jun 44–Dec 44, MRC Digital Archives.

17. Blumenson, map 4. See also VII Corps, FO 6. The corps incorrectly identified the 275th ID as the 265th ID. There were a handful of other German troops spread across the LXXXIV Corps sector. See VII Corps, FO 6, intelligence annex. Re 275th, see Hausser, "Seventh Army," 38.

18. Reardon, *Defending Fortress Europe*, 230–34. See also Kurowski, *Elite Panzer Strike Force*, 106–7; Bradley, *Soldier's Story*, 345–49.

19. Clausewitz, *On War*, 101, 104. Chapter 3, "On Military Genius," like most of Clausewitz, remains valid to the present day and will likely remain so.

20. Collins, *Lightning Joe*, 240; Craven and Cate, *Argument to V-E Day*, 228–34, number of aircraft that flew the mission at 232.

21. Collins, *Lightning Joe*, 241–42. Re effects of bombardment, see Blumenson, *Breakout*, 228–45.

22. HQ, 16th Infantry, journal for July 25–26, in RG 301-INF(16)-07: Journal, Jun 44–Aug 44, MRC Digital Archives. The 16th Infantry's journal shows how closely the 1st ID units followed the progress of the assault divisions. Fritz Bayerlein, "Panzer Lehr Division," July 24–25, 1944, ms. 902, RG 549.3, NARA, 1, 3; Wilmot, *Struggle for Europe*, 391n.

23. Bayerlein, "Panzer Lehr Division," 2.

24. Gordon, *Infantrymen*, 29–30; Baumer and Reardon, *American Iliad*, 246–47.

25. Wyman, "Journal of Events," entry for July 25, 1944.

26. Kurowski, *Elite Panzer Strike Force*, 112–13. See also Dietrich von Choltitz, "Kämpfe des LXXXIV A. K. in der Normandie vom 18.6.1944 ab," March 1947, ms. B-418, N17500.471, CARL.

27. Huebner diary, entry for July 27, 1944.

28. Huebner diary, entry for July 27; Knickerbocker et al., *Danger Forward*, 230–31. For the German assessment of the breakthrough, see Hausser, "Seventh Army." Hausser replaced Dollmann. Blumenson, *Breakout*, 252–58.

29. Lypka, *A Soldier Remembers*, 149; Ritgen, *Western Front, 1944*, 106. Ritgen identified the Panzer Lehr company commander only by his last name, Ebner.

30. E. F. Driscoll and W. H. Watson, postcombat interview by unidentified interviewer, n.d., courtesy of Steven E. Clay. See also Weidinger, *Das Reich*, 5:190–91. Weidinger is an unabashed defender of the 2nd SS, the division responsible, among other atrocities, for the slaughter at Oradour-Sur-Glane. The author's father took the family to Oradour in 1955. The recollection of the destroyed town and the horror of burned church remain crystal clear.

31. Blumenson, *Breakout*, 256–59. In chapter 22, "Opportunities and Intentions," 440–43, Blumenson reviews the intentions for both sides.

32. Blumenson, *Breakout*, 271–81; Reardon, *Defending Fortress Europe*, 241.

33. War Department, FM 17, *Armored Force Field Manual* (Washington, DC: Government Printing Office, n.d.), chart 6, p. 14. For march graphs and column computations see War Department, FM 25-10, *Motor Transport* (Washington, DC: Government Printing Office, 1942), 101–21; HQ, First Army, "Combat Operations Data First Army," November 18, 1946, N15264-2, CARL; HQ, VII Corps, Operations Memorandum 51, July 29, 1944, CARL, 1. All VII Corps orders and memos are NARA documents scanned by Dr. Stephen Bourque and donated to CARL; there are no accession numbers.

34. Clausewitz, *On War*, 314–18. Numerous examples of route overlays are present in G-3 journals; see RG 301-3.2: G-3 Journal and File, 1 Jul 44–31 Jul 44, and RG 301-3.2: G-3 Journal and File, 1 Aug 44–31 Aug 44, both MRC Digital Archives.

35. Blumenson, *Breakout*, 305–9. See also Hogan, *Command Post at War*, 110–12, re First US Army FO 2, July 28, 1944.

36. 1st ID, operations report, August 5, 1944, 30, in G-3 journal, August 1944; HQ, VII Corps, "History of the VII Corps for the Period of 1–31 July, 1944," August 9, 1944, R11799.1, CARL, 42.

37. Collins, *Lightning Joe*, 249; 1st ID, operations report, August 5, 1944, 30; HQ, VII Corps, FO 7, August 1, 1944, R13343.6, CARL.

38. Frank Murdoch, interview by Colonel John Votaw and General Paul Gorman, October 23, 1995, First Division Museum at Cantigny, Wheaton, IL; Lebda, *Million Miles to Go*, 94–95.

39. "World War II Diary of Jean Gordon Peltier," August 2, 1942–July 5, 1945, MRC 1998.79, 172–73.

40. Murdoch, interview.

41. Nauss, *Troubleshooting All the Way*, 87; G-3 journal, August 2, 1944.

42. Arthur G. Heidrick, diary, June 13, 1942–February 1, 1945, Fort Riley Museum Complex, Fort Riley, KS, entries for July 31 and August 1, 1944.

43. G-3 journal; Blumenson, *Breakout*, 444–45.

44. Blumenson, *Breakout*, 444–45; Collins, *Lightning Joe*, 249–50. Blumenson notes the 275th ID as part of the German Defense. The 1st ID G-2 reported "elements of the 116th Pz Div" in the area as well. HQ, 1st ID, Selected Intelligence Reports, vol. 1, June–November 1944, 39, in RG 301-2.0: G-2 Selected Intelligence Reports during the First Six Months of the European Campaign, Jun 1944–May 1945, MRC Digital Archives. On August 2 the 1st ID identified the 363rd ID, which had arrived in Normandy from Rouen in July. Mitcham, *German Order of Battle*, 2:71–72.

45. Reardon, *Victory at Mortain*, 65. Reardon lists Mont Joie as Hill 314. Hill 317 is used by the 1st ID in its journal and after-action report and is the altitude shown on the GSGS maps they used. Reardon believes the difference stemmed from Blumenson using modern maps. The author believes Blumenson had it right. Blumenson, *Duel for France*, 225. The author has not stood atop Hill 317; this assessment is from studying a legacy GSGS 1:1,000,000 map of the area produced by the British War office for use during the war, as well as contemporary satellite maps.

46. VII Corps, Operations Memorandum 57, August 4, 1944, CARL. These were not an innovation of VII Corps but standard practice in most units. The names to describe these daily instruction varied, but the idea was common.

47. HQ, 1st ID, overlay, annex 1 to Operations Memorandum 95, August 1944, in RG 301-3.2: G-3 Journal and File, 1 Aug 44–31 Aug 44, MRC Digital Archives; Reardon, *Victory at Mortain,* 69. The division had "swollen" to nearly two divisions' worth of combat power.

48. 1st ID, after-action report, August 1944, 10–11, in G-3 Operations Reports, Jun 44–Dec 44. See also HQ, 1st ID Artillery, after-action report, August 1–31, 1944, 2, in RG 301-ART-0.3: Artillery Operations Reports, 1 Jun 44–May 45, MRC Digital Archives. Two 155 units, the 188th FA (155 Gun) and the 957th FA (155 Howitzer) reinforced the division artillery. CCA's direct support battalion gave the division eight artillery battalions.

49. Wyman, "Journal of Events," entry for August 4–5; 1st ID, Selected Intelligence Reports, 1:39.

50. Wyman, "Journal of Events," entry for August 4–5.

51. 1st ID, after-action report, August 1944, 15–17; Clay, *Blood and Sacrifice*, 207.

52. HQ, 26th Infantry, after-action report, September 5, 1944, in RG 301-INF(26)-0.3: Reports of Operations, Jul–Sep 44, MRC Digital Archives, 3; Peltier, diary, 176.

53. 1st ID, after-action report, August 1944, 15–17; Clay, *Blood and Sacrifice*, 207. Third Army fielded four corps at this point. VIII Corps operated in Brittany while XII, XV, and XX Corps made the wide sweep. First Army controlled V, VII, and XIX Corps, turning east and then north on Third Army's left.

54. Eisenhower, *Papers*, no. 1970, 4:2049.

55. Blumenson, *Breakout*, 323–25; Baumer and Reardon, *American Iliad*, 240.

56. Baumer and Reardon, *American Iliad*, 226.

57. Gerhard Graf von Schwerin, "116th Panzer Division in Normandy," ETHINT-17, in Detweiler, Burdick, and Rohwer, *German Military Studies*, 2:4; Guderian, *From Normandy to the Ruhr*, 36.

58. Blumenson, *Breakout*, 325–28. Re Gersdorf, see Citino, *Wehrmacht's Last Stand*, 205 and, on the attitude of the German officer corps, 204–13. Re Choltitz, see Boatner, *Biographical Dictionary*, 90.

59. Wilmot, *Struggle for Europe*, 354; Blumenson, *Breakout*, 442, taken from ms. B-179.

60. Clausewitz, *On War*, 198. See also Rudolph-Christian von Gersdorf, "The Campaign in Northern France," ms. B-722, 24, www.sturmpanzer.com.

61. Citino, *Wehrmacht's Last Stand*, 261–62.

62. According to Citino, 261–62, Warlimont brought the order to Kluge personally. Warlimont, who was on the scene, claimed in his postwar memoir that he "had no new instructions." Warlimont, *Inside Hitler's Headquarters*, 448.

63. Warlimont, *Inside Hitler's Headquarters*, 447–49; Blumenson, *Breakout*, 481. See also Reynolds, *Sons of the Reich*, 72.

64. Guderian, *From Normandy to the Ruhr*, 66.

65. Citino, *Wehrmacht's Last Stand*, 260–65. See also R. von Gersdorff, "Avranches Counterattack, Seventh Army, 29 July–14 August, 1944," ms. A-921, NARA. The two SS divisions were worn down, and 2nd PZ was short tanks. Gersdorff details the effort made to assemble forces for the counterattack. This ms. is accompanied by overlays that illustrate the problems and attempts a solution.

66. Blumenson, *Breakout*, 492; Bradley, *Soldier's Story*, 492.

67. Knickerbocker et al., *Danger Forward*, 239–40; Fuller, *A Third Face*, 175.

68. Blumenson, *Breakout*, 532; Warlimont, *Inside Hitler's Headquarters*, 449.

69. Huebner diary, entries for August 18 and 21, 1944; Wyman, "Journal of Events," entries for August 17–21, 1944.

70. HQ, 26th Infantry journal, entry 384, August 21, 1944, in RG 301-INF(26)-0.3: Reports of Operations - 26th Inf Regt, 1 Jul 44–30 Sep 44, MRC Digital Archives. The 26th Infantry journal is numbered consecutively rather than by day.

71. 26th Infantry journal, entries 384–85.

72. 26th Infantry journal, entries 384–85.

73. HQ, 1st ID, G-3 after-action report, August 1944, in G-3 Operations Reports, Jun 44–Dec 44.

74. G-3 after-action report.

75. G-3 after-action report, 63–65.

76. Collins, *Lightning Joe*, 261. Re advance, see Huebner diary, entries for August 24–31, 1944; for visit to monument, see entry for August 30. On Paris, see Blumenson, *Breakout*, 590–628. The division rested and refitted from August 19–23 and then moved into assembly areas on August 24 to return to the pursuit. G-3 after-action report, August 1944, 38–42.

77. Collins, *Lightning Joe*, 261.

CHAPTER ELEVEN

Mons-Aachen

Next to our route of withdrawal, women and girls dug trenches and foxholes to provide cover against aircraft attacks.
> —*Ernst Streng, SS Panzer crewman*

As we were heading up Mons
The Krauts were on the run
You should have seen the carnage when
The fighting first was done
> —*Song of the Fighting First*

OMAR BRADLEY DESCRIBED the pursuit in the later summer of 1944 as the "headiest and most optimistic advance of the European War." At the end of August, in response to intelligence provided by supporting Air Corps pilots, he turned First Army from a northeast track, oriented along the 21st Army Group boundary, to a northern orientation (and uncoordinated violation of the British Army Group area of responsibility) intended to block the Amiens–Cambrai–Mons highway, an active German line of retreat. This resulted in the creation of the Mons pocket, an encirclement effected by the 3rd Armored and 1st Infantry Divisions. Bradley's actions reflected the army doctrine that "the object of the pursuit is the annihilation of hostile forces." According to the manual, "Effective pursuit requires leadership and the exercise of initiative." The Mons encirclement was the result of initiative shown together by Bradley, Air Force pilots, and Lieutenant General Courtney H. Hodges and his corps, division commanders, and troops.[1]

During the pursuit the Big Red One moved in alternate bounds by battalion, keeping up a pace of about twenty miles per hour when not in contact. Such a pace sounds slow but is quite fast when moving in march columns and accounting for security along the route. The pace of the pursuit extended the Allies' lines of communications to the breaking point while reducing those of the retreating Germans. How the army organized and supported the pursuit set the context for the advance to the Siegfried Line. The complex and difficult fighting needed to penetrate the Siegfried Line and then to take Aachen illustrates the confidence and the competence that the 1st Division had garnered by continually adapting and learning in the field, a process that had begun a relatively short time before in Algeria.

For the infantry, bounding forward depended on whether they did so on foot or motorized. Either way it was hard going. Reflecting on pursuing on foot, foot soldier Ralph J. Gordon remembered that his feet hurt so much that "at times I thought it would be better to cut my feet off and be done with it." Of motorized operations he wrote, "We rode in trucks following the 3rd Armored through France [and Belgium]. Riding on the tanks and trucks was definitely no joy ride, even though it was better than walking." The ride included "sweating out being shot at—that's what puts years on a man."[2]

The transition from breakthrough to exploitation seemed clear—it had come with the fall of Avranches. The transition to the pursuit, like most things in combat, was less clear. Although the 745th TB began moving on August 24, for most of the rest of the 1st ID the pursuit began the next day. The tankers road marched 156 miles to reach their assembly area. Remarkably, the tankers started out with all of their fifty-four medium and seventeen light tanks operational. En route, seven tanks ran out of fuel while five broke down. That same day Danger Forward moved fifty-five miles to catch up with the VII Corps main body. The rolling stock of the 1st ID had already been driven hard. When it reached Soissons on August 29, the division had advanced 310 miles from the beach. Continuing the pursuit from there meant following the 3rd AD while "cleaning out any enemy pockets of resistance" across Belgium to Germany.[3]

Sustaining the Pursuit: Logistics and Organization

The US Army was organized, equipped and sustained in a way that promoted initiative and flexibility. Taking the initiative requires agility, both mental and physical. Chester Wilmot, an Australian war correspondent, observed that US Army operational method reflected American culture. In the *Struggle for Europe*, he wrote, "The characteristic American resentment of authority, dating from the birth of the United States, has undoubtedly influenced command policy in their armed forces and has led to a considerable measure of independence and delegated responsibility at every level." That trait produced initiative. In his postwar memoir, Eisenhower wrote that "a qualified commander should normally be assigned only a general mission . . . and then be given the means to carry it out." So far, the World War II US Army had indeed proved both agile and flexible. This is in contrast to Bradley's assertion cited in an earlier chapter to the effect that "orders are orders."[4]

Success in pursuit requires pliable organization and effective logistics. For the first time during the war, the army's structure, organizing principles, and logistics doctrine would play out on the scale imagined in prewar maneuvers and at the Command and General Staff College. The principle of flexible organization makes its debut on the third page of FM 100-5, *Operations*: "To ensure unity of effort or increase readiness for combat, part or all of the subordinate units may be formed into one or more temporary tactical groupings."[5]

During operations in Normandy, the 1st ID routinely organized based on anticipated missions, and if necessary changed organization while in contact with the enemy. Relatively few attachments had joined the division in North Africa. In Sicily, however, systematic task organization matured, so that by the time the division landed at Omaha Beach, it expected and wanted tanks, tank destroyers, and additional artillery, including both antiaircraft artillery and the 4.2-inch chemical mortar firing high explosive, smoke, and illumination rounds. Unit after-action reports from the battalion level up cited the importance of combined arms, stemming from operating routinely with attachments or when attached to other formations such as the 3rd AD.[6]

Organization of logistics by echelon also supported flexibility. US divisions had both tactical and administrative responsibility. The 1st ID had the 1st Medical Battalion to provide immediate medical support, the 1st Quartermaster Company to manage and distribute supplies, and the 1st Ordnance Company (Light Maintenance) to provide basic maintenance. The division usually had an attached truck company and occasional detachments of ordnance and other support units. A corps had only tactical responsibility, so it had no logistics formations. Field armies had both tactical and administrative responsibility. Accordingly, they had robust logistics formations that provided most support via supply points. That is, forward units drew supplies from army ration supply points, ammunition supply points, and so on. This system allowed a corps to turn on a dime. The flexibility afforded the corps, however, placed a serious burden on divisions. Army-level truck companies hauled supplies from the ports to forward field army supply points, then trucks, organic or in support of divisions, made the runs from forward units to supply points.[7]

The Communications Zone, or COMZ, a theater organization commanded by Lieutenant General J. C. H. Lee, ran logistics from the coast to the rear boundary of field armies. That included running ports, railways, truck units, and intermodal transfer and all that implies. Two major headquarters existed within COMZ, which moved from the United Kingdom to France once 12th Army Group activated. The Advanced Section, or ADSEC, constituted the other major headquarters. COMZ units could build infrastructure as well as operate. Separate base sections established and operated logistics bases and depots. In his acerbic book *Top Secret*, Ralph Ingersoll, a staff officer who served in II Corps, First Army, and 12th Army Group, wrote of the COMZ staff that "there was the hard work of one individual, the venality of another." Ingersoll, who wrote three books during the war, including the well-received *The Battle Is the Payoff*, had sympathy for the ground troops but very little for the logisticians that took up residence in Parisian hotels.[8]

Model, Army Group B in Extremis

Hans Speidel, who served Erwin Rommel, Günther von Kluge, and Walter Model as chief of staff at Army Group B, observed that Model "showed determination combined with a gift for improvisation." Model demonstrated these traits with aplomb on the eastern front, at corps, army, and army group level. Speidel also thought him "uncouth . . . fearless in the heat of battle . . . [and a man who] thought too highly of his own ability." Finally, Speidel considered him "erratic." Model, like Kluge, came with an eastern front bias. He held "preconceived ideas and criticized his staff and the Army commanders" who might disagree, going so far as to tell Hans Speidel at Army Group B, and Günther Blumentritt, chief of staff at OB West, that he intended "to clean up the mess and to keep a tight rein." Soon after arriving, Model dressed down Sepp Dietrich at Fifth Panzer Army. Dietrich asked to be relieved, saying he was "not some little schoolboy you could pull up by his ears." Model, like Kluge, also issued orders that would have earned passing grade at the Führungsakademie but were beyond the means of Army Group B's units in the summer and fall.[9]

Model did, however, have faith in the Landsers, claiming that "no soldier in the world is better than we, the soldiers of our Führer, Adolf Hitler." Unlike either Kluge or Rommel, Model was a convinced Nazi. Despite his bias, he found his feet quickly and improvised with success similar to that he had enjoyed in the east. Once across the Seine, he was able to build a screen that provided some security for the retreat toward the Siegfried Line. Seventh Army withdrew to the rear of Fifth Panzer Army on the right, while the First Army withdrew from Brittany and took positions on the left. Seventh Army reorganized its shattered units as best it could. Model's skillful maneuvering notwithstanding, the Allies would soon force him to reconsider his "preconceived ideas" of what was possible in the west.[10]

Hodges's First Army pursued with three corps abreast, with Lightning Joe's VII Corps, now composed of the 3rd AD, 1st ID, 9th ID, and 4th Cavalry Group, on the right, V Corps in the center, and XIX Corps on the left. On VII Corps' right, Patton's Third Army advanced east at a blistering pace. With respect to "the tactical breakthrough by the British and the operational breakthrough by the Americans," Model reported to OKW, "there are no forces left with which to oppose them."[11]

As tough as the exploitation seemed to the young American infantryman Ralph Gordon, it was even tougher for his adversaries. To start with, the German infantry seldom had a ride. A US infantry division and its German counterpart were both authorized more than two thousand vehicles—some 2,100 in a US division and 2,165 in a German one. In German divisions, 1,450 of these vehicles were horse-drawn. German units moved almost exclusively at night to avoid air attacks. American ground troops who cursed the Allied airmen in North Africa had by this time become their most fervent admirers. The Sherman tank had its drawbacks, as did the half-track, but American-built armor and vehicles of all kinds proved far more reliable than their German equivalents. The odds favored the Allies during this interlude of *Bewegungskrieg*, war of movement. The Germans prided themselves on their skill in waging a war of movement, but now the Allies on both fronts were having their own back.[12]

Mêlée at Mons

During the summer of 1944 the 1st ID attacked across battlefields on which it had fought during the Great War. Early in that conflict, Kaiser Wilhelm issued a general order in which he referred to the British Expeditionary Force (BEF) as "a contemptible little army." But it was British Tommies, styling themselves "the old contemptibles," who checked the right wing of the German Army at Mons, just east of the border with France in Belgium, on August 23, 1914. Two memorial plaques can be found along the main street of the city, one commemorating the first contact with the German Army and one showing the line at Armistice: there is no more than one hundred yards between them. *Bewegungskrieg* ended early in the Great War. Not long after the fight at Mons the front stabilized, and trench warfare became the norm. Now, in September 1944, VII Corps pursued the German Army across that very ground.[13]

Generally, both VII Corps and the 1st ID provided their units with detailed estimates of the enemy, but they could not do that during the pursuit. Lieutenant Colonel Robert F. Evans, Huebner's intelligence officer, could only say that "the main enemy objective apparently was to reach the German border before American units." VII Corps reported what the troops could see for themselves: "Well defined lines of resistance are non-existent." That the enemy was fighting "a delaying action" was equally obvious. Their purpose was to reach defensible ground along their frontier, but their situation remained fluid. The VII Corps Enemy Order of Battle estimated that some two hundred tanks assigned to nine different Panzer divisions had crossed the Seine, "and are now probably regrouping in the Rouen area," well west of the corps zone. However, the 11th PZ Division, with some thirty tanks along with roughly twenty-eight thousand infantry drawn from eight understrength infantry divisions, constituted or could "constitute an immediate threat to the Corps." Enemy capabilities were far less clear than their intentions.[14]

On August 31 Hodges telephoned Collins, saying, "Joe you've got to change direction at once toward Mons to help cut off the German Seventh Army." Without an administrative tail, Collins turned the corps through nearly ninety degrees and headed north. The pursuit continued, with the 1st ID following the 3rd AD and protecting the corps' left flank. The 9th ID trailed the 3rd AD on the right, while the 4th Cavalry Group screened the corps' right flank and maintained contact with Third Army's 90th ID. Collins held the 1st ID until nearly noon, waiting for V Corps to come up on VII Corps' left. The division then advanced in jerks and stops, as battalions moved sequentially to occupy roadblocks and positions to protect VII Corps' left flank, advancing against minimal contact. At the end of the day, the 1st ID stretched some thirty miles from Marle, just south of the Belgian border, to Soissons, France.[15]

Arthur G. Heidrick, a radio operator in the 16th Infantry, reported to his diary nearly continuous movement. On September 1 he wrote that the 16th's command post "head[ed] for LAON [emphasis in original] on route N2 then, N 367." Most days his diary merely listed the names of towns through which the 16th drove at a steady pace of twenty miles an hour. The route started out northeast but then turned northwest toward Laon. Jean Peltier and the 33rd FA moved that afternoon. Soon after starting, they drove through the ruins of Tevaux, northeast of Laon, destroyed by the Germans because on the previous day one of the townspeople had shot a Landser. The German unit "lined up thirty of the men [townspeople] against a wall and shot them" in retribution. Liberation came at a cost in Tevaux.[16]

On September 2 the division continued northward, with the 18th Infantry on the left and the 26th on the right. One of the 26th Infantry's battalions raced ahead to join the 3rd AD. The 16th assumed the reserve mission. The 18th moved with its three battalions motorized, traveling in a column of battalions supported by tank destroyers and tanks. The corps advanced against no organized resistance across rolling terrain well suited to mechanized warfare and traveled on good roads, some built upon those laid down by the Roman Empire.[17]

France, Belgium, Luxembourg, and Germany are laced with rivers and streams, so bridging rivers and/or seizing bridges soon became routine. The Big Red One crossed several rivers before crossing the Seine on August 27, the Marne on the following day, the Aisne at Soissons on August 30, and still more streams as pursuit of the retreating enemy continued. Coming upon destroyed bridges and a few fleeing Germans provided more than enough excitement during the first two days of September, as fighting continued to be desultory. In the 18th Infantry, Colonel George A. Smith Jr. assigned Lieutenant Colonel Henry G. Learnard Jr.'s 1st Battalion the mission of regimental advance guard. According to FM 100-5, the advance guard achieved its mission "when after securing possession of the essential terrain features it is disposed to protect the main body."[18]

Learnard, like all of his counterparts in the 1st ID, commanded a task force formed on his infantry battalion supported by tanks, tank destroyers, and other supporting units, such as 4.2-inch mortars and antiaircraft artillery. Learnard operated as FM 100-5 required, with "speed and aggressiveness." That day his troops overran a roadblock, taking eighteen prisoners. Later they overran an antiaircraft artillery unit, taking sixty more prisoners.[19]

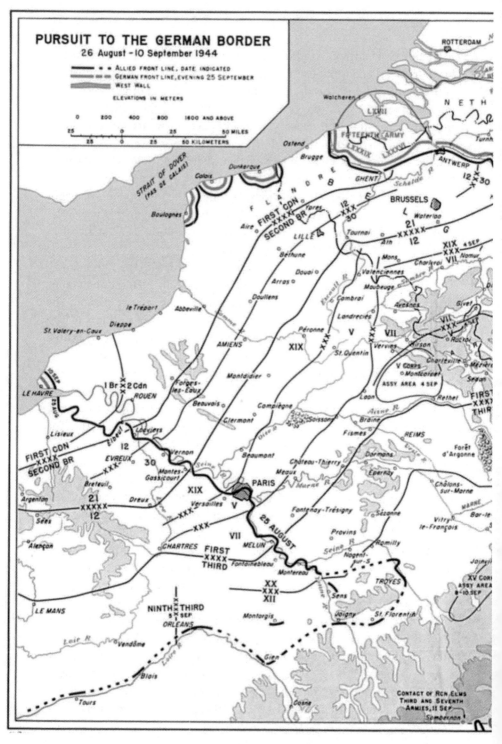

Map 16: Pursuit to the German Border, August 26–September 10, 1944. Reproduced from Blumenson, *Breakout and Pursuit*, Map XV.

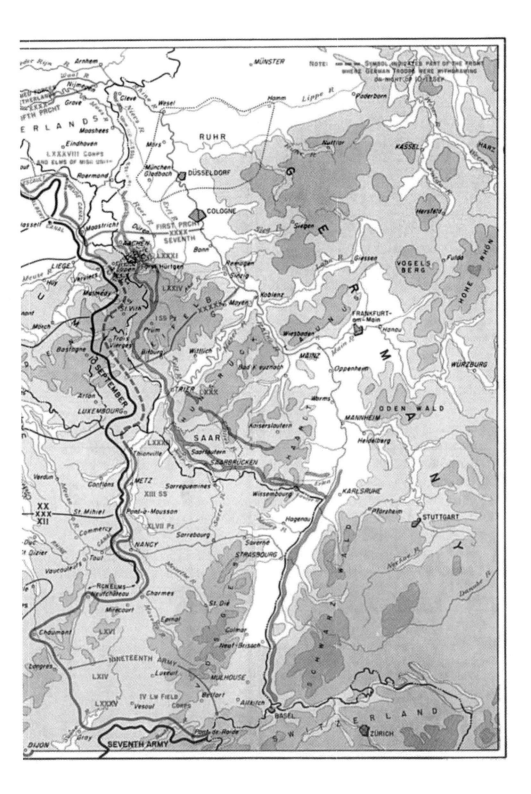

In the first week of September the 1st ID captured small groups of Germans, primarily from Panzer and Panzergrenadier units of the Fifth Panzer Army and the Fifteenth Army. Confusion and even despair among retreating Germans was evident from the intermingling of units and prisoner interrogations. An imprisoned officer spoke for many when he opined that "Germany has lost the war." Confusion manifested itself in surprising ways. A military policeman (MP) manning a nighttime traffic control point directed a Panther tank to turn right. The Panther obeyed the direction and blundered into the division motor park. The chagrined tank commander and his crew surrendered, and the Panther changed ownership. A German major attempted to lead a group of eighty Landsers on foot past Danger Forward, with the result that the major and his men ended up in the prisoner-of-war cage. On the afternoon of September 2, an MP manning the dismount point at Danger Forward accepted the surrender of six Germans who popped "out of the field across the road."[20]

The following day, as VII Corps continued northward, Learnard moved out to relieve 3rd AD units at Bavai, an ancient Roman town located at the intersection of two Roman roads, one heading more or less west to the coast and the other northeast to Mons. Bavai is less than half a mile south of the Belgian border and a dozen miles southwest of Mons. The 3rd AD had passed through both towns but had cleared neither; the armored division established roadblocks rather than defending the towns they seized. Relieving these roadblocks to free the tankers to continue on was 1st ID's mission. Huebner ordered the 16th to take control of Learnard's task force and continue the attack toward Mons. The 26th continued northward through Maubeuge, France.[21]

Learnard described the action that day as a "slam-bam free-for-all that will make it a day forever remembered by the battalion." His task force reached Bavai at 1000. Soon thereafter it encountered an enemy column. Jean Peltier's battery, in support of the task force, immediately "went into position, and with spotting planes and observers with the assaulting infantry directing fire for us, we began to lob shells up ahead about 1500 yards into the enemy columns." The air force joined in the fight as well. When Peltier reached the crossroads in town, "As far as we could see in either direction on the east-west highway were the remains of enemy materiel. . . . The ditches and the roadway were full of enemy dead. It was a burning, scattered, and completely destroyed column."[22]

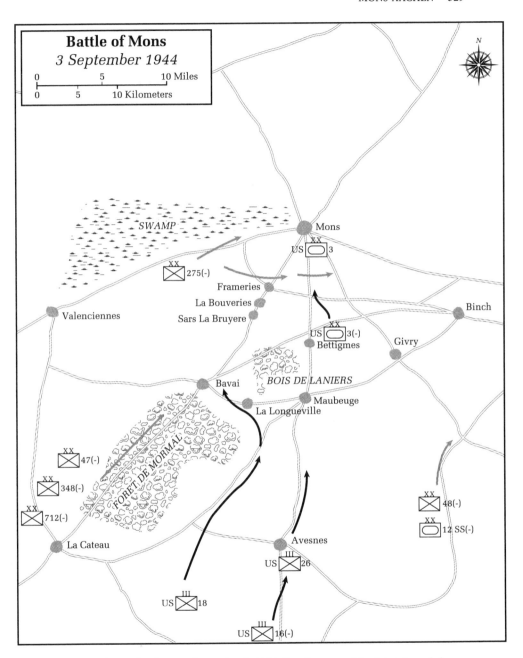

Map 17: The Battle of Mons, September 3, 1944. Based on an original sketch made by Colonel Stanhope B. Mason and used in 1st ID Reports.

Not far behind, Lieutenant Colonel John Williamson's task force consisted of his 2nd Battalion, 18th Infantry, less Company F, supported by a platoon of Sherman tanks from Company B, 745th TB, and other attachments. Williamson's troops "bounded" through Learnard at Bavai en route to secure Sars-la-Bruyère, halfway from Bavai to Mons. Williamson also had a "Ranger platoon," organized with handpicked men in emulation of Darby's Rangers. He had orders to defend the town and thus that part of the VII Corps' left flank. The village mattered, as it lay astride the next major crossroads north of Bavai. Warned of Germans in nearby woods, the battalion advance guard deployed on a broad front, with "flank guards" out three to four hundred yards on each side. The battalion moved slowly, as "the road was almost jammed by dead horses, vehicles and men of a German column caught by our Air Force earlier in the day." After a short skirmish that ended with 160 Germans surrendering, the battalion moved into the village at 2100.[23]

Williamson disposed his task force with the tank platoon in the center of the town. One tank oriented on the road toward Dour, while the remaining two oriented down the road to Bavai from the far side of the intersection, with the secondary road toward Dour. His two rifle companies organized an all-around defense. Company E oriented south and Company G north. Williamson collocated his Ranger platoon with his command post as his reserve. In support he had Captain Carlton Crouthamel's Company H (Heavy Weapons) and the regimental cannon company, with six 105-millimeter howitzers. The Company H commander positioned a section of three 81-millimeter mortars with each of the rifle companies. Williamson emplaced Company H's 30-caliber machine gun platoon to support Company E, oriented southwest along the road to Bavai. Both companies positioned listening posts beyond their positions.[24]

To this point the pursuit produced two clear facts. First, confusion reigned over which side held what town. Second, Big Red One units knew that when they stopped, they had to establish all-around defense. Jean Peltier's unit proved the point. His battery went into position in a village just inside Belgium. A local man asked if the Germans would return when the Americans moved on. Peltier asked why, to which the local "informed us that our tanks rolled through all the previous night and the civilians had put out flags and were singing and shouting. As soon as our column cleared the town, a German column came through." Of course, this caused consternation and a hasty end to the celebration. Williamson's troops completed their

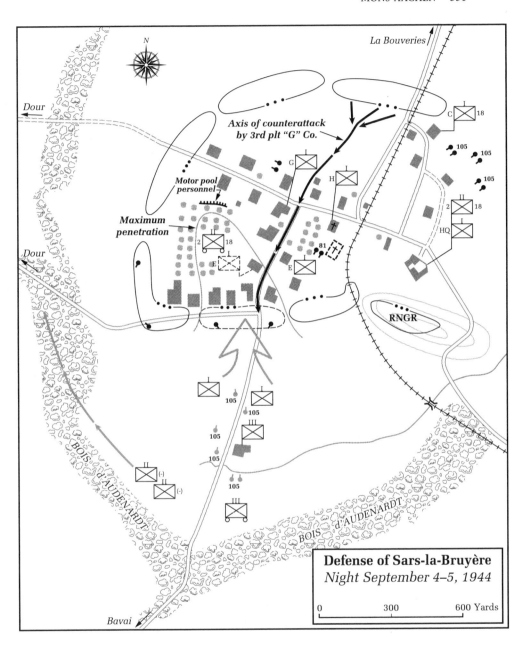

Map 18: Defense of Sars-la-Bruyère, September 4–5, 1944. Based on Major Robert E. Murphy's Personal Experience Monograph Map.

dispositions by 2200 and began digging in. Security during the pursuit could not be guaranteed for villagers or soldiers.[25]

About 2300 a Company E listening post located several hundred yards down the road toward Bavai heard "a horse drawn column in the forest to their front." Williamson believed that Company E was likely overreacting, given that the battalion had cleared the forest on the way in. Moreover, he knew that Lieutenant Colonel Elisha O. Peckham's 3rd Battalion, 18th Infantry, was defending Bavai, less than six miles south down the same road. How could an enemy column be coming from that direction? He sent his operations officer, Robert E. Murphy, to confirm or deny the report. On arrival, Murphy met with Company E's commander, Carmel DeCampo. DeCampo told him that he had withdrawn his listening post when they reported German infantry emerging from the woods along the road, and had ordered his company to "stand to" prepared to fight.[26]

Soon thereafter an intense firefight broke out. Williamson and others at the battalion command post could hear "German machine guns and machine pistols." Murphy alerted Company H and reported the situation to his commander. Williamson ordered him back to the command post. In a postwar paper written at the Infantry School, Murphy recalled that "it suddenly became apparent that this group of Germans were not of the same category" as those they had overrun or captured during the pursuit. These troops fought with purpose and support. Within fifteen minutes, DeCampo's company was in trouble. taking accurate automatic weapons fire on its positions. To compound matters, the cannon company was too close to drop rounds on the attackers. Still unclear on the situation, Williamson ordered his Ranger platoon to send a patrol to determine the size of the attacking force. He also ordered Company H to fire all six 81s in support of Company E.[27]

After the moon came up, it lit "the landscape almost like day." The Ranger platoon patrol returned and reported the enemy "moving south and east," which suggested that Germans were coming in from west of the village as well as up the Bavai road. Williamson ordered his Ranger platoon onto the ridge just south of the Bavai–Mons road. Murphy visited the battalion aid station, where the battalion surgeon reported thirty casualties and "plenty more out there." Soon after, DeCampo reported that the Germans had penetrated his 2nd Platoon, positioned astride the road. He advised that he had to withdraw his command post, as it was located in the path of the penetration. The attackers veered off the road to their left and overran the battalion motor pool, kitchens, and ammunition point. Williamson learned of this from his battalion motor officer, who arrived wounded but upright. The motor officer reported that his motor sergeant and twelve men were holding off about twenty German infantrymen, all of whom were armed with automatic weapons.[28]

Around midnight Williamson sent Murphy to Captain Gordon A. Jeffrey's Company G command post. On arriving, he and Jeffrey organized a platoon-sized counterattack supported by two tanks and supporting fire that Williamson arranged. The mission was straightforward: restore the position. Jeffrey planned to use his 3rd Platoon to attack with one squad on either side of the Bavai road, supported by two tanks moving on the road. The platoon's third squad would follow the tanks. Jeffrey estimated that the counterattack would go in at 0115. This gave the artillery forward observer time to register fires. This he accomplished from a building on the edge of the town, "as much by sound as by sight."[29]

The attack went in as scheduled. The Germans withdrew without putting up much of a fight. DeCampo reorganized his position, incorporating Jeffrey's 3rd Platoon. At 0400 the Germans tried again, this time with a company of infantry supported by artillery. Again, they penetrated along the road but were turned back by "terrific rifle fire" from the American infantry on the shoulders of the penetration. Company H's 81-millimeter mortars provided close fire support. What followed next epitomized actions in the division and corps zone that night. Shortly after 0500, the Germans surrendered. When all was said and done, Williamson's troops had killed, wounded, or captured 845 German troops, with another ninety-two dead found later. The Germans also surrendered six horse-drawn 105-millimeter howitzers, two hundred horses, and one hundred ammunition wagons. The 2nd Battalion suffered eighteen killed in action and fifty-eight wounded.[30]

During the course of 4–5 September, enemy units attempting to escape were eviscerated by fires and/or air attack. Still, some of them managed to cut off US units temporarily. Chaotic actions such as the one Williamson's troops fought at Sars-la-Bruyère occurred throughout the VII Corps zone. Reflecting on the fight, Murphy criticized DeCampo for not having assessed the situation accurately or soon enough. Without accurate reporting, Williamson could not see the battlefield. Yet at 2230, more than a half hour before the infantry attack, DeCampo did report enemy movement. Murphy admitted that the "Battalion CP," a euphemism for himself and the battalion commander, "received the report with great deal of skepticism." First, the battalion had just come through the woods from which the racket of a horse-drawn column could be heard. Second, DeCampo "was new and known to be rather excitable." Williamson sent Murphy down to see for himself, but he might have acted more quickly had he believed his company commander.[31]

Sending the patrol from the Ranger platoon reflected a continued lack of confidence in Company E. Williamson acted on the Ranger platoon's report, but Murphy admitted that "failure to completely analyze the patrol report resulted in prematurely employing the battalion reserve." Not only did Williamson commit his reserve early, he committed it where the enemy was not. That decision necessitated using the 3rd Platoon from Company G to restore the original position. Murphy concluded that he and his commander had made one other mistake: "The tanks were emplaced so deep in the position that they were unable to engage in the defense at all except in the counterattack."[32]

Williamson did not, however, panic that night, and neither did the new company commander. Williamson had made a mistake, but he was no rookie. He had served as regimental executive officer in North Africa and Sicily, taking command of the 2nd Battalion at the end of that campaign. Murphy had commanded Company H in North Africa and fleeted up to become the operations officer. All three officers made mistakes that night but acted intelligently once they understood what they were about. Seeing or sensing the battlefield requires hearing from subordinates, and sometimes requires seeing for oneself.[33]

First Army Turns East

The fighting in the first week of September demonstrated what could be achieved during the pursuit, but there was another missed opportunity to seal off a pocket of Germans and destroy them in what they called a *Kesselschlacht* (literally, "cauldron battle"). Doing so was beyond VII Corps and would have required better coordination between 12th and 21st Army Groups. Nevertheless, VII Corps destroyed a number of German units and took a great many prisoners. Huebner's diary recorded a take of four hundred on September 2. These included sixty taken by the headquarters' defense platoon as Danger Forward was "in the line." These are the same prisoners reported as eighty in the G-2 journal cited above. The next day the division took 4,200 prisoners, and another 4,153 on September 4. On September 5 Huebner visited the division prisoner-of-war cage, where he found 3,200 prisoners. The 16th Infantry took 800 more that evening.[34]

Bradley's characterization of the Mons pocket illustrates that his effort to cut off the Germans had not played out as he had hoped. He described the confusing action at Mons as one in which "neither [adversary] had been forewarned of the other and both stumbled into an unforeseen battle." Still, the 1st ID alone had processed 17,149 prisoners, including the commanding general of the 712th ID. Other VII Corps units captured thousands more. The take for VII Corps from September 3–7 amounted to 32,798. The melee at Mons added another victory to an unbroken string of victories since the breakthrough at Saint-Lô in mid-July.[35]

Optimism, even hubris, tinted many lenses with a rosy hue that September. Even Eisenhower, normally circumspect, succumbed to the idea that the war might end soon. He issued strategic guidance during the fighting in and around Mons that reflected that level of confidence. In it he asserted, "Enemy resistance on the entire front shows signs of collapse." He argued that the only way the greatly weakened enemy might avoid collapse was by pulling units from Germany and other fronts in order to man "important sectors of the Siegfried Line," concluding that "it is doubtful whether he [the Germans] can do this in time." Eisenhower supposed if they did succeed in getting troops to the Siegfried Line, they would concentrate on the sector opposite the Ruhr, north of the Ardennes. Accordingly, he directed the Allied Expeditionary Forces to strike "at the Ruhr and the Saar [south of the Ardennes], confident that he [Hitler] will concentrate the remainder of his available forces in the defense of these essential areas."[36]

Once the Big Red One reached Mons, it served, in Huebner's words, as the "pivot for the Corps." Collins began the pivot when he ordered Rose's 3rd AD to attack east on September 4. Huebner intended to follow the next day. However, First Army intervened, as Hodges felt "the situation was still too risky." He wanted to close up the First Army against the possibility of enemy counteraction. At noon on September 6 the 2nd AD relieved 1st ID so the latter could resume the pursuit. Heading toward Liege, Huebner asked VII Corps if there were "sufficient bridges to move a Division across [the Meuse] in three columns." There were, so the division advanced twenty-five miles, reaching Namur.[37]

It was, however, becoming increasingly clear that too little fuel was reaching the front to sustain the pursuit. On September 6 Huebner had a roadside chat with Collins in which he asserted, "There is a shortage of gas and [we] can barely carry out mission tomorrow." By comparison to Maurice Rose's tanks, the 1st ID used very little of the precious stuff, but still, there was little to be had. Ernie Pyle, reporting on the pursuit, succinctly described the situation in which the gas-deprived army found itself, calling it "a tactician's hell and a quartermaster's purgatory." In order to sustain operations, ADSEC showed a great deal of innovation by laying pipeline, rebuilding and then operating railways, and creating the Red Ball Express—dedicated one-way routes, one jammed with "deuce and a half" trucks heading toward the front and the other with trucks returning to the rear. Despite these herculean efforts, the Allied armies eventually outran their logistics. Through August the logisticians kept things going, even as First Army consumed more than 800,000 gallons per day. By September the rubber band had stretched too far. For the week ending September 9, First Army received 540,000 gallons of gasoline, issued 370,000 gallons, and consumed 530,000 gallons. No matter how the numbers are parsed, viewed in light of earlier receipts, the pursuit was running out of gas.[38]

Turning east had implications for the theater far above the pay grade of Huebner and Collins: they went where they were told to go. Eisenhower and his two army group commanders made decisions that would affect the lives of every soldier in the theater. The Supreme Commander's strategic vision involved a main attack north of the Ardennes Forest, a significant secondary attack oriented on Metz and Frankfurt, and still another into southern Germany All involved a run-up to, and a crossing of, the Rhine. There would be a significant and evolving debate about higher command organization and allocations of resources, which would last to the spring, and ever since in books and staff colleges. At theater level, Bernard Law Montgomery's 21st Army Group would be supported initially by Hodges's US First Army, which would advance east toward the Siegfried Line and the Ardennes. The forest physically divided 12th Army Group's zone and forces, and that would prove to be a significant problem in December. First Army would attack north of the Ardennes and cover the forest, while south of the forest Third Army attacked to the east. Lieutenant General Jacob L. Devers's 6th Army Group, composed of Seventh US Army and French First Army, would come up on the right flank of Third Army and turn east. Eventually Ninth Army, activated in August to complete operations in Brittany, would enter the line north of First Army.[39]

The Miracle in the West

Generalfeldmarschal Rundstedt returned to command OB West on September 5, a day after Eisenhower expressed his view that the Germans were on the verge of collapse. That happy vision did not, however, materialize for a number of reasons, "the psychological effect of Von Rundstedt's return on the troops" being one of them. Of Rundstedt, Oberst Bodo Zimmerman, the operations officer at OB West, said that "his return boosted [the Landsers'] morale because they trusted him and appreciated his distinguished qualities." His return did not, however, alter the unpleasant facts on the ground.[40]

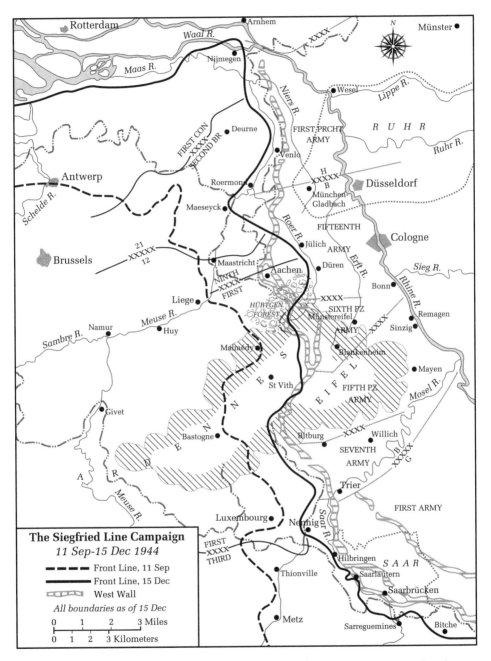

Map 19: The Siegfried Line Campaign, September 11–December 15, 1944. Reproduced
from Charles B. MacDonald, *The Siegfried Line Campaign* (Washington: Center of
Military History, 1963), Map IX.

General der Panzertrüppen Erich Brandenberger's situation as the newly appointed commanding general of Seventh Army is instructive. At the end of the first week of September, Seventh Army had no more than thirty thousand troops, with about sixty tanks under the colors of eight divisions. On September 6 the usually dour Hodges proclaimed that with ten more days of good weather, the war would be over. Yet the collapse Hodges and others anticipated did not, as mentioned, happen. Despite having been badly beaten, the Germans did not roll over.[41]

At the bottom rung the Landsers fought on. Oberst Günther Zeichhelm, Zimmerman's counterpart at Army Group B, believed that "the German Soldier was still fighting well . . . he had nothing more to lose and was searching for a last chance." In the First Army zone of action, Hodges's caution and logistics problems eased the situation of Branderberger's Seventh Army; still, it had to find units to man positions if it hoped to delay the better-equipped and more numerous Americans.[42]

Model's improvisations included manning succeeding reserve lines with rear-area troops as well as some from the Ersatzheer, or Replacement Army. Doing so bought time for reinforcements to arrive from the interior and other fronts. Equally important, German tactical and operational headquarters continued to function. Although Brandenberger was the fourth Seventh Army commander since D-Day, his staff remained stable, the headquarters coordinating reception and integration of arriving units and replacements. Eventually, effective staffs who exercised leadership produced order out of the chaos that had reigned since the fall of Avranches and the desolation at Falaise. Finally, among other reinforcements the Wehrmacht produced almost out of whole cloth, it managed to get sixteen thousand troops organized into thirty-two "Fortress" artillery battalions and to the Siegfried Line before the Allies could interfere. Once again, the Germans demonstrated what Bradley called an "astonishing capacity for recuperation."[43]

The Germans worked a good part of the miracle themselves. They scraped together units to man the Siegfried Line as well as sufficient civilian labor to repair sections of it that had deteriorated. The result was far from perfect; the 116th Panzer Division commander concluded that "we knew very well that the so-called West Wall was not in good shape . . . [but] I'm afraid the Americans were too much afraid of the Western Wall." Perhaps so, but pillboxes and obstacles along the Siegfried proved good enough.[44]

For these reasons the Allies' version of *Bewegungskrieg* wound down in mid-September. General Montgomery's plan to lay an airborne carpet across the Rhine failed, with little to show except the virtual destruction of the British 1st Airborne Division. Of that operation, Prince Bernhard of the Netherlands observed, "My country can never again afford the luxury of another Montgomery success." Benjamin A. "Monk" Dickson, the G-2 at First Army, described the consequence of the miracle in the west. The Germans "manned the Westwall with a determination that forced us to accept a static position warfare in which attrition fell heavily on both sides." In Clausewitz's terms, the pursuit had culminated.[45]

Reconnaissance in Force

Eisenhower's September 4 directive to attack on a broad front required Hodges's First Army to protect the right flank of 21st Army Group. Montgomery's group of armies attacked north of the Ardennes forest complex that stretched across the confluence of Belgium, Luxembourg, and Germany. First Army's sector straddled the great forest. That meant that VII Corps had to deal not only with Aachen but also with the northern edge of the woods. Fast running out of units, First Army assigned VII Corps a thirty-five-mile-wide zone—too wide for three divisions to cover in an attack. Collins therefore intended to drive forward on the Liege–Aachen–Düren axis with the 1st ID on the left, the 3rd AD in the center, and the 9th ID on the right.[46]

The Aachen sector of the Siegfried Line was, as Schwerin noted, rundown but still formidable. In VII Corps' zone of action the fortifications extended from forward of Aachen east to Düren. Two bands of fortifications composed the Siegfried. The first, the Scharnhorst Line, lay west of the city. The second, the Schill Line, ran north to south, just east of the city. The Schlieffen Line included a section extending through Düren along the Roer River. Although the dense woods of the Ardennes and the Schnee Eifel lay south of the corps' right flank, the forest complex included the Hürtgen Forest, just south of Aachen. Here the densely wooded, hilly ground narrowed the avenue of approach toward Düren, known as the Stolberg corridor, to less than five miles. This corridor led northeast, debouching on the Roer river plain near Düren, roughly seventeen miles east of Aachen.[47]

Collins's VII Corps ground to a halt for lack of fuel in the second week of September. That proved fortunate for General der Infanterie Friedrich August Schack and the LXXXI Corps. In command only since September 5, Schack had orders to defend Aachen, where in 800 AD Pope Leo III crowned Charlemagne as Holy Roman Emperor. As of September 9, Schack had command of the 49th, with about fifteen hundred troops; the 275th, with about

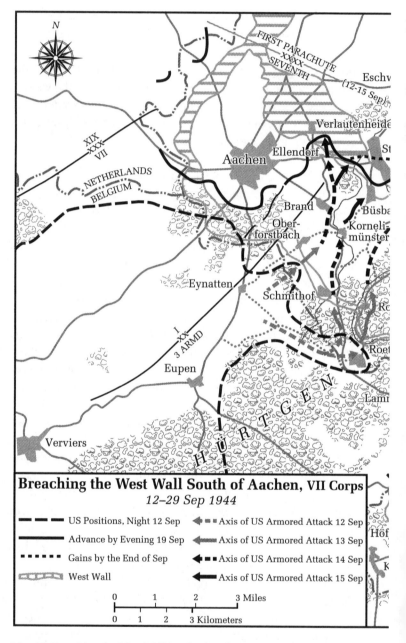

Map 20: Breaching the West Wall South of Aachen, VII Corps, September 12–29, 1944. Based on MacDonald, *The Siegfried Line Campaign*, Map III.

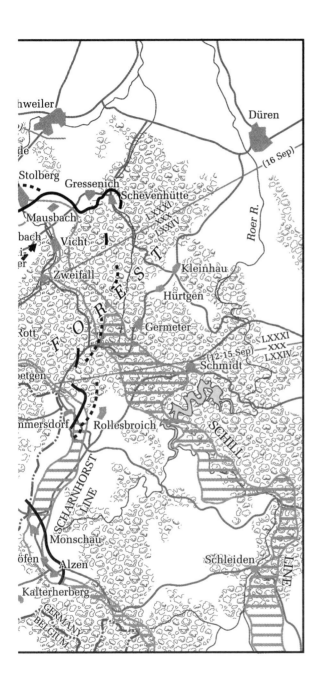

five thousand; and the 353rd ID, with fewer than three thousand. The 353rd's commander described his division as "improvised" from eight disparate units. The three, put together, did not amount to the authorized strength of a single division. Schack also had the 116th PZ, with as many as twenty tanks, and the 105th Panzer Brigade, with ten tanks and twenty half-tracks Other weakened formations, including the 9th PZ, with thirty-five tanks, also joined. Finally, Shack garnered some field and antiaircraft artillery as well, and he "concentrated every reserve available for counterattack." The Allied air forces harassed the LXXXI Corps at every turn. According to Schack, the American air force "attacked even individual motorcycle messengers and light cars." Air attack and constant fighting wore down the corps still more. When 105th PZ Brigade reached the line, it had only two tanks.[48]

Collins's VII Corps sputtered to a halt before reaching the Siegfried Line, but on September 11, with logistics improved, he sought permission to conduct a reconnaissance in force. US doctrine considered reconnaissance in force necessary if "air reconnaissance and advance detachments fail to establish the main hostile positions." Collins's idea was, doctrinally, a stretch. What he really wanted to do was sustain some momentum eastward. Hodges agreed because Monk Dickson's intelligence estimate suggested success. Hodges, too, wanted to keep pressing.[49]

Both Collins and Huebner wanted to bypass Aachen to avoid a bloody street fight. Huebner suggested to Collins that his infantry seize the high ground south of Aachen and, along with the 3rd AD, open the Stolberg corridor. Collins agreed: "If we could break [the line], then we would be just that much to the good; if we didn't, then we would be none the worse." Huebner's concept became the basis of the VII Corps plan to penetrate the Siegfried. Collins duly ordered the 3rd AD to reconnoiter in force along the Stolberg corridor, with 1st ID in echelon left. Collins sent the 9th ID to clear the northern part of the Hürtgen Forest, and ordered the 4th Cavalry Group to reconnoiter on the corps' right flank.[50]

What neither Collins nor Huebner knew is that the officer assigned to defend Aachen had hoped to give up the city in order to save it from destruction. Charged with defending Aachen, Schwerin believed he lacked the means to do so. He left a letter with a civil servant announcing his intention not to fight. When Schwerin's superiors learned of the letter, he managed to survive with his life but not with his command. Hitler wanted the city defended to the last man. Robert M. Citino notes that when the Allies culminated before the Siegfried, the German Army turned to fighting a war of position, or *Stellungskrieg.* The bloody no-holds-barred fighting that ensued in miserable conditions would last five months, until the failure of Hitler's last offensive in the West.[51]

Breaking into the Siegfried Line

Hodges intended a pause to improve his logistics situation. Collins hoped to keep pressing forward, and he convinced Hodges to allow it. Huebner duly issued a division order to conduct "reconnaissance in force to the SIEG-FRIED [emphasis in original] Line, to develop the enemy situation and be prepared to exploit any weak points in the line." The 16th and 18th Infantry led the way, with the 26th in reserve. Supplies were such that the leading regiments committed only a single battalion task force each. Roadblocks, hilly terrain, and the line itself produced slow going. Reducing pillbox-es and obstacles forced the infantry to reprise the techniques learned for Omaha Beach. Huebner was uneasy and revealed it on that first morning, coaching Lieutenant Colonel Frederick W. Gibb at the 16th on techniques he knew well enough. To ease the way forward, the air force used napalm for the first time. Danger Forward announced this by warning that planes with "flame-throwers especially designed for pill-boxes" would support the attack. The division ordered the forward regiments to mark targets for the "flame-throwers" with red smoke. The 18th objected, noting that the Germans were using red smoke, so violet was used instead. The reconnaissance of the Siegfried Line and the German Reich began on September 12, 1944.[52]

Lieutenant Colonel Edmund F. Driscoll's 1st Battalion, 16th Infantry, made the first thrust into the Scharnhorst Line. Driscoll's troops captured a number of pillboxes and were pleased to find some of them unmanned. *Baltimore Sun* correspondent Mark S. Watson, embedded in the Big Red One, believed that "we were luckier than some of the other divisions, partly because VII Corps had moved up so rapidly that the enemy did not have time to man all his West Wall defenses properly." Veterans and replacements who joined during the heady days of the pursuit presumed, for the moment, that they would penetrate the fortified zone easily. By the end of the day, reason for such optimism had waned. Driscoll had lost seven killed and eighty wounded, but he believed that his his battalion was "through most of it." That proved to be mistaken.[53]

The following day 1st Battalion, 26th Infantry, attached to Brigadier General Doyle O. Hickey's CCA 3rd AD, fought its way into the line as well. Major Francis W. Adams's troops employed skills they learned preparing for

Normandy but also did some "on the job training" on how to reduce this complex and still formidable band of fortifications. Captain Armand R. Levasseur, Adams's operations officer, observed, "The men generally realized that the picnic, wine and flowers campaign of France and Belgium was at an end." Still, "Optimism was high, in fact too high." 3rd AD patrols moved into Germany near the town of Walheim, some five miles south of Aachen, on the night of September 12–13. There the tankers prepared to penetrate the dragon's teeth, reinforced concrete pyramids up to four feet high emplaced to impede tanks and motorized infantry, and take the town of Nutheim. Adams and his infantry served as Hickey's reserve. The tankers' and infantrymen's confidence in each other had been forged during the pursuit.[54]

Hickey's tankers owed their initial penetration of the dragon's teeth to local civilians who had filled up the spaces between the obstacles with gravel in order to get their wagons to their fields. The farmers' breach enabled twenty tanks and a battalion of armored infantry to bull their way over. Once on the far side of the obstacles, antitank fire and artillery stopped them cold. Now Hickey called on Adams to assume the mission to seize Nutheim. "Little time was available to the battalion commander for reconnaissance," as the attack had to get underway soonest, Levasseur recalled. Adams looked out on the dragon's teeth from the edge of the wood from which the battalion would attack. He could not see the objective, so he consulted his map. He decided on a frontal attack through the dragon's teeth, and then veering to the southeast in order to approach Nutheim from the rear. He could tell his commanders nothing about the enemy other than that they had stopped the tankers and their supporting infantry. The battalion had artillery support, including harassing fires on Nutheim from the 3rd AD. Adams's company commanders issued their orders from the edge of the woods so that their platoon leaders could see as far forward as possible.[55]

The battalion moved out at dusk, with Captain T. W. Anderson's Company A followed by B and C. Supporting tanks planned to support by "firing into pill box embrasures." The Germans took Adams's infantry under fire as soon as they debouched from the woods, accounting for three of Company A's four platoon leaders. Once across the dragon's teeth, Anderson led the battalion using such cover as he could find. Despite high casualties Company A reduced the pillboxes covering the first barrier. As night fell, the infantry looped around as planned and surprised poorly trained Fortress troops at their supper. Though they could hear the fighting, these worthies had no local security. During the approach to Nutheim, Anderson lost his way. About 2300 serendipity led to the capture of a number of artillery and mortar pieces. Anderson oriented himself and found a way to his intended position, where the company assumed hasty defensive positions. Company A completed clearing the village at sunup and began to pass through those who would continue the reconnaissance.[56]

Major General Charles H. "Pete" Corlett's XIX Corps had not closed up, so for the moment 1st ID had an open flank. The XIX Corps with the 30th ID and 2nd AD began to move toward Aachen from Maastricht, the Netherlands. One of ten national guard divisions mobilized in 1940, the 30th had gone through nearly four years of preparation before coming ashore on D+4. The division's history reported that the crucible of training as well as the turnover of soldiers and officers had fundamentally changed "its pristine sectional and National Guard character," which was "all but buried under the influx of enlistees, Reserve Officers, Regular Army men and Officer Candidate School graduate from all sections of the country." Major General Leland S. Hobbes took command of Old Hickory, as the division styled itself, in September 1942. When it came ashore the 30th ID was a well-trained and well-led unit that fought effectively, immediately, and brilliantly at Mortain. By mid-September 1944 it was a salty, reliable outfit.[57]

In the meantime, Huebner protected his own flank and the corps by "reconnoitering" in a column of regiments, with each successive battalion assuming defensive positions as the lead advanced. Despite having aerial photographs of it, the Americans had much to learn about the composition of the Siegfried Line. Corporal Sam Fuller, who Taylor had shanghaied as his scribe, wrote one of the first reports on the line. In two succinct and chilling double-spaced pages Fuller delineated the construction and plan, including the ditches and mines that comprised the first layer. He observed that antitank ditches twelve feet wide and four feet deep lay some seventy-five yards forward of the dragon's teeth. These obstacles were supported by other devices to make them more difficult to penetrate, and together formed the second layer. Fuller reported that "concrete installations of pillboxes and emplacements" composed the final layer of the line. German pillboxes "averaged 87' in circumference, 6' in depth from top to bottom inside, and are expertly and completely covered, exclusive of turrets, with brush and long grass." Each pillbox provided separate "living and sleeping compartments."[58]

Bunkers supporting the line reached even larger proportions. Some bunkers, used as command or observation posts, extended four stories deep, with only a cupola aboveground. The German engineers who marked out the fortifications planned positions to cover obstacles that formed part of the line, with interlocking fires supported by artillery. Protected by several feet

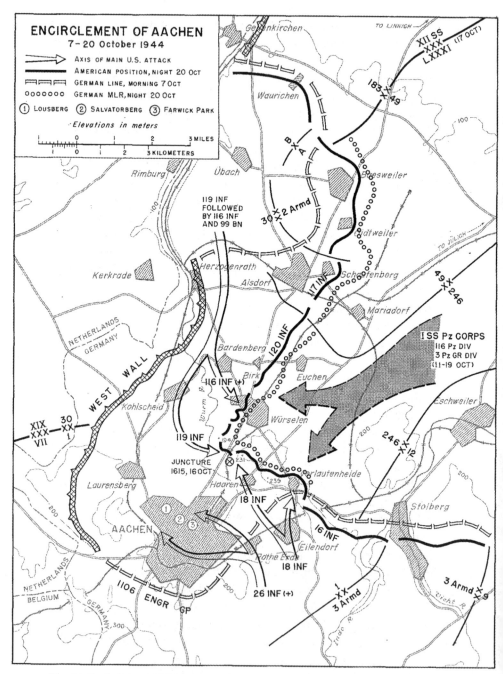

Map 21: Encirclement of Aachen, October 7–20, 1944. Reproduced from MacDonald, *The Siegfried Line Campaign*, Map 4.

of reinforced concrete, the pillboxes and bunkers were hard to crack. In the VII Corps zone, the Scharnhorst Line extended to a depth of three thousand yards. The fortifications and positions, although complex and well protected, had faults. They were blind from the rear and had embrasures that permitted no more than a fifty-degree arc of fire. The Siegfried Line, despite being undermanned and run-down, proved far more difficult to traverse than most had assumed. "The battle for the German homeland had begun for us," Fuller concluded.[59]

Operations to take the heights south, east, and north of Aachen required careful coordination and deliberate execution to cross the Siegfried Line's first and second bands. Doing so was complicated by hilly, wooded terrain broken up by streams and ravines. The warm days of late summer morphed into the cold, fog, and rain that is far more characteristic of the region than the balmy summer days the troops enjoyed during the pursuit. Wyman continued his daily visits with battalion commanders. Some days he played the role of assistant coach, and others he took requests, including the need for warmer clothing. Learnard was specific: "Need wool underwear." Gasoline remained in short supply, troubling Huebner sufficiently to take up the shortages yet again with Collings. He also gave a captain a "lecture on gasoline conservation" for using a tank to provide security for a patrol "300 yards beyond outpost."[60]

First Attempt at Circumvallation

On Wednesday, September 13, Collins issued Field Order 11, expanding the mission beyond reconnaissance. The order specified seizing an elongated oval position stretching from Aachen to Düren, "preparatory" to driving on to the Rhine. Huebner issued an overlay order at 0600 the following morning, requiring the division to attack "with a mission of taking successively the high ground" east and north of Aachen. In addition to the normally attached 103rd AAA, 745th TB, and 634th, TD Corps provided two 4.2-inch mortar companies and the 18th Field Artillery Group, composed of one 155-millimeter gun battalion and two 155-millimeter howitzer battalions. Hobbes's 30th ID, still assigned to the XIX Corps, had the mission to complete the circumvallation of Aachen by effecting a linkup with 1st ID.[61]

Collins's order is not explicit, but it reflected General Hodges's intention to take the city. A remarkable entry in Hodges's diary may explain why. Daniel P. Bolger in *Panzer Killers* asserts with good reason that Hodges took his inspiration from the "blood-begrimed fashion" of operations like that "at the Meuse-Argonne." Bolger bases his argument on a conversation between Hodges and Corlett in which the First Army commander complained that "too many of these battalions and regiments of ours tried to flank and skirt and never meet the enemy straight on." First Army under Courtney H. Hodges tended to bull straight ahead. Bolger blames Hodges for the bloody fighting that ensued, but Bradley called Hodges to order him to seize Aachen, only to learn that the army commander had anticipated him.[62]

At this juncture, Hodges might have redrawn boundaries to assign a single commander to deal with Aachen. Instead, he relied on Collins and Corlett to coordinate encircling the city and then reducing it. It is possible that Hodges did not go with a single commander because, had he assigned the mission to Collins and taken one of Corlett's two divisions, that would have left a corps headquarters unemployed. It is also possible that he did not assign the mission to Corlett because he preferred Collins. In any case, the decision taken worked; the two corps commanders did what they could, and Huebner and Hobbes made it work on the ground.[63]

In the mission to take Aachen, the 1st ID employed all of the tools it had used to penetrate the Atlantic Wall, and then some. A homemade gadget called a pole charge proved very useful. A pole charge consisted of an eight-foot pole with twenty half-pound charges of TNT affixed to one end of it. The TNT was detonated by a fuse running the length of the pole. A pole charge could be placed in the aperture of a pillbox with comparative safety and then blown. Tanks and tank destroyers were used to shoot into embrasures as well. Huebner contributed yet another tool to the fight. While serving on the staff in Washington, he played a role in acquiring three self-propelled 155-millimeter guns. He now assigned one to each of his regiments. According to Stan Mason, these guns "proved their worth through all this Siegfried Line pill box fighting," because they were accurate and could penetrate these "concrete structures with considerable ease."[64]

The 18th Infantry bunker-busting system included "direct fire of tank destroyers, tanks, small arms fire, rifle grenades and demolition charges." Suppressing the occupants by firing steadily on firing apertures enabled infantrymen to approach and kill the occupants or force their surrender using satchel charges, pole charges, or flame throwers. The infantry also used bazookas. The 26th Infantry observed that tank destroyers were a "great help with cement busters." On one occasion, the 18th Infantry reported needing "44 88-mm shells and 50 lbs of TNT" to blow in the door of a bunker. Rundown or not, the Siegfried Line was no pushover.[65]

There was still another problem to resolve in order to penetrate the forti-fied line. The Big Red One knew that when the Germans lost a position, they would counterattack and, if possible, retake it. Therefore, captured pillboxes had to be occupied or destroyed. Destroying structures with three feet or more of reinforced concrete required enormous amounts of explosives, and these, like other ammunition, were in short supply. Lieutenant Colonel Wil-liam B. Gara, who commanded the 1st Engineer Battalion, developed a solu-tion: he "thought that if we stuffed mattresses in the pill box firing ports, the buildup of pressure of even a small charge would shatter the concrete." His theory proved sound, so the 1st ID looted mattresses and blew up captured pillboxes, the remains of which can be seen even now.[66]

Hodges's decision to take Aachen, and Hitler's order to defend it to the last man, drew both sides into the rugged densely forested hills that favored the defender. Staat Forst Aachen formed part of the Hürtgen. Like the forest in the story of Hansel and Gretel, it was gloomy. The 26th found the "woods very thick you have to feel your way with patrols." On the morning of Sep-tember 14, the regiment found they had been "Neck [and] Neck with Jerries last night." The 16th described the forest as "very thick woods." They too had "to go slow."[67]

The division fought through the Siegfried Line and beyond to develop its part of the encirclement of Aachen. The 2nd Battalion, 16th Infantry, at-tacked during the night of September 15–16 to secure the thousand-yard-long ridge, speckled with the pillboxes and obstacles of the Schill Line, which extended southeast from the village of Verlautenheide to Eilendorf. Holding the ridge just about closed off the main road into Aachen. Joe Dawson, who led Company G, 16th Infantry, ashore at Omaha, issued an operations order that illustrates the value of experience.[68]

After dark on September 15, Dawson issued a concise order for his com-pany's role in seizing the ridge when he told his platoon leaders, "The enemy strengths and capabilities are unknown, as we do not know what German units are to our front." They could see the Germans moving around for themselves. Dawson described the friendly situation and identified adjacent units. Then he reviewed the mission. He stipulated what each platoon had to do and how the weapons platoon would support. This was a complex night operation, with each platoon moving on a discrete axis and in sequence. After asking for questions, he ordered his platoon leaders to "go back to your platoons and give them the dope I just gave you." Issuing the order took less than five minutes, but the attack proceeded in stages all throughout the night. By 0700 Company G held a section of the ridge, and shortly after taking it riddled an enemy unit that approached, marching in "a column of twos." As it turned out, the 2nd Battalion would hold the ridge against frequent attacks for a month.[69]

Short of ammunition, fuel, and occasionally food, the troops were tired and literally threadbare. Like the rest of the division, the clothes the Company A, 16th Infantry, troops wore "hung in tatters." Yet the "spirits of the 'doggies' were high" because they "were winning the war." Company A subsisted "mainly on food and other supplies captured from the enemy along the route of advance." Tired or not, Company A led the 1st Battalion, 16th Infantry, into Stolberg over the course of September 16–18. The encirclement of Aachen was in reach.[70]

The German LXXXI Corps fought back resolutely and with increasing effectiveness. Only the 9th and 116th PZ had mobility, and very little of that. Generalmajor Gerhard Mueller assumed command of the 9th PZ on September 8. His division headquarters and staff accounted for a considerable number of troops assigned. He had a few units "thrown together higgelty-piggelty, insufficiently equipped," some of which had no "combat experience." With roughly ten tanks, nineteen Hetzer 76.2-millimeter self-propelled antitank guns, a battalion of artillery, and some infantry and units that accreted to the division, he prepared to defend the Siegfried Line with expectations he assessed as "very modest." On the plus side, his troop commanders had "a fair knowledge of the area."[71]

The 9th PZ and its menagerie of units fought with reasonable effectiveness from pillboxes, supported by a handful of tanks and antitank guns. On September 15 a 9th PZ battle group sprung an ambush on a 3rd AD unit, destroying "seven tanks, a tank destroyer and ambulance." However weak and polyglot, the 9th PZ still had teeth. It did Mueller no good, though. He was relieved on September 16 because he had "not fulfilled expectations to stop the enemy on the West Wall."[72]

Both sides were nearing exhaustion. Haze and foul weather effectively shut down American air support for six days. Since artillery support is essential to reducing fortified positions, shortage of ammunition complicated matters. Division artillery ably supported the break-in by firing very close to the forward line of troops, applying time on target missions and counter battery fire. In doing so it used more than thirty thousand rounds through mid-September.[73]

The 1st ID successfully penetrated the first band of fortifications by September 15, and at Eilendorf had broken into the second band, or the Schill Line. The division had secured the high ground around Aachen from south of the city around to the east and then north. On the division's left flank, the 18th Infantry held the ground south of Aachen, with its right flank across the Scharnhorst Line. Left of them, the 1st Reconnaissance Troop maintained contact across a seven-mile gap between VII Corps and the 30th ID. The 26th, less one battalion attached to the 3rd AD, occupied the high ground southeast of the city, while the 16th extended east to Stolberg. Mason described the result as a "front, which on a map looked somewhat like the shape of a question mark reclining on its back, hook upwards." At roughly eight miles the main line of resistance consumed "every combat soldier in the Division, leaving no infantry reserve." Casualties, particularly in the 16th and 26th Infantry regiments, exacerbated the problem.[74]

In mid-September German reinforcements, replacements, and equipment began arriving, shifting the correlation of forces in favor of the defenders. For example, fifteen replacement tanks plumped up the 9th PZ. The 353rd ID acquired sufficient troops to take over part of the sector, enabling the 9th PZ to shorten its line. The arrival and immediate commitment of the newly reorganized, reequipped, and retrained 12th ID provided LXXXI Corps the means to counterattack. Commanded by Gerhard Engel, onetime adjutant to Hitler, the 12th was organized on the 1944 table of organization. It fielded three infantry regiments of two battalions each and a separate fusilier battalion mounted on bicycles. At 14,800 troops, it exceeded its authorized strength of 12,500. It lacked only its authorized assault guns. Model provided the 102nd Sturmgeschütz Brigade, equipped with seventeen guns, to fill out the division.[75]

On September 16 Engel committed the 27th Grenadier Regiment (GR), his lead regiment, as soon as it arrived. One battalion attacked toward Verlautenheide, a mile east of Aachen. The second came in on the left or eastern flank of the first battalion. Success would widen the passage into Aachen for supplies and reinforcement. The 1st ID shelled the 27th as it moved up. Nevertheless, the Landsers mounted "a charge in well-disciplined waves with fixed bayonets." A bayonet attack across open ground reflected inadequate training as much as it did discipline. The 16th Infantry beat the off this "old school" attack using direct fire and artillery. The 16th decimated a second attack, but at one point reported that the "situation is getting sticky."[76]

The situation had indeed gotten sticky. The 3rd AD lost two tanks to Engel's arriving 48th Grenadier Regiment. The next day Brigadier General Clift
Andrus's division artillery had the "most active day since the start of the
campaign." The artillerymen fired 226 missions, consuming 4,734 rounds
with devastating effect. At day's end, Engel reported that one of his infantry
battalions had only one hundred men remaining, or about one-fifth of their
authorized strength.[77]

Despite this success, Collins concluded that the pursuit/reconnaissance in
force had culminated. In a postwar interview he observed, "A combination
of things stopped us." The exhaustion of his units loomed near the top of
the list, but what finally stopped the corps was that the Germans held "really beautiful" positions. On September 18, Operations Memorandum 94
ordered a halt, and further required Huebner and Rose to "consolidate and
hold present position." The 9th ID was to eliminate pockets of resistance, but
was also told to "hold present positions."[78]

Crucifix Hill

From September 18 until October 8, artillery duels and clashes between
combat patrols characterized the fighting around Aachen. Stan Mason recalled that the fight had become one of "daily hacking away at closing off
[Aachen's] east side while still maintaining [the division's] position against
incessant counterattacks in the captured portion of the main Siegfried Line."
He believed that Hitler's exhortation that the "eyes of Germany are upon
you" had stiffened resolve to defend this cultural icon of the German Reich.
Generalmajor Walter Denkert, who commanded the 3rd PZG, highlighted
just what Hitler wanted: "to show the enemy that every town in Germany
would be defended to the end and not given up unless completely ruined."
Furthermore, Mason thought that the defenders recovered daily from "previous German Army disorganization."[79]

From the German point of view, *Stellungskrieg*, or war of positions, could
not produce victory, although some of the high command apparently continued to believe that firing commanders might work. On September 21,
General der Infanterie Friedrich Köchling assumed command of LXXXI
Corps in lieu of Schack, who was deemed too close to Schwerin. Defending
Aachen by fighting a war of position remained anathema, so the Germans
continued to mount counterattacks as troops became available.[80]

Huebner issued orders on October 2 to complete the 1st ID's part of the
encirclement of Aachen. Specifically, he required George Smith's 18th Infantry "to seize the high ground northeast of AACHEN [emphasis in original]."

The high ground he had in mind included a ridge east of Aachen topped by a conical peak known as Crucifix Hill, and a hill farther north named Ravelsberg. Crucifix Hill was so known for a sixty-foot stone cross erected to commemorate the lives lost in the Thirty Years' War. Both hills lay within the Schill Line and were festooned with pillboxes, including "tank turret" pillboxes, generally with 360-degree fields of fire and well protected with obstacles. The conditions met the doctrinal definition for an "Attack of an Organized Position." Accordingly, Huebner ordered the two battalions of the 1106th Engineer Group to relieve the 18th Infantry so that the troops could rest, train, and, once the plan was in hand, rehearse.[81]

Colonel Smith had only his 1st and 2nd Battalions, the 3rd Battalion being attached, for the time being, to the 26th Infantry. The division attached tanks, tank destroyers, and both 105- and 155-millimeter artillery to support the attack. Smith planned the operation in two phases. First, John Williamson's 2nd Battalion would seize Verlautenheide at the northern end of the ridge, which was already in the hands of the 16th. Then Learnard's 1st Battalion would take Crucifix Hill. Elisha O. Peckham's 3rd Battalion, once released from the 26th, would take Hill 192, northwest of Eilendorf. Huebner assigned no time or date for the attack but rather planned to attack based on the approach of the 30th ID as it attacked down the length of the Schill Line. While the 18th prepared, the air force and the division artillery hammered Aachen and nearby German positions.[82]

Smith's commanders were among what Collins described as "a fabulous group of battalion commanders in the 1st Division." They were talented and experienced. Several of Smith's commanders had served with the division since North Africa or before. Learnard and his 1st Battalion exemplify the maturity and confidence of the 1st ID's battalion-level leadership. Learnard and his staff began with a map analysis and review of Smith's plan. The following day they moved north to see Crucifix Hill for themselves. The trip revealed a daunting task. The division reported these positions defended by a German replacement battalion and the 352nd Infantry of the 246th Volksgrenadier Division (VGD).[83]

Thankfully, the regiment had a few days to rest and to receive and integrate replacements. Replacements made good losses suffered. Learnard, back at full strength, planned a deliberate attack with rifle platoons organized in assault teams, equipped with pole charges, satchel charges, Bangalore torpedoes, and flame throwers. He used his Ranger platoon as instructors. His ammunition and pioneer platoon built replicas of pillboxes against which the infantry could rehearse techniques to reduce obstacles, clear communications trenches, and take pillboxes. Located generally south of Aachen, where they had broken into the Siegfried Line, the 18th did not know the ground over which they would attack. Therefore, all of the company commanders reconnoitered routes and at least the near objective, including Crucifix Hill, on October 4. They could not see Ravelsberg beyond. The following day each repeated the drill, this time with their company's leadership.[84]

On October 7 orders came to attack at 0400 the next morning. Bobbie E. Brown's Company C, reinforced with the Battalion Ranger platoon, made the main effort to seize Crucifix Hill. Bobbie Brown was an unlikely company commander. He had very little formal education and at age forty-one was older than the division's battalion commanders. Born in 1903, he had lied about his age to enlist in the army in 1918. He had served ever since, finally earning a battlefield commission. In the summer of 1944, Lieutenant Colonel Robert H. York chose Brown to command Company C over college graduates, including those of West Point, because "he had an intense desire to kill Germans and was shrewd at finding out ways to do it." York thought Brown a consummate soldier, one who was "absolutely fearless." Brown was ready. He had good maps of pillbox locations and had trained his assault teams so that each "knew what pill box or bunker it was to assault and where they fitted into the company picture."[85]

The operation began the evening of October 7. The regiment moved on trucks and tanks to the rear of the 26th Infantry, which held the ground east of Aachen. During the move, the 26th Infantry ran all of its motors and those of their attached tanks to prevent the Germans from hearing the 18th move. They reached Brand about 2300. Not long after midnight, the 1st Battalion moved out on foot to Eilendorf, where the troops took cover in basements to wait for the 2nd Battalion to seize the line of departure at Verlautenheide.[86]

Artillery preparation fires began at 0300. The 2nd Battalion attacked at 0400, on the heels of the artillery preparation. Despite shooting flares, low-lying fog prevented the defenders from seeing their attackers clearly and inhibited an impressive counterpreparation effort. Nevertheless, the intensity of German artillery fire prompted Sergeant Earl R. Jacobsen, a tank commander, to remark that it was the "worst artillery fire I had ever seen." The tanks could not move and were "scarcely" able to return fire. Williamson's infantry broke into Verlautenheide at 0700, but it took them until noon, supported by artillery and P-47 fighters, to finally clear the village. The supporting tank platoon from Company B, 745th TB, lost three of its four tanks to mines or Panzerfaust rocket launchers. German mines and artillery stymied a second platoon of tanks.[87]

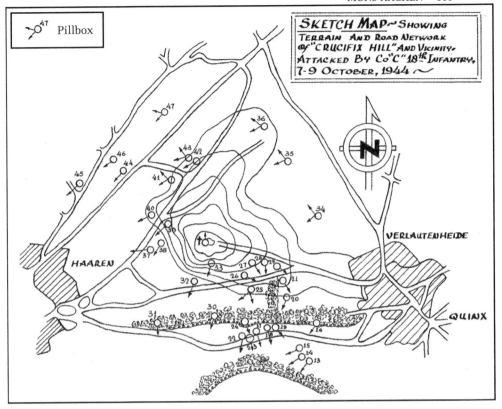

Map 22: Sketch Map Showing the Terrain and Road Network of "Crucifix Hill."
Reproduced from Captain Bobbie E. Brown's Personal Experience Monograph Map.

Field Manual 7-5, *Organization and Tactics of the Infantry Rifle Battalion*, asserts that "the approach march is conducted with a view to bringing Infantry close to the enemy in readiness for action with minimum losses." Colonel Smith ordered Learnard to follow the 2nd Battalion closely. Learnard demurred, asking to delay the approach until Williamson's troops cleared the village. Smith said no, so Learnard moved out at 1000. On reaching the line of departure he had to wait for Brown to reorganize, as Company C had taken casualties. The troops sheltered where they could while Brown positioned his forward observers and his heavy machine guns to support the assault on Crucifix Hill. He then went forward to reconnoiter his objective. He had gotten about four hundred yards forward from Verlautenheide when his adversaries opened up with machine guns and mortars.[88]

In a postwar monograph Brown reported laconically that he withdrew to the edge of Verlautenheide. There he organized for the assault, including taking control of the Battalion's Ranger platoon assigned to support the attack. Brown conferred with Learnard to assure all was ready to meet H-Hour at 1330 as ordered by regiment. At the set time the battalion attacked, heading west with Brown's Company C and the regiment's Ranger platoon on the right and Company A on the left, with Company B moving to attack Ravelsberg farther west.[89]

Wounded at the outset, the Ranger platoon leader, Lieutenant Joseph W. Cambron, remained with his troops, who began reducing their share of pillboxes. Meanwhile Brown, who had not yet committed all of Company C, set about neutralizing pillboxes and breaching obstacles. Within half an hour, Brown and Company C had put five pillboxes out of action, making it possible for him to bring forward his weapons platoon and two of his rifle platoons that had been pinned down. Although wounded three times within half an hour, Brown destroyed one bunker himself and personally led the reduction of four others. Lieutenant Cambron, wounded twice, succumbed to a third hit. Shortly after 1410, Company C reached the peak of Crucifix Hill, by now shorn of its iconic cross by artillery fire.[90]

Brown and Company C transitioned to defend the hill because, as Brown put it, "We expected a counterattack at any time." He defended the hill with his three rifle platoons along with the Ranger platoon, now led by the platoon sergeant. Within an hour the company had evacuated wounded, organized sectors of fire, and positioned heavy and light machine guns, as well as 60-millimeter mortars. At 1530 the Germans began an intense mortar and artillery barrage, supplemented by machine gun and sniper fire. While checking positions, Brown "got shot through the shoulder." Nevertheless, he stayed with his company. While enjoying a cup of hot coffee his first sergeant made on the stove that comprised part of the furnishings of the bunker, Brown sat back and let "the Aid man do some first aid work."[91]

At dusk Brown met with Captain McGregor, the battalion operations officer, who had come up to review the plan for final protective fires; they believed the Germans would try again to retake the hill. At 0400 on October 9, as expected, the Germans "attempted to retake Crucifix Hill by storm." They came in waves, "silhouetted by our artillery flares and W. P. [White Phosphorus] shells." According to Captain Brown, the men of his company "opened up with a murderous grazing fire that piled the onrushing Germans in front of their foxholes." At daylight, "more than one hundred dead [Germans] could be seen forward of the company's defensive positions." Within the position, Company C found "forty-odd dead within our 'blood rock' throwing distance." Brown's troops also took thirty-five prisoners.[92]

Success had not come cheaply. Company C lost thirty-six dead or wounded. The battalion suffered sixty dead but remained fit to fight—and fight they did. During the night of October 9–10, moving in a column with Company B in the lead and Company A trailing, 1st Battalion passed in the lee of Crucifix Hill, then turned north. Captain Jessie R. Miller led the way, with the battalion following in single file. Miller relied on his compass to maintain direction in a night so dark the battalion operations officer said that "each man could reach out and touch the back of the man in front of him without seeing him." The Americans let one German column pass on its way into Aachen and bypassed several occupied bunkers. Along the way they saw and heard Germans in or near bunkers en route to Ravelsberg. Yet when the column reached the densely wooded and heavily fortified hill, it seemed to be unoccupied. Searching the bunkers led to awakening a German officer and his troops in order to take them prisoner.[93]

Closing the Circle

Later that morning a German mess team arrived, whereupon the Americans helped themselves to hot food. Learnard's troops seized the last piece of ground needed to effect the division's part of isolating Aachen. Although the last route into Aachen had not been closed off, Huebner put the 26th to work to reduce the city. Brigadier General Wyman, who joined the division with Huebner, departed for the United States in order to take command of the 71st Infantry Division. In his stead George A. Taylor, who had followed Teddy Roosevelt in the 4th ID, returned to the Big Red One. Wyman went to a well-earned reward while Taylor stepped in without missing a beat.[94]

Huebner assigned Colonel J. F. R. Seitz the mission to take Aachen, well supported by tanks, tank destroyers, and both division and corps artillery. Each of the regiment's two assault battalions would have a self-propelled 155-millimeter gun. The IX Tactical Air Command would provide air support. Francis W. Adams, Derrill M. Daniel, and John T. Corley commanded Seitz's three battalions. Collins rated Corley as the best of what he called "fabulous battalion commanders." Seitz and his team had a good idea what they faced, as they had overlooked Aachen from the east for the better part of a month.[95]

The vista they "enjoyed enabled constant surveillance of a large portion of the city." To a lesser extent their counterparts in Aachen enjoyed the same advantage in surveilling the 26th. Because they were cheek by jowl with the Germans, "daytime patrols could not progress very far beyond our lines." The regiment began "preliminary study plans" on October 2, this after it had seized the high ground east of the city. The battalions ran daily patrols aimed at reconnoitering or taking prisoners. When the 26th wanted prisoners, they went in with robust patrols supported by armor.[96]

The German fought back with artillery, direct fire, and loudspeakers. On the latter, they blared popular American music, making "every effort to induce homesickness." They also made ludicrous claims about the damage the Luftwaffe was doing to American cities. Despite German efforts to worry them, most of the troops restored their strength at a "recreation area" where they could take a shower and sleep with both eyes closed. Getting to know the ground also proved important. In the meantime, Aachen attracted German units like a magnet does iron filings.[97]

The view enjoyed from the high ground from which they would attack allowed Corley to see into the city and as far as his ultimate terrain objective: a hill called Lousberg that loomed above Aachen on its northern edge. Daniel could see past Rothe Erde, his initial objective, and well into the city. Both men could see the railyards at the southern end of town and factories east of the city. Aachen, in fact, boasted an even larger railyard to the northwest, with a trunk line coming in from the north that looped around the southern end of town and trailed off to the northeast and the interior of the Reich. Seitz planned to attack from the east, with Daniel's 2nd Battalion leading.[98]

Derrill M. Daniel described the operational concept in a postwar paper written during his study at the Staff College course that began in the summer of 1946. He recalled that the scheme required maintaining the isolation of the defenders by mortar and artillery fire, supplemented by direct fire from tanks and tank destroyers. Huebner's self-propelled guns, or rifles, as the reports called them, helped the infantry to enter buildings via "mouse holes" blown through exterior walls that passed through interior walls and into the next building. Finally, the infantry assaulted each house, driving the enemy into the cellars, where they used "bayonets and hand grenades to destroy or capture the defenders." Inelegant but effective.[99]

On October 10, still hoping to avoid a street fight, Huebner ordered the 26th Infantry to send a party into Aachen to present the *Kampfkommandant* [battle commander], Oberstleutnant Maximilian Leyherr, with an ultimatum. That document informed Leyherr that if he did not surrender within twenty-four hours, US forces would bombard the city "ruthlessly." Lieutenant William Boehme, who spoke German fluently, Lieutenant Cedric A. Lafley, the regimental intelligence officer, and Private First Class Kenneth Kading, who carried a white flag made from a bedsheet, went into Aachen.

There they handed off the ultimatum, which was politely but firmly rebuffed. The division artillery also fired leaflet shells into Aachen, which did produce some effort by civilians to surrender, but the German Army put a stop to that. Twenty-four hours after the delivery of the ultimatum, the air force dumped sixty-two tons of bombs on Aachen. Not to be outdone, VII Corps and 1st ID Division Artillery fired more than five thousand rounds, delivering another 169 tons of explosives. On October 12 Brandenberger relieved Leyherr, and Oberst Gerhard Wilck, the unfortunate Leyherr's division commander, assumed command of the Aachen *Kampfraum*, or battle area. The fighting Mason described as "hacking away" continued unabated until October 15, when Seventh Army launched a counterattack to "prevent the junction between the American Forces."[100]

In his counterattack plan for Aachen, Brandenberger made an odd decision—odd, in that he pulled Gerhard Engel's 3rd PZG from LXXXI Corps and had Engel report to him directly. He required 3rd PZG to seize the ridge that extended from Verlautenheide to Eilendorf, and ordered I SS PZ Corps to form the right wing of the attack. At this point, I SS PZ Corps had the remnants of three divisions: the 49th ID, the 183rd VGD, and the 116th PZ. The I SS Panzer Corps sent the 116th Panzer to attack toward Würselen against the 119th Infantry of the 30th ID. Lieutenant Colonel Herbert C. Hicks's 2nd Battalion, 16th Infantry, defended the bulk of the ridge that the 3rd PZG attacked.[101]

Joe Dawson's Company G bore the brunt of the attack on what became known as Dawson's Ridge. Engel's grenadiers, supported by tracked Sturmgeschütze (literally, "assault guns," but in fact armed vehicles similar to tank destroyers), began moving into their assault positions during the night of October 14. Some of the grenadiers attacked down the boundary with Company G, 18th Infantry, on Dawson's left. The 16th Infantry reported seeing the Germans off. At 1000 hours on October 15 the 8th Panzergrenadier Regiment attacked, following an artillery preparation, with the support of three Sturmgeschütze. Prompt defensive artillery fire from the 7th FA, reinforced by two corps 155-millimeter battalions, turned back the Germans. A second German assault supported by tanks and assault guns went in at 1300, but artillery and direct fire stopped them again. But at 2300 that evening the 29th Panzergrenadier Regiment, supported by four Sturmgeschütze, overran one of Dawson's squads and got into Verlautenheide. Dawson reported his position critical at 2350. The regiment and the division both sent reinforcements. The division also alerted 3rd AD of the developing danger on their left flank.[102]

Although Dawson did not realize it, his tank destroyers had driven off the German assault guns. During the night German armor, including three captured Sherman tanks, harassed the 18th Infantry while other Panzers moved up toward Dawson and Captain Kimball R. Richmond's Company I on Dawson's right. The grenadiers, supported by about ten Panzers, renewed the assault at roughly 0630. The doughboys drove the grenadiers off, but the tanks penetrated. Just who did what to whom is uncertain, but tanks and tank destroyers moved in to support the infantry and, along with the artillery, "neutralized" two Panzers. By midmorning the German attack had petered out. Confusion reigned throughout October 15 and the early-morning hours of the next day, but artillery and determined American soldiers drove off the Germans.[103]

The next day Dawson and Kimball restored their positions. Late in the afternoon Private Frank A. Karwell led a patrol of two other privates from Company K, 119th Infantry, to make contact with 1st ID troops they could see about a thousand yards away. Karwell was wounded en route, so Privates Edward Krauss and Evan Whitis went on alone, where they climbed a hill in order to make contact with Company F, 18th Infantry. At 1815 the two privates achieved their goal. The 30th ID and 1st ID together had closed the circle. Southwest of Dawson's Ridge, the 26th Infantry could be heard fighting its way into Aachen.[104]

Taking Aachen

While the 16th and 18th Infantry regiments fought to maintain the isolation of Aachen, the 26th "hammered away, by day and night at the perimeter of Aachen." The 26th edged in to Aachen from the east because they lacked the resources to do anything else. Seitz had fewer troops to take the city than the Germans had to defend it. Oberst Wilck commanded the 246th VGD, which comprised the bulk of the troops defending Aachen. The 246th had reorganized in Prague in September with men originally classed as unfit for service, as well as wounded men returned to duty, sailors, and deferred defense workers. Wounded men returning to duty comprised the whole of Wilck's 689th Grenadier Regiment.[105]

When the 246th arrived in Aachen, it had 8,000 troops. Of these, the 1st ID estimated 3,500 were physically in the city, although the actual number may have been as high as 5,000. The 34th Machine Gun Battalion, XIX Luftwaffe Battalion, and 453rd Ersatz (replacement) Battalion already occupied positions in the city when Wilck's troops arrived. In addition to artillery support from outside the city, the 246th had eight 75-millimeter antitank guns, nineteen 105-millimeter howitzers, and six 150-millimeter howitzers. As late as October 17, LXXXI Corps reported fourteen operational Hetzer antitank guns and fourteen assault guns. Wilck may also have had five Mark IV Panzers. He disposed his three regiments with the 404th in the north, the 352nd in the east, and the 689th in the south. The remnants of Kampfgruppe Rink from the 1st SS PZ joined the defenses as well.[106]

Wilck's adjutant knew the Big Red One from the fighting in North Africa and considered it "probably the best [division] in the American Army." He argued that the 1st ID would undoubtedly attempt to seize Lousberg and Observatory Hill, which lay at the southeastern end of Lousberg. Accordingly, the defenders of Aachen made certain that these two places were "strongly held and well defended."[107]

Against the disparate defenders, Daniel's battalion, bolstered with tanks and tank destroyers, moved into "jump off" positions along the railway south of Rothe Erde. Corley's battalion, also with ample tank and tank destroyer support, came up on Daniel's right in Eilendorf. Daniel aimed to head straight west through the city, while Corley drove through the factory district. Corley's objectives included taking Observatory Hill and Lousberg, which lay nearly three miles of street fighting away. Seitz's operations officer reckoned the two battalions would have to fight "with one eye cocked over their right shoulder," sound thinking given the continuous German thrusts aiming to break through the thin lines encircling Aachen. On October 12 Corley's battalion entered the city proper. Daniel followed a day later.[108]

Regarding buildings, Daniel wanted to "KNOCK 'EM ALL DOWN [emphasis in original]." The Germans, he reasoned, could not "deliver accurate fire with buildings falling down around their ears." Both Daniel and Corley fought with combined arms teams formed at company level. Both attacked meticulously, combining the effects of all the weapons at their disposal. And both appreciated the self-propelled 155-millimeter guns, which they called "rifles." Beginning that first day, Corley's troops combined direct fire and indirect fire as well as dive bombers on single targets. Gains were measured in "rooms and houses taken," the regiment reported. Neither battalion gained more than three hundred yards a day.[109]

Ted Dobol, recently returned to duty after having recovered from wounds, learned a hard lesson in Aachen. He recalled "fighting from one house to another." As he led his platoon, supported by two tanks, his "radio man was hit in the head" by a sniper shooting from behind the advance. Dobol was in the process of deploying his infantry to deal with the sniper when he took a bullet in the shoulder. After an adjacent unit discovered the sniper and killed him, Dobol decided to go see for himself who had shot him. The sniper turned out to be "a 'punk' kid not 15 years old, with a hunting rifle with a two foot long scope." Dobol learned that day, as did the rest of 1st ID, that when fighting in a city, the experience of the soldier who kills or wounds you is irrelevant. The urban environment enables even the least capable of soldiers to fight effectively at times. Wounded for the fifth time, Dobol returned in early December.[110]

As the 26th ground its way forward, Huebner sought troops to occupy ground that the regiment had cleared. Collins solved the problem by providing 3rd AD's Task Force Hogan, composed of a tank battalion, an armored infantry battalion, and an infantry battalion from the 28th ID. The fighting rose to a crescendo from October 16 to 19, during which the 16th and 18th fought off German counterattacks in the north and northeast of Aachen, while Daniel and Corley drew near their final objectives. Still, the Germans "fought efficiently and had to be driven out of each position."[111]

On October 19 German airdrops of supplies and a rare appearance by Luftwaffe bombers demonstrated declining defensive capability and the lack of success in breaking the encirclement. That day the division advised the 30th ID, "We have the eastern part of AACHEN [all caps in original] cleaned out and the progress in town itself looks pretty good. With good luck we should clean [out] AACHEN in a day or two." The next day, with the end in sight, VII Corps sent the 1st ID a teletype message that read, "Request written report on defenses of the Siegfried line and assault methods used by your troops including infantry, artillery, engineers and tank units." Learning what worked, and passing that on, continued in the US Army.[112]

Although Corley did not know it, thanks to their use of their 155-millimeter rifle, his troops had driven Oberst Wilck from his command post in the spa Hotel Quellenhof. On October 21, continuing to operate on the principle of "sending a projo so Joe don't go," that same rifle hammered the bunker that had become Oberst Wilck's last command post. At 1205 he surrendered the city to Brigadier General Taylor. "When Americans start using 155s as snipers weapons," Wilck observed, "it is time to give up." The German colonel despaired, telling his captors, "I wish I had been killed."[113]

Then Corley's 3rd Battalion and Task Force Hogan "made a sweep of the remaining area." Since Wilck could not communicate effectively with his remaining units, a US armored car carried a German officer around to get the word out to Wilck's troops. Meanwhile the 26th Infantry gingerly continued clearing buildings. At 1656 the division reported Aachen cleared. Later in the evening, in accordance with Collins's instruction, Huebner issued Field Order 52. The mission read, "The 1st US Infantry Division holds and reorganizes on present positions, prepared for further advance to the east on Corps order."[114]

Assessing Aachen

The 1st ID learned many a lesson during the fight to reduce Aachen, including some that might seem mundane. For example, learning to protect the radiators of M10 tank destroyers with "reflectors made of armor plate" may sound trivial, but the tank destroyer proved vital in close combat in a city and as a supplement to artillery. Another lesson was that, in consolidating gains in the defense, "the infantry must 'tie in' with artillery and other supporting weapons for the defense." Though this may appear obvious, it is nevertheless an example of the reinforcement of lessons learned over time—and sometimes the hard way. The utility of combined arms led to the conclusion that "junior infantry officers must be taught the proper use of tank destroyers." They did not arrive to the front with that knowledge. Tanks supported operations against unobserved pillboxes firing on the infantry by spraying the "suspected area with machine gun fire. When a ricochet was observed, a round of 75-mm HE [75-millimeter-high explosive] on that spot would usually blow off the camouflage and expose the concrete structure."[115]

The matter of tank-infantry cooperation in woods and in the city took up several paragraphs. Chiefly the division concluded that fires supported maneuver. Bullets, main gun rounds, and artillery preceded the infantry almost always. The division artillery opined that effective use of concentrated artillery fires proved "instrumental in breaking up not less than 16 enemy attacks." The artillery fired 4,670 discrete missions during October, consuming 94,842 rounds. This round count included 3,408 rounds fired by the 634th Tank Destroyer Battalion.[116]

So just what did the fight for Aachen mean? Colonel Evans, the 1st ID G-2, sent Lieutenant Robert G. Botsford, a onetime writer for the *New Yorker*, to survey the city. Botsford spent four hours exploring and concluded that "the city is as dead as a Roman ruin, but unlike a ruin it has none of the grace of gradual decay. The end of Aachen came so suddenly and so completely that it is now of no historic interest except as an object lesson in the power and application of modern warfare." Botsford reported also on the desperate condition of the few civilians who remained in the ruined city. He ended by saying, "There is no question that AACHEN [caps in original], after the tottering buildings have been demolished by the engineers and after the rubble has been bulldozed off the main thorough fairs, will equal any of the destroyed towns and villages of Normandy." What happened at Aachen boded ill for both sides.[117]

Notes

1. Bradley, *Soldier's Story*, 407; HQ, First US Army, "Combat Operations Data First Army," September 18, 1946, N15264-2, CARL, 55; War Department, FM 100-5, *Field Service Regulations: Operations* (Washington, DC: Government Printing Office, 1941), 131–32. See also Sylvan and Smith, *Normandy to Victory*, 103; Blumenson, *Breakout*, 679.

2. Gordon, *Infantrymen*, 52–53. This quotation comes from the last days of August but applied to the ride across Belgium as well.

3. Clarence R. Huebner, diary, March 3, 1944–September 26, 1944, April 2, 1945–September 6, 1945, Stanhope B. Mason Collection, MRC 1994.26. Re tank battalion organization, see also Forty, *US Army Handbook*, fig. 11, 80. Each battalion also had six howitzers on Sherman chassis. Mygatt, *Return to La Roche-en-Ardenne*, 474; HQ, 1st ID, G-3 after-action report, August 1944, 43, in RG 301-3: G-3 Operations Reports, Jun 44–Dec 44, MRC Digital Archives. See also HQ, 745th Tank Battalion, after-action report, September 9, 1944, in "After Action Reports, June 1944–May 1945," doc. 8745, TB 101-A, DRL, 39–54. The daily report for 240001 Aug 44–250001 Aug 44 shows no tanks dead-lined. The battalion rested and did maintenance from August 18 to August 24, so began the pursuit in good shape.

4. Wilmot, *Struggle for Europe*, 463–64. The Eisenhower quotation appeared originally in Eisenhower, *Crusade in Europe*, 126.

5. War Department, FM 100-5, 3–4.

6. 1st ID, after-action reports, June, 47–48, July, 32–34, and August, 61–66, all in G-3 Operations Reports, Jun 44–Dec 44.

7. Ruppenthal, *Logistical Support*, is the compendious source on theater logistics in Europe. See also War Department, *Field Service Regulations: Larger Units* (Washington, DC: Government Printing Office, 1942), 49–57. Army Group, like the corps, had virtually no administrative responsibility. See also Bellanger, *Army Infantry Divisions*, 1:1. Chart at p.e 1 shows the basic units and gives citations for their tables of organization.

8. Ruppenthal, *Logistical Support*, 1:84–87, 213–30. See chart 6 re organization and transition ashore. The description of the Communications Zone and its foibles in Ingersoll, *Top Secret*, 204–8, is succinct and accurate. A combative left-of-center journalist, Ingersoll enlisted as a private in 1941 and ended the war as a lieutenant colonel. There are several obituaries on line.

9. Speidel, *We Defended Normandy*, 146–47; Ludewig, *Rückzug*, 124.

10. Blumenson, *Breakout*, 678; Citino, *Wehrmacht's Last Stand*, 352; Ludewig, *Rückzug*, 171.

11. Model's quotation is from Ludewig, *Rückzug*, 171.

12. Ludewig, 18.

13. The author discovered this plaque while working at NATO military headquarters during the Kosovo air war.

14. 1st ID, Selected Intelligence Reports, vol. 1, June–November 1944, 46, in RG 301-2.0: G-2 Selected Intelligence Reports during the First Six Months of the European Campaign, vol. 2, June 1944–May 1945, MRC Digital Archives; HQ, VII Corps, FO 9, August 26, 1944, annex 2, 1, and Office of the Assistant Chief of Staff, G-2 report, August 26, 1944, 3, both R13343, CARL, 9.

15. HQ, VII Corps, "History of VII Corps for the Period of 1–30 September 1944," R1179.2, CARL 9–11. The corps report mistakenly places 1st ID on the right and 9th ID on the left, but corrects that error in unit subparagraphs. 1st ID, after-action report, September 1944, 2, in G-3 Operations Reports, Jun 44–Dec 44.

16. Arthur G. Heidrick, diary, June 13, 1942–February 1, 1945, Fort Riley Museum Complex, Fort Riley, KS, entry for September 1, 1944; "World War II Diary of Jean Gordon Peltier," August 2, 1942–July 5, 1945, MRC 1998.79, 181.

17. Re Bavai, or Bagicum as it once was, see https://www.livius.org/articles/place/bagacum-bavay/, downloaded on September 13, 2021. For other map data, see GS sheet 11, Valenciennes, 1:100,000.

18. HQ, 18th Infantry, "Unit History, 1–30 September 1944," n.d., 1, in RG 301-Inf(18)-0.3: Reports of Operations, 1 Jun 44–31 Mar 45, MRC Digital Archives; War Department, FM 100-5, 114; 1st ID, after-action reports, August 1944, 45–50, 53, and 57, in G-3 Operations Reports, Jun 44–Dec 44. See also VII Corps, "History of VII Corps," 74, 77, 78.

19. Baumer and Reardon, *American Iliad*, 260–61.

20. HQ, 1st ID, G-2 periodic report, September 3, 1944, 2, in RG 301-2.0, G-2 Periodic Reports, Nov 42, 10 Jul–14 Aug 43, Sep 44; 1st ID, "The Belgian Border," 46. The incident with the Panther appears in several reports, but just what happened to the tank and its crew is unclear.

21. 1st ID, after-action report, September 1944, 4–6, in G-3 Operations Reports, Jun 44–Dec 44. I have used the spelling used in the after-action report. The town is now called Bavay. See also Bavai from https://en.wikisource.org/wiki/1911_Encyclopædia_Britannica/Bavai, accessed September 20, 2021. The author also read a French source, but *Britannica* has a shorter explanation.

22. Baumer and Reardon, *American Iliad*, 261; Peltier, diary, 184.

23. Robert E. Murphy, "The Operations of the 2nd Battalion, 18th Infantry (1st Infantry Division) at Sars le Bruyere, Belgium, West of Mons, 4–5 September, 1944," n.d., WWII Student Papers, DRL, 11–12.

24. Murphy, 11–12, map D. The howitzer battery was almost certainly from the 32nd FA, but none of the after-action reports are clear about which battery was in Sars-la-Bruyère. Baumer, map 263, 264.

25. Peltier, diary, 185.

26. Murphy, "Operations of the 2nd Battalion," 12–14; HQ, 32nd FA, "Special Report of Action," September 23, 1944, 3, in RG 301-FA(32)-03: Reports of Operations, 1 Jun 44–31 May 45, MRC Digital Archives. B Battery, 32nd FA, is likely the battery that provided support to the 18th Infantry that night.

27. Murphy, "Operations of the 2nd Battalion," 14; Baumer and Reardon, *American Iliad*, 265.

28. Murphy, "Operations of the 2nd Battalion," 14–15; Baumer and Reardon, 262–66. Baumer and Reardon's account is in greater detail than Murphy's and names commanders.

29. Murphy, "Operations of the 2nd Battalion," 16.

30. Murphy, 16–19.

31. Murphy, 12–13.

32. Murphy, 32.

33. On Williamson taking command, see Baumer and Reardon, *American Iliad*, 180. Re Murphy, see Baumer and Reardon, 23; Murphy, "Operations of the 2nd Battalion."

34. Huebner diary, entry for September 2–6.

35. Bradley, *Soldier's Story*, 408; 1st ID, Selected Intelligence Reports, 1:47; VII Corps, "History of VII Corps," 98–99. Both of these pages are numbered 3, but in sequence they are as cited.

36. Cable FWD 13765, in Eisenhower, *Papers*, no. 1933, 4:2115–16. There are a number of good sources on the debate over broad versus narrow front. In the author's opinion, both Montgomery and Bradley favored a narrow front attack as long as it was their front. Ambrose, *Supreme Commander*, is well documented and critical of Eisenhower; see book 2, chapters 12 and 13. Chester Wilmot's analysis in *The Struggle for Europe* remains a well-reasoned assessment; see chapter 24, "The Great Argument." Bradley, *A Soldier's Story*, and Montgomery, *Memoirs*, offer their respective views.

37. Huebner diary, entries for September 2 and 6; 1st ID, after-action report, September 1944, 10–13, in G-3 Operations Reports, Jun 44–Dec 44.

38. 1st ID, after-action report, 13; Ruppenthal, *Logistical Support of the Armies*, 1:489, 505, table 10, 503. Re efforts to build logistics infrastructure, see Ruppenthal, chapters 12 and 13, "Breakout and Pursuit" and "Frantic Supply." Re gasoline shortages, see also Sylvan and Smith, *Normandy to Victory*, 123.

39. See Eisenhower to Montgomery, December 1, 1944, in Eisenhower, *Papers*, no. 2145, 4:2323–25. Eisenhower rebuked Montgomery politely but firmly regarding his continued carping.

40. Bodo Zimmerman, "OB West, Atlantic Wall to Siegfried Line: A Study in Command," ms. B-672, n.d., Department of the Army, Historical Division, part 2, 176. This study was done in the immediate postwar era as an amalgamation of senior German officer monographs with commentary and criticism by other Wehrmacht officers.

41. Ludewig, *Rückzug*, 220; Hogan, *Command Post at War*, 143.

42. Oberst Günther Reichhelm, "Summary of A Gp B Engagements from the Middle of October 44 until the Middle of Apr 45," November 29, 1947, ms. B-701, N-16603, CARL, 2. Reichhelm based this assessment on touring the units in the line.

43. Ludewig, *Rückzug*, 227, 234, 253, 255, 285; Bradley, *Soldier's Story*, 343.

44. Art Chaitt, "View from the Other Side," *Bridgehead Sentinel*, June 1965, Bridgehead Sentinel Collection, MRC, 5.

45. Ryan, *A Bridge Too Far*, end matter.

46. Cable FWD 13765; Collins, *Lightning Joe*, 267–68. See also Ambrose, *Supreme Commander*, 529, referencing a SHAEF memorandum that articulates the importance of the lines of communication afforded by the broad front approach. Although critical, Ambrose concludes that Eisenhower's choice made sense.

47. Lucian Heichler, "The Germans Opposite VII Corps in September 1944," Research Section, Office of the Chief of Military History, Washington, DC, December 1952, map, p. 99. Most historians, including the official historian, mention only two lines or bands, but there were three. The Schlieffen Line ran along the Roer River. McDonald, *Siegfried Line Campaign*, 29–30.

48. Friedrich August Schack, "LXXXI Corps, 4–21 September, 1944," ms. B-816, Sturmpanzer, 10–16. VII Corps estimated the 275th ID strength at 5,000 and the 116th at 1,000. Later, when refitted for the Ardennes campaign, the 116th fielded 16,000 troops. Siegfried Macholz, "The 49th Infantry Division," 1953, ms. B-792, Sturmpanzer, 2–3, 5. The 49th was relieved on August 29 to reorganize. Macholz organized two weak battalions into a single infantry regiment with what he had on hand. On September 8 the division returned to fight. Re 353rd ID, see Paul Mahlmann, "353 Infantry Division, 9–18 Sep 44," ms. n.d., B-232, Sturmpanzer, 5. VII Corps estimated that 116th PZ had no more than 1,500 troops all told. The 275th it estimated at 5,000. HQ, VII Corps, FO 10, September 3, 1944, annex 2, in 1st ID, Selected Intelligence Reports, 1:2.

49. Collins, *Lightning Joe*, 267; Hogan, *Command Post at War*, 147–48.

50. Collins, *Lightning Joe*, 269–72; HQ, VII Corps, Operations Memorandum 91, September 12, 1944, CARL. This one-page memorandum sufficed to get VII Corps on the move. MacDonald, *Siegfried Line Campaign*, 95.

51. Citino, *Wehrmacht's Last Stand*, 345; Guderian, *From Normandy to the Ruhr*, 131–66. Guderian, like most German officers, remained bound by his oath. He clearly did not approve of his division commander and took some thirty pages to make his case. The passage is wondrous in carefully polite criticism. For Schwerin's view, see Arthur L. Chaitt, "Clarence R. Huebner, Lieutenant General USA (Retired), 1888–1972," *Bridgehead Sentinel*, March 1973, Bridgehead Sentinel Collection, MRC, 5.

52. 1st ID, after-action report, September 1944, 21–22, 25, 30–31, in G-3 Operations Reports, Jun 44–Dec 44. The order cited is FO 46, issued on September 11 and reproduced in part in the after-action report.

53. Baumgartner et al., *16th Infantry*, 155; Knickerbocker et al., *Danger Forward*, 279.

54. Armand R. Levasseur, "The Operations of the 1st Battalion, 26th Infantry (1st Infantry Division) during the Initial Penetration of the Siegfried Line in the Vicinity of Nutheim, Germany, 13–20 September 1944 (Rhineland Campaign)," Advanced Infantry Officers Course, 1947–1948, Fort Benning, GA, WWII Student Papers, DRL, 10–13. See also Weingartner, *Blue Spaders*, 1996.

55. Levasseur, "Operations of the 1st Battalion," 13–14.

56. Levasseur, 14–18.

57. Hewitt, *Workhorse of the Western Front*, 14–15, 17. Hewitt's history was first published in 1946. He claims that the 30th was one of the first four Guard divisions

mobilized. That is mistaken. It was among the first five. The 33rd Division mobilized in March. The 30th, 40th, 41st, and 45th all mobilized on September 16, 1940. See Wilson, *Maneuver and Firepower*, table 12, 157.

58. HQ, 16th Infantry, "Material from Cpl. Fuller, Outer Defenses of the Siegfried Line," n.d., box 1, Smith Papers, Fort Riley Museum Complex, Fort Riley, KS; Levasseur, "Operations of the 1st Battalion," 9.

59. Levasseur, "Operations of the 1st Battalion," 10.

60. Wyman, "Journal of Events," entry for September 9, 1944.

61. HQ, VII Corps, FO 11, September 13, 1944, R13343.11, CARL, 1. See also HQ, 1st ID, 140600B, FO 49, in RG 301-3.2: G-3 Journal and File, 1 Sep 44–14 Sep 44, MRC Digital Archives.

62. The author, like Bolger, found this entry in Hodge's diary "chilling." For Bolger's analysis, see his *Panzer Killers*, 76; Hogan, *Command Post at War*, 170.

63. Many observers believed that Collins was the fair-haired boy in First Army. Certainly he enjoyed a good reputation with Hodges and Bradley. MacDonald, *Huertgen Forest*, 8. Later during the Battle of the Bulge Montgomery wanted Collins to make the main effort to reduce the salient.

64. Mason, "Reminiscences," 240. Mason recalled that these were eight-inch self-propelled guns, but all other accounts including the Division after action report describe them as 155.

65. 1st ID, after-action reports, September 1944, 34, 38, 44, 45, in G-3 Operations Reports, Jun 44–Dec 44.

66. Mason, "Reminiscences," 226.

67. 1st ID, after-action reports, September 1944, 34–35. MacDonald uses the Hansel and Gretel reference in *Huertgen Forest*, 5.

68. "Attack to Gain High Ground Northeast of Eilendorf, 15–16 September 1944," ch. 6 of HQ, 1st ID, "World War II Combat Achievements Report," MRC 1988.31, 1–2.

69. "Attack to Gain High Ground," 1–2. This oral order is transcribed in full.

70. "The Attack on Stolberg, 16–18 September," ch. 1 of 1st ID, "Combat Achievements Report," 2.

71. Gerhard Mueller, "Report on the Commitment of the 9th Panzer Division, 11–16 September 1944," ms. B-345, Sturmpanzer, 1–3, 15.

72. Mueller, "Report"; MacDonald, *Huertgen Forest*, 87. The 9th PZ is not clearly identified. My assessment comes from Heichler, "Germans Opposite VII Corps," 43. The 9th PZ is the only unit with tanks and antitank guns capable of executing the ambush. The 9th PZ had eight operational tanks assigned or attached, six assault guns, and fifteen 75-millimeter antitank guns. Finally, the action occurred in the 9th PZ defensive sector. See also Schack, "LXXXI Corps," 31–32. Schack mentions the action, calling it a counterattack.

73. HQ, Division Artillery, after-action report, 4–6, in RG 301-ART-03: Artillery Operations Reports, 1 Jun 44–May 45, MRC. The division's organic battalions fired 27,049 rounds of 105 and 4,631 rounds of 155 ammunition in September, most of it between the 17th and 18th. Corps artillery fired 6,328 105 rounds and 541 155

rounds in support of 1st ID. Together division and corps artillery fired 38,549 rounds in September. Re weather effects on air, see Sylvan and Smith, *Normandy to Victory*, entry for September 18, 1944, 131.

74. Mason, "Reminiscences," 220–21.

75. Heichler, "Germans Opposite VII Corps," 47; Mitcham, *German Order of Battle*, 1:50–53.

76. Gerhard Engel, "First Battle of Aachen, 16 Sept–22 Sept 1944," March 27, 1945, ms. A-971, Sturmpanzer, 4–5. Engel claimed success beyond that obtained. Clay, *Blood and Sacrifice*, 215; G-3 after-action report, September 1944, 41.

77. MacDonald, *Huertgen Forest*, 88–89.

78. MacDonald, 95; VII Corps, Operations Memorandum 94, September 18, 1944, CARL.

79. Mason, "Reminiscences," 226. See also Walter Denkert, "3d Panzer Grenadier Division in the Battle of Aachen, October 1944," ms. A-971, N175001015, CARL, 2.

80. Citino, *Wehrmacht's Last Stand*, 345–49; Schack, "LXXXI Corps," 23–27, 43.

81. FO 52 is cited in total in 1st ID, after-action report, October 1944, 1–2, in G-3 Operations Reports, Jun 44–Dec 4.

82. Baumer and Reardon, *American Iliad*, 270–75. See also Bobbie E. Brown, "The Operations of Company C, 18th Infantry (1st Inf. Div.) in the Attack on Crucifix Hill, 8 October 1944 (Rhineland Campaign) (Aachen Offensive)," Infantry Advanced Officers Course, 1946–47, Fort Benning, GA, n.d., WWII Student Papers, DRL, 5.

83. Collins, *Lightning Joe*, 272; Baumer and Reardon, *American Iliad*, 275–76; Mitcham, *German Order of Battle*, 1: 200, 289–93.

84. Baumer and Reardon, *American Iliad*, 275–76. See also Brown, "Operations of Company C," 5. Brown recalled that 1st Battalion was restored to full strength. It is not clear whether that applied to the regiment as a whole.

85. Murray Illison, "Bobbie E. Brown, Medal of Honor Winner, Is Dead," *New York Times*, November 1971; Brown, "Operations of Company C," 6.

86. Brown, "Operations of Company C," 7.

87. Baumer and Reardon, *American Iliad*, 278; 2nd Battalion, 18th Infantry, "Verlautenheide, Germany, 8 October 1944," ch. 32 of 1st ID, "Combat Achievements Report," 3.

88. War Department, FM 7-5, *Organization and Tactics of Infantry: The Rifle Battalion* (Washington, DC: Government Printing Office, 1940), 36; Brown, "Operations of Company C," 9–10.

89. Brown, "Operations of Company C," 9–10.

90. Brown, 9–13.

91. Brown, 13–14.

92. Brown, 14–15.

93. Baumer and Reardon, *American Iliad*, 289–91.

94. Knickerbocker et al., *Danger Forward*, 409. General Wyman's career timeline provided by his grandson, Jed Wyman.

95. Collins, *Lightning Joe*, 272; HQ, 26th Infantry, after-action report, September 30, 1944, 5–6, in RG 301-INF(26)-0.3: Reports of Operations, Jul–Sep 44, MRC

Digital Archives. The 26th crossed into Germany on September 13 and began their attack to gain the high ground east of Aachen on September 15.

96. "Aachen, 8–20 October 1944," ch. 35 of 1st ID, "Combat Achievements Report," 1; HQ, 26th Infantry, activity report, October 1944, 1, in RG 301-INF(26)-0.3: Reports of Operations, Oct–Dec 44.

97. 26th Infantry, activity report, 1–2.

98. Impression of the views the commanders stems from terrain analysis using a 1:25,000 German military map with Allied forces overprint and the ESGS 1:100,000 Allied forces map. Both maps are in the McMaster University Map Library. The author also used the town plan map in Third Battalion, 26th Infantry, "The Infantry Battalion in Offensive Action, 'Farwick Park, Aachen,' 18 October 1944," ch. 36 of 1st ID, "Combat Achievements Report." This chapter is attributed to John T. Corley.

99. Derrill M. Daniel, "The Capture of Aachen (Personal Experience of a Battalion Commander)," Command and [General] Staff College, Fort Leavenworth, Kansas, N225317, CARL, 5. Re eight-inch self-propelled howitzers, see also Mason, "Reminiscences," 240.

100. MacDonald, *Huertgen Forest*, 307–9; Baumer, *Aachen*, 267; Mason, "Reminiscences," 234.

101. Brigadeführer Fritz Kramer, "I SS PZ Corps in the West in 1944." Sturmpanzer, 14. In his monograph Kramer did not list all of the assigned units. The list here is drawn from Guderian, *From Normandy to the Ruhr*, 213.

102. Re: 3rd PZG, see Dieckhoff, *3. Infanterie-Division*, 347, 350–51. The Division moved from Denmark to France where it fought at Metz and then moved by train to the Aachen battlefield. The 3rd PZG still reported about 8,500 troops on the strength but rated its combat readiness as suitable for defense. HQ, 16th Infantry, after-action report, November 2, 1944, 2, in RG 301-INF(16)-0.3: Reports of Operations, 1 Sep 43–31 Dec 44; HQ, 1st ID, annex 3 to G-2 periodic report 119, 1, in RG 301-2.2: G-2 Journal and File, 17 Oct 44–31 Oct 44; 16th Infantry, "History of the 3rd Panzer Grenadiers Division," October 16, 1944, in 16th Infantry, Journal, Sep 44–Dec 44. Dawson believed the attackers had six to ten tanks.

103. Dieckhoff, *3. Infanterie-Division*, 352; 16th Infantry, after-action report, 2. The 1st ID reported four Shermans, but the Germans only had three.

104. 16th Infantry, after-action report, 2. Journal entries for October 16 show that the fighting continued from 0002 through 1545. That entry refers to a directive from the G-3 per General Huebner for the 16th and 18th to back each other up in the event of a penetration. Hewitt, *Workhorse of the Western Front*, 200.

105. 1st ID, Selected Intelligence Reports, 1:67–70. Paul F. Gorman in his Institute of Defense analysis "Aachen,1944 Implications for the Command Post of the Future," January 28, 2000, argues that including a handful of SS troops, there were 5,000. 1st ID took 3,473 prisoners, so there were at least that many.

106. 1st ID, Selected Intelligence Reports, 1:67–71, 85; MacDonald, *Huertgen Forest*, 308; Hassler, *Den Westwal*, 277. Selected Intelligence Reports makes no mention of tanks, nor do the G-2 periodic reports for the last few days before the surrender.

107. 1st ID, Selected Intelligence Reports, 1:67–71, 75, 86.

108. MacDonald, *Huertgen Forest*, 309; Daniel, "Capture of Aachen," 5; Derrill McDaniel, "The Capture of Aachen," lecture presented at the Marine Corps Schools, Quantico, VA, n.d., George Taylor Papers, MRC, 1960.88.3.208, 6–11. Daniel details preparation and rehearsing in this presentation.

109. McDaniel, "Capture of Aachen," 6; 26th Infantry, operations report, 7.

110. "Theodore L. Dobol, Command Sergeant Major United States Army (Retired): Autobiography," n.d., MRC 1991.24, 15.

111. Collins, *Lightning Joe*, 273; 1st ID, after-action report, October 1944, 35; 26th Infantry, operations report, 8, 10.

112. 1st ID, after-action report, October 1944, 36, 41.

113. 1st ID, Selected Intelligence Reports, 1:85–86; Yeide, *Longest Battle*, 96.

114. 1st ID, after-action report, October 1944, 126.

115. 1st ID, after-action report, 55–57; re combined arms techniques employing tanks and/or tank destroyers, see 55–60. See also 745th Tank Battalion, after-action report, November 1, 1944, in "After Action Reports, June 1944–May 1945." The report enables tracking tank platoons as they moved from one unit to another. The 1st ID tried to maintain habitual attachments, but the 745th responded efficiently to necessary changes.

116. 1st ID Artillery, after-action report, October 1944, in RG 301-ART-03: Artillery Operations Reports, 1 Jun 44–May 45, MRC Digital Archives, 8–10.

117. 1st ID, Selected Intelligence Reports, 1:80, 82–83.

CHAPTER TWELVE

Wild Fire: The Forest Battles

The great enemy hope that the Battle of Germany would be a walk to Berlin has not been fulfilled. . . . If danger does not kill you—it strengthens you.

        —Joseph Göbbels, October 27, 1944, German Radio

Our November and early December attacks on the West Wall had been bitterly expensive in men and morale.

        —Ralph Ingersoll, Top Secret

WHILE HUEBNER'S TROOPS fought to take Aachen, General Eisenhower had considered his options for the coming winter. At the theater level he had to take decisions weeks or months ahead of execution. By the end of October, the Allies would have forty-seven divisions ashore, with six more staging in the United Kingdom. Eisenhower would have thirty infantry, two airborne, and fifteen armor divisions. Impressive, but he had serious problems as well. Logistically the Allies had ground to a halt. Units in the field lacked ammunition, winter clothes, and other supplies. Worse still, according to Eisenhower, "All divisions are very tired and completely lack fresh replacements."[1]

This chapter examines the consequences of Eisenhower's direction on the way forward. His decision led to savage fighting to clear the Hürtgen Forest that consumed equipment, supplies, and lives at a prodigious rate. Ernest Hemingway, traveling with the 4th ID, described the fighting in the Hürtgen as "Passchendaele with tree bursts." The soldiers in the Big Red One who had seen plenty of hard fighting, ranging from Longstop Hill and Kasserine Pass in Tunisia to the near-run fight at Gela, the crucible of Omaha Beach, and the bloodletting at Aachen, would now enter the meat grinder of the Hürtgen, and on its heels face the German counteroffensive in the Ardennes. New misery and more casualties. In successive battles, the division had shown tactical acumen and confidence at all levels. At Aachen, it had reached the epitome of tactical excellence. The focus here is to examine whether the 1st ID could sustain that excellence in three months of bloody fighting in the great forest complex that divided the First Army front.[2]

The problem of replacing combat losses in infantry units first arose in 1942. The issue was solved momentarily in early 1943 but remained problematic thereafter. In retrospect, it seems surprising that the US Army should suffer this problem. By no means did American units have the same level of difficulty finding replacements as the Germans did, but like them, the army had to reduce the size of its divisions and the planned end strength of the Army Ground Forces. In 1943 the War Department cut the US Army (including the Army Air Force) from a planned 7,500,000 to 7,000,000 in order to maintain production in the United States, To meet that limit, the department reduced the number of divisions from the one hundred originally planned for 1943 to ninety. Accordingly, no new divisions were activated after August 1943.[3]

American armor and infantry divisions reorganized several times during the war. Each time they became smaller but also better equipped. The infantry divisions, including the 1st ID, remained organized as designed in 1943, with 14,253 authorized. Only the 2nd and 3rd Armored Divisions remained "heavy," that is, composed of a tank regiment and two infantry regiments. The remaining armored divisions organized with three tank battalions and three armored infantry battalions, bringing their complement of tanks down from 360 to 263. The war department found replacements by reducing standards and by closing down or reducing specialty programs like the Army Specialized Training Program, which had 150,000 soldiers in Universities rather than units. Britain and its Commonwealth were tapped out as well.[4]

Carl von Clausewitz described the problem of manning any army quite nicely: "The aim will then be to take the field in the greatest possible strength. . . . In practice, the size will be decided by the government . . . the general who is to command the army in the field usually has to accept the size of his forces as a given factor. . . . Consequently, the forces available must be employed with such skill that even in the absence of absolute superiority, relative superiority is attained at the decisive point." In plain English,

Eisenhower had to do what could be done with the forces he had and in the context of competing for manpower with other theaters.[5]

On a positive note, Eisenhower reported to Marshall that Bernard Law Montgomery "has at last seen the light and is concentrating toward his west, left, flank in order to clear up the Antwerp situation." Logistics would improve once General Montgomery cleared the Scheldt estuary so the port at Antwerp could operate. Strapped logistically, and with shortages of ground troops, Eisenhower believed he had two options. He could assume the defensive in order to address the logistics problems and build up ground strength to resume the offensive in the spring. Or he could tighten his belt and, like Grant in the Wilderness, keep the pressure on by continuing the offensive with what he had. Grant's bloody Wilderness campaign in the summer of 1864 prevented Lee from sending forces against Sherman, who then cut the eastern confederacy in half with his march to the sea.[6] Grant's comparatively heavier losses were relatively less damaging to his force than Lee's losses to his. In spite of growing personnel shortages, fighting on in 1944 would deny the Germans a breathing space and force them to withhold forces from other fronts. It would also set the necessary conditions for a subsequent deliberate crossing of the Rhine. Attrition, as painful as it would be for the Allies, would do even more harm to their adversary. Thus Eisenhower decided on a campaign not unlike Grant's.

Eisenhower convened a conference in Brussels on October 18 to share his conclusions and instruct his senior commanders. He directed Montgomery to open Antwerp. He ordered Bradley to continue the drive to the Rhine and attempt to cross south of Cologne. Jacob L. Devers's 6th Army Group would attack to close up to the Rhine as well.[7]

At 12th Army Group, Bradley planned for Courtney H. Hodges's First Army to make the main effort in the center, supported by William H. Simpson's Ninth Army on his left and Patton's Third Army on his right. In the end, to find troops to continue to attack, Bradley had to assume risk. He believed the Ardennes Forest complex was the right place to do so. Therefore he assigned Major General Troy H. Middleton, in command of VIII Corps, to defend roughly eighty miles of complex terrain in Ardennes with three worn-out infantry divisions. The VIII Corps sector extended from just north of Saint-Vith, Belgium, to south of Luxembourg City. Each of Middleton's divisions had about three times the frontage they were designed to defend. Bradley assumed this risk to meet Eisenhower's objective, the "destruction of the enemy's forces west of the Rhine."[8]

Reflecting on the postwar argument of whether First Army could have avoided the bloodbath that Eisenhower's strategy produced in the Hürtgen, Joe Collins could see no way around it. Clearing the ground to reach the Roer river plain made sense then and does now. Collins defended Eisenhower's decision, but he was keenly aware of the time it took, and the costs it involved. Taking Aachen took two weeks. Clearing the forest and reaching the Roer took more than a month. Charles B. MacDonald, the author of the official history of the Siegfried Line campaign, reckoned the cost at 47,030 battle casualties, including 7,024 killed, with thousands more lost to non-battle injury or death and sickness.[9]

The German Problem

In his postwar memoir Siegfried Westphal, Rundstedt's chief of staff, described the German problem succinctly. In mid-October 1944, Army Group B reported that it had "forty-one infantry divisions and ten mobile divisions (Panzer and Panzergrenadier)." Against this there were "forty-two enemy infantry divisions and eighteen armoured divisions, as well as eighteen tank brigades." Westphal overestimated Eisenhower's strength, but not by much. More important was the Allies' advantage in equipment, tanks, artillery, and aircraft, which dwarfed that of Army Group B. Nevertheless, German combat strength in the Seventh Army and LXXXI Corps grew opposite Collins's VII Corps and 1st ID. OB West withdrew some divisions to be refitted, while new ones began to arrive to mount the counteroffensive that Hitler first imagined in August. The new Volksgrenadier divisions (VGD) reflected Germany's difficulties in manning and equipping units. The combined strength of the German field army and replacement army (the training establishment) declined from 6.55 million in 1943 to 5.5 million by war's end. Himmler, in charge of the replacement army since the July plot, culled the armed forces, industry, occupied territories, and those previously considered unfit, too old, or too young to man these new units.[10]

The 1944 Volksgrenadier divisions were organized on a reduced establishment of 10,072, down from 12,500 in the 1943 table of organization. The VGD had only seven infantry battalions. With nine infantry battalions, the American divisions had more riflemen and more supporting weapons. To offset the reduced number of infantry, the VGD had a great many automatic weapons. These included 2,064 submachine guns, far more than their American counterparts, who were authorized only 243 automatic rifles. The VGD retained three battalions of field artillery, including three

75-millimeter howitzer battalions and one 105-millimeter howitzer battalion. Finally, they all had supporting units, including antitank guns and antiaircraft artillery.[11]

Despite horrendous bombing, German industry not only continued to function but actually increased production of tanks and other heavy equipment through 1944. But to reach the front, new gear had to run the gauntlet of Allied bombing. In the fall of 1944, 2,199 tanks rolled off assembly lines bound for the western front, but only 1,371 reached units in the field to replace the 1,575 lost. Just as the German Army pared back the infantry division, so too did it reduce the complement of armor in its Panzer divisions. The regular army's Panzer divisions had an authorized complement of 103 tanks, while the SS divisions had 126 tanks authorized. Both remained robust in end strength, with 13,725 in the regular army units and 17,262 in the SS. Germany managed to build or rebuild fifty VGDs and refitted most of its SS units and regular army Panzer divisions.[12]

Despite serious problems, new formations made their way forward. While Seventh Army confronted First US Army, the 5th Panzer and newly organized 6th Panzer Army refitted units and prepared arriving units for the counteroffensive. The order of battle varied over time as OKW attempted to find units. In the end, the Germans both maintained their defense along the Roer River and found the means to mount a counteroffensive with twenty-seven divisions and three separate brigades that fielded the equivalent of a US infantry division and supporting troops.[13]

On October 24 General der Panzertruppen Hasso von Manteuffel's Fifth Panzer Army took over the part of the Seventh Army sector defended by General der Infanterie Friedrich Köchling's LXXXI Corps. Fifth Panzer Army brought no combat units, but together with LXXXI Corps it had formidable artillery. Köchling's corps artillery fielded a menagerie of German, French, and Russian artillery. This eclectic but nevertheless effective collection of guns and howitzers included two railway guns, eleven heavy guns, two dozen 76.2-millimeter fortress antitank guns, and a handful of Russian self-propelled 122-millimeter howitzers. A battalion of towed Russian howitzers and a Volks-Werfer Brigade of four more battalions of howitzers and 210- and 280-millimeter rocket artillery rounded out the corps artillery order of battle. By the end of November as many as one thousand artillery pieces could support the Landsers in the forest. In the official history, Charles B. MacDonald observed that "for once the Germans were capable of laying down massive fires."[14]

Köchling believed that because his sector was too large, the only way he could operate "with the means and forces of the Corps [was] in the form of an elastic defense." He believed that Army Group B understood that he could not be expected to hold the line without breaches. Certainly Model "visited nearly every day" and accepted the facts on the ground. Essentially the Corps could not promise to hold the ground, but it could execute a "delaying resistance" and preserve the bulk of its infantry. To defend, Köchling had, from north to south, the 246th VGD, the 3rd Panzergrenadier Division, 12th ID, 275th ID, and various combat support formations, including an assault gun brigade. The rebuilt 47th ID, now styled the 47th VGD, joined the corps on November 16.[15]

The Terrain, Weather and Plan

Hemingway's comparison of the horrendous slaughter at Passchendaele in the Great War to that in the Hürtgen is an exaggeration only in scale. The scope of misery through early February 1945 in the Hürtgen, the Schnee Eifel, and the Ardennes merits the comparison. The forest complex includes the Schnee Eifel south of the Hürtgen; the Ardennes, the third component, extends well into Belgium and Luxemburg. The forests are really a single terrain feature. In addition to the *Siegfried Line Campaign*, Charles B. Mac-Donald wrote two other books on the battles that occurred in and around these dense woods. He described the terrain succinctly as "one high plateau of ancient volcanic origin. . . . To the eyes of anyone but a geologist the region appears to less plateau than mountains." About fifty inches of rain or snow fell annually. During the winter of 1944–45 snow depth reached nearly two feet and as much as four or five feet in drifts.[16]

The area is similar to the Pacific rain forest of the American northwest. Much of Hürtgen, the Schnee Eifel, and the Ardennes is covered by what the Germans call *Hohe Venn*, in English "high fens," or upland marsh. Several rivers rise in the region, including the Roer in the Hürtgen, the Erft in the Schnee Eifel, and the Our in the Ardennes. These rivers and other streams cut ravines and gorges, creating a rugged range of densely forested hills. There are few roads in the Hürtgen. Trails and firebreaks that cut through the forest are soft and become quagmires when it rains or snows. To Pete Lypka, a jeep driver in the 16th's intelligence and reconnaissance platoon, "It seemed to rain all the time." Worse, when it did, "The roads were a sea of mud, in some places so deep [it] came up to the running board of a jeep." The trails and roads were better in the Schnee Eifel and Ardennes but not as numerous. The forests in the Schnee Eifel and Ardennes are older, formed of mixed coniferous and deciduous trees. The 1st ID terrain study reported that trees in the Schnee Eifel were "2–3 feet in diameter paced at 3–5 foot intervals." The 1st ID history, *Danger Forward,* claimed that the German general staff planted the Hürtgen as an obstacle, and that it was at least as dense as the Schnee Eifel.[17]

According to the 1st ID G-2, temperatures in November would hover around forty degrees, with seven days or more below freezing. The days would shorten from not quite ten hours on 1 November to just over eight hours by the end of the month. In December there were nearly two weeks around the winter solstice during which daylight lasted less than eight hours. Temperatures declined to the twenties in December and January during what was reputedly among the coldest winters ever in Europe. Bastogne, in the heart of the Ardennes, "enjoyed" an average of "145 days of freezing weather." December and January provided all the cold temperatures and snow anyone could want. The 1st ID prepared no detailed weather study for the months of December–February because they had been committed to the Ardennes fight unexpectedly, but its journals report plenty of miserable wet, cold weather.[18]

Early on, First Army mistakenly believed it confronted the German Seventh Army, with whom it had fought since D-Day. First Army estimated that Seventh Army controlled four corps composed of nine infantry divisions, two understrength Panzer divisions (2nd and 116th PZ), and the 3rd Panzergrenadier (PZG) Division. A dozen or more fortress battalions and a Tiger tank battalion rounded out the ground combat forces. First Army noted that its boundary with adjacent field armies proved nearly the same as those of Seventh Army, and that there was "marked similarity between Corps boundaries as well." All of this was accurate except that Manteuffel's Fifth Panzer Army, not Seventh Army, controlled LXXXI Corps.[19]

On October 26 First Army issued its field order to comply with Bradley's instructions. From north to south Hodges commanded VII, V, and VIII Corps, composed of nine infantry and three armored divisions. First Army also had a robust array of supporting units, including about forty artillery battalions. Even so, the zone of attack was too wide for the available troops. Worse still, Hodges's order required V Corps to seize the town of Schmidt to clear maneuver room so VII Corps could clear the northern half of the Hürtgen. Rather than loop around the southern flank of the forest, Hodges chose to bull straight through on roughly the same axis that had produced failure for 9th ID in October. Middleton's VIII Corps remained on the defensive, spread thinly in the Ardennes to narrow the attacking zone.[20]

Hodges's plan included "Operation Queen, the largest air-ground cooperative effort yet undertaken." He assigned the main effort to VII Corps. Collins, at the behest of Hodges, prepared two plans, one with three divisions, and a second with the addition of a fourth infantry division if one became available. Weather delayed the operation long enough to enable the 104th ID to join the Corps, making the four-division version of the plan possible. VII Corps issued Field Order 12 on November 9. The Corps intelligence estimate began with a sentence that underlined the wisdom of Eisenhower to attack where able; according to Colonel Leslie G. Carter, the VII Corps G-2, "During the last six weeks the enemy opposing VII Corps has been content to improve his defenses; to reorganize his improvised units; and to establish his supply system." This was exactly what Eisenhower wanted to prevent—giving the Germans time to restore their balance.[21]

Field Order 12 specified that VII Corps, "supported by XX Air Force will attack on order First Army in the direction Duren (F1266) [grid reference]-Koln to penetrate the enemy's main defense and seize Koln." It was ten miles to Düren and eighteen more to Köln. The corps planned to attack with 104th ID on the left, 1st ID making the main effort in the center, and the 4th ID on the right. The 3rd AD formed the reserve, prepared to exploit success in either the 1st ID or 4th ID zones. Collins provided for robust counter-flak, counter-battery, and preparation fires. Corps artillery planned to fire twenty-four concentrations to suppress or destroy ninety-five identified enemy antiaircraft guns in support of Operation Queen. These concentrations would be fired as the bombers approached their targets. The VII Corps artillery, supported by XIX Corps artillery, planned to fire 195 preparation concentrations. Twenty-nine of these would be fired on towns or known observation posts, while the rest targeted the positions of nearly four hundred artillery pieces.[22]

Huebner published his order on November 6. Collins provided the 1st Division with an additional regimental combat team (the 47th Infantry) from 9th ID. Each regiment had at least one tank company, one tank destroyer company, a 4.2-inch mortar company, and combat engineers. Finally, the corps assigned an additional artillery battalion to 1st ID Division Artillery. Huebner's order required the division to "seize crossing of the Rur [Roer] north of Duren, prepared for further advance east with the 16th Infantry on the left, the 26th Infantry on the right and 18th Infantry in reserve." The 47th Infantry would pass forward of lead regiments to take Gressenich, less than three miles from the start line. Tactically Huebner proposed to advance his regiments by alternating bounds.[23]

The dates of plans and orders illustrate parallel planning. Collins issued instructions and conferred with his commanders as the corps and division staffs planned collegially—in parallel. All but the 104th ID had worked together long enough to understand how the others thought and operated. Consequently, they could plan rapidly even when planning deliberately. The corps operations plan dated October 27 outlined both the three- and four-division options. The corps also floated an operations overlay that enabled planning as well. This was an attack planned deliberately, with time to compare notes and refine plans. Failure, if it came, would not stem from inadequate planning or coordination.[24]

In addition to a detailed terrain and weather study, division G-2 Robert F. Evans published, as he had before every deliberate attack, a detailed order of battle and estimate of enemy capability and intentions. Lieutenant Colonel Evans's estimate was quite accurate, built on his section's analysis and on estimates provided by Colonel Carter, who built on that issued by Benjamin A. "Monk" Dickson at First Army. Gross numbers of troops were generally the same at each echelon, as reports going up the chain stemmed from data submitted by units in contact based largely on prisoner interrogations and captured documents. Evans believed that the 12th had the equivalent of seven battalions in the line, each with a strength of about five hundred Landsers. "There may be as many as 30 tanks or self-propelled guns" in support, he estimated, as well as "the normal three light battalions and one medium battalion" of artillery.[25]

Evans believed the 275th defended on the left of the 12th ID and the more robust 3rd Panzergrenadier Division on the right. He estimated that the 3rd PZG had as many as sixty tracked vehicles. Finally, he asserted that the 2nd Panzer Division was refitting near Köln. Both the 9th PZ and 15th PZG were reported in the area, but their exact location was unknown. The locations of the 9th PZ, 15th PZG, and 9th SS were among "essential elements of information," as were bridges and crossings on the Roer, and any indications that the Germans might flood the Roer plain by releasing water from the dams upstream. Locating the 9th PZ was of particular interest, as Evans thought that "thirty 'Panther' tanks" were on the way to join the 9th. The tone of Evans's analysis is positive. He knew the12th ID battalions were "depleted."[26]

During the course of the war the 1st ID published observations and/or lessons in each after -action report. It also published studies that amounted to how-to memorandums. On October 31, 1944, during the planning for the Hürtgen operation, the division issued Operations Memorandum 3, "Employment of Infantry in Woods." The basis for the memorandum came from "lessons learned in fighting through thickly wooded areas . . . obtained from records and interviews with Staff Officers of the 9th Division." The memorandum, although numbered 3, was by no means the third of its kind. Lessons, training directives, and observations were collected long before the landings in Algeria and had become de rigueur. Two pithy pages followed the introduction and covered moving in forests, patrolling, overhead cover for foxholes, how to employ mortars, adjusting artillery by sound, air support, mines, and booby traps. All of this information would prove useful.[27]

Bloody Hürtgen

Weather delayed the attack until November 16, and then it began with biblical violence. First, artillery fired counter-flak targets to prepare the way for the bombers, who followed soon after those preparation fires concluded. The US Army Air Force used 1,191 heavy bombers escorted by 482 fighters to dump "4,120 tons of fragmentation bombs" on five German villages, including two in the 1st ID Zone-Eschweiler and Langerwehe. Army medium bombers dropped 150 tons on four other targets. Fighter bombers flew 352 sorties on planned targets as well as targets identified by ground controllers. The Royal Air Force attacked Düren and two other towns on the Roer with 1,188 heavy bombers escorted by 275 fighters. Not be outdone by their American cousins, the RAF unloaded 5,640 tons on their targets.[28]

Fearful of bombing short as they had at Saint-Lô, Army Air Force bombers achieved far less than hoped, with one exception. The bombers essentially destroyed an artillery battalion of the newly arriving 47th VGD, striking as the battalion was unloading at a Roer River railhead. Another of the 47th's units got hit as it moved forward. Charles B. MacDonald quoted a German sergeant who said, "I never saw anything like it. These kids [his new troops] were still numb forty-five minutes after the bombardment." According to the Army Air Force official history, "Several fortified villages were virtually obliterated." Eschweiler suffered on the same scale as the fortified villages.[29]

The coordinated bombing preparation began as promised at 1115, with troops able to see much of the deluge. At 1235 the 16th Infantry reported that bombs fell close enough to the 2nd Battalion "to throw shrapnel around the area." Unperturbed, regiment reported, "We are all set." Five minutes later the attached 47th Infantry noted, "Last bombing came in close." Furthermore the 47th command post said, "Can see arty barrage landing in gressenich right now." Bombers and howitzers pasted the enemy simultaneously to suppress and/or destroy the opposition.[30]

At 1245 the division attacked, the 16th and 26th abreast with battalions in column. The 16th aimed to take the village of Hamich while the 26th moved on Gressenich. The 47th trailed the 26th in a column of battalions, while the 18th remained in reserve. Division artillery continued preparation fires, including rocket fires from the 18th FA, a corps rocket artillery battalion. The Germans responded with effective artillery and mortar fires. At the outset of the attack, Company A, 745th TB, found just moving on the narrow forest trails difficult. Worse still, German artillery knocked out two tanks right after they crossed the line of departure. The surviving Sherman tanks found no targets and so proved of little use to the infantry. Tanks supporting the 26th and 46th did no better.[31]

Lieutenant Edmond F. Driscoll's 1st Battalion, 16th Infantry, closed on Hamich about a thousand yards from their line of departure, where he found that "the enemy was defending hamich fanatically, and had all the advantages of good terrain in the defense." Driscoll's troops beat off a counterattack of about fifty German infantry who debouched from the town unsupported by armor. German "artillery fire, however, continued in large quantities." Driscoll continued the attack after nightfall, but nothing worked. His tanks could not get up to support, and German artillery stymied his infantry. Hamich remained in the hands of the 12th ID.[32]

Major Maurice A. Belisle, S-2 of the 26th Infantry, wrote a paper about his experience in the Hürtgen while attending the Advanced Infantry Officers Course after the war. He called the paper, aptly, "Regimental Attack in Heavy Woods." Belisle remembered that "progress was extremely slow—it always is initially when hitting a prepared defensive position." To him, "It seemed as though any movement by our troops was observed." That of course produced artillery and mortar fire, of which "mortar fires was particularly accurate." Attacking at "precisely 1245," the 2nd Battalion, which was leading the attack, had made all of five hundred yards. Understrength or not, Oberst Gerhard Engel's newly designated 12th VGD put up the kind of fight Belisle expected. In his estimate of the situation issued on November 10, he had asserted that "a strong defense will be made in the heavily wooded area of the Regiment's initial advance." Belisle advised that "the first serious counterattack can be expected from Panzer elements in tactical reserve at dawn of the second day."[33]

Despite a day's hard fighting, the 1st Division failed to take its objectives. Engel's division had suffered during the battle for Aachen, but the 12th VGD gave as good as it got on November 16. Although his infantry companies had been reduced to roughly a third of their authorized strength of 142 officers and men, two replacement battalions came up toward the end of October with about 500 trained replacements each. Another 350 convalescent veterans from the division also returned. As a result, Engel's infantry battalions reached about half strength. On the plus side, he had lost very little artillery and few artillerymen. Finally, the division made good use of the time between the surrender of Aachen on October 21 and the attack on November 16.[34]

The 12th VGD dug in, built bunkers, and prepared the ground by laying "about 10,000 mines" along the few muddy trails that that led into its positions. German engineers also erected wire obstacles to canalize the Americans. The result was a line of combat outposts and strongpoints rather than a continuous front—perfectly good in terrain constricted by dense woods, deep ravines, streams, and no roads adequate for armor. The risk in this kind of defense is infiltration between strongpoints. Model's Army Group B ordered two reserve lines built along the front. The intent was to withdraw to these lines about two hundred yards to the rear of primary positions when an attack seemed eminent. That would enable the Landsers to escape what Engel called the "the drum fire [of artillery] and air raids that preceded" American attacks. Engel observed the buildup forward of his lines and the vectors of attack telegraphed by US combat patrols and artillery observation aircraft. On November 16 his efforts and that of his troops paid off and continued to do so for days.[35]

During that first day of renewed fighting, the 1st ID identified three German regiments, one each from the 12th and 47th VGD as well as the 275th ID. The 47th had just joined the fight; after being mauled at Mons, it had withdrawn to Germany, where it reconstituted as a Volksgrenadier division. It deployed to Denmark in early October and then to the Aachen sector after less than six weeks of training. In 1947 Generalleutnant Max Bork, who commanded the 47th VGD, argued that he needed two more weeks to have his division ready to fight. Instead, the 47th attempted to relieve the 12th VGD the night of November 16–17. Contact with the 1st ID impeded the effort, so Generalleutnant Köchling halted the operation. He did get one regiment of the 47th in place by sunup, allowing the 12th VGD to shorten its line. After sunup, Bork managed to get the rest of his division into position on left of the 12th VGD.[36]

Despite Bork's relative lack of confidence, the 47th did well. Correspondent Cy Peterman observed accurately that inexperienced German troops did well in the forest because "in certain spots it was simply that anyone could defend them." Hill 232, just north of Hamich, proved the point. One officer noted that from this hill "the enemy could look down our throats in Gressenich, and observe the slightest twitch in Hamich." German artillery struck with ruinous accuracy, even as German grenadiers swept the few avenues of approach with direct fire. Two-man bunkers and mines made roads and firebreaks deadly. The American infantry moved with difficulty through the dense forests. To the Big Red One troops, it seemed that "the Germans were everywhere, and in the thickness of the woods it was impossible to spot them, or divide them up so they could be developed or flanked." The rebuilt and renamed 47th did just fine in this environment.[37]

The forest and the weather proved difficult antagonists as well. In *The Guns at Last Light*, Rick Atkinson points out that rain fell in the forest on all but two days in November 1944. Gelatinous mud, cold and wet, took a toll on the troops of both sides. Immersion foot, known colloquially as trench foot, felled some 23,000 in November and December alone. The army failed to provide cold-weather gear in time by choice, because getting other supplies up seemed more important. Major General Paul R. Hawley, the senior Army medical officer in the theater, described the problem plainly: "The plain truth is that the footwear furnished U.S. troops is in general lousy."[38]

The Germans took their toll as well. The 1st ID had fared well integrating replacements at least until Aachen, but losses, coupled with very little time out of the line, had worn down units and made bringing on replacements difficult. Driscoll's 1st Battalion, 16th Infantry, illustrates the problem. When the division undertook to clear the Hürtgen, his rifle companies A, B, and C were authorized 6 officers and 187 enlisted men by the 1944 tables of organization. On November 16 Company A had 7 officers and 166 enlisted men. Company B began with 7 and 172, while Company C had 6 and 155. By the end of that day, Company B reported 6 officers and 115 soldiers present for duty. Of these, 1 officer and 34 soldiers had been wounded, and 23 were absent sick or nonbattle casualties. By the end of the next day, the company had declined in strength to 2 and 97, including fifty replacements that arrived that day. Company B's strength seesawed up and down but reached 4 and 175 on November 22. On December 10, when the battalion withdrew to a rest area, the company had declined to 6 and 128. Driscoll concluded that German artillery produced 70 percent of his wounded or killed.[39]

Replacements came from two sources: the replacement pool, and soldiers returning from hospitals. Returnees slotted in easily, as they knew their units. Those from the replacement pool were either real rookies or "retreads" who had been culled from other branches and reclassified as infantry. Frank Kolb, who commanded Driscoll's Company B, described the problem of integrating replacements vividly. Until the forest fighting, Kolb believed, "Everyone was well trained and we were a fighting machine." That machine got ground up in the forest. "In the Hürtgen there were replacements coming in. In one bunch we got sergeants and corporals from the coast artillery with technical grades." He gave the newcomers a choice: he would accept them in grade. If they "cut it, I'd let them keep it [rank]." If not, he would reduce them to private. With brand-new soldiers, "lieutenants and sergeants were just pushing and shoving everybody, trying to get them to go in the right direction." Kolb found if he could get replacements through the first two or three days of combat, they turned out all right.[40]

Despite suffering similar high casualties, the Germans fought ferociously and effectively in the forest, not only because their megalomaniacal führer demanded it but because they were fighting to defend their homeland. No matter how bad the cause, in the end the Landsers fought first for each other and then their country. The result was that while their "morale should have been shaky. It was not." They were also well led. Whatever German unit the 1st ID confronted in nearly a month's combat fought hard, often refused to surrender even when surrounded, and routinely executed suicidal counterattacks.[41]

On November 17 the 1st Battalion, 16th, fought off a particularly savage counterattack that aimed to drive the battalion from the Hamich ridge. Down to seventy effectives, Company C had an especially hard fight. A company of the 12th VGD's 48th Volksgrenadier regiment supported by five tanks came "within 20 feet" of the battalion's positions. Lieutenant James Wood's platoon was down to six men, including him. Technical sergeant Jake W. Lindsey, Wood's platoon sergeant, replaced him during the fight when Wood was cut off and taken prisoner. Lindsey personally drove off the five tanks with rifle grenades and then led the remnants of the platoon in repulsing six infantry assaults. Lindsey led the way, killing, according to witnesses, twenty enemy soldiers, three of these by bayonet.[42]

Hamich finally fell at 1300 on November 18, although some Germans remained in the immediate area. The 2nd Battalion, 16th Infantry, took Hill 232 after a prodigious artillery preparation, including 196 rockets fired on a rectangle "800 by 400 yards." Captain Maxie Zara, the division public information officer, regaled correspondents on his visit to Hill 232. It was, he said, "filled with dead. About 200 Krauts and something like 50 of our men."

He added that the artillery "chewed up the trees with the big stuff" and concluded, "Boy, you should see it."[43]

Hasso von Manteuffel, in command of the sector, had to find mobile forces to respond to the constant pressure exerted by VII Corps. He turned to the worn-down 116th PZ. The 116th decimated the 28th ID in the first major American attack in the forest, but it too had taken a beating. Withdrawn to refit due to high losses, Manteuffel now ordered the 116th to form a *Kampfgruppe*, or battle group. Manteuffel required a regiment-sized combined arms combat group. What the 116th could do was less than that. The division provided Oberst Johannes Bayer, commanding Panzer Regiment 16 and the attached 1st Battalion Panzer Regiment 24, with seventeen Mark Vs, a single Mark IV, and a command tank. A menagerie of troops and units composed the rest of the *Kampfgruppe*, with about three hundred reconnaissance and engineer troops who would fight as infantry, and three howitzers with three hundred rounds of ammunition.[44]

Naturally the Germans counterattacked to retake Hill 232. The 47th VGD's 1st Battalion, 104th Volksgrenadier Regiment, counterattacked at 1810. Bayer's *Kampfgruppe* was to support them. One of Bayer's officers, leading seven tanks with reconnaissance troops riding aboard, headed for the 1st Battalion's assembly area. The young officer got lost. First he drove into Company C, 16th Infantry, which was down by now to forty-five effectives. Backing off, he next wandered into Hamich and the 3rd Battalion, who called a fifteen-battalion time-on-target mission that along with the infantry drove the Germans out with three less tanks around midnight. During the course of the night the artillery fired 5,350 rounds.[45]

At 0530 the 1st Battalion of the 104th managed to make the planned counterattack with two of its three companies. The unsupported attack failed miserably. One of the two company commanders was the only man in his unit who was not wounded or killed. That must have been surprising to him; his captors found seven bullet holes in his overcoat. When he stopped during the attack to blow his nose, he got two more in his handkerchief. The failed counterattack destroyed the battalion.[46]

The character of combat during the first three days of the operation applied equally to the rest of the campaign. Every day proved difficult, bloody, and miserable. Huebner did what he could. On November 20 the 18th Infantry assumed the main effort. Coach told Colonel George A. Smith Jr. that he had "Div Arty [division artillery] all in front of you [fires, not guns]. Don't hesitate in using it." If you "run into resistance," he advised, "by-pass it and go around." Not much chance of that happening, but like everyone in the division, Smith used artillery and mortars lavishly. Brigadier General Clift Andrus even attached a 155-millimeter howitzer platoon to the 18th that could be used in direct fire or instant support to a unit in contact. Tanks, tank destroyers, and howitzers—whatever it took, division supplied it. On November 21 Huebner and Andrus set up a time-on-target mission in support of the 47th Infantry. Collins intervened to add more artillery. Twenty battalions "fired for three minutes upon a target area measuring approximately 300 by 500 yards."[47]

Still, there were no decisive engagements and no outright breakthrough. Fighting in the forest proved much like Aachen. Huebner described it as a "bloody inch by inch, tree-by-tree grind; casualties were heavy and gains figured in yards." On November 22 the 18th Infantry reported that one of its companies had gained about four hundred yards. The grid coordinates for that achievement showed the division had reached a depth of three miles into the forest, with a bit more than one to go to reach the northern edge. The defenestration of the Germans had not been achieved, although much deforestation had.[48]

Fewer than three dozen damaged or destroyed homes comprised Hamich. But the village lay astride a decent road leading north, so it changed hands twice, with horrific casualties. Köchling used Bayer's troops, Engel's 48th Grenadier Regiment, and other units as fire brigades and did so adroitly. In the midst of this mayhem, the 1st ID fed the doggies and their help turkey with trimmings on Thanksgiving Day, which fell on November 23. That day Huebner exhorted Colonel Smith to push on. He wanted the town of Langerwehe on the road that exited the forest. He reminded Smith, "Langerwehe is where your big fight is." The next day Smith reached the edge of the forest and reported "observation into langerwehe" a mile or so to the northeast. Jeff Seitz's 26th Infantry on the 18th's right had not yet reached the edge of the forest but was within a mile of it. In just over a week the division had managed to drive about three miles through the forest and finally could see the Roer river plain. The Roer itself flowed northwest about six miles beyond the forest. The ground sloped down toward the river, so observation extended to Luchem, the next village north, and the east-west autobahn beyond.[49]

The remainder of VII Corps had not been idle. Terry Allen, back in the harness, led the 104th ID with aplomb and reprised his penchant for night attacks. Collins assigned the 104th ID the zone on Huebner's left, hoping to stimulate some friendly rivalry—there is little evidence to suggest the privates in the line felt inspired. The 4th Cavalry Group fought attached to 1st

ID and other units as required. The 4th ID continued on the right flank of the corps. Rose's 3rd AD remained in reserve, ready to exploit any breakthrough. To secure its share of the exits from the forest, the division had to seize Merberich, a mile north of Schontal, Langerwehe, just over a mile north of the forest, and Merode, half mile or less from its edge. From there Collins wanted Huebner to seize crossings on the river.[50]

Inch-by-inch fighting continued unabated. On November 26, "six fighter-bomber squadrons" pummeled the "towns of langerwehe, schlich, jungersdorf, echts and stammelin," which had the misfortune of being just north of the forest and still defended. Hill 203, a few hundred yards south of Langerwehe, received similar attention. The Germans defended the reverse slope of Hill 203 and hung on. The 47th Infantry, supported by 3rd AD tanks, pushed northward on the right flank. Collins brought up part of the 3rd AD, promising Huebner they would pass to him. On November 27, attacking in the predawn hours with Driscoll's battalion and one from the 3rd AD, the 18th Infantry reported Hill 203 in their hands at 0900. Of course, the Germans counterattacked and were duly driven off.[51]

Captain Richard J. Lindo, who had served with the 18th Infantry since North Africa, took command of Company B, 1st Battalion, 18th Infantry, three days before the 18th finally took Hill 203. "I joined the company when it was down to 48 or 49 men," Lindo recalled. He went around and met every soldier. That night he received thirty replacements. The company attacked the next day. According to Lindo, "The poor bastards didn't have a chance, because they didn't know their sergeants or anybody else." Lindo knew what right looked like after nearly two years in the field, but neither he nor his surviving leaders had time to teach their new arrivals. The 1st ID was running down like an unwound watch.[52]

Yet the regiments kept on ticking, albeit slowly. On November 28 John T. Corley's 3rd Battalion of the 26th Infantry took Jungersdorf and was fighting in Langerwehe. Engel described this attack as "bitter" and wrote that what he had left was no longer able to stop the American advance. Per VII Corps Operations Memorandum 122, 1st ID attacked on November 29 to get out of the forest by taking (from east to west) the villages of Schlicht, Merode, and Luchem. The first two lay just north of the forest, while Luchem was nearly two miles north. The 3rd Fallschirmjäger Division (FJD) had joined the fight. That division, along with the remnants of the 12th and 47th VGD and other odds and sods Köchling could find, and battle groups from the 116th PZ, comprised the opposition. When Engel begged Köchling for more troops, the best that could be done was to combine the remnants of the 47th

VGD with those of the 12th. In just over a week, the infantry strength of the 47th VGD had been reduced to fewer than three hundred.[53]

On November 29 Lieutenant Colonel Derrill M. Daniel's 2nd Battalion, 26th Infantry, prepared to pass through Major J. K. Rippert's 1st Battalion to seize the village of Merode. Constrained by the forest, the regiment was attacking in column, with battalions passing forward as progress occurred. Late that day Private First Class Alwin E. Bulau, the loader on his platoon leader's tank, felt compelled to capture what he had seen. He sat at a German typewriter and typed an eight-page account of the attack on Merode. That morning Bulau breakfasted on C-ration ham and eggs, and coffee made with water drawn from a stream in which he had seen two dead Landsers downstream. While he and his buddy Tom, the tank's driver, were eating, their lieutenant, Leonard Novak, came by to say, "Well boys this is it. . . . We pass LD [line of departure] at 0900. Our objective is a little town called Merode."[54]

Bulau turned to preparing, as he put it, "beaucoup" main gun rounds in his ready racks. Mostly he laid in high explosive but also some armor piercing and two of a new round called "canister." These he described as being "like a big shotgun shell and is to be used on personell [sic]." He also checked his coaxial machine gun, the weapon "we use most of all." The attack started on time, with one infantry squad sticking close to the five tanks in Bulau's platoon, to protect them from *Panzerfäuste* (the German equivalent of bazookas) as they trundled down the trail leading to Merode. The platoon leader's tank was the third in column. Bulau could see the driver struggling with the steering levers to keep the tank on the muddy trail. Tom, despite the cold, had broken a sweat just getting to the LD. Whatever trouble Tom had was nothing to compared to that of the infantry. "It was hell for the doughs," Bulau wrote. "The muck is knee deep in places."[55]

The infantry and tankers advanced, with most of the infantry spread out through the forest when the fight began. Bulau could see "the assaulting company taking a beating" from snipers, rapid-firing machine guns, and tree bursts. He watched a wounded infantryman drag himself into the ditch only to have an artillery round land "on the exact spot where he was laying. . . . I don't like to even look at that spot because I know what's there." Bulau continued, "It's like that all over." The advance went on, with the "men fighting not only the enemy but fighting the mud, fighting fatigue and fighting that almost overwhelming desire to run and hide in a hole. But no these boys've got guts. They keep going until knocked down by flying steel."[56]

Late in the afternoon some of the infantry managed to get into the town, but without Bulau, his tank, or for that matter the rest of the platoon. Bulau's driver lost control, and his tank slid partway off the road and then was hit by artillery. Damaged and unable to move or even get out of the tank due to fire, the lieutenant ordered the two forwardmost tanks to continue, with the fourth tank covering them. That tank was poorly positioned to do much, given that the two tanks advancing immediately rounded a bend that led into the village and disappeared from sight. The fifth tank could not support, as it could not get around Bulau's tank.[57]

The tankers reported by radio that they could see none of the infantry. A well-aimed *Panzerfaust* soon damaged one of the tanks, which reappeared around the bend, smoking. Bulau next heard a lot of static on the radio, followed by the fourth tank's commander screaming, "Oh my god." Then it grew awfully quiet. Minutes later that tank's crew appeared, "running around the bend." The platoon leader concluded that the best they could do was to hold their position. His tank took a second artillery round on the back deck, which holed a fuel cell. Mud blocked the tank's drain plugs, so gasoline rose to a depth of "eight to ten inches" on the turret floor. Because artillery fell constantly, the crew remained aboard their explosively flammable tank, hoping not to be burned or asphyxiated by the fumes. After half an hour more, still under intense artillery fire and of no use to the infantry, the platoon decamped to the rear as best they could. Miraculously none were killed. Bulau does not say what became of the fifth tank. The 745th reported that it held the road within five hundred yards of Merode. If so, it could not fire into the town. That tank too withdrew by midnight. In a group interview right after the war, the 745th described this event as the "sorriest experience" in the whole sorry battle in the Hürtgen.[58]

Daniel's Companies E and F, and two platoons of Company H, the weapons company, did get into Merode. Not long after, determined German infantry and armor cut the road they had come down. Worse still, at least three German tanks, supported by infantry, entered the village. A half hour after midnight a worried Seitz reported to division that he feared for the troops in town, as Daniel and the rest of the battalion could not break in. Nor, with the road blocked, could the regiment reinforce. Over the next twenty-four hours the regiment and the division struggled to relieve the two companies or restore communications by carrying radios in to the besieged companies by hand. For that to happen, combat patrols had to break in. They did not. The messages recorded in the regimental journal convey a sense of foreboding and immediacy of danger that remains chilling nearly eighty years later.[59]

Huebner and Taylor came forward, as if somehow their presence might matter. Engineers and tank recovery vehicles attempted to pull out the tanks that blocked the road or build a bypass. Harassed by German fire, these efforts went for naught. Midmorning on December 1, Daniel confided to the regimental operations officer, "I can't see any reason why the men could hold out in town. . . . They didn't have any protection against those enemy tanks in town. I can't imagine them holding out." The regiment never learned precisely what happened, but when part of Seitz's 1st Battalion reached the edge of the village, they found empty foxholes and abandoned equipment. The regimental after-action report on the matter is laconic: "By midafternoon, the two companies plus the two supporting heavy weapons platoons of Company H were definitely given up as lost." The division learned from prisoners that the troops in Merode held out until they ran out of ammunition and then surrendered.[60]

The Last Act in the Hürtgen

The 1st ID never did take Merode but managed to clear other exits at Langerwehe and Jungersdorf on December 1, 1944. On December 2, Collins ordered 1st ID to attack the following day "in coordination with the 104th Infantry Division on its left to seize the Luchem area." That village lay just north of Langerwehe, south of an autobahn that ran west–east less than four more miles from the Roer. The order was no surprise, as Collins and Huebner had had this in mind for some time. Lieutenant Colonel Frederick W. Gibb had issued a warning order to Lieutenant Colonel Driscoll on November 29. Finally there seemed to be a way out of the woods, and some time to prepare.[61]

Driscoll's battalion had paid dearly for the twelve hundred yards it advanced in the first few days of the offensive. He brought his battalion out of the line on November 19 with only 380 effectives of an authorized strength of 860—35 officers and 825 men. The battalion absorbed 400 replacements and returned to the fight on November 23. It took more losses to reach Langerwehe on November 28. When Driscoll received Gibb's warning order, he was in good shape, theoretically, with 34 officers and 750 enlisted soldiers assigned. A battalion report written soon after the war argued that end strength "was a deceptive criterion on which to rate efficiency." Driscoll and his leadership had too little time "to whip what was practically a new battalion into shape." The report argued that "a handful of officers, noncommissioned officers and soldiers in each company did the fighting. . . . The main body of the company was excess baggage."[62]

On receipt of the warning order, Driscoll assembled his leadership. These included his company commanders and his artillery liaison officer.

Supporting platoon leaders from a tank platoon, tank destroyer platoon, and two antitank platoons rounded out the team. Together they planned reconnaissance and developed a preliminary concept. They also had the advantage of being able to see Luchem from Langerwehe. After two days of reconnaissance and preparation, Driscoll reassembled the team at 1155 on December 2 to issue his order.[63]

Driscoll identified the enemy as the newly arrived 3rd FJD, whose troops were, he said, "green and young." He provided grid coordinates to defensive positions, including a machine gun hidden in a haystack. Furthermore, he warned that there might be two or three tanks in the village. He also described the planned action of the 104th ID, which would attack that night. Units on his immediate left and right would not be attacking. Driscoll described the mission in a straightforward way: "We are attacking the town of Luchem tomorrow morning; at six o'clock, I believe is the best time for it. That will get us across the open ground into the edge of town before daylight." Driscoll also decided to go with no artillery preparation. The orders briefing including questions was over in "15–20 minutes."[64]

The battalion moved out the following morning as planned, with "new guys" being coached as necessary. A and B Companies led the way, moving abreast, enveloping the town from the east. Initially the paratroopers put up a good fight from well-prepared positions. Driscoll decided the affair by committing his armor. Both the tank platoon and tank destroyer platoon "roared down the road to Luchem." Most of the paratroopers surrendered when the tanks came in, but "others continued to fight and were mopped up by combined tank-infantry work." In the process they took more than a hundred prisoners.[65]

After clearing the town, the battalion prepared for the inevitable counterattack. Paratroopers, supported by six tanks or assault guns, attacked at 1430. The battalion's mortars, augmented by two captured German 120s, supported by four battalions of artillery, broke up the attack, while small arms fire took care of those who got through. Three hours later, Driscoll's troops had destroyed the better part of two companies. Success, the commander believed, stemmed from thorough planning and effective leadership at company and platoon level. Newly arrived replacements well led can produce what Driscoll thought was "a most impressive achievement."[66]

The day before the attack on Luchem, Collins told Huebner that the 1st ID had "done all that could be expected." The division would be relieved and given the opportunity to rest, less the 16th Infantry and its supporting attachments. These units remained to support the 9th ID for a short time.

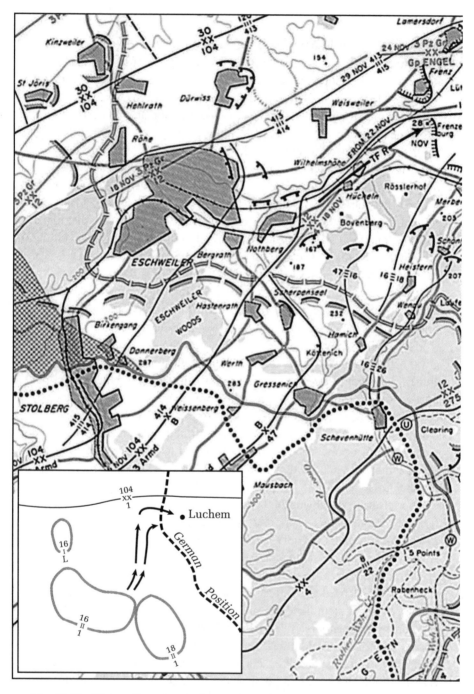

Map 23: The Hürtgen Forest, November 16–December 9, 1944. Reproduced and edited with Luchem insert from MacDonald, *The Siegfried Line Campaign*, Map VI.

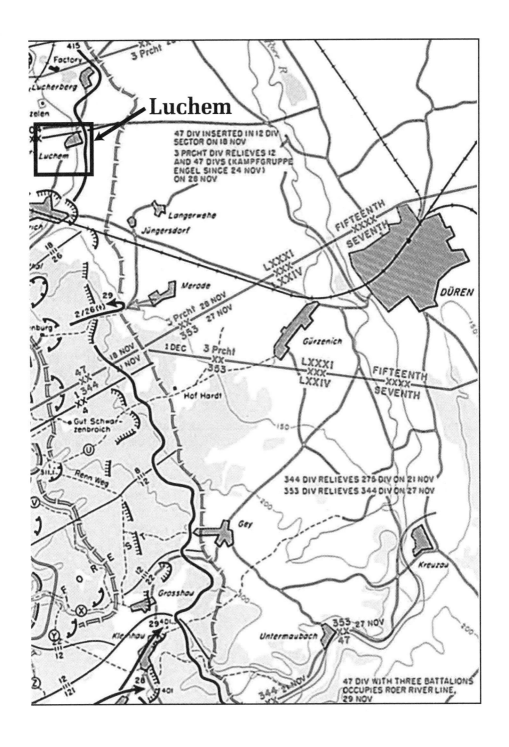

Luchem

415
Factory
(Lucherberg)
zelen
Luchem

47 DIV INSERTED IN 12 DIV
SECTOR ON 18 NOV
3 PRCHT DIV RELIEVES 12
AND 47 DIVS (KAMPFGRUPPE
ENGEL SINCE 24 NOV)
ON 28 NOV

Langerwehe
Jüngersdorf

FIFTEENTH
XXXX
SEVENTH

DÜREN

Merode
29
2/26(t)
3 Prcht 28 NOV
XX 27 NOV
353

LXXXI
XXX
XXIV

Gürzenich

18 NOV
1 NOV
1 DEC
3 Prcht
XX
353

LXXXI
XXX
LXXIV

FIFTEENTH
XXXX
SEVENTH

nburg

47
XX
344
XX
A
Gut Schwar-
zenbroich
Hof Hardt
150

SILI.
Renn Weg
8
12

344 DIV RELIEVES 275 DIV ON 21 NOV
353 DIV RELIEVES 344 DIV ON 27 NOV

U

Gef

FOREST

12
22

Kreuzau

Grosshau
X
Y

Untermaubach

353 27 NOV
XX
47

Kleinhau
294 01.
28
401

344 29 NOV
XX

47 DIV WITH THREE BATTALIONS
OCCUPIES ROER RIVER LINE,
29 NOV

The 9th ID relieved the Big Red One over the course of three days, completing the task on December 7. Two of the 16th's battalions and the regimental headquarters came out of the line on December 11, and the last on December 13. Most of the troops moved into a tent city near Aubel, Belgium, although the 18th Infantry billeted in Belgium homes in and around Plombiers. The troops enjoyed showers, USO shows and movies, and best of all sleeping warm and without fear of shelling or attack.[67]

The troops needed the rest, and their units needed time to integrate replacements, many of whom were not trained infantrymen. During just over two weeks of fighting the division had advanced not quite seven miles and barely managed to emerge from the woods. It had destroyed both the 12th and 47th VGD, but that success came at great cost. Charles B. MacDonald did the reckoning for the 1st ID in the official history. Advancing about four miles had cost 3,993 battle casualties. The 47th Infantry attached from 9th ID lost 641 more. A 3rd AD task force attached briefly lost another 101. The 26th suffered most, with 1,479. Of these 163 were killed, and 261 missing, most from the ill-fated Companies E and F. These losses do not include hundreds more nonbattle casualties, from causes including trench foot, various illnesses, and accidents.[68]

In accordance with Huebner's conviction about training and rest, both would occur in balance. Rest and maintenance took priority, but the shift to training occurred quickly. Like the rest of the division, the 26th Infantry published detailed training plans. On December 9 the regiment published the plan for December 11–23, with squad drills focused on "Target designation and Fire orders," "Creeping and Crawling," and other basic skills. The intent was to emulate the "gun drill that an artilleryman goes through." In short, fundamentals should be automatic. Battalions were told to focus training on "Squad and Platoon" combat problems. Officer and noncommissioned officer classes were to focus on "Battle Experience" and "Critique of previous actions," as well as basic leadership. There was more, much more, including schools for snipers, practice with the Browning automatic rifle, and training for cannon company and other specialists.[69]

On December 11 Huebner reported to V Corps as deputy commanding general. In January he took command of V Corps in place of Leonard T. Gerow, who assumed command of the newly organized Fifteenth US Army. Clift Andrus took command of the Big Red One in Huebner's stead. Andrus, sometimes called Mr. Chips after his similarity to the schoolmaster made famous in the movie *Goodbye Mister Chips*, had served with the 1st Division through all of its campaigns, first with his childhood friend Terry Allen, and

since October 1943 with Huebner. Donald McBurney Curtis, one of his officers, claimed that Andrus was heard to say that the basic load (ammunition
for three days' firing) for an artillery unit was "all the ammo they can carry
without having to shuttle trucks." Andrus, like Allen and Huebner, was physically courageous, cool under fire, and a proven artillery officer.[70]

Andrus was somewhat reserved and had a desert-sands-dry sense of humor. After the war he was asked a to give a short address at a soiree. He
began by saying, "My address is Quarters 1, Fort Sill." He waited for that to
sink in before continuing. He like to gather his key staff for a "quiet hour,"
have a drink, and discuss key matters at hand. He toasted always, "Here's
to us. Good men are few." When Huebner left, he took Stanhope B. Mason
with him. On January 7 Andrus brought Colonel Verdi B. Barnes, who had
served with the division from the outset of combat landing in Algeria in
command of the 33rd FA, from division artillery to replace Mason. Barnes
then served as Andrus's executive officer in the division artillery. Lieutenant
Colonel Clarence E. Beck, the G-3, served as acting chief of staff in the interim. Colonel William E. Waters replaced Andrus in the division artillery. The
division's rest would be short. The Germans were on the verge of launching
a dramatic counteroffensive that demonstrated once again their "astonishing
capacity for recuperation."[71]

Fire in the Forest Redux
German Planning and Preparation for the Counteroffensive

Hugh Cole, the US Army's official historian of the Battle of the Bulge, wrote
that Adolf Hitler was "a fanatical believer in the Clausewitzian doctrine of
the offensive as the purest and only decisive form of war." About the time of
the Mortain counterattack, Hitler announced his intention to mount a counteroffensive in the west. Preparations for the offensive continued throughout
the year in spite of Soviet and Allied offensives, culminating at the same time
First Army was fighting bloody battles in the Hürtgen and clearing Aachen.
In his postwar memoir, Walter Warlimont, deputy chief of staff of operations, OKW, wrote that "by the end of September—early October OKW's
preliminary studies had produced the conclusion that the area Monschau-
Echternach offered the best prospects" for success. Hitler decided on Antwerp as the objective with two purposes in mind: to preclude the use of the
port and separate the British and US Army Groups.[72]

OKW produced an outline plan, "Order for Assembly and Concentration
of the Attack (Ardennes Counteroffensive)." Rundstedt at OB West learned
the broad outline of the plan as OKW did its preliminary studies. Siegfried

Westphal, Rundstedt's chief of staff, was surprised by the level of detail and the promises made in terms of fuel, air support, supplies, and troops. OB West was "told verbally that about twenty infantry divisions and ten Panzer Divisions," along with combat support formations, would be available at the end of November or the beginning of December. Debate over the details of the plan continued despite Hitler's declaration that "the operation is *unalterable in every detail*."[73]

Model's Army Group B would employ three field armies in the counteroffensive. These included Fifth and Sixth Panzer Armies, respectively, commanded by Manteuffel and Dietrich, and Seventh Army, commanded by General der Panzertruppen Erich Brandenberger. Fifth Panzer Army had four corps headquarters; the Sixth had three, as did as did the Seventh. OKW and the Ersatzheer (Replacement Army) provided close to the promised number of divisions. Ten mobile divisions (Panzer or Panzergrenadier) and seventeen infantry divisions, two of which were rebuilt Fallschirmjäger divisions, the Führer Begleit (Escort) Brigade, the Führer Grenadier Brigade, and the 150th Panzer Brigade completed the ground combat forces order of battle. Considerable supporting arms, including an impressive amount of artillery and reasonable air support, rounded out the forces provided.[74]

Virtually all of the units deployed for the counteroffensive required enormous effort to rebuild. The 12th SS PZ Hitler Jugend Division was one of 1st ID's chief antagonists during the Battle of the Bulge. Badly mauled in France and the frontier fighting, the 12th SS withdrew to refit in Germany on October 14. It had to replace nine thousand officers and men killed, wounded, or missing. When it withdrew, the division turned over most of its heavy equipment to units still fighting, so it had also to replace most of its artillery, tanks, and half-tracks. Like their American counterparts, wounded SS troopers hoped to return to their original units. One noncommissioned officer quit the hospital without release and sneaked back to his unit despite having a shell fragment still in his heart.[75]

The Ersatzheer found two thousand replacements from the Luftwaffe and Kriegsmarine and others from administrative services and wherever they could be identified. Despite the situation, morale was good. Artur Axman wrote his family with great pride and patriotism about the ceremony during which he received his 12th SS sleeve band—the equivalent of a division patch. He was delighted with the speech a Nazi functionary gave describing the "previous heroic battles by our division." This did not include, of course, anecdotes about shooting Canadian prisoners in Normandy. Axman wrote that he was pleased to learn that the führer held the division in "highest esteem."[76]

When the attack came, Sepp Dietrich's Sixth Panzer Army made the main effort. The army group plan required Sixth PZ Army to pass along five routes westward through Eifel, the Hohe Venn, and finally into open ground. West of the Hohe Venn, these routes were inadequate for his five mobile divisions (4 PZ and 1 PZG). Dietrich's complaints about the mission, the inexperience of his troops, his zone, and his routes are often quoted. Speaking of the latter, he observed, "There isn't room to deploy four tanks abreast, let alone armored divisions." Nevertheless, the counteroffensive would begin on December 16, with Sixth Panzer Army attacking in the north to cross the Meuse and turn toward Antwerp. Manteuffel's Fifth PZ would attack on Dietrich's left, while Brandenberger and Seventh Army provided flank guard in the south.[77]

Fire in the Forest Redux
Rest, Reconstitution, and Training in 1st ID

The Battle of the Bulge is the largest ground battle fought by the United States in World War II. The only other battles anything like it in scale are those fought by Pershing's troops in the fall of 1918. Two thousand tanks and half a million combatants fought for six weeks in cold, snow-covered, rugged ground. The Luftwaffe mounted its last major effort in the west. The Americans suffered 80,000 casualties, including 8,607 killed in action. German casualties were slightly higher. The German Army's losses are not known with certainty, but multiple sources cite the numbers as 12,652 killed, 38,600 wounded, and 30,582 missing. Like Gettysburg, the Battle of the Bulge has almost mythic qualities and stands as a memorial to American courage. In terms of despair and misery, it was the Hürtgen rather than the Ardennes that was the Garden of Gethsemane for what some troops called the "Bloody Red One." The Battle of the Bulge served that purpose for First Army and the 28th Infantry Division that fought in the Ardennes.[78]

By no means as ravaged as the 12th SS, the 1st ID too needed time to rest, reconstitute, and train. It had days, not weeks. On December 16 Daniel's 2nd Battalion, 26th Infantry, was billeted in Aubel and executing the training plan cited above. It also had to rebuild half of the battalion. Captain Thomas J. Gendron, Daniel's operations officer, reported that by December 16 Companies E and F "had been brought up to about 100 men each." Gendron believed roughly ninety men of each company were new, while the rest had escaped the debacle at Merode. The two heavy weapons platoons had only eight survivors of sixty-four authorized. According to Gendron, only nine officers remained of those that landed on D-Day. There were of course others who had arrived since. The battalion was short heavy weapons, grenade launchers, and Browning automatic weapons.[79]

Most of the 1st Division had a week or more to rest, refit, and train. The 16th Infantry did not. First Army kept the 16th in the Hürtgen fight, attached to V Corps, until December 11, when all but the 2nd Battalion moved to the rest area. The 2nd Battalion reached the rest area on December 13. The last unit to come out, Company C, 634th TD, arrived on December 14. Nothing untoward marred December 16. "Rest and rehabilitation" continued even for the 2nd Battalion. South of the division's rest areas, the German counteroffensive began with a dazzling light show along the eastern horizon at 0530. Soon after, projectiles fired from nearly two thousand guns and howitzers impacted all along the roughly eighty miles from Monschau to Echternach. German infantry followed on the heels of the preparation fires, with searchlight beams aimed at the low clouds to provide artificial moonlight for the attackers.[80]

The Northern Shoulder

The Germans achieved complete surprise, even though the Allies had observed the buildup of reserves and identified their assembly areas. Arguments among the participants as to why the Germans proved able to surprise the SHAEF, 12th Army Group, and First Army abounded, then and ever since, in part because the pattern of assembly areas was highly ambiguous. The explanations are simple in retrospect. First and foremost, the Allies assumed the Germans could not or would not attempt such a thing; to them, it made no sense. The Allies believed that the best use of the arriving German reserves would be to defend the Reich, and consequently they discounted the possibility of a counteroffensive. Finally, the Germans practiced secrecy and executed an elaborate deception plan that the Allies bought entirely because it suited their bias.[81]

Surprise and superiority at the point of attack are nearly axiomatic in Clausewitz's theory on war. Surprise, he argues, comes from secrecy and speed. At the outset, the Germans enjoyed both, but surprise wears off and speed works both ways. On December 16 Dwight D. Eisenhower, alone among the senior commanders, recognized the danger, acting speedily and decisively. He and Bradley were together in Verdun, discussing the problem of infantry replacements, when reports of the attack arrived around noon. Eisenhower's vision and decisions that day proved that he was more than worthy of the challenge. By the end of the first day, he and Bradley had committed the 82nd and 101st Airborne Divisions, as well as the 7th Armored

Division from Ninth Army and the 10th Armored Division from Third Army. The speed of his reaction took advantage also of the demonstrated ability of the US Army to move rapidly in response to clear orders.[82]

In accordance with the then current intention to remain on the offensive, several American corps, including both V and VII Corps in First Army, had local attacks planned. None were called off, because Hodges and his staff believed the action in the Ardennes might be a spoiling attack rather than a counteroffensive. Even so, Hodges acted before the end of the day. At 1630 VII Corps ordered 1st ID to be prepared to move on six hours' notice and, with not atypical micromanagement, ordered the 26th Infantry attached to V Corps, effective midnight. At 0230 on the 17th, the 3rd Battalion, 26th Infantry, headed south from Aubel to Camp Elsenborn, a Belgian Army post some thirty miles southeast. The rest of the regiment followed soon after. Rumors of a German parachute landing caused delay, but 3rd Battalion arrived in Camp Elsenborn at 0700. Two hours later the division headed south. Gardner Botsford, the G-2 staff officer who so eloquently described the destruction of Aachen, did equally well on returning to the fight. Of the move he wrote, "The First Division—unrested and unrepaired—was ordered south to stop the Germans from coming up the main road heading to Liège."[83]

The Germans coming up the road were the I SS PZ Corps, commanded by SS Gruppenführer Hermann Priess. The corps attacked with three infantry divisions abreast to break through the recently arrived 99th ID. The 277th VGD attacked in the north toward Elsenborn, the 12th VGD in the center toward Nidrum, and the 3rd FJD in the south toward Schoppen. The 3rd FJD came west along the southern most route assigned to Sixth Panzer Army. The 1st and 12th SS PZ followed, with 1st SS on the southern or left flank and 12th SS on the right on or northern flank. On December 16 the three infantry divisions forced the 99th back but achieved no penetration. Of the fight between Engel's rebuilt 12th VGD and Lauer's 99th ID at Losheimergraben, Priess observed that "the enemy troops in occupation defended themselves fiercely and skillfully.[84]

When the 26th Infantry arrived at Camp Elsenborn, Lieutenant Colonel Edwin Sutherland was acting commander, as Colonel Seitz had gone on leave. Sutherland was fully up to the task. With Lieutenant Colonel Francis Murdoch Jr., wounded in August but now back with the regiment, absent without leave from a convalescent center and acting as his second, he traveled to the 99th ID command post. They found the post in an uproar, for very good reasons in light of events. According to Murdoch, when Sutherland

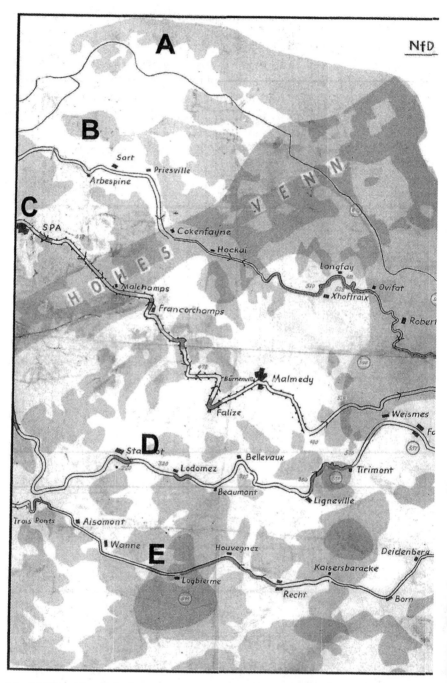

Map 24: Wegeskizze Teil I (Route sketch part I). Reproduced and edited to add
Route Letters and Elsenborn from an artifact showing the German Route Sketch for
6th Panzer Army. Original map located at the Dwight D. Eisenhower Library.

WEGESKIZZE TEIL I

PANZERVERBÄNDE

Maßstab 1:100 000

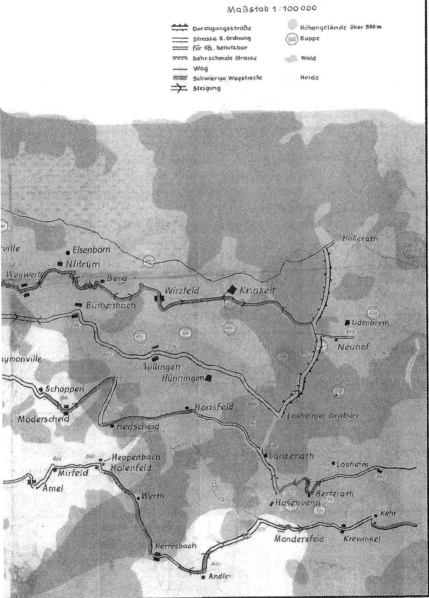

walked in, the din in the place subsided. Sutherland was an impressive figure. Tall and lean, he sported a very broad red handlebar mustache. Wearing the Blue Spade crests of the 26th Infantry and the Big Red One patch, he announced in a loud voice, "You need worry no longer. The 1st Division is here. Everything is under control."[85]

Despite Sutherland's assurances, 99th ID commander Major General Walter E. Lauer and the "Battle Babies," as his men called themselves, had earned their pay. Lauer positioned the 26th Infantry in Butgenbach, Belgium, where they blocked two of Sixth Panzer Army's routes. The 99th's stand on the Elsenborn ridge enabled the 1st ID, and eventually the 2nd ID, to arrive in time to form a shoulder along the northern flank of the German main effort. In the official history, Hugh Cole points out that army doctrine, based on Great War experience, held that if the defenders held the shoulders of penetration, it could be contained and reduced. Indeed, FM 100-5 *Operations* specified, "The shoulders must be held at all costs." First Army intended to do just that.[86]

The 26th Infantry established positions at a right angle to the 99th. The 2nd ID moved in between the depleted regiments of the 99th and the 26th while the 16th came in on the right, and the 30th ID on their right. V Corps used the 18th Infantry to sweep the rear for enemy paratroopers from the parachute assault conducted in the early morning hours of December 17. Led by Oberst Friedrich von der Heydte, the jump achieved little beyond tying up the 18th Infantry for a short time. First Army was following army doctrine; now all that remained was for the troops to arrive in time and actually hold the shoulders.

Because the 1st ID had moved "unrepaired," replacements showed up just in time to head south. Carrol Ed Beadenkopf arrived in Le Havre, France, on December 5. He and other replacements were on the French-Belgian border on December 16. "That same day a bunch of us were issued on clip of ammunition for our rifles, loaded onto trucks, and moved to a front line outfit," he recalled. As he and truckloads of disoriented replacements moved forward, they found "the roads jammed with men and equipment coming back to regroup, and the retreating troops hollered to tell us what was ahead. We went through the cities of Liege and Eupen, and arrived in the 1st Division sector at night." A colonel with a flashlight assigned Beadenkopf to Company F, 1st Battalion, 16th Infantry, the battalion decimated defending Dawson's Ridge. He joined an understrength rifle squad and was well received, but he had to learn on the job.[87]

Beadenkopf's experience getting to the front was not unusual. On arriving and joining a unit, most replacements received a warm welcome. Even during the Bulge, leaders attempted to pair rookies with veterans and do what could be done to integrate them. Veteran Private First Class William M. Lee, Company D, 1st Battalion, 26th Infantry, said he and the other veterans "felt pity and compassion for replacements . . . we tried our best to keep them alive . . . to survive and fight another day." Staff Sergeant Rocco J. Moretto in Company C recalled that "replacements we got in combat were always eager to please and paid attention to what they were told and were apprehensive. . . . On the whole replacements were quite effective, although during the Bulge and some other times we received replacements that were poorly trained." New soldiers arriving during the Battle of the Bulge often were reclassified from some other military specialty and arrived with little infantry training.[88]

The Americans built the northern shoulder more quickly than the Germans could break through or flank the defenses. Andrus and Danger Forward headed south on December 17. By 2000 that evening Danger Forward had set up in Sourbrodt, Belgium, ready to take over the sector, including the 26th Infantry. By then the 1st, 9th, and 30th ID had joined V Corps. Andrus advised Seitz, "As soon as we get tied in, we are going to take you over. Haven't got much support. Would like to get a picture of what you are doing." Seitz replied with a clear and concise situation report. 1st ID was back in the fight and would soon have all of its regiments.[89]

When alerted to move, Andrus had a problem. He needed a mobile battle group to support a V Corps tasking. He couldn't use the 745th TB because it had thirty-three of fifty-three Sherman tanks down for maintenance, battle damaged, or destroyed. Andrus solved his problem by organizing a task force around the 634th TD commanded by Henry L. Davisson, an able officer, in command since the battalion came ashore on June 30, 1944. Task Force Davisson had the 634th's staff, its reconnaissance company, the light tank company of the 745th with seventeen Stuart tanks, and four 75-millimeter assault guns, the 745th TB's 81-millimeter mortar platoon and assault gun platoon, one platoon of the 703rd TD, and two platoons from Company B, 1st Engineers.[90]

Davisson's goal was "to seize, occupy and hold the town of Weismes [Waimes is the more common spelling], Belgium until the 47th EVAC hospital had been evacuated and the ammunition in the ASP # 125 had been evacuated or until TF D relieved by friendly troops." Alfred A. Alvarez

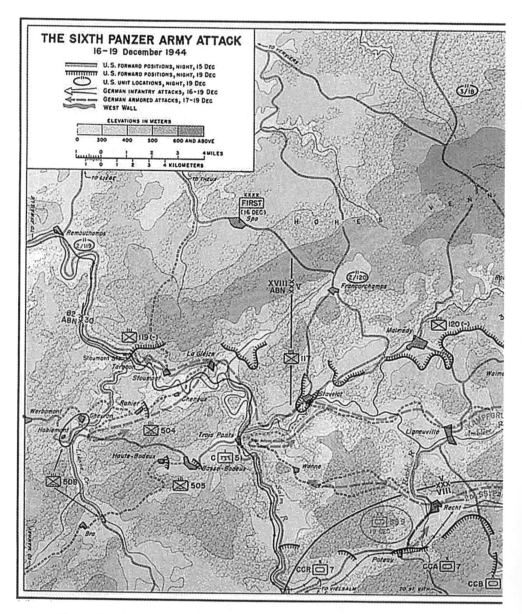

Map 25: The 6th Panzer Army Attack, December 16–19, 1944. Reproduced from Hugh M. Cole, *The Ardennes: Battle of the Bulge* (Washington: Center of Military History, 1965), Map II.

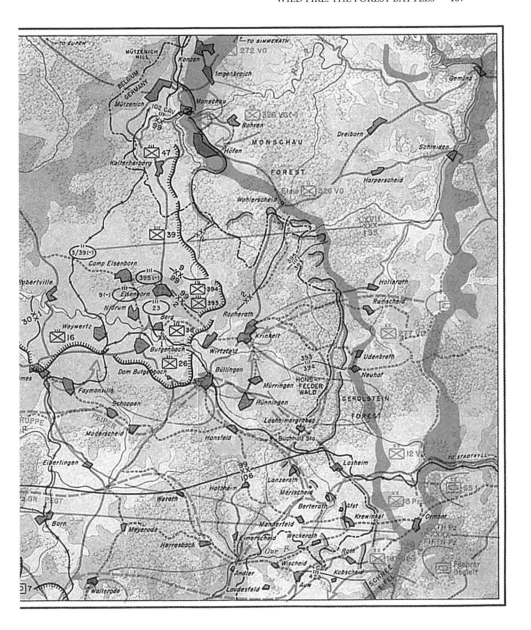

remembered Davisson as an "aggressive commander." He gave simple and clear guidance: "Recon you find 'em; engineers you fix 'em; tanks you fight 'em and TDs you finish 'em." With that guidance the motley force moved with all but the one platoon from 703rd TD who joined them en route. There was no time to waste assembling before moving.[91]

TF Davisson reached Waimes about 1700 on December 17, long after the soldiers assigned to the 47th had decamped or been captured. The task force did manage to save much of the equipment and the ASP. The following day, TF Davisson joined the 16th Infantry as it extended the defenses on the northern shoulder westward. For the 26th Infantry the fighting turned ugly at dawn on December 19. Rocco Moretto, manning an observation post, claimed that "as far as your eye could see German tanks were coming over the rise firing their machine guns as they came." Morretto and Company C had been attached to Derrill M. Daniel's 2nd Battalion defending Butgenbach, Belgium. In fact, Morretto and his squad shared the building with Daniel's command post. Thinking back on the battle, Moretto said, "There is no doubt in my mind that Colonel Daniels [sic] almost single handedly slowed down the German advance until reinforcements arrived and began to build on our positions." Daniel achieved this feat by personally directing effective fires on tanks and infantry of Kampfgruppe Kuhlman from the 12th SS.[92]

Two tanks penetrated the infantry and reached the village of Dom Butgenbach. Once there, they approached the building that Moretto shared with Daniel. Unfazed, Daniel told Moretto to keep him informed of the tanks' doings. One young soldier worked his way up onto the roof and disabled one tank with a bazooka. The second withdrew. Daniel's antitank platoon scored some kills with their British-made discarding sabot rounds. The British-made rounds afforded a velocity of 4,200 feet per second, which could penetrate six inches of armor. The 12th SS report on the action notes that the attackers received heavy antitank and artillery fire. The 560th Panzerjäger Battalion supported the attack. One company commander lost his Jagdpanzer and had to dragoon a replacement from a subordinate to continue the attack. The battalion commander also lost his combat vehicle, but the infantry suffered most. The SS withdrew with the Panzerjäger battalion, leaving about half their antitank guns ablaze on the field.[93]

Over the next several days the 26th Infantry fought off numerous attacks from the 12th SS. In several instances tanks and/or antitank guns broke through the lines, but the 26th's veterans kept themselves and their "new guys" in their holes with confidence that the regiment would restore the lines. During that first major action on December 20, the 1st Battalion exacted revenge for Merode. According to the regimental account, "There was grim satisfaction in the sight of row upon row of German Dead that lay in front of their positions; of blazing tanks that lay to their front and behind them." The 12th SS PZ duly reported that defeat. The SS renewed the attack the next day. An SS tank crewman described the chief reasons for this next defeat: "Abruptly, an almost indescribably devasting fire from the American artillery set in . . . a number of panzers took direct hits. Renewed and well-aimed anti-tank fire" joined in.[94]

The 16th Infantry moved south on December 18 to the vicinity of Waimes. The following day Lieutenant Colonel Charles T. Horner Jr., still commanding the 3rd Battalion, captured two German paratroopers (probably from the 3rd FJD) who were guarding some 47th EVAC prisoners. At first the 16th had no contact to speak of, so it sent patrols toward Faymonville, which they found "swarming with the enemy including tanks." The 16th moved in, dug in, and as Sam Fuller put it, "fought like hell and held on." In Fuller's mind and that of others, including the G-2 1st ID, this was a chance to redeem what happened at Kasserine Pass, and they did.[95]

After swanning about looking for German paratroopers, the 18th moved into the line between the 26th and 16th, straddling the north-south road that led to Schoppen. On December 22 they too stopped a 12th SS PZ attack. By December 23 the Americans had stabilized the northern shoulder, more or less. When it arrived, the 30th ID extended the line to the right of the Big Red One. The 82nd Airborne came next, along with the 3rd AD and XVIII Airborne Corps Headquarters. Priess had planned to break through with his infantry divisions and use the 1st and 12th SS PZ Divisions to exploit. Instead, attempting to break through was fast using up the 12th SS PZ. On December 20, II SS Panzer Corps took over the 12th SS and the waning effort to break through at Butgenbach in order to keep the effort on the left flank of the Sixth Panzer Army afloat. Preiss received the 21st PZ to continue westward, but the end of the advance was already in sight.[96]

The End in Sight

Obersturmbahnführer Joachim Peiper, leading the main effort with about six thousand men, 117 tanks, 149 half-tracks, and two artillery batteries, had the bulk of the 1st SS PZ Division's combat power. Peiper was strung out and pecked away at by American units as he headed west, and combat engineers denied him key bridges along the way. On December 19 the 30th ID's 117th

Infantry made contact with Peiper at Stavelot on the Amblève River and stopped him for good. Desperate efforts to break through to him continued, but effectively his moment had passed.[97]

The German counteroffensive failed in large part because their assault formations failed to take key first-day objectives, including the critical road junction at Saint-Vith, Belgium. That failure bought time for the Americans to respond. The Germans fell behind their schedule and never caught up. Better-than-expected performance by new units like the 99th ID and outstanding performance by units such as the 28th ID, another recovering veteran of the Hürtgen, contributed to slowing the Germans. Inadequate roads, poor march discipline and very bad traffic management led to both Model and von Manteuffel directing traffic to unsnarl traffic jams—or *Staus*, in German slang—of epic proportions. But most importantly, the speed with which the US Army reacted and the professionalism of the bulk of its units was more than a match for its adversaries.

The surrender of two regiments of the 106th ID in the Schnee Eifel on December 20 sent a shock through the US Army. It was a worse disaster than Kasserine Pass, and comparable only to the surrender in the Philippines. The massacre at Malmedy and other outrages perpetrated by Kampfgruppe Peiper enraged the Americans and no doubt prompted American misbehavior as well. The misery in the Ardennes did not end when First and Third Army linked up on January 16, 1945. The end of the campaign arguably should be marked when the Germans had all recrossed their start points in February, or when the 7th Armored Division retook Saint-Vith, but January 16 tied it up with a bow.[98]

On December 18, before there was any reason to be particularly optimistic, Eisenhower sent cables to Bradley at 12th Army Group and Devers at 6th Army Group. He sent a separate cable to Montgomery at 21st Army Group. In these messages he announced his intentions; specifically, "to take immediate action to check the enemy advance; to launch a counter-offensive without delay with all forces north of the Moselle." He then followed with concise orders for each of the three army groups. Eisenhower's vision during the darkest hours of the Battle of the Bulge reflected intellect and courage; he had what Clausewitz described as "glimmerings of the inner light which leads to truth and second the courage to follow this faint light where ever it may lead."[99]

On Christmas Eve, Peiper and the less than eight hundred of his original six thousand men still with him abandoned what equipment they had remaining and exfiltrated their encircled position on foot. The Americans had held the northern shoulder just as doctrine required. The army did what it else it could do, including giving its troops a Christmas dinner. In the 16th Infantry, Arthur G. Heidrick faithfully reported to his diary that dinner on Saturday, December 25, was "excellent." Bert H. Morphis in the 26th Infantry ate his standing in a stable, with "the cattle looking on. It was great."[100]

Tragedy and misery continued, abated only by moments like Christmas dinner. Nathaniel Broadhead joined the 26th Infantry on December 23. About 1500 on Christmas Eve, his squad leader came by to check on him. As he approached Broadhead's hole, he "spotted a German patrol coming." The squad leader joined Broadhead in the foxhole and "killed six Germans right in front of my eyes." Christmas Day, though, Broadhead too ate Christmas dinner. Three days later he finally had time to change his socks. When he did, he noted, "my toenails wanted to come with them." Broadhead, like thousands of others, had immersion foot. He stuck it out, and he too learned how to fight.[101]

From Christmas Day until January 15, the 1st ID daily reports generally ended with the following phrase: "The 1st US Infantry Division continued to consolidate and improve defensive positions, using mines and a barbed wire." The daily update included overlays showing the positions of units. The regiments patrolled aggressively to maintain contact with the enemy and pushed out listening and observation posts as far as one thousand yards, but the action had moved farther west. Occasionally opportune targets presented themselves. On December 27, the division artillery struck hard at a German column in which "the vehicles are bumper to bumper." Four battalions of artillery fired a time-on-target mission. An airborne artillery observer learned that the Luftwaffe had not given up when he was shot down by a fighter. "The Cub [light observation airplane] was riddled, the radio damaged but the observer lost only his bar [lieutenant's rank insignia]," the daily summary reported. The enemy dispersed. The G-2 also noted that on January 2 the division encountered "another old acquaintance," a regiment of the 12th VGD.[102]

On January 3 the First US Army returned to the offensive to reduce the salient or bulge. The attack rippled from right to left, or west to east. Collins's VII Corps led off well to the west. The XVIII Airborne Corps attacked on January 13. 1st ID and V Corps followed on January 15 to protect the left flank of the 7th Armored Division and XVIII Airborne Corps. The attack occurred in snow as much as five feet deep in drifts. The infantry struggled to move. Loaded down with the necessities of combat, they could make "no more than 300 yards without stopping to rest." But now, schooled by the hard schools of Aachen and the Hürtgen, the division's leaders and veterans knew how to operate in forests.[103]

Reflections on Fighting in Forests

New to fighting in forests in the fall of 1944, the 1st ID had become good, if not expert. Two pages of advice on how to operate in the forest garnered from the 9th ID in October grew to a far denser paper that General Taylor produced in December. In its first sentence, Taylor's study asserts that the division's tactical methods in the attack had been "in many cases wrong." German artillery proved particularly effective in forests primarily because of the proliferation of artillery observers and the use of preplanned concentrations—preplanned, because that was the likely explanation for fires that included "every type of weapon from light mortars and field pieces to large calibre railroad guns."[104]

Tactically, early on 1st ID units operated as "they had been trained to do, our troops generally used *close formations* [italics in original]. " Germans defended in a series of outposts rather than in a line, with the result that they decimated close formations with automatic weapons and artillery. The Germans exacted a high price among supporting units as they fired on areas "where they expected weapons, communications and headquarters personnel to be." The Germans had learned to anticipate American tactics as surely as the Americans knew to expect German counterattacks to retake positions.[105]

The study's conclusions had effect. Dispersion rather than close formations became the rule. The study recommended that a squad serve as advance guard for platoons moving through woods to reduce the probability of getting an entire platoon in a kill zone. Among many other findings, the study concluded that 81-millimeter mortars were the best means of providing rapid fire support and so should be "held in battery." Communications problems could not be solved with the means authorized by the table of organization and equipment. Additional radios and communicators had to be provided when attacking in forests.[106]

Reducing the Salient

Whether all of the ideas that Taylor's study defined as "correct" were applied cannot be proven with available data. What is clear is that many of these "lessons" were adopted and used during the counterattack to push the

Germans from the Bulge. To get that job done, the 1st ID infantry waded through snow drifts and through forests in their now well-defined combined arms formations. The task of the 1st ID was to clear the Ondenval corridor, a valley that ran south of the village by the same name. The 7th Armored Division passed forward and continued south while the 1st ID went on the defensive to protect the 7th AD and XVIII Airborne Corps' flank. The 7th Armored Division, led by Major General Robert W. Hasbrouck, retook the important crossroads town of Saint-Vith on January 23, just over a month from when they were finally driven out after a memorable stand against the elements of both Fifth and Sixth Panzer Armies. Earlier on January 13, units of First and Third Armies linked up at Houffalize. By the end of January, the Germans had been driven back across their start lines, and for the second time the 1st ID turned east and headed back toward the Siegfried Line and the Hürtgen forest.[107]

During the last half of January, it was the Germans who attempted to hold the shoulders so their units could withdraw. They fought gamely despite the G-2 finding evidence of low morale in some units. In his contemporary assessment, Evans asserted that "at no point did [the German] retreat without pressure, no matter whether he held good or poor defensive terrain." In more than one instance, German prisoners "expressed surprise that the Division had been able to attack at all" in the bitter weather. The weather plagued both sides. The attack to reduce the Bulge occurred primarily in forest or over open ground, with relatively few "villages or houses to shelter the troops." In some cases, units went two or three days with "no more shelter than they could dig for themselves in the frozen ground."[108]

The division did not rate high marks for integration and training during the reduction of the salient. The conditions simply did not permit it. Jim Sharp arrived with other rookies in Le Havre, France, on January 5. First by train, then by truck, then by jeep, and finally wading through snow, he made his way to the front. He and four replacements made the penultimate leg of their way forward in a jeep. They moved out after midnight during a blizzard, carrying hot chow for Company B, 18th Infantry. From where the company was feeding, they went forward on foot, each "with a hand on the shoulder of the soldier in front of him" through foot-and-a-half-deep snow, with drifts as deep as four feet.[109]

On arriving at a smoke-filled but warm dugout at the front, they met two weary, grizzled, unshaven sergeants named Zilish and Angel, their platoon leader and platoon sergeant. They were oriented on the situation and taught to say "Kommen sie hier mit hande hoch" (Come here with your hands up).

Zilish then took Sharp and James W. Rogers, his new best friend, farther forward, where he put them in a hole full of snow and gave last-minute instructions on remaining alert and the password. When he left after 0100, he advised he would see them in the morning. Rogers took the first shift on watch while Sharp slept. Morning came at 0400, when Zilish returned with white snow capes. He found Sharp dozing on watch while Rogers, who was supposed to be resting, slept. Zilish counseled Sharp about how that could get him and Rogers killed, and anyway it was a court-martial offense. Sharp took the point. He and Rogers joined their new company in an attack mounted on tanks at 0430. Nether had been on a tank, but it would not be the last time. Sharpe was grateful to Zilish, who, he believed, not only took care of him but trained him. Private Sharp learned his lessons well and ended the war as a squad leader.[110]

Lessons Old and New

When he took command in Sicily, Huebner developed a plan that Andrus stuck with: when in reserve or in rest areas, train, train, train. In rest areas, that meant rest and recreation half a day and training the other half. At the end of December an Army Ground Forces observer team published a study called "Training of Infantry Division during a Lull in Combat." Units that provided feedback all stressed the need to train when time permitted, even during short periods out of contact. As the narrative has shown, the 1st ID had experienced few lulls—a consequence of the number of divisions available. Such training as there was in the fall of 1944 was integrated with operation at unit level.[111]

The division continued to expend projectiles rather than lives. Massed artillery drove off armor attacks on three separate occasions in December. The division found that the new proximity fuses produced "everything that could be desired and the results were gratifying." Proximity fuses reliably resulted in air bursts, with devasting effects on infantry. In December the four organic artillery battalions fired 73,943 rounds of 105-millimeter ammunition and another 14,591 rounds of 155-millimeter. Corps artillery, direct support, fired 19,752 howitzer and 155 rounds. In January the artillery suffered some difficulty with recoil systems due to prolonged cold, but still managed to fire 58,917 rounds from organic battalions as well as 30,165 rounds from corps battalions.[112]

Tactically the 1st ID continued to believe in the efficacy of attacking at night or predawn. The regiments liked to bound by battalion, which enabled sustained attacks even in close terrain. They sought to envelop the enemy to take ground in the "rear of German-held positions." In the forest, digging in and building overhead cover proved essential, but the position had to be one that "could be used for active defense. The primary mission of any soldier is to be able to use his weapon effectively. His secondary mission is to provide himself proper protection so that he can continue to use that weapon." The lessons learned in the forests went from elegance in tactics to the mundane but essential preparation of good fighting positions.[113]

At the end of January, the 1st ID had been in combat 354 days. The Big Red One had reason to be proud of its achievements, but like other veteran units it was tired. Iris Carpenter, one of a very few women war correspondents, reported on the 1st ID in the Ardennes. Doing her own arithmetic, she concluded that Big Red One "had been fighting with two eight-day rest periods in eight months." She found an artillery battery in which the "gunners have been out of the line only one day since D-Day." Of course, every soldier knows that artillery is never in reserve, but they too had been worn down.[114]

From October through January the 1st ID fought in the three forests, the Hürtgen, Schnee Eifel, and Ardennes. The rugged terrain there afforded so much advantage to the defenders that even inexperienced units like the 47th VGD could grind down battle-proven units like the 1st ID.

Assessing whether the 1st ID demonstrated tactical excellence in the forests equal to the level it showed at Aachen is difficult. The pursuit, the transition at the Siegfried Line, and taking Aachen arguably showed the Big Red One at its best as a battle-tested, constantly learning organization. The fighting in the Hürtgen ground it up, just as it had other very good units such as the 4th and, most infamously, 28th ID.

General Eisenhower's decision to continue attacking through the winter meant accepting, as Grant had, a battle of attrition. Eisenhower's goals were straightforward—impose costs on the Germans they could not afford and prevent them from maintaining any reserves. By the end of 1944 the Germans were scraping the bottom of their manpower barrel, with the British not far behind. The country, if it also had to maintain war production and build the air force and navy, lacked the means to create sufficient divisions to provide for rotation. As a consequence, units could not be guaranteed time to refit, rearm, and train.

To generate the means to fight through the winter, Eisenhower and Bradley took a calculated risk in the Ardennes. General Middleton's VIII Corps had four divisions spread out on eighty miles of front, and the army reckoned a division could defend ten miles. Two of Middleton's four divisions were the 4th and 28th ID, both battered in the much-loathed Hürtgen. The

106th ID had arrived on December 10 and was untested. Finally, he had one of the two combat commands of the recently arrived 9th ID. The Germans chose the Ardennes because it was lightly defended by a combination of worn-out and new units. It was, as Charles B. MacDonald wrote in *The Siegfried Line Campaign*, "a combination nursery and old folks' home of the American command."[115]

Although the German counteroffensive, conceived long before the Allied pursuit, proved dangerous and frightening, it was always a forlorn hope. Eisenhower acted with alacrity and vision. Three days after the counteroffensive began, he turned to developing the means to take advantage of Hitler's thrust, which he did with confidence during the darkest days of the German attack. Defending the northern shoulder, veteran divisions like the 1st ID and new divisions like the 99th delayed and eventually stopped the Germans. The 1st ID took revenge on the 12th SS Panzer Division for the Kasserine Pass, and found that revenge satisfying. The division showed also that a core of effective leaders and veterans could keep new soldiers alive long enough to teach them the basics.

From the Olympian heights of SHAEF, and even the less lofty peak at division (let alone nearly eighty years later), cool analysis of what was achieved was possible. In the valleys, at company level, it was less so. Frank Kolb, whose company paid an awful price, thought that "the whole thing was useless. We never did anything there. We hardly even made contact with the enemy. Instead, we were cut down by tree-bursts of German artillery as [we] were moving up. . . . To me the Hürtgen was just a dead loss." But even Kolb hoped that it "contributed to the big picture." He and a lot of other soldiers just could not see it.[116]

Notes

1. MacDonald, *Siegfried Line Campaign*, 382–88. See also Eisenhower, *Crusade in Europe*, 324; Eisenhower to Thomas Troy Handy, in Eisenhower, *Papers*, no. 2042, 4:2229. In this cable to the deputy chief of staff of the army, he complained about Fifth US Army in Italy in particular. On the replacement problem see Keast, *Provision of Enlisted Replacements*.

2. MacDonald, *Huertgen Forest*, 4.

3. Greenfield, Palmer, and Wiley, *Organization of Ground Combat Troops*, 225–27. For a concise discussion of the difficult process of sustaining the force, see Mansoor, *GI Offensive in Europe*, 32–48.

4. Mansoor, *GI Offensive in Europe*, 42–43; Bellanger, *Army Infantry Divisions*, 1:1. See also Wilson, *Maneuver and Firepower*, chart 19, 181, and, for Armor Division, chart 20, 186. See also Forty, *US Army Handbook*, 78. For the Army Specialized Training Program, see Mansoor, *GI Offensive in Europe*, 12, 34, 41–43.

5. Clausewitz, *On War*, 196.

6. Eisenhower to Marshal, in Eisenhower, *Papers*, no. 2041, 4:2228.

7. Eisenhower, *Crusade in Europe*, 321–29; Pogue, *Supreme Command*, 310–11.

8. Bradley, *Soldier's Story*, 439; for Bradley's estimate of the situation, see 432–39.

9. Collins, *Lightning Joe*, 278–79; MacDonald, *Siegfried Line Campaign*, 417. MacDonald believes that taken together, First and Ninth US Armies suffered 140,000 battle and nonbattle casualties.

10. Westphal, *German Army in the West*, 173; Cooper, *German Army*, 485–88. Originally *Volksgrenadier* was intended as an honorific to be earned. In the end, all of these formations were given the title.

11. War Department, TM-E 30-451, *Handbook on German Military Forces* (1945; repr., Baton Rouge: Louisiana State University Press, 1990), 97–106.

12. Cooper, *German Army*, 488. Cole, *Ardennes*, 675, reports that 2,277 tanks reached the west. What matters more than the number that went west is that the number sent to the east was so low that units in the east had only two-thirds as many tanks as committed in the west. MacDonald, *Siegfried Line Campaign*, 392.

13. In *Loss and Redemption at St. Vith*, I put the number of German divisions at twenty-eight. That is a miscount. Charles B. MacDonald's order of battle is more accurate, showing twenty-seven divisions; the Escort Brigade alone had as many tanks as a Panzer division. The Führer Grenadier Brigade too was armor-heavy. Otto Skorzeny's 150th Panzer Brigade had still more tanks. MacDonald, *A Time for Trumpets*, 644–55. MacDonald's order of battle is as of December 28, 1944.

14. MacDonald, *Siegfried Line Campaign*, 394, 396. On November 15 Manteuffel's headquarters came out of the line. Fifteenth Army replaced that headquarters. Manteuffel himself remained until November 20, when General der Infanterie Gustav von Zangen replaced him.

15. Köchling's rumination about the battle are found in seven short postwar manuscripts, titled "Battles in the Aachen Sector (Sep 44–Nov 44)," mss. A-989 to A-995, Sturmpanzer. See ms. 996, "Battles in the Aachen Sector (16 Nov–16 Dec 44)," N17500.1045, 2–5. This text was in response to questions posed by US historians in Oberursel, Germany, on February 24, 1946.

16. MacDonald, *Huertgen Forest*, 4. Average precipitation varies somewhat depending on the location within these three forests. Snow depth for December 1944–45 from multiple sources.

17. HQ, 1st ID, intelligence annex 2 to FO 53, November 6, 1944, 3–4, in RG 301-3.2: G-3 Journal, 1 Nov 44–30 Nov 44, MRC; Lypka, *A Soldier Remembers*, 183; Knickerbocker et al., *Danger Forward*, 299. Trafficability, rivers, and general description of terrain are at HQ, 1st ID, "Tactical Study of Terrain," March 25, 1944, in RG 301-0.13: Operation Plan "Neptune," Mar–May 1944, MRC Digital Archives. Re the Our River, see Fontenot, *Loss and Redemption*, 56–57.

18. Winters, *Battling the Elements*, 51. See also Mavin D. Kays, "Weather Effects during the Battle of the Bulge and the Normandy Invasion," US Army Research and Development Command, White Sands Missile Range, New Mexico, 1982.

19. HQ, First Army, after-action report, November 1–30, 1944, N1149, CARL, 47.

20. First Army, 47; Hogan, *Command Post at War*, 184; MacDonald, *Siegfried Line Campaign*, 397.

21. Craven and Cate, *Argument to V-E Day*, 631–32; Hogan, *Command Post at War*, 182–84. The 104th ID moved into Stolberg corridor on November 10. HQ, VII Corps, operations plan, October 29, 1944, R13343.12, CARL. See also FO 12, November 8, 1944, R1433.12, CARL, annex 2, 1.

22. FO 12, annex 3, appendix 1 and 2.

23. HQ, 1st ID, FO 53, 060100A, November 1944, 1–2, in RG 301-3.9: Field Orders, Apr–May 44, Jul–Sep 44, Nov 44, Jan–Apr 45, MRC Digital Archives.

24. VII Corps, operations plan, October 28, 1944, 1.

25. 1st ID, intelligence annex 2 to FO 53, 1–2.

26. 1st ID, 6.

27. HQ, 1st ID, Operations Memorandum 3, "Employment of Infantry in Woods," October 31, 1944, George A. Taylor Collection, 1960.88.3, MRC.

28. Craven and Cate, *Argument to V-E Day*, 632.

29. *Huertgen Forest,* 130; Craven and Cate, *Argument to V-E Day*, 632.

30. HQ, 1st ID, after-action report, November 1944, 14–15, in RG 301-3: Operations Reports, Jun 44–Dec 44, MRC Digital Archives.

31. John M. Gaustad, "Armor in the Hürtgen Forest," Committee 7 Officers Advanced Course, Armored School, Fort Knox, KY, May 1949, WWII Student Papers, DRL, 70.

32. Edmond F. Driscoll, interview by Kenneth W. Hechler, Frant Lanze, Czechoslovakia, May 24, 1945, RG 407, NARA, 1–2.

33. Maurice A. Belisle, "The Operations of the 26th Infantry Regiment (1st Infantry Division) in the Attack on the Hurtgen Forest, 10 November–5 December 1944 (Rhineland Campaign)," Advanced Infantry Officers Course, 1949–1950, Class No. 1, Fort Benning, GA, n.d., WWII Student Papers, DRL, 11.

34. Gerhard Engel, "The 12th Infantry Division in the Third Battle of Aachen, 16 November to 5 December 1944," November 3, 1947, ms. B-764, Sturmpanzer, 2, 3.

35. Engel, 9–13.

36. Max Bork, "The 47th Volksgrenadier Division (VGD) in the West," June 1947, ms. B-602, Sturmpanzer, 3–4; Friedrich Köchling, "Battles in Sector Aachen," February 23, 1946, ms. A-996, N17500.1045, CARL, 5.

37. Knickerbocker et al., *Danger Forward*, 287, 288.

38. Atkinson, *Guns at Last Light*, 335; Cowdrey, *Fighting for Life*, 266. Atkinson cites Cowdrey also at 339.

39. Driscoll, interview, 2–3.

40. Finke, *No Mission Too Difficult*, 218–19.

41. HQ, 1st ID, "Intelligence Activities (1 Nov 1944 to 30 Nov 1944)," box 18952, folder 5, NARA, 14; 1st ID, after-action report, November 1944, in RG 301-3: G-3 Operations Reports, Jun 44–Dec 44, MRC Digital Archives; 1st ID, after-action report, June 1944–December 1944, 15, in RG 301-ART-0.3: Artillery Operations Reports, Jun 44–May 45, MRC Digital Archives.

42. Clay, *Blood and Sacrifice*, 219; Jake Lindsey, telephone interview by Albert H. Smith, May 1985.

43. Clay, *Blood and Sacrifice*, 303–4; 1st ID, after-action report, November 1944, 5–6.

44. Guderian, *From Normandy to the Ruhr*, 273–77.

45. 1st ID, "Intelligence Activities," 6–7; Guderian, *From Normandy to the Ruhr*, 273–74; 1st ID, after-action report, November 1944, 19.

46. Clay, *Blood and Sacrifice*, 219. Oberst Josef Kimbacher commanded the 104th VGR. Clay believed both battalions of the 104th VGR participated; Bork, "47th Volksgrenadier Division," reported only one battalion. See also Guderian, *From Normandy to the Ruhr*, 273–74.

47. 1st ID, after-action report, November 1944, 23, 30. MacDonald also quoted Huebner's instructions to Smith. MacDonald argues that this may have been the single "concentrated artillery" shoot during the war in Europe. MacDonald, *Siegfried Line Campaign*, 477, 479, 481; Collins, *Lightning Joe*, 276.

48. *Memorial Album: Pictorial History of the 1st Division* (San Diego, CA: Society of the First Division, 1950), cited in Weingartner, *Blue Spaders*, 88.

49. Engel, "12th Infantry Division," 15–20; G-3 after-action report, November 1944, 38.

50. The 4th Cavalry Group did number of different missions during the approach to the Roer. VII Corps, Operations Memorandums 118–20.

51. 1st ID, after-action report, November 1944, 39–47.

52. Baumer and Reardon, *American Iliad*, 306.

53. Baumer and Reardon, 55; Engel, "12th Infantry Division," 30–31; MacDonald, *Siegfried Line Campaign*, 488; Engel, "12th Infantry Division," 28–29.

54. Alwin E. Bulau, untitled ms. written shortly after first contact in the Hürtgen Forest, n.d., MRC (no acession no.), 2; Wallace J. Nichols, Howell H. Heard, Thomas Carroll, Donald English, Wallace Warden, Leonard Novak, John Lefeber, and Frederick P. Chjrgotis, interview by Kenneth J. Hechler, Cheb, Czechoslovakia, May 23, 1945, box 18952, folder 5, RG 107, NARA, 4.

55. Bulau ms., 2–3.

56. Bulau, 4.

57. Bulau, 5.

58. Bulau, 5–8. Parts of Bulau's account is incoherent or at least unclear. He was not certain of what happened to the first tank that was hit, or the second. He believed that the third tank that was to support by fire had only one gun functioning by the end of the fight, and that that was the spark that led to his lieutenant giving up on the position. He mentions a fifth tank once but never reports what became of it. See also 745th Tank Battalion, after-action report, December 1, 1944, in "After Action Reports, June 1944–May 1945," doc. 8745, TB 101-A, DRL.

59. HQ, 26th Infantry journal, November 30, 1944, 180–93, in RG-INF(26)-0.3: Reports of Operations, Oct–Dec 44, MRC Digital Archives; Seitz quotation at 181, Daniel at 183.

60. 26th Infantry journal, November 30, 1944, 183; 26th Infantry, after-action report, December 1944, 1, in Reports of Operations, Oct–Dec 44. See also 26th Infantry, after-action report, November 1944, 5, in Reports of Operations, Oct–Dec 44, re prisoner taken at 1845, reporting how the troops in Merode were cut off. Lieutenant

Colonel Corley reported to regiment at 2150 that he had seen a working party of American prisoners near Merode. See 26th Infantry journal, November 30, 1944, 192; Knickerbocker et al., *Danger Forward,* 295.

61. HQ, VII Corps, Operations Memorandum 124, CARL, 1; HQ, 1st Battalion, 16th Infantry, "The Attack on Luchem," December 3, 1944, ch. 28 of 1st ID, "World War II Combat Achievements Report," n.d., MRC 1988.31, 2. Driscoll's oral order is transcribed and in chapter 28.

62. 1st Battalion, "The Attack on Luchem," 2.

63. 1st Battalion, 3.

64. 1st Battalion, 3–5.

65. 1st Battalion, 4–6.

66. 1st Battalion, 6–7.

67. Wheeler, *The Big Red One,* 349.

68. MacDonald, *Siegfried Line Campaign,* 492. See also Wheeler, *The Big Red One,* 349.

69. HQ, 6th INF, Training Notes, no. 41, December 9, 1944, in Reports of Operations, Oct–Dec 44. See also n. 42. The regiment published a detailed range schedule for small arms, antitank, mortars, machine guns, and snipers on December 16.

70. Donald McBurney Curtis to Al Smith, November 3, 1983, Albert H. Smith Papers, MRC 1996.95.

71. Military Hall of Honor, https://militaryhallofhonor.com/honoree-record, accessed 16 January 2022; Curtis to Smith, October 3, 1983; Knickerbocker et al., *Danger Forward,* 408–9, 416; Bradley, *Soldier's Story,* 343.

72. Cole, *Ardennes,* 11, 13. The first three chapters outline the development of the Ardennes counteroffensive, and the "intelligence failure" is at 1–75. MacDonald, *A Time for Trumpets,* is an update in some ways, as he could refer to ULTRA and had access to far more veterans, including Germans. Caddick-Adams, *Snow and Steel,* is more recent and builds on earlier works. The author's *Loss and Redemption at St. Vith* examines the campaign through the lens of the 7th Armored Division, which attacked alongside the Big Red One in January 1945.

73. Westphal, *German Army in the West,* 178, 180; Warlimont, *Inside Hitler's Headquarters,* 480–82.

74. Danny S. Parker, "Order of Battle—German Army," in MacDonald, *A Time for Trumpets,* 644–55. Parker is the author of several books. The order of battle includes a brief note on each division's reconstitution. See also Mitcham, *German Order of Battle.*

75. Meyer, *12th SS,* 2:199–205. Like all of the SS divisions, the 12th SS enjoyed the benefit of being Hitler's private army, and it too had an unsavory reputation. Meyer commanded the 12th SS temporarily, for just over a month in September–October 1944. He remained with the 12th SS until the end of the war. The book is painstakingly researched, and while it is an apologist's argument, Meyer's sincerity is clear by the postwar associations he formed with his former enemies.

76. Meyer, 205–6.

77. Cole, *The Ardennes,* 19–29; MacDonald, *A Time for Trumpets,* 37

78. Fontenot, *Loss and Redemption*, 7–8. The data cited come from a number of sources. Chief among them are Cole, *The Ardennes*, MacDonald, *A Time for Trumpets*, and Winton, *Commanders of the Bulge*. In his conclusions Cole asserts only that the Germans suffered more than the Allies did. Craven and Cate, *Argument to V-E Day*, chapter 19, "Battle of the Bulge," is the standard for the history of the US Army Air Force in the Battle of the Bulge.

79. Derrill Daniel, Walter W. Nations, Thomas J. Gendron, Elmer C. Killens, Pierre Stepanian, August T. McColgen, and James E. Rea, joint interview by Forrest C. Pogue and Jose M. Topete, box 24012, folder 7, NARA, 1.

80. Fontenot, *Loss and Redemption*, xiv, 73–74.

81. "Preparations," ch. 2 of Cole, *The Ardennes*, 48–75. See also MacDonald, *A Time for Trumpets*, book 1, chapters 2 and 3, 39–80. For an entertaining, albeit bitter, defense of 12th Army Group see Ingersoll, *Top Secret*, 246–48.

82. Clausewitz, *On War*, 198; Ambrose, *Supreme Commander*, 556. See also Eisenhower, *Crusade in Europe*, 343–45, for his account of the staff work that day and the decisions taken. XVIII Corps main command post, still in the United Kingdom, was ordered to the Continent.

83. Hogan, *Command Post at War*, 209; HQ, VII Corps, Operations Memorandum 132, CARL, 1; Botsford, *Life of Privilege*, 54.

84. H. Priess, "Commitment of the I SS Panzer Corps during the Ardennes Offensive (16 Dec 1944–25 Jan 1945)," n.d., ms. A-877, N17500.1035, CARL, 6. In his postwar manuscript Priess's rank is rendered in the style of the Wehrmacht, but I have used his SS rank to identify him in the text. The 99th ID entered the line on November 11 so had time to acclimate to the front and learn its sector. https://www.99thinfantrydivision.com/organisation/, accessed 24 January 2022.

85. Weingartner, *Blue Spaders*, 92, 99.

86. Cole, *Ardennes*, 334. See also War Department, FM 100-5, *Field Service Regulations: Operations* (Washington, DC: Government Printing Office, 1941), 156.

87. Finke, *No Mission Too Difficult*, 225; on integration, and eventual capture, see 225–33. Beadenkopf did learn to fight effectively but was captured on January 15, 1945, during the fight to erase the Bulge when he and others were cut off during an attack.

88. Pallud, *Battle of the Bulge*, 224; Rocco J. Moretto, veteran's survey, Army Heritage and Education Center, Carlisle, PA.

89. 1st ID, after-action report, December 1944, 39–47, in G-3 Operations Reports, Jun 44–Dec 44.

90. HQ, 634th Tank Destroyer Battalion, after-action report, December 1944, 1, http://www.tankdestroyer.net. See also 745th Tank Battalion, after-action report, December 16, 1944, in "After Action Reports, June 1944–May 1945." It is likely that most of the deadlines and shortages stemmed from standing down for maintenance. It was not unusual for tank battalions to pull engines for maintenance when they came out of the line. On December 10 the battalion showed only two Sherman tanks down. On December 17 they were short for all reasons forty-two Sherman tanks, but on December 18 the battalion reported two Sherman tanks down. That suggests

routine maintenance on engines and setting them in order to move. The division after-action report cites a report from the 745th that alleged that none of its Sherman tanks were available. In any case, Task Force Davisson was needed.

91. Veterans of the Battle of the Bulge, *Battle of the Bulge*, 19. See also Alfred Alvarez, interview by Robert Etheridge, n.d., http://www.loc.gov/vets/, accessed July 2020. Alvarez remained in the army and retired as a lieutenant colonel.

92. Veterans of the Battle of the Bulge, *Battle of the Bulge*, 311; HQ, 26th Infantry, after-action report, January 1, 1945, 3–4, in Reports of Operations, Oct–Dec 44.

93. Weingartner, *Blue Spaders*, 107. By December 20 Seitz had returned from leave and resumed command of the regiment. HQ, 1st ID, Selected Intelligence Reports, vol. 2, December 1944–May 1945, 24, in RG 301-2.0: G-2 Selected Intelligence Reports during the First Six Months of the European Campaign, Jun 1944–May 1945, MRC Digital Archives. See also Meyer, *12th SS*, 228. The strength of the 560th in Jagdpanzers is uncertain. There were only 31 Jagdpanzer IVs so this attack seems to have been a mixed force. Just how many were lost is uncertain.

94. Weingartner, *Blue Spaders*, 104–11; Stepanian, joint interview by Pogue and Topete. See also Pallud, *Battle of the Bulge*, 42. Because the 12th SS was short tanks (78 of 184, according to Meyer, *12th SS*, 228) the 26th SS Panzer Regiment's had the 560th Panzerjäger Battalion assigned with twenty-five antitank guns built on the Panzer IV and Panzer V "Panther" chassis. See also Donald F. Rivette, "The Operations of the 2nd Battalion 26th Infantry (1st Infantry Division) at Dom Butgenbach, 16–21 December 1944," Advanced Infantry Officers Course, 1948–1949, n.d., WWII Student Papers, DRL. Rivette's monograph includes detailed sketches of the action in the early-morning hours of December 20.

95. Baumgartner et al., *16th Infantry*, 186; Fuller, *A Third Face*, 201. The G-2 called the German attack "a startling parallel" to the Kasserine Pass action.

96. Priess, "Commitment of the I SS Panzer Corps," 35; Caddick-Adams, *Snow and Steel*, 348.

97. MacDonald, *A Time for Trumpets*, 197–223, 227–30, 450–65. Peiper's Kampfgruppe began with 4,000 men, but he was joined a by a reconnaissance group that brought another 1,800.

98. MacDonald, *A Time for Trumpets*, 615.

99. Eisenhower to Bradley and Devers in Eisenhower, *Papers*, no. 2178, 4:2356; Clausewitz, *On War*, 102.

100. Cole, *The Ardennes*, 376–77; Arthur G. Heidrick, diary, June 13, 1942–February 1, 1945, Fort Riley Museum Complex, Fort Riley, KS, entry for December 25, 1944; Veterans of the Battle of the Bulge, *Battle of the Bulge*, 315.

101. Veterans of the Battle of the Bulge, *Battle of the Bulge*, 56–57.

102. 1st ID, after-action report, December 1944, 39–47; 1st ID, after-action report, January 1945, 52, in RG 301-3: G-3 Operations Reports, European Campaign, Jan 45–Dec 45; 1st ID, Selected Intelligence Reports, 2:25.

103. Hogan, *Command Post at War*, 228–29; Knickerbocker et al., *Danger Forward*, 326–27.

104. "Fighting in Woods," draft ms., n.d., George A. Taylor Collection, MRC, 1. There is no file copy of the final version of this paper, but the lessons were promulgated in one form or another, if the after-action reports and personal accounts are to be believed.

105. "Fighting in Woods," 3.

106. "Fighting in Woods," 6, 10.

107. 1st ID, after-action report, December 1944, 61. The December report's conclusions focused on the necessity of consolidation on objectives with respect to immediately "laying" in supporting weapons are explicit. 1st ID, after-action report, January 1945, 63. Taylor's report examines the difficulty of using forest trails. Paragraph one of "Conclusions" in the January report examines this problem of trails as obstacles.

108. 1st ID, Selected Intelligence Reports, December 2:26, 33. Evans's report on the conditions is at 33.

109. Jim Sharp, telephone interview with author, March 19, 2020; Sharp, *Diary of a Combat Infantryman*, 21–28. Zilish might really have been Zilic, as Sharp pronounced the name as "zil ich," which sounds like a Serb or Croat family name.

110. Jim Sharp, telephone interview with author, March 19, 2020; Sharp, *Diary of a Combat Infantryman*, 21–28.

111. Army Ground Forces Board report ETO C-481, "Training of Infantry Division during Lull in Combat," December 28, 1944, N5993, CARL.

112. HQ, 1st ID Artillery, after-action report, January 5, 1945, 17–19, and 1st ID, after-action report, January 1–31, 1945, 19–22, both in RG 301-ART-0.3: Artillery Operations Reports, 1 Jun 44–May 45, MRC Digital Archives.

113. 1st ID, after-action reports, January 1945, 67, and November 1944, 61.

114. Knickerbocker et al., *Danger Forward*, 351. Re Iris Carpenter, see https://www.encyclopedia.com/women/encyclopedias-almanacs-transcripts-and-maps/carpenter-iris-1906.

115. MacDonald, *Siegfried Line Campaign*, 612.

116. Finke, *No Mission Too Difficult*, 218.

CHAPTER THIRTEEN

Streams, the Roer, and the Rhine

> Condemned—condemned to attack and after this attack condemned
> to attack again.
>
> *—Lieutenant John Walker, 16th Infantry*

> After having thrown back the German Forces to the West Wall, the en-
> emy would aim at breaking through where possible, and finally roll up
> the German Front.
>
> *—General der Infanterie Otto Hitzfeld, LXVII Corps*

AT 1825 ON January 19, 1945, the Big Red One advised V Corps, "We are all set for the 7th Armored Division. We have full control of objectives." The 1st ID, supported by the 23rd Infantry of the 2nd ID, set the conditions for the "Lucky Seventh" to pass forward and retake the critical road junction at Saint-Vith. The following day, XVIII Airborne Corps units began relieving the 23rd Infantry so it could return to its division. Over the next several days the 1st ID patrolled actively to maintain contact with adjacent units and the 7th AD as it attacked south. A lot of jockeying around occurred to maintain a cohesive forward line, with the view that ultimately the units attacking south would turn east to reduce the salient. In addition to contact patrols, the 1st ID conducted combat patrols to maintain pressure on the Germans to their front. The division conducted limited night attacks that featured shallow envelopments designed to nip off exposed German units. The 7th AD retook Saint-Vith on January 23. The following day, as the attack paused, 1st ID crowed that all "objectives were taken by the 1st Infantry Division after skillful maneuvering, night attacks and trapping elements of 5 enemy battalions." The 23rd Infantry returned to the 2nd ID that same day.[1]

The Big Red One's bragging was not without justification. From mid-September through January the 1st ID had fought through difficult terrain against a determined enemy. It had integrated replacements on the fly, moved with precision and speed, and shown skill in maneuvering and attacking at night. Worn down but not worn out, the Big Red One stumbled at Merode, but with the briefest rest it recovered. Fortunately it suffered comparatively few casualties during the Battle of the Bulge. With no respite, the division joined XVIII Airborne Corps on January 26 to prepare for an attack that would require it to fight through the Schnee Eifel and the Siegfried Line and revisit the Hürtgen Forest yet again, cross the Roer River, close, then cross to the west bank of the Rhine and exploit the opening that offered. This chapter examines how the 1st ID transitioned from one complex mission to another while serving in three different corps.[2]

At SHAEF, Eisenhower's vision had to extend beyond the immediate to weeks or months. Accordingly, on New Year's Eve, he sent out an outline plan for resuming the offensive to Bernard Law Montgomery. Bradley and Devers received their copies soon after. The context of the operations envisioned stemmed from the fall conferences in which Eisenhower settled on a broad front strategy, modified by decisions taken in late December to restart the Allied offensive soon after closing out the Bulge. The revised strategy now called for a clear main effort north of the forest complex, led by Field Marshall Montgomery attacking to seize the Ruhr industrial region. Montgomery was to be reinforced by the Ninth US Army increased from five to ten divisions.

The divisions to bring Ninth Army up to ten divisions would come from First Army, which would retain eleven divisions. Reinforcing Ninth Army would require careful coordination and greatly reduce First Army's capacity for offensive operations. Eisenhower's directions were categorical. The Allied forces were to reduce the German salient and then take the initiative, with 21st Army Group receiving priority for resources including assignment of Lieutenant General William H. Simpson's Ninth Army.[3]

Bradley, of course, was unhappy. Assigning the main effort to Montgomery was galling. The British and Canadians fielded only fifteen divisions in northwest Europe, while the US Army boasted fifty. Even more irritating, the British press was calling for Montgomery to serve as the single ground force commander. Some in Britain argued that the Americans had needed

Montgomery to save the day in the Ardennes. Winston Churchill tamped down the furor with a brilliant speech in the House of Commons, noting accurately that "highly skilled commanders [the Americans, in this instance] handled very large forces at their disposal in a manner which I think I can say without exaggeration may become a model for military students in the future." Bradley admitted also that Eisenhower stood firm; Montgomery would command 21st Army Group and no more.[4]

Eisenhower's vision for resuming the Allied offensive had still another controversial facet that affected the troops on the ground more directly than the question of who commanded the ground forces. Contrary to the wishes of the British, the supreme commander phased the coming campaign. In the first phase he wanted all three army groups and their seven subordinate field armies to close up to the Rhine. Defeating the Germans and forcing them east of the Rhine offered several benefits. Once the Allies controlled the west bank of the Rhine, the Germans would find it difficult to envelop Allied ground forces. Closing on the Rhine would shorten the line along a readily defensible terrain feature, a fact that seemed to elude Hitler. By doing so, SHAEF could concentrate forces required to sustain the planned offensive. The Soviet winter offensive, begun on January 12, would likely ease the way for the Allies in the west. Crossing the Rhine would come in the second phase, and then 21st Army Group would take the stage.[5]

First Army issued orders to affect the wishes of 12th Army Group and SHAEF on January 25. Collins and the VII Corps staff were withdrawn to rest, so Lieutenant General Courtney H. Hodges had only Clarence R. Huebner's V Corps and Ridgway's XVIII Airborne Corps. He proposed to attack through the Eifel on a front of twenty-five miles extending from just north of Monschau to just north of Losheim. Hodges's order required the two corps to attack abreast in succession, with XVIII Airborne Corps leading off on January 29 and V Corps attacking the next day. Hodges did not designate a main effort nor did he resource one. Instead, the two corps were more less balanced. Huebner had three infantry divisions and one armored division. Ridgway had three infantry divisions, the 1st, 30th, and 84th, as well as the 82nd Airborne. For his part Ridgway proposed a "powerful attack on a narrow front, in great depth; the attack to be sustained advance by successive attacks by rested divisions, abreast." By this he meant that he would lead with two divisions abreast. When they were stopped or needed a pause, he would "leapfrog the two in the rear through them and continue the assault." The corps would drive to and through the Siegfried Line.[6]

The German Situation

In his memoir, OKW operations officer General der Artillerie Walter War-limont included a verbatim transcript of Hitler's musings in the presence of Generalleutnant Wolfgang Thomale, the inspector general of the Panzer troops. The dictator treated Thomale to his assessment over several hours during the night of December 29–30, 1944. At the outset Hitler observed, "I started this war with the most wonderful Army in Europe; today I've got a muck heap." He went on to complain at length about his generals and his troops. He found the Landsers "wretched." The army as a whole lacked "perseverance and fanatical determination." His rant continued in this vein for some time. In his view, winning was "merely a question of who can stand it longer."[7]

Soon after, his wretched Landsers and muck-heap army conducted Operation Nordwind, an almost extemporaneous second counteroffensive launched in the Vosges Mountains in January 1945. On the whole it proved more successful than the attack in the Ardennes. In *The Wehrmacht's Last Stand*, Robert M. Citino shows that Nordwind was a tactical victory against a Seventh US Army that had been both thinned out and spread out to find reinforcements for the 12th Army Group. Nordwind, Citino argues, showcased the continued tactical acumen of the German Army. But here too, "The army of the new superpower gave it all that it could handle." Hitler squandered his last well-equipped strategic reserve in the Ardennes and the Vosges.[8]

The German powers of recuperation that Bradley found astounding diminished thereafter. Many of the mobile divisions raised in 1944 and the rebuilt or newly formed Volksgrenadier divisions were consumed that winter. The manpower for another wave of infantry divisions could not be found. Instead, the Germans raised Volkssturm units, literally the "People's Storm"— poorly trained formations of "old men, and boys." Hans Kissel, in *Hitler's Last Levy: The Volkssturm, 1944–1945*, points out that a fifty-five-year-old textile salesman was one of the first conscripted for the Volkssturm.[9]

The generals that Hitler characterized as incompetent were at that moment attempting to salvage what they could from the western-front counteroffensives. Meanwhile, the Germans evacuated Warsaw on January 17. The Russian First Tank Army had reached the Oder near Frankfurt am Oder, advancing nearly 250 miles in two weeks. On both fronts the Germans struggled to generate sufficient force to forestall the Allies. Cobbling together defensive positions that might extend the war with no chance of winning, or what Charles B. MacDonald entitled the US Army's history of what followed—*The Last Offensive*—characterized the fighting in the west.[10]

German commanders on both fronts were hampered by Hitler's insistence that no ground be given up. The Russians galloping west now posed an immediate danger, so the priority of resources shifted back to the east. Siegfried Westphal, Gerd von Rundstedt's chief of staff, recalled that OB West gave up, altogether, "sixteen divisions, mostly of high quality, and a large part of the artillery to the Eastern Front." With too few troops to hold the west bank of the Rhine, Rundstedt asked to withdraw to the east bank. Hitler refused. The field marshal persisted, telling Hitler that the troops "were fed up to the back teeth with the war." Rundstedt's complaints led eventually to his being relieved of command a second time, and the stand-fast order remained in effect.[11]

Whether or not the Landsers were "fed up to the back teeth," their units were worn down. Oberst Friedrich Kittel's 62nd VGD is a good example. Decimated and reconstituted twice on the eastern front, it arrived in the west in November 1944. Paired with the 18th VGD in LXVI Corps, it helped force the surrender of two regiments of the 106th ID in the Schnee Eifel. By the end of December, the 62nd once again had to be reconstituted. In January enough replacements arrived for Kittel to rebuild his division. He complained that new arrivals were poorly trained, but he did have sufficient materiel, including ammunition, to train them. Kittel believed the division needed "a rest from fighting for eight or nine days." There was no rest for either side.[12]

Sisyphus and the 1st ID

Surely even Sisyphus would have blanched had he been asked to fight through the Siegfried Line a second time, but that is just what appeared to lie ahead for the Big Red One. The division faced that task with little rest but with relative continuity of leadership. Brigadier General William E. Waters, a 1921 graduate of VMI who had been his deputy, replaced Brigadier General Clift Andrus as commanding general of the division artillery. Among the artillery battalions only the 5th Field Artillery changed hands. Lieutenant Colonel Francis J. Murdoch Jr., who had commanded the 1st Battalion, 26th Infantry, until he was wounded in Normandy, assumed command of 3rd Battalion, 26th Infantry, from John T. Corley, who went home for a well-deserved leave. Lieutenant Colonel Charles T. Horner Jr. turned over 3rd Battalion, 16th Infantry, to Edward F. Wozenski, who had led Company E ashore at Omaha Beach. Continuity in the 1st Engineer Battalion would not be a problem and was important. Lieutenant Colonel William B. Gara, who had been with the battalion since North Africa and in command of it since Sicily, remained in command. Bill Gara and his engineers had proven themselves and would do so again, in a series of river crossings far more difficult than those conducted during the breakout and pursuit.[13]

After passing the 7th AD forward, the 1st ID continued to push the German 3rd Fallschirmjäger Division (FJD) and the 89th ID on its right to the south and east. Essentially the Germans pivoted on the town of Bullingen, pounded into rubble by both sides. By January 25 the German main line of resistance stretched north-south, oriented west. The 89th ID remained on the 3rd FJD's right. Shattered in the Siegfried Line fighting, it was partially rebuilt in time to take another beating in the Ardennes. The 89th defended with remnants of its 1056th Grenadier Regiment north of Hepscheid and 1055th Grenadier Regiment on its left or south. Lieutenant Colonel Robert F. Evans, the division G-2, believed neither battalion had a hundred infantrymen left. The 3rd FJD front extended from Heppenbach south to Valender. The G-2 believed the 5th Fallschirmjäger Regiment (FJR) held the line on the right and north with the 9th FJR on the left and 8th FJR in reserve. In contact with these two units for two weeks, Evans had developed sound intelligence on both enemy divisions.[14]

On January 28, the XVIII Airborne Corps attacked with 1st ID on the left or north and the 82nd ABN on the right. The 16th and 18th Infantry penetrated the German line north of Hepscheid and then turned south to roll up the Germans. Snow more than the enemy slowed the attack. Tracked and wheeled vehicles moved with great difficulty. The burden fell, as it almost always had, on the "poor bloody infantry." Squads rotated their point men "every 75 to 100 yards." Mines added to the misery. Medical evacuation proved possible only with light tracked vehicles known as Weasels. Ralph J. Gordon, in the 18th Infantry, noted that "it was impossible to walk more than 300 yards through that snow without a rest." Machine guns could not be set up because they sank in the deep snow. Worse still, "men that were wounded also sunk into the snow and many poor souls froze to death before anyone found them."[15]

Nevertheless, the two divisions continued fighting their way forward. On January 29 the 3rd Battalion, 26th Infantry, took Bullingen, following a time-on-target concentration of nine artillery battalions. The 18th Infantry cleared Hunningen on January 30. Not given to hyperbole, Ridgway exulted in the performance of his lead divisions. In his memoir, *Soldier*, he wrote of the attack of the 1st and the 82nd that "it was like watching two great racehorses, driving head and head to the finish line." He found that both reacted quickly and supported each other readily. On February 1 the 1st ID approached the Siegfried and the Hürtgen for the second time. That day Andrus issued orders "to continue the attack to breach the defenses of the siegfried line."[16]

The attack began badly. Shortly after 0400 on February 2, the 18th Infantry reported that its 3rd Battalion was "pretty well cut up by friendly artillery fire when they were ready to move off." It turned out that the 82nd Airborne had fired on the 18th accidentally. The 26th Infantry got off without incident. The two regiments attacked with the 18th on the right and the 26th on the left, heading northeast into the Siegfried where it crossed into the Eifel under the illumination of a full moon. At 1542 that afternoon the 18th reported having "made it through both rows of dragons' teeth, meeting heavy small arms fire." The report continued, noting that they were receiving "some light mortar fire, no artillery. Tanks and TDs [tank destroyers] moving up." At last the division's infantry would be able to employ their preferred combined arms tactics, though it took blade tanks to plow routes through the snow and Gara's engineers to improve roads.[17]

Breaking into the Siegfried is not the same as breaking through. Systematic reduction of pillboxes and mine clearing required tactics first developed for the invasion and honed in the fighting to reach Aachen. Combined arms meant using everything from bazookas and tanks to eight-inch guns in direct fire. To be of use, good tactics had to be taught and executed. New officers like new enlisted replacements usually performed well if they had time and wit to learn. In early 1945 they often had too little time.

Bert H. Morphis, a squad leader in the 26th Infantry, survived a mistake made by a new lieutenant. In a postwar survey, Morphis recounted a tragic misadventure that happened during the fight to break into the Siegfried Line, recalling that

> G-2 said the pillboxes were empty, but many of us old time squad leaders were skeptical. Unfortunately, we had a new platoon leader who had never been in combat, and he refused to listen to our pleas for caution. Early in the morning, when it was pitch black, he led the platoon on a combat patrol into an area where there were a large number of pillboxes. We passed by one without incident, until the entire platoon had passed by. Then a machinegun opened up from behind, killing about half the platoon, including the lieutenant. The poor guy never had a chance to learn, and he took a dozen others with him!

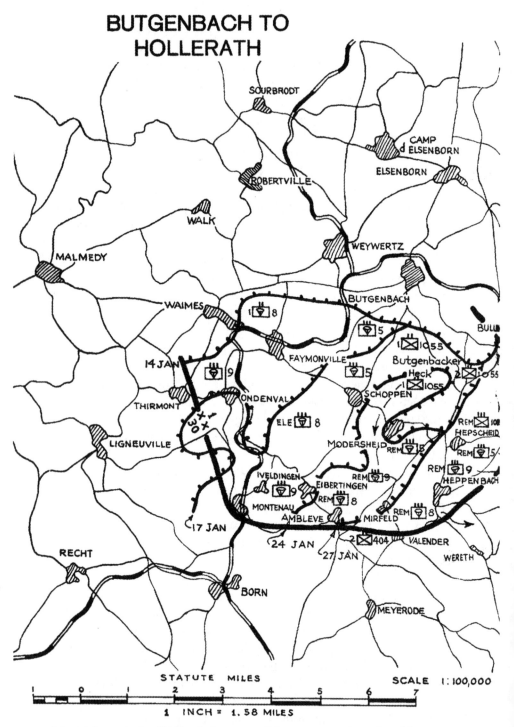

Map 26: Butgenbach to Hollerath, January14–February 5, 1945. Reproduced from 1st ID *Selected Intelligence Reports*, Volume 2.

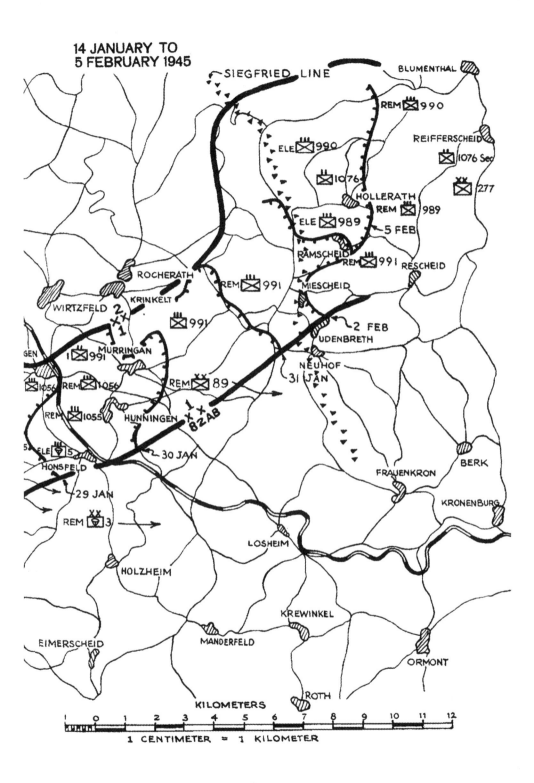

**14 JANUARY TO
5 FEBRUARY 1945**

SIEGFRIED LINE

BLUMENTHAL

REM 990

REIFFERSCHEID

ELE 990

1076 Sec

1076

277

HOLLERATH

REM 989

ELE 989

5 FEB

RAMSCHEID

REM 991

RESCHEID

ROCHERATH

REM 991

MIESCHEID

KRINKELT

WIRTZFELD

991

2 FEB

2

1

UDENBRETH

MURRINGAN

REM 89

NEUHOF

GEN

1 991

31 JAN

1056

REM 1056

REM 1055

HUNNINGEN

1
82AB

ELE 5

30 JAN

HONSFELD

FRAUENKRON

BERK

29 JAN

KRONENBURG

REM 3

LOSHEIM

HOLZHEIM

KREWINKEL

EIMERSCHEID

MANDERFELD

ORMONT

ROTH

KILOMETERS

1 0 1 2 3 4 5 6 7 8 9 10 11 12

1 CENTIMETER = 1 KILOMETER

Years after the fact, Morphis felt sorry both for the lieutenant and those whose lives his mistake cost. He viewed the incident as tragic, a kindness others might not have felt. 1st ID patrols did find some pillboxes unoccupied, but there are no reports suggesting that they should be assumed to be unoccupied. Why this officer accepted the G-2 estimate without question or mitigation in execution is hard to fathom.[18]

On January 31 Ridgway alerted the 30th and 84th ID to be prepared to pass forward of the 82nd Airborne and the 1st ID respectively, subject to on-order delays. In short, he did not plan to relieve his two thoroughbreds until absolutely necessary. The Germans of course got a vote. That day resistance stiffened among the pillboxes within the Siegfried. Both the 18th and 26th reported "heavy resistance" in the form of "intense small arms and automatic fire and some mortar and artillery fire." Still, the 1st ID and the 82nd managed to break through.[19]

As this attack was underway, the 12th Army Group G-3 ordered First Army to bring its offensive to a halt and prepare to extend its line north and provide up five divisions to Ninth Army to support 21st Army Group's assault crossing of the lower Rhine. General Bradley believed that it was essential to keep the pressure on the Germans, so he permitted the First Army offensive to continue less those divisions required by Ninth Army. In the following days divisions moved north to reinforce Ninth Army or extended their sectors to reduce the frontage in Ninth Army, and corps headquarters shuffled about. A lot of pawns had to move in order for 21st Army Group to mount the series of operations that would culminate in an assault crossing of the lower Rhine.[20]

The Big Red One was one of the pawns. Late on February 3, XVIII Airborne Corps advised Andrus that the division less the 16th Infantry would be relieved the following day. The 16th would move forward to the Roer, attached to the 8th ID, to take over the sector of one of its regiments. Having done so, Colonel Frederick W. Gibb's regiment would revert to 1st ID and prepare to receive the rest of the division when it moved up to the Roer. On the evening of February 4, the 99th ID relieved the two forward divisions rather than the 30th and 84th, as originally planned. The XVIII Airborne Corps' "Summary of Operations" intoned that "as a result of the breach of the west branch of the siegfried line in many places, the enemy commenced a withdrawal to the east."[21]

While the 16th set out for the Roer, the rest of the division moved to an assembly area near the village of Aywaille, Belgium, eighteen miles southwest of Aachen. Because of traffic on and trafficability of the roads, the 1st ID did not close on its assembly area until February 6. Two days later the Big Red One moved again, this time back in the Hürtgen near Schevenhutte, where it had mounted the attack to break out of the forest in November. Here they would plan an assault crossing of the Roer River. Mines, craters, and obstacles made moving around the forest difficult and consumed resources from both corps and division. Thankfully this time they did not have to fight for every inch of the muddy shattered forest.[22]

On February 8 German engineers damaged the discharge valves on two Roer River dams located in the Hürtgen, producing flooding and a flow rate that delayed the Ninth Army's Operation Grenade, as well First Army's plan to cross the Roer. Snow melt following a thaw exacerbated matters. By mid-morning on February 9, the 16th Infantry reported that the river had risen two feet and was "flowing so fast, it is questionable if we can use the boats [or] not." The regiment amplified its report, noting that "our people are safe. Cannot wade it [the Roer]." Nothing would happen until the Roer receded, which would prove the silver lining in this cloud.[23]

The delay bought time for detailed planning and the chance to integrate replacements. That proved true for all three regiments, including the 16th. Colonel Gibb and his regimental staff developed their crossing and follow-on operations for some three weeks. They built detailed models and planned meticulously. Andrus intended for the 16th and 26th to make the assault crossing. Accordingly, the 26th came forward on the night of February 10–11 and took over part of the 16th sector along the Roer. The 14th Cavalry Group took over another part of the sector to secure the southern or right flank. For the time being the 18th Infantry rested, trained, and prepared in its forward assembly areas.[24]

The 1st ID and its attached units benefited from this time. For example, Lieutenant Colonel Henry G. Learnard Jr. reported that in his battalion, "Replacements were absorbed and casuals returned to their organizations. Training and exercise were carried on daily in order to meld the new men into strong fighting groups with the old men, firing of all weapons was carried on and squad problems were started." The report noted with satisfaction that "the companies had their highest strength since before the invasion."[25]

On February 13 the 1st ID joined Major General John Millikin's III Corps to make the assault crossing of the Roer. That same day, the 1st Engineers provided the technical plan for the crossing. It called for ninety-two assault boats with paddles, three kinds of bridging, ten DUKW amphibious trucks, and several engineer units, including bridging detachments from the 2nd, 276th, and 994th Engineer Combat Battalions and all of the 299th Engineer

Combat Battalion.[26] The G-3 section confided in the division journal that as of midnight February 13, the 1st Infantry Division had concluded its 365th day in combat. Division units operating attached to other formations had accrued 136 more days of combat separately. The count began with the invasion of North Africa. The reckoning for detached units began on November 20, when 1st ID units were committed piecemeal by the British First Army.[27]

Brigadier General Andrus issued Field Order 65 at 1400 on February 16, specifying that the division would "attack to the east in its zone of action, force a crossing of the Roer river, seize and secure a bridgehead for further advance east and north east on Corps order." As always each of the infantry regiments organized as combined arms teams, including 4.2-inch mortars. Task Force Davisson organized in December rounded out the force. Davisson lacked infantry but otherwise his task force was a combined arms team. The III Corps provided a 155-millimeter howitzer battalion, as well as a battalion of 25-pounder British-made howitzers, and a battery of self-propelled howitzers. At two and half pages, the base order was brief. Annexes provided the necessary details of enemy dispositions and planned fires. The engineer plan laid out the scheme for the crossing and bridging efforts. The order envisioned the 16th crossing with one battalion on D-1, with the remainder of the 16th and the 26th crossing on D-Day. All that remained was for the Roer to recede.[28]

Meanwhile the division continued to prepare. The G-2 reported that the enemy order of battle on the east bank of Roer was not clear. What was clear was that they were "occupying positions along the east bank which he had many weeks to prepare." The Germans also had good observation of the west bank. As soon as American patrols appeared, they were fired on. The two sides shelled each other, with the Americans enjoying the advantage of ample ammunition. By contrast the German situation deteriorated rapidly as the OKW moved resources east. III Corps estimated that the 85th VGD, the 272nd VGD, the 353rd VGD, and the 3rd FJD were in the III Corps zone. None of these units was in good shape. General der Infanterie Friedrich Köchling's LXXXI Corps controlled the 353rd while General der Infanterie Otto Hitzfeld's LXXIV Corps had the others. In mid-February Rundstedt provided Hitler with a grim assessment. He believed that Army Group B had the equivalent of only forty-five infantry battalions. Charles B. MacDonald calculated that these amounted to the strength of "six and a half

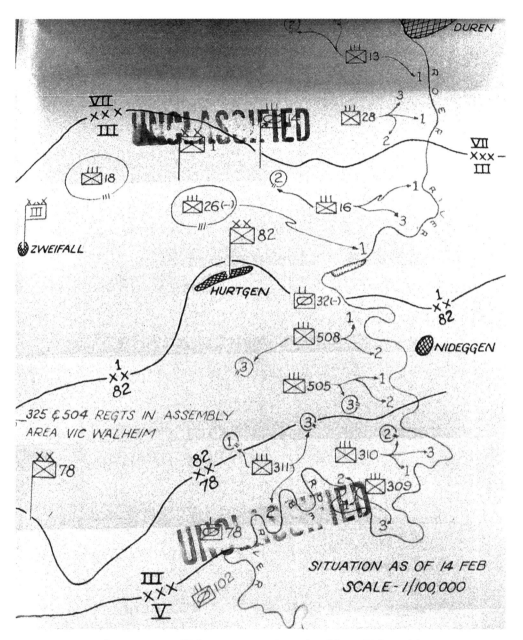

Map 27: The Situation as of February 14, 1945. Reproduced from III Corps After Action Report for February 1945.

full divisions." The available artillery ammunition amounted to "less than a third of that expended in the earlier fighting [in November]."[29]

Another change of command occurred when Lieutenant Colonel John Williamson replaced Colonel George A. Smith Jr. on February 22, when Smith left to serve as assistant division commander of Terry Allen's 104th ID. Smith had begun his service in the 1st ID during Allen's tenure. Moving to the 104th ID would mean promotion to brigadier general. Sadly, George Smith did not live to be promoted. He was killed in action a few days after his transfer. Williamson was no stranger to the division or the 18th. He had been with the regiment since the campaign in North Africa and had commanded the 2nd Battalion.[30]

The following day, the 8th ID, styled "Pathfinder," played that role in its assault crossing of the Roer. VII Corps preceded the assault with a forty-five-minute preparation fire beginning at 0245. By 0400 the 8th ID's 1st Battalion, 28th Infantry, was "well across," with the 13th Infantry starting across. During the course of the crossing in the 16th Infantry's sector along the banks of the Roer, German artillery fired 184 rounds of light and medium artillery (75-millimeter and 105-millimeter), 465 mortar rounds, and 20 rockets. The Americans responded with multiple-battalion time-on-target concentrations. The 33rd FA, one of the division's 105-millimeter battalions, fired 480 rounds in the artillery preparation and 152 more in missions during the day, this from an ammunition allowance of 800 rounds. During the fighting in the fall, and even during the Bulge, German artillery was effective partly due to their caching of ammunition for the counteroffensive and their shorter lines of communication. The weight of Allied logistics and manpower, if not yet decisive, was approaching that point.[31]

On February 23 Hodges determined that rather than all three corps conducting discrete assault crossings, 1st ID would cross on VII Corps bridges and attack south to clear the east bank. Then 1st ID would build bridges for III Corps. The process would then ripple down the line. By February 25, the 8th ID had expanded its bridgehead so that additional bridges could be built. In accordance with Hodges's innovation, III Corps and 1st ID would not have to make an assault crossing. In the wee hours that morning, the 1st ID's G-3 coordinated with Pathfinder to cross its bridges. "You have priority on use of Bridges," the 8th ID promised. Moreover the 8th ID reported, "Duren is all cleaned out." The two divisions collaborated on a complex crossing operation over multiple bridges, including footbridges. The 8th ID also facilitated the 1st ID's passage through its lines while in contact with the enemy.

VII Corps controlled the crossing while protecting the right flank of Ninth Army. A river crossing and assisting a forward passage of lines while focused in contact is easy to describe in a few sentences. It is difficult when no one is shooting at you, let alone in contact with a determined albeit weakened enemy.[32]

At 0835 Lieutenant Colonel Walter H. Grant's 2nd Battalion, 16th Infantry, headed for the bridges. At 1005 the 26th Infantry began crossing with its lead battalion, accompanied by tanks, tank destroyers, six towed 57-millimeter antitank guns, communications, and medical evacuation vehicles. Lieutenant Colonel Bill Gara's 1st Engineer Battalion and its attached engineers began putting in bridges to develop other crossing sites in the 1st ID zone. These would be used by other 1st ID, III Corps, and V Corps units. By late afternoon his engineers had one eighty-foot footbridge completed and were building a second, along with a treadway bridge. Gara was on the move, reconnoitering additional sites because he believed that with the Roer still receding, he had enough treadway left to put in still another bridge. Capacity produces momentum, which supports execution.[33]

16th Infantry Starts the Dance to Clear the East Bank of the Roer

Despite its complexity, a river crossing is a task, not a mission. Crossing the Roer all along the front was a preliminary step in defeating the German Army west of the Rhine. Once across the Roer, Grant's 2nd Battalion, 16th Infantry, would lead the 1st ID's attack south to roll up the Germans on the east bank. The 2nd Battalion's mission included clearing the villages of Niederau and Kreuzau in preparation for continuing the attack southeast or east. The 3rd and 1st Battalions initially remained on the west bank but crossed as the 2nd Battalion moved south. The rest of the division would cross in due course.

Grant knew his business. He took command of the 2nd Battalion during the pursuit. Moreover, because the regiment had been on the west bank for some time, "minute plans were worked out. Sand tables constructed, and all personnel thoroughly briefed." Aerial photographs of the target area enabled careful assessment, supported by reconnaissance "from a suitable observation point on the high ground west of the river." The attack on February 25 stemmed from detailed planning and contingencies based on considering what might go wrong.[34]

Major Albert H. Smith Jr., the regimental S-3, arranged for two self-propelled 155-millimeter howitzers to be used in direct fire on the objective

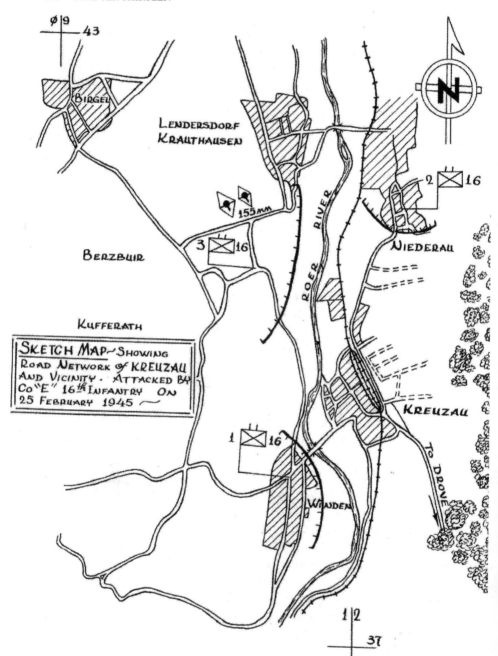

Map 28: A Sketch Map Showing the Road Network of Kreuzau. Reproduced from Combat Achievements Report, Chapter IV, "The Attack on Kreuzau," February 25, 1945, Company E 2nd Battalion 16th Infantry.

villages. According to Smith, for two days the howitzers "had been pasting specific strongpoints in Kreuzau and the high ground east of the town, using a delayed fuze [*sic*] so that rounds would burst inside of the buildings that were being hit." Gibb set H-Hour at 1200. At H-10 1st Battalion feigned an assault crossing of the river at Winden by opening up with heavy machine guns and Browning automatic rifles. The regimental commander weighted the main effort with the bulk of available combat support. He provided one platoon of Shermans, one platoon of tracked tank destroyers, one of the regiments' towed 57-millimeter antitank platoons, the two self-propelled howitzers mentioned above, one section of 4.2-inch mortars, and the fires from four artillery battalions.[35]

With this largesse, Grant built a carefully choreographed plan that would have made Busby Berkley green with envy. Grant developed detailed maneuver, fire support, obscuration, and communications plans that would support his companies, bounding by platoons, to seize and clear positions held by the 353rd VGD. As the attack began, the 7th FA, the regiment's direct support battalion, would fire concentrations on the "woods east of town and on the southeast road," leading from Kreuzau toward Drove, to harass and interdict the defenders The 4.2-inch mortars would fire smoke to screen the edge of woods. The battalion's 81-millimeter mortars would fire a rolling barrage. The two 155-millimeter howitzers remained on the west bank, prepared to suppress enemy armor, antitank guns, and automatic weapons.[36]

Grant used phase lines to coordinate the attack and planned to lead with Companies E and F abreast, with E on the left or east. The tank platoon and two tank destroyers would move with Company F along with a minesweeping team. World War II Signal Corps radios had limited frequencies. For a number of reasons, the army chose to equip different branches with radios that generally lacked the frequencies to communicate with other units. Tanks could not, with the turn of a dial, talk to the infantry they supported. Often tank platoon leaders led their platoons on foot, communicating via a "prearranged arm and hand signal system" or a telephone with a long trailing cable. In any case, combined arms attacks required careful communications planning to ensure that units could talk to each other. The 745th TB and the 1st ID had become quite good at making things work.[37]

Despite high turnover and high casualties, the 2nd Battalion, 16th Infantry, and for that matter all of the units assigned or attached to the 1st ID, had a core of experience that permitted the complexity required for organizing a crossing, assembling the force on the far side, and attacking and clearing towns. It is easy to characterize the 1st ID as battle-hardened or experienced, but that fails to consider the continual learning and teaching that has to happen to succeed. Casualties and routine turnover meant that these units, as entities, could not be described as "veteran," let alone hardened. But the small veteran core of the 2nd Battalion made sure the attack began on time and proceeded as planned. Together the veterans passed on what had become, to some extent, tribal wisdom. The companies bounded by platoon, using phase lines to pace their advance. During the last part of the attack through Kreuzau, Company F advanced with direct fire support from both Sherman tanks and tank destroyers. As a result, the battalion cleared Kreuzau by 1700 and continued the attack toward Drove.[38]

Major Smith discussed the operation in early March with a US Army combat historian. Commanders had confidence in each other and their supporting units, he explained, because the 1st ID had kept the same attachments "so long that the Bn Co's [battalion commanders] regard their tank and TD [tank destroyers] as virtually organic support." Team work and confidence permitted well-choreographed elegant plans that saved lives. As important, "the 2nd Bn had little difficulty in overrunning the defenses of Kreuzau" and Grant's troops took 112 captives from the 941st and 943rd regiments of the 353rd VGD.[39]

Despite their weakened and weakening condition, the Germans did not go belly up. They mined approaches and prepared defensive positions, fought to hold them, and counterattacked when they could. Nevertheless, both the 16th and 26th Infantry crossed that day. The 26th crossed during the late afternoon and evening, so did not get into action until the next day. Despite the rapid buildup of American forces, the 353rd VGD mounted a counterattack on February 26, supported by artillery and tanks. The 16th repulsed the counterattack and, along with the 26th, expanded and ultimately broke out of the bridgehead to get their part of Operation Lumberjack underway. By the end of the day 1st ID had pushed south on as far as Boich, some three miles from Niderau and beyond Stockheim, roughly two miles east of the Roer. The 18th Infantry crossed that same day and passed through Stockheim to carry the attack east, then northeast.[40]

The pace of operations picked up as the division exploited the breakout. Although the ground east of the Roer was comparatively flat, with good roads, it was also dotted with small towns. With little effort, German units could prepare effective roadblocks. Sam Fuller complained that the exploitation turned into "a nonstop marathon that was not to end until the Rhine had been reached. There were so many little towns that we took, I lost track of their names." He remembered that "rest was snatched in periods of minutes, not hours. Fatigue and trench foot made every step of that operation tough as hell. We looked more haggard than the Nazis we captured." Fuller suffered along with his mates, but he and most of them understood why. Keeping the pressure on left the Germans little chance "to get set for a counterattack."[41]

After breaking out of the bridgehead, the three regiments attacked abreast, with the 18th in the north, the 16th in the center, and the 26th in the south. Task Force Davisson screened the northern flank. Continuing the attack through the last night of February, the Big Red One crossed the Neffel River in stride. The 1st ID had a penchant for attacking at night, and it did so now with good reason. The S-2, S-3, and operations sergeant of the 18th Infantry provided an explanation that makes sense. First and foremost, they noted, the river plain was "flat as a billiard table." Hence there was no cover, and in this area no woods, so no concealment. "When there's no concealment or cover," they concluded, "you've got to attack at night. The primary things now are German artillery and mortar. Jerry infantry is almost a thing of the past." Major Earl Green, assistant G-3, 1st ID, echoed this sentiment.[42]

Jerry infantry was, in fact, not quite a thing of the past. When Company C, 18th Infantry, attacked the village of Pingsheim in the wee hours of March 1, German infantry supported by machine guns and five large-caliber guns pinned them down. Company C took heavy casualties, including all of its platoon leaders and fifteen noncommissioned officers. Ralph J. Gordon, working in the Company C command post, was furious. According to him, "The bastard Jerries were waiting for them. Having dug trenches around the town, they just mowed our boys down as they came across the open plain." Lieutenant Colonel Henry G. Learnard Jr. stopped the killing by maneuvering Company B in position to finish the job. It took several hours. but Learnard's infantry captured two officers, 126 Landsers, and several vehicles, as well as "4-100-millimeter guns and S.P. gun and an armored car." By day's end the division had taken three hundred prisoners from the 12th and 353rd VGD.[43]

Bonn and the Rhine

The 1st ID continued eastward against the kind of resistance that is described by those not in close combat as "sporadic." On March 3, in the village of Gymnich, the division captured a young German officer and what was left of his 8th Company, 89th Infantry, 12th VGD. Originally positioned northeast of Düren, the officer had withdrawn when the 1st ID crossed the Roer south of him and retired to the northeast with two horse-drawn 75-millimeter howitzers, six 81-millimeter mortars, four heavy machine guns, and his troops. As his company moved, four of its soldiers were killed. At Golzheim, American artillery accounted for the howitzers, machine guns, and two mortars. The officer left Golzheim with twenty-five Landsers and eventually reached Gymnich with twenty men and no mortars. There a captain ordered him to defend the village, provided him with some overlays, and left.[44]

The young officer set about building roadblocks. He rounded up some Volkssturm men, but after inspecting these "troops," he told them "to return to the cellars and wait for the Americans." The next morning an officer senior to him arrived with seventy men from the 4th Fortress Regiment and assumed command. The commander of 8th Company "retired to a cellar for the first sleep he had had since the breakthrough; when he woke up there was nobody in town but the Americans." The defense west of the Rhine was unraveling.[45]

In the midst of this, Oberst Kurt Hummel took command of the 353rd VGD. Hummel found that he "did not have a single coherent infantry regiment." He had two regimental staffs and four battalion staffs, so he had the means to exercise command. By looting his own support formations and adding Volkssturm to the division, he managed to field what he called "alarm units" of sixty to eighty soldiers. He reckoned he could maintain ten or twelve of these. He still had his four artillery battalions and some antitank guns but was short of ammunition.[46]

The day after he assumed command, Hummel lost contact with 12th VGD on his right. On March 4, the 1st ID crossed the Erft River and took the village of Weilerwist, threatening his left flank. Ordered by corps to counterattack, he did, but his inexperienced alarm units "started running around in circles as soon as they came within the orbit of the enemy's fire." By March 6 the 353rd had been forced within two miles of the Rhine and was even weaker. Although Hitler denied permission to withdraw artillery or armor east of the Rhine, the German bridgehead had become untenable. Forced north and east, the 353rd no longer opposed the Big Red One. Friedrich Köchling, whose LXXXI Corps defended just south of the 353rd, complained after the war that "had the proportion of strength been even only approximately equal, the result of the fighting would have been altogether different."[47]

Köchling's complaint aside, the 1st ID continued to advance. The 62nd VGD now blocked the way. On March 5, the 1st took part of the Vorgebirge, a ridge running more or less parallel to the Rhine, rising as much as three hundred feet above the river valley. The authors of *Danger Forward* exulted about crossing the streams west of Köln (in English, Cologne) that constituted the so-called Cologne moat and "biting into the Vorgebirge whose supposed defenses had turned out to be a hollow sham." The G-3 characterized resistance as "moderate," with the troops encountering "scattered mines." Of course, one mine makes a minefield.[48]

John P. Downing, who had fought with the 18th since North Africa, expressed his frustration and even some confusion about "moderate" resistance. Of the fighting in March, he observed, "All the people we met from North Africa to Germany just loved Americans, and yet you had to fight into every town. At present the war is strategically over and even the most stubborn German should have been able to see that the end was just a matter of time. Yet every little village had to be fought for and more people had to be killed needlessly. Nobody was mad at anybody, and still everybody [is] blowing each other's heads off." Resistance became more or less moderate, depending on who made the call.[49]

On March 6, the forward line of troops ran along the major north-south road parallel to the Rhine, roughly two miles west of the river. That day III Corps added Bonn to the 1st ID zone of action. Having taken the first major German city, the 1st ID now aimed to take the second largest German city west of the Rhine. Andrus rotated regiments during the advance to allow some rest. In part because of that, the regiments uniformly reported combat effectiveness as excellent. Maybe so, but, having cleared about dozen towns, the troops were tired. On the southern flank, the 16th Infantry had seized the village of Waldorf, less than five miles west-northwest of Bonn. In the north, the 26th was fighting at Bruhl and also embroiled in heavy fighting at the village of Pingsdorf. The intermingling of German units told its own story. For example, the 16th Infantry captured twenty-seven soldiers from sixteen different units, including the 9th PZ, 3rd FJD, and 62nd, 89th, and 353rd VGD, and one man from the 1st Don Cossack Division.[50]

First Army had largely closed up to the Rhine. Collins's VII Corps was fighting in Köln, Millikin's III Corps was just west of the Rhine, and Huebner's V Corps had reached the Ahr River short of the Rhine. The 1st ID spent March 7 coordinating the relief of a 9th ID regiment in order to gain maneuver space to attack Bonn the next day. In the north the 26th Infantry cleared Bruhl. The 16th Infantry reached Roisdorf and Alfter, less than three miles from Bonn. The 18th Infantry moved from their reserve positions to an assembly area in the 9th ID zone, "prepared to move on bonn." Bonn, like Cologne, was a university town founded by the Romans in the first century BC. It was also the birthplace of Ludwig van Beethoven, whose Fifth Symphony resonated with the Allies: its *dit, dit, dit, dah* rhythm sounded like Morse code for V, and thus Victory.[51]

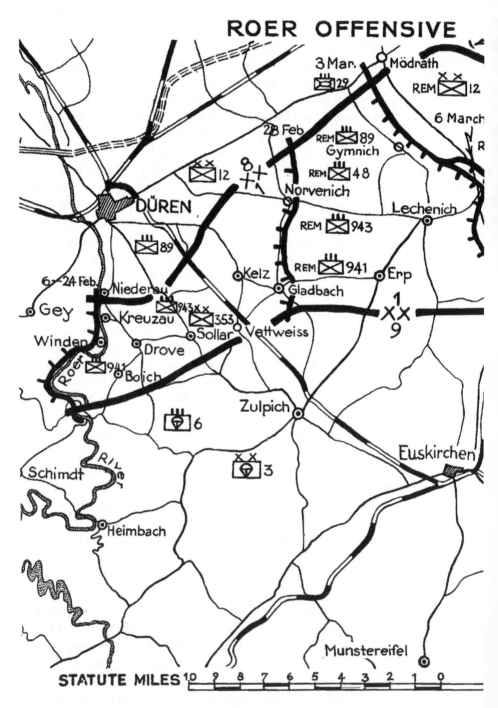

Map 29: The Roer Offensive, February 25–March 9, 1945. Reproduced from 1st ID *Selected Intelligence Reports*, Volume 2.

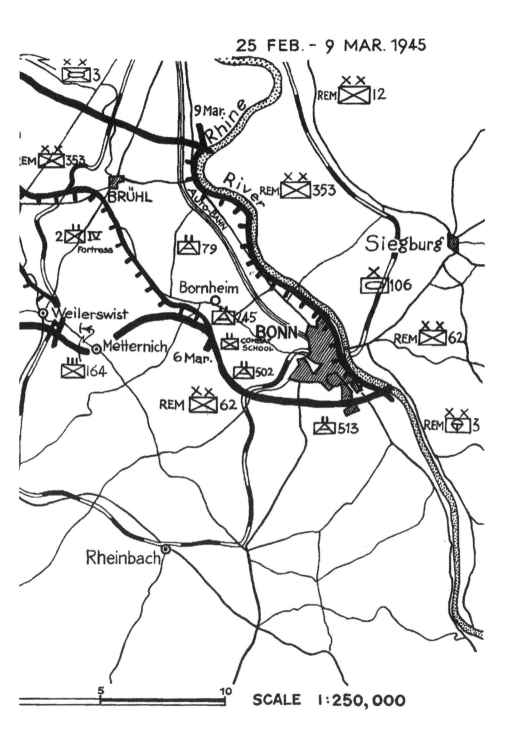

25 FEB. - 9 MAR. 1945

SCALE 1:250,000

Exploiting the breakout from the Roer bridgehead required rapid development of the situation. The deliberate planning for the crossing of the Roer could not be repeated; regimental and battalion commanders had little time to organize the attack on Bonn. Andrus kept it simple. He ordered the 16th and 18th Infantry to make the assault, with the 16th on the left, coming out of Roisdorf and Alfter, and 18th striking due east from near the village of Ollekoven. This was in every way a hasty offensive. The 16th Infantry's planning serves to make the case. Gibb passed the execute order to his regiment at 2050 March 7, with the attack scheduled for 0400. He planned to lead with his 3rd Battalion on the left or north, his 1st battalion on the right heading through the city toward the Rhine River bridge, and his 2nd Battalion in reserve. That same night he sent his intelligence and reconnaissance platoon toward the city to learn what they could.[52]

The platoon went almost a mile along the north side of the railway, running east toward the river and then turning south into the city. They found the road had not been mined. A civilian, when questioned, reported enemy trucks in the area. Once, hearing German voices from what they concluded was an outpost, they stopped. The only other information came from the G-2, who believed there were six hundred enemy in Bonn, including antiaircraft troops, some infantry, and a few tanks, and perhaps twenty thousand remaining civilians. The mission of Wozenki's 3rd Battalion was to get into the city and prevent the enemy from "coming from the north."[53]

Gibb provided the 3rd Battalion with robust support, including a medium tank platoon, a light tank platoon, two Sherman assault guns (105-millimeter howitzers), an M10 tank destroyer platoon, mine-sweeping teams, and two platoons of heavy machine guns. Andrus eschewed an artillery preparation for either regiment, hoping to surprise the defenders. The 7th FA would focus interdictory fire on the eastern end of the Rhine River bridge on order. Wozenski issued an oral order shortly after 2300. Although there had been no time for detailed preparation, the battalion had 1:25,000 maps and two versions of the city street plan as well as aerial photos. At 0330 they had coffee and sandwiches for breakfast and then moved out in a column of companies at 0400.[54]

Captain John E. McCarthy's Company K led the way, heading down the road in a column of twos. The order of march was 1st Platoon, 3rd Platoon, 2nd Platoon, followed by a Sherman tank platoon of four tanks and an assault gun, the company headquarters, the company weapons platoon, an antitank platoon from regiment, and engineers, including a minesweeper team. The Germans either knew something was up or were nervous, as "numerous flares were observed and sporadic machine gun fire heard." As the company closed on the city, the Germans opened up with machine gun fire that passed overhead. Company K crossed the railway, passed through a traffic circle at the edge of the city, and entered Bonn at 0500.[55]

As they progressed, the company surprised enemy sentries at several intersections. These they disarmed and brought along. At one point "the lead platoon marched side-by-side down the street" with a German unit. The Germans had seen a 76-millimeter armed Sherman in the attached tank platoon. With its long gun tube and muzzle brake, it apparently resembled a Panzer tank. Finally one of the Germans inquired, "What Panzer division is this?" They became prisoners of Lieutenant Robert H. Smith's 1st Platoon. The company made it to within sight of the Rhine River bridge, some five blocks south of where Rosentalstrasse reached the river.[56]

Smith had just reported to McCarthy that the bridge was intact when "all hell broke loose." Somehow the unit had passed through "a ring of tanks and self-propelled guns guarding the approaches to the bridge." The troops encountered were likely from a mix of units but mainly from the 253rd Replacement Training Regiment. The infantry scrambled for cover. Two tanks secured the intersection of Rosental and Römerstrasse, while the assault gun secured the intersection of Rosental and Wachsibleicher. The rest of the battalion blocked German units heading for the bridge, while McCarthy and his troops dealt with German traffic attempting to reach the bridge or perhaps counterattacking. In any case, within an hour Company K and the 3rd Battalion stopped Germans from getting through Bonn.[57]

McCarthy's company and attachments did a good bit of damage. The assault gun destroyed a Tiger tank. One of the Shermans knocked out a self-propelled 88-millimeter antitank gun. The infantry and regimental antitank guns accounted for two captured American Weasels, two trucks, three cars, and an ambulance hauling "food and ammunition." Once the fighting died down, Lieutenant Smith and five volunteers took the time to "clean the buildings on Rosenthal [sic] Strasse down to the river." German artillery and mortars shelled the Americans throughout the day.[58]

At 0830, Company A from Lieutenant Colonel Edmund F. Driscoll's 1st Battalion linked up with McCarthy's troops. The forward line of troops had nearly reached the Rhine bridge. Fierce resistance along Bornheimer Strasse stopped the rest of Driscoll's battalion cold. It took the 1st Battalion nine hours to clear the enemy. The 18th Infantry encountered even stiffer resistance from the replacement regiment, supported by what the G-2 described as "Grade-A troops of the flak [antiaircraft] units." Equipped with automatic

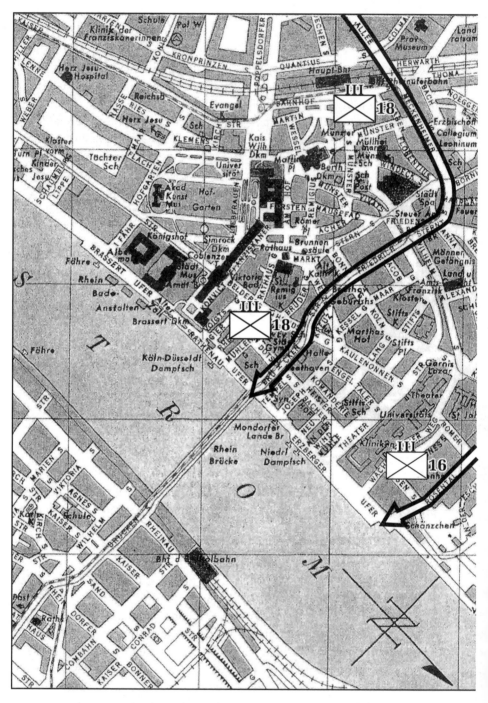

Map 30: 1st ID Attack on the City of Bonn, March 8, 1945. Reproduced from Combat Achievements Report, Chapter VIII, "The Attack on the City of Bonn, 8 March 1945," Company K, 3rd Battalion 16th Infantry.

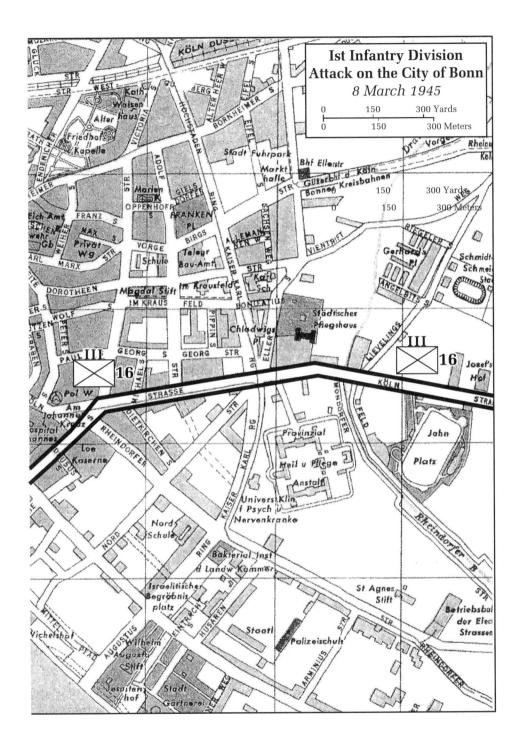

20-millimeter cannons, these units bedeviled both Driscoll and the 18th. Hearing that the bridge remained intact, Andrus ordered the 26th to pass through Gibb's regiment and take it.[59]

The chance to be first across the Rhine had passed at 1630 the day before, when the 9th Armored Division reported that Brigadier General William M. Hoge's Combat Command B had taken the town of Remagen south of Bonn, and with it the Ludendorff railway bridge. The chance to be second passed at 2115 hours, when a German engineer captain blew up the Rhine bridge in Bonn. When he was captured and interrogated that day, the G-2 learned that he had not "slept for three days, worrying whether he would be able to blow the bridge at precisely the right moment." The G-2 concluded ruefully, "He succeeded admirably." The division finished clearing the city the next afternoon at 1410, taking 733 prisoners. German civilians constituted a new problem, and a large one. Until closing on the Rhine, the 1st ID had dealt with relatively few civilians, but there were 50,000 in Bonn alone, and 100,000 others encountered during the approach to the Rhine. Many of these were refugees from west of the Roer. Coping with civilians and screening them would be a growing burden.[60]

The 1st ID, and for that matter First Army, enjoyed a remarkable twelve days from the breakout from the Roer bridgehead on February 26 and March 10. They crossed the Köln plain at a pace that, compared to operations since mid-September, constituted breakneck speed, and took 5,163 prisoners. On March 10 the 1st ID returned to VII Corps and turned to defending the west bank of the Rhine, which permitted some time for "rehabilitation and training for future operations." The troops were dead tired, and many suffered from trench foot or worse. Lieutenant John Baumgartner, who had joined just before the attack on Bonn, described his unit as a "company of walking dead men." In Bonn, Big Red One troops captured a distillery. Ralph Gordon recalled that on a rest day, "the company got a huge whiskey ration, and everyone was in their glory getting so drunk we didn't know where we were—nor did we care." Rehabilitation comes in many guises.[61]

Integrating a New Kind of Replacements

Receiving replacements continued, but with a wrinkle. Casualties were light in the fighting from the Roer to the Rhine, but nevertheless the division's infantry companies remained understrength. On March 7–8, for example, the 16th Infantry received 7 officers and 58 replacements, 21 of these returning from hospitalization. Company F of the 16th was "fat" with 5 officers

and 171 enlisted men assigned, so they were short only 1 officer and 15 enlisted soldiers. With only 4 officers and 144 enlisted soldiers, Company C
was in the worst shape, and the shortage of infantry replacements had not
improved. Eisenhower took what for the time was a bold decision: in early
January he sent a cable to Marshall, telling the chief that he intended to afford black soldiers serving in the Communications Zone the opportunity to
fight as infantrymen. Originally he planned to form independent infantry
battalions, but in the end that proved impossible, given the time it would
take to train specialists. He therefore advised Marshall in February that he
would form only infantry platoons. Early that month nearly five thousand
black soldiers assigned to the Communications Zone volunteered to fight as
infantrymen. Many of these men were noncommissioned officers in support
specialties but accepted demotion to serve in the infantry. They took accelerated infantry training and formed platoons led by white platoon leaders and
platoon sergeants who volunteered to serve with them.[62]

Black Americans were already serving in "colored" combat units led, with
few exceptions, by white officers. Black Americans had fought and died for
their country since the revolution without ever being accorded the unqual-
ified respect they both earned and deserved Black men and women who
served in World War II did so with no more assurance of equal treatment
than their forbears. Yet they volunteered to serve. On March 11, 1945, a platoon of black Americans joined each of the 1st ID's three infantry regiments.[63]

On their arrival the 18th Infantry undertook integrating these replacements. Brigadier General George A. Taylor led the way, briefing the new men
on the history and achievements of the Big Red One. Colonel Williamson
mandated that these soldiers would receive equal treatment in all matters.
He assigned the new platoon to Lieutenant Colonel Learnard's 1st Battalion.
Learnard assigned the platoon to Company B, commanded by Richard J.
Lindo, who noted that most of these men "had taken a bust from master
sergeant, first sergeant down to private, to prove themselves. This they did,
because I could not keep these people from being heroes and from killing
Germans whether I had them in the attack or in reserve." Lindo thought they
"were some of the most magnificent soldiers I had ever seen." To Lindo they
showed "that the color of your skin on your face didn't mean a damn thing."[64]

Jim Sharp, now a hardened veteran of two months in combat, served in
Lindo's outfit. According to Sharp, two soldiers, one from Louisiana and
one from Alabama, were outspoken in their opposition to the idea of fighting alongside black soldiers. But most of the troops in Company B had not

"grown up around segregation and therefore did not feel the same way." In any case Sharp concluded that "after a few days in battle they proved themselves to be good soldiers like the rest of the company." They remained with Company B through the end of the war and beyond.[65]

The Rhine Bridgehead

While the 1st ID enjoyed a few days of relative ease on the west bank of the Rhine, First Army moved what it could to expand the bridgehead at Remagen. Hodges, thought pedestrian by the likes of George Patton, acted with alacrity. He called Bradley immediately to let him know about seizing the bridge and asked to exploit this success. Bradley responded, "Hot Dog, Courtney, this will bust him wide open. . . . Shove everything across it Courtney, and build up the bridgehead up tightly." Eisenhower's G-3, Lieutenant General Harold R. "Pink" Bull, present at 12th Army Group, was nonplussed. He objected that a bridgehead at Remagen was not in the plan, which focused on 21st Army Group making the crossing. Bull was rightly concerned about weakening the main effort. Bradley called Eisenhower. Unlike Bull, the supreme commander proved enthusiastic, but he too had misgivings based on the high palisades of the east bank and because there was no favorable exit east.[66]

Six miles east of the Remagen bridgehead, an autobahn ran south from Köln to Frankfurt. Reaching the autobahn would enable moving north and out of the mountains or south to Koblenz and a maneuver corridor that ran east toward the Giessen. The autobahn running from Frankfurt to Kassel went through Giessen. The terrain and the autobahn afforded rapid movement. Going north and then east to Giessen was the shortest way out of the mountainous region. However one got there from Giessen, the First Army could move north and perhaps envelop German forces on the east bank of the Rhine. Eisenhower authorized Bradley to use five divisions, which would not interfere with the grand plan to which Pink Bull had referred.[67]

In *The Last Offensive*, Charles B. MacDonald points out that neither side had anticipated or even considered an American crossing in this area, precisely because there was no exit, and the terrain favored the defender. The Remagen bridge lay in the sector of the German Fifteenth Army, commanded by General der Infanterie Gustav von Zangen, who had General der Artillerie Walter Lucht's LXVI and Hitzfeld's LXVII Corps immediately available. Though both had limited means, they had good terrain to defend. But neither had the means to reduce the rapidly growing American bridgehead. Generalleutnant Fritz Bayerlein's LIII Corps mounted the main opposition and had the best chance to reduce the bridgehead. Bayerlein, formerly commander of Panzer Lehr, had more recently led Korpsgruppe Bayerlein, defending a sector north of Köln. On March 9 Walter Model assigned him command of the LIII Corps and the task of reducing the bridgehead and restoring the defense. On March 11 Generalfeldmarschall Albert Kesselring showed up at the LIII Corps command post to announce that he now commanded OB West in place of Rundstedt, whom the führer relieved for a second and final time.[68]

Bayerlein's order of battle sounded impressive. He had the 9th, 11th, and Panzer Lehr Panzer Divisions as well as the 106th Panzer Brigade. He had two infantry formations, the well-equipped and up-to-strength 130th Infantry, with about two thousand troops, the 340th VGD, with no more than two hundred troops, and the 208th Artillery Regiment. Finally, he had an antitank battalion, a mortar battalion, and an assault battalion. All told, LIII Corps had about sixty tanks, twenty pieces of artillery, fifteen antitank guns, twenty mortars, ten assault guns, and perhaps ten thousand troops, or less of everything than would have been found in a full-strength Panzer division, and far fewer infantry than in a full-strength infantry division.[69]

Despite their comparative weakness, the Germans had an important advantage. The Americans had to cross a river, assemble, and expand the bridgehead under fire. Little had changed since Clausewitz devoted a chapter of *On War* to river crossings. The Prussian theorist pointed out that "the very difficulty involved in taking up a position beyond a river also greatly increases the possibility of effective defense." He concluded that forcing a river crossing "always weakens and dislocates the offensive," and cited the difficulties the Austrian Army suffered "on the lower Rhine in 1796." In 1945 the Rhine did not prove an insurmountable problem; rivers don't, but they do provide obvious advantages to the defender, and did so in this case.[70]

While the 1st ID enjoyed a few days of comparative respite, III Corps struggled to expand the bridgehead at least beyond the range of observed artillery fire. It took more than a week for the 9th, 78th, and 99th IDs to hammer their way forward to a depth of not quite three miles. This provided scant room for more troops, but more troops were coming anyway. The 1st ID was one of the five divisions that Eisenhower could spare for Bradley's use east of the Rhine. Hodges called VII Corps forward. In turn, Collins ordered the Big Red One to lead the corps across, and the 8th ID relieved Andrus's troops in the Bonn sector. The G-3 operations report described what happened next without emotion: "At 0400A [March 16], the 26th Infantry, in trucks, reinforced by the 33d and 957th Field Artillery Battalions, moved out of their assembly areas to cross the RHINE river in the 3d Corps sector and by 1835A, the combat team closed in its assembly area." This laconic entry marked an historic second crossing of the Rhine for the 1st Infantry Division, which had first crossed the river in 1918.[71]

The division, less the 16th Infantry, crossed the river and moved up on the right of the 78th ID to seize objectives east of the Köln–Koblenz autobahn. Andrus attacked with the 18th on the left, the 26th on the right, and the 1st Battalion, 16th Infantry, in reserve. The remainder of the 16th stayed on the river's west bank. The attack went in at 0250 on March 17 and immediately encountered "intense small arms, tank and rocket fire." The defending troops came from a heterogenous collection of units, including a training unit, a Kampfgruppe from 3rd FJD, tanks from 3rd Panzergrenadier Division, and a battalion from the 9th PZ. Small villages abounded among rugged hills, often with places names ending in *scheid* or *berg*, denoting ravine or gorge in the first instance and hill or mountain in the second. The enemy fought back with desperation and expended 4,500 rounds of artillery. Nevertheless, both regiments took objectives east of the autobahn.[72]

Naturally, in addition to lavish expenditure of scarce ammunition, the Germans also mounted a counterattack using five assault guns carrying infantry. They were driven off with damage to three of their vehicles, and the division artillery swept the ground clean of enemy infantry. The Big Red One's infantry battalions continued the attack, maneuvering by company, but it was slow going. The 33nd FA, supporting the 18th Infantry, fired 1596 high-explosive rounds in fifty-nine missions, while the 18th Infantry used artillery to suppress the enemy and enable maneuver, in some cases firing smoke to screen movement. Remarkably, a 105-millimeter artillery round struck a Tiger tank with "no noticeable effect." Of course, that observation fails to account for what the tank's occupants felt—most of those who have been under fire would say that what does not kill you does not necessarily make you stronger.

By nightfall the division held the autobahn along three miles of its length, between the villages of Ruttscheid to Windhagen. By no means had a break-out occurred. Breaking out would require fighting across miles of ridges and hills, some of which were seven hundred feet or higher above the river level. In the *Scheid*, or ravines, ran streams, all of which had to be crossed, complicated by peaks that rose three or four hundred feet on either side.[73]

Of the day's fighting, Bayerlein wrote, "Strong enemy attack in the sector of 9 PZ and 340 VGD advancing beyond the Autobahn between Orscheid and Windhagen. Windhausen, Stockhausen and Willscheid lost [to the 1st

ID]." Collins crossed the river and visited the 1st and 78th to check on their progress. Reflecting on the visit, he wrote that Andrus "was proving a good successor to Huebner." He was also favorably impressed with Major General Edwin Parker and his Lightning, so known for their shoulder flash, which featured a bolt of white lightning on a red background. VII Corps now included the 1st, 8th, 78th, and 104th Infantry Divisions. The 3rd AD and 4th Cavalry Group completed the order of battle. Several days passed before the rest of corps found room to cross.[74]

With Apologies to Lord Moran, an Aside on the Anatomy of Courage

The 1st Division's infantry continued to push forward alongside the fresher and well-led 78th. Soldiers grow old in combat before their time. For some old soldiers, their age was showing. Even men of proven courage like Ted Dobol, who had earned three silver and two bronze stars, found his will to fight challenged. Wounded for the third time in the Hürtgen Forest, Dobol recovered in time to enjoy a stateside leave that he certainly had earned. He returned in time to cross the Rhine with his home in Company K, 26th Infantry. As he crossed the river, he wrote, "The sound of artillery and the rattling of machine guns came back to me after my trip to the USA. A couple of times I wished I had never returned to the states for a visit as it was hard to accept the reality of being back."[75]

In his seminal study *The Anatomy of Courage*, Lord Moran, a professional soldier and medical officer, tried to account for courage and how to preserve it. Moran served as medical officer in a battalion of the Royal Fusiliers for three years in combat during the Great War. He kept a journal and studied the problem of shell shock, later known as combat or battle fatigue and now as post-traumatic stress disorder. He continued that effort during World War II, even writing about it aboard a bomber over the Libyan desert. Moran concluded that courage can be used up. He asked the fundamental question, "How is courage spent in war?" Moran believed that courage is "will-power whereof no man has an unlimited stock; and when in war it is used up, he is finished."[76]

Moran believed courage was used up in fighting, but also in exhaustion brought on by intense effort or exposure. March in the highlands of the Rhine is cold and wet. Climbing those hills under fire and with little rest wore fit men down. All of this Moran chronicled in the first two parts of his book. In part 3 he considered the "Care and Management of Fear." In it, he asked how courage could be preserved. His conclusions seem obvious now and were generally understood in World War II. Dr. Joseph Bradley, who joined the 1st ID during preparation for the invasion of France, certainly understood the problem of combat fatigue and did what he could to prepare troops and mitigate the stress. Rest, the support of numbers, cohesion, discipline, and good leadership all preserve courage. There were numbers, cohesion, discipline, and effective leadership in the 1st ID, but there was too little rest.[77]

Jim Sharp witnessed the sad end of a proven combat veteran. After crossing the river, Sharp's company huddled in the railway tunnel on the east bank. "It was obvious from the tremendous noise battles [were] being fought nearby, that we would soon have to join them [the others fighting]," he remembered. A sergeant standing next to him began to "shake and mumble." This man had "just come back from the hospital after being wounded." The sergeant told Sharp that he'd told the hospital authorities, "I am not ready to go back into combat yet." Sharp tried to console the sergeant, who wanted to go with the company but simply could not. Sharp, already a veteran, grew up even more in that dark tunnel. Although "I had never seen 'battle fatigue,'" he wrote, "it was obvious to me that he was not fit for the battle we were going to be fighting." Sharp reported the sergeant to a medic, who evacuated a good man whose courage had been used up. Sharp never saw him again.[78]

Breakthrough East and North toward the Ruhr

Collins's Operations Memorandum 177, issued on March 19, ordered the 1st ID to "relentlessly push" to seize the First Army bridgehead line. Superfluous language and occasional tactical meddling characterized the aggressive corps commander. Still, Andrus knew what was expected. He described the division's battle to expand and break out of the bridgehead as "one of the most grueling experiences in its battle starred career." The battle grew, according to "Mr. Chips," until "every man was on the front line . . . it was bitter fighting." Leroy Stewart, an infantryman in the 26th, remembered that "we lost a lot of men and equipment. [But] the push never stopped." The division attacked day and night. Stewart understood that "the idea was never to give the Jerrys time to rest and regroup." He thought the plan worked, "but we didn't get much [rest] either."[79]

During the fighting to expand the bridgehead, the corps attacked northeast, but as more units crossed the river, the vector shifted north. That shift toward the Sieg River, which joined the Rhine north of Bonn, reflected Collins's influence with Hodges. Bradley intended to attack with all of

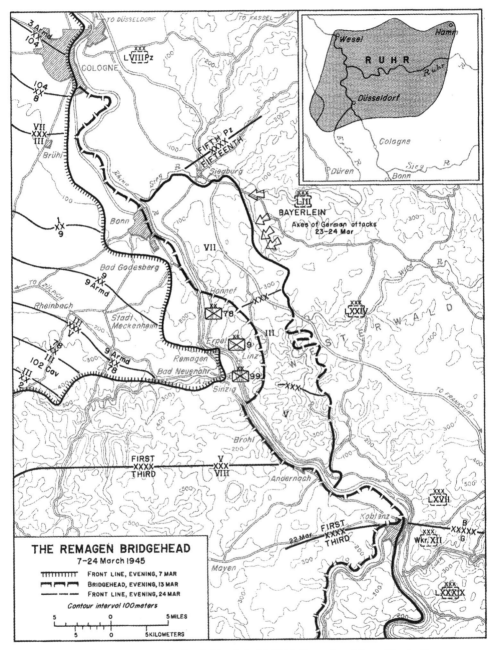

Map 31: The Remagen Bridgehead, March 7–24, 1945. Reproduced from Charles B. MacDonald, *The Last Offensive* (Washington: Center of Military History, 1993), Map 3.

12th Army Group once Montgomery's 21st Army Group crossed the Rhine. Hodges planned to attack with his three corps, VII, III, and V, from north to south. Collins's part of the plan featured moving to the Sieg and then turning east along the southern bank, with Maurice Rose's 3rd AD making the main effort. The 1st ID would attack on the Armor Division's left to protect the corps' northern flank, the 3rd AD would be in the middle, and the 104th ID on the right. The 78th would follow 1st ID to extend flank protection. The 7th Armored Division reverted to III Corps, and the 8th ID remained on the west bank. Montgomery's set-piece crossing of the Rhine occurred successfully on March 23–24. The day before, and far to the south, Patton's 5th ID had crossed the Rhine at Oppenheim south of Mainz. For a change, Patton's diary reflects gratitude for success rather than braggadocio.[80]

In any case VII Corps attacked northeast, with 3rd AD leading at 0500 on March 25. They encountered stiff resistance because a few days before, Army Group B had reinforced the Remagen sector. The 512th Jagdtiger (a turretless antitank gun on a Tiger chassis) as well as the 506th and 654th Jagdpanzer Battalions joined the defense. These units moved into the LVII Corps sector in support of the 62nd, 363rd, and 89th Regiment of the 12th VGD. Soon after, LIII Corps assumed command of the entire sector. Bayerlein's three weakened Panzer divisions assembled to make a last effort to reduce the bridgehead. Before he could attack, Bayerlein had to attempt to shield Altenkirchen from Rose's tanks. This proved hard to do with American fighter bombers working over any Germans who used any of the roads.[81]

In his recollection of March 25, Ralph Gordon wrote, "The German resistance broke, and we attacked like rabid dogs, breaking right through the German line." He was right, the 3rd AD raced eastward ahead of the infantry divisions. The Big Red One had a hard fight to reach the south bank of the Sieg River, while the 78th moved up to free up flank security units of the 1st ID. That day Major Frank Colaccio, one of the old soldiers from before the invasion of North Africa, now in command of the 2nd Battalion, was wounded driving over a land mine. On March 27 the division turned east well behind 3rd AD and moved along the south bank of the Sieg. Maurice Rose, operating well to the front, had turned his division north. Confusion was the order of the day as the Americans overran small pockets of German defenders. Exploiting a breakout is never as neat as blue arrows on a map suggest.[82]

That afternoon Maurice Rose entered the small village of Rehe, some twenty-five miles east of Altenkirchen. Just ahead, he could see Germans. Rose got his jeep stopped, dismounted, grabbed his .45-caliber Thompson submachine gun, and prepared to fight. Behind him a second jeep and scout car slowed to a stop. Some fifteen Germans took Rose and his party under fire. The Americans killed three, and the rest surrendered. That same afternoon Collins ordered Rose to turn north. The 3rd AD reached Marburg that night and Giessen the next day. Heading north, VII Corps would link up with Ninth Army and might cut off Army Group B.[83]

The pace for the 1st ID accelerated. On March 28 Jean Peltier and the 33rd FA moved through Altenkirchen, where Peltier saw the devastation wrought by US bombers and perhaps some by the 3rd AD as they went through. The 33rd kept moving past abandoned German equipment and the detritus of a beaten army—beaten on the ground and from the air. The regiments reported taking prisoners from units hitherto unknown to the 1st ID. Ralph Gordon recalled that the 18th moved a hundred miles on the last two days of March and still had not caught up with the 3rd AD. The breakthrough become a breakout. Exploitation was becoming pursuit. The G-3 after-action report noted that the division was moving as fast as it had "across France and Belgium in the early fall of 1944."[84]

The tenor and tempo of pursuit can be seen in the 16th Infantry journal for March 30. Colonel Gibb's troops were moving fast, using checkpoints to report locations quickly. The journal reflects not only the speed of movement but the effort to coordinate and pass information. Overrunning roadblocks and shooting up retreating Germans is one thing, but getting killed in the chaos is another. Cross talk helped reduce the likelihood of friendly fire or being ambushed by a rear guard. At 1715, the regimental S-2 passed a message to the G-2. It was old news but good news, garnered from the 3rd AD liaison officer traveling with the regiment. The S-2 advised that the 3rd AD had jumped off at 0900 for Paderborn. "In the last 2 days they took 10,000 PWs [prisoners of war], destroyed 420 trucks, 20 Sps [self-propelled guns], 5 trains, 8 planes and so on. No report on any tanks." The 3rd AD also seized an aircraft plant in full production. The G-2 had heard the news and added more detail. At 1740, the G-3 advised that the 26th would lead the next day. The 3rd AD certainly was living up to its moniker of Spearhead.[85]

At dusk that day, in the muddle that accompanies a pursuit, Maurice Rose again ran into a group of Germans near Paderborn, a major training base for both German Army and SS Panzer units. Here, instead of a handful of German infantry, he encountered SS tankers aboard four Tiger tanks. To escape, Rose and his party tried to drive past the tanks, but one blocked their passage. What followed turned ugly. Possibly through miscommunication, or plain meanness, the Germans killed Rose as he and his small command team attempted to surrender. They did a good job of it, hitting him fourteen times with submachine gun rounds. Pursuit leads to the greatest gains, but even so it is not without cost.[86]

From Andrus to the privates, the 1st ID had the sense that the end, if not in sight, was not far off. Unit journals remained suitably professional, but they clearly convey the sense of the tide flowing toward victory at last. With it, though, came a sense of confusion. Complaints of other units not being where they claimed to be produced frustration and perhaps unease. Units lost contact with one another, all of which generated danger. Exhaustion is the handmaiden of pursuit. Gibb's S-3 spoke with Driscoll during the day. The message was short: "The Colonel wants you to go to bed." Driscoll responded, "I will be up sometime today."[87]

The Germans too knew the end was coming. Generalleutnant Wend von Wietersheim, commanding the 11th PZ, observed that "once the enemy had crossed the Rhine at any point neither the bulk of the German people nor the bravest individual soldier believed—especially in view of the previous failures—that the overall military defeat could be averted." This of course affected "the fighting morale of the troops, especially in the case of the shattered and badly mixed units." Perhaps, but that did not mean that the high command proposed to give up. Model issued orders to Bayerlein to take the remnants of Panzer Lehr and the 3rd Flieger Division (a Luftwaffe unit converted to infantry) and counterattack against 3rd AD south of Paderborn. Bayerlein thought the idea was crazy and referred to Model's headquarters as a *Narrenhaus*—literally, a madhouse. Still, he followed orders and got nowhere.[88]

The 1st ID's Assessment

Clift Andrus made the 1st ID his own during the Battle of the Bulge. In February and March, however, he really came into his own as a combat commander. The instrument that Huebner left was a good one. Andrus showed he knew how to care for it and how to use it. The division's monthly report for March began by observing that it "took part in several various types of maneuver and employment." Indeed, it had. Breaking out of the Roer bridgehead stemmed from a deliberate attack based on good intelligence, employing everything from patrols to aerial photography. The advance to the Rhine, on the other hand, required rapid movement with limited knowledge of the enemy. During that phase the 1st ID attacked night and day, bounding battalions to maintain the pace.

The 3rd Battalion, 16th Infantry, employed a similar technique at battalion level in the attack on Bonn. That attack showed particular sophistication in the way that Wozenski used his supporting arms. Andrus, an artilleryman, decided not to fire an artillery preparation but instead attacked at night, with both attacking regiments holding fire until forced to do otherwise. Bonn fell quickly, and the Germans were just barely able to blow up the bridge. Soon after, the division motorized, using trucks, and moved quickly to crossing sites on the Rhine, joining III Corps to expand the bridgehead. This required coordinating with the 8th ID to assume the defense of the west bank, and similar coordination to move into assembly areas in the 78th ID sector while planning and executing motor and foot movement. Andrus's G-3, Lieutenant Colonel Clarence E. Beck, wrote in his report that all of this occurred "with very little incident and can be considered an excellent movement of troops due to the long experience in this type of operation that the division had since being overseas."[89]

Beck's claim is fair, but staff work provides the necessary detail. Execution depends on effective leadership from top to bottom. New troops had to be told what to expect. Integration and training of replacements during February and March occurred during two very short intervals before the crossings of the Roer, the many streams between the Roer and the Rhine, and the many streams on the far bank of the Rhine. The work of the engineers in crossing streams and rivers seemed routine, then and now, only because Bill Gara's 1st Engineers and their many colleagues at corps were so good at what they did that their feats appear in the daily journal but not in Beck's report. Instead, Beck focused his observations on combined arms tactics. In particular, he noted that when the infantry uses darkness to advance, leaving its noisy tanks and tank destroyers behind, those units must depend on guides from the infantry.[90]

The notion of using artillery and mortars firing smoke and high explosive to screen movement and suppress enemy opposition had become so de rigeur that Beck does not mention it either. Fire and movement and attacking at night were standard operating procedure in 1st ID with the occasional exception, such as the night attack on Bonn. Beck did note, however, the efficacy of airpower in combination with artillery. To make the maximum effective use of artillery, "all infantry officers should have as a part of their training, instruction in adjusting of artillery fire by forward observer methods and should be able to do this in case of emergency."[91]

Despite knowing how to motorize on the fly, the division could not keep up with the 3rd AD. Beck complained that despite using all organic transport, and even taking trucks from the cannon company, there was insufficient transport to motorize the infantry because truck companies could not be found. This complaint, though legitimate, was a consequence of the amount of traffic within the bridgehead and during the early days after the breakthrough. On a positive note, Beck revisited the tried-and-true utility of highly mobile, relatively small combined arms task forces when the infantry cannot be fully motorized. During the breakout, a task force composed of the division reconnaissance troop, a tank platoon, and a motorized infantry company supported by mortars and machine guns proved able to take towns and hold them until the main body of infantry could catch up.[92]

The G-3 concluded his report by noting that during March the division "encountered the stiffest opposition yet met since the fighting in the hurtgen forest." The division took its objectives, but "with considerable loss of personnel and equipment." Hürtgen Forest, not Kasserine Pass, Omaha Beach, or the Bulge, remained the standard of misery for old soldiers in the Big Red One.

Notes

1. HQ, 1st ID, after-action report, January 1945, 37–49, in RG 301-3: G-3 Operations Reports, European Campaign, Jan 45–Dec 45, MRC Digital Archives. There is some confusion on just when the 23rd Infantry returned to 2nd ID. HQ, XVIII Corps (Airborne), "Summary of Operations," March 1, 1945, R11476, CARL, 9, reports that the 23rd was relieved by the 508th Parachute Infantry on January 21, which was the condition of their return. That did not occur. The 23rd returned to the 2nd ID on January 24; see 1st ID, after-action report, January 1945, 49.

2. 1st ID, after-action report, January 1945.

3. Eisenhower, *Papers*, no. 2211, 4:2388; Pogue, *Supreme Command*, 385–87, 417. Eisenhower passed the outline plan to Bradley on New Year's Day.

4. Bradley, *Soldier's Story*, 487–89. See also Ambrose, *Supreme Commander*, 571–89.

5. Ambrose, *Supreme Commander*, 572. For Eisenhower's view on events, see Eisenhower, *Crusade in Europe*, 356–67. For Montgomery's view, see Montgomery, *Memoirs*, 283–98; *Supreme Command*, 385–91, 407–13.

6. Hogan, *Command Post at War*, 239–40. See also HQ, First Army, after-action report, January 1–21, 1945, CARL, 51–52; XVIII Corps, "Summary of Operations," 19; Ridgway, *Soldier*, 127.

7. Warlimont, *Inside Hitler's Headquarters*, 496.

8. Citino, *Wehrmacht's Last Stand*, 420.

9. Citino, 408; Kissel, *Hitler's Last Levy*, image at 35.

10. Citino, *Wehrmacht's Last Stand*, 432–35.

11. Citino (421–46) describes the miracle in the west as "epic in its way, but an empty one," leading to disaster in the east. See also Westphal, *German Army in the West*, 190.

12. Friedrich Kittel, "Report on the Ardennes Offensive," June 1946, ms. B-028, Sturmpanzer, 28–29. The title of this ms. is misleading, as it contains a supplement that addresses post-Ardennes fighting.

13. The bulk of the data here comes from Knickerbocker et al., *Danger Forward*, 409–18.

14. 1st ID, Selected Intelligence Reports, vol. 2, December 1944–May 1945, 26–33, in RG 301-2.0: G-2 Selected Intelligence Reports during the First Six Months of the European Campaign, Jun 1944–May 1945, MRC Digital Archives. See also 1st ID, G-2 Periodic Report 220, January 25, 1945, and 26th Infantry, interrogation report on eighty-one prisoners of war (date illegible), both in RG 301-2.2: G-2 Journal and File, 1st Inf Div (ETO), 25 Jan 45–31 Jan 45, MRC Digital Archives.

15. Knickerbocker et al., *Danger Forward*, 331; Ralph J. Gordon, *Infantrymen*, 99–100. Re time of attack, see 1st ID, after-action report, January 1945, 57; MacDonald, *Last Offensive*, 63–67.

16. Ridgway, *Soldier*, 127–28; 1st ID, after-action report, February 1945, 5, in G-3 Operations Reports, Jan 45–Dec 45.

17. 1st ID, after-action report, February 1945, 5–7. Like the Germans before them, the Americans suffered traffic jams, but on the whole they resolved them more quickly. American combat engineers also worked hard to improve and/or repair roads.

18. Bert H. Morphis, veteran's survey, n.d., US Army Heritage and Education Center, Carlisle Barracks, PA.

19. 1st ID, after-action report, January 1945, 60. The relief took more than a day, so moving to the assembly area took the better part of two days.

20. 1st ID, after-action report, February 1945, 17–22; Sylvan and Smith, *Normandy to Victory*, 285–92; Hogan, *Command Post at War*, 240–45. MacDonald, *Last Offensive*, 185–91, lays out the general scheme for Operation Lumberjack.

21. MacDonald, *Last Offensive*, 135–40; Ridgway, *Soldier*, 132; XVIII Corps, "Summary of Operations," 13. In his memoir Bradley articulates the case for continuing the offensive with limited means. See Bradley, *Soldier's Story*, 495–97.

22. MacDonald, *Last Offensive*, 191–92; 1st ID, after-action report, February 1945, 18–19. Jean Peltier confided in his diary that when the 33rd FA moved forward on January 31, it took the battalion all day to traverse the ruins of Bullingen. "World War II Diary of Jean Gordon Peltier," August 2, 1942–July 5, 1945, MRC 1998.79, 230.

23. 1st ID, after-action report, February 1945, 21. First Army's belated fears about the Germans blowing the Schwammenauel and Yrft dams led to the ill-fated attack by the 28th ID to seize them. The 78th ID finally reached the dams on February 10, too late to prevent the Germans from damaging the discharge valves. Exactly when they did this is not clear. See MacDonald, *Last Offensive*, 80–84; Clay, *Blood and Sacrifice*, 228–23.

24. 1st ID, after-action report, February 1945, 11, 17–25. Units moved forward in increments to the west of bank of the Roer as VII Corps permitted.

25. 1st ID, after-action report, February 1945; HQ, 26th Infantry, "Regimental Activities for February 1945," March 21, 1945, 2, in RG 301-INF926(26)-0.3: Reports of Operations, European Campaign, 1 Jan 45–31 Mar 45, MRC Digital Archives; HQ, 1st Battalion, 18th Infantry, "Record of Events for Month of February 1945," March 3, 1945, 2, in RG 301-INF(18)-0.3: Reports of Operations, 1 Jun 44–31 Mar 45, MRC Digital Archives. See also reports for 2nd and 3rd Battalions.

26. 1st ID, after-action report, February 1945, 26.

27. 1st ID, 28, 31.

28. HQ, 1st ID, FO 56, February 1945, 1, in G-3 Operations Reports, Jan 45–Dec 45. See also annex 2, "Engineer Plan for Crossing the Roer River."

29. 1st ID, Selected Intelligence Reports, 2:46; MacDonald, *Last Offensive*, 141; HQ, III Corps, G-2 periodic report no. 76, February 24, 1945, 1, and 1st ID, G-2 periodic report no. 247, February 23, 1945, 1, both in RG 301-2.2: G-2 Journal and File, 1st Inf Div (ETO), 23 Feb 45–28 Feb 45, MRC Digital Archives. Units moved around continuously during this period. The German corps sectors are from HQ, 12th Army Group, Assistant Chief of Staff, G-2, "The Destruction of the German Armies in Western Europe, June 6th 1944–May 9th 1945," N10099, CARL, chart following 24.

30. Baumer, *Aachen*, 333, 336.

31. HQ, 1st ID, G-3 journal, February 23, 1945, 1, in RG 301-3.2: G-3 Journal and File–1st Inf Div–European Campaign, 1 Feb 45–28 Feb 45, MRC Digital Archives; 1st ID, G-2 periodic report no. 247, 1. The division's general support battalion, the 5th FA, averaged 279 rounds per day in February. HQ, 5th Field Artillery, after-action report, March 2, 1945, 2, in RG 301-FA(5)-0.3: Reports of Operations, Jan 45–May 45, MRC Digital Archives; HQ, 33rd Field Artillery Battalion, after-action report, March 1, 1945, 6, in RG 301-FA(33)-0.3: Reports of Operations, 1 Jun 44–31 May 45, MRC Digital Archives.

32. Hogan, *Command Post at War*, 249; 1st ID, G-3 journal, February 25, 1945, 2, in G-3 Journal, 1 Feb 45–28 Feb 45.

33. G-3 journal, February 25, 1945, 6–8; Richard Alber Williams and Rocco (Rocky) Moretto, *Men of Iron: A Tribute to Courage* (self-published, 2011), 127.

34. "The Attack on Kreuzau, 25 February 1945," ch. 4 of 1st ID, "World War II Combat Achievements Report," n.d., MRC 1988.31, 1.

35. "Attack on Kreuzau," 2; Albert H. Smith Jr., interview by Franklin Ferriss, March 15, 1945, Bornheim, Germany, RG 407, NARA, courtesy of Steven E. Clay. Captain Ferriss conducted six interviews bundled together as "From the Roer to the Rhine, 25 Feb–9 March 1945." See also "Attack on Kreuzau," 2–3.

36. "Attack on Kreuzau," 3–4.

37. "Attack on Kreuzau," 3–5; William R. Campbell, "Tanks with Infantry," Advanced Officers Class No. 1, Fort Knox, KY, February 25, 1947, 4. According to his title page, Campbell's paper describes "methods learned and employed by the 1st U.S. Infantry Division and the 745th Tank Battalion in tank-infantry team work."

38. "Attack on Kreuzau," 5–6; Smith interview.

39. Smith interview; 1st ID, "Combat Achievements Report," ch. 4, p. 6.

40. MacDonald, *Last Offensive*, 184–85; 18th Infantry, "Record of Events," 2.

41. Fuller, *A Third Face*, 203.

42. Sam Carter, Edward McGregor, and David W. Parker, interview by Franklin Ferriss, March 14, 1945, and Earl Green, interview by Franklin Ferriss, April 4, 1945, both RG 407, NARA, courtesy of Steven E. Clay.

43. 1st ID, Selected Intelligence Reports, 2:57–58; Gordon, *Infantrymen*, 104.

44. 1st ID, Selected Intelligence Reports, 2:58–59.

45. 1st ID, 58–59.

46. Kurt Hummel, "Report of Fighting Engaged in by the 353 Infantry Division West and East of the Rhine and South of Cologne, from 2 to 22 March 1945," ms. B-098, Sturmpanzer, 1–2.

47. Hummel, 2–5; General der Infanterie Friedrich Köchling, "Battles between Roer and Rhine, At the Rhine Sieg and in the Rhine-Rhur-Sieg Pocket," ms. B-614, Sturmpanzer, 36. The 1st Engineers put in two treadway bridges and a bailey bridge and then took down one of the treadway bridges to have it available for the next stream. 1st ID, 1st Engineer Battalion, Combat, S-3 periodic report, 1, in RG 301-3.2: G-3 Journal and File, European Campaign, 1 Mar 45–31 Mar 45.

48. G-3 after-action report, April 1945, 2–7, in G-3 Operations Reports, Jan 45–Dec 45; MacDonald, *Last Offensive*, 194–95; Knickerbocker et al., *Danger Forward*, 374.

49. From John P. Downing's unpublished memoir, quoted in Baumer and Reardon, *American Iliad*, 335.

50. G-3 after-action report, March 1945, 6–7, in G-3 Operations Reports, Jan 45–Dec 45; HQ, 16th Infantry, after-action report, April 1, 1945, 1, in RG 301-INF(16)-0.3: After Action Report, Combat Team 16, MRC Digital Archives. See also 26th Infantry, "Regimental Activities of the 26th Infantry for the Month of March," April 1, 1945, 3, in Reports of Operations, European Campaign, 1 Jan 45–31 Mar 45; Baumgartner et al., *16th Infantry*, 124. All of the regimental journals note that Bonn became an objective for the 1st ID on March 7; 0200 is given as the time the order came. There is, however, no corresponding entry in the division journal for that or any other time on March 7. A flurry of messages allude to Bonn, but none are specific.

51. MacDonald, *Last Offensive*, 185–207; G-3 after-action report, March 1945, 8.

52. "The Attack on the City of Bonn," ch. 8 of 1st ID, "Combat Achievements Report," March 8, 1945, 1. See Clay, *Blood and Sacrifice*, 231–33, for a narrative of the regiment's attack.

53. "Attack on the City of Bonn," 1–2.

54. "Attack on the City of Bonn," 2–3. The battalion issued its order at about 2300. Captain McCarthy issued his order at 2400.

55. "Attack on the City of Bonn," 2–3.

56. "Attack on the City of Bonn," 3.

57. "Attack on the City of Bonn," 3. See also Clay, *Blood and Sacrifice*, 231. Steven E. Clay argues that the Germans tanks and assault guns that Company K encountered were with the replacement training regiment. The combat achievement report has them coming into the city. The confusion that night was sufficient to make either possible, but my judgment is that most of those systems destroyed were from outside of the city, There was at least one tank that played the role Clay asserts.

58. "Attack on the City of Bonn," 3–4.

59. Clay, *Blood and Sacrifice*, 232; 1st ID, Selected Intelligence Reports, 2:60–61; Baumer and Reardon, *American Iliad*, 335–36.

60. 1st ID, Selected Intelligence Reports, 2:61; G-3 after-action report, March 1945, 8–11. Re Remagen bridge, see HQ, III Corps, after-action report, April 1, 1945, N12029, CARL.

61. G-3 after-action report, March 1945, 22; 1st ID, Selected Intelligence Reports, 2:62; Clay, *Blood and Sacrifice*, 233; Gordon, *Infantrymen*, 107.

62. Daily casualty report, March 7–8, in RG 301-INF(16)-0.3: Reports of Operations, Jan 45–Dec 45, MRC Digital Archives; Eisenhower, *Papers*, no. 2218, 4:2394, no. 227, 4:2409, and no. 2276, 4:2474; Wheeler, *The Big Red One*, 373; Gordon, *Infantrymen*, 107.

63. 1st ID, after-action report, April 1, 1945, 2, in G-3 Operations Reports, Jan 45–Dec 45. It is not entirely clear when each of these platoons joined its company.

64. Richard J. Lindo, oral history transcript, October 15, 1990, D-Day Project, National World War II Museum, New Orleans; Baumer and Reardon, *American Iliad*, 340. See also Clay, *Blood and Sacrifice*, 233.

65. Sharp, *Diary of a Combat Infantryman*, 60.

66. Hogan, *Command Post at War*, 250–51; Bradley, *Soldier's Story*, 510–15; Eisenhower, *Crusade in Europe*, 379–80; Ambrose, *Supreme Commander*, 618–20; Sylvan and Smith, *Normandy to Victory*, 325–27. Eisenhower's recollection of the call almost certainly is taken from Butcher, *Three Years with Eisenhower*, 768.

67. Bradley, *Soldier's Story*, 512; Eisenhower, *Crusade in Europe*, 379–80; Ambrose, *Supreme Commander*, 618–20.

68. MacDonald, *Last Offensive*, 220–21. In fact, on March 7 both corps had troops still on the west bank and in danger of being encircled. Fritz Bayerlein, "Remagen Bridgehead LIII Corps," March 26, 1946, ms. A-970, CARL, N-17500.1098, 3. See also Spayd, *Bayerlein*, 195.

69. MacDonald, *Last Offensive*, 220–21. Re order of battle, see Bayerlein, "Remagen Bridgehead," 7.

70. Clausewitz, *On War*, 532–34.

71. G-3 after-action report, March 1945, 15.

72. G-3 after-action report, 16–17. The after-action report is not very helpful for this attack. 1st ID, Selected Intelligence Reports, 2:62–65, is far better, as are the three regiments after-action reports and journals. HQ, 16th Infantry, after-action report, March 1945, 17, in Reports of Operations, Jan 45–Dec 45. The 18th Infantry reports are done at battalion level all within RG 301-INF(18)-0.3. The regimental summary lacks detail. There is no agreement on when the attack started. Reported times vary from 0200 to 0250.

73. 1st ID, Selected Intelligence Reports, 2:65; HQ, 33rd Field Artillery, after-action report, April 1, 1945, 9, in Reports of Operations, Jun 44–May 45.

74. Bayerlein, "Remagen Bridgehead," 5. Re VII Corps order of battle, see HQ, VII Corps, Operations Memorandum 175, March 14, 1945, R13343.6, CARL, 1. For the addition of the 7th Amored Division, see VII Corps, Operations Memorandum 177, March 19, 1945, CARL.

75. "Theodore L. Dobol, Command Sergeant Major United States Army (Retired): Autobiography," n.d., MRC 1991.24, 29.

76. Moran, *Anatomy of Courage*, xvi.

77. Moran. Part 3 begins at 151 and has four chapters: "Selection," "Discipline," "The Support of Numbers," and "Leadership." Re cohesion, or the support of numbers, see 174–79.

78. Sharp, *Diary of a Combat Infantryman*, 68–69.

79. VII Corps, Operations Memorandum 177, CARL, 1; Weingartner, *Blue Spaders*, 119. Quotations are from *Memorial Album: Pictorial History of the 1st Division* (San Diego, CA: Society of the First Division, 1950) and Leroy Stewart's memoir, *Hurry Up and Wait*, both cited in Weingartner, *Blue Spaders*, 119.

80. Collins, *Lightning Joe*, 308–11; MacDonald, *Last Offensive*, 266–69, 284–89; Bolger, *Panzer Killers*, 280–81; Blumenson, *Patton Papers*, 659–60. See also HQ, VII Corps, FO 18, March 23, 1945, 1; Hagan, map 16.

81. Bayerlein, "Remagen Bridgehead," 6; Spayd, *Bayerlein*, 198. See also Hogan, *Command Post at War*, 256–57.

82. Gordon, *Infantrymen*, 109; 1st ID, after-action report, March 25, 28–30; Baumer and Reardon, *American Iliad*, 341–42.

83. Bolger, *Panzer Killers*, 288–95.

84. Peltier, diary, 49–50; Gordon, *Infantrymen*, 110; G-3 after-action report, March 1945, 34.

85. HQ, 16th Infantry, journal, March 30, 1945, March 1945, in RG 301-INF(16)-0.7: Journal, European Campaign, Jan 45–May 45, MRC Digital Archives, 8.

86. MacDonald, *Last Offensive*, 352; Bolger, *Panzer Killers*, 312–13.

87. 16th Infantry, journal, 5.

88. Wend von Wietersheim, "Rhineland-Part V, 6–21 Mar 1945: The Battles of the 11. Panzer Division at the Remagen Bridgehead," Allendorf, Germany, October 26, 1946, ms. B-590, N17594, CARL, 3; Spayd, *Bayerlein*, 199.

89. G-3 after-action report, March 1945, 41.

90. After-action report, 41.

91. After-action report, 43–44.

92. After-action report, 42.

CHAPTER FOURTEEN

The Race to the Finish Line

They sent us up into the Harz
And said to clean them out
A hundred thousand trees in there
And each one hid a kraut.
—Song of the Fighting First

Once again, the German troops fought valiantly for their country, however, it was [a] futile battle, and both the command and troops lacked enthusiasm.
—Oberst Günther Reichhelm, 1st general staff officer, Army Group B

SERGEANT JOHN LEBDA, who had moved from a rifle platoon to a safer job serving as company motor sergeant in the 26th Infantry, perceived that the end of the war was not far off. "Now it was time to be more cautious and not take chances," he concluded. Having survived three landings, Lebda proposed to survive the war. Even so, he was elated when "on Easter Sunday [April 1, 1945], we took off for Berlin down their autobahn using all four lanes traveling at full speed." Even though Lebda and the 26th were not actually en route to Berlin, they were moving rapidly north toward the Ruhr industrial zone. The 16th Infantry had moved out the night before, and while the 26th was motoring north, the 16th took the towns of Rüthen and Steinhausen, southwest of German Panzer training areas at Sennelager, near Paderborn but east of the Ruhr region. The 16th and the rest of the 1st Division would form blocking positions on the eastern side of what most historians call the Ruhr pocket, known in VII Corps as the Rose pocket in honor of the 3rd AD's deceased commander.[1]

Whether or not the end of the war was nigh, for those still fighting in it, survival remained uncertain. Ralph J. Gordon's close friend Frank "Pete" De Pietro was seriously wounded on the last day of March. Ralph wondered if his buddy Pete would recover. He did not. No one could say just how long the dying and suffering would last, or who might die next. On Easter Sunday, the war had just over a month to go, but of course no one knew that at the time. But if the dying and suffering continued much as it had since day one of the conflict, the character of the fighting had changed in a number of ways.[2] Tracking and assessing how the division and its troops coped with these changes is the focus of this chapter.

Easter Sunday 1945 was the 412th day of combat for the Big Red One. The 1st ID had fought impressively in an array of difficult operations, terrain, and weather since landing on the beaches of Algeria on November 8, 1942. There was a certain continuity in operations, but methods had continually changed; combat techniques are dynamic, depending on immediate circumstances and conditions. Perhaps the most important change after the breakout from the Remagen bridgehead was the dramatic decline in Germany's capability to generate sufficient forces to develop a coherent front. Without time to regroup or generate reserves, the Germans generally fought from roadblocks protected by mines.

Once they began fighting in Germany, the Allies required specialized civil affairs units charged with the task of establishing infrastructure to govern captured German towns and villages. However, the civil affairs units could not operate until combat forces had established security. Naturally, the task of security grew larger as the Allies advanced. Tactical units needed not only to secure enemy towns but also to vet "civilians" to weed out Nazi officials, German soldiers attempting to blend in with civilians, and would-be partisans who might wage guerrilla war in the American rear. The US Army Counterintelligence Corps, which traveled with units like the 1st ID, began the vetting process. Although occupation had not become the primary focus of the fighting formations, transitioning captured territory to military government took increasingly more time and effort. Finally, the advancing Allied forces had to communicate with Russian forces to avoid the possibility of unintentional fratricide among Allied forces. As the war neared its end, political agreements on occupation zones played an important role in operational and tactical decisions.[3]

Eisenhower's plans for crossing the Rhine put the main Allied effort in 21st Army Group, but he also mapped out a simultaneous supporting effort by 12th Army Group. When 9th AD, assigned to III Corps, seized the Ludendorff bridge, Eisenhower and Bradley immediately acted to execute a double envelopment of the Ruhr industrial region with Ninth Army, still attached to Bernard Law Montgomery, attacking east and First Army attacking north from the Remagen bridgehead. Eisenhower cabled orders to that effect to his senior commanders on March 25, 1945. In accordance with those orders, VII Corps had hastened north, with 3rd AD in the lead. To enhance speed, 3rd AD took risks with its own security.[4]

On Easter Sunday, the 16th Infantry seized several towns north of the Ruhr River along the eastern edge of the industrial zone. The regiment took Rüthen, Hämmern, and Steinhausen and oriented west to block the retreat eastward of Army Group B. Just after noon, 3rd AD linked up with 2nd AD from Ninth Army. That feat occurred because Lightning Joe Collins, exhibiting commendable initiative and chutzpah, phoned Lieutenant General William H. Simpson at Ninth Army to ask him to shift a combat command of the 2nd AD toward Lippstadt. Collins needed help because 3rd AD had run into the feisty SS troops who had killed Rose and were now putting 3rd AD at some risk. The opportunity to encircle Army Group B was too good to pass up, and it also reflected a strategic shift at SHAEF. The plan Eisenhower issued on March 25 instructed 21st Army Group to release Ninth Army, and thus the SHAEF main effort, to 12th Army Group once the encirclement was completed.[5]

First and Ninth Army units met at Lippstadt on the Lippe River, roughly ten miles west of Paderborn, where they had originally intended to meet. Ninth Army closed off the north, First Army the east and south. The newly formed German Fifteenth US Army defended the west bank of the Rhine, forming the western part of the pocket in which Model and Army Group B now found themselves. Within the pocket, the Ruhr industrial zone, the heart of German heavy manufacturing, lay prostrate before the western Allies. In The Last Offensive, Charles B. MacDonald described the zone as a triangle, the base of which is the east bank of the Rhine from "Cologne northward to Duisburg." From Duisburg, the northern leg of the triangle ran east "along the Lippe River to Dortmund." The final leg stretched southwestward more or less along the Ruhr to Cologne.[6]

German officers had been trained to believe in Bewegungskrieg, or war of movement, but now they lacked the means and authority to follow that

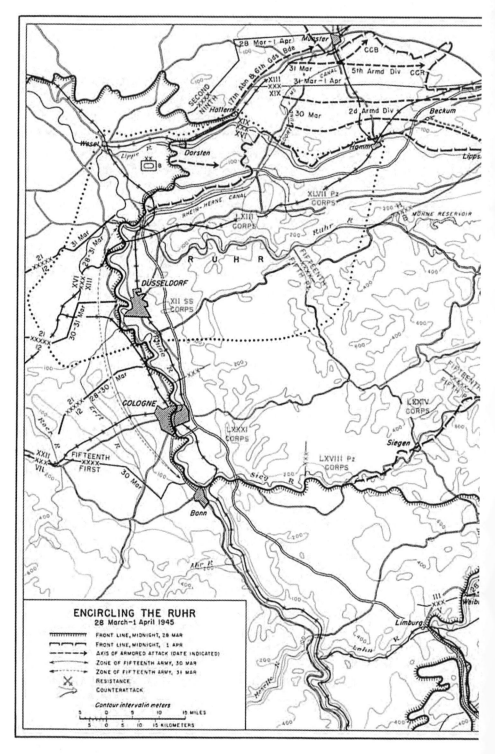

Map 32: Encircling the Ruhr, March 28–April 1, 1945. Reproduced from MacDonald, *The Last Offensive*, Map XIII.

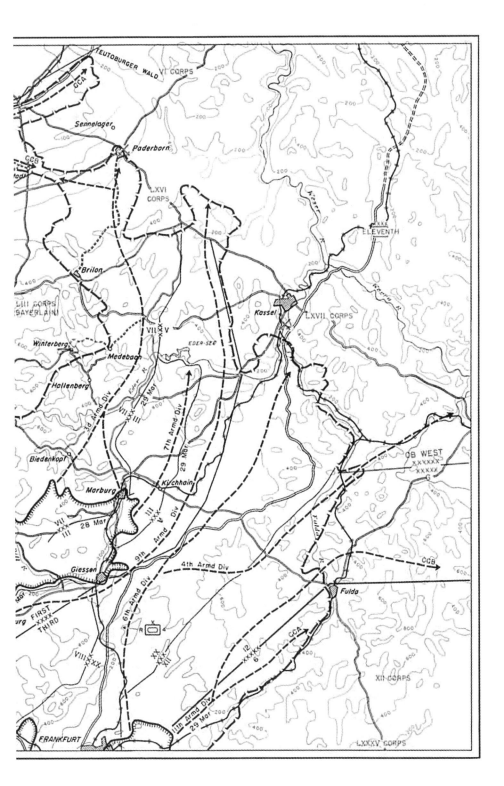

strategy. Hitler's stand-fast orders prevented Generalfeldmarschall Albert Kesselring at OB West from managing the battle as he would have liked. Kesselring "felt like a concert pianist who is asked to play a Beethoven sonata before a large audience on an ancient, rickety and out-of-tune instrument," he wrote.[7] The result, according to Generalmajor Carl Wagener, Model's chief of staff, was that Army Group B was "restricted to blocking of villages, bridges and important roads. The command was no longer in a position to direct battle and movements." Moreover, he concluded that Army Group B lacked freedom of action of any kind because "OB WEST itself had no freedom of action." In any case, the Americans surrounded Army Group B. Wagener argued in a postwar monograph that had Army Group B had the freedom to do, so it would have "given up the Rhein front and . . . concentrated all forces on a decisive attack on the flank of one of the enemy forces that had broken through." He believed the way out was to attack either south or east. Even after the war, Wagener believed Bewegungskrieg had been the only hope for Army Group B.[8]

Model did what he could, reorienting Bayerlein's LIII Corps and ordering him to mount an attempt to break out toward Kassel from positions in the southeast quadrant of the pocket. Model also reoriented LXVII Panzer Corps and the 116th PZ in the northeastern quadrant. Bayerlein ordered the 116th PZ to counterattack toward Munster, and Kesselring did what he could, directing the newly reconstituted Eleventh Army to attack from outside the pocket. Wagener worried that if the efforts to break in and break out failed, Army Group B would be "sacrificed for the imaginary defense of the Ruhr.[9]

Tightening the Noose

OKW, Hitler, and for that matter Model never fully grasped the flexibility and speed with which the US Army could act. Not only could the Americans move quickly, but they also could sustain continuous, rapid, and lengthy operations. The Allied air forces owned the skies above, scourging German units that attempted to move in daylight, so Allied ground forces could move with impunity. Postwar interviews of German general officers promoted better understanding of the history of the war but also provided those men with a forum to air their grievances. As noted in previous chapters, many of them argued that the American army was not very good and could not have won without its material advantages, including first-rate air forces, unlimited ammunition, and good equipment. Their assertion has some merit, but they of course presumed that they had beaten Poland exclusively because of their excellence rather than the material advantages they had enjoyed in that campaign. As for the American forces that the Germans currently faced, deuce-and-a-half trucks and superb air forces clearly enabled their mobility and tactical success, but so did their flexible thinking and continuous innovation.

Collins's VII Corps demonstrated just how much better the US Army had become since it first encountered Germans at the Kasserine Pass. On April 2, John Lebda and the 26th arrived on the eastern edge of the encirclement. One battalion joined the 4th Cavalry Group to extend the barrier, preventing escape by the enemy. When the lead battalion of the 18th Infantry arrived, it was attached to the 26th Infantry to thicken the barrier. All three battalions of the 18th had driven a hundred or more miles to get within hailing distance of the 3rd AD, now commanded by Brigadier General Doyle O. Hickey. With the 1st ID's infantry employed to prevent German units from fighting their way out, the First and Ninth Army were using the Germans' preferred method for destroying large enemy formations—a Kesselschlacht, or cauldron battle. The 116th PZ, various remnants, and part of LIII Corps were the antagonists. Within days the noose around them was well tightened.[10]

The prizes within the Rose pocket included Army Group B, all or part of First Parachute Army, Fifth Panzer Army, and Fifteenth Army, seven corps headquarters, nineteen divisions, and various corps and army troops. Model desperately needed to affect a breakthrough to keep lines of communications open. Accordingly, he assigned Bayerlein's LIII Corps, composed of what was left of Panzer Lehr, the 3rd PZG, the 176th VGD, the 506th Schwere Panzer Abteilung (heavy tank battalion), and the 654th Schwere Panzerjäger Abteilung. The order of battle looked better than it was. Panzer Lehr had no more than twenty tanks and fifteen antitank guns, along with Panzergrenadier regiments, each down to about three hundred Landsers. The 3rd PZG had roughly the same number of infantry as Panzer Lehr, no tanks, and ten assault guns. The 176th VGD had roughly one thousand infantry. The Panzerjäger Abteilung had perhaps as many as ten antitank guns, and the tank battalion no more than ten King Tiger tanks.[11]

Bayerlein attempted, without success, to break out on the evening of April 1. He mounted his attack from just east of Winterberg toward the town of Medebach, in the southeast portion of the pocket. The Eleventh Army, with remnants of two corps, tried to break in as well. The SS Ersatz Brigade Westfalen, formed from SS replacement training battalions and the Army's 508th Schwere Panzer Abteilung, was the largest formation assigned to Eleventh

Army. The brigade may have had as many as forty tanks and assault guns remaining after an earlier fight with the 3rd AD. Assigned to LXVI Corps, they too failed.[12]

On April 2 the 1st Division thickened the eastern side of the pocket. That day 16th Infantry units attacked both west and east to generate depth in which to operate. All three regiments enjoyed success, but not without confusion stemming from the intermingling of friendly and enemy units. Prisoners taken that day reflected the unraveling of Army Group B. They came from a hodgepodge of units, including rear-echelon repair and various logistics formations. The 16th Infantry took 342 prisoners from forty-two units, along with Hungarians, 2 female soldiers, and 35 Landsers who attempted to elude capture by wearing civilian clothes.[13]

Jean Peltier, traveling with his battery, reported encountering German civilians in his diary. Not surprisingly, he found them "very sullen in their attitude," but noted they had "put white flags of surrender in the windows of almost every house." Rain fell that day, making life miserable. Peltier's battery oriented their guns west, reminding him, "We had surely done a lot of firing to the rear since we broke out of Normandy." Indeed, they had. The day ended on a happy note when the 3rd Battalion captured "sixty thousand cases of four star cognac." The 3rd Battalion shared their largesse, as they "passed it around to the whole division."[14]

Bayerlein's weakening LIII Corps again attacked southeast with little success, this time actually giving up some ground to 9th ID. Ridgway and his XVIII Airborne Corps Headquarters rejoined First Army as more troops became available to reduce the pocket. On April 3 the day passed quietly in the 1st ID sector. Unit journals reported consolidating positions and patrolling to round up any Germans lurking about. With more troops available, Hodges issued orders for III and XVIII Corps, with four divisions each, to attack to reduce the pocket. V and VII Corps were to prepare to attack east, with 3rd AD, 1st ID, and 104th ID working for Collins. Hodges assigned the 9th AD and the 2nd and 69th ID to Huebner.[15]

Crossing the Weser

Control of Ninth Army passed from General Montgomery to Bradley and 12th Army Group on April 4. In possession of forty-five US divisions, Bradley now had the means both to reduce the pocket and renew the offensive eastward. Bradley left Fifteenth Army on the west bank of the Rhine, "as a semioccupation army." He also left eighteen divisions to deal with Army Group

B and turned the rest east along a two-hundred-mile front from Hanau in the south to Duisburg in the north. At the outset First Army would orient on Leipzig, attacking with VII Corps on the left and V Corps on the right. Fighting through the Harz Mountains, the last terrain obstacle between VII Corps and the Elbe, would be the penultimate "campaign" of the war.[16]

The 8th AD arrived the following day, freeing 1st ID to attack east with VII Corps. Andrus ordered 16th Infantry into an assembly area late that day—and to be prepared to move on the next. The 18th and 26th remained in place until the 8th AD completed occupying positions west of them. Collins issued Field Order 20 on April 7, ordering an attack to "seize a bridgehead on the Weser River and advances . . . prepared to exploit to the east." The two infantry divisions would attack to seize crossing sites, with the 1st ID on the left and the 104th ID on the right. Once across, the 1st ID would assist forward passage of the 3rd AD and then "push east from the Corps bridgehead in conjunction with 3rd AD."[17]

There was, however, a wrinkle. To assure the security of the corps rear in the event of a successful enemy breakout from the Rose pocket, Collins had the 1st ID organize Task Force Taylor, commanded by Brigadier General George A. Taylor. More accurately, the corps commander gave Taylor verbal orders to secure the corps rear as it reoriented to attack east. Collins's instructions included specifying task organization, continuing his inclination to reach down inside assigned divisions and issue orders that bypassed intermediate divisional headquarters. The task force included the 26th Infantry less Lieutenant Colonel Frank Dulligan's 1st Battalion. Dulligan had taken over from Francis J. Murdoch Jr. when the latter took command of the 26th Infantry from J. F. R. Seitz. Seitz left on April 7 to become assistant division commander in the 69th ID. Task Force Taylor also included Colonel John C. McDonald's 4th Cavalry Group, composed of the 4th and 24th Cavalry Squadrons, the 759th Light Tank Battalion, two artillery battalions, and a combat engineer battalion. Taylor commanded what amounted to a bobtailed division with the teeth necessary to deal with any likely threat to the corps rear. The task force dispersed on April 8, once other units had moved into its sector.[18]

Rapid changes to task organization remained essential to keep pace with changing conditions. By the spring of 1945, three of the four divisions assigned to VII Corps had worked together long enough that they could operate on verbal orders, followed up by written orders that mounted to artifacts. The 104th ID, the most recent to join the club, had been in theater since

September. Terry Allen and his staff knew the drill as well, so the corps could maintain momentum no matter how dynamic the situation. Similarly, the divisions had developed standard operating procedures that permitted rapid development of orders.

As the troops attacked east, they unearthed non-German civilians used as forced labor. Releasing these unfortunates from the labor camps was not sufficient, as many of them were emaciated and ill. Leroy Stewart, an infantryman in the 26th, described the problem: "As we would take [a] town and find these D.P.s [displaced persons] as we called them . . . the first thing we did was get them food and fix them up with something to wear. If we could find something in German homes for them, we gave it to them." This problem grew exponentially and came to include situations far worse.[19]

The 16th and 18th Infantry moved to assembly areas just west of the Weser. On April 7 they reconnoitered the river, looking for suitable crossing sites. Unlike the Roer crossing, this would not be a deliberate crossing, with detailed reconnaissance of the far side. The corps intended for the two infantry divisions to cross in stride, using assault boats. Lieutenant Colonel Bill Gara's engineers, who supported the hasty reconnaissance, would man the boats to get the infantry across. With too few boats to cross both regiments at once, the 18th would go first. Once the far side was secured, and the enemy pushed beyond direct fire range, corps engineers would follow to put in six bridges, including four able to support tanks, including the new T-26 heavy tank. These beauties sported 90-millimeter guns that could take on anything the Germans had but required the emplacement of bridges that could support their forty-ton weight.[20]

The terrain on the other side of the Weser favored the defender. High wooded hills dominated the far side, rising as high as 450 feet above the level of the river and, farther east, as high as 900 feet. Accordingly, the attacking units prepared for the worst. VII Corps estimated that SS replacement battalions from the Westphalia Brigade would provide the bulk of enemy troops prepared to "fight a rear guard action." With that in mind, the 18th began to cross the river in the "late hours of 7 April. By 0545B [B is the time zone] they were fighting in the town of Lauenforde and by 1300B reported the town cleared." At 1000 on March 8, Andrus called Lieutenant Colonel Frederick W. Gibb at the 16th's command post. "Are you all fixed on the river?" he asked, and Gibb replied, "Yes sir." Andrus and Gibb discussed the dense fog on the Weser and the fact that Colonel John Williamson of the 18th had two companies in in Lauenforde and "beaucoup people [Germans] killed." Andrus went on to add that the soldiers of the 18th "were running into SS and kids from 14 to 16 years of age." Andrus urged Gibb to get a patrol across the Weser to see what the far side was like.[21]

Fifty minutes later the G-3, Lieutenant Colonel Clarence E. Beck, called, asking Gibb if he could cross early. The 18th Infantry was reporting light resistance, as was the 104th Division crossing upstream. Gibb's S-3 then called Lieutenant Colonel Edmund F. Driscoll at the 1st Battalion and asked if he could go early. Driscoll responded, "I wanted to jump last night." Accordingly, the regimental S-3 started planning for a crossing at 1530 using a footbridge that Company A, 1st Engineers, planned to put in. In the middle of all this Gibb advised his 2nd Battalion commander, Lieutenant Colonel Walter H. Grant, that he was to give up a captain to the 106th ID to become a battalion S-3. Routine matters had to occur routinely.[22]

By 1300, the 18th Infantry had driven more than a mile east along about two miles of front. At 1324 Andrus, every bit as aggressive as his predecessor, met with Gibb at the 16th's planned crossing site. He found Gibb stalled, waiting on assault boats. Here Andrus discovered that the engineers had not come forward, apparently intending to wait until the far side had been fully cleared. Andrus called Beck with a short message: "I want you to get on the Engineers. They seem to think they cannot put the bridge up until it is safe." The 16th Infantry began crossing at 1500, using three assault boats. In two and half hours the regiment's 1st and 2nd Battalions were across, and taking the town of Fürstenberg for good measure.[23]

The crossing continued, primarily on boats, as the footbridges could not withstand the Weser's strong current. Heavy equipment crossed by raft until engineers completed a treadway bridge on April 8 and still more bridges later in the day. General Hickey's 3rd AD crossed the following day and drove east. Ralph Gordon watched the tankers cross the river for five hours in what seemed to him an awesome display of power. He was not alone in his awe. "[T]he German people just gazed at all, unable to believe what they saw." With all the major combat forces finally across, it was time to get on with it. The units assigned to Task Force Taylor also crossed on April 9. The 26th Infantry returned to division control. VII Corps attached the 4th Cavalry Group to the 1st ID to serve initially as advance guard and then to protect the corps' left flank. Andrus attached one of Gibb's battalions to the cavalry.[24]

The 1st ID would protect the corps' left flank with the 4th Cavalry Group and maintain contact with the Ninth Army's XIX Corps, attacking east along the northern edge of the Harz Mountains. Andrus planned to sustain the offensive using the well-tried system of rotating the regiments, with two up front and a third in reserve. That afforded some rest and eased the problem of maintaining the pace logistically. The 4th Cavalry Group covered the division's front as an advance guard. Colonel John McDonald organized three task forces built on his two squadrons, the 4th and 24th Cavalry Squadron, and the 759th Light Tank Battalion. All three had infantry, tanks, and tank destroyers as well as cavalry scout cars. The 26th Infantry trailed the cavalry on the left, securing the corps flank. Collins determined to use the 3rd AD south of the Harz Mountains, with the 104th ID in support. He tasked 1st ID with clearing the Harz. As of April 9 the G-2, Major John H. Lauten, concluded, as had VII Corps, that the "enemy was in the process of organizing some sort of order out of the chaos." The corps had crossed the Weser in two days' time, but that still gave the German Eleventh Army time to gather reinforcements and reorganize remnants of units to defend the mountains.[25]

Some sense of what that "order" might be came when the 4th Cavalry Group captured Generalmajor Paul Goerbig, along with his briefcase, which contained order-of-battle information, including the strength of VI Corps, formed from the Wehrkreis VI military district. He confirmed the presence of the Eleventh Army, though he used its old designation, Eleventh Panzer Army. The organization remained weak, with about two thousand troops assigned to the 466th Ersatz Division, commanded by Generalleutnant Friedrich Karst, the weakened SS Westphalian Brigade, which may have still had forty tanks and remnants of other units. The 166th VGD brought in from Denmark was the only other significant formation composed of three regiments formed from replacement units.[26]

The Harz Mountain Fortress

On April 8, as VII Corps crossed the Weser, OKW designated the Harz Mountains, Germany's the northernmost range, as a Festung (fortress). The designation meant little more than another stand-fast order. General der Artillerie Walter Lucht's Eleventh Army would defend the Festung. The mountainous terrain, densely wooded, with few roads, certainly provided great advantage to the defenders; the division G-2 thought it more formidable than that of the Ardennes. Furthermore, he believed that the terrain in the Harz Mountains was even worse than that of the Hürtgen, a view shared by Andrus. For his part, Collins thought this assertion represented some "exaggeration." Nonetheless, General Collins described the terrain in some detail, writing in Lightning Joe, "The mountains, with heights up to 3,700 feet, run generally eastward between the Leine and Saale Rivers."[27]

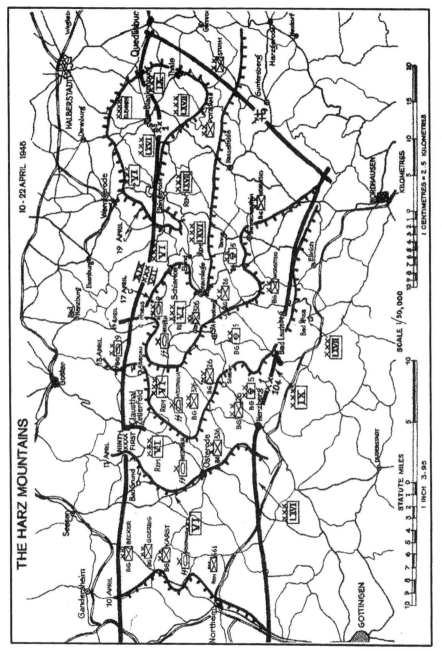

Map 33: The Harz Mountains, April 10–22, 1945. Reproduced from 1st ID *Selected Intelligence Reports*, Volume 2.

Few others who fought in the Harz Mountains would agree with Collins. Captain Felder F. Fair, who commanded Company B, 26th Infantry, shared G-2's belief that the Harz Mountains were a more difficult place to fight than the Ardennes. He described the range as "an area as difficult and forbidding militarily as it was scenic in peace time," not to mention that it constituted "approximately 1,000 square miles of heavily wooded, and very mountainous terrain." Captain Steve F. Phillips, also assigned to the 26th Infantry, shared Fair's view. Perspective matters. Lightning Joe did not hump the Harz Mountains carrying a rifle, but Fair and Phillips certainly did. Collins viewed the mountains from a broader perspective than did the young captains or, for that matter, the 1st ID. Both perspectives are valid, given the different concerns of their holders.[28]

Meanwhile Kesselring and OKW entertained the hope that Eleventh Army could delay the American advance "until a stronger organized striking force could come to the rescue." According to Kesselring, only the newly reactivated Twelfth Army could retrieve the situation. Twelfth Army was formed on April 10 with three subordinate corps and ten newly organized divisions under the command of General der Panzertruppen Walter Wenck. The divisions were formed in part from officer candidates and various "Reich labor services" units. They were, Wenck reported, poorly equipped and lacked training, but "these troops possessed a magnificent fighting spirit because of their youth." Moreover, their officers were "exceptionally good."[29]

After crossing the Weser, VII Corps next conducted a rapid crossing of the Leine River. The 1st ID G-2 characterized the resistance there as "varied from bitter opposition put up by the SS men from the Westphalia Brigade to near collapse on the part of many of the straggler units." VII Corps put it differently, concluding that "members of the Wehrmacht surrendered quite readily; but the SS troops [we] encountered continued to offer bitter resistance." What neither corps nor division intelligence understood was just how many German units were reorganizing or being formed in the Harz Mountains.[30]

The initial estimate presumed that VII would face one corps composed primarily of remnants. Instead, they would meet the units mentioned above, along with several reorganized divisions and newly built formations, organized in four corps. As they encountered the enemy, the 1st ID G-2 described two of the corps, the VI and IX, as "little more than a formless body of troops." Eventually the 1st ID also identified LXVI and LXVII Corps, both of which, while in better shape, were "up to the level of German corps in the Wehrmacht's salad days." 1st ID confronted three veteran albeit weakened divisions, the 26th VGD, the 326th VGD, and the 5th FJD. After the fact, the G-2 estimated that the Eleventh Army had as many as a hundred thousand troops. In his memoir, Collins wrote that there were seventy thousand assigned. Either way, the 11th Army was a formidable force for the 1st ID to face alone, and even after the 9th ID joined the fight. The 83rd ID from Ninth Army's XIX Corps operated on the northern edge of the mountains. The 3rd AD and 104th ID attacked along the southern edge. There were, it seemed, still plenty of Germans to go around.[31]

John McDonald, commanding the 4th Cavalry Group with 1st Battalion 26th Infantry attached, intended to operate by "smashing through or bypassing resistance." On April 10 the 4th Cavalry Group moved twenty-five miles east and seized Northeim, ten miles west of Osterode, a town on the western edge of the range. The infantry and McDonald's cavalry swept east, clearing the ground of the enemy by working in "close conjunction." The following day the cavalry group joined the 1st ID. McDonald and the 1st ID worked pretty well together. Lieutenant Colonel Francis J. Murdoch Jr., a cavalryman himself, was particularly effective working with the 4th Cavalry Group. By the end of the day, the division artillery had closed up to positions just west of Northeim.[32]

On April 12 the cavalry squadron operating in the north came up against "felled trees, road craters and blown bridges." These obstacles enabled single German tanks and antitank guns to knock out several of the squadron's tanks and force it to fight dismounted. Even with an infantry company attached, the squadron needed help. Murdoch and 26th Infantry passed through and joined the battle. In the center the 749th task force took Osterode. Congestion more than the enemy slowed things down. The congestion stemmed from three units, including 4th Cavalry, 3rd AD, and a battalion of the 18th Infantry, all of which had orders to seize the town. Colonel John Williamson, commanding the 18th, asserted that pileups of this nature happened whenever "top commanders run around and issue orders without telling their G-3s who and what they ordered." Williamson did not say who he thought was the offender. In the south the 24th Cavalry task force attacked southeast along the southern edge mountains and looked for good crossing sites on the Sose River.[33]

Murdoch advanced his companies by bounds. Whichever one was in the lead "sent out tank hunting teams equipped with bazookas." Murdoch's infantry cleared roads for the cavalry by rousting out tanks and killing them. Then they did it all over again, as required. Murdoch believed his combat team killed forty tracked vehicles over the course of the campaign. But it was, he admitted, "slow work"—so slow it attracted the dour attention of Collins, who called Verdi B. Barnes, the 1st ID chief of staff, to get things moving or fire the regimental commander. Andrus heard of the contretemps but backed up his commander. His observation to Barnes upon hearing the details was, "I don't give a damn what Joe Collins says; I run this division." Presumably he was more circumspect with Collins in person.[34]

First and Ninth Armies were in the process of creating a second pocket. The 83rd in the north and 3rd AD in the south were on the verge of encircling the Harz Mountains, and with them the Eleventh Army. In fact, Collins was bringing up the 9th ID to attack north to complete the circle. On April 12, despite slow going, the 26th took Clausthal-Zellerfeld. The 16th, driving in the south, seized the town of Herzberg. The 3rd AD complicated that operation as it fought through Herzberg in order to use the road east. Gibb was stymied. At 0630 he asked Andrus, "What do you want me to do?" Andrus replied, "Do not move until you get the dope from me to move." That order to move having come later that morning, the 18th advanced in the center but lost four tanks to an a particularly effective "88." Beck characterized resistance as "moderate to heavy" because the "terrain was highly suitable for defense."[35]

That same day, April 12, 1945, President Franklin Delano Roosevelt died at Warm Springs, Georgia. Word of Roosevelt's death reached Joseph Goebbels, Hitler's propaganda minister, late that evening. Goebbels and Hitler both believed in the efficacy of astrology. Goebbels concluded that FDR's death illustrated the accuracy of the Reich's horoscope, which had predicted that in "the second half of April we [the Reich] were to experience a temporary success." The prediction went on to prophesize that the war would end in August, and "in 1948 she [the Reich] would rise again." Goebbels called Hitler with the good news: "I congratulate you! Roosevelt is dead! . . . It is the turning point."[36]

The day of Goebbels's turning point, VII Corps continued eastward with 1st ID roughly halfway through the mountains. In the north, Company F, 2nd Battalion, 26th Infantry, had a sharp fight to take the town of Altenau. The company, like most of those in the 1st ID, was understrength. The company had two officers, First Lieutenant Webb W. Chestnut in command, and another lieutenant who led the weapons platoon. The rifle platoon leaders included one staff sergeant and two technical sergeants. These three noncommissioned officers were under grade. Their ranks would ordinarily have made them no more than squad leaders.[37]

At 0900 Chestnut led the company through Clausthal-Zellerfeld, taken by John T. Corley's 3rd Battalion only a few hours earlier. The mission required Company F to clear the ridges that lay between Clausthal-Zellerfeld and Altenau and then take the town. Chestnut advanced with his 3rd Platoon on the left side of the road leading toward Altenau. The 1st Platoon moved on the right side of the road. Both platoons had a light machine gun squad in support. Chestnut and his runner followed the 1st Platoon with his radio operator, and his 2nd Platoon moved along the road to provide security for a heavy machine gun platoon, 60-millimeter mortars, and three tanks.[38]

Five hundred yards east of Corley's battalion, "a pocket of enemy soldiers who were guarding the road" opened up with machine gun and small arms fire. By this point in the war, however, an ambush of this kind was old news to Corley and his men. The company responded immediately. The 1st Platoon broke farther right and moved up to "a wooded ridge and lay down covering fire for the remainder of the company." Chestnut ordered his 3d Platoon south of the road to envelop the position. Undiscovered self-propelled guns stopped them cold. Chestnut then brought up his tank platoon "so that they could fire through the trees." The tankers knocked out the guns and then attacked down the road with the 2nd Platoon in support. This enabled the 3rd Platoon to overrun the enemy, taking twenty-five of them prisoner.[39]

The company next came upon a roadblock built around a captured Sherman tank protected by land mines. Chestnut's troops ran off the Sherman with bazookas, cleared the mines, and continued east in pursuit of the tank. Finally the Germans stopped the company at "a major road block formed by a blown-out overhead railway trestle." Chestnut and his platoon leaders retired to cover, where they planned their next move. The 2nd Platoon would "secure the road block" while the rest of the company made "a flanking movement to the horseshoe-shaped town of altenau." Chestnut positioned his weapons platoon overlooking the town and sent a reconnaissance patrol forward, where it located and broke up a tank killer team armed with a Panzerfaust antitank explosive launcher. The company then went in hard, supported by its machine guns, 60-millimeter mortars, tanks, and artillery. The envelopment cut off the enemy's retreat from the town, resulting in a brisk skirmish. Chestnut's tankers destroyed the captured Sherman. Overall the company killed or captured thirty-five Landsers and fifty SS troops and secured the town.[40]

Jean Peltier's battery moved into Altenau to keep up with the attacking infantry. Finding a position for his howitzers proved difficult, thanks to the rugged ground. He finally laid all four weapons oriented east on the crushed rock of an uncompleted road running north-south. The position was awkward in that it required firing over houses just forward of where the guns were laid. The first time the battery fired it blew out all of the windows of said houses, with the roadbed passing the concussion of the howitzers' blasts directly into the artillerymen. "We really got shook up when we fired thereafter and we did plenty of firing." Of their targets, Peltier observed that "for a totally disorganized enemy, whose position was very rapidly becoming untenable, the Germans were really making things difficult for us."[41]

Fighting at company level, albeit with battalion supporting fires, characterized operations in the Harz Mountains. The conditions often led to ambush or other surprises. Corporal Sam Fuller, for one, had such an experience. Hardly an optimist about the war, Fuller nevertheless "sensed the war was winding down." Rumors abounded to the effect that the Germans would be "surrendering at any moment." Fuller remembered his sergeant warning him and the others "to ignore all the hearsay. . . . One bullet, either random or well aimed, could still rip off your head." His sergeant's warning proved prescient. While Fuller was attacking with his company toward Sankt Andreasburg, a sniper's bullet just missed him, killing a soldier to whom he was speaking at the time. The enraged infantrymen cornered the sniper only to find that "he was just a kid, not more than ten years old!" The sergeant spanked the child on his bare behind. Of the scene Fuller wrote, "All that would be left of Hitler's thousand-year Reich was a river of children's tears."[42]

Lieutenant Colonel Henry G. Learnard Jr.'s 3rd Battalion, 18th Infantry, fought attached to 3rd AD. Learnard led a task force formed on two of his rifle companies mounted on tanks or deuce and half trucks. The task force, as part of 3rd AD, drove along the southern edge of the Harz Mountains and then north toward Dessau, east of the mountains. Learnard's troops had what he called "three big fights before it was over[,] Köchstadt, Alten and north of Dessau." Ralph Gordon, who had served in Learnard's battalion since just before D-Day, and three other soldiers had become close. He lost one of his two close friends, Pete De Pietro, who was hit by shrapnel on the last day of March, and then his best friend, Ben Ackerman, on April 16 in Kochstedt. That morning, as Ben passed en route to the fight, Ralph had yelled over to him, "Take it easy kid." Word that Ben had been killed in what turned out to be his last fight reached Ralph later. Gordon really did not believe it until, traveling with his company command group, he reached the town. On arriving, he saw "Ben lying there on the road."[43]

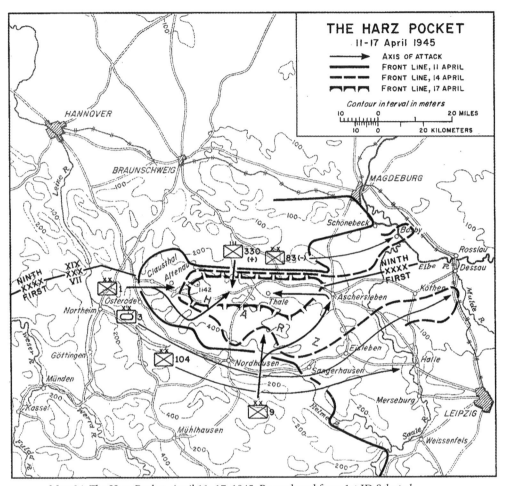

Map 34: The Harz Pocket, April 11–17, 1945. Reproduced from 1st ID *Selected Intelligence Reports*, Volume 2.

The painstaking, dangerous, and decidedly nonlinear clearing of the Harz Mountains continued against the "rat's nest of road blocks." Lieutenant Clifford Chandler, commanding Company I, 18th Infantry, affirmed that the "enemy defended fanatically from well-prepared positions particularly at road blocks." In his zone, "the blocks were generally so placed that their flanks were sheer cliffs or dense woods." Chandler therefore often had to resort to frontal attacks. The G-3 after-action report for April 18 noted that "opposition encountered was in some few sectors light, however, the majority of the units encountered determined opposition by organized units in the form of enemy infantry with supporting weapons and numerous road blocks of the same variety run into since entering the harz mountains." Additionally, "small groups of two or three stragglers were picked up over the entire area."[44]

Whether or not the end of the war was near, the Germans in the mountains remained willing to fight, and there were still plenty of them. The division artillery fired 165 missions that day. The weather was clear, enabling the air force to fly three major missions, including one "against a column estimated at approximately 150 enemy vehicles." Despite fierce resistance put up by both organized formations and small groups, the Germans lost. Not all of them were killed. Big Red One units took 3,100 prisoners that day.[45]

First and Ninth Armies continued the attack east while reducing the Ruhr pocket. Continuous attacks from the air and ground rendered Army Group B units unable to fight. Heinz Günther Guderian, the Panzer general's son, wrote that as of April 14, in the 116th Panzer Division "there could no longer be talk of regulated battle conduct," and the division "now had no more battleworthy tanks."[46]

That same day the Americans cut the pocket in two; what remained of the 116th was trapped in the smaller eastern half. Generalfeldmarschall Model could not bring himself to surrender. Instead he dissolved the army group by order effective April 17. Mass surrenders soon followed. Model remained in the pocket, where on April 19 he committed suicide rather than be taken prisoner. Some 317,000 Germans who remained in the pocket surrendered, more than had surrendered to the Soviets at the Battle of Stalingrad. The Americans had become competent at, if not masters of, operations at scale.[47]

That same day the 1st Division began to turn northeast, with the 9th ID coming up on its right or eastern flank. By then the 4th Cavalry Group had returned to corps control. The 16th Infantry took Elbingerode that day, pinching out Murdoch's regiment to the west. The 26th had to clear the several high peaks in the mountains, but a company of the 26th Infantry managed to take Brocken, at 3,747 feet the highest peak of them all. The 18th Infantry attacked toward Thale while maintaining contact with 9th ID.[48]

On one of the hills taken by the 1st Battalion, 26th Infantry, SS troops counterattacked successfully, forcing the battalion to leave behind several of its wounded. When it retook the hill, they discovered that the SS had murdered their wounded, having slit their throats. John Lebda recalled what happened next. Two SS, an officer and a private, were captured. A sergeant asked the SS man why his outfit had murdered the American wounded. By way of answering, the SS officer spat in the sergeant's face. According to

Lebda, the sergeant and a couple of troopers marched the two SS men away and shot them. Retaliation incidents of this kind were rare in the Big Red One, but occur they did.[49]

Having reached the limit of advance, the fighting for 1st ID declined over the next few days. The euphemism for confirmation that an area has been cleared is "mopped up." Clearing is usually associated with the size of units that may be missed. In this instance the idea was to find everyone, and by this point the Germans began surrendering en masse. On April 20, 1st ID took 10,000 prisoners. On April 23 a patrol from another unit captured the Eleventh Army's commander, General Lucht, along with his staff, thereby effectively ending the fighting in the Harz Mountains.[50]

That day, while processing prisoners, the Big Red One discovered that "hidden away under a bushel of generals, colonels and other elevated brass was the 1st Division's 100,000th prisoner of war taken during the present war." This worthy was a twenty-eight-year-old sergeant from Magdeburg who claimed to have been captured and escaped both at Falaise and Remagen. After his unit was overrun, the sergeant "dug himself a hide-out nest in the woods," intending to evade capture and find a unit to join. He was caught when he left his hidey hole to find water. The G-2 made the point that this man contradicted the assumption many made that the Germans would fold up at any moment.[51]

The challenge of processing prisoners taken during the fighting taxed transportation, logistics, and patience. The 1st ID took 30,343 of the 73,490 prisoners captured during the two weeks of fighting in the Harz Mountains, including ten general officers. In addition, three corps commanders and two division-level battle group commanders went into the cage. Other units captured eleven more generals, including the Eleventh Army commander.

Thanks to Simpson's Ninth Army having taken a bridgehead on the Elbe and the arrival there of the 3rd AD, the enemy's forlorn hope that their Twelfth Army would relieve the Eleventh came to naught. For his part, Simpson hoped to go on to Berlin, but Eisenhower declined the opportunity for at least three reasons. First, Bradley reckoned the cost to take Berlin at 100,000 casualties. And once the city was captured, the western Allies would have to turn it over to the Russians per the Yalta agreement. Lastly, SHAEF had concerns about the Alpenfestung, the national redoubt that the Nazis were supposedly building in the Austrian Alps, to which Germany's troops and government might retreat.[52]

What little chance Twelfth Army may have had to break into the Harz Mountains evaporated on April 23, when Hitler directed it to attack to relieve Berlin. In his memoir Kesselring wrote that he believed Twelfth Army could be a kind of deus ex machina, Germany's only hope of restoring the situation. To believe that, he had to have believed at the time that the Twelfth Army was indeed miraculous, but he later asserted he had been misled about this "glorified phantom body." Whether or not that was so, what William Shirer called the Götterdämmerung (or "twilight of the gods") of the Reich was well underway. The Russians were literally at the gates, and the only reason the Western Allies were not as well is because Eisenhower chose not to continue beyond the postwar political boundaries already agreed upon.[53]

The End of the Road in Cheb

The possibility of OKW withdrawing troops into a German national redoubt had been raised months earlier. Allegedly the SS would "man" the redoubt. The idea seemed consistent with the appearance of SS units on the southern flank, and SHAEF decided to take it seriously. After the fact, Bradley professed to be "astonished we could have believed it [the existence of a redoubt] as innocently as we did." Nevertheless, at the time the threat seemed real, and despite the success of the Italian campaign, troops attacking into Austria from the south would likely not be able to prevent enemy troops from escaping into the redoubt. Precluding that possibility meant sending Patton's and Devers's forces southeast, which in turn required First Army to spread out and fill the gap created.[54]

With its work done in the Harz Mountains, the 1st ID had become available for another mission. On April 24, VII Corps ordered the division into an assembly area near Blankenheim, just east of the Harz Mountains, to rest, or so Andrus believed. The order did, however, state that the division should be "prepared for further movement." Of the move, Andrus wrote, "Only part of the units had reached the 'rest area' when orders came sending the division off on its last battle where it relieved another division near the Chec [sic] border." Those orders to move arrived on April 27.[55]

What followed produced fighting of "spotty intensity," according to the commanding general, but it was "the last place where the Germans were putting up a fight." The division moved some 130 miles down, toward the border between Czechoslovakia and Germany. Cold War soldiers would recognize the names of the towns near where 1st ID crossed the border: Grafenwöhr, Hof, and Weiden.[56]

Despite the war winding down, or perhaps because of it, transportation to motorize the division remained problematic. Trucks were being used to support displaced persons and liberated slave laborers. Although most of the prisoners of war walked to where they would be held, some trucks supported their movement as well. At 0645 on April 27, the 16th Infantry complained to Lieutenant Colonel Beck, "You have us down for 65 trucks for the move today. We can't move on that many trucks." Beck promised, "I will call you back." Regiment and division explored several alternatives. In the end, Beck could not find more trucks, so the infantry doubled up where possible, and some rode the 130 miles or so standing up. With time running out, the S-3 read the order over the phone to the 7th Field Artillery, including the details of serial, march speeds, intervals, and so on. No matter what, 1st ID made the time set to cross the initial point, as did the 16th and 26th Infantry. Only sixty-two of the sixty-five promised trucks reached the 16th, but no one was left behind. The 18th Infantry and its supporting artillery moved the next day.[57]

The regiment crossed its initial point at 1100, on time, and closed in to Selb, Germany, not quite twelve hours later. The 26th Infantry left an hour earlier and closed their new area around 2000. On arriving in the area, 1st ID passed from VII Corps to VIII Corps. The attached armor and tank destroyers moved on the 28th and closed the same day. The 745th TB and the 643th TD moved to assembly areas near Marktleuthen, Germany, some 152 miles away. The tank and tank destroyer companies rejoined the infantry regiments they supported.[58]

While the 18th Infantry, 634th, and 745th moved south, the 16th and the 26th relieved the 97th ID. Murdoch's 26th Infantry moved in on the northern or left flank, while Gibb's 16th moved into the center. The 18th Infantry closed on April 28, as did the last two battalions of artillery. By midafternoon Murdoch and Gibb had assumed responsibility for their new sectors. The following day, the 18th completed the relief. That day a detachment of ten officers and 140 Czechoslovak soldiers arrived, planning to proceed to Cheb.[59]

On the last day of April, the 1st ID pushed patrols eastward and made contact with the enemy, with division artillery firing twenty-one missions on observed targets. Once again, the Germans demonstrated that regardless of dire conditions, many of them would still fight. In October, after the frustration of culminating on the Siegfried Line, Eisenhower commented to Roosevelt's press secretary that "people of the strength and war-like tendencies of the Germans do not give in; they must be beaten to the ground." Throughout the first four days of May, 1st ID made "minor shifts and improvements of the line." The response from Division Benicke, an extemporized formation named for its commander, varied from "stiff fighting at isolated roadblocks and strong points" to completely undefended towns. Officer candidates from the officer candidate school at Milowitz, Czechoslovakia, were, according to the G-2, among "the best quality troops encountered by the Division."[60]

There were two major German formations operating in what the Germans thought of as the Sudetenland and others as western Czechoslovakia. It was, of course, the German-speaking Sudetenland that had been ceded to Germany at Munich. Now, some six and half years later, XII Wehrkreis, newly styled as XII Corps and commanded by General der Artillerie Herbert Osterkamp, constituted the main antagonist of the 1st ID. XIII Corps, also formed from a Wehrkreis, served in the area as well. Virtually all the German units in the area were organized from stragglers and Volkssturm.

Generalmajor Kurt von Berg commanded such a unit. He and his division staff moved into the area in mid-April. Once arrived, they set about collecting stragglers, whom they fed, armed, and organized into units to return to the front. Berg also made contact with the rear area of an eastern front field army retiring toward his rear area. General der Infanterie Karl Weissenberger, commanding the XIII Corps near Pilsen, performed similar tasks, forming battle groups of a few hundred men. He believed that "the troops still did good things, although they were in no way up to their tasks."

These improvised units did what they could. "The enemy defended strategic road junctions and village strong points bitterly," the G-2 reported, "making good use of small arms and automatic weapons fire." Yet these efforts had no chance to achieve anything beyond extending the misery on both sides. One last attack had to be made. At V Corps, General Huebner issued that order, at least as it applied to V Corps. He required the Big Red One, reinforced by Combat Command A, 9th AD, to attack the 97th ID on its right "to eliminate all enemy resistance, protect north flank of V Corps, maintain contact with VIII Corps elements on the north and be prepared to seize karlsbad on Corps order."[61]

The division duly crossed the line of departure at 0600 May 6, with 16th and 26th abreast along nearly 30 miles of front. The attack angled northeast toward Karlsbad. The 1st ID and CCA 9th AD made "slow progress against defended road blocks, panzerfausts and antitank gunfire and difficult terrain." The division advanced about six miles, taking several towns and 1,400 prisoners on its 441st day of combat. That day proved to be the last combat operation of World War II for the Big Red One.[62]

It was not, however, the last day of combat. That came the next day and ended more with a whimper but not entirely without a bang. Jim Sharp, now leading a squad, had a comparatively quiet day, mostly accepting the surrender of German troops who were ready to quit. Three Germans he captured advised Sharp that there was a German Army camp just up the road, so he and two other soldiers went to investigate. While rooting around the camp, they came under fire. Sharp "had heard rumors that the war was about over, so we got out of there in a hurry." Neither Sharp nor anyone else who had made it this far could see any point in being killed at the end of the war. It was not a day for aggressive initiative.[63]

On May 7 at 0815, while continuing to advance on Karslbad, the 1st ID received the following order: "all troops to halt in place and maintain defensive positions. effective at once. details to follow. cg, v corps." At 1030 the division received a copy of Eisenhower's official message detailing the German surrender. The message specified that hostilities would cease at one minute after midnight on May 9.[64]

For some soldiers the end involved ceremonies and joyous celebrations with Czech civilians, newly released Allied prisoners, and official "linkups" with the Russians. But the detritus of the end included the human flotsam and jetsam of prisoners and displaced persons, and the starting and stopping of postwar occupation. Eclipse, the code name for the postwar operations, was published, then rescinded, and published yet again. For Jerry Nauss and other wiremen, May 8 was a busy day. The next day, though, Nauss and a buddy drove their jeep from Schoenbach, where they were stationed, to Karlsbad to meet with the Russians. "As we drove along," he remembered, "we passed convoy after convoy of German soldiers going westward to surrender to the Americans. Several German Divisions specifically asked to surrender to the 1st Infantry Division, which we considered a very nice compliment." Of course, they would have preferred to surrender to any American division than to any Russian unit.[65]

Conclusions on How to Fight

For the first time since the invasion of Algeria, the division after-action report covered a partial month. Instead of reporting lessons on the week of

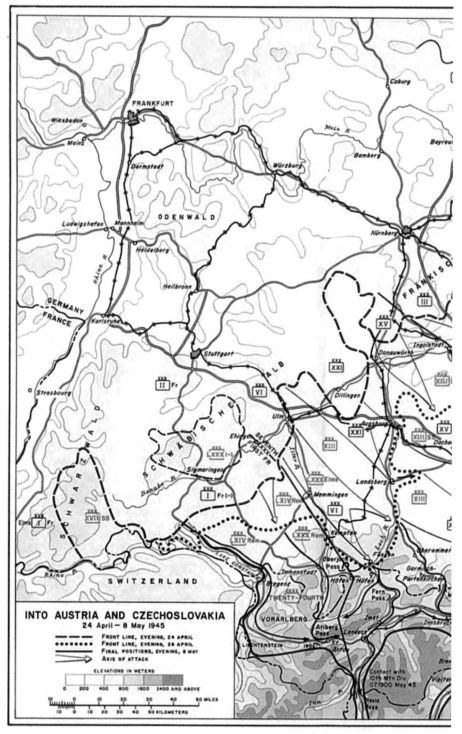

Map 35: Into Austria and Czechoslovakia, April 24–May 8, 1945. Reproduced and edited to add Cheb and Karlsbad, from MacDonald, *The Last Offensive*, Map XVI.

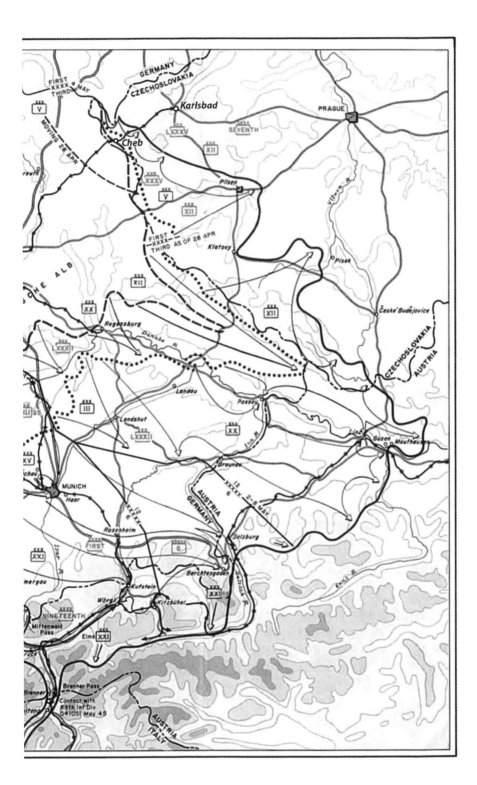

combat in May, the G-3 produced overarching conclusions or lessons from the whole of its combat experience. The report began with the claim that the 1st ID was "probably closer than any other division to being a potential text-book on the art of modern infantry fighting." Lieutenant Colonel Beck made a good case with a summary of the division's operations from the beginning in North Africa. He recalled that the Big Red One had done three assault landings and fought in the desert, cities, compartmented terrain, deep woods, and deep snow, had reduced part of the Siegfried Line, and had faced three different armies, including those of Vichy France, Italy, and Germany. It executed just about every kind of offensive mission, including both hasty and deliberated attacks, exploitation, and pursuit. The division learned hard lessons on how to wage defensive fights at Longstop Hill and Kasserine Pass. It applied those lessons on the beach at Sicily and at Butgenbach. It could and did fight outnumbered and win.[66]

Beck organized the immediate conclusions published on May 31 into six broad categories that considered operations at the division level: Artillery-Infantry Coordination; Air-Ground Coordination; Naval Support with Ground Troop Landings; Employment of Combat Engineer Battalion; Employment of Reconnaissance Troop; and Signal Problems.[67]

The 1st Division used artillery to break up enemy attacks, destroy enemy artillery, screen movement, support maneuver, harass the enemy, interdict enemy movement, and prepare enemy positions for attack. The report concluded, "The infantry and artillery during the course of almost three years combat have grown to rely on each other and work in very close harmony." This is an understatement: the US Army and the 1st Division absolutely took advantage of flexible, formidable, and ample artillery. The Big Red One, like other Army units, employed artillery lavishly and to good effect.[68]

Until the advent of unmanned aerial vehicles, the light observation L-4 "Cub" airplane provided a capability that US artillery with few exceptions had not enjoyed since or rather until the proliferation of unmanned aerial vehicles. The Cub was organic to the artillery battalions. It provided an "air OP [observation post]" that "proved of particular value in terrain where ground observation was limited." In hedgerow fighting the Cub "was for all practical purposes the only means of observation." Cubs flown by "artillery trained pilots proved to be most versatile in not only observing for the artillery but in such things as working with Air-Ground support and acting as eyes for a motorized column."[69]

The section on air-ground coordination acknowledges the "long tortuous period of development from no close air support to the present efficient and effective system." The bitterness evident in North Africa had become a happy if imperfect partnership at the end of the war. At Aachen, Army Air Force fighter bombers were brilliant, "in one case strafing a counter attack 50 yards in front of our troops." The air force routinely "intercepted and disorganized" enemy forces on the move. According to Beck, there were still "bugs to be ironed out." The division report offered no explicit recommendations but concluded that close air support "should be developed to its fullest capabilities in the future."[70]

Those in 1st ID who had made all three landings, including most of the senior leadership, well understood the benefit of naval gunfire support. The key, according to the 1st ID, was the Shore Fire Control Party, who went ashore with the assault forces. These Shore Fire Control Parties added capability, since they enabled naval gunfire support during and after landings. However, communications problems and the relative fragility and lack of flexibility of the era's radios proved problematic. Army and navy frequency-modulated or crystal radios were not compatible. Overlapping frequencies had to be found and procedures developed. The solutions arrived at worked. Naval gunfire helped repulse the Herman Göring Division on the beach at Gela, Sicily, thus saving the beachhead.[71]

Discussion of the employment of the 1st Engineer battalion reflected the conviction that the division had too few combat engineers. Engineers did route reconnaissance, maintained roads, laid and recovered mines, supported mine clearing, helped emplace wire and other obstacles, and carried out mobility/countermobility tasks. The division recommended developing a robust pioneer platoon organic to every regiment. It also recommended not using the combat engineers in their secondary mission of fighting as infantry. Finally, 1st ID wanted organic bridging. Since the First Gulf War in 1991, the US Army has addressed this problem by providing every brigade, the formation that replaced the regiment, with a combat engineer battalion.[72]

The section on the employment of the reconnaissance troop is arguably the most detailed. The infantry division reconnaissance troop was small and lightly armed, authorized six officers and 149 enlisted soldiers. The three reconnaissance platoons each fielded three Greyhound armored cars armed with a 37-millimeter cannon and six jeeps, three of which had pedestal-mounted machine guns. The reconnaissance troop could conduct reconnaissance, man out posts, and screen movement. The division often used the troop to maintain contact with adjacent units, which it did effectively, but it lacked the combat power to conduct other cavalry missions such as guard or cover; the cavalry groups in support of each recon corps handled those missions. The recon troop could and did, however, overwhelm or bypass German roadblocks.[73]

The end of the war was in some ways anticlimactic. For many it was disorienting—one minute attacking and the next being ordered to cease fire and the next receiving further orders for transition to less dangerous if no less important work. Soon after the war, Clift Andrus oversaw the production of a seventy-page pamphlet entitled "The First, 1917–May 1945." It begins with a short introduction of less than one hundred words that concludes with the division motto: "No mission too difficult, sacrifice too great. Duty First!" The author (or authors) of the booklet described the atmosphere at the moment the ceasefire order came, at 0815 May 7: "Nobody cheered . . . the forward units of the Division just stopped in place and dug in, ready to take up the defense if necessary."[74]

The next day the doggies learned that World War II, or at least their part in it, was over. The anonymous author continued, "When the last shot was fired (who fired it nobody knows, and nobody cares very much) . . ." In fact, somebody did know and care. The 26th Infantry journal claimed that Staff Sergeant Jerome W. Gunderson was the last Big Red soldier to fire a shot in World War II, at 0905 on May 7. And even if politicians and generals had declared the end of the war, the killing and wounding did not stop on a dime. The personnel officer for the 1st ID reported two killed, two wounded in action, and sixteen sick on May 8. In the final week of the war the division lost seventy-seven killed in action and twenty-five wounded.[75]

For Ralph Gordon the first day of peace was bittersweet. He mourned the loss of his friends Pete De Pietro and Ben Ackerman, both lost in the last weeks of the war. Gordon's memoirs of the war conclude with these words: "If only Ben and Pete could have seen this day, it would have been something to remember, but for them, it came too late." It also came too late for many thousands of other soldiers whose shoulder patches had borne a big red "1."

Notes

1. Lebda, *Million Miles to Go*, 125, 128.

2. Gordon, *Infantrymen*, 110, 112.

3. HQ, 1st ID, G-3 after-action report, April 1945, 2, in RG 301-3: G-3 Operations Reports, European Campaign, Jan 45–Dec 45, MRC Digital Archives.

4. Eisenhower, Papers, no. 2354, 4:2541, dated March 25, 1945. See also no. 2334, 4:2526, March 13, 1945, to Bradley. Eisenhower planned originally for an advance toward Frankfurt. Eisenhower, *Crusade in Europe*, 392; Ambrose, *Supreme Commander*, 609–11. Ambrose argues that Eisenhower desired at least subconsciously

to "give Bradley the leading role in the [last] campaign." This attitude was based on Eisenhower's confidence that Bradley would act more decisively than Montgomery.

5. G-3 after-action report, April 1945, 2–3; MacDonald, *Last Offensive*, 359; Zumbro, *Battle for the Ruhr*, 239–40. Zumbro's account of the Ruhr fighting is particularly good for understanding the German perspective, including that of individual German soldiers whom he interviewed.

6. MacDonald, *Last Offensive*, 18.

7. Kesselring, *A Soldier's Record*, 305; Citino, *Wehrmacht's Last Stand*, 437.

8. Carl Wagener, "The Battles of Army Group B on the Rhein Up to Its Dissolution, 22 Mar–17 Apr 45," ms. B-593, March 25, 1946, N17500.587, CARL, 22, 26 and 36. Wagener joined Army Group B from Fifth Panzer Army, where he had also been chief of staff. An experienced general staff officer, he wrote several useful postwar monographs at the behest of his captors.

9. Guderian, *From Normandy to the Ruhr*, 435; Wagener, "Battles of Army Group B," 37; Herman Floerke, "LXVI Corps (30 Mar–4 Apr 45)," 4 March 1947, ms. B-393, 383, N17500.400-A.2, CARL, 27–36. Floerke is an unsympathetic character; his manuscript reads like a defense at a court-martial. Kesselring, *A Soldier's Record*, 300–301.

10. HQ, 12th Army Group, Assistant Chief of Staff, G-2, "The Destruction of the German Armies in Western Europe, June 6th 1944–May 9th 1945," N10099, CARL, 26; HQ, 18th Infantry, after-action reports for 1st, 2nd, and 3d Battalion, April 1945, all in RG 301-INF(18)-0.3: Reports of Operations, 1 Jun 44–31 Mar 45, MRC Digital Archives. The 1st Battalion traveled 111 miles, the 2nd Battalion 110 miles, and the 3rd Battalion 120 miles.

11. Fritz Bayerlein, "The LIII Corps in the Ruhr Pocket Eastern Front," ms. B-396, October 1, 1946, Sturmpanzer, 3–8, 14.

12. MacDonald, *Last Offensive*, 359–62; Wagener, "Battles of Army Group B," 38–39. See also Floerke, 5–7, 47–58 re SS Ersatz Westfalen Brigade. The heavy tank battalion was equipped with King Tiger tanks, many of which failed because the tanks were new and had not gone through the breaking-in process.

13. 16th Infantry journal, April 2, 1945, 8, in RG 301-INF(16)-0.7: Journal, European Campaign, Jan 45–May 45, MRC Digital Archives.

14. "World War II Diary of Jean Gordon Peltier," August 2, 1942–July 5, 1945, MRC 1998.79, 250–51. Peltier's battery traveled eighty-nine miles on April 1, 1945.

15. Bayerlein, "LIII Corps," 2–6; HQ, First Army, after-action report, April 1–30, N11419, CARL, 1–2; Sylvan and Smith, *Normandy to Victory*, 357–58.

16. Bradley, *Soldier's Story*, 528–29; Hogan, *Command Post at War*, map 17, 260–61.

17. G-3 after-action report, April 1945, 7; HQ, VII Corps, FO 20, April 7, 1945, N13343.20, CARL, 2. The Weser River, formed from the Fuld and Werra Rivers, rises near the city of Münden and flows north to empty into the North Sea at Bremerhaven. https://www.britannica.com/place/Weser-River.

18. Knickerbocker et al., *Danger Forward*, 419; Weingartner, *Blue Spaders*, 120–21; HQ, VII Corps, Operations Memorandum 191, April 7, 1945, CARL, 1. See also VII

Corps, after-action report, April 1945, R1179.10, CARL, 33; G-3 after-action report, April 1945, annex B, 1. The new heavy tanks were still technically prototype tanks, thus the "T" designation.

19. Leroy Stewart's memoir, *Hurry Up and Wait*, quoted in Weingartner, *Blue Spaders*, 120.

20. G-3 after-action report, April 1945, 13; 16th Infantry journal, April 8, 1945, 1; VII Corps, FO 20, 3. The comment on the shortage of boats is an inference drawn from the after-action reports.

21. G-3 after-action report, April 1945, annex B, 1; 16th Infantry journal, April 8, 1945, 1; Baumgartner et al., 16th Infantry, 255; Baumer and Reardon, *American Iliad*, 345–46.

22. 16th Infantry journal, April 8, 1945, 2.

23. 16th Infantry journal, 8.

24. G-3 after-action report, April 1945, 12–15.

25. Knickerbocker et al., *Danger Forward*, 409; HQ, 1st ID, Selected Intelligence Reports, vol. 2, December 1944–May 1945, 78, in RG 301-2.0: G-2. It is likely that Evans joined Huebner at V Corps, given that Huebner brought him to 1st ID in the first place. Lauten's tenure extended through the end of the war.

26. Selected Intelligence Reports, 2:78–80. The intelligence reports do not specify who captured Goerbig, nor does the division after-action report, but it was likely the 4th Cavalry Group. On the organization of the 466th Ersatz Division, see Generalleutnant Friederich Karst, "466th Replacement Division, Feb–Apr 1945," MS. B-319, April 14, 1946, Sturmpanzer, 1–4. See also Order of Battle Notes, annex B to VII Corps FO 20, April 7, 1945; 4th Cavalry Group, after-action report, April–May 1945, in RG 407: Report of Operations, CAVG4, NARA, courtesy of William S. Nance. The 759th Light Tank Battalion rounded out the 4th Cavalry Group.

27. 1st ID, Selected Intelligence Reports, 2:79–80; Kesselring, A Soldier's Record, 314; Collins, Lightning Joe, 321.

28. Felder L. Fair, "Operations of Company B, 26th Infantry, 1st Division in the Reduction of Positions in the Harz Mountains, 17–18 April 1945," Advanced Infantry Officers Course, Fort Benning, GA, 1947–48, 4, and Steve F. Phillips, "The Operations of the 26th Infantry (1st Infantry Division) in the Battle of the Harz Mountains, 13–22 April 1945," Advanced Infantry Officers Course, Fort Benning, GA, 1948–1949, 4, both in WWII Student Papers, DRL. Both officers quote 1st ID, Selected Intelligence Reports, vol. 2. Caddick-Adams also cites Fair in ch. 16 of *Fire and Steel*.

29. Walter Wenck, "Report on the 12th Army Compiled for 'Historical Div. US Army," ms. B-394, CARL, 1–2; Kesselring, A Soldier's Record, 314.

30. 1st ID, Selected Intelligence Reports, 2:80; VII Corps, after-action report, April 1945, 31.

31. 1st ID, Selected Intelligence Reports, 2:80.

32. 4th Cavalry Group (Mechanized), after-action report, April 1945, in RG 407: Report of Operations, CAVG4, courtesy of William S. Nance, 3–4; G-3 after-action report, April 1945, 17.

33. 4th Cavalry Group, after-action report, 4; Edward McGregor, interview by Kenneth Hechler, Lazne Kynzvart, Czechoslovakia, May 25, 1945, in RG 407, NARA. Williamson did ask not to be quoted.

34. Frank Murdoch, interview by Colonel John Votaw and General Paul Gorman, October 23, 1995, First Division Museum at Cantigny, Wheaton, IL. The interview is used in Weingartner, *Blue Spaders*. They identify the colonel as coming from corps. That is incorrect, as the transcript refers to Berti, which is simply the transcriptionist mistaking Berti for Verdi. See also McGregor interview.

35. MacDonald, Last Offensive, 391; G-3 after-action report, April 1945, 21; 16th Infantry journal, April 12, 1945.

36. Shirer, *Rise and Fall*, 1108–10.

37. HQ, 1st ID, "World War II Combat Achievements Report," MRC 1988.31, ch. 1.

38. 1st ID.

39. 1st ID.

40. 1st ID, 2–3.

41. Peltier, diary, 55.

42. Fuller, A Third Face, 211–12.

43. Baumer, *Aachen*, 351; Gordon, *Infantrymen*, 113.

44. G-3 after-action report, April 1945, 35; Clifford Chandler, interview, Lanzne Kyunzvart, Czechoslovakia, May 25, 1945, RG 407, NARA.

45. G-3 after-action report, 35.

46. Guderian, *From Normandy to the Ruhr*, 463–65; Citino, *Wehrmacht's Last Stand*, 444; MacDonald, *Last Offensive*, 362–72.

47. Guderian, *From Normandy to the Ruhr*, 464–67; MacDonald, *Last Offensive*, 362–67. A few units of the 116th had moved east before the 1st ID and other units closed the pocket. Those units surrendered at various times. Some were cut off by the 26th INF near Bad Grund; others made it farther east. One maintenance unit made it to the Elbe. Guderian, 472–77.

48. G-3 after-action report, April 1945, summary of Phase III, 39–45; MacDonald, *Last Offensive*, 404.

49. Lebda, *Million Miles to Go*, 129.

50. MacDonald, *Last Offensive*, 404–5; 1st ID, Selected Intelligence Reports, 2:85–87.

51. 1st ID, Selected Intelligence Reports, 2:98.

52. On Eisenhower's reasoning, see Ambrose, "Controversy with the British," ch. 20 of *Supreme Commander*, 632–48. The British objected in part because Eisenhower shifted the main effort to Bradley and with it Ninth Army. They also objected to Eisenhower communicating to Stalin his intention not to attempt to take Berlin. In fact, the Combined Chiefs of Staff had authorized direct coordination. The British assumed that meant with Stalin's staff, not Stalin. In any case, Eisenhower was within his rights to decide not to take Berlin. Re the German national redoubt, see "The Myth of the Redoubt," ch. 17 of MacDonald, *Last Offensive*, 407–42.

53. Kesselring, *A Soldier's Record*, 317–18; "Goetterdaemmerung: The Last Day of the Third Reich," ch. 31 of Shirer, *Rise and Fall*, 1107–43.

54. Bradley, *Soldier's Story*, 536–37.

55. VII Corps, Operations Memorandum 202, 1, and Operations Memorandum 205, 1, both CARL; Andrus, letter, in *Memorial Album: Pictorial History of the 1st Division* (San Diego, CA: Society of the First Division, 1950), copy in MRC, call no. Unit History 05-1-1950.

56. Andrus, letter, 4.

57. 16th Infantry journal, April 27, 1945, in RG 301-INF(16)-0.7: 16th Infantry, European Campaign, Jan 45–May 45, MRC Digital Archives.

58. G-3 after-action report, April 1945, 49; HQ, 634th Tank Destroyer Battalion, after-action report, April 1945, 9, http://tankdestroyer.net; HQ, 745th Tank Battalion, after-action report, May 1, 1945, 16, in "After Action Reports, June 1944–May 1945," doc. 8745 TB 101-A, DRL.

59. G-3 after-action report, April 1945, 50–51.

60. 1st ID, Selected Intelligence Reports, 2:99. Benicke had a division headquarters with no troops. He was ordered in mid-April to form a division from various units in the Karlsbad area. He had school troops including artillery trainees, an officers' training school, and some "dispersed units." See Fritz Benicke, "Central Europe Task Group," June 1946, ms. B-165, N17500, CARL.

61. G-3 after-action report, May 1945, 5; 1st ID, Selected Intelligence Reports, 2:100.

62. G-3 after-action report, 5–8.

63. Sharp, *Diary of a Combat Infantryman*, 133.

64. G-3 after-action report, May 1945, 10.

65. Nauss, *Troubleshooting All the Way*, 196.

66. G-3 after-action report, May 1945, 12.

67. G-3 after-action report, 17–25.

68. G-3 after-action report, 18.

69. G-3 after-action report, 18.

70. G-3 after-action report, 19.

71. G-3 after-action report, 20–21.

72. G-3 after-action report, 22–23.

73. G-3 after-action report, 24–28. The report argues that the troop could not screen or do reconnaissance missions until it received armored cars in the UK. The table of organization and equipment changed over time. The one discussed here is T/O &E 2-27, in effect from 1943 to 1945. Bellanger, Army Infantry Division, 1:16–24.

74. HQ, 1st ID, "The First, 1917–May 1945," n.d., RG 301.0: History—The First, 1917–May 1945, MRC Digital Archive, 56.

75. 1st ID, "The First"; G-1 after-action reports, May 1945, 1, in RG 301-1: G-1 Operations Reports, 8 Nov 1942–14 Apr 1943, Jul 1943–Mar 1944, Jun 1944–May 1945, 1 Jul–31 Dec 1948, MRC Digital Archives.

CHAPTER FIFTEEN

Conclusion

Since the war began in AFRICA
When we fired the starting gun
There's none can beat the record of
THE FIGHTING BIG RED ONE
—Song of the Fighting First

I had no feeling that the war would ever be over, really. For me it lasted only two years . . . that was darned near 10 percent of my life.
—Frank Kolb, 16th Infantry

CLIFT ANDRUS WROTE a summary of combat operations of the Big Red One during his tenure in command that served as the preface for a pictorial history of the 1st ID in World War II, which would be published shortly after the end of the war. At the end of the summary, he wrote that several high-point soldiers had approached him, ambivalent about leaving the division. They wondered whether they should "go home or stay with the Division to the end." He told all of them, "By all means go home as a reward for a dangerous and difficult duty done in a superior manner." Less than a week after V-E Day, the 1st ID held a formation to say farewell to 600 high-point men. Having led the way in combat, these men deserved to lead the way home.[1]

What Became of the World War II Big Red One Soldiers
The war ended in May 1945 in Europe only. Many units, including General Hodges's First Army headquarters and Terry Allen's 104th ID, prepared to

redeploy to the Pacific to join the invasion of Japan. The 1st ID found itself operating at a frenetic pace both to demobilize soldiers and to get on with the business of occupation, the division spreading out to cover the US occupation zone in southern Germany and western Austria. In fact, the Big Red One did not return home in until 1955.

Whether a soldier returned early or later on, all of those who fought had earned "the reward for a dangerous and difficult duty done in a superior manner." John Lebda was one of those who went home early in the demobilization process. John married his pen-pal sweetheart and then went on to attend the University of Pittsburgh, from which he graduated in 1950. The army recalled him during the Korean War, and he served in Japan. After that he returned home, this time for good, to run a successful business and raise two children. John died on February 21, 2012.[2]

Jim Sharp, who joined the division on a bitterly cold night in January 1945, ended the war as a squad leader. During the war crimes trials in Nuremberg he served as a sergeant of the guard. He met and acquired the autographs of all of the Nazi officials on trial, including Göring, Alfred Jodl, and von Ribbentrop. He went home in 1946 and took advantage of the GI Bill to get his degree at Kansas State University in Manhattan, Kansas. After graduation he ran a business and raised a family. Jim lives in Manhattan, Kansas.[3]

There were a good many 1st ID soldiers who chose not only to stay in the army but also to stay in the 1st ID. Ted Dobol is easily the most famous of those, given that he served all but his last assignment with the Big Red One. He finished his career at the US Military Academy, and died on November 25, 1996. Thomas O. Beauchamp also ran the long course with the 1st ID. Beauchamp joined the army in 1912 and served in the Philippines and on the Mexican border with the 8th Cavalry. In 1917 he volunteered to join the 1st ID. He remained in the Big Red One for the rest of his long and distinguished career. In the forty-seven years he served in the division, he rose through the enlisted ranks to become a chief warrant officer. Known as "Mr. First Division," Beauchamp retired in September 1954. Thereafter he made his home in München, Germany, where he died on April 11, 1971.[4]

The experiences of officers who chose to leave the army were not unlike those of Lebda and Sharp. Those officers who chose an army career went on to a succession of schools and operational assignments. Many of them saw combat in Korea and/or Vietnam. For example, Albert H. Smith, who joined the 16th Infantry as second lieutenant in 1940, ended the war as a major and the regiment's operations officer. He attended the usual army schools, graduating from the Army War College in 1960. He served twice more in the

1st ID, first as commander of the 1st Battalion, 18th Infantry. In Vietnam he served as an assistant division commander. He retired as a major general and served as honorary colonel of the 16th Infantry. Smith died in 2005.[5]

Of the three wartime division commanders, only Clarence R. Huebner advanced beyond Major General. Terry Allen brought the 104th ID back to the United States to prepare it for the invasion of Japan. Once Japan surrendered, Allen went about demobilizing the division, which deactivated on December 20, 1945. He retired in early 1946 and made his home in El Paso, Texas, where he worked for an insurance company. Terry Allen died on September 12, 1968. Clift Andrus commanded the Big Red One until May 1946. He then commanded the US Army Field Artillery School at Fort Sill, Oklahoma, served in the Pentagon, and finally was deputy commander of Second Army until he retired in October 1952. Andrus made his home in Washington, DC. He died on September 29, 1968.[6]

Clarence Huebner deactivated V Corps at Fort Jackson, South Carolina, in September 1945. He returned to Germany in August 1946 and served in senior positions in military government and the US European Command. As a lieutenant general he served as the first postwar commander of Seventh Army and US Army Europe from May 1949 to August 1950. After a brief stint as special assistant to the chief of staff, he retired in November 1950. In retirement he served as the civil defense commissioner for New York State. He also served as president of the Society of the First Division. Huebner died on September 23, 1972.[7]

Not all of the Big Red One veterans thrived after World War II. The infamous incidents of Patton abusing soldiers suffering from combat fatigue, including Charles Kuhl of the 1st ID, showed how little was known about what we now call post-traumatic stress disorder (PTSD). The army understood that combat fatigue was a problem, but it did not know how to treat it. It is impossible to know how many World War II veterans suffered from PTSD.

Joe Dawson, who earned a Distinguished Service Cross (DSC) for his actions on Omaha Beach, suffered from combat fatigue and was taken out of combat because of it. John T. Corley earned a DSC in command of 3rd Battalion, 26th Infantry, and a second while commanding the 24th Infantry in Korea. In 1966 he knew something was amiss and checked himself into Walter Reed Army Medical Center. There he was diagnosed with depression. Al Smith, who served in 1st ID with Corley, visited him at Walter Reed to tell him on behalf of the chief of staff that he was to retire either medically or normally, but he would retire. Corley, a proven combat leader in two wars, chose to retire normally.[8]

Bobbie E. Brown's story is sadder still. Brown, who earned a battlefield commission, later commanded Company C, 18th Infantry. He won the Medal of Honor leading Company C in the fight to seize Crucifix Hill on October 8, 1944. Not long thereafter, Brown was concussed by a German mortar round and evacuated. After treatment he returned to the field, leading Company C until the end of the war. He returned to the United States in August 1945. Having been wounded thirteen times during his thirty-four of years of service, he spent much of 1945 through 1947 in and out of hospitals. Lacking a formal education and still suffering the effects of his injuries, Brown had no future in the US Army. In 1952, at the age of forty-nine, he retired, having served since the age of fifteen. He then worked as a janitor at the US Military Academy. In constant pain and almost certainly suffering PTSD, Brown committed suicide on November 8, 1971, in Highland Falls, New York.[9]

Gaining and Maintaining Tactical Excellence during World War II

This section revisits the central question raised in this narrative: that is, whether the 1st ID "adapted to dynamic battlefield conditions" by "innovating and altering behavior." The cumulative argument of this book establishes that the 1st Division did just that. The division built a reputation for excellence within the American forces, allies, and the enemy. This reputation was based on growing effectiveness in use of combined arms and nurtured by the division's senior leadership through the creation of an environment that supported individual and unit-wide learning, innovation, and adaptation. The principal insight is that learning and adjusting in battle depends on a leadership that learns from and matures with combat experience.

Describing the training and operations of the 1st ID during the interwar period is important to this narrative because it sets the tone and context for everything that followed. The National Defense Act of 1920 reorganized the service departments and armed forces for expansion to assure success in any future war. Twenty years later, funded and supported by the draft, the departments rapidly mobilized large naval, ground, and air forces able to engage in global war. For mobilization of ground forces, the act provided for nine corps areas, with one regular, two National Guard, and three US Army divisions. This organization provided a basic structure within which to assemble a massive wartime force. There were other important changes reviewed in chapter 1. Perhaps most important for this study is that the US Army's school for professional military education produced officers well prepared to mobilize and lead the army of World War II, in spite of having experienced interwar military life in a much smaller and less capable version of the army.

After the Great War the army suffered from many constraints, not least of which was a postwar abhorrence of war on the part of the public and politicians, which resulted in a policy of national isolation from overseas entanglements. Then, like everyone else, the army suffered financially from the effects of the Great Depression. Indeed, budget cuts severely limited tactical training, readiness, and acquisition. They also hurt soldiers directly through reduction in pay and, early in Franklin D. Roosevelt's tenure, the forgoing of an entire month's pay. However, all was not lost during these difficult years, and in retrospect the army benefited from its participation in some of the New Deal programs. For example, the Civilian Conservation Corps (CCC) provided a leadership and mobilization laboratory for the army. Young officers had the chance to work with many of the men they would later lead in combat. Major Alexander N. Stark Jr. won a national award for best-run CCC camp. He commanded the 26th Infantry in North Africa and was promoted at the conclusion of the campaign. The Citizens' Military Training Corps (CMTC), mentioned in chapter 1, also provided leadership opportunities. The CMTC provided unpaid volunteers military training at Citizens' Military Training Camps, including one at Plattsburg, run by the 26th Infantry.[10]

Once one is sent to war, tactical lessons are learned in the context of doctrine, structure, equipment, the particular environment, and the enemy. During World War II the 1st ID fought in nine campaigns in two theaters, across a range of terrain in all types of weather, and against three different armies, as well as under both British and American command. Like other divisions, it provided experienced soldiers to units preparing for employment in return for newly minted soldiers. It benefited from that practice prior to the invasion of Sicily, when it received veterans from 3rd ID, and it reciprocated after Sicily to leaven the 3rd ID as it prepared for the invasion of Italy. This practice, although beneficial, produced turbulence within units, as did the loss of men killed, wounded, or missing. Routine reassignment and promotions also produced turbulence while rewarding soldiers who performed well.

The original structure of units and supporting doctrine altered in practice. It is clear that senior officers and field grade officers who had attended advanced courses at the Command and General Staff College and the War College had read and understood the role of doctrine. It is not as clear whether this was so in the case of junior officers and noncommissioned officers, who were lately civilians. In their cases, however, it is abundantly clear that they learned from their seniors. Field Manual 100-5, *Field Service Regulations, Operations*, published May 22, 1941, provided the institutional baseline. That document explicitly permitted variation in the application of doctrine, which provided "a firm basis for action." On the other hand, the manual asserted that "set rules and methods must be avoided." Doctrine was meant to inform and describe how something might be done, all things being equal, rather than prescribe what must be done in any particular case. The 1st ID applied lessons and adjusted.[11]

A Record of Excellence

In the opening paragraph of the division's last monthly after-action combat report, that of May 1945, Lieutenant Colonel Clarence E. Beck asserted that "the 1st Infantry Division is probably closer than any other division to being a practical text-book on the art of modern infantry fighting." It was a bold assertion, but not without merit. Eisenhower, who like Marshall believed Distinguished Unit Citations should rarely be awarded to divisions, thought that the 1st ID might be one of a few actually worthy of that honor. In the end, in compliance with departmental policy, the division did not get the award commonly referred to as a Presidential Unit Citation, but many of its subordinate units did, including all three regiments, with two of them receiving multiple awards. During World War II the 1st ID complied a long list of achievements and a well-earned reputation for excellence.[12]

Despite not being awarded the Distinguished Unit Citation, the 1st Infantry Division earned its share of honors. It received campaign streamers for Algeria–French Morocco, Tunisia, Sicily, Normandy, Northern France, Ardennes, Rhineland, and Central Europe. France awarded the 1st ID the Croix de Guerre with Palm for Kasserine and Normandy. Belgium honored the division with its Croix de Guerre for Mons and Eupen-Malmedy. In total, 1st ID soldiers earned 20,752 awards, which included 16 Medals of Honor, 161 Distinguished Service Crosses, 4 Distinguished Service Medals, 6,116 Silver Stars, 79 Legion of Merit awards, 14,138 Bronze Stars, 162 Soldier's Medals, and 76 Air Medals. During World War II the 1st ID served 443 days in direct combat as a whole. It suffered 4,325 killed in action, 1,241 missing, and 15,457 wounded in action. Casualties amounted to 21,023, not including nonbattle casualties.[13]

Drew Middleton wrote the last section of *Danger Forward*'s last chapter. Middleton, like the other journalists who helped write this book, had served alongside the 1st ID. In *Danger Forward* he relayed that he had formed his impression "of a great fighting division" on "a hill side and in an olive grove" in Tunisia. But it was an RAF fighter pilot who had first pointed Middleton's attention toward the excellence of the Big Red One. Peeved at the British air defense artillery that had just shot him down, he suggested to Middleton that if he wanted a good story, he should go see the 1st Division: "They're bloody good," he said. "Bloody good." Thereafter a Gurkha officer asserted that he thought better of the Big Red One than "the guards, really I do. Almost as good as our chaps, you know." When Middleton saw the division preparing for the invasion of France, he described it as "adult," confident and ready.[14]

Middleton interviewed a German general staff officer who said simply, "Where the First Division was, there we would have trouble." The division's debut against the German 10th Panzer Division on Longstop Hill resulted in some controversy with the British but not the Germans. Hans Lüke, author of *Grenadier Regiment 69*, argued that the Americans on Longstop fought resolutely, noting, "The American attacks again and again: The fight rages hard and ruthlessly."[15]

The Efficacy of Combined Arms

Maneuver and the effective use of combined arms characterized 1st ID combat operations that grew better over time. The Big Red One was not alone in learning in combat how best to apply combined arms, and doing so far beyond what the army had imagined possible before the war. The first page of the section "Arms and Services," in the second chapter of the 1941 FM 100-5, discusses combined arms operations. The manual calls infantry the arm of close combat, but notes that when confronting an "organized defensive position . . . [or] a force of the combined arms," it has to be reinforced by "artillery, tanks, combat aviation and other arms."[16]

When the army reorganized from the square division of four regiments organized in two brigades to the triangle division composed of three regiments, it did so conceiving of the regiments as teams. From the beginning, regiments organized as teams formed within the means organic to the division. A regiment would have combat engineers attached from the 1st Engineer Battalion, and it might parcel out the cannon company or its organic antitank company. Each regiment had a direct support field artillery battalion that it thought of as its own, even if the division artillery retained the authority to position that battalion and use it to support other units as it deemed necessary.

The army planned to provide additional resources as needed. These included tanks, tank destroyers, and field and antiaircraft artillery. In North

Africa the division received attached tank destroyers and antiaircraft artillery but had little opportunity to develop relationships with these formations. Tank units were attached as well. In North Africa and Sicily, the 1st Division and others came to regard the routine attachment of the same combat and combat support formations as a necessity after the landings in Normandy. The institution as a whole learned the lesson of routinely organized robust combined arms teams. The 745th Tank Battalion, the 634th Destroyer Battalion, and the 103rd Anti-Aircraft Artillery Battalion became routine members of the division and formed part of its regimental combat teams. Routine association produced frequent observations on how to improve combined arms operations and the training to do so.[17]

Leadership and Learning in the Big Red One

Observations or innovations that do not translate into operational results are irrelevant. For an organization to demonstrate learning, it must go on to apply that which it has learned as well as use it to think critically about how it might improve its methods. There is clear evidence that the 1st ID was such an organization. Meaningful learning within the division occurred because leadership, including junior and noncommissioned officers, actually used it to adjust the division's behavior. Moreover, the 1st ID and other divisions promoted from the ranks, enriching the officer corps with experienced junior officers. Doing so may have had the effect of "teaching" newly arrived lieutenants more quickly, although that is not demonstrable in this study.

Unit maneuvers at scale supported learning. As noted in chapter 2, George Marshall believed such exercises provided a "combat college of troop leading." But the amphibious maneuvers in which the 1st ID participated may have been more instrumental. The requirements of living aboard crowded vessels not designed for amphibious operations and the early paucity of purpose-built landing craft required effective leadership and the efficiency that resulted from meticulous planning and rehearsal. Second Lieutenant Charles Hangsterfer said it best: "With all the makeshift equipment we had to use we learned a lot about the problems of assault landings."[18]

Training and experimentation with amphibious techniques prepared the division for the landings in Algiers, which became the model for amphibious operations in the Mediterranean and European theaters of war. Insufficient resources, and the melding of differing operational techniques developed in the Pacific and Mediterranean, put the landing at Omaha Beach at risk, but training and effective leadership saved the day.[19]

On Omaha Beach, small unit leaders like Jimmie Monteith, John Spalding, and Joe Dawson adapted on the fly. Technical Sergeant Philip Streczyk, Spalding's assistant boat section leader, worked effectively alongside his lieutenant, breaching obstacles and keeping the section on the move. These young men knew what had to be done and did it. Monteith was awarded the Medal of Honor posthumously. The other three earned the Distinguished Service Cross (DSC), along with five other soldiers in Spalding's boat section.[20]

In the early hours of the landing, junior leaders were materially aided by cool heads such as George Taylor, who walked about under fire organizing small groups and getting them moving. With an equally cool head, Willard Wyman managed the sequencing of the landing and did so calmly and with a remarkable patience, given the state of communications available to him. These men and others like them are why the 1st ID got off Omaha Beach and went inland. Many unsung noncommissioned officers and soldiers played their roles to the hilt. Leadership is not possible without followers.

Tactical acumen with respect to vision on the battlefield is sometimes explained as *coup d'oeil*, or insight at a glance. Another way to express this is the ability to "see" the battlefield. It is crucial in combat and stems from a number of things. Critical assessment of experience garnered in training and combat is key to developing this ability. Practical and thoughtful application of doctrine helps develop intuition and inductive reasoning in combat conditions. Unit cohesion based on confidence in the unit leader's competence can promote *coup d'oeil*. Confident subordinates will react to orders quickly, or act with insight in the absence of orders. The ability to see the battlefield in a way that affords insight also comes from accurate reporting.

All of these factors came together on June 6, 1944, for several reasons. One is that the 1st ID conducted postoperation "critiques," determining what happened, why, and what could be done better, a habit that began in peacetime and continued during the war. Terry Allen landed a well-trained division ashore in Algeria, and it improved progressively, thanks to these thoughtful after-action critiques that informed future training. Clarence Huebner brought a systematic approach to the problem of learning. He, like Allen, believed in training hard, but he also strove to correct some eccentricities the 1st ID had developed. He established standards and checked to see that they were met. Huebner's "Notes on Leadership" describe clearly what he expected of platoon leaders—and he made it a point to check that his young officers met that standard.[21]

Clift Andrus, as his nickname "Mr. Chips" implies, not only looked like the title character in the film *Goodbye, Mr. Chips* (1939) but, like that character, was also less effusive than Terry Allen. Nor did Andrus assume the role of hardheaded disciplinarian that Huebner had to play. Andrus's manner was, by comparison to both of the others, quiet and deliberate. He made frequent visits to his units, approaching them by way of asking "What can I do to support you?" Since he had served with the 1st ID since before Torch, he both knew the division well and was well known within it.[22]

Every echelon down to battalion published lessons learned, advice, and directives based on perceptions of experience in training and combat in *Army Talks* and *Yank*, which offered tips on everything from maintenance to foot care. War Department, Army Ground Forces observations, and after-action reports from the British Army all made their way into the hands of the men of the 1st ID and applied the lessons they imparted, as evidenced by their appearance in postwar donations to museums as well as mentions in memoirs and diaries. "The German Soldier in Defense," published in July 1943, and "Employment of Infantry in Woods" of October 1944 are two of many studies done in the 1st ID.

Battalion and regimental commanders in the 1st ID contributed to learning as they learned themselves. George A. Taylor, who commanded both the 16th and 26th Infantry in combat, considered carefully what he had learned in Tunisia and Sicily. In September 1943 he wrote a detailed report for the Army Ground Forces entitled "Observations on Infantry." In it Taylor covered the problem of infantry in combat from soup to nuts. Perhaps his most powerful insights were on psychology and physical conditioning. He separated his discussions on these because the army did so, but it is clear that he had a depth of understanding that the army needed to consider. "Psychology is the most neglected item in the military profession and less attention is paid to it than any other subject," he asserted point-blank. The man who advised his soldiers that there were only two kinds of men still on the beach—"the dead and those who are about to die" understood well the combat infantryman's lot.[23]

The 1st ID was fortunate in that many of its battalion commanders came from within its ranks. John T. Corley, whom Collins thought "one of the best of a fabulous group of battalion leaders," joined the 26th Infantry as a lieutenant. Corley's friend and teammate Tom Gendron met him when they reported new officers in 1940. Gendron described Corley as a "great Irish fighter, a Brooklyn Irish fighter." Indeed, he was. Including his service in Korea, Corley earned two Distinguished Service Crosses, eight Silver Stars, four Bronze Stars, and a Soldier's Medal. He was far more than brave; he was reflective, and earned the admiration of his soldiers.[24]

Reflecting on the fighting in Sicily, Ted Dobol claimed that the 26th Infantry had a special spirit and high morale. He attributed some of that high morale to Terry Allen but also in particular to Corley and his regimental commander at the time, John W. Bowen. In postcombat interviews, postwar surveys, and memoirs, battalion leadership in the 1st ID received high marks. Regimental commanders and the three division commanders received fewer accolades, as they were more remote, but they too earned high marks. Clarence Huebner never captured the heart of his troops as had Terry Allen, but he certainly earned their respect. Dobol, who came to have a lifelong friendship with Huebner, had the utmost respect for him. The commanding general need not be every soldier's friend, but knowing one's job and doing one's best for those he leads was and still is more than enough for the troops.[25]

As we have seen, Huebner believed that while in rest periods, half the day should be spent training and the other in recreation. Training during rest periods focused at small unit level, marksmanship, and combined arms practice. In preparing for the cross-Channel invasion the division focused on tank-infantry cooperation and landing team tactics for breaching obstacles and destroying field fortifications. The schedule of training and rehearsals was demanding, but Huebner still made sure his soldiers had time to rest and relax. He understood intuitively that both training and rest were important to sustaining combat readiness. Huebner and Lord Moran would have understood one another.[26]

Surveys conducted at the Army Heritage and Education Center asked veterans to comment on officer leadership. There are too few of these records (seventy-four from infantry regiments in the 1st ID) to draw conclusions with certainty except to say the veterans by and large believed they had good leaders at all levels. The quality of officer leadership by source of commission produced the most variation. Some swore by West Point officers, others by graduates of Officer Candidate School (OCS), those commissioned from the ranks, or those commissioned via Reserve Officers' Training Corps.

Lieutenant Colonel Francis J. Murdoch Jr. reflected on the matter in a postwar interview. He recounted his assessment of three of his company commanders in the 1st Battalion, 26th Infantry; later he commanded the

3rd Battalion and then the regiment. Each of these officers approached leadership differently, but all were effective. One of them joined the battalion right from OCS as just as it was preparing to invade France. On his first field training exercise, the lieutenant showed up with "a field manual sticking out of his pocket." The old salts took him for a book soldier, and consult the book he did, but he also proved to be an "outstanding" leader in combat. Murdoch believed it was because he applied the doctrine but altered it to "fit the particular situation." That, after all, is exactly what FM 100-5 suggested. This officer later commanded a company until wounded.[27]

Captain Allan B. Ferry commanded Murdoch's Company C. According to Murdoch he was "very deliberate and very much interested in tactics," and Murdoch thought him "like a school marm," but he trained a "real fine outfit" and his soldiers thought "the world of him." Three of Company C's lieutenants had battlefield commissions and all had come "off the streets of New York." They were the essence of what one German prisoner complained of when he asserted that the 1st ID were "thugs from New York." They were enthusiastic and worked well with both the schoolmarm and the company. Together with Captain Ferry, they made Company C a first-rate unit.[28]

Lieutenant Don Lister took command of Company C when Ferry was captured. Lister had risen from the ranks, starting his career as a Browning automatic rifle man and moving up over time to become a platoon sergeant. He received his battlefield commission when the unit ran short of officers. Ferry wanted Lister instead of a new lieutenant. Lister served as a platoon leader until he took command of Company C. He was in command when Company C was attached to Colonel John MacDonald's 4th Cavalry Group during the Harz Mountains fighting. Afterward, MacDonald claimed that Lister's company "was the most aggressive and fightingest outfit he had ever seen." Murdoch thought Company C was a very good unit and one whose cohesion held. For years afterward the company held annual reunions. One of the veterans attributed their cohesion to Ferry and Lister.[29]

Murdoch believed a lot of the success the 1st ID enjoyed came from the "high proportion of officers—more than half in the line companies—who had come from the ranks," and this from a West Point graduate. Of course, the company commanders who took the division to war had been commissioned elsewhere. Those who survived were field-grade officers or battalion commanders by war's end. What mattered is that the best of them, whatever their source of commission, learned while doing and applied those lessons learned in the next fight.[30]

Learning, Adapting, and Innovating

There is no need to restate conclusions offered in earlier chapters, but it is appropriate to suggest the major tendencies the 1st ID developed during the war. It also is appropriate to acknowledge that other units reached many of the same conclusions and adopted similar behaviors.

In much of the fight in Tunisia, maneuvering to a position of advantage by employing wide envelopment proved possible. Maneuver was, however, far less feasible when fighting in the mountains of Sicily. Maneuver proved possible in the European Theater of Operations, but not at the scale of the eastern front. Tactically the 1st ID favored envelopment. Generally, the regiments and battalions avoided frontal attacks. In his detailed "Observations on an Infantry Regiment in Combat," George Taylor wrote that too much was made of the "theory of envelopment." He believed it should only be attempted with detailed reconnaissance, and then it must be "aggressively conducted."[31]

Most battalion commanders bounded or leapfrogged companies when attacking. Regimental commanders tended to attack with two battalions abreast but did rotate or bound the third battalion as needed. The principle is simple; sustaining an attack is easier when units have some respite to resupply. That, however, is only possible when bounding companies. Often battalions made their approach to objectives in column. The combat achievements report is replete with examples. That attack on Crucifix Hill, as discussed in chapter 11, began with 1st Battalion, 18th Infantry, approaching the objective in a column of companies.[32]

Attacking at night or in the predawn hours is an attribute or pattern of operation that the Big Red One made its own under Terry Allen. Both Huebner and Andrus continued that approach because it worked. Allen trained and fought the 104th ID the same way when he brought it to Europe. General Collins, at VII Corps, sought to take advantage of this inclination and stimulate competition by pairing the two divisions when he could.

Generally, the division preferred to time attacks so that units assaulted their objective just before or at the break of dawn. Supporting tanks and tank destroyers were of little use during darkness but were essential for continuing the attack in daylight or to repulse the inevitable German counterattack, so tracked vehicles generally joined at dawn or shortly after. The division did use tanks at night, but doing so required special effort. In a paper written at the Armored School at Fort Knox in 1947, Major William R. Campbell reviewed "methods learned and employed by the 1st U.S. Infantry Division and the 745th Tank Battalion, in tank-infantry teamwork." He asserted that using tanks at night worked best when preceded by daylight reconnaissance and executed with careful coordination. Using tanks at night "gave the attacking infantry a defense against machine guns, built up his morale an[d] unnerved the enemy." Campbell admitted, though, that firing a tank at night "was not too accurate." To say that the tank telescope was inadequate for use at night is an understatement. Nevertheless, the tankers could adjust by using tracers to achieve "burst on target." Campbell believed it was important also to have tanks on hand to prepare for the inevitable counterattack.[33]

Campbell also covered other techniques the 1st ID and its tankers had developed during the fighting, including the best approaches in supporting infantry in the attack. The tactic for street fighting, developed on the battleground in Aachen, is of particular interest. The tanks needed infantry to provide "all around security" from the threat of Panzerfaust rocket fire, so the "infantry preceded [sic] by at least 100 yards" to clear the enemy from both sides of the street. In return tanks provided machine gun and main gun fire as required by the infantry against known enemy positions, "and on all positions thought to be occupied by the enemy." The latter is of course the essence of suppressive fire. At each intersection, supporting tanks "placed fire on all corners of the intersection."[34]

Campbell also described tactics for supporting infantry in attacking small towns as well as the best means of supporting the infantry in the defense. He argued that the light tank company should be employed as a whole, and used as a "light striking force" in the absence of enemy armor or antitank guns. Contrary to maneuvering the medium tanks at night, Campbell found that light tanks could be used to go in ahead of the infantry at night. He believed the 745th TB and the infantry they supported became a cohesive team during the fighting in the hedgerows, but the bond had begun to form during training, a sense of community that grew stronger over time. Finally, he believed that living in the field together sealed the bond.[35]

The 1st ID, like every other army division, happily expended artillery rounds—and did so lavishly—for interdiction, suppression of enemy fire, counterbattery and observed fire, and to destroy enemy targets. The 1st Division believed its artillery was good, very good, but the division could also be subtle in its use of fires. Stan Mason described just one instance. At El Guettar the division artillery wreaked havoc on the 10th Panzer Division by using a sophisticated technique he called "scissors and sweep," known doctrinally as Sweep and Zone. Andrus, an artilleryman, attacked Bonn with no artillery preparation. Attacking at night, he aimed to surprise the Germans.

It worked. Instead of preparation fires, the artillery prepared concentrations to interdict the approaches to Bonn from the east bank of the Rhine to preclude the Germans from rapidly reinforcing the defenders.[36]

In *Men against Fire*, S. L. A. Marshall asserted that too few soldiers fired their weapons. While it appears that he estimated, or perhaps even invented, the statistics used to make his case, the assertion seems to have been borne out in the 1st ID, at least by anecdotal evidence. Different techniques were used to get soldiers to fire in the direction of the enemy, even if they had no identifiable target. Doing so suppressed the enemy—they kept their heads down. Before World War II, soldiers trained on aimed fire at observed targets. Aimed rifle fire is a good thing, but suppressive fire against possible targets is a war winner. In any case, the number of small arms rounds fired suggests that many more soldiers fired a few rounds, or a relative few fired many rounds.[37]

The 1st ID appears to have solved that problem, but again the conclusion is based on anecdotes from memoirs, surveys, and interviews. Live fire training to a large degree solved the problem of soldiers not firing their weapons. Commanders had various ways in which they addressed that problem. One of Murdoch's company commanders had each soldier "fire a clip of ammunition" when they began an attack. Murdoch did not believe that technique necessary but did not overrule his company commander. He believed in fire and movement with platoons and companies, and that stemmed from training.[38]

Integration of Replacements

Integrating replacements into units in combat has been part of the narrative herein since the early chapters. As we have seen, the business of bringing in and successfully integrating replacement officers, noncommissioned officers, and soldiers was crucial to maintaining a readiness to fight. This is something that the 1st ID understood well. Huebner introduced the systematic means of doing so with a school for replacements that taught the history and traditions of the unit they were about to join and assured they knew how to use their weapons. Imparting tribal wisdom within companies and below was the business of sergeants. At the division level, the process was more formal. In August 1943 Wyman confided to his diary that Huebner intended to receive replacements with ceremony that would conclude with "awarding of the Divisional shoulder insignia."[39]

Whenever possible the 1st ID did take the time to arrange a "ceremonious reception of replacements." Even when that was not really doable, units did what they could. The vignette in chapter 9 of Jerry Nauss arriving at the 1st ID is typical of the experience of 1st ID soldiers arriving in combat. He was well treated. Within days his commander met with him. The old salts did hold him at arm's length for a few days, but he soon came to be one of them.[40]

The effective integration of replacements proved difficult once ashore in France, because the division seldom enjoyed a hiatus from the line. Christopher Cornazzi, a staff sergeant who enlisted in 1940, recalled that "when possible [replacements] were trained by a combat platoon sergeant in the rear." The old soldiers generally took care of the new men. John S. Kubala went straight into the line, but the "veterans tried to help me as much as possible." His experience was not unusual. Ted Lombarski, a twenty-six-year-old first sergeant, helped acclimate his new commander, Captain John Finke. Finke was no rookie, but he did not know the company. Together, Lombarski and Finke led Company F, 16th Infantry, ashore in the first wave on June 6, 1944.[41]

FINIS

During the course of its active duty during World War II the Big Red One learned, adapted, and showed the capacity for innovation, even from the early days of the war, by helping to carry out amphibious operations at scale by inventing, or at least improving on, tank–infantry–tank destroyer combined arms combat tactics. And the 1st Division did so in the context of theater, field army, and corps echelons. The Allied air forces and the Army Air Force grew alongside the ground formations. Bitter complaints about the quality of air support early in the war transitioned by the end of the fighting in Europe to deep respect for the airmen, who provided close support, enabled the ground forces to move with impunity, and denied their adversaries daylight movement.

The reputation the division earned during World War II was a great one. The Big Red One's journals, after-action reports, and lessons learned reflect not only what the division learned but how it did so in concert with supporting arms and within the corps and army formations. The partnership of the 1st ID with the 3rd Armored Division is emblematic of the US Army's agility. Moreover the division moved between several corps without losing a step. That, too, stemmed from the growth at all echelons. In North Africa, II Corps stumbled at first but was surefooted in Sicily, as were III, V, and VII Corps in France, Belgium, German and Czechoslovakia.

Soldiers learned to fight at the tip of the spear, where it counted most. Soldier surveys done for the Army Heritage and Education Center and for

Cornelius Ryan and Stephen E. Ambrose are rife with stories of survival based on learning personally or as a result of training. Lewis C. Smith wrote to Ambrose of his experience joining the 1st ID with a group of replacements arriving in the United Kingdom in November 1943. Smith was one of only four of that tranche who survived the war. He recalled that none of the veterans of North Africa or Sicily remained; "They were all gone either killed, wounded or sent home, or what have you [reassigned, for example]." He and the other three who arrived with him "were the oldest men left in the company." Two of them were squad leaders—they learned to fight, and because they had, Company I, 3rd Battalion, 16th Infantry, and others like it remained viable throughout the hard fighting from June 6, 1944, to May 8, 1945.[42]

In the context of learning from the bottom up and the top down, the 1st ID flourished as it became increasingly adept at applying lessons learned during WWII combat—so much better that by war's end it arguably had become an expert infantry division. Shortly before the invasion of Normandy, Huebner hosted a dinner for the commanders of the 16th Infantry. After the meal he asked the commander of 2nd Battalion, 16th Infantry, "Is there anything you might want or suggest that might help or make [crossing the beach] easier?" Herbert C. Hicks Jr. responded that he wanted more light machine guns rather than the mix of heavy machine guns he was authorized. Hicks had scrounged light machine guns above his authorization. On arriving in Sicily, Huebner required that these weapons be turned in as excess to requirements. Now he said, "I have also learned in nine months and am not ashamed to admit it." There and then Huebner told the division's supply officer, "Get them back for him."[43]

Notes

1. *Memorial Album: Pictorial History of the 1st Division* (San Diego, CA: Society of the First Division, 1950), copy in MRC, call no. Unit History 05-1-1950, 8.

2. Lebda, *Million Miles to Go*, 138–65.

3. Jim Sharp, telephone interviews, March 6 and 19. See also Sharp, *Diary of a Combat Infantryman* and *Sergeant of the Guard.*

4. "Theodore L. Dobol, Command Sergeant Major United States Army (Retired): Autobiography," n.d., MRC 1991.24; "Mr. First Division Retires," *Bridgehead Sentinel*, October 1955, Bridgehead Sentinel Collection, MRC, 11, 25, 27; US Department of State, Report of Death of an American Citizen, Munich, Germany, February 11, 1971. Beauchamp died in the US Army Hospital in Munich.

5. "Albert H. Smith Jr.," obituary, *Washington Post*, August 29, 2005, https://www. legacy.com/us/obituaries/washingtonpost/name/albert-smith-obituary?id=5538461

Author's personal knowledge re Smith's tenure as honorary colonel of the 16th Infantry.

6. Astor, *Terrible Terry Allen*, 321, 328–29, 359; Re Andrus, see "Andrus, Clift 'Mr. Chips,' " https//ww2gravestone.com; Military Hall of Honor, ID 2071, https://www.militaryhallofhonor.com.

7. Department of the Army, Office of the Adjutant General, Official Statement of Military Service of Clarence Ralph Huebner; Arthur L. Chaitt, "Clarence R. Huebner, Lieutenant General USA (Retired), 1888–1972," *Bridgehead Sentinel*, March 1973, Bridgehead Sentinel Collection, MRC.

8. Kingseed, *Omaha Beach to Dawson's Ridge*, 219–22; Michael Corley, conversation with author, April 23, 2022, Junction City, KS.

9. Murray Illson, "Bobbie E. Brown, Medal of Honor Winner, Is Dead," *New York Times*, November 11, 1971.

10. Dickson, *Rise of the G.I. Army*, 9, 23–42; re Starke, see 37. Budget issues for the army are well known; see Dickson, 1–16.

11. War Department, FM 100-5, *Field Service Regulations: Operations* (Washington, DC: Government Printing Office, 1941), ii.

12. HQ, 1st ID, G-3 after-action report, May 1–8, 1945, part 2, "Conclusions," 12–29, in RG 301-3: G-3 Operations Report, European Campaign, Jan 45–Dec 45, MRC Digital Archives.

13. Knickerbocker et al., *Danger Forward*, 406–8.

14. Knickerbocker, 398–400.

15. Knickerbocker, 403; Lüke, *Grenadier Regiment 69*, 413. Translation provided by Mark Reardon.

16. War Department, FM 100-5, 5.

17. Knickerbocker et al., *Danger Forward*, 423–29, shows what units were attached and when. The 745th TB was attached from June 6, 1944, through V-E day. The 634th TD dates of attachment are not in the annex on attachments. Curiously, the 634th's reports do not mention to whom they were attached. The 634th's operations journal shows them joining the 1st ID in July and remained attached until after V-E day. The 103rd AAA was attached briefly in June 1944. It rejoined the division in February 1945 and remained until after V-E day.

18. Finke, *No Mission Too Difficult*, 10–11.

19. Lewis, *Omaha Beach*, makes this case explicitly and compellingly.

20. Knickerbocker et. al., *Danger Forward*, 408. On Spalding's boat section, see John Spalding, interview by F. C. Pogue and J. M. Topete Herve, Belgium, February 9, 1945. Re Monteith and Dawson, see chapter 9 of this book.

21. HQ, 1st ID, "Notes on Leadership," October 14, 1943, MRC 1960.88.3.599.

22. Frank Murdoch, interview by John Votaw and Paul Gorman, October 23, 1995, First Division Museum at Cantigny, Wheaton, IL. Murdoch is cited here and elsewhere because he was asked specifically to compare and contrast leaders.

23. George A. Taylor, "Observations on an Infantry Regiment in Combat," Report No. 31 Observers Board ETOUSA, September 24, 1943, MRC 1960.88.3.313, 1, 10.

24. Thomas Gendron, interview by Michael Corley, April 20, 1977, Scottsdale, AZ. See also Gendron, unattributed interview, August 10, 1995, McCormick Research Center, Orlando, FL.

25. Re Allen and Huebner, see Albert H. Smith Jr., "Allen and Huebner: Contrast in Command," n.d., MRC 1996.95.1, a compilation of articles, documents, and short passages by veterans of the 1st ID.

26. HQ, FUSAG (1st Army Group, later renamed 12th Army Group), Immediate Report no. 10 (Combat Observations), July 24, 1944, N3080, CARL, 1; Clarence R. Huebner, interview by Julian S. Dayton, July 24, 1944, N3080, CARL, 1–3.

27. Murdoch interview.

28. Murdoch interview. See also World War II Prisoners of War Data File, Records of World War II Prisoners of War, documenting the period from December 7, 1941 to November 19, 1946, RG 489, NARA. Ferry was captured on or about September 18, 1944 in the Stolberg corridor.

29. Murdoch interview. Quoted as modified by Paul Gorman in Weingartner, *Blue Spaders*, 122.

30. Murdoch interview.

31. Taylor, "Observations," 14

32. HQ, 1st ID, "Combat Achievements Report," ch. 11, "The Attack on Crucifix Hill," 2–3.

33. William R. Campbell, "Tanks with Infantry," Advanced Officers Class No. 1, Fort Knox, KY, February 25, 1947, WWII Student Papers, DRL, 8. Campbell is not listed as assigned to the 745th Tank Battalion and was an infantry officer. This monograph appears to reflect his assessment of his own experience with the 745th TB.

34. Campbell, 6.

35. Campbell, 6–10.

36. Mason, "Reminiscences," 89.

37. Mansoor, *GI Offensive in Europe*, 257–63. A number of historians have challenged Marshall, but none more thoroughly or succinctly than Mansoor.

38. Murdoch, interview.

39. Wyman, "Journal of Events," entries for August 17, 18, 19, 1943.

40. Nauss, *Troubleshooting All the Way*, 33–35.

41. Christopher Cornazzi and John S. Kubala, veteran's surveys, n.d., US Army Heritage and Education Center, Carlisle, PA; Finke, *No Mission Too Difficult*, 174–77.

42. Lewis C. Smith, oral history transcript, D-Day Project, National World War II Museum, New Orleans.

43. Statement prepared by Herbert C. Hicks Jr. for Major General Albert H. Smith, USA retired, MRC 1996.95.

APPENDIX 1

Tactical Symbols

ECHELON

I	COMPANY	XX	DIVISION
II	BATTALION	XXX	CORPS
III	REGIMENT	XXXX	ARMY
X	BRIGADE/ COMBAT COMMAND	XXXXX	ARMY GROUP

FORMATION

SELF–PROPELLED ANTITANK

ANTIAIRCRAFT ARTILLERY

ARMOR / PANZER

ARMORED INFANTRY / PANZERGRENADIERS

ARMORED FIELD ARTILLERY

ARTILLERY

ARMORED RECONNAISANCE

MOTORIZED RECONNAISANCE

ARMORED ENGINEER

ENGINEER

INFANTRY

MOTORIZED INFANTRY

HEADQUARTERS AND HEADQUARTERS COMPANY

QUARTERMASTER

LOGISTICS

MEDICAL

MAINTENANCE

MILITARY POLICE

BAND

SIGNAL

TRANSPORTATION

MODERN US ARMY THREAT FORMATION SYMBOL

APPENDIX 2

1st Infantry Division Organization Chart

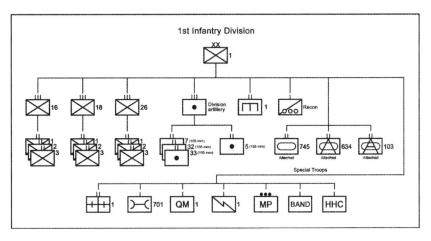

The table of organization shown above reflects the basic triangle division design, based on three infantry regiments. The structure of American infantry divisions changed over time to accommodate shortages in available manpower. In 1940 the triangle division boasted 15,345 troops assigned. By 1943 the triangle division had declined to 14,253 officers and men. However, task organizing was a hallmark of the US Army in World War II. Attaching tank, tank destroyer, and antiaircraft battalions became more or less permanent. The 745th Tank Battalion and 634th Tank Destroyer Battalion served with the 1st Infantry Division from D-Day until the end of the war. Combat engineers and 4.2-inch chemical mortar battalions were routinely attached as missions required them. The division gave up regiments with their supporting arms to other units or received similar attachments. In particular, the 1st Infantry Division and 3rd Armored Division organized and operated together with great success.

Table of Ranks through Lieutenant Colonel

US Army	German Army	SS
General of the Army	Generalfeldmarschall	Reichsfürhrer
General	Oberstgeneral	Oberstgruppenführer
Lieutenant General	General der (Infanterie etc.)	Obergrüppenführer
Major General	Generalleutnant	Grüppenführer
Brigadier General	Generalmajor	Brigadeführer
No Equivalent	No Equivalent	Oberführer
Colonel	Oberst	Standartenführer
Lieutenant Colonel	Oberst Leutnant	Obersturmbannführer

Select Bibliography

Archives and Manuscript Collections

Colonel Robert R. McCormick Research Center, First Division Museum at Cantigny Park, Wheaton, IL. Many 1st ID documents are searchable online in the MRC Digital Archives, https://www.fdmuseum.org/researchers/digital-archives/, organized by RG numbers. Others are cited as MRC, followed by accession numbers if available. The MRC also houses the bulk of the Stanhope B. Mason Collection of 1st Infantry records and documents; the Albert H. Smith Papers, at MRC 1996.95.1, a collection of personnel file extracts and letters from various officers who served with the division during World War II; and the George A. Taylor Collection.

Cornelius Ryan Collection of World War II Papers, Mahn Center for Archives and Research Collections, Ohio University. Includes questionnaires completed by veterans that Ryan used to research his book about D-Day, *The Longest Day*, many of them digitized and searchable at https://www.ohio.edu/library/collections/digital-archives/cornelius-ryan-wwii.

D-Day Project, National World War II Museum, New Orleans. Transcripts of oral history tapes made by D-Day veterans of D-Day sent in response to a solicitation by Stephen E. Ambrose. Most of the transcripts are undated.

Donovan Research Library, Maneuver Center of Excellence, Fort Benning, GA. Includes the World War II Student Paper Collection, digital copies of student papers from Fort Benning and Fort Knox, KY, which can be found online at https://www.benning.army.mil/Library/Donovanpapers/wwii/.

Ike Skelton Combined Arms Research Library, Fort Leavenworth, KS

Military History Institute, US Army Heritage and Education Center, Carlisle, PA

Sturmpanzer. This site, managed by Richard Hedrick, provides resources for individuals researching topics relating to the German Army in World War II. http://www.sturmpanzer.com/research/tools/fms_Index.aspx.

Books

Afiero, Massimiliano. *The 17th Waffen-SS Panzergrenadier Division Götz Von Ber-lichingen*. Atglen, PA: Schiffer, 2018.

Ambrose, Stephen E. *Citizen Soldiers: The US Army from the Normandy Beaches to the Bulge to the Surrender of Germany, June 7, 1944–May 7, 1945*. New York: Simon and Schuster, 1997.

———. *D-Day, June 6, 1944: The Climactic Battle of World War II*. New York: Simon and Schuster, 1994.

———. *The Supreme Commander: The War Years of General Dwight D. Eisenhower*. Garden City, NY: Doubleday, 1969.

Astor, Gerald. *Terrible Terry Allen, Combat General of World War II: The Life of an American Soldier*. New York: Ballantine, 2003.

Atkinson, Rick. *An Army at Dawn: The War in North Africa, 1942–1943*. New York: Henry Holt, 2002.

———. *The Day of Battle: The War in Sicily and Italy, 1943–1944*. New York: Henry Holt, 2007.

———. *The Guns at Last Light: The War in Western Europe, 1944–1945*. New York: Henry Holt, 2013.

Barnett, Correli. *The Desert Generals*. Edison, NJ: Castle, 2004.

Baumer, Robert W. *Aachen: The US Army's Battle for Charlemagne's City in World War II*. Mechanicsburg, PA: Stack Pole, 2015.

Baumer, Robert W., and Mark Reardon. *American Iliad: The 18th Infantry Regiment in World War II*. Bedford, PA: Aberjona, 2004.

Baumgartner, John W., Al de Poto, William Fraccio, and Sammy Fuller. *The 16th Infantry, 1861–1946*. 3d ed. Holbrook, NY: 16th Infantry Regiment, 1999.

Bellanger, Yves J. *The US Army Infantry Divisions, 1943–1945*. 2 vols. Solihull, UK: Helion, 2002.

Blair, Clay. *Ridgway's Paratroopers: The American Airborne in World War II*. Garden City, NY: Dial Press / Doubleday, 1985.

Blaxland, Gregory. *The Plain Cook and the Great Showman: The First and Eighth Armies in North Africa*. London: William Kimber, 1977.

Blumenson, Martin. *Breakout and Pursuit*. Washington, DC: Office of the Chief of Military History, 1961.

———. *The Duel for France, 1944*. Boston: Da Capo, 1963.

———, ed. *The Patton Papers, 1940–1945*. Boston: Houghton Mifflin, 1974.

Blumenson, Martin, and James L. Stokesbury. *Masters of the Art of Command*. Boston: Da Capo, 1975.

Boatner, Mark M., III. *The Biographical Dictionary of World War II*. Novato, CA: Presidio, 1996.

Bolger, Daniel P. *The Panzer Killers: The Untold Story of a Fighting General and His Spearhead Tank Division's Charge into the Third Reich*. New York: Caliber, 2012.

Botsford, Gardner. *A Life of Privilege Mostly: A Memoir*. London: Granta, 2006.

Bradley, Omar N. *A Soldier's Story*, New York: Popular Library, 1964.

Brown, John Sloan. *Draftee Division: The 88th Infantry Division in World War II.* Lexington: University Press of Kentucky, 1986.

Butcher, Harry C. *My Three Years with Eisenhower: The Personal Diary of Captain Harry C. Butcher, USNR.* New York: Simon and Schuster, 1946.

Bykofsky, Joseph, and Harold Larson. *The Transportation Corps: Operations Overseas.* Washington, DC: Office of the Chief of Military History, 1957.

Caddick-Adams, Peter. *Fire and Steel: The Battle of the Bulge, 1944–45.* New York: Oxford University Press, 2022. Author's review copy.

———. *Snow and Steel: The Battle of the Bulge, 1944–45.* New York: Oxford University Press, 2015.

Calhoun, Mark T. *General Lesley J. McNair: Unsung Architect of the US Army.* Lawrence: University Press of Kansas, 2015.

Cameron, Robert S. *Mobility, Shock, and Firepower: The Emergence of the U. S. Army's Armor Branch, 1917–1945.* Washington, DC: Center of Military History, 2008.

Capa, Robert. *Slightly Out of Focus.* New York: Modern Library, 1999.

Carell, Paul. *Invasion! They're Coming! The German Account of the D-Day Landings and the 80 Days' Battle for France.* Atglen, PA: Schiffer Military History, 1995.

Center for Air Force History. *The AAF in Northwest Africa: An Account of the Twelfth Air Force in the Northwest African Landings and the Battle for Tunisia. Wings of War Series No. 6.* Washington, DC: Center for Air Force History, 1992. This is a reprint of the original Army Air Force Wings at War series.

Center of Military History. *Order of Battle of the United States Land Forces in the World War, American Expeditionary Forces.* Vol. 1, *General Headquarters, Armies, Army Corps, Services of Supply, Separate Forces.* Vol. 2, *Divisions.* Washington, DC: Department of the Army, 1988.

Churchill, Winston S. *The Second World War: The Hinge of Fate.* New York: Bantam, 1962.

Cirillo, Roger. *Kasserine Pass Battles.* 2 vols. Washington, DC: Center of Military History, n.d. Online at https://history.army.mil/books/Staff-Rides/kasserine/kasserine.htm.

Citino, Robert M. *Blitzkrieg to Desert Storm: The Evolution of Operational Warfare.* Lawrence: University Press of Kansas, 2004.

———. *The Wehrmacht Retreats: Fighting a Lost War, 1943.* Lawrence: The University Press of Kansas, 2012.

———. *The Wehrmacht's Last Stand: The German Campaigns of 1944–1945.* Lawrence: University Press of Kansas, 2017.

Clausewitz, von Carl. *On War.* Edited and translated by Michael Howard and Peter Paret. Princeton, NJ: Princeton University Press, 1984.

Clay, Steven E. *Blood and Sacrifice: The History of the 16th Infantry Regiment from the Civil War through the Gulf War.* Chicago: Cantigny First Division Foundation, 2001.

Cline, Ray S. *Washington Command Post: The Operations Division.* Washington, DC: Office of the Chief of Military History, 1951.

Coakley, Robert W., and Richard M. Leighton. *Global Logistics and Strategy.* Washington, DC: Office of the Chief of Military History, 1968

Coffman, Edward M. *The War to End All Wars: The American Military Experience in World War I,* Madison: University of Wisconsin Press, 1986

Cole, Hugh M. *The Ardennes: Battle of the Bulge.* Washington, DC: Center of Military History, 1965.

Collins, J. Lawton. *Lightning Joe: An Autobiography.* Baton Rouge: Louisiana State University Press, 1979.

Condell, Bruce, and David T. Zabecki. *On the German Art of War: Truppenfuhrung.* Boulder, CO: Lynne Rienner, 2001.

Cooper, Matthew. *The German Army, 1933–1945: Its Political and Military Failure.* New York: Stein and Day, 1978.

Cowdrey, Albert E. *Fighting for Life: American Military Medicine in World War II.* New York: Free Press, 1994.

Craven, Wesley Frank, and James Lea Cate. *Europe: Torch to Point Blank, August 1942–December 1943.* Vol. 2 of *The Army Air Forces in World War II.* Chicago: University of Chicago Press, 1949.

———. *Europe: Argument to V-E Day January 1944 to May 1945.* Vol. 3 of *The Army Air Forces in World War II.* Chicago: University of Chicago Press, 1951.

Daniel, J. Furman, III. *Patton: Battling with History,* Columbia: University of Missouri Press, 2020.

Darby, William O., and William H. Baumer. *We Led the Way: Darby's Rangers.* San Rafael, CA: Presidio, 1980.

Dastrup, Boyd L. *King of Battle: A Branch History of the U. S. Army's Field Artillery.* Washington, DC: Center of Military History, 1992.

D'Este, Carlo. *Bitter Victory: The Battle for Sicily, 1943.* New York: E. P. Dutton, 1988.

———. *Decision in Normandy.* London: Penguin, 2004.

Detweiler, Donald S., Charles Burton Burdick, and Juergen Rohwer, eds. *World War II German Military Studies.* 24 vols. New York: Garland, 1979.

Dickson, Paul. *The Rise of the G.I. Army, 1940–1941: The Forgotten Story of How America Forged a Powerful Army Before Pearl Harbor* New York: Atlantic Monthly Press, 2020.

Dieckhoff, Gerhard. *3. Infanterie-Division, 3. Infanterie-Division (Mot.), 3 Panzergrenadier-Division.* Göttingen: Erich Börries, 1960.

Dupuy, Trevor N. *A Genius for War: The German Army and General Staff, 1807–1945.* Garden City, NY: Military Book Club, 1977.

Eisenhower, Dwight D. *At Ease: Stories I Tell to Friends.* New York: Avon, 1968.

———. *Crusade in Europe.* Garden City, NY: Doubleday, 1948.

———. *The Papers of Dwight D. Eisenhower: The War Years.* Edited by Alfred Chandler Jr. and Stephen E. Ambrose. 5 vols. Baltimore: Johns Hopkins, 1970.

Eisenhower, John S. D. *The Bitter Woods: The Battle of the Bulge.* New York: G. P. Putnam's Sons, 1969.

Ewing, Joseph H. *Twenty-Nine, Let's Go: A History of the 29th Infantry Division in World War II.* Washington, DC: Infantry Journal Press, 1948.

Fey, Will. *Armor Battles of the Waffen-SS 1943–1945.* Winnipeg: J. J. Fedorowicz, 1990.

Finke, Blythe Foote, ed. *No Mission Too Difficult: Old Buddies of the 1st Division Tell All About World War II.* Chicago: Contemporary Books, 1994.

Fontenot, Gregory. *Loss and Redemption at St Vith: The 7th Armored Division in the Battle of the Bulge.* Columbia: University of Missouri Press, 2019.

Forty, George. *US Army Handbook, 1939–1940.* Stroud, UK: Alan Sutton, 1998.

Forty, Simon. *American Armor, 1939–1945: Portfolio.* Harrisburg, PA: Stackpole, 1981.

Frieser, Karl Heinz, with John T. Greenwood. *The Blitzkrieg Legend: The 1940 Campaign in the West.* Annapolis, Maryland: Naval Institute Press, 2005.

Fritz, Stephen G. *Front Soldaten: The German Soldier in World War II.* Lexington: University Press of Kentucky, 1995.

Fuller, J. F. C. *Machine Warfare: An Inquiry into the Influence of Mechanics on the Art of War.* Washington, DC: Infantry Journal, 1943.

Fuller, Samuel. *A Third Face: My Tale of Writing, Fighting and Filmmaking.* With Christa Lang Fuller and Jerome Henry Rudes. New York: Alfred Knopf, 2002.

Fussell, Paul. *The Boys' Crusade: The American Infantry in Northwestern Europe, 1944–1945.* New York: The Modern Library, 2003.

Gabel, Christopher R. *Seek, Strike and Destroy: US Army Tank Destroyer Doctrine in World War II.* Fort Leavenworth, KS: Combat Studies Institute, 1985.

———. *The US Army GHQ Maneuvers of 1941.* Washington, DC: Center of Military History, 1991.

Garland, Albert N., and Howard McGaw Smyth. *Sicily and the Surrender of Italy.* With Martin Blumenson. Washington, DC: Center of Military History, 1965. https://history.army.mil/html/books/006/6-2-1/CMH_Pub_6-2-1.pdf.

Gavin, James M. *On to Berlin: Battles of an Airborne Commander 1943–1946.* New York: Viking Press, 1978.

George, Robert H. *Ninth Air Force: April to November 1944.* Army Air Forces Historical Studies No. 36. Washington, DC: Army Air Forces Historical Office, 1945.

Gordon, Ralph J. *Infantrymen.* Self-published, 2012.

Gorman, Paul F. *The Secret of Future Victories.* Washington, DC: Institute for Defense Analysis, February 1992.

Greenfield, Kent Roberts, ed. *Command Decisions.* Washington, DC: Center of Military History, 1987.

Greenfield, Kent Roberts, Robert Palmer, and Bell I. Wiley. *The Organization of Ground Combat Troops.* Washington, DC: Center of Military History, 1947.

Gross, Gerhard P., and David T. Zabecki. *The Myth and Reality of German Warfare: Operational Thinking from Moltke to Heusinger.* Lexington: University Press of Kentucky, 2016.

Guderian, Heinz Günther. *From Normandy to the Ruhr: With the 116th Panzer Division in World War II*. Bedford, PA: Aberjona, 2001.

Hamilton, Nigel. *Master of the Battlefield: Monty's War Years, 1942–1944*. New York: McGraw-Hill, 1983.

Harding, Edwin F., ed. *Infantry in Battle*. Washington, DC: Infantry Journal, 1939. Facsimile reprint, US Army Command and General Staff College.

Harrison, Gordon A. *Cross-Channel Attack*. Washington, DC: Office of the Chief of Military History, 1951.

Hassler, Timm. *Den Westwal halten oder mit dem Westwall untergehn*. Aachen, Germany: Helios, 2013.

Hastings, Max. *Overlord*. Norwalk, CT: Easton Press, 1984.

Heller, Charles E., and William A. Stofft, eds. *America's First Battles, 1776–1965*. Lawrence: University Press of Kansas, 1986.

Hewitt, Robert L. *Workhorse of the Western Front: The Story of the 30th Infantry Division*. Las Vegas: Combat Books, 2020.

Hogan, David W., Jr. *A Command Post at War: First Army Headquarters in Europe, 1943–1945*. Washington, DC: Center of Military History, 2000.

Holland, James. *Sicily '43: The First Assault on Fortress Europe*. New York: Atlantic Monthly Press, 2020.

Houston, Donald E. *Hell on Wheels*. Novato, CA: Presidio, 1977.

Howe, George F. *Northwest Africa: Seizing the Initiative in the West*. Washington, DC: Office of the Chief of Military History, 1957.

Huebner, Clarence R. Diary, March 3, 1944–September 26, 1944, April 2, 1945– September 6, 1945. Stanhope B. Mason Collection, MRC 1994.126.

Ingersoll, Ralph. *The Battle Is the Payoff*. New York: Harcourt Brace, 1943.

——. *Top Secret*. New York: Harcourt, Brace, 1946.

Jackson, W. G. F. *Alexander of Tunis as Military Commander*. New York: Dodd, Mead and Company, 1971.

——. *The Battle for North Africa, 1940–43*. New York: Mason/Charter, 1975.

Jeffers, H. Paul. *Theodore Roosevelt Jr.: The Life of a War Hero*. Novato, CA: Presidio, 2002.

Johnson, David E. *Fast Tanks and Heavy Bombers: Innovation in the US Army, 1917–1945*. Ithaca, NY: Cornell University Press, 1998.

Johnson, Franklyn A. *One More Hill: The Big Red One from North Africa to Normandy*. Wheaton, IL: Cantigny First Division Foundation, 2010.

Kershaw, Alex. *The Bedford Boys: One American Town's Ultimate D-Day Sacrifice*. New York: Da Capo, 2003.

Kesselring, Albert. *Kesselring: A Soldier's Record*. New York: William Morrow, 1954.

Kingseed, Cole C., ed. *From Omaha Beach to Dawson's Ridge: The Combat Journal of Captain Joe Dawson*. Annapolis, MD: Naval Institute Press, 2005.

Kirkpatrick, Charles E. *An Unknown Future and Doubtful Present: Writing the Victory Plan of 1941*. Washington, DC: Center of Military History, 1990.

Kirkland, William B. Jr. *Destroyers at Normandy: Naval Gunfire Support at Omaha Beach*. Washington: Naval Historical Foundation, 1994.

Kissel, Hans. *Hitler's Last Levy: The Volksturm 1944–1945*. Translated by C. F. Colton. Solihull, UK: Helion, 2005.

Knickerbocker, H. R., Jack Thompson, Jack Belden, Don Whitehead, A. J. Liebling, Mark Watson, Cy Peterman, Iris Carpenter, Col. R. Ernest Dupuy, and Drew Middleton. *Danger Forward: The Story of the First Division in World War II*. Washington, DC: Society of the First Division, 1947.

Koch, Oscar W. *Intelligence for Patton*. With Robert G. Hays. Atglen, PA: Schiffer Military History, 1999.

Kreidberg, Marvin A., and Merton G. Henry. *History of Mobilization in the United States Army, 1775–1945*. Washington, DC: Department of the Army, 1955.

Krepinevich, Andrew F., Jr. *The Army and Vietnam*. Baltimore: Johns Hopkins University Press, 1986.

Kurowski, Franz. *Elite Panzer Strike Force: Germany's Panzer Lehr Division in World War II*. Mechanicsburg, PA: Stackpole, 2011.

Lambert, Ray, and Jim DeFelice. *Every Man a Hero: A Memoir of D-Day, The First Wave at Omaha Beach, and a World at War*. New York: William Morrow, 2019.

Lebda, John F. *Million Miles to Go*. Victoria, BC: Trafford, 2001.

Lewis, Adrian. *Omaha Beach: A Flawed Victory*. Chapel Hill: University of North Carolina Press, 2001.

Liddell-Hart, B. H. *The German Generals Talk*. New York: HarperCollins, 2002.

———, ed. *The Rommel Papers.* New York: Da Capo, 1953.

Liebling, A. J. *The Road Back to Paris*. New York: Random House, 1997.

Ludewig, Joachim. *Rückzug: The German Retreat from France, 1944*. Edited by David T. Zabecki. Lexington: University Press of Kentucky, 2012.

Lüke, Hans. *Die Geschichte des Regiments 69*. Hamburg, Germany: Herausgegeben der Traditionsgemeinschaft, 1986.

Lypka, Demetrius "Pete." *A Soldier Remembers: A Memoir of Service in the 1st Infantry Division, 1941–1945*. Chicago: Cantigny First Division Foundation, 2007.

MacDonald, Charles B. *The Battle of the Huertgen Forest*. Philadelphia: University of Pennsylvania Press, 2003.

———. *The Mighty Endeavor: American Armed Forces in the European Theater in World War II*. New York: Oxford University Press, 1969.

———. *The Siegfried Line Campaign*, Washington, DC: Center of Military History, 1963.

———. *A Time for Trumpets: The Untold Story of the Battle of the Bulge,* New York: William Morrow, 1985.

Mansoor, Peter R. *The GI Offensive in Europe: The Triumph of American Infantry Divisions, 1941–1945*. Lawrence: University Press of Kansas, 1999.

Marshall, S. L. A. *Men against Fire*. 1947. Reprint, New York: William Morrow, 1968.

Mason, Stanhope B. "Reminiscences and Anecdotes from World War II." N.d. MRC 1994.126.

Matloff, Maurice. *Strategic Planning for Coalition Warfare, 1943–1944.* Washington, DC: Center of Military History, 1959.

Matloff, Maurice, and Edwin M. Snell. *Strategic Planning for Coalition Warfare, 1941–1942.* Washington, DC: Chief of Military History, 1953.

Maycock, Thomas J. *The Twelfth Air Force in the North African Campaign: 11 November 1942 to the Reorganization of 18 February 1943.* Maxwell Air Force Base, AL: Army Air Forces Historical Office, January 1946.

McManus, John C. *The Dead and Those About to Die: D-Day: The Big Red one at Omaha Beach.* New York: Penguin, 2014.

Meyer, Hubert. *The 12th SS: The History of the Hitler Youth Panzer Division.* 2 vols. Mechanicsburg, PA: Stackpole, 1994.

Miller, Robert A. *Division Commander: "Dutch" Cota Fighting General.* Spartanburg, SC: Reprint Company, 1989.

Milner, Mark. *Stopping the Panzers: The Untold Story of D-Day.* Lawrence: University Press of Kansas, 2014.

Mitcham, Samuel W., Jr. *German Order of Battle.* Vol. 1, *1st–290th Infantry Divisions in WWII.* Vol. 2, *291st–999th Infantry Division, Named Infantry Divisions, Special Divisions in WWII.* Vol. 3, *Panzer, Panzer Grenadier, and Waffen SS Divisions in WWII.* Mechanicsburg, PA: Stackpole, 2007.

Molony, C. J. C. *The Campaign in Sicily 1943 and the Campaign in Italy, 3rd September 1943 to 31st March 1944.* Vol. 5 of *The Mediterranean and Middle East.* With F. C. Flynn, H. L. Davies, and T. P. Gleave. London: Her Majesty's Stationery Office, 1973.

Montgomery, Bernard Law. *The Memoirs of Field-Marshal the Viscount Montgomery of Alamein.* Cleveland: World Publishing, 1958.

Moorehead, Alan. *The March to Tunis: The North African War, 1940–1943.* New York: Harper & Row, 1965.

Moran, Lord [Charles McMoran Wilson, 1st Baron Moran]. *The Anatomy of Courage.* Garden City Park, NY: Avery, 1987.

Morrison, Samuel Eliot. *The Invasion of France and Germany, 1944–1945.* Boston: Little Brown, 1984.

———. *Sicily-Salerno-Anzio, January 1943–June 1944.* Vol. 4 of *History of the United States Naval Operations in World War II.* Boston: Little, Brown, 1957.

———. *The Two-Ocean War: A Short History of the United States Navy in the Second World War.* Boston: Little, Brown and Wood, 1963.

Mygatt, Philip Sherman. *Return to La Roche-en-Ardenne: A Love Story.* Privately published, 2019.

Nauss, Lovern "Jerry." *Troubleshooting All the Way: A Memoir of the 1st Signal Company and Combat Telephone Communications in the 1st Infantry Division, 1944–1945.* Wheaton, IL: Cantigny First Division Foundation, 2005.

Ossad, Steven L. *Omar Nelson Bradley: America's GI General 1893–1981.* Columbia, MO: University of Missouri Press, 2017.

Pallud, Jean-Paul. *Battle of the Bulge: Then and Now.* London: After the Battle, 1984.

Perret, Geoffrey. *There's a War to Be Won: The United States Army in World War II.* New York: Random House, 1991.

Playfair, I. S. O., and C. J. C. Molony. *The Destruction of the Axis Forces in Africa.* Vol. 4 of *The Mediterranean and the Middle East.* London: Her Majesty's Stationery Office, 1966.

Pogue, Forrest C. *George C. Marshall: Ordeal and Hope, 1939–1942.* New York: Viking, 1966.

———. *The Supreme Command: European Theater of Operations.* Washington, DC: Center of Military History, 1989.

Porch, Douglas. *The Path to Victory: The Mediterranean Theater in World War II.* New York: Farrar, Straus and Giroux, 2004.

Pyle, Ernie. *Brave Men.* New York: Henry Holt, 1944.

Reardon, Mark. *Defending Fortress Europe: The War Diary of the German 7 Army in Normandy, 6 June to 26 July 1944.* Bedford, PA: Aberjona, 2012.

———. *Victory at Mortain: Stopping Hitler's Counteroffensive.* Lawrence: University Press of Kansas, 2002.

Reynolds, Michael. *Steel Inferno: 1 SS Panzer Corps in Normandy.* New York: Sarpedon, 1997.

———. *Sons of the Reich: II SS Panzer Corps, Normandy, Arnhem, Ardennes, Eastern Front.* Havertown, PA: Casemate, 2002.

Ridgway, Matthew B. *Soldier: The Memoirs of Matthew B. Ridgway.* As told to Harold H. Martin. New York: Harper and Brothers, 1956.

Ritgen, Helmut. *Western Front, 1944: Memoirs of a Panzer Lehr Officer.* Winnipeg, Manitoba: J. J. Fedorowicz, 1995.

Ruppenthal, Roland G. *Logistical Support of the Armies.* Vol. 1, *May 1941–September 1944.* Washington, DC: Office of the Chief of Military History, 1956. Vol. 2, *September 1944–May 1945.* Washington, DC: Office of the Chief of Military History, 1959.

Ryan, Cornelius. *The Longest Day: June 6, 1944.* New York: Simon and Schuster, 1959.

———. *A Bridge Too Far.* New York: Simon and Schuster, 1974.

Schick, Albert. *Combat History of the 10. Panzer Division, 1939–1943.* Winnipeg, Manitoba: J. J. Fedorowicz., 2013.

Schifferle, Peter J. *America's School for War: Fort Leavenworth, Officer Education, and Victory in World War II.* Lawrence: University Press of Kansas, 2010.

Schrijvers, Peter. *The Crash of Ruin: American Combat Soldiers in Europe during World War II.* New York: New York University Press, 1998.

Senger und Etterlin, Frido von. *Neither Fear Nor Hope: the Wartime Career of General Frido von Senger and Etterlin, Defender of Cassio.* Novato, CA: Presidio, 1989.

Severloh, Hein. *WN 62: A German Soldier's Memories of the Defence of Omaha Beach Normandy, June 6, 1944.* Garbsen, Germany: H. E. K. Creativ Verlag, 2019.

Sharp, Jim. *Diary of a Combat Infantryman: From the Bulge to Bavaria.* Manhattan, KS: Ag Press, 2010.

———. *Sergeant of the Guard at Nuremberg.* Manhattan, KS: Ag Press, 2012.

Shirer, William L. *The Rise and Fall of the Third Reich*. New York: Simon and Schuster, 1960.

Showalter, Dennis. *Hitler's Panzers: The Lightning Attacks That Revolutionized Warfare*. New York: Berkley, 2009.

Smith, Walter Beddell. *Eisenhower's Six Great Decisions: Europe, 1944–1945*. New York: Longmans, 1956.

Spayd, P. A. *Bayerlein: From Afrikakorps to Panzer Lehr; The Life of Rommel's Chief of Staff Fritz Bayerlein*. Atglen, PA: Schiffer, 2003.

Speidel, Hans. *We Defended Normandy*. London: Herbert Jenkins,1951.

Steinhoff, Johannes, Peter Pechel, and Dennis Showalter. *Voices from the Third Reich: An Oral History*. New York: Da Capo, 1994.

Sylvan, William C., and Francis G. Smith Jr. *Normandy to Victory: The War Diary of General Courtney H. Hodges and the First US Army*. Edited by John T. Greenwood. Lexington: University Press of Kentucky, 2008.

Uffner, Raphael L. Major. "Recollections of World War II with the First Infantry Division." N.d. MRC 1997.98.

Van Creveld, Martin. *Fighting Power: German and U.S. Army Performance, 1939–1945*. Westport, CT: Greenwood, 1982.

Veterans of the Battle of the Bulge. *The Battle of the Bulge: True Stories of the Men and Women Who Survived*. Reading, PA: Aperture, 2014.

Warlimont, Walter. *Inside Hitler's Headquarters, 1939–1945*. New York: Frederick A. Praeger, 1964.

Weidinger, Otto. *Das Reich*. Vol. 5, *1943–1945: The 2. SS-Panzer Division "Das Reich"; The History of the Original Division of the Waffen-SS*. Translated by Klaus Scharley and Fred Steinhardt. Winnipeg, Manitoba: J. J. Fedorwicz, 2012.

Weigley, Russell F. *Eisenhower's Lieutenants: The Campaign of France and Germany, 1944–1945*. Bloomington: Indiana University Press, 1981.

———. *History of the United States Army*. Bloomington: Indiana University Press, 1984.

Weingartner, Steven, ed. *Blue Spaders: The 26th Infantry Regiment, 1917–1967*. Wheaton, IL: Cantigny First Division Foundation, 1996.

———. *The Greatest Thing We Have Ever Attempted: Historical Perspectives on the Normandy Campaign*. Wheaton, IL: Cantigny First Division Foundation, 1998.

Westphal, Siegfried. *The German Army in the West*. London: Cassell, 1951.

Wheeler, James Scott. *The Big Red One: America's Legendary 1st Infantry Division from World War I to Desert Storm*. Lawrence: University Press of Kansas, 2007.

Whitehead, Don. *Combat Reporter: Don Whitehead's World War II Diary and Memoirs*. Edited by John B. Romeiser. New York: Fordham University Press, 2006.

Whiting, Charles. *Poor Bloody Infantry*. London: Stanley Paul, 1987.

Whitlock, Flint. *The Fighting First: The Untold Story of the Big Red One on D-Day*. Boulder, CO: Westview, 2004.

Wilmot, Chester. *The Struggle for Europe*. Old Saybrook, CT: Konecky & Konecky, 1952.

Wilson, John B. *Maneuver and Firepower: The Evolution of Divisions and Separate Brigades.* Washington, DC: Center of Military History, 1998.

Winters, Harold A. *Battling the Elements: Weather and Terrain in the Conduct of War.* With Gerald E. Galloway Jr., William J. Reynolds, and David W. Rhyne. Baltimore: Johns Hopkins University Press, 2020.

Winton, Harold R. *Corps Commanders of the Bulge: Six American Generals and Victory in the Ardennes.* Lawrence: University Press of Kansas, 2007.

Wyman, Willard G. "Journal of Events from August 14, 1943 to November 19, 1944." Manuscript. Courtesy of Jed Wyman.

Yeide, Harry. *Steel Victory: The Heroic Story of America's Independent Tank Battalions at War in Europe.* New York: Ballantine, 2003.

———. *The Longest Battle, September 1944 to February 1945: From Aachen to the Roer and Across.* St. Paul, MN: Zenith, 2005.

Zumbro, Derek. *Battle for the Ruhr: The German Army's Final Defeat in the West.* Lawrence: University Press of Kansas, 2006

US War Department Field Manuals

Field Service Regulations, 1923. Washington: US Government Printing Office, 1923.

FM 6-20 *Field Artillery Field Manual Tactics and Technique.* Washington: US Government Printing Office, 1940.

FM 7-5: *Organization and Tactics of Infantry: The Rifle Battalion.* Washington: US Government Printing Office, 1940.

FM 7-40: *Rifle Regiment,* Washington: US Government Printing Office, February 9, 1942.

FM 17: *Armored Force Field Manual,* Washington: US Government Printing Office, n.d.

FM 17-100: *Armored Command Field Manual, The Armored Division,* Washington: US Government Printing Office, 15 January 1944.

FM 100-5: *Field Service Regulations: Operations.* Washington: US Government Printing Office, May 22, 1941.

Louisiana State University. Reproduction of TM-E 30-451: *Handbook on German Military Forces,* Louisiana State University Press, Baton Rouge, 1990.

Index

A